"It is becoming more and more widely accepted that successful human settlements must be planned. Economic development guided by no more than the principle of the most rapid achievable rate of growth does not . . . produce settlements in which the citizen can live with acceptable standards of security and happiness. Over-concentration of people, uncontrollable environmental pollution, blatant differences of opportunity between region and region, between place and place: all these evils are in no way self-correcting.

"Good human settlements, it must be repeated, depend upon positive policy, not upon the residual result of decisions directed toward other, usually economic goals."

Barbara Ward
Human Settlements: Crisis and Opportunity

BASIC ORGANIZATION OF THE TEXT

CONTENTS

PREFACE

The North American City, Second Edition, is an attempt to portray the broad scope and varied nature of the geographer's interests in, and contribution to, the study of cities. It is primarily intended as a textbook for introductory courses in urban geography for undergraduates—principally at colleges and universities in North America. Since the book is self-contained, few assumptions are made about the reader's background in human geography. Hence it is designed to cater to the needs of the growing number of students from other disciplines taking courses in urban geography, as well as to the needs of geography majors and honors students. For the former, the book ought to illustrate the importance of the spatial viewpoint in urban study. For the latter, the aim is to develop a broad and sound understanding of modern urban geography and, in so doing, to lay the foundations for more advanced study in geography relating to the three main themes treated in the book—the organization of city systems, the internal structure of urban areas, and urban problems, policies, and planning.

The presentation mainly emphasizes human geography as the study of the spatial organization of human activity. Stress is firmly placed on the functional organization of cities and urban regions rather than on details of the evolution and form of specific urban places. Throughout the text, the major concern is consequently with theories and generalizations about the locations of people and their activities, the interaction between them, processes at work, and behavior in urban and regional space, and with key issues, problems, and policies relating to the human consequences of urbanization.

Second Edition Revisions

In addition to the usual tidying up of loose ends, updating statistical data, and adding more recent references, a number of important changes have been made in this Second Edition of *The North American City*. The first of these relates to the important new trends that have emerged in urban geography since the first edition of the book was written. Significant among these have been the increasing interest in behavioral problems, the growing emphasis on policy issues, and the mounting concern for the fate of the individual in an increasingly complicated urban environment. In revising the text, these newer interests have been incorporated in the discussion wherever appropriate.

Second, the organization and content of the final part of the book has been substantially altered. The three original chapters have been extensively rewritten and enlarged, and two entirely new chapters have been added. One of these deals with housing problems and policies, and we thank Dr. John Holmes for writing this; we are convinced that his excellent contribution has added significantly to the strengths the book already possesses. The other focuses on urban policies and planning at the regional and national scales. Transportation and pollution problems are now discussed in greater depth as a separate chapter, while the treatment of local government fragmentation has been expanded and complemented with new material on the current crises in financing local government activity within cities.

Third, the topics covered in the first seven chapters have been rearranged into a more coherent whole, and, in the rewriting, a more direct emphasis has been placed on the functional–spatial organization of the city system. The chapters on the economic base and growth of cities, the location of manufacturing, and city types and functions have been extensively revised to fit more comfortably into the general theme of the first part of the book.

In addition to these major changes, many smaller alterations have been made throughout the text as part of the general improvement of the volume. Several chapters have been shortened, for example those dealing with cities as service centers and with the commercial structure of urban areas. The material that originally appeared in the Appendices has been deleted from the Second Edition. Although the discussion still focuses inevitably on the United States, much more Canadian material has been included, and more attention is paid to similarities and differences in the urban environments of the two countries. Finally, a number of superfluous illustrations have been deleted and a great many new illustrations added to retain what many users of the book have considered one of its strongpoints—visual interest and clarity.

Organization of the Second Edition

In revising *The North American City*, the structure used in the first edition has been retained. The Introduction is designed to present students—and particularly those with little background in geography—with an idea of the scope and nature of urban geography, the diversity of approaches and emphases that are employed, and the methodological framework within which much contemporary research in the subject takes place. A key component in this chapter is the introduction of basic locational, organizational, and behavioral concepts and considerations.

The topics dealt with in subsequent chapters are arranged under three main themes to form the main parts of the book. Part I, "The City System," concentrates on the aggregate characteristics of cities and their roles in the organization—particularly economic organization—of regions and national territories. The six chapters are devoted to concepts, simple theoretical statements, and broad generalizations relating to the urbanization process, the evolution of urban patterns, functional specialization and city types, urban growth mechanisms, location, and the complex patterns of spatial interaction that bind cities together into a complicated, functional whole referred to as the city system.

In Part II, "The Internal Structure of Urban Areas," the emphasis shifts to the ways cities are themselves spatially organized. Patterns in the residential, social, commercial, and manufacturing structure of cities are discussed, and the importance of the theories of urban land use and spatial behavior are stressed. Although systems in themselves, cities are also characterized by complex internal patterns of interaction in which the role of transportation and mobility are critical. The way in which transportation has affected the growth and internal structure of urban areas is explicitly dealt with in a prefatory chapter to this part of the book, and this theme is implicit in much of the ensuing discussion, particularly in the concluding chapter which deals specifically with principle intraurban movements—the journeys to work and shop.

Part III is entitled "The Urban Dilemma." Here the emphasis shifts away from concern with spatial regularities to a discussion of selected key issues and urban problems, many of which clearly have a spatial component. Hence in this final section the concern is not with urban geography as a theoretical science but as an applied science, rich in its potential contribution to the solution of contemporary urban problems. The five chapters deal with transportation and pollution, housing, local government fragmentation and fiscal squeeze, urban and regional policies, and the urban future. The relationship between geography and planning is made more explicit, and the need for a certain measure of control over the future development of the urban environment is stressed.

The kinds of topics dealt with in this final part of the book are already the subject of a very extensive literature, and we are the first to admit that it has only been possible here to skim the surface of what are, after all, extremely complicated problems—each of which could indeed be the basis of a book in its own right. Nevertheless, in isolating a set of major problems and identifying solutions and policies, it is very much hoped that a useful, albeit admittedly incomplete, framework is presented that will stimulate further discussion in the classroom. The emphasis given in Part III of the book is, then, to the application of the geographer's craft in helping to make a better urban environment for ourselves and for future generations.

In acknowledging the help of the many people who contributed to the success of the first edition and, we hope, to this Second Edition of *The North American City*, we would like to thank particularly our colleagues at Queen's and Aarhus. They, and our many friends in the profession, have given us excellent advice, and we wish we could have incorporated all their suggestions. Finally, Maurice would like to think Marilynn, Maurine, and Harry for their continuous emphasis on the inherent humor that is to be found in all situations, and Barry expresses his appreciation to Ulla and those others who have endured the disruptions to normal routine that continued work on the book has involved.

Maurice Yeates   Barry Garner

ACKNOWLEDGMENTS

Since the material cited below is also listed alphabetically by author in the references section located at the back of the book, the reader will find it easier to consult that section for further information about particular source material used in the text.

The Authors and Publisher wish to express their thanks to the following for permission to reprint or modify material from copyright works:

The American Academy of Political and Social Science for Figs. 1–4 and 5, pp. 8–9 and 11, from *The Annals*, Vol. 242, 1945 (Paper by C. D. Harris and E. L. Ullman).

The American Geographical Society of New York for the following from the *Geographical Review*: Figs. 2–9, p. 92 and Table 1, p. 88, Vol. 33, 1943 (Paper by C. D. Harris); Fig. 7, p. 232, Vol. 46, 1956 (Paper by E. J. Taaffe); Fig. 1, p. 185, Vol. 46, 1956 (Paper by R. T. Novak); Fig. 1, p. 165, Vol. 55, 1965 (Paper by A. Pred); Fig. 2, p. 361, Vol. 56, 1966 (Paper by G. Carey); Table II, p. 219, Vol. 56, 1966 (Paper by B. E. Newling); Figs. 6–10, pp. 313 and 322, and Tables II and III, pp. 315 and 329, and to quote from p. 329, Vol. 57, 1967 (Paper by J. Borchert); Fig. 4, p. 630, Vol. 58, 1968 (Paper by J. Simmons); and the map on p. 3, *Focus*, Vol. 20(6), 1970.

Edward Arnold (Publishers) Ltd., London, for Fig. 5.4, p. 119, from *Locational Analysis in Human Geography* by Peter Haggett, 1965; and to quote from p. 298 from *Explanation in Geography* by David Harvey, 1969.

The Association of American Geographers for the following from *Annals of the Association of American Geographers*: Fig. 6, p. 324, Vol. 44, 1954 (Paper by C. D. Harris); Table 1, p. 147, Vol. 49, 1959 (Paper by B. J. L. Berry); Fig. 3, p. 8, Vol. 54, 1964 (Paper by B. J. L. Berry); Fig. 5, p. 358, Vol. 62, 1972 (Paper by J. Borchert); and for information from pp. 9 and 11 from *Air Pollution*, Resource Paper No. 3, by R. A. Bryson and J. E. Kutzbach, 1968.

Basic Books Inc., Publishers, New York, for Table 8.2 "Financing of selected urban services, 1970-71," p. 228 from *Economics and Urban Problems: Diagnoses and Prescriptions*, 2nd and enlarged edition, by Dick Netzer, 1974. © 1970 and 1974, Basic Books, Inc.

The Brookings Institution, Washington, D.C., for Table 16, p. 243 from *The Metropolitan Transportation Problem* by W. Owen, 1966 (revised edition).

The Bureau of Business and Economic Research, The State University of Iowa, to quote from p. 15 of the *Iowa Business Digest*, 1960 (Winter) (Paper by E. N. Thomas).

The Canadian Association of Geographers and the Authors for the following from *The Canaidan Geographer*: Fig. 2, p. 4, Vol. 2, 1958 (Paper by R. Mackay); and Tables 3 and 4, pp. 216 and 220, Vol. 10, 1966 (Paper by L. J. King).

The Editor of the *Canadian Review of Sociology and Anthropology* for Table 1, pp. 166-167, Vol. 6, 1969 (Paper by T. G. Nicholson and M. H. Yeates).

The Center for Urban Studies, University of Chicago, for Fig. 3.7, p. 91 from *The Impact of Urban Renewal on Small Business* by B. J. L. Berry, S. J. Parsons, and R. H. Platt, 1968.

The Centre for Urban and Community Studies, University of Toronto, for Fig. 12, p. 185, from *Readings in Airport Planning*, edited by R. Soberman, 1972 (Paper by E. Hauer).

The Chicago Area Transportation Study for map 12, p. 21; Figs. 15 and 24, pp. 35 and 48; and Tables 4 and 6, 37 and 47, from the *Final Report*, Vol. 1, Survey Findings, 1959.

The Detroit Metropolitan Area Traffic Study for map 4, p. 33, from *Report, Part I*, Data Summary and Interpretation, 1955.

The Editor and the Authors for the following from *Economic Geography*: Tables 1 and 2, pp. 204 and 302, and to quote from p. 219, Vol. 30, 1954 (Papers by R. Murphy and J. E. Vance, Jr.); Figs. 3, 12, 13, 14, 15, pp. 27, 33, 35-37, and Table 1, p. 22, Vol. 31, 1955 (Paper by R. Murphy, J. E. Vance, Jr., and B. Epstein); Figs. 1, 2, 10, pp. 192, 197, and 204, Vol. 31, 1955 (Paper by H. J. Nelson); Figs. 3, 4, 5, 7, 8, 9, pp. 287, 290, 292, 296, 298-299, Vol. 31, 1955 (Paper by H. L. Green); Table 2, p. 150 and Fig. 3, p. 310, Vol. 34, 1958 (Papers by B. J. L. Berry and W. L. Garrison); Fig. 5, p. 9, Vol. 38, 1962 (Paper by E. J. Taaffe); Figs. 6, 7, 8, pp. 325-326, and 328, Vol. 38, 1962 (Paper by P. J. Smith); Fig. 3, p. 170, Vol. 39, 1963 (Paper by H. A. Stafford, Jr.); Figs. 6, 7, 14, 15, 30, and 31, pp. 219, 221, and 231, Vol. 41, 1965 (Paper by R. A. Murdie); and Figs. 1, 2, pp. 60-61, Vol. 41, 1965 (Paper by M. H. Yeates).

The Federal Reserve Bank of Kansas City, for Table 1, p. 4, from the *Monthly Review*, Vol. 37, 1952.

Gustav Fischer Verlag, Stuttgart, W. Germany, for Figs. 27 and 86, pp. 118 and 448, from *The Economics of Location* by A. Lösch, 1954.

C. W. K. Gleerup Publishers, Lund, Sweden, for Fig. 2, p. 129 from *Proceedings of the I.G.U. Symposium on Urban Geography, Lund, 1960*, edited by K. Norborg, 1962 (Paper by E. L. Ullman and M. F. Dacey).

Hakkert Publishing Company Ltd., Toronto, for Table 10, p. 60, from *Programs in Search of a Policy* by M. Dennis and S. Fish, 1972.

Harvard University Press, Cambridge, for Fig. 9, p. 63, from *Streetcar Suburbs: The Process of Growth in Boston* by S. B. Warner, Jr., 1962.

R. F. Latham for information from *Urban Population Densities and Growth, with Special*

Reference to Toronto, unpublished M.A. thesis, Department of Geography, Queen's University, Canada, 1967.

Macmillan Company of Canada Ltd., Toronto, for various tables from *Canada's Urban Axis* by M. H. Yeates, 1975.

McGraw-Hill Book Co., New York, for Figs. 5 and 6, pp. 102 and 107, from *The Metropolitan Community* edited by R. D. McKenzie, 1933 (Paper by R. E. Park and C. Newcomb); and data from p. 167 from *Fundamentals of Forestry Economics* by W. A. Duerr, 1960.

The Maryland-National Capital Park and Planning Commission, Washington, D.C., for the diagram on p. 20 of *On Wedges and Corridors*, 1964.

The Massachusetts Institute of Technology Press, Cambridge, for Table A–5.3, p. 23, from *Principles and Techniques of Predicting Future Demand for Urban Transportation* by B. V. Martin, F. W. Memmott, and A. J. Bone, 1961.

Methuen and Co. Ltd., London, for Fig. 10.1, p. 365 from *Models in Geography* edited by R. J. Chorley and P. Haggett, 1967 (Paper by F. E. I. Hamilton).

The Author and the Editor, *Tijdschrift voor Economische en Sociale Geographie* for Figs. 2 and 3, pp. 232–233, Vol. 56, 1965 (Paper by K. R. Cox).

Northwestern University Press, Evanston, for Figs. 1.1, III.3A through 3F, pp. 6 and 22–23, and Tables II.1, p. 9, and V.6, p. 88, from *The Peripheral Journey to Work* by E. J. Taaffe, B. J. Garner, and M. H. Yeates, 1963.

The Authors and the Department of Geography, Northwestern University for the following from *Studies in Geography*: Figs. 2, 16, and 19, pp. 14, 55, and 61. No. 10, 1965 (Paper by J. L. Davis).

The Ohio State University Research Foundation for Table 20, p. 40 from *The Shopping Center versus Downtown* by C. T. Jonassen, 1955.

The Pergamon Press, Oxford, to quote from p. 80, *Urban Geography: An Introductory Analysis* by J. H. Johnson, 1967.

Prentice-Hall Inc., Englewood Cliffs, N.J., for Figs. 1.3, 1.4, 2.1, 2.8, 2.9, 2.11, 2.16, 2.21, and 2.23, pp. 6, 27, 32, 33, 36, 38, 49, and 52, and to quote from pp. 34–35 from *Geography of Market Centers and Retail Distribution* by B. J. L. Berry, 1967.

The Public Administration Service, Chicago, for Fig. 49 from *Urban Renewal and the Future of the American City* by C. A. Doxiadis, 1966.

The RAND Corporation, Santa Monica, for Fig. 2, p. 15, and Table 10, p. 46, from *A Multiple Equation Model of Household Locational and Trip Making Behaviour*, Memorandum RM–3086–FF by J. F. Kain, 1962.

P. H. Rees for Fig. 4, p. 47 from *The Factorial Ecology of Metropolitan Chicago*, unpublished M.A. thesis, Department of Geography, University of Chicago, 1960.

The Regional Plan Association, New York, for Chart 3, p. 10 from *Anatomy of a Metropolis* by E. M. Hoover and R. Vernon, 1959; Table 22, p. 131 from *Freight and the Metropolis* by B. Chinitz, 1960; and to quote from pp. 19 and 113 from *1400 Governments* by R. C. Wood, 1961.

The Regional Science Association and the Authors for the following from *Papers and Proceedings of the Regional Science Association*: Table 1, p. 113, Vol. 4, 1958 (Paper by B. J. L. Berry and W. L. Garrison); Tables 1 and 3, pp. 242 and 247, Vol. 4, 1958 (Paper by I. Morrissett); Fig. 6, p. 165, Vol. 6, 1960 (Paper by D. Huff); Fig. 2, p. 39, Vol. 7, 1961 (Paper by J. E. Nystuen and M. F. Dacey); and Figs. 1, 3, 4, 7, 10, 11, 14, 15, and 17, pp. 66, 71, 79, 81, 83, 89, 91, and 95, and Tables 1, 4, 5, and 6, pp. 70, 77, 78, Vol. 9, 1962 (Paper by B. J. L. Berry, H. G. Barnum, and R. Tennant).

The Commission on Geography, Pan American Institute of Geography and History, The Author, and the Editor for Fig. 4 from *Revista Geografica*, Vol. 15, No. 42, 1954 (Paper by R. A. Kennelly).

The Planning Division, Rhode Island Development Council, for data on p. 51 of *Metropolitanization and Population Change in Rhose Island*, Planning Division Publication No. 3 by S. Goldstein and K. B. Mayer, 1961.

The Royal Statistical Society and the Author for Diagrams on p. 492 from the *Journal of the Royal Statistical Society*, Series A, No. 114, 1951 (Paper by C. Clark).

St. Martins Press Inc., New York, for Fig. 18, pp. 175–176, and to quote from p. 73 from *The Human Consequences of Urbanization* by B. J. L. Berry, 1973.

Scientific American Inc., for the diagram on p. 30 of A. J. Hagen-Smit, "The Control of Air Pollution," *Scientific American*, Vol. 210(1), 1964. Copyright © 1964 by Scientific American, Inc. All rights reserved.

The Scripps Foundation, Miami, Ohio, for material on pp. 121–124 from *Suburbanization of Manufacturing Activity within Standard Metropolitan Areas*, Studies in Population Distribution, No. 9, by E. M. Kittagawa and D. J. Bogue, 1955.

The Editor of the *Southeastern Geographer* for Fig. 1, p. 33, Vol. 8, 1964 (Paper by C. E. Browning); and the Table on p. 31, Vol. 12, 1968 (Paper by A. W. Stuart).

Stanford University Press, Menlo Park, and the Board of Trustees of the Leland Stanford Junior University for Fig. V.14, pp. 42–43, and Table II.1, p. 4 from *Social Area Analysis: Theory, Illustrative Applications and Computational Procedures* by E. Shevky and W. Bell, 1955. Copyright 1955 by the Board of Trustees of the Leland Stanford Junior University.

The Editor of the *Town Planning Review* and the Author for Fig. 17, p. 175, Vol. 22, 1961 (Paper by J. P. Reynolds).

The Editor of *Traffic Quarterly* for Fig. 2, p. 209, Vol. 26, 1972 (Paper by J. Plewes and M. H. Yeates).

The Editor of the *Transactions* of the Institute of British Geographers for Fig. 3, p. 27, No. 51, 1970 (Paper by B. J. L. Berry).

The Twentieth Century Fund, New York, for Fig. 3, p. 26, from *Megalopolis* by J. Gottmann, 1961.

The University of Chicago Press for Charts I and II, pp. 51 and 55, from *The City* by R. E. Park, E. W. Burgess, and R. D. McKenzie, 1967 edition. © The University of Chicago. All rights reserved.

The Editors and the University of Chicago Press for the following from the *American Journal of Sociology*: Chart X, p. 78, Vol. 35, 1929 (Paper by R. E. Park); Table 1, p. 153, Vol. 60, 1954 (Paper by W. Isard and P. Kavesh); and to quote from p. 156, Vol. 56, 1950 (Paper by R. G. Ford); and for Fig. 1, p. 239 from *Economic Development and Cultural Change*, Vol. 4, 1956 (Paper by C. H. Madden). © The University of Chicago. All rights reserved.

The Editor and the Authors for the following from *Research Papers*, Department of Geography, University of Chicago; Figs. 3, 10, 11, and 12, pp. 14, 32, 64, and 68, and Tables 1, 2, 6, 19, 49, 50, 51, and B1, pp. 17, 20, 42, 43, 65, 133, 135, and 228, from No. 85, 1963 (Paper by B. J. L. Berry); Table on p. 3 from No. 86, 1963 (Paper by B. J. L. Berry and R. J. Tennant); Fig. 18, p. 78 from No. 90, 1964 (Paper by M. Helvig); Fig. 8, p. 28 from No. 104, 1966 (Paper by J. Simmons); to quote from p. 188, from No. 111, 1966 (Paper by B. J. L. Berry); Fig. 29, p. 169, Table 34, p. 164, and to quote from p. 76, from No. 116, 1969 (Paper by R. A. Murdie); and for Table 10, p. 95 from No. 155, 1974 (Paper by B. J. L. Berry).

The University of Nebraska Press for Table 5.2 and data from pp. 40, 47, 53, 98, and 106 from *The Industrial Structure of American Cities* by G. Alexandersson, 1956.

The University of North Carolina Press for Fig. 2 from *The Urban South* edited by R. B.

Vance and N. J. Demerath, 1954 (Paper by R. B. Vance and S. Smith).

The University of Pittsburgh Press for Tables 21, 22, 23, pp. 65, 67, and 69, from *Portrait of a Region* by I. S. Lowry, 1963.

The Editors and the University of Reading Press for Figs. 70, 74, 75, and 76, pp. 325, 329, and 330, from *Essays in Geography for Austin Miller* edited by J. B. Whittow and P. D. Wood, 1965 (Paper by M. H. Yeates).

The University of Washington Press and the Authors for Table 11.8, p. 221, from *Studies of Highway Development and Geographic Change* by W. L. Garrison, B. J. L. Berry, D. F. Marble, J. D. Nystuen, and R. L. Morrill, 1959; and for Fig. 2.6, p. 21, and Tables 2.1 and 2.2, pp. 16 and 20 from *Studies of the Central Business District and Urban Freeway Development* by E. M. Horwood and R. R. Boyce, 1959.

The Editor and the University of Wisconsin Press for the following from *Land Economics*; Tables 1, 2, and 3, p. 106, and footnote 3, p. 105, Vol. 52, 1964 (Paper by J. H. Niedercorn and E. F. R. Hearle).

The Urban Land Institute, Washington, D.C., for the Table on p. 43 of *Metropolitanization of the United States* by J. P. Pickard, 1959.

John Wiley and Sons Inc., New York, for Figs. 8 and 12, pp. 67 and 73 from *Location and Space-Economy* by W. Isard, 1956.

The Authors and Publisher also acknowledge the use of material from United States Government noncopyright publications, and especially for Figs. 28 and 40, pp. 77 and 115, and to quote from p. 76 of *The Structure and Growth of Residential Neighborhoods in American Cities* by Homer Hoyt, Federal Housing Administration, 1939. Use of material from Canadian Government and province of Ontario noncopyright publications is also acknowledged: Figs. 31, 40, 41, and 42, pp. 47, 52, and 53 from *Report No. 1*, Metropolitan Toronto Area Regional Transportation Study, 1966; Fig. 12, p. 97 from *The Changing Face of Toronto* by D. Kerr and J. Spelt, 1965; and for Fig. 5, p. 95 and Table V, p. 89 from *The Geographical Bulletin*, Vol. 7(2), 1965 (Paper by J. W. Maxwell).

THE NORTH AMERICAN CITY

1
INTRODUCTION TO URBAN GEOGRAPHY

The geographer's viewpoint is a *spatial* one. His focus has been traditionally on the content of areas, their similarities and differences, the interactions and relationships between them, and the behavior and processes that give rise to distributions, patterns, and structure in the organization of space. A very general description of the objective of study in human geography might be, then, that it seeks to *describe and explain* patterns in the spatial organization of human activity. This statement can be divided into two parts: (1) the first part, which is italicized, and (2) the remaining part about spatial organization. Breaking the statement up in this way is helpful because it distinguishes between two fundamentally distinct, but necessarily related, parts of geography. Thus the second part (2) is concerned with what geographers do—with the definition of the subject—while the first part (1) concerns how they do it. This is the basic difference between the philosophy of geography and its methodology (Harvey, 1969).

In this chapter we shall look at both of these aspects as they relate to the subject matter of urban geography. On the one hand, the chapter is a brief introduction to urban geography as it exists today; on the other, it is an introduction to the rest of this book, since the emphasis in much of what follows has its roots in the viewpoints presented here.

THE NATURE OF URBAN GEOGRAPHY

In starting the study of a new subject at college or the university, it helps at the outset to have some general idea of what the subject is all about, in the same way that it helps to have a map when driving in an unfamiliar city. Without the map, "we see the sprawling new suburbs, the bustling freeways, the pockets of decay, but find it hard to get an overall impression of the [city's] structure or to know where we are" (Haggett, 1972, p. xix). It is not easy to draw the "map" we need of urban geography, for it is a broad and diffuse subject. In fact, it can be likened to a "Los Angeles of academic cities in that it sprawls over a very large area, it merges with its neighbors, and we have a hard time finding the central business district [downtown]" (Haggett, 1972, p. xix). But then, this is not altogether surprising when we consider just how complex the urban pattern is, that cities are studied from many different points of view in other disciplines besides geography, and that a variety of approaches and emphases are possible in the study of urban areas by geographers.

Urban areas, then, can be thought of as a laboratory in which studies are undertaken by researchers from many different disciplines. Consequently urban geography merges and overlaps with the urban-oriented parts of many other disciplines. Figure 1.1 shows this overlap for some of the more important cognate sciences, the core of which can be thought of as comprising the interdisciplinary science of planning. This overlap points to a fundamental premise concerning the definition of subjects, namely that they are identified by the kinds of questions asked and the concepts and processes stressed rather than by the kinds of phenomena that are studied. In its simplest form, the distinctively geographical question is: *"Why are spatial distributions structured the way they are?"* (Abler, Adams, and Gould, 1971). Hence the integrating concepts of the geographer are spatially oriented and relate to spatial interaction and organization, and to spatial processes (Berry, 1964a). Thus although there may often be a close resemblance between the work of urban geographers and, for example, that of some urban sociologists, the fundamental difference between the kinds of studies each undertakes results from the fact that the geographer is essentially concerned with the behavior and processes that give rise to patterns in the *spatial organization* of society (Morrill, 1974a).

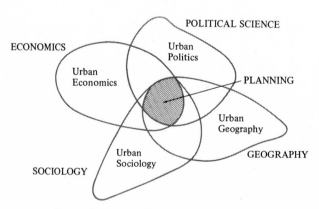

Fig. 1.1 The overlap of urban-oriented sciences.

In a similar way, there may be overlapping of the different systematic branches of human geography, each of which may in part focus on the study of urban areas. This is shown in Figure 1.2 for the principal branches of human geography. Thus an economic geographer may be concerned with the location of industry. He can study this general problem with special reference to the industrial structure of urban areas, either looking for patterns in the distribution of industry between them or looking for patterns and processes at work in the location of industry within them. Similar urban bias may be characteristic of the work of political and social geographers, and so on. Hence just as planning may be thought of as being at the core of the overlap between different sciences, so urban geography can be thought of as an area of convergence of the various systematic branches of human geography. It is largely because of this that urban geography is not so much a well-defined subject on the basis of the facts it deals with as it is an area of inquiry in which the inquiry is spatial and the area urban.

Approaches to Urban Geography

The easiest way of defining urban geography is to describe what urban geographers do. On the basis of *what* is done, two main approaches can be identified. First, there is the study of problems relating to the spatial distribution of cities themselves and the

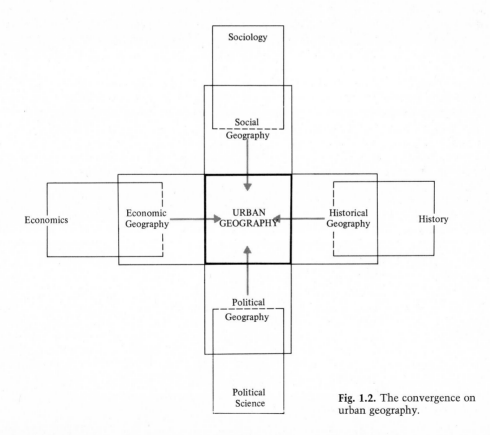

Fig. 1.2. The convergence on urban geography.

complex patterns of movement, flows, and linkages that bind them together in space. Studies in this category are concerned with the *city system*. Second, there is the study of patterns of distribution and interaction within cities — the study of their internal structure. Studies in this category are concerned with the *city as a system*. Although these two main approaches to urban geography can be, and often are, studied independently of each other, they are not completely unrelated. This is because changes in the internal structure of cities often result from the processes and changes operating in the overall urban pattern of which they are an integral part. A succinct definition of urban geography which recognizes the link between these two approaches within the subject is, then, that *urban geography is the study of "cities as systems within a system of cities"* (Berry, 1964b).

A useful way of generalizing about the different kinds of study that fall within each of these two main approaches is to use the notion of a "geographical matrix" (Berry, 1964a). Such a matrix is outlined in Figure 1.3. It comprises a number of rows and columns. Although in reality there is an infinite number of both, it is normally possible to define a fixed number of them, which is meaningful in the context of a given problem. The columns in the matrix refer to places; we can refer to them generally as urban areas. The rows refer to characteristics — the variables or attributes to be used in study — which have been grouped in the diagram into the main systematic branches of human geography. The intersection of a given column and row defines a *cell* (as shown for the intersection of column *i* and row *j*), which contains a *geographic fact*. This is an observation of a single characteristic recorded by its location at a single place at a given point in time. At any other point in time the fact could be different, for variation occurs in time as well as space. The addition of the time dimension is therefore essential. Without it it is impossible to describe changes in spatial patterns or to study the processes operating in space. Changes through time can easily be incorporated if we think of slices cut through various time periods. Each slice represents a matrix containing the same characteristics about the same places — but as they occurred in the past. The set of time-space matrices shown in Figure 1.3 is about the closest we can come to drawing, as it were, our map of urban geography.

Approaches to the City System

In studies of this kind, urban areas are treated as discrete entities in space. Concern is with their aggregate characteristics and attributes. Facts in the cells of Figure 1.3A might be, for example, relative location, population size, total employment, major economic functions, crime rates, incoming telephone calls, and so on. A column in the matrix is therefore an inventory of general information about a particular city for a given point in time. When the contents of the rows are the basis for study, concern is with the same characteristic as it occurs in a number of cities. Emphasis is on patterns of location, interaction, and spatial variation within the urban system. Studies of this kind, like all work in geography, can be undertaken at different *scales* — for example, at the national, regional, or local scales. Scale, or the size of the study area, determines the number of cities (which columns in the matrix) and often the kinds of characteristics to be included in the study.

Study of the content of the rows need not, of course, be confined to the present. Similar kinds of studies can be undertaken for different times in the past (see Pred,

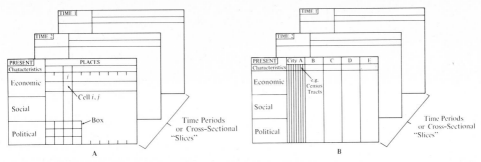

Fig. 1.3. The "geographic matrix" in urban geography as applied to the study of the city system (A) and the internal structure of cities (B). (*Source*: after Berry, 1964a, Fig. 3.)

1966, 1971). In this way a picture can be built up of the changes that have taken place in the urban system and of the way in which the urban pattern has evolved through time. The historical perspective is important for identifying the processes that have been, or that still are, operating in space, a knowledge of which is fundamental in understanding why spatial distributions are structured the way they are.

Another approach is that of comparative study, either of the columns or of the rows in the matrix. Comparison of two or more columns amounts to the study of similarities and differences between individual cities (see Weber, 1958). Alternatively, the characteristics in two or more rows might be compared in order to study interurban differences in, for example, economic and social characteristics (see Nelson, 1957). A further possibility is to take a number of adjacent rows and columns that comprise boxes of the matrix (Figure 1.3A) and look at their contents. In essence this involves both of the above approaches and may lead to the classification of cities (see Chapter 7), interregional comparisons of urban patterns, and so on.

Comparison between rows in the matrix can also be undertaken to identify the ways in which different characteristics vary together in space. The identification and analysis of spatial relationships and associations form a central part of all work in urban geography. It is one of the basic ways by which we are able to explain why and how spatial patterns and structures are the way they are. All of these alternative approaches to the study of urban systems are explicit or implicit in Part I of this book. The six chapters are devoted to concepts and generalizations relating to the urbanization process, the evolution and distribution of settlements, their functional specialization and economic structure, and the interrelationships that bind them together into a complex, functional whole — the urban system.

Approaches to the City as a System

Only a slight modification of our geographic matrix is needed to illustrate the approaches to the study of the internal structure of urban areas. For this we can think of each city as having a number of columns associated with it, as shown in Figure 1.3B. These columns could represent, for example, census tracts within the city or any other small areas we choose to delimit. In this way the characteristics can be recorded at different locations within the urban area. By adding the slices through different time periods, we can adopt the same basic approaches discussed above in studying patterns *within* urban areas. Thus, for example, study of the cells in a particular row for a given city would amount to study of the intraurban variation of the selected characteristic, for example, population density, income, housing quality, and so on. When the cells in an entire row(s) are included, comparisons of the internal spatial variation of the characteristic(s) can be made between cities. Analysis of relationships between characteristics in boxes of the matrix essentially constitutes what is known as factorial ecology (see Chapter 11). With other permutations and combinations, the result is a rich diversity of possible approaches and themes in studying the internal geography of urban areas.

These are the kinds of approaches treated in Part II. Patterns in the residential, social, commercial, and manufacturing structure of cities are discussed, and the importance of the theories of urban land use and spatial behavior are stressed. As systems in themselves, cities are also characterized by complex internal patterns of interaction in which the role of transportation is critical. The way in which transportation has affected the growth and internal structure of urban areas is explicitly dealt with in a prefatory chapter to the section; and it is implicit in much of the ensuing discussion, particularly in the last chapter, which deals specifically with intraurban movements.

Emphases in Urban Geography

Just as there is diversity in approach, so there is considerable variation in emphasis in urban geography. The question of emphasis and what is stressed is related to the objectives and purpose of study — to the individual's philosophy of (urban) geography. The important thing about the philosophy of a science is that it is ultimately a matter of opinion; hence there is plenty of room for disagreement between individuals about what the emphasis and objectives of study ought to be. Because of this, contemporary urban geography is characterized by a number of points of view (Taaffe, 1974). Three of these are particularly important.

The first is the emphasis on *man-land relations*, which was typical of early studies in urban geography during the first quarter of this century. Emphasis tended to focus on specific details of individual towns and cities, the main objective being to identify associations between the absolute location of places, their character, and the physical environment. At this time, the closest associations of geography were with geology and history, and it was perhaps natural that the major stress was on the *morphology*, or form, of settlements and their historical development (for example, see James, 1931; Taylor, 1942). In recent years, interest in man-land relations and ecological studies has been revived in geography accompanying the growing concern with environmental problems such as air and water pollution in cities and urban regions.

The second is the emphasis on *areal differentiation* which was characteristic of work after about 1940 (Hartshorne, 1939). Within this framework, a key objective of much of the work in urban geography was the description of distributions and patterns in areas, particularly land use patterns within urban areas. Stress was placed on synthesis — on the way various physical, economic, and social characteristics existed together to differentiate cities themselves, and areas within them, from each other (Smailes, 1953). This is still one of the important emphases in urban geography today (Murphy, 1974), and one that is found at various places in this book.

The third is the emphasis on *spatial organization*, and it is this that is stressed in

Parts I and II of this book. This more recent development stems essentially from the reaction against the isolationism characteristic of the early growth of geography (see Ackerman, 1963). It is associated with the conceptual and quantitative revolution that gathered momentum during the late fifties (Davies, 1972). The principal result of this was that greater stress was placed on "the search for order" in spatial arrangements and behavior. In urban geography it led to a stronger emphasis on generalizations concerning urban patterns, the structure of cities, spatial interaction, and processes and behavior in space. The concern with order and generalization was accompanied by greater concern for hypothesis testing, model building, and the development of theory together with the increased use of mathematical and statistical methods. Work in urban geography became more analytical and abstract as the methodology of the subject changed.

The kind of urban geography presented in this book is, therefore, just one of a number of alternative viewpoints that could be adopted. It is characterized by a strong emphasis on function and organization of urban systems rather than on the morphology and form of urban patterns. The physical environment plays only a minor role in the discussions. Man-land relations in the traditional sense have been supplanted by what may be called man-man relations — a shift in emphasis resulting from the concern with the behavior of individuals and the functional-spatial patterns of relations among people. The detail of history characteristic of early studies is replaced by the emphasis on the relationships between space, time, and processes at work.

Urban geography is, however, not only an academic subject concerned with developing theories about spatial organization. It is also a subject rich in its potential contribution to the solution of contemporary urban problems. To an increasing extent the emphasis in urban geography is a more practical one that stresses the application of the results of research in planning and their relevance for policy making. In this connection, many urban geographers are becoming increasingly concerned with questions relating to the fate of the individual and particular groups of people in the urban environment, with problems of "social justice and the city" (Harvey, 1973). The way in which cities are spatially organized is in large part conditioned by the way society itself is organized. Many of today's acute urban problems can perhaps be solved only by changing the structure of society (some geographers argue that a radical change is needed). In this context, a newer *activist* emphasis has lately emerged in the work of a growing number of urban geographers (Kasperson and Breitbart, 1974). In large part this is a reaction against the essentially value-free nature of most of the work in mainstream urban geography (Buttimer, 1974). For this group, the urgency for undertaking studies of a more prescriptive nature is stressed so that endorsement of the status quo is not the basis for policies and planning in the future as it has largely been in the past (Eichenbaum and Morrill, 1974).

The concern with problems, policies, and planning in the urban context is taken up in Part III. Here the emphasis is on what many social philosophers have termed the "urban dilemma." The relationships between urban geography and planning are explicit, and the necessity for a certain measure of control over the development of urban environments is stressed. It is in the final part of this book, then, that emphasis is given to the application of the geographer's craft in helping to make a better urban environment for ourselves and for future generations.

CONCEPTS AND CONSIDERATIONS

Just as the facts used in urban geography are common to other subjects, so are most of its concepts. There are, in fact, very few truly geographic concepts: distance, location, and accessibility are perhaps the most important (Nystuen, 1963). For the rest we are dependent on other subjects, particularly economics and sociology, and to an increasing extent psychology and political science. The many concepts from these subjects are presented in their appropriate contexts throughout this book. At this point it is sufficient to draw attention to some of the more general concepts and considerations that are important for the study of spatial organization.

The Role of Distance

Distance is fundamental for any understanding of spatial organization. In fact, it has been suggested with very good reason that geography itself is a "discipline in distance" (Watson, 1955). It is certainly true that the concept of the "friction of distance" is one of the important cornerstones on which a considerable part of contemporary urban geography is constructed. As such it is a consideration that runs throughout this text. Distance is a fundamental consideration because it separates locations from each other, thereby necessitating various kinds of flows, movements, and linkages between them that are collectively referred to as *spatial interaction*. A considerable part of man's technological effort has been directed at inventing ways of reducing the barrier effects of distance (see Chapters 2 and 8). This history of transportation and communication is thus essentially one of successive reduction in the inconvenience of distance. Although this has certainly been achieved for many kinds of spatial interaction, the effects of distance can never be completely removed. It still constitutes an important constraint on the movement of people and, to a lesser degree, flows of goods and information (see Chapter 3).

Distance is a fundamental factor because of the costs involved in overcoming it. These costs are an important consideration in the collective and individual decision-making processes underlying spatial patterns. Decisions are often made with the express purpose of minimizing distance costs, thereby giving rise to "centripetal forces" in space. These forces tend to bring things together to result in various forms of agglomeration (see Chapter 5). Cities themselves can be thought of as having resulted from the operation of centripetal forces; the emergence of "downtown" as the major retail-service complex within urban areas is another example. At the same time distance affords the opportunity for spatial separation. Hence centrifugal forces exist that operate in opposition to the centripetal ones to result in dispersion in space. Spatial organization owes much to the interaction of these opposing sets of forces, which are consequently an important framework for understanding why spatial distributions are the way they are.

Locational Concepts

In discussing where things are, we are explicitly concerned with location. However, it is often difficult to talk meaningfully about location without at the same time considering distance. The two are very closely interrelated. Location can be described in absolute or relative terms. Absolute location is given by a grid reference; for example, in terms of degrees of latitude and longitude. In discussing the site of a town or a shopping center we are essentially referring to absolute location. Although it is useful to know exactly where things are, thinking in terms of absolute location is not very helpful in understanding why they are there.

Because of this it is usually more productive to use the concept of *relative location*. By relative location we mean the location of something with respect to the location of selected other things. In a general way it approximates the traditional geographical concept of *situation*, and for all intents and purpose we can think of them as synonymous. Thus, for example, patterns in the distribution of manufacturing can be more readily understood by looking at the location of plants in relation to the sources of raw materials, other linked activities, and the markets in which products are sold (see Chapter 5).

Relative location is expressed in terms of direction and distance. Distance is normally thought of in miles or kilometers — in absolute terms. However, it is often more rewarding to think of distance in other ways; for example, in terms of money, time, or effort. Transformation of distance in this way creates *relative space*. Plotting locations in relative space reveals "true" relative locations and often enables a better understanding of patterns of location and interaction, as well as changes in these through time.

It is in terms of relative space that we are able to grasp what is perhaps the most important locational concept of all, that of *accessibility*. By accessibility is generally meant the "ease of reaching a place." All locations are accessible to some degree, but some locations are much more accessible than others (Garner, 1967). How accessible a particular location is depends largely on its position in transportation and communication networks (Ingram, 1971). In this sense, it is often useful to think of locations as nodes of varying degrees of connectivity in networks of different kinds. Changes in the structure of networks may often bring about an increase or decrease in the accessibility of particular locations through time, to result in changes in their importance. This is particularly true, for example, in the evolution of urban patterns (see Chapter 2). Newer forms of transportation and communication reduce time-distance relationships and often improve the accessibility of certain locations as places converge on each other in relative space (Janelle, 1969). Accessibility is a fundamental concept for understanding spatial patterns and it is a basic building block in many theories of spatial organization; for example, the land-use theories discussed in Chapter 9.

Organizational Concepts

The fact that locations are linked together through various forms of spatial interaction is what gives rise to the concept of *systems* in spatial organization. Simply put, a system is a "set of objects together with the relationships between the objects and their attributes" (Hall and Fagen, 1956). A spatial system can therefore be thought of as one in which the objects are locations, their attributes the activities at them, and the relationships between them some kind of spatial interaction. This is basically what is meant when we talk of cities as systems. Systems thinking is increasingly important as a framework for studies in urban geography (Robson, 1973). The most important systems concept from our point of view is perhaps that of *interdependence* (Warneryd, 1968). What goes on at one location often has repercussions at other locations. For example, the growth of one particular city may bring about stagnation in a number of others (see Chapter 2); the opening of a new major shopping center affects the viability of existing retail outlets in its vicinity as shopping patterns change (see Chapter 12), and so on. Positive and negative effects of decisions and behavior are transmitted in space. It is in this context that concepts such as *multipliers, feedbacks, spillovers,* and so on assume special significance in urban geography, particularly for discussions of growth in the urban system (Pred, 1973) and the location of economic activity (see Chapter 5).

Another important concept relating to the organization of space is that of *hierarchical structure.* Hierarchies are a basic feature of the way society is organized, especially for administrative purposes; for example, the army, corporations, government. Consequently, there is an important hierarchical component in spatial patterns. The essense of hierarchical organization is that objects are placed at different levels (Philbrick, 1957). For example, we can think of cities or shopping centers as occupying different levels in a hierarchy on the basis of their functional importance (see Chapters 6 and 12). Position in a hierarchy can be thought of in terms of a vertical dimension; position in space in terms of the horizontal dimension. The two are closely interrelated; the higher the level in a hierarchical structure, usually the larger the space over which the object—a city, for example—dominates (see Chapter 3).

The idea that cities dominate surrounding areas is the basis for the concept of the *nodal region.* A nodal region comprises a central point or focus with which a surrounding area is linked on the basis of a given kind of spatial interaction. Examples are a town and its trade area, a factory and its labor shed, the circulation areas of local newspapers (Fig 1.4B), and so on. Administrative regions such as states, provinces, school districts, and so on can also be thought of in part as nodal regions. They are different in one

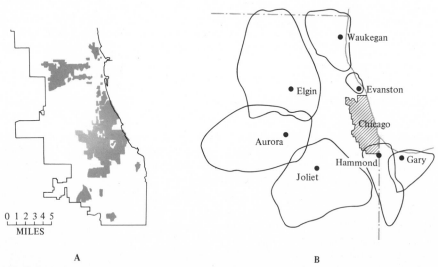

A   B

Fig. 1.4. Uniform and nodal regions in urban geography: (A) nonwhite areas in the city of Chicago, (B) newspaper circulation areas in the Chicago metropolitan area. (*Source:* after Berry, Parsons, and Platt, 1968, Fig. 3.7, and Park and Newcomb, 1933, Fig. 5.)

important respect, however: their boundaries are fixed and discrete. The boundaries of other kinds of nodal regions are determined by the researcher. How and where the boundaries of regions are drawn are essentially matters of classification (Grigg, 1965). Problems in delimiting nodal regions are taken up in connection with the discussion of cities and interaction in Chapter 3. Nodal and administrative regions are hierarchically structured, and they constitute an important feature of the spatial organization of the urban system. Another type of region characteristic of spatial patterns is the *uniform region*. Delimited on the basis of spatial distributions, boundaries are drawn to delimit areas possessing a high degree of internal homogeneity in terms of either one particular characteristic (single-factor regions) or many characteristics taken together (multifactor regions). An example of a single-factor, uniform region is the nonwhite area of a city (Fig. 1.4A); other examples are explicit in the discussion of the internal structure of cities in Part II of this book.

Behavioral Concepts

Although geographers have traditionally been interested in spatial behavior, it is only recently that the study of behavior has been treated explicitly by urban geographers. In the so-called behavioral approach, the emphasis is on the human actors of a system rather than on the objects of the system within which behavior takes place, the goal being to find process-oriented explanations of human activity (Golledge et al., 1972). As a result, a number of exciting new concepts, considerations, and methods have been introduced into urban geography from social psychology and political science. Important among these are those relating to preferences and choice, diffusion and information spread—particularly at the micro scale space searching and learning, decision making, and perception of the environment (Downs, 1970). The emphasis on individuals and small groups is especially relevant in studying behavior within urban areas; for example, in residential site selection (see Chapter 10) and in the study of journey to work and shopping patterns (see Chapter 15). Particularly important concepts include those of *activity and action spaces* (Horton and Reynolds, 1971), and *place utility* (Wolpert, 1965). These and other behavioral concepts are elaborated at various places in Parts II and III.

METHOD IN URBAN GEOGRAPHY

We noted above that with the shift in emphasis in urban geography to the study of spatial organization, work became more analytical and abstract as the methodology of the subject changed. By the methodology of study we mean the conceptual framework within which study is undertaken. Much of current research in urban geography is undertaken within the framework of the scientific method.

The Search for Order

With the adoption of the scientific framework for study, geography became *nomothetic*; the search for laws, regularity, and order in spatial structure became the principal objective. The important thing about order—or chaos, for that matter—is that it is relative to the individual researcher. Order is a concept of the mind. Thus if "we ask of a given region whether its settlements are arranged in some predictable sequence, or its land-use zones are concentric, or its growth cyclical, the answer largely depends on what we are prepared to look for and what we accept as order" (Haggett, 1965, p. 2). In urban geography the search for order is reflected in an increasing concern for generalization, higher degrees of abstraction, and a greater problem orientation.

The Concern with Generalization

We noted above that early studies in urban geography were for the most part concerned with detailed descriptions of towns. Stress was on case studies. The prevailing view was *idiographic*. Since the particular combination of detail making up the urban area differed from city to city, each place was considered to be unique. The concept of uniqueness has played a key role in traditional geography. In a scientific geography, however, it is illogical because it does not permit explanation or the prediction of phenomena; and for science these are the essential concerns. Hence "science is diametrically opposed to the doctrine of uniqueness. It is willing to sacrifice the extreme accuracy obtainable under the uniqueness point of view in order to gain the efficiencies of generalization" (Bunge, 1962, pp. 8–9). Consequently, in most contemporary studies in urban geography much of the fascinating detail about places is purposely sacrificed so that general similarities, regularities, and order in spatial structure may be identified.

More Abstract Study

The identification of regularities in spatial distributions requires that study is undertaken at fairly high levels of abstraction, for it is only in this way that order can be perceived among all the confusing detail. This means that a more selective approach must be adopted in choosing the variables and characteristics thought to be significant in a given context. By restricting choice, greater clarity can be achieved, and the identification of order and chaos is made easier. In this book much of the interesting detail has been sacrificed in this way, and greater attention is given to regularities in spatial structure that have been identified at fairly high levels of generalization.

Abstract study results in another important way: through the use of mathematics. The language of mathematics is more precise than words alone. Hence the use of mathematics makes possible a more precise definition of things and a clearer and more objective identification of underlying relationships and regularities. Abstraction is achieved, then, on two fronts—through greater simplification and through more frequent use of mathematical symbols and arguments. The fundamental objective of both is the formulation of theory and models.

The Concern with Problems

To the layman a problem is something that requires solution. In urban geography such a problem might be, for example, where to locate a new shopping center. The solution to a practical location problem such as this can be arrived at in fundamentally different ways. On the one hand, the solution could be reached intuitively, on the basis of the skill and subject-matter knowledge of the researcher. Alternatively, the problem could be solved by recourse to a theory. For much current work in urban geography, it is this concern with theory that constitutes the overriding problem. This first involves establishing significant relationships by formulating and testing hypotheses. Increasingly the methods of statistical inference are used for this. Once significant relationships have been identified, the problem becomes that of explaining why they are there. The basic problem is consequently that of answering the questions Why? and How?

Stages in Study

There are three distinct but complementary stages in the scientific approach to study: (1) description, (2) explanation, and (3) prediction. Explanation occupies the central position; it is the heart of scientific endeavor. It is necessarily preceded by description, and it leads logically to prediction.

Description

A number of aspects are included under the general heading of description, all of which have to do with the arrangement of facts so that they can be used meaningfully in later study. First there is the question of selecting those facts that are relevant to a given problem. This involves observation in its broadest sense. In many cases where data are not readily available, observation directly involves field study and selection of facts. As Harvey has remarked (1969, p. 298):

> Reality presents the observer with a vast inflow of information. It is the function of observation techniques to select and order this information in a way that makes it manipulable and comprehensible. This process is a kind of search procedure. . . . Clearly, the way in which reality is searched, the particular set of filters (some might call them blinkers) which we use, has an enormous influence upon the kinds of questions we ask and the kinds of answers we are able to give.

Quite clearly this notion of searching reality implies that we have some kind of hypothesis in mind at the outset and in connection with which we are collecting information. Hence in this case we are structuring reality in order to test hypotheses about it. An alternative approach is to search reality in order that hypotheses may be identified. This approach has been characteristic of much urban geographical research. Vast amounts of information are collected, which are then sifted through in the hope of identifying significant hypotheses. Clearly this is not a very efficient way of undertaking study.

Description also involves the problem of defining the observed facts so that a specific meaning can be attached to them. Lastly there is the organization or classification of the facts into some meaningful system. Classification has held a dominant place in the literature of urban geography since it underlies virtually everything we do. Several attempts to classify cities, for example, are discussed in Chapter 7.

Prediction

In science, prediction is usually couched in terms of conditional statements such as "If X, then Y." This simply states that if X occurs, then it should result in, or be associated with, the occurrence of Y. For example, imagine a proposal has been made to build a bypass around a small town in an attempt to reduce traffic congestion in its center. If this were done, it would probably bring about a marked change in the flow of traffic through the town, which might very well have an impact on the town's business. Clearly the planner wants to know whether constructing the bypass will have an adverse effect on the local business community, and if so, how serious this would be.

Obviously the planner cannot experiment by constructing the highway so as to observe what happens. The planner could, however, shed some light on the problem if there were a theory about the impact of bypasses on local business communities, for then the theory could be used to predict the likely effects of constructing the new highway. The theory might tell him, for example, that if the bypass (X) is constructed, there will in all probability be an increase in business turnover (Y) in the town's center. The planner would like to predict the possible outcome of his decisions in order to avoid making mistakes. It is quite clear from this example that prediction is possible in a scientific sense only when we have an adequate theory for the given situation. It is because of this that prediction follows explanation to form the logical third stage in study.

Explanation

The critical stage in study is quite clearly that of explanation. The quest for explanation is the quest for theory. Theories are thus at the heart of explanation in science. Generally speaking, explanation can be viewed as any satisfactory answer to a why or how question. Most of the questions asked in geography have no single answer. There can often be a number of alternative explanations (and hence theories) for the same set of events, each of which may satisfy different researchers. The important point is that explanations should be plausible.

Different explanations for the same events are possible because explanation can be arrived at in alternative ways. In the idiographic context of early studies in urban geography, *genetic* explanation was stressed. This form of explanation consists of a set of declarative sentences about past events which, taken together, describe how the existing situation came about. Although genetic explanation is still found in the work of urban geographers, it is less important because it assumes that events or places are unique. The main forms of explanation in urban geography today are based on logical deductive arguments couched in either *deterministic* or *probabilistic* terms. Deterministic explanation is based on the classic notion of direct cause and effect between events and the specification of necessary and sufficient conditions for their occurrence. In terms of the specific causal factors chosen, one and only one explanation is, by definition, possible. Many events, particularly those associated with behavior in space, are much less predictable, however. For these, explanation must be less specific and couched in terms of probability. In this case, it is accepted that a range of outcomes is possible, each of which can be associated with a given level of probability. A third form of explanation is found to an increasing extent in current work, namely *functional* explanation. In this, events are explained in terms of the functions that objects fulfill in a system. Despite the fact that a number of thorny conceptual problems are associated with functional explanation (see Langton, 1972), it will probably become increasingly important in the future as more studies in geography are undertaken in a systems framework.

MODELS

To bridge the gap between description and explanation, scientists use models. There is a good deal of variation among philosophers of science as to exactly what models are. In everyday language the word "model" has at least three meanings. As a noun it signifies a representation, as, for example, in the case of a model railroad. For many of us this is perhaps its most familiar meaning. As an adjective the word implies an ideal, as, for example, a model home. As a verb, to model means to demonstrate, as, for example, the modeling of new fashions in a fashion show.

In its scientific usage, the concept of a model implies all three meanings. Hence a model is an idealized representation of a part of reality, which is constructed so as to demonstrate certain of its properties. This is the way in which the concept of a model is used in this book. A more catholic view would be, however, that models are primitive theories, laws, hypotheses, hunches, structured ideas, a relation between things, an equation, or a synthesis of data, and sometimes this much broader interpretation is implicit in geographical study (see Chorley and Haggett, 1967) and at times in this book.

Types of Models

An overview of the main types of models used in geography is shown in Table 1.1. The experimental models, in which the properties being investigated are translated into some tangible structure, and the natural models, in which some other circumstance is used as an analogue, are seldom used in urban geography and therefore will not be discussed at any greater length here (see Chorley, 1964). The models most commonly used in urban geography are the graphical and mathematical ones.

Graphical models are the simplest kind of models and have been widely used in studies in urban geography for a long time. They take the form of generalized maps, diagrams, or graphs. As such they are essentially descriptive and consist of a stylized representation of a part of reality as it is or is thought to be. An example is the concentric zonal model of urban form discussed in Chapter 9. Sometimes they are *normative* and portray what ought to be under certain stated conditions. A good example of this is Christaller's model of the settlement pattern of an area discussed in Chapter 6. Many other examples of graphical models will be encountered in the discussions that follow.

Mathematical models have found their place in urban geography more recently. They are abstract and symbolic; the properties of the real world are represented by numbers, relations, equations, and formulas. A basic distinction can be made between *deterministic* and *stochastic* (probabilistic) models which are used in connection with the corresponding forms of explanation discussed above. Geographers have now developed some very sophisticated mathematical models of urban and regional systems (see Wilson, 1974). However, for the most part they are relatively simple; good examples are the gravity and potential models discussed in Chapter 3. Although mathematical models may at first glance appear difficult to understand, with a little patience and willingness the ones presented in this book should not present any real difficulties.

Stages in Model Building

Model building and use is essentially a decision-making process. The principal stages of this are shown in Figure 1.5 to consist of a series of stages (the boxes) linked together in sequence by a series of transformations (connecting lines). Together, these form a circuit starting and ending with the part of the real world under study. Four major stages in the model-building process can be identified.

(1) A simplified version of the real world is first derived by the process of abstraction. This is where huge amounts of information are discarded, where the deadwood is pruned away to reveal what are believed to be the significant variables and relationships in a given situation. It is also at this stage that the subjective element in model building comes to the fore and that assumptions under which the model is meant to hold are made. What is selected as significant for a given problem depends largely on the values and beliefs of the researcher. Consequently, important factors may unknowingly (or purposely) be excluded and "red herrings" often introduced.

Table 1.1. A GENERAL TYPOLOGY OF MODELS USED IN GEOGRAPHY

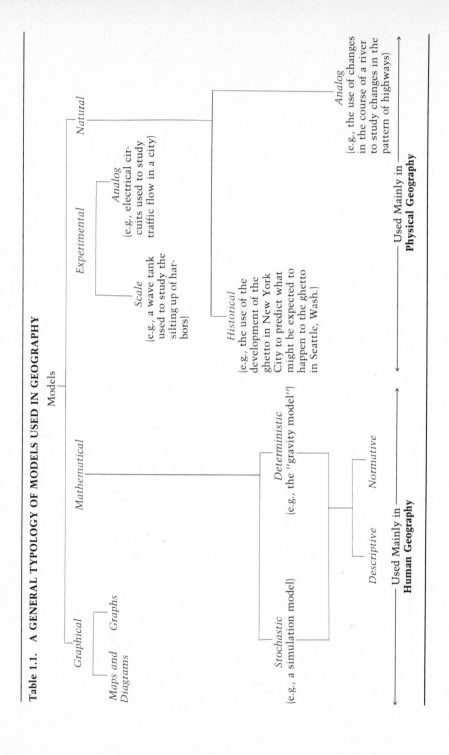

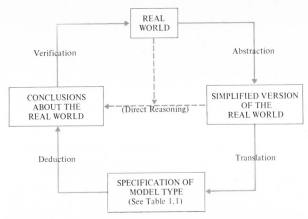

Fig. 1.5. An outline of the stages in model building and use.

The assumptions are usually made to simplify the framework within which the events take place. A common assumption in geographical research is that of an *isotropic surface* (see Chapter 6). It is important for us to remember that it is not always appropriate to criticize these simplifying assumptions on the grounds that they are unrealistic. If in evaluating a model it is felt that something important for the problem has been assumed away, then it must be demonstrated that the conclusions or hypotheses resulting from the model are contradicted by the facts.

(2) The simplified version of the real world is next translated into an appropriate analogue. This is essentially the decision to choose one of the various model types or subtypes shown in Table 1.1. The particular type selected will depend partly on the nature of the problem and partly on the researcher's interests. The underlying objective remains, however, of translating the circumstances being studied into an analogous form that is either simpler to handle, more accessible, or more easily controllable.

(3) Conclusions can now be made from the model about the real world. These may take the form of a set of implications, a number of testable hypotheses, or a set of actual findings. The way in which these are derived depends directly on the type of formal model used. Thus if an experimental model (i.e., a wave tank) was used, observations would be derived by actual experimentation. When mathematical models are used, the conclusions are obtained as a result of the logic of mathematical argument.

(4) The final stage is that of verification—comparing the results of the model with what is known to exist in the real world. Often the findings are verified simply by visual comparison. It is becoming increasingly common, however, to use statistical inference in verifying models. This essentially amounts to a set of rules enabling us to say with a specified level of probability how closely the conclusions from the model match the real world. The great thing about the use of these statistical techniques is that different researchers using the same sets of information should come to the same conclusions.

It is on the basis of using the methods of statistical inference that scientists are able to agree on whether the postulates of the model can be considered a significant explanation of the situation in the real world. If the results of the model can be satisfactorily verified, then the model might be proposed as a theory to be applied in similar situations elsewhere. Hence it is that models are not exactly the same as theories, but can be a useful stage in the formulation of them. As Chorley states (1964, p. 128):

> A model becomes a theory about the real world only when a segment of the real world has been successfully mapped into it, both by avoiding the discarding of too much information in the stage of abstraction. . . . and carrying out rigorous interpretation of the model results into real world terms.

In concluding this brief discussion of models and their development, two points are worth emphasizing. First, models or theories can never be proven to be true. To say that "I have proved that my model is correct" is a meaningless and impossible statement. Models or theories can be shown to be either consistent with the facts or refuted by them, but they can never be proved correct. Second, model building is a reiterative process. The first pass through the circuit may result in conclusions at variance with the real world. The researcher must then ask a number of questions concerning why this is so. Have the significant relationships been identified? Has the most appropriate form of model been used? Is there an error in the calculations? and so on. The answers to questions of this sort may result in modification of the initial model to result in a second, third, and subsequent passes through the circuit, each one of which brings the model closer and closer to reality without sacrificing its generality. It is in this way that good models, those that may eventually stand as theories, are ultimately developed. The models referred to in this book often represent the final result, although in some cases only an initial one, of this reiterative model-building process.

Urban geography today, then, is a broad and diffuse subject. The main emphasis in this book on the spatial organization of urban systems is a comparatively recent one, and of course is not without its shortcomings. However, it is felt that the concepts, considerations, techniques, and models introduced will enable a good understanding of why urban spatial distributions are structured the way they are. It is hoped that this understanding will make it easier to comprehend the complex nature of many important contemporary urban problems and the difficulties planners and politicians face in attempting to solve them.

PART
1

THE CITY
SYSTEM

2
THE EVOLUTION
OF
URBAN PATTERNS

Despite considerable differences in their physical environments and cultural histories, the technically advanced nations of the world today have one thing in common: they are, with some variation, all highly urbanized. Moreover, they have become so in the recent past. Urbanization is a relatively new phenomenon, dating essentially from the beginning of the nineteenth century. Even before 1850 no society could be described as predominantly urbanized; and by 1900 only one—Great Britain—could be so regarded. Yet today, scarcely 75 years later, all the industrialized nations are highly urbanized, and throughout the world the urbanization process is accelerating rapidly.

Quite clearly something dramatic occurred to bring about so radical a transformation of the distribution of population in such a short span of time. The purpose of this chapter is to look more closely at the main forces that lay behind the process of urbanization, to trace in general terms the evolution and spread of large cities in the United States and Canada, and to discuss some of the main features of the present-day system in North America.

THE URBAN TRANSFORMATION

The complex process of social and economic change whereby a society is transformed from an essentially rural to a predominantly urban one is called *urbanization*. The stage the process has reached in a particular country at a given point in time is indicated by the *level* of urbanization, defined as the proportion of the total population living in urban places. Clearly, this in turn depends on the way in which places are defined as urban in official statistics. There is no universally accepted definition of urban places, and considerable differences exist from country to country in the definition used. Thus, for example, in Denmark places with 200 inhabitants are called urban; in Korea a place with less than 40,000 is not. In Canada, places are officially designated as urban if they have at least 1,000 inhabitants, while 2,500 is the critical figure in the United States.

The increasing level of urbanization since 1790 is shown for the United States and its four major census regions in Table 2.1. Except for the decade 1810–1820, when events were interrupted by the War of 1812, every federal census since 1790 has reported a growing number of people living in urban places. The same has been true of Canada since about 1870. In the United States the process of urbanization was a very gradual one throughout most of the nineteenth century, mainly because the growth of the urban population in the eastern states was continually being offset partly by the opening up of new rural territory to the west. Despite this, by 1870 the nation was 25 percent urbanized; only 50 years later, in 1920, over half the total population was urban. Today the proportion is about 75 percent. In Canada about 72 percent of the population in 1971 lived in incorporated cities, towns, and villages with more than 2,500 inhabitants.

Within a country, the level of urbanization often varies considerably at a given point in time from one region to another, as is shown for the United States in Table 2.1 (cols. 3–6). The Northeast region, which today is the most highly urbanized, was more than 50 percent urbanized by 1880; the North Central and Western regions, together with the nation, by 1920; while the South failed to reach this level before the mid-fifties. Moreover, within each major census region, marked differences also occurred in the level of urbanization of individual states at each census period. These differences are shown for selected dates in Figure 2.1. For example, whereas Rhode Island and Massachusetts were both more than half urbanized by 1870, Mississippi was still predominantly rural and the least urbanized of all states in 1960 (37.7 percent urban). In 1970, Vermont and West Virginia were the least urbanized, with 32.2 and 39.0 percent, respectively, and were the only two states to have experienced an absolute decline in urban population in the decade 1960–1970. In terms of the level of urbanization, therefore, many states lag behind those in southern New England by 50 to 60 years, while some states in the deep South lagged until recently by more than a century (Lampard, 1968).

Although the increase in the level of urbanization in the United States and Canada, as in other countries, can in part be explained by growth in the number of urban places (see Table 2.1, col. 1), the most important factor has been the growth in their size. Significant in this respect was the emergence of urban places in the United States with more than 250,000 inhabitants by 1840 and of the cities with populations of a million by the end of the nineteenth century. By 1970, nearly 70 percent of the national population lived in places with at least 50,000 inhabitants designated as "standard met-

Table 2.1.   TOTAL NUMBER OF URBAN PLACES AND LEVELS OF URBANIZATION, UNITED STATES, 1790 to 1970

Date	Number of Cities ≥2500 (1)	Percent Population Urban				
		U.S. (2)	North-east (3)	South (4)	North-Central (5)	West (6)
1790	24	5.1	8.1	2.1	—	—
1800	33	6.1	9.3	3.0	—	—
1810	46	7.3	10.9	4.1	0.9	—
1820	61	7.2	11.0	4.6	1.1	—
1830	90	8.8	14.2	5.3	2.6	—
1840	131	10.8	18.5	6.7	3.9	—
1850	236	15.3	26.5	8.3	9.2	6.4
1860	392	19.8	35.7	9.6	13.9	16.0
1870	663	25.7	44.3	12.2	20.8	25.8
1880	939	28.2	50.8	12.2	24.2	30.2
1890	1348	35.1	59.0	16.3	33.1	37.0
1900	1740	39.6	61.1	18.0	38.6	39.9
1910	2262	45.6	71.8	22.5	45.1	47.9
1920	2722	51.2	75.5	28.1	52.3	51.8
1930	3165	56.1	77.6	34.1	57.9	58.4
1940	3464	56.5	76.6	36.7	58.4	58.5
1950	4054	59.6	75.4	44.6	61.1	59.9
New definition						
1950	4284	64.0	79.5	48.6	64.1	69.5
1960	5445	69.9	80.2	58.5	68.7	77.7
1970	6435	73.5	80.4	64.6	71.6	82.9

[a] States included in each major census region are shown in Figure 2.1.
Source: U.S. Bureau of the Census. *U.S. Census of Population: 1970. Number of Inhabitants, United States Summary*, Tables 7 and 20. (Washington, D.C.: U.S. Government Printing Office, 1971.)

ropolitan statistical areas" (smsa's), and 67.5 percent of all Americans lived in smsa's larger than 100,000; the corresponding figure for Canada was 47.5 percent in 1971 living in "census metropolitan areas" (cma's) larger than 100,000.

General Factors in Urban Growth

The increase in level of urbanization and the accompanying growth of cities in North America since 1800 is a reflection of profound changes that occurred in the economic and social organization of society, caused initially by the Industrial Revolution. Although the details of change are complex indeed, a number of general factors can be identified that have permitted the growth of large cities.

An obvious first prerequisite was an efficient agricultural system able to produce surplus quantities of food to sustain the urban population. In this respect the United States was in the fortunate position of having extensive areas of virgin agricultural land that could be brought into use throughout most of the nineteenth century. Even an extensive agriculture was able to produce vast surpluses. From the latter part of the nineteenth century onward, improvements in farming technology and method permitted a substantial reduction in the number of people needed to work in agriculture, thereby

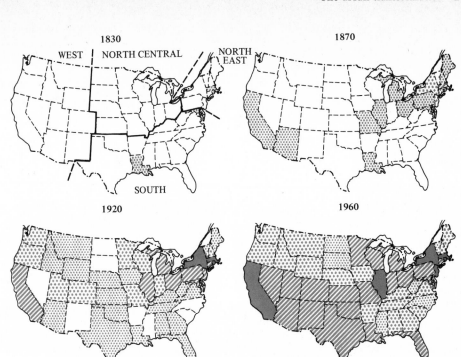

Fig. 2.1. Levels of urbanization in the United States at selected time periods. (*Source*: U.S. Bureau of the Census, *Census of Population, 1960. Number of Inhabitants, United States Summary*, Table 10.)

releasing surplus labor to fill the growing number of jobs in the cities. Following the widespread use of the tractor and other mechanized equipment after about 1920, the proportion of the total population living on farms in the United States decreased from 30 percent to only 5 percent in 1970 (Chinitz and Dusansky, 1972). By 1971, only 6.6 percent of the Canadian population was classified as rural farm dwellers.

A second basic prerequisite for urban growth was the scientific discoveries and mechanical inventions that made possible power-driven machinery. The introduction of the steam engine after about 1830 was without doubt the most important, since it made possible the concentration of production into bigger factories requiring large numbers of workers. With the introduction of steam power, coal replaced wood and water as the primary source of industrial energy; and thereafter urbanization rapidly became synonymous with industrialization on a large scale. As the scale and complexity of industry increased, a division of labor became a necessity; and strong agglomerative forces based on external economies favored concentration of production and distribution in cities (see Chapter 5). Of course, not all urban growth was based on the development of manufacturing. Many smaller places grew up solely as collection and distribution centers for their surrounding areas.

Since 1920, employment in the service, or tertiary, sector of the labor force has been the most important single factor in the growth of cities. Until then, employment in the primary (agriculture, forestry, and mining) and secondary (manufacturing) sectors had dominated the structure of national employment and contributed most to the growth of cities. Since 1920, however, their share has been less than half and falling rapidly accompanying the phenomenal growth of white-collar occupations. The growth of this sector of the labor force has been the most important single factor in the growth of cities, especially the large metropolitan areas, in the twentieth century.

A third important factor was the development of an efficient transportation system. This was essential not only to bring into the cities food and raw materials for the growing industries, but also to distribute the finished products. Moreover, cities could grow in size only if there were a proper intraurban transportation system enabling mass movement of people between home and work places. The growth of cities in the last 150 years has therefore been dependent on a series of technological changes in transportation. Especially important was the introduction and spread of the railroads after about 1850. Although the impact of the railroads on the spread of cities was dramatic, the widespread use of the automobile in the twentieth century has been a phenomenal force in reshaping the internal structure of urban areas and the decentralization of people and jobs within them.

Fourth, demographic and social factors have played important parts in city growth. Until relatively late in the nineteenth century, cities—and especially the largest ones—experienced a natural decrease in population; the number of deaths exceeded the number of births in them. Growth in urban population depended largely on the migration of people from rural areas to the growing cities, and in North America, on immigration from abroad (Ward, 1971). Since the turn of the century, however, improvements in medicine and urban sanitary conditions have resulted in a natural increase in city population. Today, urban growth is largely self-generating. Although migration is still important, it is the movement of people from small cities to larger ones rather than rural-urban migration that has become the most significant mechanism in urban population growth in recent decades (Gibbs, 1963).

Although it is the economic opportunities of the city that have exerted the greatest pull on migrants, the social advantages of life in the city have played a contributing role. The prospective excitement of city life has exerted a persuasive influence on migration patterns throughout the period of rapid urban growth. Today the wide range of cultural facilities found in the larger metropolitan centers is important because it encourages a highly educated cadre to live in them. It is from the ranks of these people that key personnel are recruited, which in turn means that the larger cities have become increasingly attractive as the locations for employment in the now rapidly growing administrative and service sectors of the economy.

THE METROPOLITAN UNITED STATES

The structure of the present urban system is the cumulative result of a growth process that rapidly gained momentum after the early decades of the nineteenth century. By about 1920 to 1930, the basic features of the present urban pattern dominated by large metropolitan centers had jelled. In the same period the national economy completed its transition from a commercial-mercantilist base to an extremely complex industrial-capitalist one (Pred, 1965), the spatial dimension of which was dominated by the emergence and consolidation of a core area, the *heartland*, and its evolving relationships with the peripheral regions—the *hinterlands*. Against this background, two general factors have been particularly important in molding the pattern of growth, spread, and spatial integration of the urban system. The first of these was a series of resource-converting and space-adjusting changes in the technology of industrial processes and transportation. Together these brought about a continual reappraisal and definition of the national resource base. Second, there was a series of great migrations that sought to exploit the newly appreciated and changing resource base on which large-scale urban growth and the development of a spatially integrated urban system were based.

The Stages of Growth

From an analysis of major technological innovations, Borchert (1967) has identified four critical epochs in the evolution of the metropolitan pattern (Table 2.2), and has provided us with a fascinating series of maps that show the growth and spread of cities since 1790 (Figs. 2.2–2.6). On these maps cities are classified by population size into five orders (size classes), the lower limits of which are higher at each epoch to take account of the increasing scale of urban growth through time. For example, the threshold for a fourth-order city in 1790 was 15,000 inhabitants; this would have made it a sizable city at that time. However, to maintain its status as a fourth-order city it would need a population of at least 250,000 in 1960. The fact that cities were able to increase in population size is closely related to the changes that took place in their internal structure. Although these are not discussed here, it should be kept in mind that changes in transportation technology also had a profound impact on the form and spatial extent of cities during each epoch (see Chapter 8).

The Sail-Wagon Epoch, 1790–1830

In 1790 the major cities were ports along the Atlantic coast and on the navigable rivers. The exceptions were Worcester, Mass., and Pittsburgh. The largest cities were New York (33,181), Philadelphia (28,522), and Boston; together with Baltimore and Charleston, S.C., these contained just over half of the nation's urban population (Fig. 2.2). The economic orientation of the larger cities was primarily commercial, and they

Table 2.2.   CRITICAL STAGES IN THE EVOLUTION OF THE
CITY SYSTEM, UNITED STATES, 1790–1970

Epoch	Major Innovation	Stimulus	New Territories
Sail and wagon 1790–1830	–	Agricultural settlement	Eastern Midwest
Age of steam 1830–1870	Steam engine in land and water transportation	Agricultural settlement, small-scale manufacturing, mining, canals	Midwest, Lakes states, Gulf Coast
Steel 1870–1920	Steel and electricity	Large-scale manufacturing, mining, tertiary activity	High Plains, West Coast, South
Automobile era 1920–1970	Automobile, airplane	Tertiary activity, amenity resources	Gulf Coast, South, Southwest

SOURCE: Based on Borchert (1967).

functioned as centers of trade and finance for relatively small-sized agricultural hinterlands. They were, in fact, the mercantilist outposts of England, and as such could be
regarded as a peripheral part of the European city system at that time.

The first decades of the nineteenth century saw the beginning of modest independent urban growth (Table 2.3). The higher order towns were becoming the outlets for
capital accumulated from commercial agriculture and the centers from which the
development of the interior proceeded. Arable land was the resource that counted, and
the infant regional economies were developing a certain archetype: "a good deepwater
port was the nucleus of an agricultural hinterland well adapted to the production of a
staple commodity in demand on the world market" (Berry and Horton, 1970, p. 22).

Despite the spread and consolidation of the network of post roads and turnpikes
within the settled areas, distance overland was still an effective barrier to movement,
especially for goods. Pittsburgh was, for example, still four days' travel from New York
City in 1830. It was in this epoch that the short-lived boom in canals occurred, especially in New York, Pennsylvania, and Ohio. The most successful of all the canals was
without doubt the 350-mile Erie Canal, between Albany and Buffalo, which, when
opened in 1825, created a through waterway between the Atlantic and the Great Lakes.
Consequently water transportation was still dominant and apart from the new cities in
the Great Valley, the boom cities of the period were closely tied to inland waterways
and the extension of the agricultural frontier (Fig. 2.3). The higher order cities on the

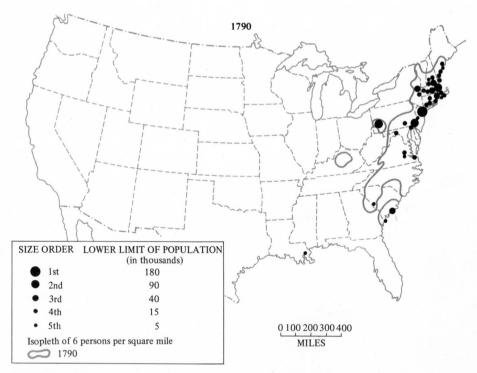

Fig. 2.2. Distribution of major towns in the United States, 1790. (*Source*: after Borchert, 1967, Fig 6.)

Atlantic coast continued to dominate the infant urban system, and by 1830 the role of New York City as the nation's commercial and financial center had been permanently secured.

The Age of Steam, 1830–1870

During this period the Appalachian barrier was penetrated and extensive urban growth occurred for the first time in the Midwest. By 1870 New York City had emerged as the nation's only first-order center, one-quarter of the nation's population was urban, and there had been a rapid growth in both the number and population size of cities of all orders (Table 2.3). This minor urban revolution was made possible by the development of an integrated inland transportation system, which permitted the commercial exploitation of the agricultural, mineral, fuel, and power resources of the newly settled territory. The keys to urban growth during this epoch, then, were the developments that occurred in transportation technology; this was the era of the steamboat and of the emergence of the railroad.

The first decades of the epoch were the heyday of the river towns on the Ohio-Mississippi-Missouri system, particularly New Orleans, Cincinnati, and St. Louis. St. Louis doubled its trade with New Orleans, which even by 1835 had a larger volume than New York City. By 1850 New Orleans had become the nation's third largest city, a

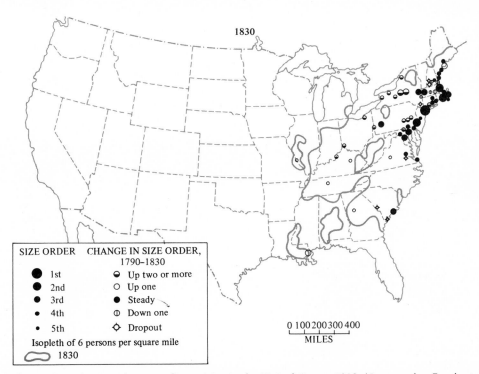

Fig. 2.3. Distribution of metropolitan cities in the United States, 1830. (*Source*: after Borchert, 1967, Fig. 7.)

rank it was to lose shortly afterward as a result of the shifting alignment of trade and economic growth brought about by the rapid development of the railroad network. In 1850 there were 9,000 miles of track; by 1860 this had swelled to 31,000; and by 1870 to 53,000 miles. The continent had been spanned, and the basic framework of America's future railroad network had been laid down. However, in the initial period of extensive spread, the limitations of technology—the iron rails and light equipment—essentially made the railroads complementary to the waterways for long-haul traffic. As a result, most of the boom cities of the epoch were the great ports and particularly those serving as the gateways to the agricultural regions of the Midwest (Fig. 2.4). The importance of St. Louis and Cincinnati was reinforced, while by 1870 Chicago had emerged as the nation's most important railroad center, the terminal of 11 trunk and 20 branch and feeder lines. Elsewhere in the northeastern region, the railroads acted as a new stimulus to urban growth as the settled areas of the interior, and hence their products, were brought closer to the east. But new resources were becoming important and a different set of locational forces was coming into play there.

These were related to the newer materials and energy sources on which the continued growth of small-scale manufacturing industry was increasingly based. Although the steam engine had been applied to industry early in the epoch, its impact was local-

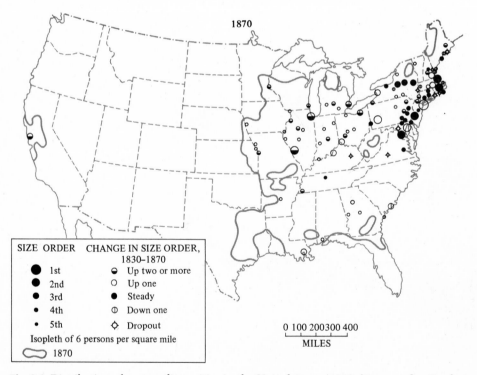

Fig. 2.4. Distribution of metropolitan cities in the United States, 1870. (*Source*: after Borchert, 1967, Fig. 8.)

Table 2.3. NUMBER OF CITIES AND TOTAL POPULATION BY SIZE ORDER, UNITED STATES, 1790–1970

Size Order	1790	1830	1870	1920	1960[a]	1970
NUMBER OF CENTERS						
First	0	0	1	1	1	1
Second	3	3	6	4	6	9
Third	8	8	14	16	19	28
Fourth	20	29	33	51	70	84
Fifth	8	12	37	75	82	107
TOTAL	39	52	91	147	178	228
TOTAL POPULATION (THOUSANDS)						
First[b]	—	—	2,171	8,490	14,760	16,178
Second	514	1,120	3,301	10,364	28,826	36,513
Third	499	784	3,627	13,918	26,493	35,572
Fourth	530	1,812	2,533	12,829	30,473	34,867
Fifth	95	300	1,826	6,972	12,647	15,524
SMSA TOTAL	1,638	4,016	13,458	52,573	113,199	138,655
U.S. TOTAL	3,929	12,866	39,818	105,711	179,323	203,121

[a] Includes only SMSA's over 80,000 in 1960 and 1970.
[b] 1960 and 1970 population totals are for the New York–Northeastern New Jersey Standard Consolidated Areas.
SOURCE: Borchert (1967), p. 315, Table 2.

ized owing to the high costs of transporting coal over long distances. Consequently, water was still the dominant source of power for the developing industries, and even as late as 1870 water wheels still provided approximately half of the inanimate energy for manufacturing. However, as first the railroads and then newer types of manufacturing industry developed and spread, there was a growing demand for coal and iron, the relative locations of which rapidly emerged as a major factor in industrial location by the end of the period. Boom cities appeared in the anthracite region of Pennsylvania, and Pittsburgh attained second-order status for the first time. Detroit, Cleveland, and Buffalo grew significantly, and throughout the Northeast the railroads added a new dimension to urban growth. The heartland of North America was now beginning to take shape. Outside this area there was relatively little growth of large cities. Fourth- and fifth-order cities had grown up along the Missouri River; San Francisco had attained second-order status; and New Orleans was still the only large city in the South.

The Steel Epoch, 1870–1920

The key to urban growth in this epoch was the development in manufacturing and its ancillary activities. Initially based on the growth of the iron and steel industry, the development of manufacturing was stimulated by a series of further inventions, such as the electric power station (1882) and the gasoline motor (1883), which passed into general use by the turn of the century. At the same time, significant changes occurred in the organization of industrial and commercial interprises with the formation after 1870 of limited-liability joint stock companies. Backed mainly by the large financial houses, these new companies permitted the development of market-oriented manufacturing industry on a scale never before experienced.

Urban growth based on manufacturing would have been impossible without the extension and consolidation of the railroad network. By 1910 there were some 240,000 miles of track in operation and gauges had been standardized. Steel rails replaced iron, and steel made possible the construction of larger locomotives and heavier equipment. This in turn permitted longer and cheaper hauls of raw materials, particularly coal. The average freight charge per ton-mile was reduced from 3.31 cents in 1865 to 0.70 cents in 1892; and the average length of haul increased from 110 miles per ton in 1822 to 250 miles per ton in 1910 (Pred, 1965).

Changes in the pattern of cities during this period are shown in Figure 2.5. Although many smaller ports on the Ohio-Mississippi-Missouri river system, the Hudson River, and along the New England coast declined, as did small industrial cities at important water-power sites along the Mohawk and Merrimack rivers, the picture elsewhere was generally one of unprecedented growth and spread based on industrialization and the exploitation of new resources. Urbanization had jumped to the West Coast and by 1920 Seattle, Portland, San Francisco, and Los Angeles had developed into sizable urban centers. Inland, Salt Lake City and Denver had reached metropolitan status by the end of the epoch. New cities grew up in conjunction with the exploitation of new

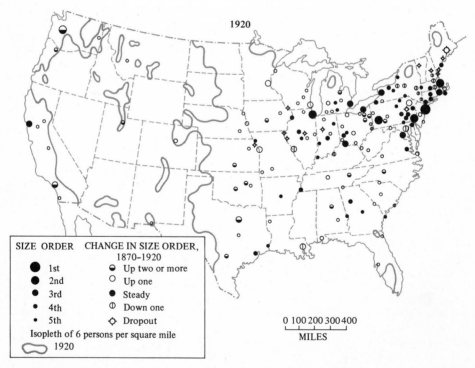

Fig. 2.5. Distribution of metropolitan cities in the United States, 1920. (*Source*: after Borchert, 1967, Fig. 9.)

minerals, such as Butte copper, the Lake Superior iron ores, and the lead and zinc deposits of northeastern Missouri. Others grew in conjunction with the spread of farming into the Great Valley of California and on the prairies of Texas and Oklahoma. As agriculture boomed, service centers and agriculturally oriented manufacturing followed; and the hierarchy of smaller sized central places emerged to become a distinctive feature in the urban pattern throughout America, especially in the Midwest (see Chapter 6). In the South, Birmingham (founded in 1871) rose to metropolitan status as its iron and steel industry expanded, and it was soon the focal point for a series of smaller satellite mining and smelting cities. Elsewhere in the region, the growth of the textile industry became a major urbanizing force, but only on a small scale. Despite these developments, however, the South remained still predominantly rural in 1920 (Table 2.1).

Spectacular as the expansion of settlement and the growth of cities were in the new territories of the West, the most significant changes in the urban pattern occurred in the older settled areas of the East, particularly in the area bounded by the Lake Superior iron ores, the Pennsylvania coalfields, and the financial and entrepreneurial resources of the Northeast—in the heartland of the American manufacturing belt. Here the close juxtaposition of coal, iron ore, and growing rural and urban markets provided the impetus for the large-scale, concentrated growth of cities based on manufacturing and processing industries serving the national market. Accompanying the growth of the iron and steel industry, clusters of boom cities appeared on the coalfields of western Pennsylvania, West Virginia, and eastern Kentucky in response to the demand for bituminous coal. Outside the coalfield areas, the expansion of manufacturing and the distributive trades enabled Chicago, Cleveland, Detroit, and Buffalo to grow and maintain their high-order status. A cluster of boom cities emerged between Pittsburgh and Lake Erie, while many new fourth- and fifth-order manufacturing cities grew up rapidly in Michigan, Ohio, Indiana, and southern Wisconsin (Fig. 2.5). In this epoch, the five largest cities increased their share of the national population faster than in any other; the population size of the third-order cities rapidly increased; the fourth-and fifth-order cities registered their greatest growth in the period up to 1920 (Table 2.3); and the basic features of a metropolitan United States had been established.

The Heartlands and the Hinterlands

The evolution of the urban pattern up to 1920 and its subsequent elaboration in the decades immediately following must be seen as part of the growth and spatial integration of the national economy. In this context, the relationships between the urban-industrial heartland and the subnational economies of the peripheral hinterlands formed a major, underlying spatial-organizational theme. As cumulative urban-industrial specialization intensified, the heartland became increasingly dependent on the products of the hinterlands, each of which found its comparative advantage in narrow and intensive specialization in a few resource subsectors. As a result, the spatial dimension of the national economy became a "great heartland nucleation of industry and the national market [surrounded by] the resource dominant regional hinterlands specializing in the production of resource and intermediate outputs for which the heartland reaches out to satisfy the input requirements of its great manufacturing plants" (Perloff and Wingo, 1961, p. 211). Flows of raw materials inward and of finished products outward articulated the whole into a spatial economic system dominated by the largest cities.

The evolution of the urban pattern closely reflected these relationships. Aided by a number of initial advantages, large-scale industrial growth was concentrated increasingly in the cities of the heartland. This in turn became the focus around which the subsequent growth, spread, and functional specialization of the major regional centers was organized. As we have seen, by 1920 these included New Orleans in the South, Minneapolis in the mid-continental plains, and San Francisco in northern California. By 1940 Los Angeles dominated southern California and Kansas City had emerged in the central plains. Since then, Seattle has become the focus of the Pacific Northwest and Dallas, Houston, and Phoenix have emerged as regional centers in Texas and the Southwest. A process of "circular and cumulative causation" strengthened and maintained the "relationship of the national heartland to the hinterlands — of the core to the periphery — and the new metropolitan centers that emerged [outside the heartland] did so in consequence of the over-all growth, outward spread, and spatial integration of the national economy" (Berry and Horton, 1970, p. 35).

Recent Developments

Since 1920, and particularly after World War II, large-scale metropolitan growth has continued to be the dominant trend (Table 2.4). By 1970, 69 percent of the total population of the United States lived in metropolitan areas, and almost 75 percent of this total lived in smsa's with more than 500,000 inhabitants. Recent patterns of growth and spread reflect an alteration in locational forces associated with (1) changes in the composition of the labor force, particularly the growth of employment in white-collar occupations since World War II; (2) rising real incomes and higher individual mobility; and (3) the spectacular advances in technology which have permitted a newer form of economic and spatial organization: "instead of heavy crude products, light and increasingly complex ones; instead of coal, electricity; instead of the universal railway, increasing dependence on the motor vehicle; instead of concentration in congested centers, freedom of location through improved communications" (Hall, 1966, p. 24). People and jobs, it could now be argued, were free to locate almost anywhere. The latest phase in the evolution of the urban pattern has been characterized, then, by three main trends:

Table 2.4. **POPULATION CHANGE IN STANDARD METROPOLITAN STATISTICAL AREAS, 1940–1970**

	Number of Areas				Population (Thousands)			
smsa Size	1970	1960	1950	1940	1970	1960	1950	1940
3,000,000 or more	6	5	5	3	37,710	31,763	25,789	16,476
1,000,000–3,000,000	27	19	10	9	42,946	29,818	16,628	16,210
500,000–1,000,000	32	29	21	16	21,936	19,215	14,439	11,057
250,000– 500,000	60	48	44	36	19,761	15,829	15,209	12,008
100,000– 250,000	92	89	89	76	14,973	14,498	15,046	12,075
under 100,000	26	22	43	72	2,091	1,761	3,205	5,005
Total	243	212	212	212	139,419	112,885	89,317	72,836

1. Increasing deconcentration of national growth.
2. Spectacular decentralization at the more local scale.
3. The emergence of supermetropolitan or *megalopolitan* areas at the regional level.

Figure 2.6 shows the changes that had occurred in the city system by 1960, and which have continued essentially up to the present. Deconcentration of urban growth, especially since 1950, reflects the increasing importance of amenity resources in the location of newer types of "footloose" industries, the rapidly growing "quaternary" sector (e.g., research and development establishments), and the non-job-oriented population. Consequently, growth has occurred to an increasing extent in the "outer rim" of the country at locations "relatively well endowed with such amenities as advances in technology have reduced the time and costs involved in the previous heartland-hinterland relationships" (Berry and Horton, 1970, p. 35).

As a result, new or higher-order cities appeared in the oilfield areas of western Texas and the Gulf Coast. An almost spectacular growth of metropolitan centers had taken place in Florida, the Southwest desert, and southern California, while all the cities on the West Coast except Seattle had moved up one or two ranks in size order by 1960. In the decade 1960–1970, the SMSA population of the West major census region increased by a further 28 percent, in Arizona by 42 percent, and in Nevada by a staggering 86 percent. By 1970 California had emerged as the nation's most metropolitanized state, with 93 percent of the population living in SMSA's. The strong trend toward urbanization and metropolitan growth in the South census region during the past 15 years is reflected in a 37 percent increase in metropolitan population in Florida, 30 percent in Maryland, and 26 percent in Delaware and Georgia respectively. In contrast, the average rate of metropolitan population growth in the states comprising the Northeast and North Central census regions was only about 10 percent during the 1960–1970 decade.

The effects of technological developments on reducing the constraints of geographic space that underlie this deconcentration of urban growth have also profoundly affected the form and structure of metropolitan areas themselves (see Chapter 8). Modern forms of communication and transportation, especially the automobile and truck,

Percentage Change			
1960–70	**1950–60**	**1940–50**	**1940–70**
18.7	23.2	56.5	128.9
44.0	79.3	2.6	164.9
14.2	33.1	30.6	98.4
24.8	4.1	26.7	64.6
0.3	3.2	16.3	24.0
18.7	−45.0	−35.9	−58.2
23.5	26.4	22.6	91.4

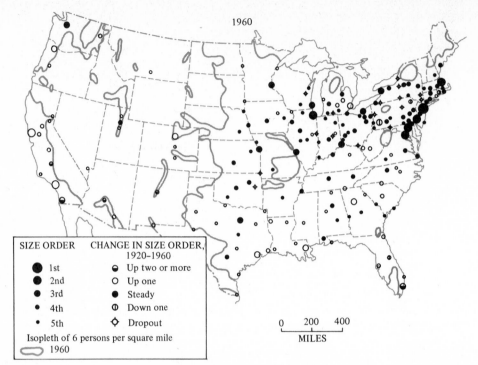

Fig. 2.6. Distribution of metropolitan cities in the United States, 1960. (*Source*: after Borchert, 1967, Fig. 10.)

have caused decentralization, sprawl, and declining overall densities to become the dominant spatial processes in the growth and spread of metropolitan areas at the local-regional scale. Whereas lower densities are typical of the younger metropolitan areas, whatever the age of cities, overall densities have declined significantly in recent decades as even the oldest cities have responded to changing technology and increasing affluence.

Between 1950 and 1970 the average density of all urbanized areas in the United States declined from 5408 persons per square mile to 3376; in the central cities the decline was from 7786 to 4463 (Berry, 1973b). In the decade 1950–1960, the population of the central cities of the 212 SMSA's increased by only 10 percent compared with a growth of 49 percent in their outlying suburban parts. This trend has been especially marked in the older metropolitan areas that grew in the period of rapid industrialization at the end of the last century. The central cities of Baltimore, Boston, Philadelphia, Pittsburgh, Chicago, Detroit, and St. Louis have all experienced declining populations. Of the 21 central cities with populations exceeding 500,000 in 1960, 15 lost population in the 1960–1970 decade. The picture is the same for jobs and many urban institutions, which have also been suburbanizing to an increasing extent.

The process of decentralization has been accelerating at such a pace that virtually all recent metropolitan growth has been concentrated in rapidly extending, and often newly annexed, suburban territory; so much so, in fact, that terms like "city," the continuously built-up "urbanized area," and even the current census definition of the SMSA have perhaps all been superseded by the changing realities of daily urban life. The process of decentralization has created metropolitan areas of a newer and even larger kind, which Berry (1968a) has termed "Daily Urban Systems"—which in many cases extend for more than 100 miles from the traditional city centers (Fig. 2.7). The core-oriented urban structure implied by terms like "central city" is rapidly disappearing. Instead, "today's daily urban systems appear to be multi-nodal multi-connected social systems in action. The essence of any such system is its linkages and interactions, as changed by changing modes of communication" (Berry, 1973b, p. 55). More than 90 percent of the national population lived within these systems in 1960; today the figure is almost certainly as high as 95 percent.

Megalopolis

The continued sprawl and physical coalescence of adjacent metropolitan areas resulting from decentralization, and the complex overlapping of "daily urban systems," have, since about 1950, given rise to metropolitan growth and spread at a new and increasingly larger geographic scale. Nowhere in the world does the scale of this newer form of urban growth match that found today along the now almost continuously urbanized seaboard of the United States between Boston and Washington, D.C. To capture

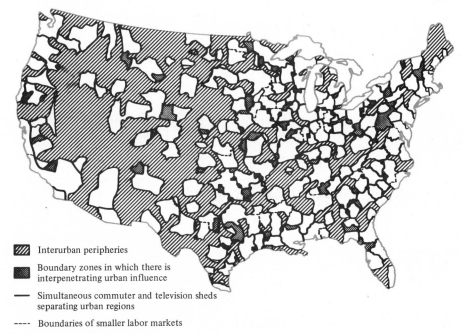

▨ Interurban peripheries

▪ Boundary zones in which there is interpenetrating urban influence

— Simultaneous commuter and television sheds separating urban regions

---- Boundaries of smaller labor markets

Fig. 2.7. "Daily Urban Systems" of the United States, 1960. (*Source*: after Berry, 1970, Fig. 3.)

the very special significance of this new form of supermetropolitan region, Gottmann (1961) coined the term *Megalopolis.*

The dimensions of Megalopolis are staggering. Today it stretches for more than 600 miles from north to south. Varying in width between 50 and 150 miles, it extends over an area of more than 55,000 square miles (Fig. 2.8). In 1970 it was the home of about 37 million Americans. Thus about 20 percent of the total population of the con- terminous United States are concentrated in an almost continuously urbanized region that accounts for only about 2 percent of the national territory. Within the region are five of America's largest metropolitan areas—Boston, New York, Philadelphia, Balti- more, and Washington, D.C.—besides another dozen or so smaller ones ranging in size from 200,000 to 800,000. In spite of recent trends toward lower density developments, the overall density of land use means that population densities are still invariably high; in 1970, the average was over 500 persons per square mile.

The high level of population concentration reflects the wealth of economic opportunities that Megalopolis has accumulated. In 1970, about 12.8 million were employed in the region—almost 23 percent of the total number of persons employed in the entire country. As Gottman (1961) pointed out, there are not very many nations in the world today with labor forces much larger than this. Moreover, the labor market has traditionally catered to the white-collar occupations; hence blue-collar jobs have tended to be underrepresented. As a result, per capita income is still on average among the highest in the country; and despite the recent urban-economic growth in other regions, Megalopolis is still today the largest market in the United States for well-paid labor.

Here, too, the scale of problems associated with supermetropolitan growth have reached their climax (Browning, 1974). Chief among these are those associated with deprivation, deterioration, and congestion. A surprisingly large segment of the popu- lation is socially and economically deprived; for these the quality of life and living con- ditions fall far below the average. It is also this group that feels most acutely the deterio- ration of the urban environment. The problems of an aging and dilapidated housing stock, of the ghetto and the slum, shortages of open space and inadequate recreational facilities, and the general running down of social facilities have reached their extreme proportions in the older central cities of the region, and particularly in New York City. And it is, of course, in the older central cities that most of the socially and economically deprived Americans are forced to live. Problems of deterioration are closely bound up with those of congestion; high residential densities and overcrowding, traffic snarls on the ground and increasingly in the air, overfilled parks and crowded beaches are just some of the more obvious ones. Although the problems associated with congestion are naturally greatest in the innermost parts of the metropolitan areas, it is becoming increasingly clear that these problems are also likely to emerge to an increasing degree in the area of sprawling suburbs too.

Of course, the specific characteristics and problems of Megalopolis stem in large part from the long tradition of urban growth and concentration in this particular region. However, many of the problems are more general and typical of large-scale, intensive urban development. Today megalopolitan growth is well under way, albeit at lesser scales and densities, between Pittsburgh and Cleveland; Chicago and Detroit; along the east coast of Florida; and in the Far West between Los Angeles and San Diego. And

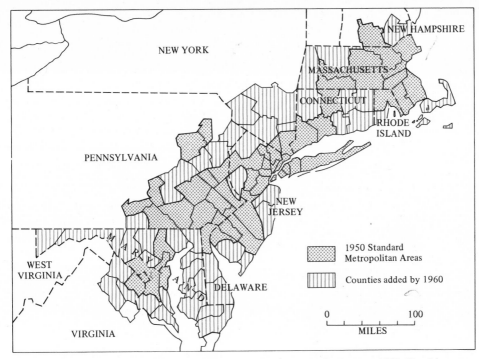

Fig. 2.8. Megalopolis as delimited by Gottmann, 1960. (*Source*: Gottmann, 1961, Fig. 3.)

urban growth at such gigantic scale, and all that this implies, is expected to become even more pronounced in the future (see Chapter 20). Megalopolitan growth has, then, from many viewpoints now emerged as the "new order in the organization of inhabited space."

METROPOLITAN CANADA

Canada is also a highly urbanized and industrialized country today, with an urban system dominated by large metropolitan centers. However, the scale, age, spatial pattern, and historical development of the present-day urban system differ in a number of important respects from those in the United States. In large part this reflects the different cultural, political, and economic framework within which urbanization has taken place in Canada. For example, the fact that the country is dominated today not by a single large metropolis, but by two metropolitan areas of almost equal size (Montreal and Toronto), is a direct result of the traditional rivalry between the English- and French-speaking sections of the country.

With a population of only 22.4 million in 1974, the scale of urban growth in Canada is necessarily smaller in absolute terms. Whereas Canada could boast only three metropolitan areas with more than one million inhabitants in 1971 (Montreal, Toronto, and Vancouver), there were 33 SMSA's of comparable size in the United States in 1970. Moreover, in 1971 Canada had only 22 metropolitan areas larger than 100,000, whereas in 1970 there were 217 SMSA's of similar size in the United States. In Canada a place with at least 25,000 inhabitants must be considered a large and relatively important city in the urban system today.

The growth of large cities and particularly the metropolitan areas has also occurred considerably more recently in Canada, where it has essentially been a post-1940 phenomenon. While there were only 8 cities larger than 100,000 in 1941, the number had increased to 22 in 1971. Finally, the growth and spread of the urban pattern have been influenced to a much greater extent by the limitations imposed by physical geography, which have confined the main areas of settlement to the southernmost part of the country in a relatively narrow zone adjacent to the boundary with the United States. As a result, the urban pattern is a much simpler, linear one, oriented east-west with its focus in the Great Lakes–St. Lawrence lowlands of central Canada (Fig. 2.9).

Evolution of the Urban Pattern

Although the Canadian urban pattern has been molded by the same general factors as those that have influenced the United States—changes in the technology of transportation and industrial processes, changes in the national resource base, great migrations, and heartland-hinterland relationships—their significant effects have generally been felt later. Consequently, the growth of large cities has, until very recently at least, generally lagged behind that in the United States, often by several decades. This lag effect is, for example, well illustrated by developments in transportation, which we have seen were a crucial factor in determining the pattern and growth of cities in the United States, particularly during the nineteenth century. Thus the Erie Canal, which cut Montreal's hinterland at least in half, was completed in 1825, but it was not until 1848 that a comparable water route had been developed from Lake Erie to tidewater in Canada. In 1860 there were only 1,800 miles of railroad in Canada compared to 31,000 miles in the United States, and Chicago had been linked to New York long before a

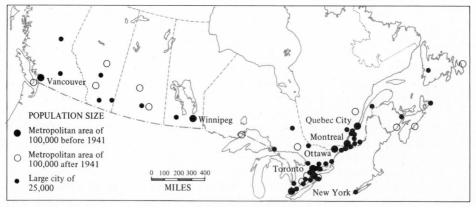

Fig. 2.9. Metropolitan areas and large cities in Canada, 1971.

railroad of any significant length had been constructed in Canada. Finally, while San Francisco had been connected to the east coast by railroad in 1870, a comparable transcontinental rail net was not completed in Canada until 1885, when the CPR reached Vancouver (Warkentin, 1968).

The difference in the timing of the growth and spread of large cities between the two countries was, of course, very much to Canada's disadvantage, especially during the formative years of urban growth in the nineteenth century. Because of this, the evolution of the urban pattern and the development of the Canadian economy have, in many important respects, been influenced and conditioned by events in, and relationships with, the United States. Particularly important were the effects of commercial and industrial competition from the already well-established cities across the border. An important result of this was that urban-industrial developments in the Canadian heartland, and particularly in southern Ontario, have taken place very much in the economic shadow of the American manufacturing belt (Ray, 1965).

Expansion and Consolidation, 1871–1921

At the beginning of the period, the population of Canada was only about 4 millions—97 percent of whom were concentrated in the central and eastern parts of the country, in southern Ontario, the Quebec lowlands, and the Atlantic Provinces. The western part of the country was at this time still virtually empty. Settlement was predominantly rural, and a complete network of small service centers existed in central Canada. Only seven cities had more than 25,000 inhabitants. Montreal (122,000) dominated the urban pattern at this time, and it was the country's undisputed commercial, financial, and manufacturing center. Quebec City and Toronto, both with about 59,000 inhabitants, were the only other relatively large cities.

In the following 50 years, Canada experienced its first economic boom (1896–1913), and the national economy was transformed from one almost completely dependent on the supply of staples for world markets to one based increasingly on processing and manufacturing industries. By 1921 the population of the country had grown to 8.8 millions. Key factors in the economic transition were the opening up of the western plains for the cultivation of wheat (in the period from 1901 to 1911, 73 million acres of farmland were brought under cultivation in the three Prairie Provinces); the extension and consolidation of the railroad network; and the exploitation of resources of the Shield.

These developments had a profound effect on the spatial pattern and growth of the larger cities, of which an additional six had reached 100,000 by 1921. The most noticeable change in the spatial pattern was the growth of cities in the western part of the country. Vancouver (117, 217 in 1921) became a major seaport on the west coast and Winnipeg (179, 087 in 1921) consolidated its role as the gateway to the western agricultural regions. Victoria, Edmonton, Calgary, Regina, and Saskatoon had all emerged as the major subregional service or administrative centers in the western part of the country. In the Atlantic Provinces far to the east, however, the urban pattern experienced only slight growth during the period. Halifax (58,000), St. Johns, and Saint John were the main regional centers. Although manufacturing developed on a small scale and an iron and steel industry had been established at Sydney and New Glasgow, proper industrialization never really took place. In this respect the Atlantic Provinces resembled western Canada. The changing spatial relationships within the country that accompanied the growth in the west and the long distance to the main markets in central Canada reinforced the region's peripheral location and acted as a brake to economic and urban growth.

The most significant developments, then, occurred in central Canada, and particularly in southern Ontario. Endowed with a number of initial advantages, especially its proximity to the American manufacturing belt, the region experienced rapid industrialization after 1890. Toronto's nodality in the regional transportation system made it the natural focus of urban-industrial development, and assured its rapid growth. By 1921 it had a population of over 500,000, making it the primate center for English-speaking Canada and a serious challenger to Montreal as the nation's foremost city. Elsewhere in southern Ontario, Hamilton, with its iron and steel industry, reached 100,000 by 1921; three cities had exceeded 25,000; and a large number of lesser places were emerging as small manufacturing centers on which their subsequent growth was to be increasingly based (Spelt, 1972).

In Quebec, conditions up to 1921 were generally not so favorable for industrialization as they were in Ontario. Nevertheless, Montreal and to a lesser extent Quebec City continued to grow in part by the addition of manufacturing and processing activities. By about 1890, Montreal had become the Chicago of the Canadian railroad system. After 1900 it was increasingly the focus for the growth of small manufacturing centers in the surrounding hinterland, and with a population of 618,500 in 1921 it was still Canada's largest city.

By the end of the period, then, the basic framework of present-day metropolitan Canada dominated by Montreal and Toronto had emerged; the winners and losers in the economic competition for growth had almost all been identified; and the foundations for the Canadian heartland had been laid down in central Canada (Simmons and Simmons, 1969).

Subsequent Developments, 1921–1971

During the past 50 years, and especially since 1940, the national economy has become more tightly integrated as heartland-hinterland relationships have intensified, and increasingly more diversified accompanying the continued growth of processing and manufacturing industries and employment in the service sector (Ray, 1969). Significant new mineral resources have been exploited; the rate of population growth has been explosive compared to the previous period; and the growth of larger cities and metropolitan areas has been phenomenal, especially in the heartland.

In eastern Canada, the trends emerging by 1921 have since been reinforced by subsequent events. The economy of the Atlantic Provinces proceeded from retarded growth through stagnation to relative decline; since the 1960s the region has become an economic backwater and Canada's problem area. The urban pattern, which has been relatively stable in the past 50 years, has become a poorly articulated satellite of the central Canadian system concentrated on Montreal and Toronto. Growth has been concentrated increasingly in the three traditional centers—Halifax, St. Johns, and Saint John—all of which had populations larger than 100,000 by 1971.

In the Prairie Provinces, the pattern of the larger cities dominated by Winnipeg continued more or less unchanged until 1940. Since then, the discovery of significant mineral resources (notably oil, natural gas, potash, and industrial minerals) has provided the basis for considerable industrial development. The growth of Edmonton and Calgary has been particularly impressive, and by 1971 both cities had populations over 400,000. Saskatoon and Regina have also experienced significant growth, albeit at a smaller scale, but by 1971 they too had qualified as metropolitan areas with populations larger than 100,000. Although Winnipeg is still the largest city in the prairies, it has lost its role as the region's primate city and its rate of growth has been much slower than that of its western rivals (Burghardt, 1971). Farther west, Vancouver has continued to grow as a major seaport on the Pacific coast, and by 1971 it ranked third in size behind Montreal and Toronto with a metropolitan area population of over one million. Today it is not only the major regional focus of the western part of Canada, but together with Victoria it is also the center of a rapidly growing local urban region that already is developing the characteristics typical of smaller scale megalopolitan development.

Since 1921, however, the most significant feature in the continuing evolution of the urban pattern has been the dramatic urban expansion in the heartland of central Canada, and particularly the sustained, rapid growth of Montreal and Toronto, both of which had metropolitan area populations of over 2.5 million by 1971. Within the heartland a significant difference in urban concentration had emerged between Quebec and Ontario. In Quebec, where industrialization became especially rapid after about 1950, growth has been largely concentrated in Montreal. However, by 1971 both Quebec City and Chicoutimi-Jonquiére had more than 100,000 inhabitants, and eight other places had populations greater than 25,000. Most of these were located in southwestern Quebec in the vicinity of Montreal (Fig. 2.9). However, despite these developments, the growth and spread of larger cities was considerably less pronounced in Quebec than in southern Ontario.

Here, by contrast, urban growth has been spectacular. By 1971 there were, in addition to Toronto, eight metropolitan areas larger than 100,000, and 10 other cities larger than 25,000 (Fig. 2.9). A salient feature in the urban pattern has been the strong concentration of rapidly growing cities in the crescent-shaped area around the western end of Lake Ontario, extending from Toronto in the east to Welland in the west—the area traditionally referred to as the "Golden Horseshoe." A second major concentration extends in a corridor southwestward to Windsor (Whebell, 1969). Within this region a number of urban growth complexes have been identified, the largest of which is an extended Toronto-Hamilton complex called Lake Ontario, with a population of over three millions. Others with populations of about 250,000 include Kitchener-Guelph, London–St. Thomas, Windsor, and a Niagara complex based on St. Catherines, Niagara Falls, and Welland (Bourne and Gad, 1972).

Today, then, the heartland extends from Windsor in the west to Quebec City in the east (Yeates, 1975). Despite the recent developments in Quebec, the continuing expansion of the heartland westward in southern Ontario toward the contiguous parts of the American manufacturing belt in upstate New York and in Michigan has been the dominant trend. The region is now a part of the development of a Great Lakes megalopolis extending from Chicago to Quebec City and linking the Midwest to the eastern megalopolis along the Atlantic coast.

THE LOCATION OF CITIES

An interesting question arising from the review of the evolution of urban patterns in North America is why cities grew up where they did. In discussing the location of cities, geographers have traditionally differentiated between the *site* and the *situation*. The site is the precise features of the terrain on which the settlement began; situation is usually taken to mean the physical conditions and human characteristics of the surrounding country (Dickinson, 1948). In some respects site approximates the concept of absolute location, while situation is closely linked to that of relative location. The built-up areas of today's cities usually bear very little relationship to their original sites, which were for the most part selected without any idea of, or consideration for, the scale of urban growth that was often to take place at them. Site selection was often strongly influenced by factors in the physical environment. Things such as the need for shelter and good supply of drinking water, freedom from floods, and perhaps good defensive positions were prime considerations. Often great care was taken in the selection of the initial site for settlement. This was the case, for example, in the founding of Charleston and Philadelphia, and later in the location of Washington, D.C. More often, however, settlements grew up at particular locations more by chance than anything else, and their subsequent growth had very little to do with their initial site or situation.

Madison, the state capital of Wisconsin, is a good case in point. At first sight the location of this city seems a good example of the role of physical factors; however, the history of the choice of site reveals that the human rather than the physical factor was the most important.

> In 1836 the Wisconsin Territorial Legislature was obliged to choose a site for a permanent capital. A total of sixteen localities were considered, all of them owned by speculators, who energetically advanced the claims of their own land. The decision to locate the capital on its present site was taken by 15 votes to 11, and this decision owed more to intrigue than to any careful assessment of site and situation [Johnson, 1967, p. 80].

Although the sites of initial settlements were significant, their situation was usually the more important locational consideration, since this had a more direct bearing on the functions they performed and on their subsequent growth. Physical factors were also important in the situational context, particularly as these related to movement. Thus we have seen from the discussion of the spread of cities that many of today's urban giants originated as small settlements on navigable rivers, on good harbors, or at the entrance to passes through difficult terrain. Junction points in the transportation networks of the time were especially important, and locations were frequently selected at river confluences, bridging points, and crossroads. Particularly important were the junctions where different types of transportation came together—the so-called break-of-bulk points at which goods and materials had to be transferred, commonly after processing, from one means of transportation to another. It is not difficult to appreciate how the initial site and situation could affect subsequent development of city function, particularly of these transport-oriented cities.

As technology advanced, so new locational forces became important; and location became more directly related from the start with the functions settlements were to perform. Thus with the early growth of manufacturing, new settlements grew up at water-power sites. The planned mill towns of the Boston Associates in the 1840s at Lowell, Lawrence, Chicopee, and Holyoke in Massachusetts, and at Manchester and Nashua in New Hampshire, are good examples. Later with the spread of the railroads, junctions of different lines became important growth points. In the West the operating needs of the railroads themselves dictated the locations where many new settlements grew up at watering stops or in conjunction with car and locomotive repair shops. As coal became increasingly important, new mining settlements grew up on the coalfields; and older settlements assumed new significance. Similarly settlements were founded in conjunction with the opening of new mineral ore deposits. Most recently, in the age of leisure, a different natural resource—climate—has influenced location and subsequent development of settlements to result, for example, in the growth of resort cities in Florida and California.

URBAN SIZE CHARACTERISTICS

As the urban pattern evolved in North America and significant changes took place in the spatial distribution of cities, the process of growth also brought about significant changes in their sizes. The size of a city can be measured in various ways, two of which are particularly important—number of inhabitants and number of functions. Obviously these are not completely unrelated; the larger a city's population, the greater the range of functions it usually performs. The population and functional size characteristics of cities are what underlie two important but separate aspects of the structure of urban systems: rank-size relationships and the urban hierarchy.

Rank-Size Relationships

Rank-size relationships are inherent in the ranking of cities on the basis of their population sizes. The nature of the relationship for a particular country can be identified by constructing a graph like the one shown in Figure 2.10. On this, the metropolitan areas of Canada and the United States have been plotted in descending order by their population sizes on the Y axis, and by their corresponding rank on the X axis, both of which are scaled in logarithms. The resulting pattern is rather interesting. In both countries the distribution of city sizes forms a smooth progression approximating a straight line. This intriguing empirical regularity, which is typical of many countries in the world, results from what is known as the *rank-size rule* (Zipf, 1949). This states that if all cities are ranked in descending order of population size, the population of the rth ranking city will be $1/r^{th}$ the size of the largest city in the country. The rule can be stated mathematically as follows:

$$r \times P_r^q = K$$

where r is the rank of a particular city, P_r is the population size of that city, and q and K are constants. When q has a value of 1.0, the value of K is equal to the population size of the largest city (P_1), and the formula can be restated simply as:

$$r \times P_r = P_1$$

Some examples will make this clear. In 1970 the largest SMSA (P_1) in the United States was New York, which had a population of 9,019,500. According to the rule, the population of the fifth-ranking SMSA (P_5) ought to be 1,801,870. Detroit was the fifth-ranking SMSA in 1970, but its actual population was 4,200,000. In Canada, the largest metropolitan area in 1971 was Montreal, with a population of 2,743,208. The fifth largest was Winnipeg, and according to the rule it should have a population of 548,641; its actual population was 540,262.

On the basis of these two cases, we might be tempted to conclude that the rank-size rule applies in Canada but not in the United States. But that would be very unscientific of us and we would in fact be wrong. Deviations from the "expected" populations are to be expected, and these are sometimes quite marked for the top-ranking cities even when the overall city-size distribution is in accordance with the rule. In testing whether a particular city-size distribution agrees with the rank-size rule or not, all cities in the system must be included (remember that only the top 22 cities are shown in Fig. 2.10 for Canada), and the comparison between the actual and theoretical patterns needs to be couched in probability terms. When this is done, it turns out that the rule does hold for the United States, but not so well for Canada.

The deviation of actual from expected rank-size city distributions has prompted a number of researchers to investigate the conditions under which the rank-size rule holds. The results from these studies have been far from conclusive, although a number

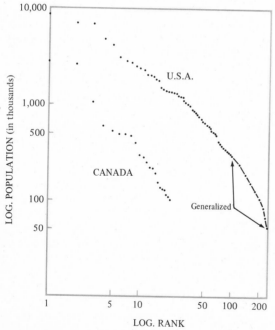

Fig. 2.10. Rank-size relationships for the 243 SMSA's in the United States, 1970, and the 22 CMA's in Canada, 1971.

of significant correlates have been identified. Stewart (1958) suggests, for example, that the rule appears to hold fairly well for industrialized countries, principally because of the large size of some industrial centers; for areas with high rural population densities; and for areas where population is well distributed spatially. In a more recent study, Berry (1961) noted that the rank-size regularity appeared to be typical only of larger countries that have a long tradition of urbanization and that are politically and economically complex.

The fact that some of these characteristics are not typical of Canada, particularly the lack of a long tradition of large-scale urbanization, may contribute toward explaining why the rank-size rule does not hold so well there. However, a more important factor must be the existence of the twin cultures that we have already noted as the reason for the growth of Montreal and Toronto as top-ranking cities of almost equal population size—clearly not in accordance with the rank-size rule. Moreover, urban development in French-speaking Quebec has taken place more or less independently from that in the rest of Canada, and this further complicates the rank-size relationships at the national scale.

Explaining why the rank-size regularity occurs is a more difficult problem. Some of the alternative explanations have been reviewed by Berry and Garrison (1958d), and among these the most plausible, but by no means the most easily grasped, is that offered by Simon (1955). Noticing that rank-size distribution approximates many probability distributions, among them the Yule and Pareto, Simon argues that the linear regularity of city sizes is generated by a stochastic process. In this, many forces affect the size of cities, often in a random fashion within the context of growth proportionate to size of city (Beckmann, 1958).

Implicit in this explanation is often the notion that cities are integrated through linkages and interchanges into a system, the "steady state" of which is the log-linear rank-size regularity noted in Figure 2.10. The plausibility of this explanation is further enhanced by the stability of the rank-size relationship through time. Thus for the United States, Figure 2.11 shows that the general growth of cities since 1790 has not occurred independently of the total population system of which they are a part. Consequently the distribution of the city sizes at each census period has generally approximated the linear form of the rank-size distribution. However, as indicated for Los Angeles, Baltimore, Savannah, Ga., and Hudson, N.Y., within the fairly stable overall distribution of cities there is often marked divergence in the growth rates of individual places. This is expected because of the factors operating to bring about the differential growth of cities in time.

The Urban Hierarchy

Whereas the rank-size rule postulates a continuous distribution of cities on the basis of their population size, the concept of the urban hierarchy postulates a ranking of cities into size classes on the basis of their functional importance, which is normally measured by the numbers and kinds of services they provide (see Duncan et al., 1960, chap. 3). The concept of the hierarchy can thus be thought of as a vertical dimension that complements the spatial dimension of the urban system; cities have not only a location in space, but also a position at a particular level in the hierarchy.

In its structure the hierarchy of cities can be likened to a pyramid. The pyramidal

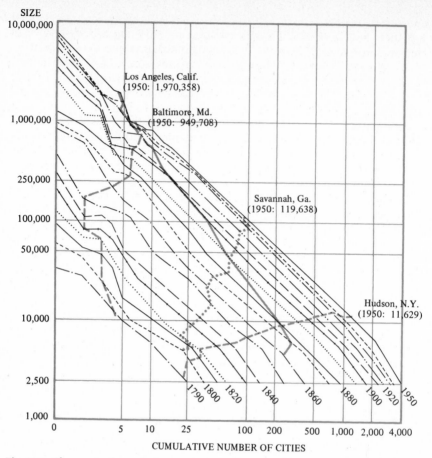

Fig. 2.11. Changes in the rank-size regularity in the United States, 1790–1950. (*Source*: after Madden, 1956, Fig. 1.)

shape results from the fact that there is a greater number of smaller cities than large ones in the urban system (see Table 2.1). Thus the number of cities at each level (order) in the hierarchy decreases as one moves upward through it. Conversely, their functional structure becomes increasingly more complex. For not only do larger cities provide a wider range of functions, they also perform increasingly more specialized roles in the city system. It is in this way that the series of distinct city-size classes takes on a more functional meaning.

When we add the spatial dimension to this, the notion of an urban hierarchy becomes an important feature in the organization of the urban economic system. The heartland and hinterlands are, for example, articulated into a national system through the hierarchy of metropolitan centers, large cities, and smaller towns. Flows of goods, materials, services, people, funds, decisions, and even innovations appear to diffuse outward and downward from heartland metropoli to those in the hinterland; from larger centers to smaller ones in the regions; and outward from urban centers across their surrounding urban fields (Ray, 1972).

Each city is the center of a nodal region, the size of which increases according to the level in the hierarchy (see Chapter 3). It is the few high-order centers that provide very specialized functions for large regions, while the increasing number of smaller cities at successively lower levels provide more general services for increasingly more local hinterlands. Hence the cities at different levels in the hierarchy are not independent but are interrelated. Specifically, cities of a given order have an autonomy over those at lower levels, but in turn are dominated by larger, higher order centers. Moreover, higher order centers perform the functions characteristic of centers at each of the lower levels in the hierarchy.

Identification of the number of levels in the hierarchy is essentially a problem in classification, the object of which is to divide the continuous distribution of city sizes into meaningful functional classes. Consequently the number of levels proposed depends on many factors, particularly the purpose for which the hierarchy is being identified. Because of this it is important to keep in mind that there is no single, best specification of the urban hierarchy. Thus, for example, the hierarchy of metropolitan organization shown in Figure 2.12 is only one of a number of alternatives that could be suggested for the South.

For the United States, Philbrick (1957) has suggested a hierarchy with seven distinct levels. At the pinnacle sits New York, the first-order national metropolis and world city. The influence of New York is thus nationwide, through such things as the financial activities on Wall Street, the advertising activities of Madison Avenue, and

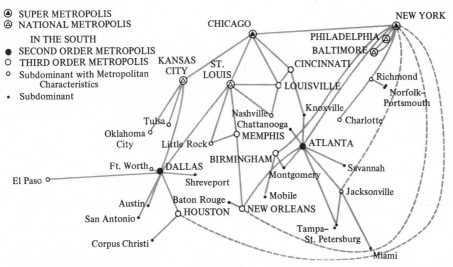

Fig. 2.12. Hierarchical metropolitan organization of the South. (*Source*: after Vance and Smith, 1954, Fig. 2.)

the decisions made in the headquarters offices of many of the country's largest business organizations. Next are the second-order centers, which include Los Angeles, San Francisco, Chicago, Detroit, Boston, and Philadelphia—each of which acts as a major regional metropolis for a vast portion of the United States market. Typical of the third-order, subregional level are cities like Seattle, St. Louis, Minneapolis, Salt Lake City, New Orleans, and so on. Borchert (1972) lists 20 third-order centers altogether. Each of these subregional centers is the focus of a surrounding urban field containing centers at the lower end of the hierarchy: the cities, towns, villages, and hamlets (see Chapter 6).

Concluding Remarks

The evolution of the urban patterns of North America has been part of a continuous process of economic and social change that has been taking place during the past 150 years. In this relatively short time span, a relatively simple pattern of towns and villages has been transformed into a complex and tightly integrated urban system dominated by large metropolitan centers. And the trend toward increasingly large-scale spatial concentration shows every sign of continuing. We have, however, only touched upon some of the more obvious factors that have influenced the development of the present-day patterns, and many important questions have necessarily remained unanswered. However, one thing has clearly emerged: many features of the contemporary urban pattern are rooted in the past, and to gain a deeper understanding of many aspects of the present-day spatial organization it is imperative that events are considered in both time and space.

3
CITIES
AND
INTERACTION

Cities do not and cannot exist in isolation. The people and activities in them are connected with those in other places by a complex pattern of flows, movements, transactions, and linkages that are collectively referred to as spatial interaction. It is because of the interaction between cities that we can think of them as being organized into a system, an important characteristic of which we have noted is its hierarchical structure. In this chapter attention is therefore focused on patterns of intercity interaction and on the relationships between city and surrounding regions. Pertinent concepts and considerations are discussed and some of the simple models of interaction are introduced.

SOME BASIC CONSIDERATIONS

To begin with, it is perhaps appropriate to look at the different kinds of interaction, the magnitudes involved, the basis for interaction, and the various ways in which interaction helps shape patterns of urban spatial organization.

51

Toward a Typology of Interaction

Many frameworks can be used to classify the various kinds of interaction. A useful starting point is that suggested by Haggett (1972), based on the way physicists differentiate between the three methods of heat transfer: convection, conduction, and radiation. In the first category are those forms of interaction requiring movements and the physical transfer of elements. Included here are the movements of goods and materials to industries and markets, commodity shipments, the dispatch of mail and parcels, and so on. Movements of people also fall into this category. The second, conductive category includes the various kinds of transactions between cities. These are not normally characterized by a physical transfer of mass, but rather by a system of accounting. The various kinds of financial transactions between cities is a good example. Credits in one city are matched against debits in another simply through a bookkeeping procedure, thereby maintaining a balance of payments. The third category includes the flows of information and the diffusion of ideas and innovations. These do not involve a physical transfer of mass, nor do they require that books be balanced, and hence this form of interaction perhaps resembles radiation in a general way. Contacts and linkages between cities are therefore expressed in three main ways: through the movements of goods and people, a wide range of transactions, and the flow of information.

A further differentiation between the various forms of interaction is possible on the basis of the networks within which they occur. Physical movements take place in transportation networks—the railroads, navigable waterways, highways, and airplanes. We noted the significance of transportation in the growth and spread of cities in the previous chapter, and today railroads and highways are the most important surface links connecting cities. On the other hand, transactions and flows of information take place primarily within communication networks—via the telephone and teleprinter circuits, over the air waves of radio and television broadcasting, and so on. Often, however, it is the network of personal contacts that matters most particularly for certain kinds of diffusion processes (Hägerstrand, 1968). Cities can thus be viewed as nodes of varying importance in different kinds of networks. The way networks are spatially structured and overlap each other often helps shape patterns of interaction between cities (Haggett and Chorley, 1969). Generally speaking, the more connected a city is in a network, the higher its accessibility, and the more important it can be expected to be as a focus of particular kinds of interaction (Marchand, 1973).

Further subdivisions are possible based on the type of movements, their nature and purpose, the volumes and distances involved, their periodicity, modes used, and so on. In discussing movements of people Morrill (1974a) has added a further distinction based on the degree of permanency of movement, and he differentiates between temporary, transient, and permanent moves. The latter category is migration, which throughout history has played an important role in shaping the city system as well as being one of the principal mechanisms in the diffusion of ideas, culture traits, customs, and other forms of social behavior. Migration is consequently another component in the matrix of interaction. When all these aspects are put together, it is hardly surprising that the nature, extent, and patterns of interaction in the city system are inordinately complex.

The Volume of Interaction

In highly urbanized societies such as the United States and Canada, the total volume of intercity interaction can only be described as phenomenal. In fact, there is most certainly a connection between the magnitude and intensity of interaction of all kinds and the level of urbanization of countries in view of the fact that interaction is not entirely divorced from the level of technological development. Moreover, the volume of all kinds of interaction has increased in the comparatively recent past at a staggering rate. Some of the more obvious reasons for this are the continued concentration of people and activities in larger urban areas; the increasing complexity and scale of contemporary economic and social organization; and the increased level of mobility and spatial awareness resulting from improved living standards and technological developments in transportation and communication. In fact, it is difficult to conceive of any change, technical, economic, political, or social, that does not ultimately have some direct effect on the volume and pattern of interaction between cities.

A general impression of the total magnitudes of intercity freight and passenger traffic for the United States is given in Tables 3.1 and 3.2. Since 1940 the volume of intercity freight movements has increased by a staggering 200 percent to an all-time high of 1.9 billion ton-miles. The increase in passenger traffic is equally dramatic: from 500 billion passenger-miles in 1950 to 1.2 billion in 1970. Exact details of intercity flows of information and transactions are more difficult to obtain, but a general idea of the magnitudes involved can be obtained from the following national statistics. In 1970 the U.S. Post Office handled an estimated 87 billion pieces of domestic mail, compared to 45 billion in 1950. In 1970 the number of long-distance telephone calls averaged 27 million per day compared to only 7 million in 1950. There were in 1970 5339 commercial broadcasting stations in the United States compared to 2336 in 1950. Finally, an indication of the volume of migration between large cities is given by the fact that of the 6.9 million people who moved in the period 1970–1971, 4.4 million moved between SMSA's in different states.

Tables 3.1 and 3.2 also give some idea of the relative importance of the different

**Table 3.1.   VOLUME OF DOMESTIC INTERCITY FREIGHT TRAFFIC
BY TYPE OF TRANSPORTATION, U.S.A., 1940–1970**

		Percentage of Total Volume by				
Year	Total Volume[a]	Railroads[b]	Motor Vehicles	Inland Waterways[c]	Oil Pipelines	Airways[d]
1940	651	63.2	9.5	18.1	9.1	0.002
1950	1,094	57.4	15.8	14.9	11.8	0.029
1960	1,330	44.7	21.4	16.6	17.2	0.058
1970	1,936	39.8	21.3	16.5	22.3	0.170
Percentage point change 1940–1970		−23.4	+11.8	− 1.6	+13.2	+0.168

[a] In billions of ton-miles. A ton-mile is the movement of one ton (2000 lbs.) of freight for one mile.
[b] Includes electric railways, express, and mail.
[c] Includes Great Lakes, Alaska for all years, and Hawaii beginning 1960.
[d] Includes express, mail, and excess baggage for domestic services.
SOURCE: U.S. Bureau of the Census, *Statistical Abstract of the United States, 1973*, Table 884. (Washington, D.C.: U.S. Government Printing Office.)

kinds of networks for movements of people and goods. For freight traffic, the railroads dominate. This is expected, since the railroad network is flexible and particularly suitable for the transportation of heavy and bulky goods. Next in order of relative importance come oil pipelines, the highway network, and inland waterways. The use of airways for freight traffic is still insignificant, despite the fact that it has become relatively more important since 1940. Changes in the relative importance of the different networks are much as expected and largely reflect the increased competition of newer forms of transportation. Thus the traditional importance of waterways and railroads has declined. This is particularly noticeable in the case of railroads, which in 1940 accounted for nearly two-thirds of intercity freight traffic. Conversely the highway and oil-pipeline networks have become relatively more important since 1940.

Comparison of these figures with those shown in Table 3.1 for intercity passenger traffic clearly points up the basic differences between the networks for flows of people. For these, the highway network is supreme and the use of the automobile is dominant. The only other important mode for passenger traffic is the airlines, which are becoming increasingly more important. The railroad and inland waterways are relatively insignificant for passenger traffic, and much of the flow by railroad is accounted for by intercity commuting.

Complementarity

What is it, then, that brings about such large volumes of interaction? A primitive explanation might be that since cities are separated from each other by distance, interaction in large quantities is necessary to link them together. But this is in itself not sufficient, for distance does not generate interaction; rather, it helps shape the patterns that result. A next step, therefore, must be to recognize that cities differ from one another in the functions they perform, the opportunities they offer, and their population structures. Particular kinds of industry are found in certain cities and not in others; certain cities are wholesaling centers, others banking centers, and so on; some

Table 3.2. VOLUME OF DOMESTIC INTERCITY PASSENGER TRAFFIC BY TYPE OF TRANSPORTATION, U.S.A., 1950–1970

Year	Total Volume[a]	Percentage of Total Volume by				
		Private Automobiles	Airways[b]	Commercial Motor Carriers	Railroads[c]	Inland Waterways[d]
1950	508	86.2	1.9	5.2	6.4	0.2
1960	784	90.1	4.3	2.5	2.7	0.3
1970	1,185	86.6	10.0	2.2	0.9	0.3
Percentage point change 1950–1970		+0.4	+8.1	−3.0	−5.5	+0.1

[a] In billions of passenger-miles. A passenger-mile is the movement of one passenger for the distance of one mile.
[b] Includes domestic commercial services, private, and business flying.
[c] Includes electric railways.
[d] Includes Great Lakes.
SOURCE: U.S. Bureau of the Census, *Statistical Abstract of the United States, 1973*, Table 885. Washington, D.C.: U.S. Government Printing Office.

cities have important cultural and recreational facilities while others may be seats of government and centers of administration. People living in one city have friends and relations scattered throughout the city system. Organizations have their headquarters in one city, from which they direct and control their branches located at other places. Thus the difference in locational patterns of people, activities, and organizations is a major factor explaining why the potential for intercity interaction exists. However, neither distance nor differences in spatial distributions are enough to account for the fact that interaction actually takes place. Something else is still needed for a complete explanation. Ullman (1956) has suggested that this something else is *complementarity*. This concept states quite simply that the potential for interaction between two cities is realized only when there is a supply of some kind at one of them and a demand of some kind at the other. Specific complementarity between cities in supply-and-demand terms is therefore the underlying basis for spatial interaction. Admittedly Ullman was writing about flows of commodities, and the concept in its pure form is most applicable to the movement of goods and materials within the urban system. However, since supply-and-demand relationships can assume many forms, the notion of complementarity can be broadened to account for movements of people, transactions, and flows of information. The bases for interaction, then, are the various forms of complementarity relationships that exist between the spatially separated activities, people, and organizations within the city system.

The Importance of Interaction

Interaction plays a number of crucial roles in shaping the form and structure of the city system. Three of these are particularly important. First, interaction performs an *integrating* function. Because activities and people are separated from each other in space, interaction is needed to link them together. Thus it is through the movements, flows, and transactions between cities and regions that they are joined together into a unified whole. The importance of an integrated city system was noted as one of the prerequisites for the existence of rank-size regularities in city-size distributions. Second, interaction permits *differentiation* within the city system. It is necessary for a spatial division of labor, enables a high degree of freedom of choice in location, and makes possible the functional specialization of cities and regions (see Chapter 7). Without interaction, for example, specialization within the framework of the heartland-hinterlands would not have been possible. Third, and most important, interaction is the medium of spatial *organization*. The various kinds of movements, flows, and transactions between cities are the expressions of linkages, relationships, and above all interdependencies within the city system (Warneryd, 1968). Because of these, what goes on in one city or in one part of the system often affects what goes on in other cities and other parts of the system. It is very much in terms of relationships and interdependencies that cities are articulated into the complex functional whole we refer to as the city system, in which the largest metropolitan centers have traditionally played a dominant organizing role.

Interaction and Change

Interaction is also important in bringing about change and the reorganization of the city system. The diffusion of ideas and innovations is one of the major ways changes are transmitted through the city system. In this connection, patterns in the flow of information are particularly important. But so is migration (Morrill, 1965a). Migration has traditionally been a principal mechanism in the spread of technology, culture, and social customs, and hence it plays an important part in the process of change. Migration makes cities more cosmopolitan; it also contributes to many of their problems, especially social ones.

Migration is also important in helping to bring about differential growth in the city system. Without the large-scale relocation of population through migration and immigration, the rapid growth of cities during the closing decades of the last century would not have been possible. Although today the population growth of cities is to a large extent self-generated, migration continues to play an important role in the process of growth and change. The rapid urbanization of California since the 1950s and the more recent growth of large cities in the Southwest and Florida attests to this. Moreover, the large-scale migration of blacks from the South to the major cities of the North in the post–World War II period has been instrumental in bringing about fundamental changes in the urban pattern.

Intercity interaction patterns are normally thought of as a response to locational decisions; interaction between cities is generated by the activities carried on in them. Changes in the activities thus bring about changes in the level of interaction between them. However, there are good grounds for supposing that interaction itself is self-generating, especially when high levels of interaction already exist between cities, particularly large metropolitan centers (Pred, 1973). This is because, under certain conditions, the already existing interaction gives rise to demands for improvements in the transportation and communication networks. If these demands are realized, and after some time has elapsed, the improved connections result in further increases in the level of interaction.

As a result of alterations to the structure of the networks, changes are brought about in the relative location of cities and their importance as nodes in the network. Some cities become more accessible, others perhaps less so. Travel times are reduced and the barrier effects of distance on movements are decreased. As a result of this space-shrinking process, "time-space convergence" occurs (Janelle, 1969). The effects of this are not, however, spread evenly throughout the city system. Rather they seem to benefit the more distantly spaced cities more than the smaller, intervening ones. For example, Janelle found in his study that the minutes saved per mile (average convergence) as a result of transportation improvements in the Midwest between 13 smsa's was 0.51 for Detroit, 0.49 for Chicago, 0.42 for Grand Rapids, and only 0.34 for Port Huron, the smallest city included. Detroit's relative accessibility was increased considerably, therefore, as it was pulled closer to, and became better integrated with, the system than the others. As a result of the spatial reorganization of the city system brought about in this kind of way, some cities become "better" places at which to locate various kinds of activities, and in turn this leads to higher levels of interaction between them and other cities. The deconcentration of urban growth from the core to the periphery in the United States is part of a current reorganization of the city system made possible by the time-space converging effects of transportation and communication improvements.

THE GENERATION OF FLOWS

As a response to locational decisions, interaction in the city system is generated by the characteristics of cities involved. The level and nature of interaction between specific cities results from many factors. Position in transportation and communication networks may exert a generating effect. Specific kinds of complementarity between cities may result in large volumes of particular kinds of movements, as is often the case with commodity flows (Ullman, 1957). Variation in *place utility*—the individual's perception of the social, economic, and environmental attractiveness of different cities—has been suggested as an important factor in explaining patterns of intercity migration (Wolpert, 1965). The locational patterns of major job-providing organizations is important in generating flows of information and transactions between particular cities (Pred, 1974a). Over and above these specific kinds of considerations, however, the generation of intercity interaction is affected to a large extent by a number of more general factors. Three of these are particularly important: the population and functional sizes of cities, their social and (especially) economic diversity, and their degree of spatial separation.

That population size is an important factor in the generation of interaction between cities is self-evident. The more people living in a city, the greater the probability that a large number of them will interact with people living in other cities. Moreover, population size is a fairly good indicator of the social and economic diversity of cities and their importance in the urban hierarchy. Thus Chicago or Toronto generates a considerably greater volume of interaction of most kinds than, for example, Des Moines, Iowa, or Kingston, Ontario, simply because they are bigger and functionally more important in the city system.

The way that functional specialization affects the generation of flows between

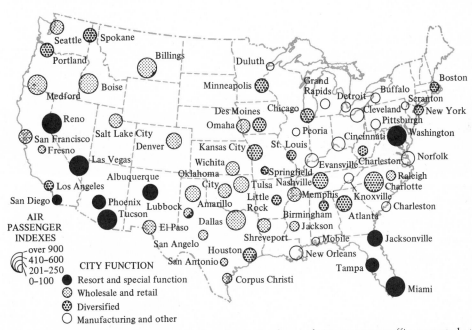

Fig. 3.1. The relationship between city function and volume of air passenger traffic generated at selected U.S. cities. (*Source*: Taaffe, 1956, Fig. 7.)

cities is illustrated by the results of a study of air transportation and the urban pattern in the United States shown in Figure 3.1 (Taaffe, 1956). On the map, cities are plotted as circles proportional to the number of passengers generated per 1000 inhabitants (the air-passenger index), and they are shaded according to their dominant function in the Harris classification of cities discussed in Chapter 7. If all cities generated the same volume of air-passenger traffic per 1000 inhabitants, each circle on the map would be the same size. Clearly this is not the case. Close inspection of the map reveals that variation on the air-passenger index is highly correlated with city function. Thus the resort and special-function cities have an extremely high average index of 679. Wholesale cities have an average index of 442. In contrast, the nine manufacturing cities have an index of only 234. Diversified cities, which can be thought of as representing a division of the wholesale and manufacturing functions, fall between these two types, with an index of 345.

The degree of spatial separation between cities affects interaction because of the friction of distance. All things being equal, we would expect larger volumes of interaction between cities the closer they are in space. However, the attenuating effects of distance are counteracted in varying degrees by city size and functional specialization. Specifically, the total volume of interaction between pairs of cities has been shown to be directly proportional to their sizes (and implicitly their functional structure) and inversely proportional to the physical distance separating them. This relationship is, in fact, the basis of the simple gravity model discussed later in the chapter.

Distance, however, takes on a different meaning depending upon how we look at it. It can be measured in a variety of ways; for example, in terms of money costs, time, even effort, as well as miles. As it relates to interaction, however, the more abstract concept of *functional distance* is perhaps more important. Functional distance has been defined as a "summary descriptive measure . . . of the attenuation effect of nodal properties (i.e., the characteristics of cities) upon internodal interaction" (Brown and Horton, 1970, p. 77). Thus functional distance is comparable to that of *social distance* as applied to interpersonal relations (see Chapter 11). Lesser functional distance between a pair of cities indicates a greater level of interaction between them, and also, in the context of migration, perhaps a greater difference in their place utility (Brown, Odland, and Golledge, 1970).

The general correspondence between the actual volume of flows between cities and that expected on the basis of their size and separation appears as a widespread feature of intercity interaction patterns. An example is presented in Figure 3.2, taken from a study of telephone calls between Montreal and samples of cities in (1) Quebec Province, (2) the rest of Canada, and (3) the United States (Mackay, 1958). For each of the three sets of cities, the close correspondence between the actual volume of calls (x axis) and that expected on the basis of city size and distance (y axis) is clearly visible. What is more interesting, however, is that each of the three sets of cities form distinct regimes on the graph. This reflects the influence that political boundaries have on intercity interaction. Thus the volume of calls between Montreal and other cities in Quebec is five to ten times higher than that between Montreal and cities with corresponding P/D values in English-speaking Canada. The effect of the international boundary is even more striking. Comparison of the actual and expected volume of telephone calls indicates that the United States cities are in effect 50 times farther away from Montreal than is indicated by their physical distance. This suggests that because of language and

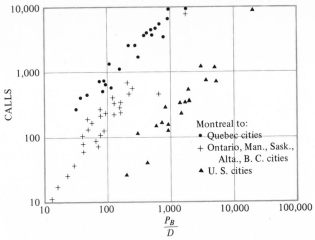

Fig. 3.2. The relationship between actual and expected number of telephone calls from Montreal to sample cities in Quebec, English-speaking Canada, and the United States. (*Source*: Mackay, 1958, Fig. 2.)

perhaps because of its position in the hierarchy, functional distance is much smaller between Montreal and cities in the Quebec subsystem than it is between it and cities in the United States.

DISTANCE-RELATED CONCEPTS

The Friction of Distance

Implicit in the foregoing discussion is the idea that overcoming distance takes time, costs money, or requires effort. Although developments in transportation and communication have significantly reduced the effect of distance, and time-space convergence brings cities closer together, the costs of overcoming distance cannot be removed completely and they continue to be an important consideration in decisions about location and a major factor in shaping interaction patterns. These costs are what underlie the concept of the *friction of distance*, the effect of which is to give rise to distance-decay regularities in spatial organization. Interaction and distance are therefore inversely related; the volume of interaction declines with increasing distance, as shown in Figure 3.3. Although distance decay is a general characteristic of all spatial interaction, some kinds are more sensitive to distance than others (Simmons, 1972). On graphs like those shown in Figure 3.3, sensitivity to distance is indicated by the slope of the line that best fits the scatter of dots—the steeper the slope, the greater the frictional effect of distance, and hence the rate of distance decay.

Transferability

Differences in sensitivity to distance are most clearly revealed when actual physical movements are involved. For people the degree of sensitivity largely depends on the frequency and purpose of trips; for goods it depends on the type of product being moved. The fact that different kinds of goods move with unequal ease is related to differences in their *transferability*. The transferability of a given product depends on its specific value—its value per unit weight. Table 3.3 shows a good example of the way specific value relates to transferability. The generalization stemming from the relationship shown is that low-value-per-unit-weight products generally move over shorter distances whereas higher-value-per-unit-weight products can withstand higher transport costs and hence can be moved over longer distances. Although the concept of transferability is directly applicable to flows of goods, it can be thought of as a general feature of spatial interaction. For example, a kind of transferability effect is typical of shopping trips; people are normally prepared to travel only short distances to obtain low-value items, but much farther to purchase more expensive goods and services (see Chapter 6).

Transferability relates basically to the economics of distance—to dollars and cents. The details of the relationship between dollars and distance are extremely complex and vary with type of interaction, mode of transportation, and characteristics of the transportation and communication networks involved. In some circumstances costs of movement may be more or less independent of distance because transportation

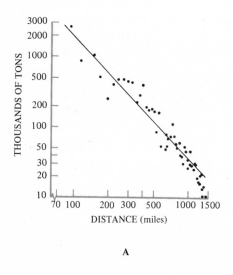

A

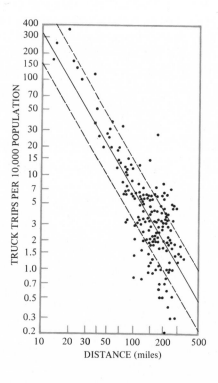

B

Fig. 3.3. Distance-decay regularities for Class I railroad shipments in the United States (A) and the number of truck trips in the Chicago region (B). (*Source:* after Helvig, 1964, Fig. 18, and Isard, 1956, Fig. 12.)

Table 3.3. RELATIVE TRANSFERABILITY OF THREE TIMBER PRODUCTS

	Veneer Logs	Pulpwood	Mine Props
Specific value[a]	150	20	5
Maximum railroad haul in miles	400	100	25

[a]Dollars per ton.
SOURCE: Duerr (1960), Table 10.

companies have the ability to manipulate rates and prices charged. In this way distance decay may be increased or decreased and transferability radically altered (see Chapter 5).

Least Effort

Since the costs attached to distance cannot be avoided altogether, attempts can at least be made to reduce them as much as possible. This notion of least movement has occurred in various forms in many disciplines, ranging from classical physics to operations research. In the social sciences, it was introduced by Zipf (1949) as the "principle of least effort." Although he defined effort in a rather special way, urban geographers regard effort as any inconvenience related to distance. In this way, the principle can be more generally interpreted as that of *distance minimization*.

Distance minimization forms a basic building block for many location and interaction models in urban geography (Yeates, 1963). In its strictest sense, the concept assumes that human beings are rational, that economic factors govern their behavior, and that decisions are made to minimize distance costs. Although this is a convenient argument for conceptual purposes, empirical observations suggest that interaction patterns rarely correspond to this ideal. This is illustrated in Figure 3.4 for patterns of interstate flows of aluminum bar. The actual flow pattern is shown in Figure 3.4A; that which would occur if the total distances, and hence costs, involved were minimized is shown in Figure 3.4B. Comparison of the two maps clearly indicates that actual flows are far from optimal, implying that interaction is considerably more complex than envisaged by the principle of least effort.

Human beings are not entirely rational creatures who act wholly within an optimizing framework. But neither are they fools who completely disregard the effect that distance has on their spatial behavior. Although distance may actually not be minimized in spatial interaction, it is fair to assume that attempts are made to reduce its inconvenience as much as possible. Hence distance-minimization behavior tends to reinforce distance-decay regularities and is an important element underlying patterns in various kinds of spatial interaction.

Intervening Opportunities

A concept allied to distance minimization is that of *intervening opportunities*. These can be thought of as acting in two ways to result in a kind of place substitution. First, as a direct way of reducing the costs associated with distance, nearby places are substituted for those farther away. This effect of intervening opportunities is a partic-

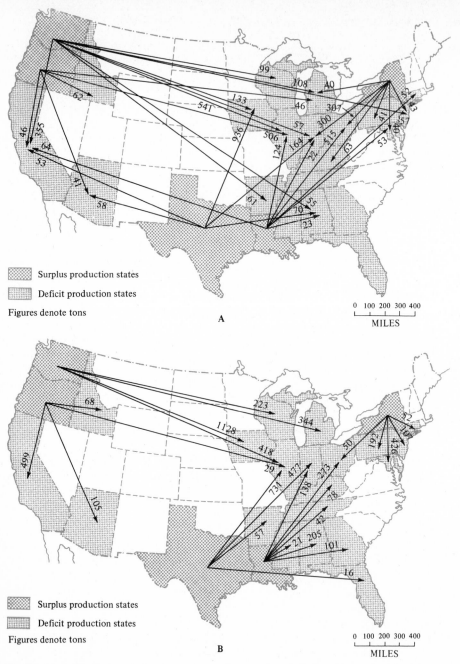

Fig. 3.4. Interstate flows of aluminum bar, United States. The actual pattern of flows (A) bears little resemblance to that which should occur if all distances were minimized (B). (*Source*: Cox, 1965, Figs. 2 and 3.)

ularly noticeable feature of the pattern of commodity flows. For example, at the end of the last century, few forest products moved from the Pacific Northwest to the Eastern Seaboard, despite the existence of cheap water transportation between the two regions. This can be explained by the fact that the then extensive forest resources of the Great Lakes region were better placed to serve the demands for timber in the urban East. The Great Lakes region acted as an intervening opportunity for the supply of forest products, which made possible a considerable reduction in the delivered price of timber in eastern cities.

Second, intervening opportunities can be thought of as a kind of filter affecting movements, particularly the movements of people, and one that indirectly brings about place substitution. For example, there would most probably be a much higher degree of interaction between Boston and Philadelphia were it not for the fact that New York is located between them to siphon off what might otherwise be through traffic. The filter effect of intervening opportunities is a particularly important factor in understanding migration patterns, and is generally important in reinforcing distance-decay regularities.

INTERACTION AND THE CITY SYSTEM

The emphasis in the discussion so far has been on interaction between cities themselves; on the pattern of point-to-point connections in space. There is, however, another set of patterns — the point-to-area connections arising from the interaction between cities and their surrounding regions. Both are explicit in interaction patterns. If we now introduce the notion of the urban hierarchy and allow for variations in geographic scale, then the organization of the city system can be described in broad outline as follows: (1) Positioned at the highest levels in the hierarchy is a national pattern of metropolitan centers, each of which is the capital of an extensive hinterland "carved out of the slab of intermetropolitan space" (Borchert, 1972). (2) Within each of the hinterlands is a regional pattern of cities occupying the intermediate levels in the hierarchy. Each of these cities is the center of a surrounding region containing (3) a pattern of smaller settlements at the lowest levels of the hierarchy, each of which is the focus for a surrounding local area. Within the complex pattern of interaction that links everything together, the dominant paths are those across the national territory between the metropolitan centers, those downward through the hierarchy, and those radiating outward from cities into their surrounding regions.

Pattern Components

Nodal Regions

Explicit in the above description is the idea that the organization of the city system is focal in character (Philbrick, 1957). Each city is the focus of a surrounding area, the center of a *nodal region* (tributary or trade area) over which it exerts a gradient of influence similar to the field effect of a magnet. With increasing distance from the city, its influence weakens in accordance with the factors giving rise to distance-decay regularities, and eventually the influence of another city becomes dominant over the closer area surrounding it. The size of each nodal region depends on the number of goods, services, and opportunities provided by its center (the size of the magnet), which in turn is a function of its level in the urban hierarchy. The tributary area of a village is obviously smaller than a town's. Moreover, since the number of places decreases upward, the system comprises a large number of small nodal regions at its base and progressively fewer but more extensive ones at the successively higher levels in the hierarchy.

Nesting

If the nodal regions are delimited for all places within the metropolitan hinterlands and superimposed on a map, the result would resemble something like a layered mosaic of overlapping regions of varying size. Each layer corresponds to cities and functions at the various levels in the urban hierarchy. Thus *nested* within the hinterland of a metropolis (e.g., New Orleans) is a number of large nodal regions centered upon each of the larger cities (e.g., Mobile, Ala.). In turn, nested within these is a number of smaller nodal regions associated with the smaller places. And so this nested arrangement continues downward through the hierarchy. In reality, of course, the ideal pattern of nested nodal regions is warped and blurred by irregularities in the size and spacing of cities, their functional structure, and so on; but it is far from completely destroyed (see Chapter 6).

Dominance

Since a city's influence over the surrounding space is gradational and theoretically continuous, a particular part of that space may fall under the influence of more than one center (Fig. 3.5). The edges of nodal regions are not therefore sharp and marked by a definite boundary, as is the case, for example, with administrative areas. Rather, the influence of a center is represented by a series of isopleths of decreasing value outward from the center, any one of which could be selected as the basis delimiting the boundary of its nodal region. However, since the influence of one city over a particular part of the surrounding space is usually stronger than that of any of its competitors, in practice the boundaries of nodal regions are chosen in such a way as to delimit the region over which a particular center exerts a dominating influence. *Dominance* over surrounding regions is therefore an important characteristic of all cities, although the term has traditionally been reserved for the role played by metropolitan centers in the organization of their hinterlands and as dominant nodes in patterns of interaction within the city system.

An example of the dominance of a few large metropolitan centers in the pattern of interaction within the city system is shown in Figure 3.6, which is taken from a study of air-passenger traffic in the United States (Taaffe, 1962). Only the 13 cities shown on the maps by open circles are dominated by cities other than the nine major centers designated in the key. In this study dominance was defined as follows: city A dominates city B if it accounts for more air traffic to and from city B than does any other city. Thus Chicago dominates New York because it accounts for more passengers to and from it than does any other of the cities included in the study. The pattern of dominance in air traffic is, in fact, so well developed that every city on the map is ultimately linked to one of five major cities: New York, Chicago, Los Angeles, San Francisco, and Dallas–Houston.

These cities are at the top of the urban hierarchy defined on the basis of dominance in air-passenger flows. Note, however, that a different urban hierarchy would be identified if total number of passengers emplaned had been used as the defining criterion. Thus the hierarchical component in patterns of dominant flows may not be coincident with the urban hierarchy derived from the characteristics of cities themselves. For example, in the urban hierarchy defined by dominant migration flows between the largest 100 smsa's in the United States, Paterson and Newark, N.J., are positioned together with major cities like New York, Detroit, and San Francisco at the highest level, whereas they would occupy considerably lower levels in the urban hierarchy identified on the basis of population size and services provided (Brown, Odland, and Golledge, 1970).

Propinquity

The frictional effect of distance can be expected to give rise to a marked propinquity, or nearness, component in patterns of spatial interaction. Distance-decay regularities and the nested pattern of nodal regions explicitly recognize this fact. Evidence in support of this has been presented in a number of studies (for example, Clayton, 1974), and is also revealed in Figure 3.6. The air-traffic hinterlands of the dominant cities are clearly regional in character; the strongest links are with cities in the same general part of the country. Good examples are the cluster of cities centered on Seattle and the dominance of Chicago in the Midwest. The one exception is New York. Although it clearly dominates the Northeast, included in its hinterland are a number of cities much farther away than might be expected (e.g., Miami). This distortion can most certainly be accounted for in part by the special position of New York as the national metropolis.

The propinquity and hierarchical components in interaction patterns are closely interrelated; the one tends to reinforce the other. This is particularly clear in the pattern of information flows accompanying the diffusion of innovations. Numerous stud-

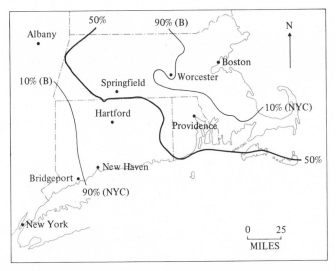

Fig. 3.5. Overlapping influence of New York City and Boston in southern New England, measured by telephone calls. (*Source*: after Green, 1955, Fig. 5.)

ies have shown that the largest cities in the system are, for a number of reasons, most often the earliest adopters of innovations, which thereafter diffuse downward through the urban hierarchy to the smaller places (Hudson, 1969; Pyle, 1969; Pred, 1971). Thus, although the first television station opened in the second largest city in America in 1940 (Chicago), the second opened the following year in New York, and thereafter TV stations diffused downward through the hierarchy so that in general the smaller the place, the later the arrival of a local station (Berry, 1970). However, superimposed on this pattern of hierarchical diffusion, and tending to blur its detail, was a strong propinquity effect. The smaller cities that established local TV stations at a very early date were those located closest to an early adopting large city.

Scrambling

Although dominant flows within the city system are largely hierarchical and characterized by a nearness component, it must be remembered that a considerable part of the total pattern of interaction between cities takes place without any regard for propinquity or hierarchy—but is what Borchert (1972) has aptly termed "scrambled" and confused. This is to be expected because many movements, flows, and transactions take place within the structure of organizations or reflect special cases of complementarity. Thus, to take an example, transactions between correspondent banks reflect "links between parent and branch plants, raw material producers and processors,

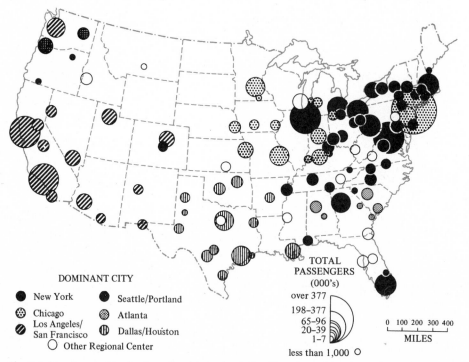

Fig. 3.6. Dominant cities in the urban hierarchy defined in terms of numbers of air passengers generated. (*Source*: Taaffe, 1962, Fig. 5.)

migrants and home relatives or businesses, specialized distributors and major industrial plants" (Borchert, 1972, p. 362), and the resultant patterns are in their detail essentially nonregional and nonhierarchical. Further evidence of this aspect to interaction patterns has been collected by Pred (1973) in the context of flows of information in the city system. Thus, although we can identify major components in patterns of interaction, it is well to bear in mind that these are broad generalizations of main trends, and that in its detail the pattern of interaction in the city system is inordinately complex and seemingly without spatial rhyme or reason.

Metropolitan Regions

The role of the national pattern of metropolitan centers and regions in the organization of the city system and national territory has been aptly summarized by Berry (1966, p. 188) as follows:

[There is] a set of metropolitan regions within which exchanges of each area are dominantly to and from the metropolitan centers, perhaps via smaller nodes in the urban hierarchy. Each region also has certain specialties that it provides for the nation as a whole—either based upon major resource complexes, or industry in the metropolis and its satellites. Flows of these specialties between regions hold them together in a national economy although the preponderance of them are routed between the metropolitan centers. Thus it is the inter-metropolitan linkages that hold the economy together.

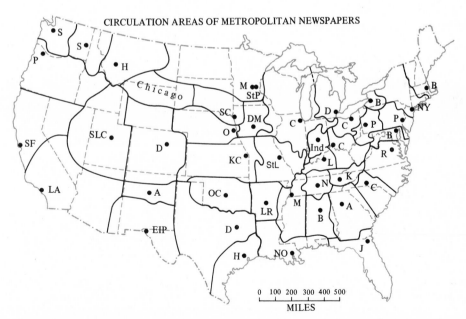

Fig. 3.7. Metropolitan regions in the United States based on newspaper circulation, 1933. (*Source:* after Park and Newcomb, 1933, Fig. 6.)

The dominance of these major centers is the outgrowth of the historical evolution of the urban pattern discussed in Chapter 2. Their present size, economic wealth, and cultural influence are in themselves enough to assure their continued domination of the national interaction matrix. Moreover, because of marked spatial bias in the interdependencies between the metropolitan centers, the predominance of intermetropolitan flows, and hence dominance of the centers themselves, appears to be reinforced through time (Pred, 1973).

The dominance of a metropolis over its surrounding hinterland is largely based on its role as a center for the organization of the regional economy: distribution, production, business services, and particularly finance (Kerr, 1968). In addition, however, because of its connections with the rest of the world, it is also a prime importer and a major center for the diffusion of culture, technology, and information throughout its hinterland, thereby making it more cosmopolitan. A good summary measure of the extent of the region over which the metropolis exerts a dominating influence in the organization of the regional economy is the degree to which it acts as the focus for financial transactions (see Duncan et al., 1960). The pattern of migration fields centered on the metropolitan centers is perhaps a rough guide to their role as foci in culture diffusion (Borchert, 1972). An early attempt to delimit metropolitan regions on the basis of newspaper circulation, perhaps a fair measure of the flow of local information, is shown in Figure 3.7.

The pattern of third-order metropolitan regions in the United States delimited on the basis of dominant correspondent banking links is shown in Figure 3.8 (Borchert, 1972). Since banks in smaller cities are linked to correspondents at a number of higher

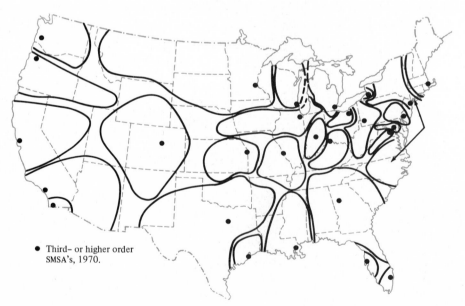

• Third– or higher order
SMSA's, 1970.

Fig. 3.8. Third-order metropolitan regions, United States, 1967, delimited on the basis of correspondent banking linkages. (*Source*: after Borchert, 1972, Fig. 5.)

order places, the dominant cities in the pattern of connections can be identified as those at which the number of accounts is greatest. Thus although Salt Lake City, for example, has links with correspondent banks in a number of third-order centers, it has most of its accounts in Denver. Denver is thus the dominant third-order metropolis for Salt Lake City, and consequently falls within its hinterland. In the same way, the dominant second-order metropolis can be identified; for Salt Lake City it is Chicago. In this way, then, every lower order city in the country can be assigned to its dominant second- or third-order metropolis, and the extent of the metropolitan regions established.

The nodal regions of third-order centers vary considerably in size, shape, and orientation. This is not unrelated to the spacing of the high-order metropoli themselves and the density of activity in the spaces surrounding them. In many ways the details of the pattern must be explained in terms of past developments—the process of urban growth discussed in the previous chapter. However, the major components in the pattern of spatial organization are evident. There are clear propinquity effects, and the 28 third-order regions nest within those of the eight second-order metropolitan centers. For these the pattern of regions is much simpler: New York, Chicago, and San Francisco between them dominate the pattern of linkages over most of the country.

The Subregional Pattern

The way in which the metropolis is connected to the hierarchy of smaller places within its hinterland is shown in Figure 3.9 for the metropolitan region based on

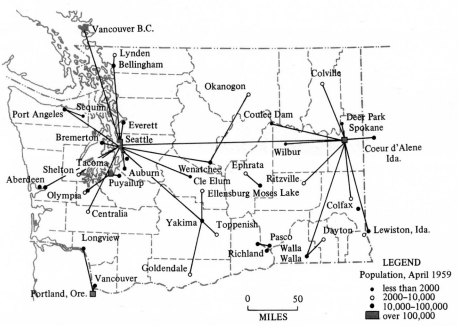

Fig. 3.9. Nodal structure in state of Washington, United States, based on the flow of telephone messages. (*Source*: Nystuen and Dacey, 1961, Fig. 2.)

Seattle. This map is based on dominant links in the pattern of telephone calls (Nystuen and Dacey, 1961). The existence of nodal organization characterized by propinquity and the hierarchical component in the pattern of linkages are clearly illustrated. A good example is the chain of connections starting at Dayton in the southeast corner of the region and proceeding upward in the urban hierarchy through Walla Walla, Spokane, and on to Seattle—the regional metropolis and dominant city. Major nodal structures are based on Seattle, Tacoma, Spokane, and Yakima—and the extent of the structures is closely related to the size of the centers. In a similar study in central Canada, the cities of Toronto, Ottawa, and Montreal were found to be dominant centers in the pattern of telephone calls there. Within the Toronto region, London and Kitchener appear as minor foci in the organization of the regional urban hierarchy, and the main pattern components discussed above are clearly apparent (Simmons, 1972).

WARPING AND DISTORTIONS

On a perfectly uniform plane and if distance minimization were the controlling force in interaction, then the ideal shape of nodal regions would be a perfect circle. Given all the imperfections of the real world, it is perhaps not surprising to find that this ideal is only rarely found. In reality, as shown in Figure 3.8, nodal regions generally tend to be more amoeba-like, with lobes and indentations. Nevertheless, despite these distortions, there is abundant evidence suggesting that they often approximate something like a circular form. Under certain conditions, however, the shapes of service areas have been noted to depart quite markedly from anything like a circular form. Haggett (1965) has drawn attention to two commonly found types: truncated and distorted nodal regions.

Truncation occurs when the influence of a center is constrained by barriers. Perhaps the classic example of this was that given by Lösch (1954) for the financial sphere of influence of El Paso, Texas, reproduced here as Figure 3.10. On the map each dot represents a bank keeping an account at a central bank in El Paso. The presence of the international boundary restricts this city's influence to the south, so that the extent of the field on the Mexican side is only about half that of the corresponding part in Texas.

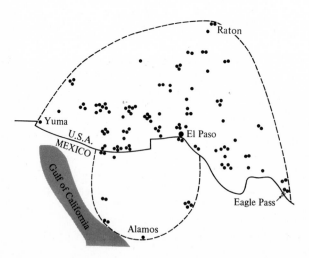

Fig. 3.10. A truncated service area: the financial sphere of influence of El Paso, Tex. (*Source*: Lösch, 1954, Fig. 86.)

In effect the cities south of the border are much farther away from El Paso than is indicated by their physical distances. Barrier effects are not only confined to political boundaries, but can result from natural barriers, such as unbridged rivers, extensive swamps, mountain ranges, and artificially induced economic barriers like tolls.

Distortion occurs for a variety of reasons. A common example is the elongation of nodal regions in the direction away from a competing center. This is particularly evident in the pattern of newspaper circulation areas in South Dakota. Figure 3.11 shows how the fields for Aberdeen, Huron, and Mitchell are considerably more extensive in a westerly direction, away from the competing influence of Sioux Falls and Watertown and the larger centers off the map to the east. The elongation of metropolitan regions is also evident on Figure 3.8; those of Minneapolis and Portland, Ore., are particularly good examples.

Spatial competition between cities for control over intervening space is therefore one of the important factors in distorting hinterlands and nodal regions. Large cities, by virtue of their stronger influence, encroach on the territory closer to smaller neighbors, which as a result dominate an even smaller area than might otherwise be the case. This effect is shown in Figure 3.12 for the hinterland boundary between New York City and Boston. The boundaries shown in Figure 3.12A indicate the lines of equal attraction (the median or 50 percent boundary) between the two cities for five selected indices, and an attempt has been made to generalize these by a single line — the modal boundary. That New York's hinterland is pushed closer to Boston is clear on both maps.

Reilly's Law

The way that the size of competing cities influences the location of the hinterland boundary between them was formalized many years ago by Reilly (1931) as the "Law of Retail Gravitation." Using the theory of gravitation from Newtonian physics as an

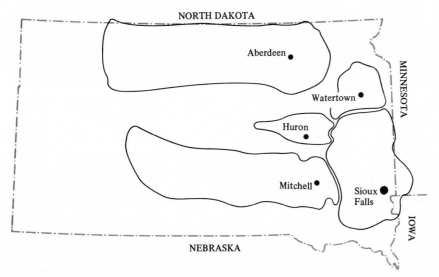

Fig. 3.11. Distorted service areas: newspaper circulation areas in South Dakota. (*Source*: after Park, 1929, Chart X.)

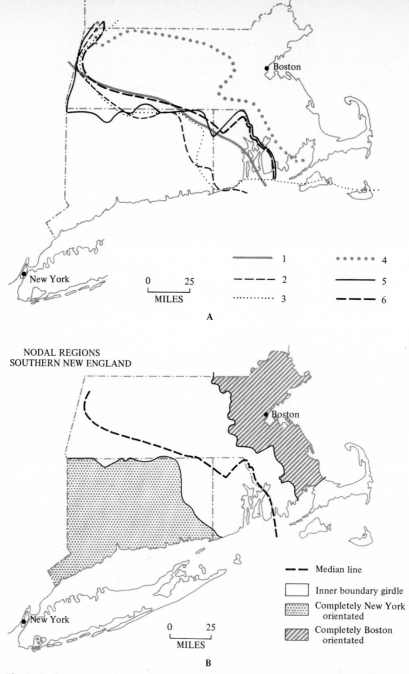

A

NODAL REGIONS
SOUTHERN NEW ENGLAND

— — — Median line

☐ Inner boundary girdle

▦ Completely New York
    orientated

▨ Completely Boston
    orientated

B

Fig. 3.12. Competition between New York City and Boston. (A) The modal boundary (6) is based on the median boundaries for (1) railroad coach passenger flows, (2) newspaper circulation, (3) telephone calls, (4) business addresses of directors of manufacturing firms, and (5) correspondent banks. (B) The resulting hinterlands for New York City and Boston. (*Source*: after Green, 1955, Figs. 3, 4, 5, 7, 8, and 9.)

analogy, Reilly argued that two cities attract retail trade from the intermediate area in direct proportion to their population size and in inverse proportion to the square of the distance between them. The breaking point, or boundary of equal attraction, between two competing cities can be determined quite simply from the following formula:

$$\text{Breaking point from city } A = \frac{\text{Distance between } A \text{ and } B}{1 + \sqrt{\dfrac{\text{Population of city } B}{\text{Population of city } A}}}$$

An example will make clear the application of this restatement of Reilly's Law. In 1960 the urbanized areas of St. Louis (city A) and Kansas City (city B) had populations of 1,667,693 and 921,121 respectively. These two cities are located 252 miles apart. Using the Reilly formula, the breaking point between them is

$$\frac{252 \text{ miles}}{1 + \sqrt{\dfrac{921,121}{1,667,693}}}$$

which equals 144.6 miles. St. Louis would therefore be expected to capture retail trade in the area up to 144.6 miles in the direction of Kansas City. The fact that Kansas City dominates over a smaller distance is consistent with that expected because of spatial competition between cities of unequal size.

INTERACTION MODELS

The importance of the various kinds of interaction for spatial organization and the many regularities found in flow patterns have led to the development of a wide range of interaction models. Excellent reviews of many of these are found in Isard (1960, 1974), Olsson (1964), and Wilson (1974). In this section we shall concentrate on the more elementary gravity models, a derivation of them known as potential models, and the intervening opportunity model.

The Gravity Model

The gravity model is the oldest, simplest, and most widely used of all interaction models. Although variations of it have been used since the first half of the nineteenth century (Carrothers, 1956), it was not until the 1940's that it was given the more general form by which it is recognized today. Based on ideas from Newtonian physics, the gravity model postulates that interaction between two centers of population varies directly with some function of the population size of the two centers, and inversely with some function of the distance between them. We have already seen one form of this, the Law of Retail Gravitation proposed by Reilly (1931), discussed above.

In mathematical form, a general expression for the gravity model is:

$$I_{ij} = \frac{(W_i P_i)\,(W_j P_j)}{(D_{ij}^b)} \qquad\qquad (3.1)$$

in which

I_{ij} = the volume of interaction between places i and j
W_i and W_j = empirically determined weights

P_i and P_j = the population sizes of places i and j
D_{ij} = the distance between places i and j
b = an exponent measuring the friction of distance

If we forget for the moment the problem of the weights attached to the values of P (the masses), and assume as Reilly did that b, the exponent of distance, is 2, then knowing the two population sizes and the distance between places i and j, we can compute the expected interaction between them. For example, if the population of city i is 5,000 and the population of city j is 10,000, and D_{ij} is 10 miles, then:

$$I_{ij} = \frac{(5,000)\ (10,000)}{10^2} = 500,000$$

Obviously, application of the gravity model in empirical studies is not quite so simple as this example suggests. The usefulness of the model is very closely related to the ways in which the masses and distance are measured, and also to the values that are given to the exponent of distance and the weights in equation 3.1.

Mass and Distance
Although the population size of cities has most commonly been used as the measure of mass in the gravity model, other measures have been used in empirical studies. Clearly the particular measure used depends on the problem under consideration. For example, Isard (1960) suggests that in studies of intermetropolitan migration, urban employment opportunities or income may be a better measure than population size. Similarly, in the context of a marketing problem, total dollar volume of sales of a city may be a more appropriate measure of mass than population. Other possiblities include value added in manufacturing, number of families, economic opportunities, total number of retail outlets, and so on.

Different ways of measuring distance are justified because different things are more or less relevant for different types of interaction. Thus, although mileage is the most common way of measuring distance, other possibilities are driving time, the cost of travel, effort or energy required to overcome the frictional effect of distance, number of traffic lights, and so on. Although some of these may be more logical in a given situation, many studies have shown that they only marginally improve the performance of the model in empirical study. Thus one of the conclusions arrived at in a study of freight movements by railroad between cities in Canada was that "distance measured in cost does not perform significantly better than distance measured in terms of miles" (Ray, 1965, p. 66).

The Weights
The problem of weighting the masses in the gravity model is a very difficult one. In many applications, the weights attached to the population are set equal to 1.0, but many studies have shown that the model's performance can be greatly improved if other values are selected. The basic reason for attaching weights to the masses is to bring out the differences in the population size. For example, the average Chinese farmer does not make the same contribution to sociological intensity as someone living in the Los Angeles metropolitan area (Dodd, 1950). Following this line of argument, it has been suggested that when population is used as the mass, it should be weighted by indices measuring differences in sex, age, income, occupation, years of schooling, and

so on. However, the essence of the gravity model is its simplicity; and although some kind of weighting may be necessary, this very quickly makes the model cumbersome and difficult to work with.

The Distance Exponent

Perhaps the most important problem in applying the gravity model is the choice of the value for b, the distance exponent. From a theoretical standpoint, it has been argued that the value of the exponent should be either 1.0 or 2.0. The latter value was preferred by Reilly. Empirical studies have shown, however, that the value of the distance exponent may lie anywhere in the range 0.5 to 3.0. For example, Ikle (1954) found values of 0.69 for trips by car between downtown Dallas and the rest of the city; 2.57 for automobile trips between Fort Wayne, Ind., and selected counties in that state; and 1.07 for airline trips between cities in the United States.

Variation in the value of the distance exponent is to be expected because the frictional effect of distance depends on the type of interaction. As we have seen, different products move with unequal ease, hence differences in transferability are reflected in the value of the distance exponent. It is not surprising to find, therefore, that several studies have demonstrated that there are marked differences in the value of b by type of trip. Thus Carroll and Bevis (1957) found lower b values for journeys to work than for shopping and school trips in Detroit. It is also clear from other studies that the value of the exponent varies through time, a fact that may reflect time-space convergence associated with transportation improvements.

The Potential Model

The gravity model enables us to calculate the expected interaction between a pair of cities. However, if we are interested in the interaction between place i and all other places including itself, then a number of calculations must be made and the results summed. Thus the expected interaction between place i and place 1, or I_{i1}, must be added to that between place i and place 2 (i.e., I_{i2}), and so on. This can be represented in equation form as follows:

$$\sum_{j=1}^{n} I_{ij} = \sum_{j=1}^{n} \frac{(P_i)(P_j)}{D_{ij}^b} + \frac{(P_i)(P_i)}{D_{ii}^b} \tag{3.2}$$

in which the symbols have the same meaning as in equation 3.1 and D_{ii} is some average radius of the area occupied by the place. Since P_i may be factored from the right-hand side of equation 3.2, by dividing both sides by P_i we get:

$$\sum_{j=1}^{n} \frac{I_{ij}}{P_i} = \sum_{j=1}^{n} \frac{P_j}{D_{ij}^b} + \frac{P_i}{D_{ii}^b} \tag{3.3}$$

Now the numerator on the left-hand side of equation 3.3 is the total interaction of place i with all other places including itself. When we divide this by the value of P_i, the total interaction associated with place i is expressed on a per capita or a per unit mass basis. Expressed in this form, the total interaction at place i is known as the *potential* at i, and is usually designated as $_iV$. By definition, then, the potential at place i is given by:

$$_iV = \sum_{j=1}^{n} \frac{P_j}{D_{ij}^b} + \frac{P_i}{D_{ii}^b} \tag{3.4}$$

The interpretation to be given to the population potential at a place is not yet entirely clear. It may indicate a kind of aggregate accessibility of the place to all others in the system. In this sense the potential at a place may be regarded as an index of likely interaction. Because of this, the concept of potential has mainly been used as a descriptive device (Stewart, 1950). Since potentials may be calculated for many different points in space, it is possible to plot them on a map. Interpolation between the mapped points then enables contours of equal potential to be drawn. An example of the kind of surface that results from this mapping is shown in Figure 3.13 for the United States.

It is interesting to compare this map with Figure 2.6, showing the distribution of metropolitan areas in 1960. The dominance of New York City is clearly brought out. East of the Sierras, every contour line closes round New York. In this part of the country, all other major cities are local peaks on the downward slope away from the national metropolis. West of the Sierras, three local peaks occur. One centers on Seattle, and the other two on San Francisco and Los Angeles. An example of the use of such a potential surface for more analytical purposes is presented in Chapter 5.

The Intervening-Opportunity Model

This approach to modeling interaction was proposed by Stouffer (1940) as an alternative to the gravity formulation. Stouffer argued that no necessary relationship existed between interaction and distance as it had been used in the gravity and other interaction models. Rather, he suggested that in the context of migration, the number of people moving a given distance is directly proportional to the number of opportunities at that distance and inversely proportional to the number of intervening opportunities. This relation can be expressed as follows:

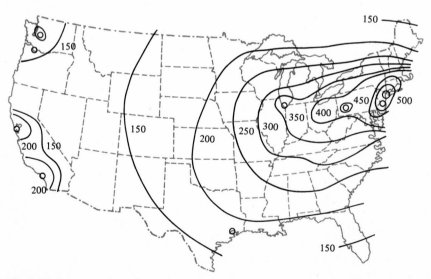

Fig. 3.13. Contours of equal population potential in the United States, 1940. (*Source*: Isard, 1956, Fig. 8. Adapted from *Theory in Marketing* by Reaves Cox and Wroe Alderson, eds., published by Richard D. Irwin, Inc., 1950, under the sponsorship of the American Marketing Association.)

$$M_{ij} = (N_j/N_{ij})K \qquad (3.5)$$

in which

M_{ij} = the expected interaction between places i and j
N_j = the number of opportunities at place j
N_{ij} = the number of opportunities intervening between places i and j
K = a constant

The main problem in applying the intervening-opportunities model is defining the opportunities in a suitable way. In his original presentation, Stouffer used the number of migrants that had earlier moved into the area. However, this involves a certain circularity in reasoning. Despite this, application of the model has shown that better predictions of interaction may be obtained in certain situations than the more straightforward gravity type of model (see, for example, Haynes, Poston, and Schnirring, 1973).

4
THE ECONOMIC BASE
AND
GROWTH OF CITIES

As a general rule the basis for cities is economic, and their population size is largely a reflection of the functions they perform. It follows from this that change in the population size of cities is in some way or other related to—perhaps even conditioned by—corresponding changes in their functional structure. A fundamental concern in urban geography is, therefore, with the way these two things are related, in the context of both the evolution of the urban pattern and the structure of the present-day city system. On the one hand this involves discussion of the general factors relating to urban growth, decline, and change; on the other it necessitates a consideration of the mechanisms whereby change in the functional structure of cities translates into changes in their population size. We shall begin to explore some of these problems in this chapter by looking at the urban economic base, elementary input-output models, and the way these relate in a general way to growth and change in the city system.

THE BASIC-NONBASIC CONCEPT

It was observed that one of the basic reasons for interaction between cities is the fact that they specialize in different activities; there is a spatial division of labor in the city system. Like countries, cities must export and import, and hence they are centers of trade engaged in the exchange of goods and services with each other. For in order to exist, a city must sell part of the product of the gross labor of its inhabitants elsewhere in order to import not only the necessary foodstuffs but also the raw materials for further production. However, not all production is exported; part is sold within the city itself and therefore does not earn income for the city from outside. This distinction between that part of the production of goods and services that a city sells beyond its borders and that part that is consumed locally is what lies at the core of the basic-nonbasic concept (Andrews, 1953; Pfouts, 1960).

The Meaning of Economic Base

The economic-base concept states that the reason not only for the existence but also for the growth of a city lies in the goods and services it produces and sells beyond its borders. The more goods and services a city can produce and sell beyond its immediate environs, the more income it will earn, the more viable it becomes, and the more growth will be generated. Thus the economy of a city can be divided into two parts. The *basic* (or city-forming) sector refers to the goods and services produced within the city but sold beyond its borders; the *nonbasic* (or city-serving) sector refers to the goods and services produced and sold within the city itself (Blumenfeld, 1955). Thus it is the basic sector that relates to urban growth.

In terms of the basic-nonbasic concept, economic activity in a city can therefore be expressed as a simple equality:

$$\text{Total activity in the city} = \text{Total in basic activities} + \text{Total in nonbasic activities}$$

or, symbolically, as:

$$(TA) = (BA) + (NBA)$$

This equality can be expressed in income terms as:

$$\text{Total income of the city} = \text{Total income derived from basic activities} + \text{Total income from nonbasic activities}$$

Therefore, if half the income of an urban area originates in nonbasic activities, the other half must come from basic activities.

These two proportions can be expressed as a ratio that is termed the *basic-nonbasic ratio*. In the example cited above, if half the income comes from basic activity and the other half comes from nonbasic activity, the ratio can be written 1:1. Alternatively, if a quarter of the city's income comes from basic activity, then three-quarters must come from nonbasic activities, and the ratio is 1:3. By convention, the basic side of the ratio is written first and is represented as unity.

Empirical Estimates of the Basic-Nonbasic Ratio

Most estimates of the basic-nonbasic ratio have been based on employment data rather than income because this is usually more difficult, if not often impossible, to obtain for cities. Using an employment definition, the equality can be simply rewritten as:

$$\text{Total employment in a city} = \text{Total employment in basic activities} + \text{Total employment in nonbasic activities}$$

The ratio can be calculated in either of two ways. The first way is to estimate the total employment in a city's basic and nonbasic activities and then to express these as a ratio. Thus for 1961 it was estimated that basic employment in Gainesville, Fla., totaled 12,171, whereas the nonbasic employment totaled 17,097. This gives a basic-nonbasic ratio of 1:1.4, which states that for every five basic workers in Gainesville in 1961 there were seven nonbasic workers.

A second method is to calculate for a given time period the changes in employment in a city's basic and nonbasic activities and to express these changes as a ratio. Both ways of estimating basic-nonbasic ratios are illustrated in Table 4.1 for Wichita, Kansas, for 1940 and 1950. From this table it can be calculated that the basic-nonbasic ratio in 1940 was 1:2.5, and in 1950 1:2.0; however, when the employment changes in the decade 1940–1950 are used to calculate the basic-nonbasic ratio, the result is 1:1.6. Thus one of the weaknesses of the basic-nonbasic ratio is that its numerical value may vary depending on the method used to calculate it.

It can be hypothesized that there should be some regularity in the trend of the basic-nonbasic ratio with city size. As cities get larger, a greater proportion of the total employment is engaged in the production of goods and services that are sold within the settlement itself. Thus it follows that the basic sector of a city's total labor force should get smaller with an increase in its population size. Consequently the basic-nonbasic ratio should become larger and larger as the population of a city increases. Despite the intuitive appeal of this hypothesis, the results of empirical studies indicate that such trends are difficult to discern. Because of this the usefulness of the basic-nonbasic ratio in practical situations has been seriously questioned by several researchers (for example, Lane, 1966).

Discussion of the Basic-Nonbasic Concept

Although the basic-nonbasic concept is recognized as a gross oversimplification and hence is of limited analytical value, it nevertheless has a certain appeal and is accepted as a useful device for descriptive purposes. Moreover, since the concept explicitly recognizes the existence of spatial relationships, its potential usefulness for

Table 4.1.   BASIC AND NONBASIC EMPLOYMENT IN WICHITA, KANSAS, 1940 AND 1950

Component	1940 Employment	1950 Employment	1940–1950 Employment Change
Nonbasic	37,148	59,325	22,177
Basic	14,943	29,250	14,307
Total	52,091	88,575	36,484

Source: Federal Reserve Bank of Kansas City (1952), p. 4.

geographic study have not gone unnoticed. Thus, for example, Alexander (1954) has drawn attention to the fact that:

1. The concept brings into sharper focus the economic ties of cities or regions to other areas. Furthermore, the composition of a city's or region's basic activity may be quite different from that of its total economic structure. Since it is the basic activity that is important for the existence and economic growth of a city or region, the explicit identification of such activity is significant in distinguishing between city types and regions.

2. The concept makes possible a more satisfactory classification of cities. Since basic activities express the link between cities and their surrounding regions, identification of these activities offers a more realistic basis for the classification of cities in terms of their functional specialization (see Chapter 7).

3. The concept provides a basis for classifying individual businesses. For example, two firms might be engaged in manufacturing, but because of the location of their markets one could be predominantly basic and the other essentially nonbasic or service activity.

The limitations of the basic-nonbasic concept are both practical and conceptual (Isard, 1960). A primary difficulty concerns the unit of measurement used in calculating the basic-nonbasic ratio. Employment figures have usually been used, but these give a poor indication of income because of differences in wage levels between workers. Consequently, the use of employment figures is questionable whenever the basic-nonbasic ratio is used to estimate the amount of income brought into a city. Moreover, even if it is possible to use some sort of income data—for example, payrolls—a further difficulty arises because of the fact that unearned income is ignored, and unearned income in some cities may be very large, particularly in some of the retirement cities and holiday resorts.

Another set of problems is associated with the identification of the basic and nonbasic components itself. Firms themselves can rarely be classified as basic or nonbasic, since usually part of their total production is sold outside the city and part is consumed locally. It is therefore necessary to determine which proportion of a firm's employment or payroll is related to its role as a basic activity and which part is associated with its nonbasic function. In this context another difficulty arises owing to the linkages between activities. Many firms are subsidiaries feeding other firms; for example, coal can be mined locally and sold for fuel to a local steel producer who exports finished steel products. The question then arises whether the coal mine is a basic or nonbasic activity. In most studies it would be regarded as a nonbasic activity because its output is locally consumed.

A fundamental practical problem arises in connection with the way cities themselves are delimited. Quite clearly the distinction between basic and nonbasic activities depends on where we draw the boundary between city and surrounding region, since it is in terms of this boundary that the term "exports" takes on specific meaning. In turn, the size of the base area is one of the important factors governing the numerical value of the basic-nonbasic ratio (Roterus and Calef, 1955). For example, a firm that is essentially basic within the city of Chicago may be predominantly nonbasic if the state of

Illinois is used as the base area. Ultimately, if the world is taken as the base area, then all activities are nonbasic.

Moreover, the choice of base area is not unrelated to the way in which commuters are handled in connection with the definition of basic and nonbasic employment. If workers originate outside the area delimited as the city, then strictly speaking they should not be counted as part of the city's employment because their wages represent an export of the city's income. Therefore the problem associated with the delimitation of the base area in terms of which basic and nonbasic employment, income, and activity are defined is crucial, and one that has no single or best solution. In addition to such rigid statistical definitions as "urbanized areas" and smsa's, other possibilities include concepts such as *functional economic areas* (Fox and Kumar, 1965; Berry, 1967) and "daily urban systems" (Berry, 1968a). The best one can aim for is the adoption of a standardized way of delimiting urban areas, since this at least enables meaningful comparisons to be made between different cities.

The conceptual limitations are rather more subtle than the practical ones, but equally important since they mainly concern the way that the basic-nonbasic ratio relates to the growth of cities. Although this aspect is taken up again later in the chapter, some of the main difficulties can be outlined at this stage of the discussion. It is important to remember that the basic-nonbasic ratio is in fact an average over the whole range of economic activity in the city. Increases in some kinds of activities may, however, generate greater growth than similar increases in other activities. Consequently, the ratio fails to distinguish between the greater and lesser growth-generating capacity of different activities. Furthermore, the ratio fails to take into account the feedback effects in the growth process. For example, it can be argued that city size itself creates growth. Large cities demand a greater range of services, which are subsequently established in them to satisfy these needs. These firms might export part of their final product even though they were established as city-serving activities. The fact that a firm is partially a basic activity may therefore be quite incidental to its primary function, which is to provide goods and services for the city itself (Richardson, 1972a).

MINIMUM REQUIREMENTS AND THE ECONOMIC STRUCTURE OF U.S. CITIES

A number of attempts have been made to estimate in more general ways the expected proportion of a city's economic activity that is city-serving and that which is city-forming and growth-inducing. Two of these attempts—those by Alexandersson (1956) and Ullman and Dacey (1962)—will be discussed here.

The Use of the Fifth Percentile in an Employment Array

Alexandersson used the 1950 census of population to obtain the occupations of employed persons by industry groupings for 864 cities and urbanized areas with populations of 10,000 or more. For each city he calculated the percentage of employed persons working in each of 35 employment groupings (see Table 4.3). Then, for each employment group, the cities were arrayed by these percentages from the lowest to the highest; and the percentage at the fifth percentile was designated as the k value for that employment group.

As an example, consider the employment array for wholesale trade—one of the four employment groupings in the trade category. Table 4.2 shows that Sanford, Fla., is the city with the largest proportion of its total employment in this industry group. It therefore ranks number 864 and is the 100th percentile in the ranked array. The city with the smallest proportion (0.01 percent) of its employment in wholesale trade is Richland, Wash. Out of a total of 864 cities, the fifth percentile corresponds to the 43rd city in the array, which in 1950 had 1.4 percent of its employed persons in wholesale trade. Thus only 5 percent of all the cities had 1.4 percent or less of their employed persons working in wholesale trade and 95 percent of the cities had more than 1.4 percent of their employed persons working in this industry group. The k values calculated in this way for the 35 employment groupings are listed in Table 4.3. Cumulative frequency distributions (ogive curves) for wholesale trade and four other industry groups are shown in Figure 4.1. The more concentrated an industry is in a small number of cities, the closer the curve will be to the vertical axis and the more sharply it will change direction.

Alexandersson considered that these k values indicate the minimum percent of employment one would expect in a given industry group in any city. The fifth percentile was chosen after some experimentation. Alexandersson tried using the first percentile city, but found that this gave a distorted picture because cities at the lower end of the distribution showed highly abnormal employment patterns. The fifth percentile cities, however, seemed in fact to exhibit more the characteristics that were expected of most settlements. It is interesting to note that the k values add up to 37.7 percent (Table 4.3), which implies a basic-nonbasic ratio of 1:0.6. Of course, the sum of the k values does not represent the minimum requirements of *all* cities in the United States, because those at the bottom of the array represent the minimum amount. Consequently, the figure of 37.7 percent can be interpreted as the minimum percentage of employment that is to be expected on the average to serve the requirements of a city itself in the United States. Employment in excess of this figure therefore constitutes a city's basic employment.

Table 4.2. **EMPLOYMENT ARRAY: WHOLESALE TRADE, 1950**

Percentile	Rank	Settlement	Percent of Employed Persons in Wholesale Trade
100	864	Sanford, Fla.	18.7
	863	Suffolk, Va.	16.9
	862	Mercedes, Tex.	16.7
5	43		1.4
	4	Kannapolis, N.C.	0.4
	3	Kings Park, N.Y.	0.2
	2	Oak Ridge, Tenn.	0.2
	1	Richland, Wash.	0.01

SOURCE: Alexandersson (1956), p. 98; and Morrissett (1958), pp. 240–241.

Table 4.3.   *K* VALUES AND NATIONAL PERCENTAGES, U.S.A., 1950

Employment Groupings	k	National Percentage
Mining	0	.9
Construction	3.5	6.2
Durable manufacturing	0.3	15.9
Furniture, and lumber and wood products	0	1.3
Primary metal industries	0	2.6
Fabricated metal industries	0	1.8
Machinery, except electrical	0.1	2.9
Electrical machinery, equipment and supplies	0	1.8
Motor vehicles, and motor vehicle equipment	0	2.0
Transportation equip., excl. motor vehicles	0	1.1
Other durables	0.2	2.4
Nondurable manufacturing	1.6	14.2
Food and kindred products	0.7	3.0
Textile mills products	0	2.2
Apparel and other fabricated textile products	0	2.4
Printing, publishing, and allied industries	0.7	2.1
Chemicals and allied products	0.1	1.3
Other nondurable goods	0.1	3.2
Transportation and utilities	2.9	9.2
Railroads and railway express service	0.4	2.9
Trucking and warehousing	0.5	1.3
Other transportation	0.5	2.0
Telecommunications	0.6	1.4
Utilities and sanitary	0.9	1.6
Trade	14.2	22.6
Wholesale trade	1.4	4.4
Food and dairy products and milk retailing	2.7	3.5
Eating and drinking places	2.1	3.6
Other retail	8.0	11.1
Services	15.2	30.8
Finance, insurance, and real estate	1.8	4.5
Business services	0.2	1.1
Repair services	1.1	1.6
Private households	1.3	3.3
Hotels and lodging places	0.3	1.1
Other personal service	2.1	3.0
Entertainment and recreation services	0.7	1.2
Medical and other health services	1.8	3.6
Education service	2.6	3.9
Other professional and related services	1.2	2.2
Public administration	2.1	5.3
Total	37.7	100.0

Source: Morrissett (1958), Table 1.

Variations in k

It has previously been suggested that large cities should have more nonbasic activities than smaller cities. Morrissett (1958) has used the k values from Alexandersson's study to examine this hypothesis and to investigate regional variations in the minimum requirements of U.S. cities. After 123 of the cities originally included in Alexandersson's study had been omitted because of their rather special functional structure (e.g., college towns and administrative cities such as Washington, D.C.), the remaining 741 cities were divided into seven size categories in two regions—the Northeast, and the South and West, as shown in Table 4.4.

From this table it can be observed that the sums of the k values increase with city size both in the Northeast and in the South and West of the United States. In other words, large cities do tend to have more of their total economic structures devoted to service activities than small cities (the basic-nonbasic ratio for cities with more than one million inhabitants in the South and West is 1:2.4). Furthermore, the service (or nonbasic) component seems to be higher in the cities of the South and West than in those of the Northeast. This is because the employment structure of cities in the Northeast is dominated far more by manufacturing than that of cities in the South and West. Manufacturing cities are more concerned with basic activities, exporting their finished products to other cities in North America and the rest of the world.

Reading across the rows of Table 4.4, one can also observe that the k values for individual employment categories increase with size of city. In other words, all activities tend to become more city-serving in the larger settlements. It can therefore be concluded that the economic structure of cities becomes more city-serving as their size increases and that regionally there is more specialization in cities in the Northeast than in those of the South and West. The increase in size of the basic-nonbasic ratio implied

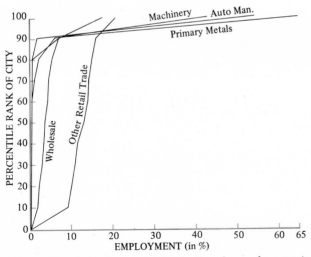

Fig. 4.1. Cumulative frequency distributions for employment in five industrial groupings in cities in the United States, 1950. (*Source*: based on information from Alexandersson, 1956, Table 5.2.)

Table 4.4.   K VALUES ($P_{.05}$) BY REGION AND CITY SIZE, U.S.A., 1950

	Alexanderson's k	Northeast Population[a]							South and West Population[a]						
		10	25	50	100	250	500	1000	10	25	50	100	250	500	1000
Mining	0	0	0	0	0	0	0	0	0	0	0	0	0	0	0
Construction	3.5	2.4	2.7	3.0	3.4	3.8	4.0	4.2	4.2	4.4	4.6	5.0	5.7	6.1	6.4
Durable Mfg.															
Furniture	0	0	0.1	0.1	0.2	0.3	0.4	0.4	0.1	0.1	0.1	0.2	0.4	0.5	0.5
Prime Metals	0	0	0	0.1	0.1	0.3	0.5	0.4	0	0	0	0	0.1	0.2	0.3
Fab. Metals	0	0.1	0.1	0.1	0.2	0.5	1.1	1.4	0	0	0.1	0.2	0.3	0.4	0.7
Machinery	0.1	0.1	0.2	0.3	0.5	0.9	1.0	1.0	0.1	0.1	0.1	0.1	0.2	0.4	0.8
Elec. Mach.	0	0	0.1	0.1	0.1	0.2	0.7	0.7	0	0	0	0	0	0.1	0.2
Mot. Vehic.	0	0	0	0	0	0.1	0.3	0.3	0	0	0	0	0	0.1	0.1
Transport. Eq.	0	0	0	0	0	0.1	0.1	0.2	0	0	0	0	0	0	0.1
Other dur.	0.2	0.2	0.3	0.4	0.6	1.0	1.3	1.3	0.1	0.1	0.2	0.3	0.6	0.8	0.8
Nondurable Mfg.															
Food Mfg.	0.7	0.5	0.6	0.8	1.0	1.4	1.8	1.8	0.7	0.8	0.8	1.0	1.3	2.0	2.7
Textile Mfg.	0	0	0	0	0	0	0	0.1	0	0	0	0	0	0	0.1
Apparel	0	0	0	0	0.1	0.2	0.2	0.2	0	0	0	0	0.2	0.5	0.6
Printing	0.7	0.5	0.6	0.7	0.8	1.1	1.4	1.4	0.6	0.7	0.7	0.9	1.1	1.3	1.3
Chemicals	0.1	0.1	0.1	0.1	0.1	0.3	0.6	0.7	0	0.1	0.1	0.1	0.2	0.4	0.6
Other Nondur.	0.1	0.1	0.1	0.2	0.3	0.6	1.2	1.5	0	0	0.1	0.1	0.2	0.5	0.8
Mfg. not spec.	—	0	0	0	0.1	0.1	0.1	0.1	0	0	0	0	0.1	0.1	0.1
Transp. & Util.															
Railroads	0.4	0.4	0.4	0.4	0.4	0.5	0.7	0.9	0.3	0.4	0.5	0.7	1.1	1.2	1.5
Trucking	0.5	0.4	0.4	0.5	0.6	0.8	0.9	1.0	0.5	0.5	0.6	0.7	0.9	1.0	1.2
Other Transp.	0.5	0.4	0.5	0.5	0.5	0.6	0.8	1.1	0.5	0.6	0.7	0.8	1.0	1.4	2.1
Telecom.	0.6	0.5	0.6	0.7	0.7	0.8	0.9	1.1	0.8	0.8	0.8	0.9	1.0	1.1	1.4
Utilities	0.9	0.7	0.8	0.8	0.9	1.1	1.3	1.3	0.8	0.9	0.9	1.0	1.1	1.2	1.4
Trade															
Wholesale	1.4	0.9	1.1	1.3	1.6	2.2	2.8	3.0	1.4	1.6	2.1	2.7	3.8	4.7	5.1
Food Stores	2.7	2.7	2.7	2.7	2.7	2.8	2.8	2.9	2.7	2.7	2.7	2.7	2.7	2.8	2.8
Eating	2.1	1.9	2.9	2.0	2.1	2.5	2.8	2.9	2.1	2.2	2.3	2.4	2.7	2.9	3.0
Oth. Retail	8.0	7.2	1.5	7.9	8.3	8.9	9.2	9.2	9.0	9.2	9.4	9.9	10.6	10.8	10.8
Services															
Fin. and Ins.	1.8	1.5	1.6	1.7	1.9	2.3	2.6	3.0	1.7	1.9	2.1	2.4	3.2	4.1	4.7
Bus. Serv.	0.2	0.2	0.3	0.3	0.4	0.6	0.7	0.7	0.2	0.3	0.3	0.4	0.6	0.7	1.0
Repair Serv.	1.1	1.0	1.0	1.0	1.0	1.1	1.2	1.2	1.1	1.2	1.2	1.3	1.5	1.5	1.6
Private HH.	1.3	0.8	0.9	0.9	1.0	1.3	1.4	1.4	0.8	0.9	1.1	1.2	1.9	1.9	1.9
Hotels	0.3	0.2	0.2	0.2	0.3	0.4	0.5	0.5	0.3	0.4	0.4	0.5	0.8	1.0	1.0
Oth. Pers. Ser.	2.1	1.7	1.9	2.0	2.0	2.0	2.0	2.0	2.2	2.2	2.3	2.4	2.5	2.5	2.5
Entertain.	0.7	0.5	0.5	0.6	0.8	0.8	0.8	0.8	0.8	0.8	0.8	0.9	0.9	0.9	1.0
Med. Ser.	1.8	1.6	1.7	1.9	2.1	2.5	2.7	2.7	1.5	1.8	2.0	2.2	2.6	2.8	2.8
Education	2.6	2.2	2.2	2.3	2.4	2.6	2.6	2.6	2.9	2.9	2.9	2.9	2.8	2.8	2.7
Oth. Prof.	1.2	1.0	1.1	1.2	1.3	1.5	1.6	1.6	1.2	1.2	1.3	1.4	1.6	1.9	1.9
Pub. Admin.	2.1	1.7	1.9	2.0	2.2	2.4	2.6	3.0	2.3	2.4	2.5	2.6	3.0	3.2	3.7
Total	37.7	31.5	34.1	36.8	40.7	48.6	55.6	58.7	38.9	41.2	43.7	47.9	56.8	64.3	71.0

[a] In thousands.

Note: The values in italics are those for which $k \geqq \dfrac{\text{national percentage}}{4}$. The k values were read from smoothed curves.

SOURCE: Morrissett (1958), Table 3.

by this is due to the fact that there are greater possibilities for interindustry linkages in larger cities. Large urban areas have a diversity of economic activities that both produce for and purchase from other local activities.

Morrissett also used the fifth-percentile values to obtain some idea of the degree to which activities are distributed ubiquitously — that is, found in all cities — and the degree to which they are sporadic — that is, found only in a few places. An activity was considered to be sporadic if its k value was less than one-quarter of the national percentage. Alternatively, activities with k values one-quarter or greater than the national percentage were considered to be ubiquitously distributed. The ubiquitous activities are shown in italics in Table 4.4; and the general distribution of the italicized figures indicates that as city size increases, more and more activities are classified as ubiquitous in all regions. It can therefore be concluded that the economic structure of large cities is much more diversified than that of small cities. Moreover, owing to their greater total of k values, large cities tend to be like each other, whereas considerable differences in economic structure can be expected among small cities.

The Ullman-Dacey Minimum-Requirements Approach

Ullman and Dacey (1962, 1969) approached the problem of identifying the basic-nonbasic structure of cities in the United States in another way. Cities were first classified on the basis of their population into size groups, and then for each employment category the city in each group that had the lowest percentage of its employment in that category was found. This percentage was considered to represent the minimum requirement for the activity for all cities in that particular size group.

Using this method, Ullman and Dacey calculated the minimum requirements for 14 employment categories in six size groupings of American cities. The graphs of these minimum requirements plotted against city size are shown in Figure 4.2. The straight lines on the graphs indicate that on average the minimum requirements for each of the employment categories increase with city size, but at different rates. With these graphs, the minimum requirements can be calculated for any city with more than 10,000 inhabitants in the United States.

For example, Sioux City, Iowa, had a population of 100,000 in 1960 and should therefore have 0.6 percent of its total labor force in agriculture serving the city itself, 1.8 percent in wholesale trade, 1.9 percent in durable manufacturing, 3 percent in nondurable manufacturing, 3.4 percent in construction, and 3.8 percent in transportation. As we read farther along the graph to the highest proportion, we see that 13 percent of the total labor force should be employed in retail trade serving the city itself. In the same way, figures can be estimated for the service activities shown on the other graph. Thus if the total labor force of a city is known, it is possible to calculate the percentage that one would expect to find in nonbasic activities in a city of any size. Once the nonbasic part of the total is determined, the basic-nonbasic ratio can be calculated.

The minimum-requirements approach is very useful in that, like Morrissett's use of Alexandersson's k values, it emphasizes the changing economic structure of cities with city size. However, by taking the minimum value in an employment category, there is a very strong danger that an urban area with an abnormal employment structure may be selected to give the minimum requirement for that particular size group. For example, in the group of 14 cities with over one million inhabitants, Washington,

D.C., with 2.3 percent of its employment in durable manufacturing, had the smallest percentage in this employment category, and hence this figure was selected as the minimum requirement for all other cities in this size group. Obviously Washington, D.C., by its very nature as the capital of the United States, is bound to have a quite abnormal employment structure. However, the technique of fitting regression lines to the data, as shown in Figure 4.2, tends to average out these kinds of abnormalities.

All these approaches to evaluating the economic base of settlement, however, disregard the fact that it is the flow of money into the settlement that generates economic activity and growth. The employment definition of the basic-nonbasic ratio is at best a poor substitute for detail concerning the actual money flow within the urban economy. Furthermore, the use of money flows emphasizes that a city is, in fact, an economic system (like an individual family household) that has to be financially solvent if it is to be viable.

MULTIPLIERS

The concept of the *multiplier*, which is a fundamental part of the mechanism of urban growth, is based on the circular flow of income in the city system. Central to the basic-nonbasic concept is the idea that money flows into a city as a return from the sale of exports. We also noted that with its emphasis on exports, the concept does not recog-

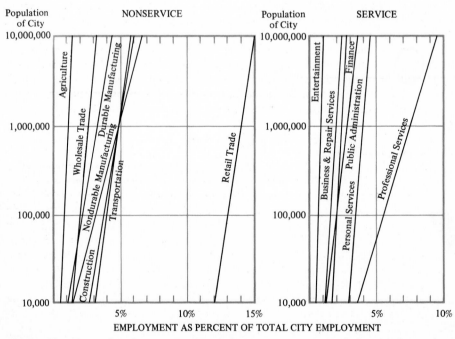

Fig. 4.2. The relationships between city size and minimum requirements for 13 industry types for U.S. cities. (*Source*: Ullman and Dacey, 1962, Fig. 2.)

agais

nize other ways by which income may flow into a city—the example of unearned income was cited, and to this can be added investment inflows, government spending, and so on. At the same time, money flows out of the city—the example of wages paid to commuters was cited, but more important is the outflow of money connected with the purchase of imports of goods and services and so on. If we now assume that at a given time period income and expenditure are balanced so that a state of equilibrium exists, then the concept of the multiplier can be illustrated.

Suppose that a new industrial plant representing an investment of three million dollars is constructed in the city. Clearly there will be an increase in local expenditures, if only because of the wages paid out to the labor force employed at the plant. Part of this income will be passed on to other activities in the city as workers and businessmen spend it on local goods and services and so on. In turn, the incomes of the shopkeepers and tavern owners will be increased, and part of this income will again be fed back into the city's economy through their own consumption. Several rounds of increases in income and expenditure will be created within the city in this way as the initial effect of the new industrial plant "multiplies" itself through the local economy. At the same time, however, money is being withdrawn from the city—through savings, taxes, and especially the purchase of imports. Ultimately, then, a point will be reached where the level of outflow reaches the three million dollars of the original investment, and the multiplier stops as a new state of equilibrium is attained.

In this process, the growth in income in the city created by the new investment will have exceeded the original three million dollars by a finite amount. The multiplier can be defined, then, as the ratio of the change in income to the permanent change in expenditure that created it (see Lloyd and Dicken, 1972). Thus if we imagine that the total growth in income at the city had been 4.2 million dollars, then the numerical value of the multiplier would have been 1.4. In a recent study of the impact of the Boeing Company on the regional economy of the Puget Sound area, Erickson (1974) has calculated that the effect of 500 million dollars of new investments by the company in the region from 1963 through 1967 had a total income multiplier effect of 1.9.

The Economic Base Multiplier

The calculation of multipliers based on income and expenditures in the city system is complicated and made difficult by the fact that the necessary data on money flows are often not available. As a result, attempts have been made to calculate simple multipliers using figures on employment (Tiebout, 1960). The simplest of all multipliers based on employment is that calculated from the basic-nonbasic ratio of cities. If the basic-nonbasic ratio is constant, a unit increase (U) in basic activity will yield an increase in total employment equal to the product of U and the sum of the figures comprising the basic-nonbasic ratio. Thus if the ratio is 1:3, an increase of 10 in basic employment will yield a total increase in employment of 40 workers, or $10 \times (1 + 3) = 40$. Thus the basic-nonbasic ratio is a crude form of economic multiplier known as the export-base multiplier (Tiebout, 1956), and in an urban context is known as the *urban economic multiplier*.

The validity of this form of multiplier depends on the assumption that nonbasic employment is a constant function of total employment in a city, or $(NBE) = v(TE)$, which can be rewritten as $(TE) = \frac{1}{v}(NBE)$, where v is a parameter indicating the constant relationship between nonbasic and total employment. Therefore,

$$(TE) = \frac{1}{1-v}(BE) = m(BE)$$

where m is the multiplier (Berry, 1967b). In the basic-nonbasic ratio used as an example above, m equals 4 and v is 0.75. Thus m may be written variously as

$$m = \frac{1}{1-v} = \frac{1}{1 - \frac{(NBE)}{(TE)}} = \frac{TE}{BE} = 1 + \frac{NBE}{BE}$$

As a consequence, the multiplier m links the basic component to total activity, and the constant v links the nonbasic component to the total. But the implication of the term "multiplier" is that changes in the amount of basic employment *cause* changes in the amount of total employment.

Some researchers have made extensive use of the economic-base multiplier for projection purposes (Hoyt, 1961; Andrews, 1953). By evaluating future prospects for expansion in basic activities within a city and then applying multipliers derived from basic-nonbasic ratios calculated from its existing industrial composition, they have forecast the impact of expansion of the basic sector on total activity within the city.

INPUT-OUTPUT MODELS

As we have noted, a major limitation of the basic-nonbasic concept is its emphasis on the aggregate effects of increases in urban economic activity. Moreover, although conceptually the concept relates to income changes, its practical application has largely been confined to changes in employment. An alternative technique that incorporates the real-world pattern of money flows is *input-output analysis* (Leontief et al., 1953; Miernyk, 1965). A major advantage of this technique is that it explicitly considers individual sectors in the urban economy and, moreover, it recognizes that because of interdependencies, an increase in production in one sector is likely to result in increases in other sectors because of the linked nature of activities within cities or regions.

A Simple Model

Assume the existence of an area that has no trade connections with the outside world and experiences no growth of any kind. The economy of the city or region can be subdivided into a number of sectors. These will be simplified to six major sectors of economic activity: agricultural and extractive industries, manufacturing industry, transportation, housing, financial, and all others. Presume that a census is taken showing the value of output for each of these sectors and also the amount that each sector purchases from every other.

If the census records purchases made by each sector from every other sector, then a matrix can be constructed as shown in Table 4.5. By reading down the columns of this table we can see how much each sector purchases from every other. Thus, for example, the agricultural and extractive sector bought 20 million dollars' worth of inputs from itself, 10 million dollars' worth from industry, 5 million dollars' worth from transportation, 30 million dollars' worth of inputs from housing, 5 million dollars' worth from the financial sector, and 10 million dollars' worth from all others, making a total of 80 million dollars' worth of purchases by the agricultural and extractive sector. Likewise, the purchases by the transportation sector are 5 million dollars from the agricultural extractive sector, 5 million dollars from industry, 15 million dollars from transportation, 10 million dollars from housing, 15 million dollars from the financial sector, and 10 million dollars from all others, for a total of 60 million dollars' worth of purchases.

On the other hand, by reading across the rows of Table 4.5 we can see how much each sector sells to every other. Thus, for example, the agricultural and extractive sector retained 20 million dollars for its own use, had sales of 25 million dollars to industry, 5 million dollars to transportation, 20 million dollars to housing, 5 million dollars to the financial sector, and 5 million dollars to all others, for a total of 80 million dollars' worth of sales. Thus with perfect data in a closed system, total sales should equal total purchases. In this particular case the total purchases (80 million dollars) equals the total sales (80 million dollars) for the agricultural and extractive sector. It will be seen from Table 4.5 that all inputs equal all outputs in this very simple system. A table of this kind is known as an *input-output* table.

Advantages of Input-Output Tables

Input-output tables of this type obviously have many advantages. In the first place, they record concisely a large amount of information about the economy and the intersectoral relationships between various major groupings of economic activities. Furthermore, the table provides a framework for data collection, it reveals gaps, and it shows how they can be filled. For example, if it is not known how much the housing sector purchases from the financial sector, it is a simple operation to add up all the

Table 4.5. INPUT-OUTPUT FLOW (IN MILLIONS OF DOLLARS) IN A HYPOTHETICAL URBAN REGION

Industry Producing \ Industry Purchasing	Agriculture and Extractive	Industry	Transportation	Housing	Finance	All Others	Total Gross Outputs
Agriculture and extractive	$20	$ 25	$ 5	$ 20	$ 5	$ 5	$ 80
Industry	10	40	5	40	10	15	120
Transportation	5	10	15	15	10	5	60
Housing	30	25	10	5	10	30	110
Financial	5	10	15	10	5	5	50
All others	10	10	10	20	10	10	70
Total Gross Inputs	$80	$120	$60	$110	$50	$70	$490

other purchases, and, knowing that inputs equal outputs, subtract inputs from the output of 110 million dollars' worth of goods, to find that housing purchases 10 million dollars from the financial sector.

These tables also facilitate a comparison of the magnitudes of sectors and show where further subdivisions might be illuminating. For example, the totals for the financial sector and the transportation sector are reasonably small, but for the industry and housing sectors the totals are very large. These sectors might be further subdivided. The industry sector, for example, might be subdivided into durable and nondurable manufacturing, as in Table 4.4. The housing sector might well be subdivided into high-cost housing and low-cost housing. The most important use of input-output tables, however, is that they offer a technique for projecting the impact of an increase in economic activity in any one or more sectors.

The Use of Input-Output Tables for Projection

Consider the financial column of Table 4.5. The column lists the inputs of each sector of the economy of the region into the financial sector. At the bottom of the column is the total value of inputs, which equals the total value of outputs of the financial sector. If this figure is divided into each figure in the column, then the cents' worth of inputs per dollar of output in the financial sector is obtained. For example, in the financial sector each dollar of output required 10 cents' worth of inputs from the agricultural sector, 20 cents' worth of inputs from the industrial sector, 20 cents' worth of inputs from the transportation sector, 20 cents' worth of inputs from the housing sector, 10 cents' worth of inputs from the financial sector, and 20 cents' worth of inputs from the all-others sector.

Similarly, values for the cents' worth of input per dollar of output can be calculated for each of the other sectors (columns), and this information can be used to construct a new matrix, as shown in Table 4.6. The values in this table can be used for purposes of projection if it is assumed that they remain constant through time. In this sense they can be regarded as constant production coefficients.

Suppose that consumption in the housing sector is to increase by 10 million dollars over a period of X years. What impact will this increase in consumption have on the economy of the entire region? To begin with, it is assumed that these housing

Table 4.6.   CENTS' WORTH OF INPUTS PER DOLLAR OF OUTPUT

Industry Producing	Agriculture and Extractive	Industry	Transportation	Housing	Finance	All Others
Agriculture & extractive	$ .25	$ .21	$ .08	$ .18	$ .10	$ .07
Industry	.12	.34	.08	.37	.20	.22
Transportation	.06	.08	.25	.14	.20	.07
Housing	.39	.21	.17	.04	.20	.43
Financial	.06	.08	.25	.09	.10	.07
All others	.12	.08	.17	.18	.20	.14
Total Inputs	$1.00	$1.00	$1.00	$1.00	$1.00	$1.00

expenditures are allocated in accordance with their proportions in Table 4.6. Thus, a further 1.8 million dollars will be spent in the agricultural and extractive sector, 3.7 million in the industrial sector, 1.4 million in the transportation sector, 0.4 million in the housing sector itself, 0.9 million in the financial sector, and 1.8 million in all other sectors.

These can all be considered final demands, and as a consequence the housing row can be eliminated from the projection. This is because the magnitude of disposable income over X years has already been implied, and accordingly so has the total of inputs required to earn this income. Thus, not to remove the housing row would lead to double counting (Isard, 1960). Similarly the housing column is eliminated, for the total of housing expenditures by time X has also been implied.

The Projection

In order for the housing sector to consume the various quantities listed above, these themselves have to be produced. Thus the extra 1.8 million dollars (see Table 4.7) in the agricultural and extractive sector has to be produced, and the first column of Table 4.6 indicates the dollar value of inputs that is required from every industry to produce this. Therefore, if we multiply each of the entries in the first column of Table 4.6 by 1.8 million dollars, we obtain the inputs from every industry that are required to produce this total output. Similarly, the additional 3.7 million dollars production necessary in the industrial sector has to be produced, and the dollar value of inputs required to produce this output can be calculated by multiplying down column 2 of Table 4.6 by 3.7 million dollars. Likewise the 1.4 million dollars from the transportation sector, the 0.9 million dollars from the financial sector, and the 1.8 million dollars from the all-others sector have to be produced; and the inputs required for this output can be calculated by cross-multiplying down the respective columns. If these inputs are now added up by type of input, we obtain the first round of input requirements (Table 4.7).

These first-round input requirements are directly required to produce the final demand items that housing is calculated to consume at time period X. However, these first-round input requirements also have to be produced; and the input required to produce these outputs can be obtained by a multiplication procedure similar to that used to obtain the first-round input requirements. The inputs required to produce 1.555 million dollars of output in the agricultural and extractive sector can be obtained by multiply-

Table 4.7.   FIRST-ROUND INPUT REQUIREMENTS

	AE	I	T	H	F	AO	Total Outputs
AE	$ 450,000	$ 777,000	$ 112,000		$ 90,000	$ 126,000	$1,555,000
I	216,000	1,258,000	112,000		180,000	396,000	2,162,000
T	108,000	296,000	350,000		180,000	126,000	1,060,000
H	–	–	–		–	–	
F	108,000	296,000	350,000		90,000	126,000	970,000
AO	216,000	296,000	238,000		180,000	252,000	1,182,000
Total Inputs	$1,800,000	$3,700,000	$1,400,000		$900,000	$1,800,000	$6,929,000

Table 4.8.   SECOND-ROUND INPUT REQUIREMENTS

	AE	I	T	H	F	AO	Total Outputs
AE	$ 388,750	$ 454,020	$ 84,800	–	$ 97,000	$ 82,740	$1,107,310
I	186,600	735,080	84,000	–	194,000	260,040	1,460,520
T	93,700	172,960	263,000	–	194,000	82,740	808,000
H	–	–	–	–	–	–	–
F	93,300	172,960	265,000	–	97,000	82,740	711,000
AO	186,600	172,960	180,200	–	194,000	165,480	899,240
Total Inputs	$1,555,000	$2,162,000	$1,060,000	–	$970,000	$1,182,000	$4,986,070

ing this figure down the first column of Table 4.6 to obtain the figures in the first column of Table 4.8. In a similar fashion, each of the output requirements in Table 4.7 has to be produced; and these can be calculated as explained previously and added to produce the second round of input requirements. Thus the second round of input requirements is necessary to produce the first round. As this second round of input requirements has to be produced, a third round must also be calculated (Table 4.9).

The round-by-round requirements have been calculated and added to produce the figures in Table 4.10. It should be noticed that after the fourth round these figures converge, a situation that is bound to occur inasmuch as the housing row and columns have been deleted. This convergence of the data means that the projection does not have to continue indefinitely, and in this particular example, the round-by-round projections have been discontinued at the sixth stage. By this time it is estimated that 10 million dollars of consumption in the housing sector by time period X will have resulted in a further increase of 2.1 million dollars in other economic activities. Thus over this time period the multiplier has been 3.12.

INTERREGIONAL INPUT-OUTPUT MODELS

The simple one-region input-output model discussed in the previous section can be expanded into a more complex interregional input-output model to incorporate regional

Table 4.9.   THIRD-ROUND INPUT REQUIREMENTS

	AE	I	T	H	F	AO	Total Outputs
AE	$ 276,828	$ 306,709	$ 64,640	–	$ 71,100	$ 62,947	$ 782,224
I	132,877	496,577	64,640	–	142,200	197,833	1,034,127
T	66,439	116,842	202,000	–	142,200	62,947	590,428
H	–	–	–	–	–	–	–
F	66,439	116,842	202,000	–	71,100	62,947	519,328
AO	132,877	116,842	137,360	–	142,200	125,894	655,173
Total Inputs	$1,107,310	$1,460,520	$808,000	–	$711,000	$899,240	$3,581,280

Table 4.10. INPUT REQUIREMENTS BY ROUND FOR $10 MILLION OUTPUT IN THE HOUSING SECTOR IN A HYPOTHETICAL URBAN REGION

	First	Second	Third	Fourth	Fifth	Sixth	Total
AE	$1,555,000	$1,107,310	$ 782,224	$ 557,752	$ 399,731	$ 260,034	$ 4,662,051
I	2,162,000	1,460,520	1,034,127	740,698	531,903	382,219	6,311,467
T	1,060,000	808,000	590,428	426,998	307,563	221,234	3,414,223
H	–	–	–	–	–	–	–
F	970,000	711,000	519,328	375,065	270,057	194,229	3,039,678
AO	1,182,000	899,240	655,173	472,560	339,947	244,410	3,793,330
Total	$6,929,000	$4,986,070	$3,581,280	$2,573,073	$1,849,201	$1,302,115	$21,220,749

differences in concentration of economic activity. For example, in the hypothetical model presented by Isard and Kavesh (1954), a model with respect to three regions has been developed, and this is presented in Table 4.11.

In this model there are two metropolitan regions and one broad agricultural region, which in spatial terms links the area around the two metropolitan regions into one unit. Each region has nine major sectors of economic activity (Table 4.11). There is, however, one basic variation in economic activity among the three regions; and it is this activity that provides the export base of the economy of each area. For example, in Metropolitan Region 1, heavy manufacturing is the basic activity, and it exports goods to Metropolitan Regions 2 and 3. In Metropolitan Region 2, light manufacturing is the basic activity, and all other activities are nonbasic. In the third region, agriculture is the basic economic activity, and it supplies the necessary foodstuffs for the two metropolitan areas. Concomitantly, this region imports heavy manufactured goods and light manufactured goods from the two metropolitan regions. Each region is self-sufficient in the other eight sectors of economic activity.

The assumption that each region is self-sufficient in eight sectors of economic activity and has only one sector of basic activity is, of course, unrealistic. The model is, however, simplified by this assumption; and in Table 4.11 the cents' worth of input per dollar of output is entered to illustrate that an input-output model of this kind can be developed into a table that can be used for projection purposes.

Thus the basic-nonbasic concept and the concept of the urban economic multiplier can be developed into a sophisticated procedure for projecting the impact of future expansion or development of one sector, or group of sectors, of industry in one or more regions. One of the chief problems with this kind of model is that it is difficult to construct. The amount of data needed is immense; and if many sectors of industry are being considered, the storage-space requirement in computers is also very great. The interregional input-output model does, however, emphasize in a very real way the economic interdependencies between sectors and regions, and that, because of nonlocal multiplier effects, changes in the level of economic activity in one region may bring about changes in the level of economic activity in other regions. The model also recognizes that an increase in demand in one sector of economic activity has repercussions in all other sectors in other regions, and moreover it provides a basis for calculating the multiplier effects of an increase or decrease in economic activity in any sector in any region.

Table 4.11.   HYPOTHETICAL INTERMETROPOLITAN TRANSACTIONS TABLE, CENTS'

	Metropolitan Region I:								
Industry Producing	Heavy Manufacturing	Power and Communication	Transportation	Trade	Insurance and Rental	Business and Pers. Serv.	Educational and Other Serv.	Construction	Households
	(1)	(2)	(3)	(4)	(5)	(6)	(7)	(8)	(9)
Metropolitan Region I:									
1. Heavy manufacturing	33	1	3	1		9	1	18	3
2. Power and communication	1	11	3	2	8	4	2		1
3. Transportation	2	2	5	1	1	1	2	4	3
4. Trade	1		2		2	3	5	9	12
5. Insurance and rental activities	1	1	3	5	7	5	4	2	12
6. Business and personal services	1	1	2	7	1	4	2	3	3
7. Educational and other basic services							1		10
8. Construction		4	6		10		1		
9. Households	34	58	58	63	53	46	50	40	1
Metropolitan Region II:									
10. Light manufacturing	4	1	2	2	1	14	15	4	20
11. Power and communication									
12. Transportation									
13. Trade									
14. Insurance and rental activities									
15. Business and personal services									
16. Educational and other basic services									
17. Construction									
18. Households									
Region III:									
19. Agriculture and extraction	6	5	4	1	2		4	18	6
20. Power and communication									
21. Transportation									
22. Trade									
23. Insurance and rental activities									
24. Business and personal services									
25. Educational and other basic services									
26. Construction									
27. Households									

Note: The columns do not add up to 100 owing to rounding and the fact that all values less than 0.01 have been deleted.
Source: Isard and Kavesh (1954), Table 1.

WORTH OF INPUTS PER DOLLAR OF OUTPUT

Industry Purchasing

Metropolitan Region II:									Region III:								
Light Manufacturing	Power and Communication	Transportation	Trade	Insurance and Rental	Business and Pers. Serv.	Educational and Other Serv.	Construction	Households	Agriculture and Extraction	Power and Communication	Transportation	Trade	Insurance and Rental	Business and Pers. Serv.	Educational and Other Serv.	Construction	Households
(10)	(11)	(12)	(13)	(14)	(15)	(16)	(17)	(18)	(19)	(20)	(21)	(22)	(23)	(24)	(25)	(26)	(27)
2	1	3	1		9	1	18	3	1	1	3	1		9	1	18	3
28	1	2	2	1	14	15	4	20	6	1	2	2	1	14	15	4	20
1	11	3	2	8	4	2		1									
2	2	5	1	1	1	2	4	3									
2		2		2	3	5	9	12									
1	1	3	5	7	5	4	2	12									
2	1	2	7	1	4	2	3	3									
							1	10									
	4	6		10		1											
25	58	58	63	53	46	50	40	1									
21	5	4	1	2		4	18	6	28	5	4	1	2		4	18	6
									1	11	3	2	8	4	2		1
									3	2	5	1	1	1	2	4	3
									2		2		2	3	5	9	12
									4	1	3	5	7	5	4	2	12
									1	1	2	7	1	4	2	3	3
																1	10
										4	6		10		1		
									40	58	58	63	53	46	50	40	1

A MODEL OF CITY GROWTH

The process of urban growth is complex, varies in its details in both space and time, and involves the interplay of factors and mechanisms that are not as yet completely understood. However, by the use of concepts like the multiplier it is possible to outline the general way in which urban growth takes place (Thompson, 1965a). An important element in the growth process is what Myrdal (1957) called the "principle of circular and cumulative causation." As it applies to the growth of cities, this simply states that a given change in functional structure brings about supporting, rather than contradictory, changes. Thus once something triggers growth in a city, powerful forces come into play which further encourage its growth by attracting additional activities to it. As a result, growth is cumulative and often gathers speed at an accelerating rate; in short, growth breeds growth.

Of the many kinds of functions that may bring about increases in the populations of cities, the most important is the growth of manufacturing and industry. As we have seen, most of today's large metropolitan areas owe their present status to the early development of industry there, particularly during the period of rapid industrialization (1870–1920), when the basic features of the city system in North America were established. Under these conditions, Pred (1965) has used the idea of "growth breeding growth" to explain increases in city size in the following way: First imagine an isolated city, whose economy is based on commerce and trade, which imports goods not locally produced from other places. Then imagine that a new large-scale factory is constructed in the city. Sooner or later this event evokes two simultaneous, circular chains of reaction, as outlined in Figure 4.3.

The first of these is based on the income and employment multiplier effects discussed above. The new factory and the increased purchasing power of its workers create new local demands. This results in the development of a host of new business, service, trade, construction, transportation, professional, and other white-collar jobs. The net result is that the population size of the city increases, which in turn means that the city becomes large enough to support a more specialized manufacturing activity—it attains one or more new local–regional *thresholds* (Chapter 6). These new thresholds will support new manufacturing functions, as well as making possible the enlargement of the existing ones. Once these new factories are constructed, a second round of growth is started, and eventually still higher local and regional thresholds are achieved. And so the process continues in a circular and cumulative manner until it is halted or impeded.

The second reaction, which occurs simultaneously, tends to reinforce the first. It is based on the increased amount of interpersonal interaction derived from the expanding city population. This "enhances the possibilities of technological improvements and inventions, enlarges the likelihood of the adoption of more efficient managerial and financial institutions, increases the speed with which locally originating ideas are disseminated, and eases the diffusion of skills and knowledge brought in by migrants from other areas" (Pred, 1965, p. 166; see also Feller, 1973). Once these new inventions or innovations are adopted, new or enlarged industry results, which brings about further population growth, and so the process continues in a circular and cumulative fashion until it is diverted or hindered. It is through the multiplier effect implicit in these two reactions that growth in the population sizes of cities is brought about. Although the model is based specifically on the expansion of manufacturing activity and is consequently most applicable in the context of industrialization, the general features of the model offer a plausible basis for understanding urban growth under other conditions.

If the process of circular and cumulative growth of cities functioned flawlessly, then every city would expand indefinitely, or at least until natural resources ran out. From our discussion of the spread of cities we noted, however, that only some cities expanded rapidly during the period of industrialization; others grew only moderately, while many declined or stagnated. Quite clearly, then, within an interacting system of cities in an expanding spatial economy, the circular and cumulative growth process does not persist indefinitely. Factors operate to halt or impede the process in some cities and to prevent it from ever starting in others.

The Urban Size Ratchet

An important factor reinforcing the circular and cumulative growth process in some cities and not in others is the size of the city itself. It appears that once a city has attained a certain critical size—the figure of 250,000 has often been mentioned—the chances of continued growth are improved and contraction becomes highly unlikely. Thus varying with the "degree of isolation of the urban place, the nature of its hinterland, the level of industrial development in the country, and various cultural factors, a growth mechanism, similar to a ratchet, comes into being, locking in past growth and preventing contraction" (Thompson, 1965a, p. 454).

Several reasons have been suggested to account for the operation of the size ratchet in urban growth. First, as we have already noted from the study of k values, city size is associated with increased diversification of urban economic structure, which tends to ensure that local growth rates are at least as high as the national average. Sec-

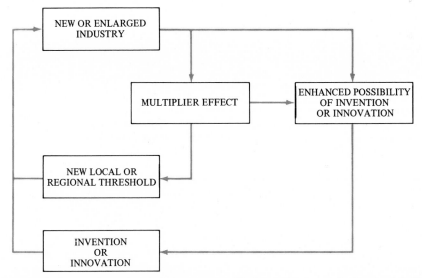

Fig. 4.3. The circular and cumulative process of industrialization and urban growth. (*Source*: after Pred, 1965, Fig. 1.)

ond, irreversible growth after some critical size is associated with increased political power; larger cities are in a stronger position to exert political pressure and to bargain for government contracts and support. A third factor is the large amount of fixed capital that has been invested in larger cities—hence they have a better developed infrastructure that can favorably influence location decision making. Finally, as stressed in Pred's model discussed above, industrial creativity can be expected to be greater in a larger city and as a result it is more likely to give birth to new activities at critical points in its life cycle.

Even if the urban size ratchet hypothesis is a valid one, so that the decline of cities above a critical size is highly unlikely, it does not follow that cities above this size will continue to expand indefinitely, or that all large cities will grow at the same rate. Other factors besides size govern urban growth. Moreover, the larger cities become, in general the slower their rate of growth compared to smaller cities. This suggests that the rate of growth depends on a fine balance between the opposing forces of advantages of agglomeration on the one hand and costs of congestion and diseconomies of scale on the other (Richardson, 1972b).

DIFFERENTIAL URBAN GROWTH

In accounting for the observation that some cities grow and become relatively more important than others, it is useful to think of cities as being in competition with each other to attract functions. In competition, those cities with some kind of initial advantage stand a better chance than those unable to attract specific types of activities to them, and hence to grow in population size. Often the initial advantage for settlement growth resulted from the natural advantages of site and situation. For example, there is no question that the initial growth of Toronto was linked to its location in an area where the hinterlands of Montreal and New York overlapped. Hence it was protected against becoming completely subservient to either port, and could more easily become the focal point of a rapidly expanding region of its own (Spelt, 1972). The early growth of New York was certainly aided by the fact that it had good access to the interior via the Hudson-Mohawk corridor, and hence it was able to build up an important import and export trade with the expanding settlements to the west. Conversely, other cities on the East Coast, such as Boston and Philadelphia, found it much more difficult to exploit the interior because of physical barriers, and they consequently suffered in the competition for trade and the accompanying growth of ancillary activities. Yet despite their initial disadvantages, these cities have emerged as major metropolitan areas. The differential growth of cities therefore cannot be explained solely on the basis of the physical aspects of location.

Local enterprise is often a significant factor bringing about growth. This is well illustrated by events in Baltimore. In 1827 bankers in the city concluded that a railroad over the mountains and into the Ohio Valley would be the best means of capturing a share of the western trade that the Erie Canal was diverting in increasing amounts to New York. Within five months a group of local businessmen had prepared a plan, obtained a company charter, raised 3.5 million dollars of capital, and engaged a competent engineer to start construction of the Baltimore and Ohio Railroad. Before this enterprise was five years old, freight was rolling into Baltimore in a volume that gave her undisputed commercial control of most of Maryland; and by 1850, when the iron tracks reached the Ohio Valley, the Chesapeake Bay port had attained a position as an outlet for western produce that only New York and New Orleans could challenge (Green, 1965).

Regardless of whether initial advantage stemmed from location or from local enterprise, one thing is clear: initial advantage and differential city growth are very closely related to changes in accessibility, particularly those brought about by changes in the transportation system. Thus we have noted that, in the period from 1790 to 1860, accessibility to hinterlands was related to navigable waterways; and it was at favorable locations along these that large cities emerged. The coming of the railroads drastically altered the pattern of accessibility to result in the decline of those river towns that did not receive a railroad connection and to change the locational advantages of those that did.

The impact of the railroad was widespread. Figure 4.4 shows the effect the railroad had on the growth of small service settlements in southwestern Iowa. In 1868, on the eve of the opening of the railroad through the area, a rudimentary pattern of small hamlets had developed (Fig. 4.4A). These were located in association with the distribution of woodlands, which had influenced the settlement pattern of the pioneer farmers. Figure 4.4B shows the pattern eleven years later. The railroad stations became the locations with initial advantage for further growth. Places in the vicinity of stations were abandoned as business moved into the station towns. Size differences emerged among these as some successfully captured small processing activities to tie in with their collection and distribution functions. Others were designated county seats, which gave them initial advantage for further growth. Despite the changes in accessibility brought by the railroads, however, none of these rural service centers ever developed into very large cities.

As suggested by the model, large-scale urban growth was initially dependent on the multiplier effects of manufacturing industry; and it is in connection with the location of manufacturing that the railroads had their most pronounced impact. The rail-

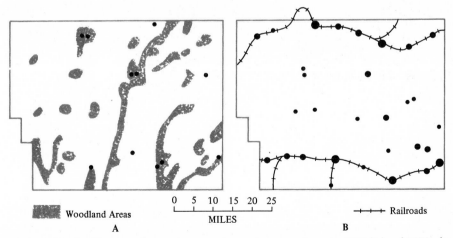

Fig. 4.4. The distribution of service centers in southwestern Iowa in 1868 (A) and 1879 after the coming of the railroad (B). (*Source*: Berry, 1967a, Figs. 1.3 and 1.4.)

roads, by lowering delivery prices of finished goods, enabled industries to increase the size of their markets and to obtain raw materials from greater distances. In turn production on a larger scale became feasible, which tended to favor the agglomeration at and growth of the already efficiently producing centers where small-scale industry may have originally grown up simply by chance. As a result, the lucky cities gained in population as the circular-cumulative process of growth got under way, while growth at the inefficient and non-producing centers was impeded or delayed until a later time.

The changes in initial advantage associated with the coming of the railroads have been stressed because, as we have seen, it was in the period from 1850 to 1920 that the basic features of the present-day urban pattern was established. However, factors other than the railroad aided or created initial advantages. Often growth was triggered by a change in the production process or local inventions, and the availability of capital and local entrepreneurial initiative was also important. Often changes in accessibility and in production occurred together in some cities, which subsequently very quickly generated their own conditions for sustained growth as the multiplier effects got under way, the critical size was reached, and the urban ratchet took effect.

Since about 1940, differential urban growth has resulted from changes in the national pattern of employment, especially the growth of the white-collar occupations; changes in locational requirements of newer types of industry; and the greater freedom in choice of location made possible by further advances in communications and transportation technology. Berry and Horton (1970) suggest that the most recent differences in relative growth of cities can be attributed to two principal factors: an industry mix effect whereby cities grow most rapidly if they have a large share of their workers in the nation's rapid-growth industries, and a competitive shift effect whereby the rapid-growth industries grow most rapidly in cities located in regions having the resources they need. It is the latter effect that underlies the deconcentration of growth in recent decades and the rapid expansion of cities in Florida, Arizona, Texas, and California.

5
CITIES AS CENTERS OF MANUFACTURING

Since the process of urbanization is intimately related to that of industrialization, the evolution of the North American city system has been very closely linked to the development of manufacturing—a relationship that has been explicitly recognized in various contexts in the previous chapters. Thus we have noted that the rapid growth and spread of large cities within the heartland-hinterland framework in the period after 1870 was conditioned to a large extent by industrial developments; that flows, movements, and transactions related to the spatial distribution of manufacturing and its ancillary activities are major features of interaction patterns within the city system; and that manufacturing not only is an important element in the economic base of many cities, but also plays a critical role in the process of urban growth through the multiplier effects and interdependencies it generates. No discussion of cities would be complete, therefore, without specific consideration of their role as centers of manufacturing, and it is to selected aspects of this that we now turn. On the one hand, discussion focuses on the general factors affecting the location of manufacturing activity; on the other, on the reasons why employment in manufacturing varies between cities and their industrial profiles differ.

THE PATTERN OF MANUFACTURING CITIES

Manufacturing is found in virtually all cities. However, its importance, measured by the proportion of the total labor force employed, varies markedly from city to city, ranging from as little as 5 percent in some to more than 65 percent in others (Nelson, 1955). When a high proportion of a city's labor force is engaged in manufacturing, it can be designated a "manufacturing city." The spatial distribution of manufacturing cities identified in this way by Harris (1943) and Nelson (1955) for the United States are shown in Figure 5.1. On both maps account is taken of the fact that some cities are more specialized in manufacturing than others. Manufacturing is more important in the cities shown by solid dots (M′) than by the open circles (M) in Figure 5.1A, and in the cities shown by solid dots (+3) than by crosses (+1) in Figure 5.1B (see Chapter 7).

The patterns on both maps are roughly the same. Manufacturing cities are predominantly concentrated in the American manufacturing belt (the heartland) and in the southwestern part of the United States, particularly along the Appalachian Piedmont ("fall-line" cities). There is a noticeable absence on both maps of cities with a concentration of employment in manufacturing west of the Mississippi, although it should be remembered that accompanying the deconcentration of urban growth toward the periphery since about 1950, manufacturing is now more important in the economic structure of many cities—particularly in California, Texas, and Florida—than it was when these maps were originally prepared. However, despite the minor changes associated with more recent developments, the distribution of manufacturing cities today is much the same as shown on the two maps. Moreover, the pattern has been remarkably stable over a very long period of time.

It is interesting to compare Figure 5.1 with Figure 5.2, Harris' map of "market potential" for the United States—a summary measure of accessibility to consumers analogous to the concept of population potential discussed in Chapter 3. Although New York had the highest market potential in 1950, there is a broad area covering the Eastern Seabord from Boston to Washington, D.C., and extending westward to Chicago, which has 80 percent or more of the market potential of New York City (Harris, 1954). Maps of population potential produced by Warntz (1965) tend to suggest that this pat-

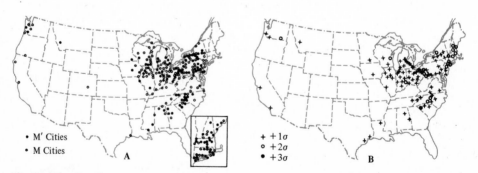

• M′ Cities
• M Cities

A

+ +1σ
o +2σ
• +3σ

B

Fig. 5.1. The distribution of manufacturing towns as classified by Harris (A) and by Nelson (B). (*Source*: after Harris, 1943, Fig. 2, and Nelson, 1955, Fig. 2.)

tern has hardly changed in recent years. Clearly, the heavy concentration of manufacturing cities in the heartland coincides with the area of highest market potential, an observation that led Harris (1954, pp. 315–316) to conclude:

> A large and very significant fraction of manufacturing in the United States is not tied to local raw materials, local markets, or to current regional differences in power or labor costs; this segment . . . appears to be concentrated in areas having maximum accessibility to national or regional markets.

Studies of the distribution of manufacturing cities in Canada reveal the same general relationship. The heaviest concentration of manufacturing cities identified by Maxwell (1965) occurs in the heartland of central Canada, which is also the area of highest market potential (Ray, 1969).

Differences Between Cities

The spatial distribution of manufacturing cities shown in Figure 5.1 does not, of course, tell us anything about the way particular types of manufacturing are distributed within the city system, or about the considerable differences that exist between cities in their manufacturing makeup. The different types of manufacturing are not distributed uniformly throughout the city system. Some types are relatively concentrated and may be found only in a handfull of cities; others are more widely dispersed and are found in many cities in various parts of the system. This was touched upon in the previous chapter in the discussion of k values and Morrissett's distinction between ubiquitous and sporadic activities (see Table 4.4). Moreover, linkages between different kinds of industries give rise to well-developed associations in the spatial distribution of manufacturing (Wood, 1969). As a result, some cities have a broad manufacturing base while others are more specialized; some cities are characterized by one kind of industry mix, other cities by another.

Considerable differences exist, therefore, in the industrial profiles of cities, as Duncan et al. (1960) have shown in their penetrating analysis of 50 major cities in the United States. However, they also demonstrate how difficult it is to generalize about these differences, and short of presenting detailed tables for each city, only very general

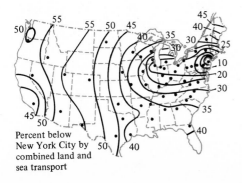

Percent below
New York City by
combined land and
sea transport

Fig. 5.2. Market potential surface for the United States based on combined land and sea transportation. (*Source*: Harris, 1954, Fig. 6.)

pictures of a city's industrial profile can be painted. Thus, for example, New York is a center for the manufacturing of nonstandardized goods such as clothing (especially fur goods and millinery), toys, sports equipment, pens, cosmetics, notions, luggage, jewelry, etc., while metalworking and metal products are relatively underrepresented. In contrast, Chicago specializes in many kinds of metalworking activities and in heavy manufacturing, besides radio and television sets, musical instruments, and plastic products. The industrial profile of Los Angeles is dominated by motion-picture making, ordnance, and aircraft; that of Boston by footwear manufacturing, electronic components, scientific instruments, special machinery, textiles, and rubber products; while Philadelphia is noted for the manufacture of certain kinds of textiles and clothing products, petroleum products, and plastics (Bergsman et al., 1972).

Moreover, although the overall pattern of the distribution of manufacturing cities themselves has remained relatively stable over a long period of time, changes are continually taking place in the distribution of particular types of manufacturing activity. Advances in the technology of industrial processes, new kinds of products, developments in transportation and communication, changes in industrial organization, and so on bring new locational forces into play. As a result, the competitive position of particular regions and individual cities has been altered—sometimes quite radically—through time, and this is often reflected in their changing industrial profiles as older industries drop out and newer ones enter. However, the large size of investments in plant and machinery typical of many types of manufacturing activity as well as many other considerations often makes relocation unfeasible except under the most pressing circumstances or without massive government assistance. Consequently *inertia* is a major factor perpetuating well-established patterns in the distribution of certain kinds of manufacturing in cities long after their original competitive advantage has disappeared.

GENERAL FACTORS AFFECTING THE LOCATION OF MANUFACTURING

Manufacturing involves the assembly of goods and materials (inputs) at a factory where they are combined with the factors of production required to undertake the process of manufacture. As a result of this process, the utility of goods and materials is changed and their value increased. The resulting products (outputs) are then marketed. This sequence of events involves the movement of inputs and outputs to and from factories, which consequently incurs transportation costs. It is important to remember that the inputs are not always raw materials, but often the outputs of other manufacturing plants, and that goods produced are not always sold directly to consumers (final demand), but often to other manufacturing firms for which they then constitute an input. The manufacturing of raw materials into final products is, then, often a complex process involving many kinds of linked manufacturing activity and often many individual firms.

The location of manufacturing is affected by myriad economic and noneconomic factors. Important among these are the nature of the material inputs, the particular combination of factors of production, the market, and transportation costs. Other important influences at work include agglomeration and external economies, public policy, and personal preferences. The relative importance of these factors varies between different industries as well as firms. In this connection a useful distinction can be made between three main types of industrial activity: extractive, processing, and fabricating. It is the latter two that are normally considered as manufacturing. Moreover, the various factors have changed in importance through time. Consequently, many features of the present-day distribution of manufacturing in the city system are legacies of former epochs during which locational decisions were made within the framework of a rather different set of technological, economic, and spatial relationships than exists today.

Material Inputs

The importance of materials, and especially raw materials, in attracting manufacturing has traditionally been emphasized in industrial location analysis because the cost of assembling them at the plant is a large and continuing item of expenditure (Stevens and Brackett, 1967). Materials are not spread evenly over the earth's surface but are localized in space. Because of this, the distribution of extractive industries—for example, mining—is easily explained because extraction has to take place where the raw materials are located. The distribution of mining towns in the United States identified from an analysis of employment data by Harris (1943) and Nelson (1955) are shown in Figure 5.3. The majority of places shown on Harris' map are the coal-mining towns located in Colorado, southern Illinois, and the Appalachian areas of West Virginia and Pennsylvania. The remaining towns are associated with the extraction of iron ore in Michigan and Minnesota, and copper at Butte, Montana. In addition to these, the oil cities of Texas, Oklahoma, and Kansas are shown on the more recent map by Nelson.

The attraction of manufacturing industries to raw-material locations was particularly important during the nineteenth century in North America. For example, the early location of the wool and textile industry in New England is commonly attributed to the abundant local supply of raw wool in the region. More recently, the location of the pulp and paper industry close to forested areas such as New Brunswick, Canada; the fruit and canning industry near truck farms and orchards in California; and the cheese and butter processing industries in dairying regions such as Wisconsin reemphasize the importance of raw materials on location, especially for many processing activities. A

Fig. 5.3. The distribution of mining towns as classified by Harris (A) and by Nelson (B). (*Source: after Harris, 1943, Fig. 7, and Nelson, 1955, Fig. 10.*)

materials location is largely related to the ease and cheapness with which the materials can be transported. In turn, this is a function of the nature of the materials themselves—on their specific value, their bulk, weight, perishability, and so on, but also on the way they enter into the process of manufacture.

The latter is particularly important and is related to the distinction made by Weber (1929) between "pure" and "gross" materials. Pure materials enter into the finished product to the extent of their full weight. Examples of this type of material are yarns in the textile weaving industry and components, such as tires, steering wheels, and light bulbs, in the automobile manufacturing industry. In contrast, gross materials impart only a proportion or none of their weight to the finished product. Most raw materials fall into this category. An extreme type of gross material—at the opposite end of the scale from the pure materials—is fuel, which adds no weight to the finished product. There are, however, many types of gross materials between fuel and the pure materials—for example, mineral ores in the metalliferous industries and wood in the furniture industry. Gross materials, then, have traditionally exerted a strong pull on industry because a materials location avoids unnecessary transportation costs. On the other hand, pure materials, because of their higher specific value and hence transferability, often permit considerable choice in location, particularly for many kinds of fabricating industries and especially those referred to as "footloose."

Sources of Fuel and Power

Since there are very few modern industries that do not use some form of powered machinery, sources of fuel and power may influence the location of manufacturing. In early industrial North America, water and coal were the fuel and power resources that counted most, and their location played a significant role in shaping patterns of manufacturing distribution and urban growth. Today the main source of power for most industries is electricity, and this can be transmitted from place to place at relatively little cost. Although the nature of certain industries makes them sensitive to costs of power and hence sources of abundant cheap power continue to play a significant role in their location (for example, the location of aluminum smelting in the Pacific Northwest and the Tennessee Valley in the United States and in the St. Maurice and Saguenay river valleys in Canada), the influence of power sources on the location of manufacturing is generally less important now than it has been in the past. In part this is also because a greater variety of sources of fuel and power are available today, and very often one type can easily be substituted for another. Nevertheless, some regional variation in the costs of different kinds of fuel and power does still exist; for example, coal is less expensive than oil in the northern and eastern parts of America, whereas oil is cheaper than coal in the South and West. Regional variation in the price of fuel and power may sometimes be important, therefore, in choosing between alternative sources as well as between alternative locations.

The Factors of Production

Once materials have been assembled at the factory, they must be combined with the factors of production required to undertake the process of manufacture. Conventionally listed as land, labor, capital, and enterprise, these may be combined in different industries. Moreover, substitution between the various factors is often possible, that between capital and labor being the most common. Hence some industries are *labor-*

intensive and use large amounts of labor compared to the other factors; others may be *capital-intensive* and highly mechanized with relatively few workers, and so on.

Land

Although the availability and price of land are very important in determining the location of manufacturing within urban areas (see Chapter 14), evidence suggests that these are also quite important considerations at the regional scale. Thus average costs of industrial land vary, often significantly, between cities in different parts of North America. For example, in Canada the cost of a 10-acre industrial site in 1962 varied from 30,000 to 40,000 dollars per acre in Montreal to 20,000 to 30,000 in Toronto, 10,000 to 15,000 in Hamilton, 4,500–6,500 in Winnipeg, and 6,000 to 11,000 in Vancouver (Smith, 1971). In the United States, Fuchs (1962) has suggested that a high correlation exists between the availability of land on the one hand and manufacturing employment and value added on the other at the state level of aggregation. Regional variation in the availability and cost of industrial land may therefore be an important locational consideration, especially for those activities that require very large sites, such as the many hundreds of acres required for modern iron and steel plants and oil refineries. Moreover, the general trend is for many other kinds of manufacturing plants to use greater amounts of land today than in the past. In part this is because vast areas have to be provided as parking lots for workers' automobiles; in part it is due to the increasing importance of assembly-line production methods, which need large expanses of flat land, and also because land is needed in increasing amounts for stockpiling and as reserves for future expansion.

Labor

The availability of labor and its productivity are vital factors in every industrial activity, though labor requirements are by no means the same for all industries. Some types of manufacturing require large volumes of cheap unskilled labor, whereas others require skilled labor and are not so concerned with the price. Thus the location of industries with a high labor-to-capital ratio is likely to be strongly influenced by the costs of labor and its productivity, whereas those with a low labor-to-capital ratio are more likely to be influenced by other factors. It is generally considered that much of the recent growth of manufacturing in the Southeast of the United States can be explained partially by the availability of large quantities of low-cost labor found there. On the other hand, although wages in southern California are extremely high, the rapid growth of modern electronics industries there can be explained in part by the availability of a large pool of highly skilled technical workers.

Firms requiring a large labor force with a wide range of skills will obviously find this easier to obtain in a major metropolitan area than in a small town. Other firms may gravitate to an existing concentration of a particular kind of manufacturing activity when workers with specific skills form an important part of their labor force. Firms needing large amounts of female labor may be attracted to locations where male employment predominates, such as in a mining town. Spatial variations in the cost of labor are particularly important for those industries that are labor-intensive. Often wage rates for similar quality workers are much lower in one region than in another, while the quality and productivity of workers in one region may be much higher for the same wage rate than in others, and so on.

The overall influence of labor is, however, difficult to establish, and in fact rarely does the availability of labor alone influence the location of most manufacturing activity. Increasing mechanization, automation, and substitution of capital is certainly reducing the importance of the labor factor in North America today. Moreover, labor-cost differentials, in theory at least, have a short-run effect. In the long run, the migration of labor should tend to even out differences in costs between regions—a process that has been speeded up as the result of the negotiation of uniform wage rates by labor unions. However, significant local advantages in terms of cost, quality, and quantity of labor still exist, and for certain kinds of manufacturing these may continue to influence location decisions.

Capital

Although particular kinds of activities may be easier to finance in some localities than others, spatial variation in the availability and cost of capital is not very pronounced today. Most manufacturing concerns, and particularly larger ones, can easily raise capital in the national money market by issuing stocks and shares. However, as Thompson (1968) has pointed out, local supplies of capital may be important for small firms and those just starting up. Thus, for example, "a man going into business for the first time may be able to get backing from friends and relatives in this home town, as well as from local banks where his personal capabilities and credit standing are known, but if he went to another city he might be refused support" (Smith, 1971, p. 38). Although there is evidence to suggest that in the past industrial growth may have been inhibited in capital-scarce regions, the availability and cost of obtaining capital are generally not as influential factors in choosing locations for manufacturing in North America today.

The Markets

The markets for the outputs of the manufacturing process may either be other firms (in the case of components and semifinished goods) or consumers (in the case of final products). The importance of the market in the location of manufacturing—and particularly for firms selling to final demand—has long been recognized and is growing in general importance relative to other factors. This is because an increasingly large proportion of modern industrial activity is devoted more to the production of consumer goods than producer goods and to the fulfillment of desires for these goods created by the "North American way of life." This demand is kept buoyant by large-scale advertising, without which effective demand for certain kinds of products would not exist, and by continuous changes in fashions and styles. As urban societies are much more likely to accept and in fact encourage changes of this type, it is likely that consumer demand will show little sign of abatement in the future. Thus market considerations are likely to increase in importance.

Although it is difficult to evaluate precisely the effect of the market on the location of manufacturing activities, two considerations are involved: the nature of the product and demand for it, and transportation costs. Demand for particular products varies from place to place, depending on the nature of the product and the number, type, and distribution of consumers and competitors. Transport costs are important because they add to the market price of the product. Hence proximity to the market, if it is concentrated, or a central location, if it is dispersed, is not only an advantage but in some cases a necessity. Consequently, many firms show a distinct preference today for locations in or near major metropolitan areas, and especially those in the heartlands, where we have already noted that market potential — both for consumers and for other firms — is greatest (Figs. 5.1 and 5.2). Of course, the market itself is not the only advantage of a location in a large city or metropolitan region like Megalopolis; but the large, concentrated, and increasingly affluent body of consumers found in cities is a persuasive reason for the relatively rapid growth of manufacturing activity in cities in general and large cities in particular.

Some Other Considerations

Although materials, markets, and factors of production are traditionally viewed as the most important economic factors affecting the location of manufacturing in general, other factors may be important in specific cases. The effect of amenities (e.g., climate and natural recreational resources) on industrial location is growing in importance (Ullman, 1954), especially for newer types of manufacturing such as the aerospace and electronics industries. Fuchs (1962), for example, has shown that states with warmer climates have experienced a relatively greater rate of growth in manufacturing employment during the past 30 years. Moreover, building costs are normally lower in regions with warmer climates, since the need for insulating large buildings is eliminated, thereby lowering initial investment and maintenance costs. Differences in levels of taxation may also affect locational decisions, and although these are not generally so important at the regional scale (Wonnacott, 1963), tax differentials between municipalities within major metropolitan areas have played an important role in shaping patterns of intraurban manufacturing (Hoover and Vernon, 1959). Even reorientation of foreign trade patterns has in some cases brought about changes in the location of industry, particularly of those that are heavily dependent upon either export markets or imported raw materials (Fuchs, 1962).

In recent decades, public policy and government activity have become increasingly important factors affecting the location of manufacturing in North America. Particularly significant are government expenditures for defense purposes, which have risen to almost half of the national budget of the United States during the past decade. These expenditures have not been spread evenly across the country, and the impact of defense spending has been both positive and negative. A recent study by Bolton (1965) indicates that defense purchases have encouraged a rapid growth of certain types of manufacturing in the West and South, but have had a very small effect on industrial expansion and location in the North and East, except for Connecticut. This is because much of modern defense spending is related to the development of sophisticated armaments and missile systems requiring technologically advanced industries that are less likely to be located in the older industrial areas.

A second way in which government has affected the location of manufacturing is through regional development policies that are concerned with alleviating either areas of unemployment or areas of slow growth and economic stress through programs of "tax holidays" and capital grants (Yeates and Lloyd, 1970). Thus in Canada the federal government attempts to attract industry to locate in the Maritime Provinces and in the slow-growth areas of Quebec and northern Ontario and the Prairie Provinces. Similarly in the United States federal programs are in effect to promote industrial growth in Appalachia. At a more local level, state and local governments also attempt to attract manufacturing with tax inducements, low-interest loans, free land, or cheap buildings. As a result of these programs at all levels of government, it is becoming increasingly apparent that public policy in general is an important factor determining the location of manufacturing and that it will increase in importance as the growing need for planning is recognized.

THE INFLUENCE OF TRANSPORTATION COSTS ON LOCATION

Transportation costs, by affecting what a firm has to pay for its material inputs and the costs of sending outputs to the market, play a fundamental role in determining the location of manufacturing. Very few firms can afford to ignore transportation costs in choosing locations, and for many the largest difference between the costs of alternative locations will be the size of the total freight bill. This will vary from industry to industry, depending on the types of materials and products involved, the kind of transportation needed, the structure of freight rates, and so on. Thus transportation costs are subject to a wide range of complicating factors. Nevertheless, transportation costs exhibit a much greater degree of spatial regularity than most of the other costs affecting the location of manufacturing, and hence they can be used as a basic theme for tying together some of the many factors discussed above—particularly the influence of materials and markets—into more general, simple theoretical statements. To reveal some of the more obvious ways by which transportation costs affect locational choice, we shall proceed with some simple models by way of example.

Imagine the simplest of situations: a firm that uses only one source of material input and sells its product in one area (e.g., a given city), and that the material source and the market are separated in space. On the basis of the transportation costs involved, the firm then has to decide whether to locate at the source of materials, at the marketplace, or at an intermediate location between the two. Let us now assume that the manufacturer chooses a location that minimizes the total freight bill. This is not an unreasonable assumption to make, because transportation costs simply add to the price of the finished product at the market. There are, of course, some industries for which society is prepared to carry high transportation costs in order to have them located far away

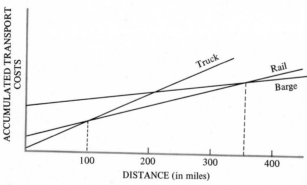

Fig. 5.4. Transport costs increase linearly with distance.

from inhabited areas; for example, the manufacture of explosives and noxious products. Let us also assume that transportation costs increase linearly with distance, as in Figure 5.4, which shows general cost curves for three modes of transportation: railroad, barge, and truck. From the diagram it is observed that water transportation is the cheapest for long hauls—those beyond 360 miles. Rail transportation is cheapest for medium hauls—distances between 100 and 360 miles; and truck transportation is the cheapest of all for short hauls of less than 100 miles. For our purposes, however, we shall assume that there is only one means of transportation connecting the materials and the market, and that this is the railroad.

It is also assumed that a given quantity of raw material yields the same quantity of finished product. In other words, the materials are pure materials, hence they do not incur any weight loss in manufacturing. In the first set of models to be discussed, this assumption is kept rigid and various assumptions concerning transportation costs are relaxed. In the second series of models to be discussed, gross materials are used; that is, weight loss is allowed to occur.

Case 1: Linear Transportation Costs

If transportation costs increase linearly with distance and the cost of shipping the raw materials (R) from the source (SR) to the market (MP) is exactly the same as shipping the finished product (P) from MP to SR, then since transportation costs increase linearly with distance at the same rate for both R and P, the same total transportation cost is incurred at any location between the raw-material source and the marketplace.

This situation is indicated in Figure 5.5 by the line T.T.C. (total transport costs). This line is calculated by constructing two transportation cost lines, one for raw materials, with its origin at SR, and one for finished products, with its origin at MP. The line from SR indicates the cost of transporting R, and that from MP indicates the cost of transporting P. Thus if the manufacturing firm locates at SR, the transportation charge will be a = TTC. If the firm locates at MP, the transportation charge will be y = TTC. If the firm locates at X, the transportation costs will be b for transporting the raw material to X and x for transporting the finished product to MP. It is obvious that x + b = TTC. In this particular situation, therefore, the manufacturing concern can locate anywhere.

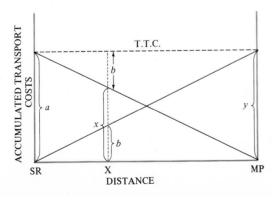

Fig. 5.5. The effect of equal costs of transport for raw materials and finished products, assuming transport costs are linearly related to distance.

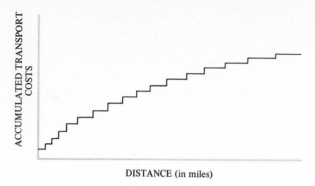

Fig. 5.6. Freight rate zones result in a stepped, curvilinear transport cost function.

Case 2: Curvilinear Transportation Costs

In reality, however, transportation costs increase at a decreasing rate with distance, as shown in Figure 5.6. This is because the freight-rate structure increases by zones. Thus a certain amount is paid for the first few miles, an additional amount for the next few miles, and so on. The width of each zone increases with distance from the point of shipment. As a result, the average freight-rate structure is actually curvilinear and not linear.

In this situation, if the same quantity of raw materials yields the same quantity of finished products and the freight-rate curves for both the raw material and the finished product are the same, the manufacturer can locate either at the raw-material location (*SR*) or at the marketplace (*MP*). However, the industry cannot locate at any point in between, because at intervening locations the total costs of transportation (*TTC*) will be higher than those incurred at either *SR* or *MP* as shown in Figure 5.7.

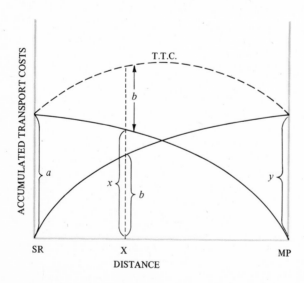

Fig. 5.7. The effect of equal transport costs for raw materials and finished products, assuming a curvilinear relationship between transport costs and distance. Compare this diagram with Fig. 5.5.

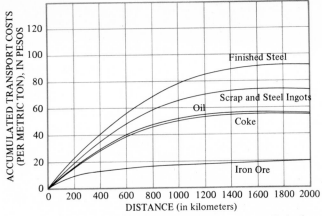

Fig. 5.8. Transport costs for finished products are normally higher than those for raw materials and partially finished products. (*Source*: Kennelly, 1954–1955, Fig. 4.)

Case 3: Unequal Transportation Costs

Transportation costs are usually higher per ton for finished products than they are for raw materials. Figure 5.8 illustrates this quite clearly for Mexico. In this case finished steel has much higher transportation costs per ton than scrap and steel ingots, which in turn have much higher costs than those for oil, coke, and iron ore. One important reason for these differences is that as manufactured goods have increased in value owing to the process of manufacture, transportation costs constitute a lower proportion of the total value of the product than they do for raw materials. Manufactured goods are therefore capable of bearing a higher transportation charge (Hoover, 1963). Consequently, transportation companies charge higher freight rates for these goods.

In Figure 5.9 the freight-rate curve for the finished product is therefore steeper than that for the raw material. Consequently the transportation charges per ton will be

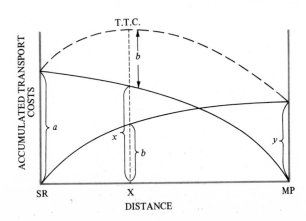

Fig. 5.9. The effects of higher transport costs for finished products than for raw materials, assuming a curvilinear relationship between transport costs and distance. Compare this diagram with Fig. 5.7.

lower if the industry locates at the marketplace than if it locates at the raw-material location. Thus, in a situation where a given quantity of raw material yields the same quantity of finished product, the industry will locate at the marketplace, for the total cost of transportation will be least at that location.

Case 4: Variation in Weight Loss

Thus far we have assumed that the material inputs used are pure materials that incur no weight loss in the manufacturing process. We have previously indicated that the concept of weight loss as developed by Weber refers to the weight by which a given unit of input is reduced during the manufacturing process. Thus a weight loss of 40 percent would indicate that a given quantity of input was reduced in weight by 40 percent in the manufacturing process.

In this particular case let us assume that the freight rates per ton of a manufactured product average for the total distance between SR and MP 20 dollars per mile. The freight rates for raw materials (R) average for the same distance 15 dollars per mile. Let us assume that 1,000 tons of raw material are to be processed into finished product (P), the amount of which will vary according to the weight loss in the production process.

If the manufacturing firm establishes itself at the marketplace, it will always have to transport 1,000 tons of materials to MP. As a consequence, the total transportation cost will be 15,000 dollars per mile. If the weight loss is 20 percent and the firm locates at SR, 1,000 tons of raw material will yield 800 tons of finished product and the total cost of shipping this amount will be 16,000 dollars per mile. Thus with a weight loss of 20 percent, the firm will gain an advantage of 1,000 dollars per mile by locating at the marketplace. However, with a weight loss of 40 percent, 1,000 tons of R yields 600 tons of P. As the cost of transporting this amount at the manufactured product rate is 12,000 dollars per mile, the firm will gain an advantage of 3,000 dollars per mile if it locates at the raw-material site. Consequently, given the transportation cost structure for finished products and raw materials, the higher the weight loss, the more likely it is that a firm will locate at the source of inputs, taking only transportation costs and weight loss into consideration.

Special Cases

Within this framework of transportation costs and weight loss, location decisions are further complicated by a number of irregular or unusual situations that tend to distort the regularity of transportation-cost gradients used in the above examples. Important among these are transshipment points, in-transit freight-rate privileges, and basing-point systems.

Transshipment Points

These occur whenever goods or materials have to be transferred from one type of transportation to another; for example, from ship or barge to railroad or truck, as at a port. Transshipment points are also break-of-bulk points, since the goods being shipped usually have to be broken down into smaller units for subsequent transportation: the contents of the hold of an ocean-going vessel would fill many railroad cars or trucks, for example. Transshipment and break of bulk cause additional costs to be incurred (an extra terminal charge in the course of a journey), which result in a marked step upward in the transportation-cost gradient. Consequently, transshipment points often attract manufacturers because the additional costs can be avoided by locating at them even though the freight rate in shipping the manufactured product to the market will be higher. The attraction of these locations is particularly strong for those types of manufacturing using raw materials with a high weight loss. Moreover, firms often choose break-of-bulk sites, and especially ports, because raw materials can be collected there easily from many locations. In fact, in the days before the development of the railroad, inland cities could not grow very large because transportation costs were at a maximum at these locations. Thus "it is no accident that the large cities of antiquity grew where they had access to sea-going ships and usually they developed at the mouth of rivers where they also had access to downriver transportation" (Gilmore, 1953, p. 23).

In-Transit Freight-Rate Privileges

The regularity of transportation-cost gradients is also distorted by the many kinds of deals transportation companies may make with favored customers or industries. In-transit freight-rate privileges are one of the most common. This system enables manufacturers to undertake production at an intermediate location between the source of raw materials and the market without incurring higher costs in transporting the manufactured goods from the factory to the marketplace. The rate paid is the same as if the raw materials had been transported directly to the marketplace and the process of manufacture undertaken there instead.

In-transit privileges can usually be traced back to some historical sequence. An industry may have located at a particular place because the raw materials were originally there, but later became exhausted. When the railroad system expanded farther into the hinterland, the owners of the industry and of the railroad might well have come to some agreement concerning in-transit freight-rate privileges which was at that time of mutual advantage to both parties. The railroad would not want to lose the business and would not want to waste the facilities that it may have built at the manufacturing plant. In turn the manufacturing company might not want to uproot itself and incur costs of relocation. It is quite obvious, however, that if this situation continues for many years, the added costs of these freight-rate privileges has to be paid by somebody; and if it is not by the manufacturing company, then it is by the railroad company, and whoever pays will pass these costs on to other users.

Basing-Point Systems

The basing-point system was a pricing policy that developed in the United States in the late nineteenth and early twentieth centuries. Under this system,

> all production of a certain commodity is regarded as originating from a single point, a uniform price at the factory is set for all producers irrespective of their costs, and the price quoted to any customer is this price plus the cost of transportation that *would* have been incurred if the consignment had originated at the basing point [Smith, 1971, p. 67].

Since the basing-point system is primarily a price-fixing device, it is now illegal.

The most often cited example of the basing-point system is that known as "Pittsburgh plus"—an arrangement that was used for some time in the marketing of steel in the United States. At the turn of the century, the greatest concentration of steel production in America was in Pittsburgh. Consequently steel producers in Pittsburgh were a very powerful group, and they were able to fix the pricing system so that all shipments of steel, regardless of where they were produced, were charged to the customer as if they had originated from Pittsburgh. This system, of course, protected steel producers in Pittsburgh from the competition of those with lower production costs at other locations. Thus even if steel was produced more cheaply in Chicago than in Pittsburgh and sold in Chicago, the buyer would pay the cost of transportation as if it were produced in Pittsburgh and transported from Pittsburgh to Chicago. In order to conceal this situation, the only prices quoted for steel were the delivered prices; and the customer was not allowed to pick up the steel for himself.

The inhibiting effects of the Pittsburgh-plus system on the location of the iron and steel industry and other manufacturing have been hotly debated (Stocking, 1954). However, it certainly had a retarding effect on the development of manufacturing in parts of the South because local firms were prevented from taking full advantage of the cheap steel being produced at Birmingham. Moreover, since the system protected the competitive advantage of Pittsburgh producers, it probably encouraged the agglomeration in the region of other steel-using activities. On the other hand, by creating artificially high delivered prices at distant locations, the system may have encouraged the growth of the steel industry in places far away from Pittsburgh. For example, a steel producer in Los Angeles sells to the Los Angeles market at a price that includes a fictitious transportation cost from Pittsburgh. This extra cost to the consumer is extra profit to the company and can be used to offset the costs arising from other disadvantages of a location in Los Angeles.

AGGLOMERATION AND EXTERNAL ECONOMIES

Although spatial variation in the factors discussed so far may cause manufacturers to choose one region over another—for example, a location in the heartland instead of one in the hinterlands—other factors must be introduced to explain why an urban location is so attractive and why firms decide to locate in one particular city instead of another. As a general rule, the concentration of manufacturing in cities and urban regions provides firms with collective benefits they would not enjoy at an isolated location. These benefits take the form of *external economies* resulting from agglomeration as distinct from economies in production that are internal to the firm or industry itself. External economies relate, therefore, to the advantages that firms enjoy because of their *locational* association and linkages with other activities in a larger scale cluster of economic activity. The exact nature of external economies due to agglomeration are not easy to define, and as Smith points out, the main benefits of a location in a city or an urban region may in fact arise from a mass of intangible factors "which the manufacturer almost instinctively knows (or imagines) will increase his efficiency, or lower his total costs" (Smith, 1971, p. 87). Nevertheless, some of the more obvious advantages of a location in a city, especially a large one, have been well documented.

Urbanization Economies

The benefits arising from the agglomeration in cities of firms from many different industries are described as urbanization economies, the potential for which increases with size of city. An obvious advantage of an urban location is its well-developed *infrastructure* — the real capital invested in utilities, roads, transportation, as well as various commercial facilities, educational and research establishments, and so on, which firms can make use of more cheaply than if they had to provide them themselves. Benefits may result because of the sheer size of the local market, while production linkages with other firms in the city or surrounding region permit economies in transfer costs. Since a wide range of skilled and unskilled labor is found in large cities, training costs may be reduced for some firms and short-term demands for extra manpower can more easily be met. Although wages are generally higher in large cities, this is offset by higher productivity (Mera, 1973). Moreover, managerial skills are more abundant and the level of creative entrepreneurship is higher in large cities (Thompson, 1968).

Other advantages of agglomeration in cities include the ease with which firms are able to obtain supplies at short notice, which reduces the need to carry large inventories of materials and components. Moreover, certain kinds of inputs may even be cheaper in cities. Large amounts of available industrial and commercial floor space make it easier to cover short-term fluctuations in production needs and storage requirements. Economies of large-scale purchasing and transportation are possible because groups of firms can share the services of freight forwarders and transportation agencies. Short-term demands for credit and working capital, especially from smaller firms, can be met more easily, and individual firms enjoy the benefits of a wide range of specialized services in cities — such as plant maintenance and surveillance, accountancy, advertising, market research, and so on — all of which permit savings in cost.

On the other hand, urbanization economies may turn into diseconomies in the largest cities as costs begin to rise and efficiency is reduced. Competition between firms may force up the cost of land and labor. Transportation facilities are often overloaded and congestion creates difficulties. Shortages of space may hinder expansion; pollution and crime become major problems (see Chapter 16); and forces of disagglomeration become increasingly important as firms decentralize to the suburbs and neighboring smaller communities.

Localization Economies

In addition to the general benefits resulting from agglomeration in cities, additional economies are possible when firms in the same industry, or a set of closely related industries, concentrate at the same place. These localization economies arise in a variety of ways. The traditional concentration of a given industry in a particular city may result in a labor force with particular skills and special educational institutions geared to the industry in question. Research institutes, marketing organizations, and other collective facilities may be formed jointly by firms in the industry to provide services that individual units would not be able to provide themselves. A wide range of supporting and ancillary activities serving the particular needs of the industry are likely to be present: machine builders and repairers, suppliers of components, special services, and so on. Localization economies may be especially important for firms producing nonstandardized products subject to rapid fluctuations in demand, since rapid communication between production units is possible. This is a particularly important advantage for those industries comprising many small-scale units, such as the clothing industry in New York.

When added together, the benefits of a location in a city specializing in a given industry or set of closely related industries may offer firms considerable cost advantages over alternative locations. Moreover, localization economies are, of course, an important factor explaining why the industry profiles of different cities—especially smaller ones—are dominated by a particular industry or industry cluster (Richter, 1969). Typical examples are glass and glass products at Toledo, Ohio, Nashville, and Waco, Tex.; precision instruments at Ann Arbor, Mich., and Rochester, N.Y.; electronics at Binghampton, N.Y., and Manchester, N.H.; rubber products at Akron, Ohio, Jackson, Mich., and Des Moines, Iowa; and appliances and furniture at Fort Smith, Ark., Grand Rapids, Mich., and Greenboro, N.C. (Bergsman et al., 1972).

HISTORICAL ACCIDENT AND PERSONAL PREFERENCES

The fact that firms choose to locate in particular cities cannot always be explained solely in terms of economic calculations based on the kinds of factors discussed above. The choice of one city over another is often the result of chance, historical accident, and the personal preferences of decision makers. Thus Ford's choice of Detroit as the location for his first automobile factory owes more to personal reasons than to economics. In some cases industries grew up at a given city because a particular invention occurred there or because an entrepreneur simply liked the look of the place. The locational advantages of a particular city will, moreover, most certainly have changed through time, accompanying the evolution of the city system and changing spatial relationships. Hence it is often necessary to reconstruct the past in order to appreciate how earlier economic and noneconomic factors influenced the location of manufacturing. However, regardless of whether the location of a particular type of manufacturing in a given city resulted from chance or accident—and its continued existence there owes more to inertia than to anything else—once established, it may have acted as a strong attractive force for the location of subsequent activities in the same city, where they could take advantage of urbanization economies in general and localization economies in particular.

The role played by personal and behavioral factors in the location of manufacturing in cities has almost certainly increased in importance during past decades. This is related in part, of course, to the greater locational freedom permitted many firms today as a result of modern improvements in transportation and communication and associated time-space convergence within the city system. Consequently, for many firms differences in costs between alternative locations in a given region may be minimal, and entrepreneurs can afford to choose one city over another for basically noneconomic reasons—for example, because of the excellent opportunities it offers for recreation or its cultural and social activities. Moreover, it is important to remember that since the framework within which locational decisions are made is a very complex one indeed, decision makers rarely have complete information—economic or whatever—about all possible locations, and this tends to reinforce the role of personal preferences in choosing a location in one particular city instead of another (see Pred, 1967, 1969).

INDUSTRY PROFILES AND DIFFERENTIAL GROWTH

The mix of industries that makes up a city's industry profile is one of the important factors accounting for differential growth within the city system. Some cities grow because they have an above-average concentration of industries that are growing rapidly in the nation as a whole (an *industry-mix* or structural effect). Others grow not because they have a preponderance of rapid-growth industries, but because of changes in the overall locational patterns of particular industries represented in them. As a result, employment in an industry may grow faster in a particular city or urban region because the industry is growing faster there than in other places, even though the industry itself may be a slow-growth one in the nation as a whole (a *competitive* effect). And of course many cities grow in part simply because the national economy itself is growing (a *comparative* effect). Total growth in employment in manufacturing in a city is built up of these three components, the identification of which is the basis of what is called *shift and share analysis* (Dunn, 1960; Perloff et al., 1960).

The components of growth for a given industry in a particular city or urban region can be represented symbolically as follows:

$$G_i = N_i + P_i + D_i \tag{1}$$

where

G_i = the absolute growth in employment in the industry during the period
N_i = growth of industry i compared to the national growth in that industry
P_i = growth of industry i attributable to the industry-mix effect (also known as the *proportional shift*)
D_i = growth of industry i attributable to the competitive effect (or the *differential shift*)

The share of growth accounted for by each component can be identified easily as follows:

$$N_i = E_t \times r \tag{2}$$
$$P_i = E_t \times (r_i - r) \tag{3}$$
$$D_i = E_t \times (r_{ij} - r_i) \tag{4}$$

where

E_t = the employment in the industry at the start of the period
r = the national growth rate for the economy as a whole
r_i = the national growth rate for industry i
r_{ij} = the growth rate for industry i at city (urban region) j

An example will make this clear. If employment in a given industry in a city in 1960 (E_t) was 40,000, and for the decade 1960–1970 r was 0.15, r_i was 0.25, and r_{ij} was 0.40, then:

$$N_i = 40,000 \times 0.15 = 6,000$$
$$P_i = 40,000 \times (0.25 - 0.15) = 4,000$$
$$D_i = 40,000 \times (0.40 - 0.25) = 6,000$$

and by summation, the total growth in employment in the industry (G_i) in the city from 1960 to 1970 is therefore 16,000. By performing similar calculations for every industry in the city and summing the results, the total growth in employment can be disaggregated into the three components and their relative importance ascertained.

Explaining differences in the relative importance of each of the components of growth is not always an easy job. Explaining growth arising from the industry-mix effect (P_i) and the comparative effect (N_i) does not normally present too much of a problem. However, the reasons for the competitive effect (differential shift) are often more difficult to isolate, although they are perhaps the most interesting for geographical analysis. Among the general reasons accounting for a high competitive component in the growth of particular cities may be local advantages with respect to

1. The availability of factors of production
2. External economies of agglomeration
3. Good access to markets for products

Public policy may be responsible in certain cases, since competitive advantage may be artificially increased as a result of planning policies (Smith, 1969). On the other hand, the diseconomies in large cities noted above may counteract these advantages to dampen the competitive effect in certain cities.

AN EVOLUTIONARY MODEL OF CITY GROWTH

An impressionistic generalization of the process of growth of cities which recognizes the importance of their industrial structure and the economic base concept has been presented by Martin (1969; see also Thompson, 1965b). Martin's model is a long-run theory of internal growth and it casts some light on the reason why economic base ratios, discussed in the previous chapter, tend to change over time and with city size. Four categories of activities are identified in the model:

Type A. Basic industries that are the original implantations.

Type B. Nonbasic industries that develop in the city as a result of some kind of linkage with the original implantations, and basic industries that are attracted to the city because of the availability of external economies created by the type A group. Thus this group depends on the industrial environment created by the industries that originally grew up in the city—the type A basic group.

Type C. Firms and institutions, both public and private, which cater to the special needs created by growing urban areas. Examples include water plants, associated services, electricity generating plants, public transport facilities, the construction industry, and so on.

Type D. Services and institutions that serve the essential urban needs of the population. The activities in this group are basically the service functions related to the central place function of cities (see Chapter 6).

A dynamic view of the growth of cities identifies three stages:

1. The stage of original implantations
2. The stage of linked implantations and external economies
3. The metropolis stage

Since type D activities develop more or less automatically as population grows, the model does not have to account for these. Furthermore, the evolutionary model is not chronologically mutually exclusive; even if the city has attained stage 2, it can still attract firms belonging to stage 1, although the order of appearance of the stages cannot, of course, be inverted.

The first stage is characterized by the implantation of private firms and public institutions that choose a particular city for reasons other than the size of the existing population in the city or the presence of other firms. If firms of this type continue to enter and if those already there continue to grow, then these firms establish the settlement as a *growth pole*. These firms are, then, the basic industries that provide the foundation for employment and urban growth.

The city enters stage 2 when new firms are attracted because of the activities that already exist there. The second stage is hence an outcome of the first and is brought about by the development of internal markets for intermediate products and external economies. Internal markets are created by linked industries. External economies are possible because the original stage 1 implantations have created the facilities and services that have become part of the city's infrastructure. Thus stage 2 is characterized by the implantation of firms of type B and a few of type A, while accompanying growth there has of course been the concomitant development of the type D service functions.

The third stage is a direct consequence of the two preceding ones. It is recognized by the appearance of external diseconomies and the presence of the many nonbasic activities (types C and D) needed to satisfy the demands of the urban population. The external diseconomies of water and air pollution, traffic congestion, slums, high crime rates, and so on are not internalized by the firms or institutions within the urban area; but they do appear in the rising costs of providing utilities and of local administration. In a sense these diseconomies create further growth because the population of the urban area is forced to spend part of its income on goods and services to reduce these ill effects of city size. The evolutionary model suggests, therefore, that the diseconomies of large cities may not in fact always impinge upon the growth of metropolitan areas.

The economic facets of a model of this type have been investigated and substantiated by Pred (1966) for the United States in the nineteenth century. In addition, as was noted in the previous chapter, an important feature of the model was the idea that growing urban areas possess an additional advantage in that the "possibilities of invention and innovation within industries" is "enhanced by an intensifying network of interpersonal communications and confrontations" (Pred, 1966, p. 84). This innovation aspect of urban industrial growth is placed in a probabilistic context by Thompson (1965b), who points out that if a town of 50,000 people is likely to produce an industrial innovator once every 10 years, then a city of half a million may produce one per year.

Thus it is not just the introduction of basic industries into cities that encourages growth. Growth of large cities is in large part self-generating, partly because of the operation of the urban ratchet effect but also because they have a predominant nonbasic component that shields them against short-run fluctuations in employment in basic industry (Thompson, 1965a, 1965b). Furthermore, economies of scale and the oligopolist nature of much of modern industry work in favor of a small number of very large cities and against the development and growth of industry at smaller places.

6
CITIES
AS
SERVICE CENTERS

Whereas primary and secondary activities tend to be localized in space, tertiary activities are more widely dispersed within the city system and are found in varying amounts in all cities. The most ubiquitous of all tertiary activities are those connected with the distribution and exchange of goods and services. Without exception, cities are market centers concerned with either the collection of goods from or the distribution of goods and services to the people living in the surrounding areas and beyond. For some cities this marketing function may be overshadowed by other, more specialized roles that they play in the economic organization of society. But for innumerable others, and especially the smaller settlements in agricultural regions, this is often their dominant and only reason for being in the landscape. These are called *central places*. In this chapter we shall discuss the role of settlements as central places, examine some of the spatial regularities that are apparent in the provision of goods and services from them, and review the models generally known as central-place theory.

THE HIERARCHY OF CENTRAL PLACES

Strictly speaking, central places are "neither more nor less than a cluster of retail and service establishments located in a place that provides a convenient point of focus for consumers who visit them to purchase the goods and services they need" (Berry, 1967a, p. 3). The retail and service businesses they provide are known as *central functions*, and these are supplied by *establishments* (retail stores and service offices). When more than one central function is provided by a single establishment, each is counted separately and called a *functional unit*. For example, a drugstore is a central function; it is provided by an establishment that may comprise a number of functional units (drugs, lunch counter, hardware, and so on.)

In visiting marketplaces on a regular basis, consumers want locations that permit them to conduct their business with a minimum amount of effort. Hence central places must be highly accessible to, and be located at points central to, their tributary areas. This quality of location is referred to as *centrality*. The centrality of a place is thought to be reflected by its size measured in terms of the number of central functions it provides. Thus the larger the functional size of a place, the greater its centrality.

The interrelationship between the levels of functional size and their corresponding levels of centrality is what underlies the organization of central places into a hierarchy, the essential features of which are as follows:

1. Higher level places offer more central functions, have more establishments and functional units, and normally are larger in population size than lower level places.

2. Places at a given level in the hierarchy perform all the functions of lower level places plus a group of central functions that differentiates them from, and sets them above, the lower level places.

3. The distribution of central places is related to the levels in the hierarchy. Higher level places occur less frequently in the landscape than lower level places; they are spaced more widely apart and serve larger trade areas and tributary populations than the lower level places.

The hierarchy of central places emerges as the fundamental feature in the spatial organization of marketing on account of differences in both the supply of and the demand for various goods and services. On the demand side, goods and services are purchased with different frequencies, and consumers differ in the proportions of their incomes they spend on the various goods and services available. On the supply side, some central functions can be supported in greater numbers than others, because of their lower *thresholds*, or entry requirements.

The Threshold Concept

The establishments providing central functions are small firms, and like all firms they must operate at a profit if they want to stay in business. To do this, they must realize enough sales to cover at least their operating costs, including a reasonable wage for the entrepreneur. The minimum sales that an establishment must secure in order to survive is called its *threshold*. This varies in size, largely depending on the operating scale of the central function.

Because of the practical difficulties of measuring thresholds, population has been used as a substitute for sales in empirical studies. Moreover, since it is difficult to talk about the minimum population required to support an individual establishment, it is usual to refer to the average establishment for a particular type of central function. Operationally, then, the threshold is defined as the minimum population needed to support a given type of central function. It is only by satisfying this threshold that the central function can appear in the landscape. In this way, the different central functions can be thought of as being arrayed along a continuum of threshold size, as shown, for example, in Table 6.1, which presents empirical estimates of threshold sizes for 52 activities in Snohomish County, Washington (Berry and Garrison, 1958a, 1958b).

Variation in the size of thresholds is perhaps the most important clue in understanding why some central functions are found more often than others in a region. For threshold size is directly related to ubiquity. Hence lower threshold functions can enter the system more easily and occur more frequently than higher threshold functions (Fig. 6.1). Moreover, since the threshold of a given central function is partly a response to the frequency with which it is demanded, thresholds are directly related to the notion of centrality. It follows that the higher the threshold for a central function, the greater the

Table 6.1.   THRESHOLD SIZES FOR 52 CENTRAL FUNCTIONS IN SNOHOMISH COUNTY, WASHINGTON, 1958

Central Functions	Threshold Size	Central Functions	Threshold Size
Filling stations	196	Freight lines and storage	567
Food stores	254	Veterinarians	579
Churches	265	Apparel stores	590
Restaurants and snack bars	276	Lumberyards	598
Taverns	282	Banks	610
Elementary schools	322	Farm implements	650
Physicians	380	Electric repair shops	693
Real estate agencies	384	Florists	729
Appliance stores	385	High schools	732
Barbershops	386	Dry cleaners	754
Auto dealers	398	Local taxi services	762
Insurance agencies	409	Billiard halls and bowling	789
Fuel oil dealers	419	Jewelry stores	827
Dentists	426	Hotels	846
Motels	430	Shoe repair shops	896
Hardware stores	431	Sporting goods stores	928
Auto repair shops	435	Frozen food lockers	938
Fuel dealers (coal, etc.)	453	Sheet metal works	1076
Drugstores	458	Department stores	1083
Beauticians	480	Optometrists	1140
Auto parts dealers	488	Hospitals and clinics	1159
Meeting halls	525	Undertakers	1214
Feed stores	526	Photographers	1243
Lawyers	528	Public accountants	1300
Furniture stores	546	Laundries and laundromats	1307
Variety stores, 5 & 10	549	Health practitioners	1424

SOURCE: Berry and Garrison (1958a), Table 2.

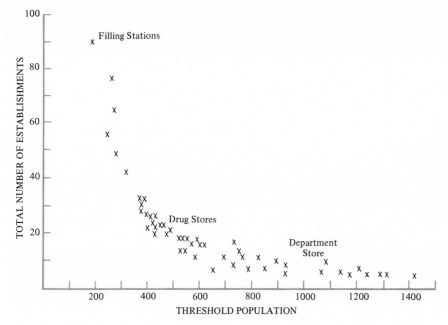

Fig. 6.1. The relationship between the frequency of occurrence of central functions and threshold size, Snohomish County, Washington. (*Source*: Berry and Garrison, 1958b, Fig. 3.)

level of centrality it needs in space. It is for this reason that the higher threshold functions are located at higher level central places in the hierarchy.

The Range of a Good

The threshold concept has been discussed in terms of the people actually residing in central places. But part of the minimum population needed to support a given function at a central place will be scattered in the area around it—and after all, it is to serve these consumers that central places exist. For these people, an additional cost is involved in acquiring the goods and services they need, arising from the journey they must undertake to the central place. This travel cost, measured as a combination of money, time, and effort, must be added to the cost of the good at the market. The actual price paid for a good, the delivered price, will consequently vary directly with distance from the central place. The delivered price will therefore increase directly with the length of the shopping trip, as shown in Figure 6.2A.

Because of this, consumers are normally not willing to travel very far to obtain items they need frequently. Less frequent purchases can often be postponed, "so that a single longer trip can accomplish several things—not only shopping, but socializing, entertainment, politics, and so on" (Berry, 1967a, p. 3). The maximum distance the dispersed population is prepared to travel to purchase a good from a central place is called the *outer range* of the good. Conceptually the outer range will have an ideal limit, which marks the locations where the price of the good is so high that demand for it is zero (see Fig. 6.2B). In practice, however, it is more useful to refer to the real limit of the outer range of a good, which coincides with locations at which the net reward to the consumer of a purchase is equal to the cost of obtaining it (Golledge, 1967). In addition, each good will also have an inner range, which incorporates its threshold requirement.

The outer range (real limit) delimits the service area of a central place for the good or central function in question. The service area will be different for each of the central functions and may also be different for the same central function at each central place, because of the competition in the supply of the good from other centers. Christaller (1966) suggests that some of the other factors influencing the outer range for a particular business type are the price of the good at the central place, the number of inhabitants of the central place itself, the density and distribution of the population surrounding central places, and the income and social conditions of the consuming population.

The Emergence of Hierarchies

Together the concepts of the threshold and the range of a good may be used to demonstrate how hierarchies of central places emerge in the landscape. Imagine that n different central functions are to be provided in a region and that these are ranked from 1 to n in order of increasing threshold requirements—as, for example, in Table 6.1. The nth central function, with its largest threshold, will require the largest market area to support it. Translated into spatial terms, its inner range will have the greatest diameter (see Fig. 6.2B). In the Snohomish County example, a health practitioner with its threshold of 1424 people would represent the nth central function, while filling stations with thresholds of only 196 would represent central function 1.

Following the argument presented by Berry and Garrison (1958c), we can imagine that central function n will be provided from the A-level central places. As many A centers can be supported in the region as there are threshold sales to support establishments supplying this central function. Since these are competing with each other spatially, they will be distributed so as to minimize consumer movement in order to satisfy their thresholds most efficiently. The question then arises as to how the $n-1$th central function will be provided (in Table 6.1, central function $n-1$ corresponds to

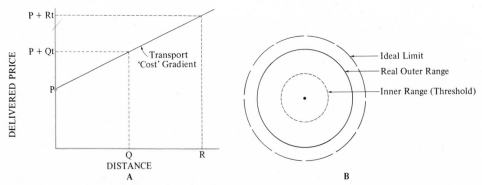

Fig. 6.2. The range of a good. (A) The delivered price of a good increases with distance traveled to purchase it. (B) Spatial expression of the ranges of a good.

laundries, with a threshold of 1307). Presumably these will also be supplied from the *A* centers, since they have sought out locations of greatest centrality in the region. In addition advantages will be gained from clustering together with the higher threshold functions at the *A* centers because of consumers' multiple-purpose shopping trips. In the same way, central functions $n-2$ through 1 will also be provided from *A* centers.

Some of the n central functions may, however, be supplied from smaller central places than the *A* centers. These smaller places will arise whenever there is a large enough demand to satisfy thresholds of lower order functions outside the threshold market areas of the *A* centers. Imagine, for example, that such a situation exists for central function $n-i$. Because there are enough sales in the region outside the threshold market areas for $n-i$ provided at the *A* centers, greater efficiency will be reached if this function is provided from a second level of central place, which we can call *B* centers. Berry and Garrison (1958c) refer to function $n-i$ as a *hierarchical marginal good* because it is just possible for it to be provided from the next lower level of centers in the hierarchy. These *B* centers will also provide all lower threshold functions below the hierarchical marginal good; that is, they will provide functions $n-(i+1)$ through 1.

A new set of centers can come into existence for every hierarchical marginal good in the system. For example, if function $n-j$ (with lower threshold requirements than business type $n-i$) is another hierarchical marginal good, it can be supplied from a third set of centers which we can call *C* centers. By the same arguments as above, these *C* centers will be able to provide all lower threshold functions as well.

The cumulative hierarchical structure that builds up in this way is shown in Table 6.2. In the table the set of functions supplied from each level of central place is indicated by the X's. Thus, in the ideal case, the *A* centers will provide all central functions; the *B* centers will provide all functions with thresholds equal to or lower than $n-i$; the *C* centers those functions with thresholds equal to or less than that of $n-j$; and the *M* centers will be able to supply only the lowest threshold functions below $n-k$. Hence the *C* places and people in the trade areas of the *C* centers rely upon either *B* or *A* centers for goods $n-i$ through $n-(j-1)$ and upon the *A* centers for goods n through $n-(i-1)$. Similarly, the *B* centers will rely upon the larger *A* centers for the provision of goods n through $n-(i-1)$. According to the premise that each center locates central to the maxi-

---

Table 6.2. THE SUPPLY OF n GOODS FROM m CENTRAL PLACES

Goods

Centers	$n^{+a}, n-1, n-2, ...$			$n-i^{+}, n-(i+1), ...$		$n-j^{+}, n-(j+1), ...$		$n-k^{+}, n-(k+1), ... 1$	
A	X X X X	X	X	X X	X	X..	X	X	X X
B		X	X	X X	X	X..	X	X	X X
C				X	X	X..	X	X	X X
.						.		.	. .
.						.		.	. .
M						X		X	X X

^{a} The symbol $^+$ denotes the hierarchical marginal good.

mum trade area it can command, all levels of central places will be located at places from which they can serve most efficiently the tributary areas with the goods and services they provide. Because of this, we would expect the higher level centers with their greater needs for centrality to be spaced more widely apart than the more closely spaced smallest level centers in the hierarchy.

An Empirical Example

Central-place hierarchies have been recognized in innumerable studies of service centers in small regions (see Berry and Pred, 1964). One of the most comprehensive studies to date was that undertaken by Berry in southwestern Iowa (Berry, Barnum, and Tennant, 1962). This nine-county study area, shown in Figure 6.3, is a homogeneous and highly productive farming region typical of the mixed crop-livestock economy of the corn belt. Rural population densities average 15.5 persons per square mile, increasing to 20.4 persons per square mile close to Omaha–Council Bluffs and decreasing to 12.7 persons per square mile in Adams County, the poorest part of the study area.

The level of settlements in the hierarchy was established by the use of a method called *direct factor analysis,* which was applied to data matrices recording the presence and absence of central functions at each place. Application of this method not only ensured greater objectivity in classification, but also avoided the need for preselecting functions thought to be characteristic of centers at the different levels in the hierarchy, as had been the case in many earlier studies (see, for example, Brush, 1953). The hierarchy identified in southwestern Iowa (Fig. 6.3) has the numerical sequence: 35 hamlets, 36 villages, 20 towns, eight cities, and one regional capital. Actually, as Berry

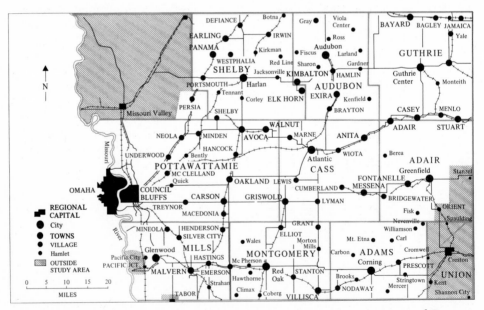

Fig. 6.3. A hierarchy of central places in southwestern Iowa. (*Source*: Berry, Barnum, and Tennant, 1962, Fig. 1.)

(1967a) points out, Council Bluffs is probably a regional city and Omaha a regional metropolis in the context of Philbrick's (1957) terminology, discussed in Chapter 2, for in other parts of the country these levels have distinct locations in the spatial system. With the exception of the hamlets, the sequence is consistent with the notion that lower order centers occur more ubiquitously in the landscape than higher order centers. The fact that hamlets, once the basic feature of the settlement pattern in agricultural regions, occur less frequently than expected partly reflects the decline in rural population in this area during the past decades. For as the number of rural dwellers has decreased, so it has become more difficult for functions in these smallest centers to satisfy their thresholds. Together with the increased mobility of the rural farm population and the associated shift in patronizing villages and higher order centers, many of the hamlets have disappeared from the landscape as service centers (see Hodge, 1965).

The size characteristics of typical centers at different levels of the hierarchy identified from the factor analysis are shown in Table 6.3. The hamlets, which are omitted from the table, had fewer than 100 inhabitants, seldom more than four to six retail businesses, and usually provided only a general store and a filling station. Villages, with 10 to 26 central functions, provided low-threshold convenience goods for which there is frequent demand (Table 6.4). Towns, having from 28 to 50 central functions, provide—in addition to the functions performed at the village level—a selection of higher threshold activities of the sort indicated in Table 6.4. Although functionally more complex than the lower level villages, which cannot profitably provide the higher order functions, the towns are characterized by a simpler set of functions than the cities. In southwestern Iowa these had in every case more than 55 central functions, including more specialized higher threshold activities as well as those typical of lower level centers, and they have well-developed central shopping districts whose major attractions include such functions as clothing stores, shoe stores, florists, and jewelers (Table 6.4).

An indication of the importance of service provision at the city level is total tax-

Table 6.3.   SIZE CHARACTERISTICS IN THE HIERARCHY OF CENTRAL PLACES IN SOUTHWESTERN IOWA, 1960: SELECTED EXAMPLES

	Level of Center	Population	Number of Central Functions	Functional Units
City				
	Red oak	6421	90	312
	Atlantic	6890	92	411
Town				
	Griswold	1207	50	102
	Anita	1273	50	84
	Villisca	1690	43	90
	Oakland	1340	49	97
Village				
	Lewis	501	24	43
	Elliott	459	26	42
	Stanton	514	21	28

Source: Berry, Barnum, and Tennant (1962), p. 81.

able sales. In 1960 Atlantic and Red Oak, for example, had sales of 16 million dollars and 14 million dollars respectively. This compares with total sales of between 2 and 2.5 million dollars at the town-level centers. The dominance of Council Bluffs–Omaha in the region is indicated by the high level of sales there, which approached 70 million dollars in Council Bluffs alone. The larger size that this reflects is illustrated by the fact that in Council Bluffs there were over 1100 retail and service establishments in 1960, including an array of department stores, specialty shops, professional services, and cultural facilities — high-threshold functions that require very high degrees of centrality in the landscape.

Table 6.4.   CENTRAL FUNCTIONS TYPICAL OF LEVELS IN THE HIERARCHY OF CENTRAL PLACES, SOUTHWESTERN IOWA, 1960

(A) The Village-level functions

Gas and service station	Meeting hall
Automobile repair	Hardware
Bars	Farm materials
Restaurants	Farm sales
Grocery	Farm implements
Post Office	Oil fuel bulk station
Local government facility	Barber
Church	Beauty shops

(B) The Town-level functions

Furniture	Doctors
Appliances	Dentists
Variety	Building services
General clothing	Building materials
Drugstores	Radio-TV sales and service
Banks	Movers and haulers
Insurance agents	Funeral home
Real estate	Veterinarian
Telephone exchange	Automobile accessories
Cleaners	Farmers' cooperatives

(C) The City-level functions

Women's clothing	Newspaper publisher
Men's clothing	Office of labor union
Shoes	Sales of new automobiles
Jewelry	Sales of used automobiles
Florist	Specialized automobile repairs
Supermarket	Automobile wrecking
Bakery	Cleaners and laundry (operator)
Liquor store	Self-service laundry
Other medical practice (e.g., op-tometrists)	Shoe repairs
	Plumbing
Lawyer	Fixit
Hotel	Movies
Motel	Indoor amusements (billiards, etc.)
County government	Drive-in eating places

SOURCE: Berry, Barnum, and Tennant (1962), Tables IV–VI.

STRUCTURAL RELATIONSHIPS IN THE HIERARCHY OF SERVICE CENTERS

One of the fundamental features of the hierarchy of central places is that higher level centers have more central functions, larger populations, a greater number of establishments and functional units, and, as we shall see below, larger trade areas encompassing more people. The existence of these kinds of structural regularities in the hierarchy in southwestern Iowa is clearly indicated by the high correlation coefficients between the relevant variables shown in Table 6.5.

The Population: Central Function Relationship

A number of studies have examined the relationship between the population size and number of central functions of places. The results of these studies have established this to be curvilinear (or linear when population is transformed into logarithms), indicating that as settlements become larger they add fewer new functions for each new increment in population. Thomas (1960, p. 15) has suggested one explanation for the curvilinear nature of this relationship:

> there may be definite limits to the functional complexity of urban places. As cities become larger, greater numbers of establishments and [central] functions are formed within them. Once a certain level is reached, however, establishments are added much more rapidly than functions. This suggests that to a considerable extent the greater numbers of people found in larger places do not desire different kinds of functions, but merely convenient access to the same ones.

Figure 6.4 illustrates the nature of the relationship in two studies. For small towns in southern Illinois, Stafford (1963) found that the variation in number of central functions at places was very highly correlated ($r = 0.89$) with variation in their population size (Fig. 6.4A). Similar high positive correlations are typical in the three areas of the American Midwest studied by Berry, Barnum, and Tennant (1962). When the hamlets are excluded from the calculations, correlations of 0.95, 0.93, and 0.91 are found in the

---

**Table 6.5. STRUCTURAL RELATIONSHIPS IN THE
HIERARCHY, SOUTHWESTERN IOWA, 1960**

Correlation Coefficients[a]

		P	*LP*	*F*	*LF*	*CF*
P	Population of center	X	—	.98	—	.89
LP	Log. of population		X	—	.96	.95
F	No. of functional units			X	—	.93
LF	Log. of functional units				X	.98
CF	No. of Central Functions					X

[a] Pearson product moment correlation coefficients. The maximum value that these can attain is 1.0; the closer the value to this, the higher the degree of correlation between the two variables.
SOURCE: Berry, Barnum, and Tennant (1962), Table 1.

---

southwestern Iowa, northeastern South Dakota, and Rapid City, N.D., areas respectively (Fig. 6.4B).

The reason for omitting the hamlets from the relationships in the latter areas is made clear from a closer look at the graph for southwestern Iowa (Fig. 6.4C). Clearly two distinct trends are apparent. First, there is the marked log-linear trend of the relationship between population size and numbers of central functions at the village-level places and above (i.e., at places with more than 10 central functions). Second, there is a different kind of relationship between the variables for the smaller hamlets, with from one to eight central functions and populations of fewer than 100. For these places the relationship is weak indeed and apparently does not conform with that typical of the larger level centers. Rather, the hamlets are contained within an equipossible area on the graph reflecting their position of decline in the settlement pattern.

In southwestern Iowa no place appears to deviate markedly from the general trend of the population-size–central-function relationship. The scatter of points about the

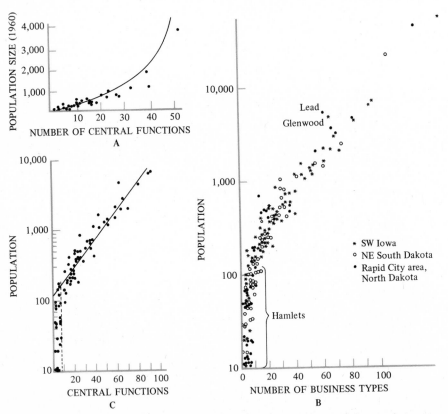

Fig. 6.4. The relationship between the number of central functions and the population size of central places in (A) southern Illinois, (B) selected Midwestern areas, and (C) southwestern Iowa. (*Source*: Stafford, 1963, Fig. 3; Berry, 1967a, Fig. 2–11; and Berry, Barnum, and Tennant, 1962, Fig. 3.)

line of average relationship is much as we would expect, given the imperfections of the real world. Often, however, certain places stand out on account of their significant deviation from the line of best fit, because they have either a greater or a smaller number of central functions than expected from their population size. Tourist centers in recreational areas are typical of the former, since they usually have a wide range of functions in addition to those normally required by their local populations. On the other hand, places may have fewer functions than expected from their population size; for example, when the usual regularities are distorted by the impact of an expanding metropolitan community (Berry and Garrison, 1958a). For, "as the commuting range of the metropolis shifts outwards, previously independent central places are drawn within the web of intrametropolitan relations" to become part of its "Daily Urban System" (Berry, 1960). The result is a population-function imbalance at nearby places as they increasingly become suburbs for the larger centers.

The Central Function: Functional Units Relationship

Figure 6.5 shows the log-linear relationship between number of functional units and central functions. The graph is similar to that shown in Figure 6.4C for population and number of central functions in that two distinct areas can be recognized: (1) the equipossible containing the hamlets, and (2) the log-linear relationship for the higher level centers (villages and above). However, unlike the relationship shown in that graph, the trend of the relationship in Figure 6.5A is not maintained throughout the scatter of points. Instead, the overall scatter may be broken down into several regimes, each with its own significantly different log-linear trend.

These discontinuities in the overall trend are clearly associated with the hierarchical structure. Figure 6.5B shows that the different regimes correspond to the different levels of places in the hierarchy. These are set within the broader framework of city-size regularities that are characteristic of aggregative analysis. This is consistent with the findings of the factor analysis used by Berry to classify centers in this region. These revealed an overall pattern of general size relationships with discontinuities associated with groups of centers and associated kinds and numbers of central functions indicative of the hierarchical structure (Berry, Barnum, and Tennant, 1962).

CONSUMER TRAVEL AND THE HIERARCHY

The shopping patterns of dispersed rural populations and the inhabitants of the central places themselves provide the means whereby the structural components of the hierarchy are welded together into a central-place system. Figures 6.6 to 6.9 illustrate typical patterns of consumer travel for different order goods and services within a small part of the southwestern Iowa area shown in Figure 6.3. On the maps, desire lines (straight lines from farm residence to marketplace) are used to indicate the shopping trips of rural farm dwellers. The shopping trips for the urban residents (those living at the central places themselves) are shown by wheels; if a good or service is obtained within the center itself, a spoke is added to the wheel, and if it is obtained from another center, an arrow is drawn linking the two centers.

The pattern for clothing purchases (Fig. 6.6) indicates the way Council Bluffs, Red

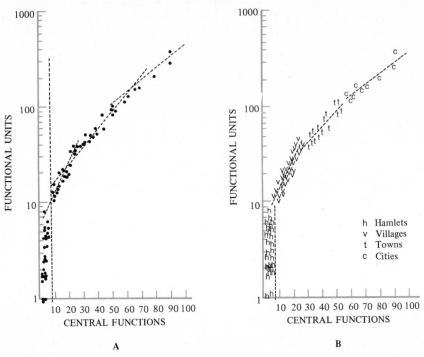

Fig. 6.5. The relationship between central functions and functional units in southwestern Iowa. Several regimes appear to be present on the graph (A), each of which corresponds to a distinct class of central places (B). (*Source*: Berry, Barnum, and Tennant, 1962, Figs. 4 and 7.)

Oak, and Atlantic dominate the provision of city-level goods. The trip patterns for urban residents and farm families are almost identical and are consistent with the notion of distance minimization in spatial interaction. The tendency for larger places to attract customers over longer distances is reflected in the way the regional capital (Council Bluffs) extends its influence into the western part of the study area. Figure 6.7 shows the travel patterns for furniture, a town-level good. The main difference between this map and that for clothing purchases is the emergence of the town of Griswold as a focus in the pattern of consumer movements, particularly for the farm families surrounding it (Fig. 6.7B). Griswold, located on the watershed between the market areas of the higher level centers for clothing, is able to secure enough sales to make the supply of furniture profitable. The hierarchical structure is clearly expressed in these patterns; drawing power is noticeably related to level of center. The regional capital attracts over longer distances, followed by the two cities of Atlantic and Red Oak, which draw from intermediate surrounding areas, while the small towns (Griswold, Oakland, and Villisca) attract sales only from local areas.

In contrast to the patterns for high-order shopping goods, Figure 6.8 shows the different picture for a high-order convenience good—dry cleaning. Although the trade areas of Atlantic, Red Oak, and Griswold are more or less unchanged for this good, the

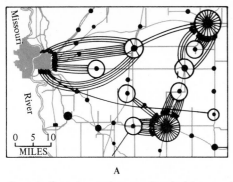 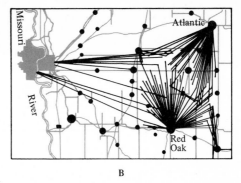

Fig. 6.6. Shopping preferences for clothing, southwestern Iowa: (A) urban dwellers, (B) rural dwellers. (*Source*: Berry, Barnum, and Tennant, 1962, Fig. 17.)

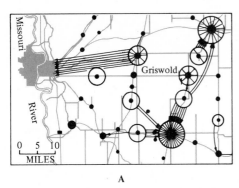 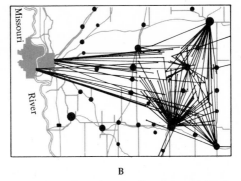

Fig. 6.7. Shopping preferences for furniture, southwestern Iowa: (A) urban dwellers, (B) rural dwellers. (*Source*: Berry, Barnum, and Tennant, 1962, Fig. 15.)

influence of the regional capital in the area has disappeared. Rural and urban consumers seem to travel to the nearest center. Thus the town of Oakland attracts consumers from the local area for dry cleaning in a way that was not possible for furniture sales. Dry cleaning is a relatively frequently demanded good, and hence consumers are not prepared to travel long distances for it.

What happens to the pattern when thresholds can be satisfied from a village location is shown for the purchase of groceries in Figure 6.9. Groceries are an example of a true convenience good for which there is a high frequency of demand and consumers are normally prepared to travel only short distances to purchase them. Hence on the maps urban residents prefer to shop for groceries where they live, while farm families travel to the nearest centers providing this order good. The small village trade areas have been created at the expense of the cities rather than the towns, and consequently their trade areas are much smaller for this order good. Clearly, the reach of centers is directly related to their size; villages attract fewer farmers than towns, but over shorter distances. Towns in turn have smaller trade areas than the cities.

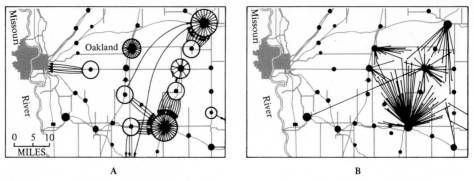

Fig. 6.8. Shopping preferences for dry cleaning services, southwestern Iowa: (A) urban dwellers, (B) rural dwellers. (*Source*: Berry Barnum, and Tennant, 1962, Fig. 14.)

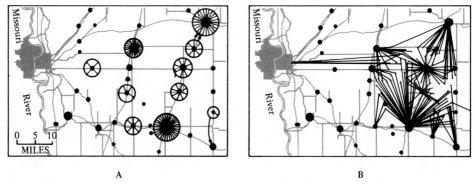

Fig. 6.9. Shopping preferences for groceries, southwestern Iowa: (A) urban dwellers, (B) rural dwellers. (*Source*: Berry, Barnum, and Tennant, 1962, Fig. 11.)

In summary, the maps indicate the close agreement between the patterns of consumer movement and the structure of the hierarchy in the area. Higher level places attract consumers over longer distances than lower level places, consistent with their higher degrees of centrality. Moreover, the trade areas of the higher level centers are more extensive than those of lower level places for goods of similar order. The trade areas for centers at any level for goods of a given order seldom overlap, and where they do, it is usually at the margins between centers, where consumers have a distinct choice of patronage (Golledge, 1967). In general, consumers do seem to be systematically selecting the closest central place for the purchase of goods of different orders. This is made possible by the fact that, as thresholds drop, establishments providing goods can squeeze into the interstitial areas between the larger centers. Finally centers do appear to be located central to the areas they dominate in the provision of goods and services, although the maps do show exceptions to this because of the boundaries of the area chosen for the shopping survey. As Berry states, "If a system is defined as an entity comprising interacting interdependent elements, then we certainly seem to be dealing with a central place system of markets, consumers, and the multiple interactions and interdependencies among them" (Berry, 1967a, p. 13).

Factors Affecting Consumer Travel

The various factors influencing the distances traveled by rural dwellers to central places for the purchase of goods and services can be summarized under three headings: (1) the characteristics of the individual and his spatial preferences (Rushton, 1969, 1971a), which are in part a function of his (2) movement imagery, and (3) behavior-space (Huff, 1960).

Individual Characteristics

Included under individual characteristics are the usual factors such as age, sex, income, and education, which are generally implicit in the notion of socioeconomic status. By and large, the higher the status of individuals, the greater their price willingness and the more prepared they are to travel to purchase goods. Thus, for example, Berry has noted from his studies in the Midwest that low-income groups tend to patronize closer centers than higher income groups in the purchase of central goods (Berry, Barnum, and Tennant, 1962). Within the central-place system, the low-income consumers tend to visit the small lower level centers and only occasionally visit centers at higher levels. Conversely, higher income groups frequently travel longer distances to purchase both convenience and shopping goods from the higher level centers.

Movement Imagery

Huff defines movement imagery as "the perceived movement of the consumer from one region to another in his quest for a desired goal object" (Huff, 1960, p. 163). The consumer's movement imagery is affected by factors such as means of travel, travel time, and the general opportunity costs involved in overcoming the frictional effects of distance in different ways. And it is this notion that accounts, in part, for the significant relationship found in empirical studies between frequency of trip and distance traveled for convenience goods.

Behavior Space

This is essentially that part of the total central-place system that individuals perceive as potential sources for satisfying their demands for goods and services. At any given moment of time the individual's behavior space will be conditioned by the information he has acquired about the structure of the central-place hierarchy from previous personal experience and from outside sources of information, such as advertisements. By and large, the ability of a place to satisfy consumer demands will depend on the number of establishments and central functions it provides—its centrality. This is borne out in empirical studies that have found size of center to be the most significant factor influencing the distance traveled in the purchase of goods and services.

An example

The way these general factors affect travel patterns is well illustrated in a study in southwestern Ontario (Murdie, 1965). Alongside the modern Canadian settlement in this area, there exists a considerable Mennonite population, many of whom still cling to the "Old Order." The simplicity of their home life is reflected in the low demand for goods, and the traditional horse-and-buggy remains as the sole means of transportation for day-to-day affairs. Moreover, their information level is low because their main contact with the modern order is only via local newspapers. Hence we might expect the Old Order Mennonites to have markedly different behavior spaces and movement imagery than modern Canadians whenever their particular culture affects the demands for goods and services.

That this is the case is clearly shown in Figures 6.10 and 6.11. The travel patterns to banks are generally the same for both groups (Fig. 6.10). Banks are typical of less ubiquitous services that have developed in the central-place structure more recently and long after the establishment of the first Mennonite settlements in the region. Old Order Mennonite demand for this and similar services is affected very little by the cultural traditions and church doctrine of the group. However, when these traditions do affect demand—as for clothing, for example—quite different travel patterns result, as shown in Figure 6.11. In contrast to the pattern for modern Canadians, which is dominated by trips to Kitchener (the regional capital), the Mennonite pattern is much more localized and reflects the fact that most of their clothes are made at home from yard goods. Thus for them, style, choice, and comparative shopping are unimportant; and their demand for yard goods is easily satisfied by the relatively unspecialized stores in the nearest hamlets, villages, and towns.

The difference in spatial behavior of the two groups is clearly apparent on graphs showing the distances traveled to purchase clothing and yard goods, respectively (Fig. 6.12). The graph for modern Canadians fits the now well-documented regularities in consumer behavior, namely that distance traveled is directly related to the size of central place. However, the graph for the Old Order Mennonites clearly shows that the centrality of a place has little effect on distances traveled; these people travel to the nearest supply point regardless of size—on average a distance of about six miles. Clearly, then, the Mennonites exhibit markedly different space preferences because of their different behavior space resulting from their cultural doctrine (especially its effect upon demand for goods) and the inability of their Old World transportation to overcome the friction of distance.

Trade Areas

The maximum trade area for a given center will be a function of the highest threshold good provided from it. Since higher order goods and services are provided from higher level centers, larger places will have larger trade areas encompassing larger total populations. This is shown for centers at different levels in the hierarchy in southwestern Iowa in Figure 6.13.

Several points about the graph should be noted. First, centers at the different levels in the hierarchy occupy distinct regimes within the overall scatter of points similar to the steplike pattern shown in Figure 6.5. These regimes are marked by upper limits corresponding to the maximum economic reach of the different level centers. The villages, serving on average a radius of about five miles, have maximum market areas of about 90 square miles. In this area they reach between 500 and 600 consumers, which with their own populations makes a total population served of about 1,100. The towns serve an area with a maximum radius of about eight miles, have trade areas of up to 200 square miles containing total populations of about 4,200. Cities have maximum trade areas of approximately 1,000 square miles containing 20,000 consumers, to give total populations served of about 30,000.

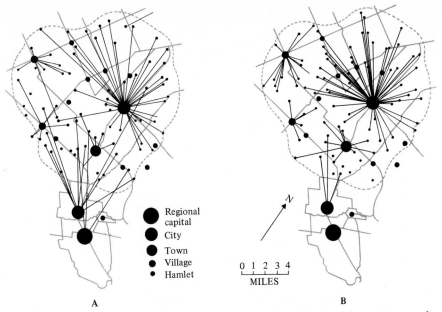

Fig. 6.10. Banks used by (A) "modern" Canadians and (B) Old Order Mennonites, southwestern Ontario. (*Source*: Murdie, 1965, Figs. 6 and 7.)

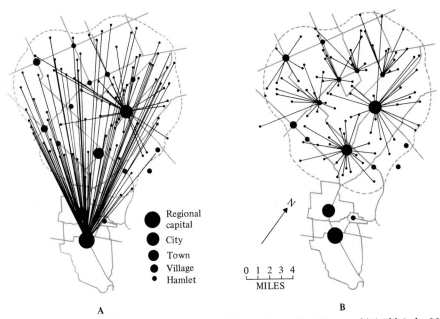

Fig. 6.11. Shopping preferences for clothing of (A) "modern" Canadians and (B) Old Order Mennonites, southwestern Ontario. (*Source*: Murdie, 1965, Figs. 14 and 15.)

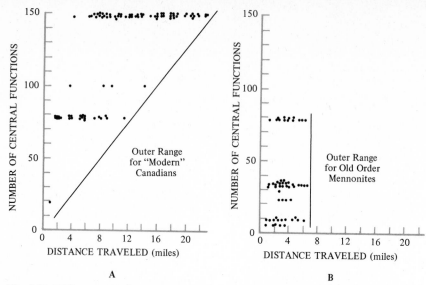

Fig. 6.12. Differences in the ranges of clothing and yard goods in southwestern Ontario. Whereas the distances traveled by "modern" Canadians (A) are related to the size of center visited, the distances traveled by Old Order Mennonites (B) are independent of size of center. (*Source*: Murdie, 1965, Figs. 30 and 31.)

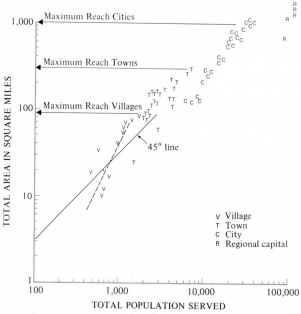

Fig. 6.13. The relationship between the size of trade areas and total population serviced by central places. (*Source*: Berry, 1967a, Fig. 2–1.)

Second, the relationship between size of trade area and total population served is double logarithmic. Hence the line drawn on the graph at an angle of 45° traces out a line of equal population densities. The overall scatter of points lies very close to this line, indicating the relationship between the size of trade area and density of population within this area. However, the separate regimes of the different level centers slope upward at angles greater than 45°—as shown, for example, by the dashed line for the trend of the villages. These therefore must serve areas with different population density characteristics. The villages at the upper end of the regime have larger trade areas than those at the lower end, but larger areas with lower density of population. This pattern is created because rural population densities decline with distance away from the urban centers, and, other things being equal, centers with larger trade areas will therefore have lower density of population (Berry, 1967a).

Systematic Variation in Hierarchies

Figure 6.13 indicated that local variation in population density in southwestern Iowa had a direct effect upon the size of trade areas of centers. For any given level of center, larger trade areas were associated with lower population densities. If the hierarchy is sensitive to these local conditions, it is realistic to expect that variations will occur in the central-place structure in association with regional variations in popu-

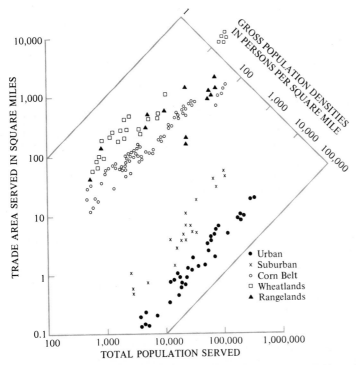

Fig. 6.14. Relationships between the size of trade areas and total population serviced by central places vary according to the density of population. (*Source*: Berry, 1967a, Fig. 2-8.)

lation density. That this is so is indicated in Figure 6.14. On this graph, the relationship between trade-area size and total population served by centers is given for the centers in southwestern Iowa ("Corn Belt") together with comparable data for centers in four other areas of contrasted density. These range from the low densities of two to five persons per square mile in the rangelands of southwestern South Dakota and the densities of between six and nine persons per square mile in the wheatlands of northeastern South Dakota through to the high densities of part of the city of Chicago ("Urban" on the graph).

The centers in the hierarchies of the different areas show a high degree of systematic variation under the different density conditions. The graph indicates the significant increase in the size of trade areas with decreasing population densities. The only exception to this occurs in the rangelands, which include the higher density mining and recreational areas of the Black Hills.

When the different levels in the hierarchy are indicated as in Figure 6.15, another interesting feature emerges. The different levels of the hierarchy in the five regions are so consistent that their upper limits can be indicated by straight lines. These slope backward to the right and indicate that trade areas increase in size with decreases in population density but at a slower rate than the decline in population density. The

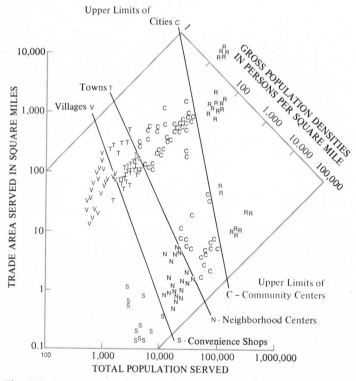

Fig. 6.15. Systematic variation in the hierarchy of central places is related to differences in the density of population. (*Source:* Berry, 1967a, Fig. 2–9.)

result is that the total population served by centers at a given level in the hierarchy also decreases.

This has a direct effect on the satisfaction of thresholds at centers. Functions with the highest thresholds at any given level of the hierarchy are forced to move up to the next higher level. Berry argues from this that a reduction is brought about in the population sizes of the centers themselves, because their economic base has declined with the loss of the higher threshold functions (Berry, 1967a). Thus the upper limit in population size of towns in southwestern Iowa is about 1700; in the rangelands of South Dakota, towns do not exceed about 500 population. Because of this, the towns in South Dakota are no longer able to support the following central functions: furniture stores, appliance stores, variety stores, insurance and real estate agents, movers and haulers, funeral homes, doctors, and dentists. Similarly, the lower threshold functions of farm implement dealers, barbershops, and beauty salons are no longer found at the village level as they are in southwestern Iowa, but have moved up to become town-level functions in South Dakota.

Berry (1967a, pp. 34–35) explains this upward shift in the level of functions as follows:

> To maintain a given array of activities, market areas must increase in size in direct proportion to the drop in population densities; the maximum distance consumers are willing to travel to the center must increase in similar proportion to the density decline. Evidently consumers are willing to travel farther where densities are lower, for movement will generally be easier where people are fewer and congestion is less, so that the economic reach of centers does increase. The change is less than proportionate, however, so center's functions must adjust to the declining numbers of consumers that can be reached within the trade areas of increasing radius. Similarly, at very high densities, congestion will not completely localize consumer movements, so that business centers of any given level within cities reach more consumers and are functionally more complex than their rural counterparts.

Thus, systematic variations in the hierarchy can be incorporated into the central-place system through the concepts of the threshold and range of the good.

THE CENTRAL-PLACE THEORY

The empirically observed regularities discussed above suggest that they may be formalized in a more abstract way. This was recognized as long ago as 1933 by Christaller, whose name today is synonymous with *central-place theory*. The ideas he presented were subsequently taken up by Lösch, who formulated them in a more rigorous way and developed them further.

Christaller's k-3 System

Christaller's model of a central-place system is based on what he calls the *marketing principle* (Christaller, 1966). To get rid of as many of the complicating influences acting on settlement patterns as possible, Christaller developed his ideas for an abstract area with the following characteristics:

1. The area is featureless plain, devoid of any natural or man-made features.
2. Movement is possible in any and every direction.
3. Population, and by implication purchasing power, is continuously and uniformly distributed.
4. Consumers act rationally according to the principles of distance minimization.

The first three of these characteristics describe what is generally referred to as an *isotropic surface* (Muller and Diaz, 1973).

If on this abstract surface consumers are to be supplied from central places with a given good, according to assumption 4 the trade areas for the good will be circular. If it is further assumed that the good is to be provided from as many central places as possible, the maximum possible size of the circular trade areas will be equal to the inner range for the good, since an area of this size will contain just enough consumers to satisfy its threshold. The most efficient packing of these trade areas in the plain is shown in Figure 6.16A. In this way, the total area of the plain that is not served by a central place is at a minimum, and the number of central places and trade areas is at a maximum. Two important features of the resulting pattern are that (1) central places are distributed according to a triangular-hexagonal pattern and (2) each trade area is tangential to six others.

However, with this arrangement consumers living in the shaded interstitial areas will not be provided with the good in question. Therefore the circular trade areas must overlap, as shown in Figure 6.16B. Consumers living in the areas of overlap may now choose which center they will visit, and from assumption 4 above they will choose the closest center. The result is a bisection of the areas of overlap and the circular trade areas are replaced by hexagonal ones, as shown in Figure 6.16C. This geometric pattern, in which the number 3 takes on special significance, forms the basis of Christaller's *k*–3 system.

So far the discussion has been in terms of the provision of only one good. In reality a number of goods and services are provided. The question is how the different order goods will be provided within the framework of the hexagonal pattern. The answer is shown in Figure 6.17, which was developed by Christaller in the following way:

The locations of the highest order good were selected as a starting point. Since

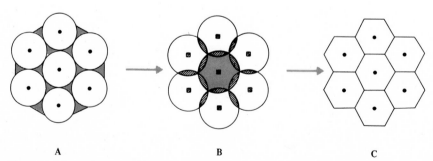

A   B   C

Fig. 6.16. The emergence of hexagonal trade areas: (A) the most efficient packing of circular trade areas on the plain, (B) overlapping circular trade areas, (C) hexagonal trade areas covering the plain completely and without overlap.

this good has the largest threshold requirement, it will also have the largest hexagonal trade area. The places from which this good is provided (primary centers) are shown in the diagram by the large solid dots, and their trade areas by the thick solid lines. Christaller considered these locations to be the sites of central places from which all lower threshold goods are also provided. It follows that the minimum size of trade areas required to support these successively lower goods will be progressively smaller than that for the highest order good. One of these lower order goods will have a threshold size just large enough for it to be provided from a new location, and an enterprising businessman could establish himself there. The trade area for this good will be a hexagon exactly equal in size to the trade area for the same good provided from the primary centers. In terms of the previous discussion, this good is an example of a *hierarchical marginal good*. Since the existing centers already provide all goods down to this order, the only location possible from which the threshold for this good can be satisfied is the midpoint between three of the original primary centers. The locations of these secondary centers are shown in the diagram by the large open dots and their trade areas by the heavy dashed lines. These secondary centers will provide all goods having thresholds smaller than that of the hierarchical marginal good typical of centers at this level. By repeating the argument a third, fourth, and succeeding times, the pattern fills out to give a system of nested trade areas and a hierarchy of different level centers. By definition, each higher level center in the hierarchy provides all goods supplied from successively lower level centers plus a group of higher order functions that set it above the lower level centers in the system. For reasons of clarity, only the three largest sized centers in this kind of hierarchy are shown in Figure 6.17.

From the geometrical properties of the hexagonal-triangular pattern, the following generalizations about the $k-3$ system can be made:

   1. The frequency of occurrence of the different levels of central places follows the progression, from large to small, 1, 2, 6, 18, 54, 162 . . . n.

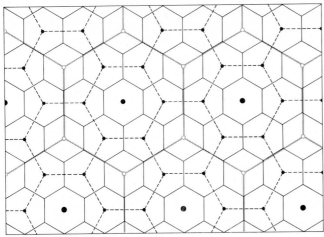

Fig. 6.17. A part of the Christaller K=3 settlement pattern. Only the three largest levels of centers are shown on the diagram.

2. Each lower level center is located at the midpoint between three higher level centers, thereby giving rise to a uniform pattern in which centers are distributed in the form of a triangular lattice.

3. The distance between centers at a given level is equal to $\sqrt{3}$ times the distance between the centers immediately below them in the hierarchy.

4. Every higher level center is surrounded by a ring of six centers of the next lower level in the hierarchy, and these are located at each corner of its hexagonal trade area. Each lower level place is therefore served equally by three centers of the next higher level in the hierarchy—hence the $k=3$ system.

5. The trade area of a higher level center is exactly three times larger than that of the next lower level centers. It comprises its own trade area at this lower level, plus one-third of the trade areas of each of the six surrounding centers (see Fig. 6.17).

6. In this way, the progression of trade areas from largest to smallest is 1, 3, 9, 27, 81, 243 . . . m.

The Löschian Landscape

Lösch's (1954) contribution to central-place theory was essentially two fold. First, he provided a more explicit and rigorous economic argument of the rationale underlying hexagonal trade areas. The more rigorous analysis of supply and demand was based on the economic theory of the firm, and this made possible a more exact specification of the spatial demand cone for a given good. Lösch was also able to prove mathe-

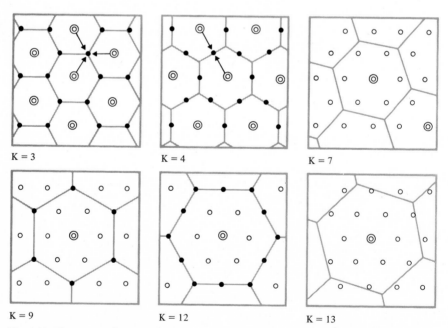

Fig. 6.18. The six smallest size trade areas in the Löschian landscape. (*Source*: After Lösch, 1954, Fig. 27.)

matically that the hexagon is the most advantageous shape for trade areas, since it requires a smaller amount of land to generate a given level of total demand than any of the possible alternatives (i.e., a triangle or a square). Consequently hexagons enable the best possible packing of trade areas in a region to the mutual advantage of both consumers (through distance minimization) and producers (because the largest number of independent enterprises is possible).

Second, in building on Christaller's initial ideas, Lösch demonstrated that a more general central-place system could be developed in which the $k=3$ system is just a very special case. This more general system can be derived by rearranging the hexagons and by changing their size and orientation. The six smallest possible hexagonal trade areas are shown in Figure 6.18, and the series continues with sizes 16, 19, 21, 25 . . .

Lösch developed his economic landscape from a different starting point than Christaller. He first assumed that the featureless plain was covered by a pattern of small nucleated settlements (hamlets) instead of a continuous distribution of population. He then built up the central-place pattern in the reverse order to Christaller by beginning with the location of places providing the lowest instead of the highest order good. This basic good is assumed to be provided from a number of villages, as shown in Figure 6.19. Lösch then argued that if the different thresholds are considered to be multiples of the size of the basic hexagons, goods requiring market areas from one to three times this size will be located in a $k=3$ pattern, goods requiring four times its size will locate in a $k=4$ pattern, those requiring from five to seven times the basic trade area size locate in a

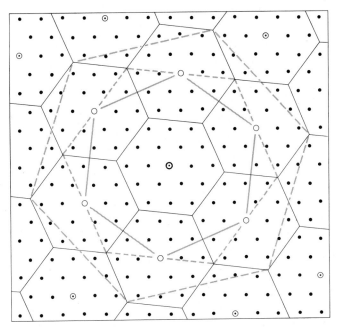

Fig. 6.19. The overlap of the three smallest size trade areas in the Löschian landscape. The map also shows the basic hexagons served by the central villages and the triangular lattice of small nucleated settlements covering the plain.

k–7 pattern, and so on up through the different orders of goods. In this way the land-scape is covered by networks of hexagons of different sizes. An example of the three smallest market area sizes in the Lösch system is given in Figure 6.19. Since it is possible to obtain these only by changing their orientation (see Fig. 6.18), it should be clear that the different order goods can be supplied from different sets of centers, depending on the way the hexagonal network of a given size is laid down.

To overcome this problem, Lösch introduced a further requirement: the amount of agglomeration of activities at central places in the system must be the maximum possible. To satisfy this requirement, one central village in the basic hexagonal network is arbitrarily selected as a starting point. For convenience let us call this A. The increasingly larger sized hexagonal networks are superimposed over the basic pattern, so that one of the centers in each of these larger networks coincides with A. Then the different hexagonal networks are rotated (with their centers fixed at A) until there is maximum coincidence of all other centers in the pattern. The particular rotation about place A needed to give this maximum degree of agglomeration is illustrated in Figure 6.20 for the 10 smallest sized hexagonal networks.

The rotation of the hexagonal trade area networks gives rise to a central-place system with interesting characteristics. Since every activity is provided from A, this can be thought of as the metropolis in the system. Radiating from the metropolis will be six $60°$ sectors, as shown in Figure 6.21A. The pattern of central places within each of the six sectors will be the same. The details of the pattern for one of the sectors are shown in Figure 6.21B. In the diagram, the numbers refer to the different order of goods provided from each place; the lowest order good is numbered 1, and the market area for this corresponds to the basic hexagons used as the starting point in building up the pattern. Number 2 refers to the next highest order good, which is associated with the trade areas of the $k=3$ type, and so on up the scale. The different order goods and their corresponding market area sizes are shown in Table 6.6. Using the diagram and the table, we have the following information about the different centers:

1. The total number of goods provided
2. The types of goods provided
3. The number and size of trade areas served

This can be illustrated by taking the places along the transect from A to B in Figure 6.21B as an example. By definition, every place provides good 1 and is consequently the center of a trade area corresponding to the basic size of a hexagon in the system (see Fig. 6.19). Above this level there is considerable variation between places in the number and kinds of goods provided by them. For example, the closest place to A provides only good 1 and serves only a basic-sized trade area. The place next to it provides goods 1 and 3 and is therefore at the center of a basic-sized trade area and one of $k=4$; the place next

---

Table 6.6.   ORDERS OF GOODS AND CORRESPONDING TRADE AREA SIZES IN THE LÖSCHIAN ECONOMIC LANDSCAPE

Order of good	1	2	3	4	5	6	7	8	9	10	...n
Size of trade area needed $K =$	basic	3	4	7	9	12	13	16	19	21	...m

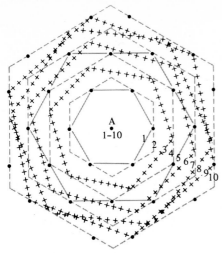

Fig. 6.20. The exact orientation of hexagonal trade areas necessary for the maximum agglomeration of central functions at central places.

to this provides goods 1, 2, and 5 and is consequently at the center of a basic-sized trade area, one of $k=3$ and one of $k=9$; and so on outward from A.

On the basis of the numbers of goods provided from each place, another interesting feature of the Löschian landscape is shown in Figure 6.21B. Each sector can clearly be divided into two parts; one in which centers are relatively specialized in the provision of goods and one that is devoid of well-developed central places. The result is an economic landscape centered on a multifunctional metropolis and comprising six 30° sectors with many well-developed central places (city-rich sectors) and six 30° sectors with few such places (city-poor sectors), as shown in Figure 6.21C.

Christaller and Lösch Compared

It is clear that although Christaller and Lösch start out with similar initial assumptions concerning the triangular pattern of settlement distribution and hexagonal-shaped market areas, their subsequent reasoning results in two completely different central-place patterns. The basic reason for this is that Christaller starts with the location of the highest threshold good and proceeds downward from this, whereas Lösch begins with the most ubiquitous, lowest threshold good and subsequently builds upward. On the basis of the resulting different patterns, it has been suggested that Christaller's model is really relevant only for the geography of tertiary activity, whereas the more flexible Loschian model is also relevant for the geography of secondary, market-oriented manufacturing activity.

The most important difference between the two systems is, however, in the type of hierarchy each postulates. In Christaller's model, all places at the same level provide not only the same number of central functions, but also the same kind of functions. Thus a very rigid kind of hierarchical system is proposed. The Löschian hierarchy is much more variable: centers at the same level provide the same number of central functions, but do *not* necessarily provide the same kinds of functions. Thus the order of goods is not strictly related to the level of places from which they are provided, and hence lower order goods may be absent and higher order goods present at smaller centers. Although this more flexible structure is not quite so appealing conceptually as Christaller's hierarchy, it does correspond more to the real-world structure of service centers, particularly to the hierarchy of shopping centers found within urban areas, which is discussed in Chapter 12.

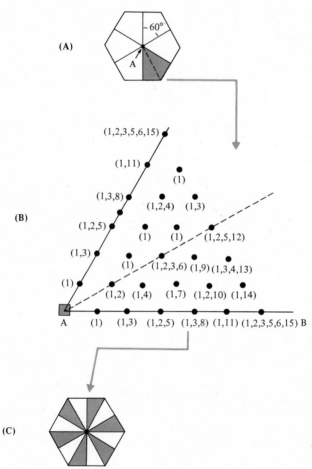

Fig. 6.21. Details of the Löschian economic landscape: (A) six sectors around the metropolis; (B) details of the location, size, and functional structure of places in one of the sectors; (C) "city rich" and "city poor" sectors.

7
CITY TYPES AND FUNCTIONS

Implicit in the discussion so far has been the notion that cities differ in their economic makeup and social characteristics, and in the roles they play in the city system. These differences can in part be traced back to regional variations in the local resources on which growth was based during the early development of the urban pattern, and in part to subsequent shifts in the competitive advantage of regions brought about by continually changing locational forces. Recognition of different types of cities necessitates their classification, and it is to this traditional and important aspect of urban geography that we turn now. We shall look at some of the ways in which cities have been classified by urban geographers, paying particular attention to what is called *functional town classification* and the identification of the basic dimensions of the city system.

THE PURPOSES OF CLASSIFICATION

In the introductory chapter we noted that, as part of the descriptive stage in study, classification is a basic procedure used to organize facts. Without classification of some sort it would be impossible to give names to things or to transmit information about them. But there is very little to be gained from the organization of facts for its own sake;

there must be a purpose. Hence classification is a means to an end—a means of organizing facts within the context of a specific problem.

The purpose of classifying cities is twofold. On the one hand it is undertaken in order to search reality for hypotheses. In this context the recognition of different types of cities on the basis of, for example, their functional specialization may enable the identification of spatial regularities in the distribution and structure of urban functions and the formulation of hypotheses about the resulting patterns. On the other hand, classification is undertaken to structure reality to test specific hypotheses that have already been formulated. For example, to test the hypothesis that cities with diversified economies grow at a faster rate than those with more specialized economies, cities must first be classified on the basis of their economic structures so that diversified and specialized types can be identified.

However, in reviewing the literature on functional town classification, we notice that the specific objectives of almost all schemes are difficult to discern and that "too often it appears that a major purpose of [such] studies (if not *the* major purpose) has been the development and presentation of a different classificatory methodology as an end in itself" (Smith, 1965a, pp. 539–540). Most attempts at classifying cities have, then, more often than not proved to be ends in themselves rather than points of departure for further analysis of the structure of city systems.

GENERAL CITY TYPES

The simplest way of classifying cities is to identify the distinctive role they play in the city system. These schemes are qualitative in nature and are often highly intuitive. Of the many classifications of this sort, a good example is that undertaken by Aurousseau (1921). From general observation he identified six types of cities based on the dominant functions they perform: administration, defense, culture, production, communications, and recreation. Although it was noted that cities may perform a combination of these general functions, it was common to find that one of them dominated to indicate the major role a city plays in the organization of space.

A similar type of general classification was that proposed by Harris and Ullman (1945), who recognized three general types of cities: (1) *central places* performing a wide range of services for local hinterlands; (2) *transportation cities* performing break-of-bulk and allied activities for larger regions; and (3) *specialized-function cities* dominated by one activity, such as mining, manufacturing, or recreation, and serving wider national, even international markets. They too point out that most cities represent a combination of all three factors, although the relative importance of each one often varies from city to city.

The significance of this very general threefold division is the way it relates to the location of cities. This is shown in idealized form in Figure 7.1. The overall pattern within the city system can be thought of as being made up of three layers superimposed on top of each other (Fig. 7.1A). The hierarchy of central places forms the basic layer. Ideally these tend to be evenly spaced throughout the productive territory, as shown in Figure 7.1B, although, as we have seen, the regularity of the pattern is distorted by the unevenness of the distribution of population. Since cities are dependent on transportation, the symmetry of the central-place arrangement is further modified by the pattern of routes. In turn, these give rise to the second layer of cities in the system. The development of cities at focal points or breaks of transportation creates a linear element along rail lines, rivers, and coasts (Fig. 7.1C). The specialized-function cities form the third layer. These occur singly or in clusters in conjunction with localized resources, such as coalfields, mineral deposits, water-power sites, and so on, to result in a clustered element in the pattern as shown in Figure 7.1D. In discussing the evolution of the city system in North America we noted how this general model of the urban pattern based on the three main types of cities developed in reality.

FUNCTIONAL SPECIALIZATION

When Pittsburgh is recognized as a "steel town" or Detroit as the "automobile capital of the world," explicit recognition is given to the existence of city types on the basis of their functional — and usually economic — specialization. As the size of cities increases, however, their economic structure becomes increasingly more complex and the urban economy is usually based on a broader mix of activities, as was noted in Chapter 4. Consequently they become more difficult to differentiate on the basis of their dominant economic activities. This multifunctional character of cities notwithstanding, it is common to find the urban economy dominated by one or more major economic activities. Classifications of this type attempt, therefore, to identify these dominant activities and to group together cities that are most similar to each other in terms of their functional specialization.

A common assumption in functional town classification is that the city's labor force is the best single indicator of the structure of the urban economy. Groups of cities

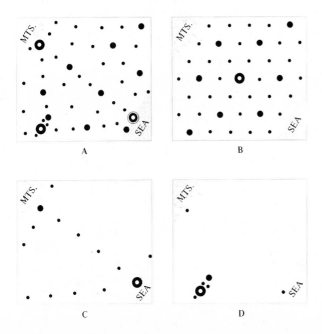

Fig. 7.1. Layers in the settlement pattern of a region. Ideally the overall pattern (A) can be thought of as comprising evenly spaced central places (B), transport centers (C), and specialized-function settlements such as mining towns and resorts (D). (*Source*: Harris and Ullman, 1945, Figs. 1–4.)

with similar functional specialization have therefore been most frequently identified from the analysis of employment profiles. Specialization in a given activity is said to exist when employment in it exceeds some critical level. For it is only when an abnormally large proportion of the city's labor force is employed in a particular activity that it becomes a distinguishing feature in functionally differentiating that city from others in the system.

The major difficulty of this approach is deciding at what point an economic activity becomes important enough in the city's economy for it to be considered as one of its specializations. The fundamental problem is, then, to define the critical level of employment necessary for specialization in a given activity to exist. There is no single or even best solution to this problem, and in the literature on the functional classification of cities there is little agreement on either the magnitudes of these thresholds or the ways by which they should be chosen. In the last resort, definitions of specialization depend very much on the methods used in classification and the decisions of the researcher. To illustrate this, some examples of functional town classification in America and Canada are reviewed.

The Harris Classification

In an early classification of 605 American cities, Harris (1943) identified 10 functional types (see Table 7.1) from an analysis of their employment profiles supplemented with data on specific occupations. In assigning cities to one of the 10 classes, the critical levels of employment needed for specialization were arbitrarily identified from an intuitive analysis of the employment profiles of what Harris believed to be well-defined functional types. A complete list of the criteria established to define specialization for each of the 10 functional types is given in Table 7.1, and the results of the classification are presented in Table 7.2 (see also Fig. 7.3). As might be expected, the most important types are manufacturing, diversified, and retail, which together accounted for over 80 percent of the cities. Specialization in manufacturing was the most important single type, accounting for 43.5 percent of the cities included in the study. This was true for both the larger metropolitan districts (with more than 50,000 inhabitants) and the smaller cities (10,000 to 50,000 inhabitants).

Harris' classification has been widely used as the basis for further studies in urban geography, in spite of its shortcomings. Two weaknesses in particular should be stressed. First is the essentially intuitive way in which Harris defined specialization; the validity of the criteria listed in Table 7.1 is open to question, and it has been said that Harris failed to identify the well-recognized types on which these were based (Mayer, 1954). Second, cities were permitted to specialize in only one type of activity. As a result, the labels attached to many urban settlements often hid more about their functional specialization than they revealed. For example, although New York City and Chicago are the nation's two principal wholesale cities and both are important manufacturing, transportation, and educational centers, specialization in these functions is not revealed in the classification. Both are considered simply as diversified cities. For these and many other large urban centers, the idea of attaching a single descriptive label is highly dubious.

Nelson's Service Classification

Nelson (1955) attempted to overcome these shortcomings by using a more objective, statistical definition of specialization to classify 897 cities in the United States. As

Table 7.1.   CRITERIA USED BY HARRIS TO IDENTIFY ECONOMIC SPECIALIZATION

Manufacturing Cities, M' Subtype.
Employment data: manufacturing employment equals at least 74% of total employment in manufacturing, retailing, and wholesaling.
Occupation data: manufacturing and mechanical industries contain at least 45% of gainful workers.
Note: A few cities with industries in suburbs were placed in this class if the percentage for the occupation data reached 50%.

Manufacturing Cities, M Subtype.
Employment data: manufacturing employment equals at least 60% of total employment in manufacturing, retailing, and wholesaling.
Occupation data: manufacturing and mechanical industries usually contain between 30% and 45% of gainful workers.

Wholesale Cities (W).
Employment data: employment in wholesaling is at least 20% of the total employment in manufacturing, wholesaling, and retailing and at least 45% as much as in retailing alone.

Transportation Cities (T).
Occupation data: transportation and communication contain at least 11% of the gainful workers, and workers in transportation and communication equal at least one-third the number in the manufacturing and mechanical industries, and at least two-thirds the number in trade.
Note: This definition applies only to cities of more than 25,000 for which such figures are available.

Resort-Retirement Cities (X).
No satisfactory statistical criterion was found. Cities with a low percentage of the population employed were checked in the literature for this function.

Retail Cities (R).
Employment data: employment in retailing equals at least 50% of the total employment in manufacturing, wholesaling, and retailing and at least 2.2 times that in wholesaling alone.

Diversified Cities (D).
Employment data: employment in manufacturing, wholesaling, and retailing is less than 60%, 20%, and 50% respectively of the total employment in these activities; and no other criteria apply.
Occupation data: with few exceptions, manufacturing and mechanical industries contain between 25% and 35% of the gainful workers.

Mining Cities (S).
Occupation data: extraction of minerals accounts for more than 15% of the gainful workers.
Note: This definition applies only to cities of more than 25,000 for which such figures are available. For cities between 10,000 and 25,000 a comparison was made of mining employment available by counties only, with employment in cities within such mining counties. Published sources were consulted to differentiate actual mining towns from commercial and industrial centers in mining areas.

University Cities (E).
Enrollment in schools of collegiate rank (universities, technical schools, liberal-arts colleges, and teachers' colleges) equals at least 25% of the population of the city in 1940.
Note: Enrollment figures were obtained from *School and Society,* 52 (1940): 601–619.

Political Cities (P).
Cities that were state capitals, plus Washington, D.C.
Note: The political function is clearly dominant in only 16 of these; in the rest it is overshadowed by trade and industry.

SOURCE: Harris (1943), Table 1.

a result, cities could be more realistically classified according to their specialization in more than one function, and it was possible to identify the degree to which cities specialized in the various activities.

The classification was based on employment figures for nine main activity types expressed as a percentage of the city's total labor force. Frequency distributions based

Table 7.2. SUMMARY OF THE RESULTS OF THE HARRIS CLASSIFICATION

Activity Type	Totals	Metropolitan Districts		Other Cities	
		No.	%	No.	%
(M') Manufacturing	118	25	17.8	93	20.0
(M) Manufacturing	140	38	27.1	102	22.0
(D) Diversified	130	33	23.6	97	21.0
(R) Retail	104	12	8.6	92	20.0
(T) Transportation	32	14	10.0	18	4.0
(W) Wholesale	27	11	7.9	16	3.0
(X) Resort-retirement	22	5	3.6	17	3.6
(E) Educational	17	–	–	17	3.6
(S) Mining	14	1	0.7	13	2.8
(P) Political	1	1	0.7	–	–
Totals	605	140	100.0	465	100.0

Source: Harris (1943) mimeographed list of results.

on all cities for each of these activities are shown in Figure 7.2. The basic characteristics of these distributions can be summarized by two simple descriptive statistics: (1) the arithmetic mean, a measure of the central tendency or average of the distribution, and (2) the standard deviation, an absolute measure of the variation about the mean. Specialization was said to exist if the proportion of a city's labor force in a given activity exceeded the average for all cities by at least one standard deviation. These critical values are shown on the graphs in Figure 7.2 by the Greek letter σ. Thus, for example, a city must have at least 43.1 percent of its labor force employed in manufacturing for this activity to be one of its specializations. Cities that did not on this basis qualify for specialization in any of the nine activities were called diversified.

Standard deviations were also used as the basis for indicating the degree to which a particular city specialized in a given activity. Three classes were recognized corresponding to one, two, and three standard deviations above the mean value respectively (see Fig. 5.1B). Thus, for example, Shenandoah, Pa., with 41 percent of its total work force engaged in mining, exceeds the value of the mean for this activity by more than three standard deviations, indicating its extreme degree of specialization in this activity, and consequently it is classified as a class 3 mining city.

The aggregate results of the classification presented in Table 7.3A show that although three-quarters of the cities specialized in only one activity, specialization in two or even three activities is not uncommon. El Centro, Calif., is really multifunctional, specializing in five activities: retail trade (class 3), wholesale trade (class 3), personal services, public administration, and finance (all class 1). Table 7.3B shows the total number of cities recorded by activity and degree of specialization. Nearly a third of the 897 cities do not specialize in anything in particular and are best represented as diversified cities. Manufacturing appears most often as the activity in which cities specialize, followed by retailing, finance, and wholesaling.

There also are marked variations in the degree of specialization in the given activities. Apart from mining, most cities have only a low degree of specialization in a given activity. The textile area of Brandon-Johnson, N.C., is the only city with a large enough proportion in manufacturing to warrant classification as a class 3 manufacturing city. Conversely, the extreme specialization typical of mining communities is well brought

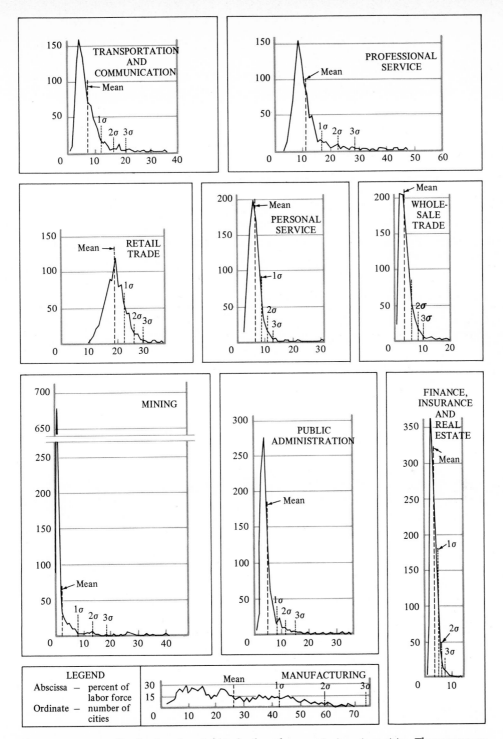

Fig. 7.2. Frequency distributions for nine kinds of employment in American cities. The percentage of a city's labor force is given on the *X* axis, and the number of cities, or frequency, is plotted on the *Y* axis. (*Source*: Nelson, 1955, Fig. 1.)

Table 7.3 SUMMARY OF THE RESULTS OF NELSON'S CLASSIFICATION

(A) Number of Functions in Which Cities Specialized

Number of Activity Groups

	1	2	3	4	5	Totals
No. of cities	679	149	62	6	1	897
Percentage of total (897)	75.7	16.6	6.9	0.7	0.1	100.0

(B) Number of Cities by Activity Type and Degree of Specialization

			Degree of Specialization				
	Totals		1 S.D.		2 S.D.		3 S.D.
Activity	No.	%[a]	No.	%	No.	%	No.	%
Manufacturing	183	20.4	153	83.6	29	15.8	1	0.6
Retail trade	137	15.3	110	80.3	21	15.3	6	4.4
Finance, etc.	123	13.7	93	75.7	13	10.6	17	13.7
Wholesale trade	107	11.9	73	68.2	21	19.6	13	12.2
Transportation	96	10.7	51	53.1	22	22.9	23	24.0
Personal services	92	10.3	57	61.9	24	26.1	11	12.0
Public administration	85	9.5	45	52.9	19	22.3	21	24.8
Professional services	81	9.0	42	51.8	16	19.7	23	28.5
Mining	46	5.1	12	25.1	12	26.1	22	47.8
Diversified	246	27.4	—[b]	—	—	—	—	—

[a] States included in each major census region are shown in Figure 2.1
[b] Not applicable.
Source: U.S. Bureau of the Census. *U.S. Census of Population: 1970. Number of Inhabitants, United States Summary*, Tables 7 and 20 (U.S. Government Printing Office, Washington, D.C., 1971).

---

out by the fact that just under one-half of cities specializing in this activity are in class 3. Levels of such extreme specialization as this are not noted for the other types, although it is significant that about a quarter of the cities specializing in professional services, transportation, and public administration are characterized by this high degree of specialization.

Despite what appears to be a more objective method in city classification, we cannot say that the results presented by Nelson are better or worse than those of Harris. Both schemes must be evaluated independently on the basis of whether they adequately do the job for which they were intended. Since the concept of specialization is a relative one, any definition of it must be considered arbitrary. In this context, Nelson's attempt to reduce the subjective element is worthy of praise, even though the subjective element in classification cannot be altogether removed (Johnston, 1968). Notwithstanding, the use of the standard deviation to identify specialization has been criticized on the grounds that the frequency distributions shown in Figure 7.2 are not normal and hence the arithmetic mean and standard deviation have little meaning. This would, however, not appear to be a condemning criticism because Nelson's use of these statistics was purely descriptive. The technical problems of normality become problems only in the context of statistical inference.

Maxwell's Classification

In both Harris' and Nelson's classifications, figures for total employment were used to identify a city's functional specialization. In Chapter 4, however, we noted that the total employment of a city can be broken down into two parts: its nonbasic and basic components. Since it is a city's basic employment—the workers producing goods and services for export—that is directly related to growth and its general well-being, it perhaps makes better sense to identify functional specialization from an analysis of a city's basic rather than its total employment. Harris did in fact recognize this implicitly by assigning higher percentages to some functions than to others in defining the thresholds for specialization (see Table 7.1). In this way he attempted to "rule out local service employment in activities that exist merely to serve workers employed in the primary (i.e., basic) activities" (Harris, 1943, p. 87). Explicit recognition of this problem is found, however, in Alexandersson's (1956) classification of American cities and in Maxwell's (1965) classification of 80 cities in Canada.

To identify basic employment, Maxwell used the minimum requirements method developed by Ullman and Dacey (1962) discussed in Chapter 4. By the use of graphs similar to those shown in Figure 4.2, the minimum requirements in each of 13 major activities were calculated for each city and then summed to give the total nonbasic employment. Subtraction of this sum from the city's total employment then enabled the basic component to be recognized. One important advantage in using this kind of approach is that changes in nonbasic, and hence basic, employment with city size are taken into account. The practice of using a single threshold in defining specialization for all cities—as, for example, in Nelson's classification—has been criticized on the grounds that one presupposes that approximately the same proportion of the labor force is engaged in a given activity in cities regardless of their size (Hadden and Borgatta, 1965).

The functional structure of cities was described by three measures: a city's dominant function, its distinctive functions, and an index of overall specialization. The *dominant* function was simply defined as the activity having the largest share of a city's basic employment. Thus each city was initially characterized by a single function in the same way that cities in Harris' classification were allowed to specialize in only one activity. As in Harris' classification, manufacturing was the most important function, dominating the employment structure of 61 of the 80 cities in Canada (see Table 7.4). Only five other functions were dominant in at least one city: mining and extraction (six cities), transportation (five cities), government service (five cities), retail trade (two cities), and community services (one city).

Describing the functional structure of cities by a single label in this way, and especially in view of the fact that manufacturing was overwhelmingly important as a dominant function, tends, as we have seen, to cover up many of the distinct and often unique features of their functional structure. For although they may not be dominant, many activities are nevertheless important enough to become distinctive features of a city's economic structure. To identify the *distinctive* functions in each city, Maxwell used the same approach as Nelson; excess employment was measured in terms of standard deviation units above the mean employment for all cities in a given activity. For

Table 7.4. DOMINANT FUNCTIONS AND SPECIALIZATION INDEXES OF CANADIAN CITIES

City			City		
Periphery : Heartland	Specialization Index	Dominant Function	Periphery : Heartland	Specialization Index	Dominant Function
Charlottetown	1.16	Retailing	St. Hyacinthe	3.96	Manufacturing
Rimouski	1.36	Community service	Victoria	4.01	Govt. service
Prince Albert	1.40	Manufacturing	Woodstock	4.14	Manufacturing
Brandon	1.41	Transportation	Cornwall	4.16	Manufacturing
Penticton	1.44	Transportation	Guelph	4.22	Manufacturing
Saskatoon	1.51	Manufacturing	Jonquière	4.40	Manufacturing
Moncton	1.55	Transportation	Shawinigan	4.53	Manufacturing
Moose Jaw	1.56	Transportation	St. Catharines	4.56	Manufacturing
Saint John	1.67	Manufacturing	Sault Ste. Marie	4.70	Manufacturing
Chicoutimi	1.72	Manufacturing	Sydney	5.21	Manufacturing
St. John's	1.75	Manufacturing	Kitchener-Waterloo	5.36	Manufacturing
Truro	1.77	Manufacturing	Windsor	5.41	Manufacturing
Fredericton	1.86	Govt. service	Peterborough	5.42	Manufacturing
Barrie	1.87	Manufacturing	Halifax	5.46	Govt. service
Medicine Hat	1.97	Manufacturing	St. Jean	5.55	Manufacturing
Winnipeg	2.00	Manufacturing	St. Jérôme	5.56	Manufacturing
Belleville	2.04	Manufacturing	Victoriaville	5.59	Manufacturing
Thunder Bay	2.08	Manufacturing	Brantford	5.67	Manufacturing
Regina	2.09	Govt. service	Hamilton	5.88	Manufacturing
Quebec	2.11	Manufacturing	Drummondville	6.24	Manufacturing
St. Thomas	2.14	Manufacturing	Granby	6.28	Manufacturing
Kingston	2.17	Manufacturing	Grand'Mère	6.34	Manufacturing
London	2.17	Manufacturing	Valleyfield	6.39	Manufacturing
Chatham	2.26	Manufacturing	Welland	6.54	Manufacturing
North Bay	2.35	Transportation	Trail	6.86	Manufacturing
Edmunston	2.35	Manufacturing	Galt	7.14	Manufacturing
Vancouver	2.40	Manufacturing	Oshawa	7.50	Manufacturing
Brockville	2.71	Manufacturing	Magog	7.56	Manufacturing
Owen Sound	2.73	Manufacturing	Ottawa	7.84	Govt. service
Orilla	2.74	Manufacturing	Arvida	8.99	Manufacturing

City

Periphery : Heartland	Specialization Index	Dominant Function
Joliette	2.88	Manufacturing
Pembroke	3.41	Manufacturing
Toronto	3.51	Manufacturing
Trois Rivières	3.52	Manufacturing
Sherbrooke	3.61	Manufacturing
Niagara Falls	3.62	Manufacturing
Trenton	3.63	Manufacturing
Stratford	3.87	Manufacturing
Sarnia	3.90	Manufacturing
Montreal	3.92	Manufacturing

City

Periphery : Heartland	Specialization Index	Dominant Function
Sorel	10.93	Manufacturing
Lethbridge	11.69	Retailing
Edmonton	14.96	Manufacturing
Calgary	17.21	Manufacturing
Rouyn	612.92	Extraction
Sudbury	918.63	Extraction
Thetford Mines	1139.76	Extraction
Timmins	1400.66	Extraction
Glace Bay	1697.89	Extraction
New Waterford	1952.46	Extraction

SOURCE: Maxwell (1965), Table V.

example, whereas manufacturing dominates the functional structure of Winnipeg, Manitoba, wholesale trade, finance, transportation, and recreation are its distinctive functions. As a general rule, the distinctive functions of Canadian cities, particularly those dominated by manufacturing, relate to their importance as central places and transportation centers.

Indexes of Specialization

Although urban functional specialization has been most commonly described in terms of a single dominant function (i.e., Harris) or a number of distinctive activities (i.e., Nelson), a number of attempts have been made to measure overall specialization using a single index (Rodgers, 1957; Berry, 1972). In this approach, a city's actual employment profile is compared with an idealized one thought to represent a balanced employment structure. The level of specialization in a given city is then measured in terms of the deviation of its actual employment profile from the model. In his study, Maxwell employed an index developed by Ullman and Dacey (1962) which uses the distribution of the nonbasic employment among the various functions in a city as the model of balanced structure. If the city's actual employment is distributed among activities in the same proportion as the nonbasic employment, a situation of least specialization is said to exist. Thus the greater the deviation from the nonbasic employment profile, the more specialized the city becomes.

The index of specialization (S) is calculated as follows:

$$S = \Sigma_i \left[\frac{(P_i - M_i)^2}{M_i} \right] \div \frac{(\Sigma_i P_i - \Sigma_i M_i)^2}{\Sigma_i M_i}$$

where P_i is the percentage of a city's total labor force employed in activity i, and M_i is the minimum requirement (percent nonbasic employment) in that activity. Large deviations from the minimum requirement are accentuated in the numerator, and the denominator reconciles the index to city size. A value of 1.0 indicates a situation of least specialization. The indexes of specialization calculated in this way for the 80 Canadian cities are shown in Table 7.4.

City Types in Canada

From the foregoing analysis, Maxwell loosely identified five major types of cities in Canada on the basis of the index of specialization, urban population size, and the importance of basic employment in wholesale trade and manufacturing (Fig. 7.3). The five types identified were:

1. *Specialized manufacturing,* including 31 cities with high specialization indexes and large proportions of their basic employment in manufacturing but with few workers in wholesaling.

2. *Regional capitals* (type I), in which manufacturing is relatively unimportant; the 17 cities included in this group are dominated by activities reflecting their role as central places.

3. *Special cities* — eight cities that are highly specialized but which have a small proportion of their basic employment in both wholesaling and manufacturing.

4. The four major *metropolitan centers* of Winnipeg, Vancouver, Toronto, and Montreal.

5. *Regional capitals* (type II), in which manufacturing is relatively important.

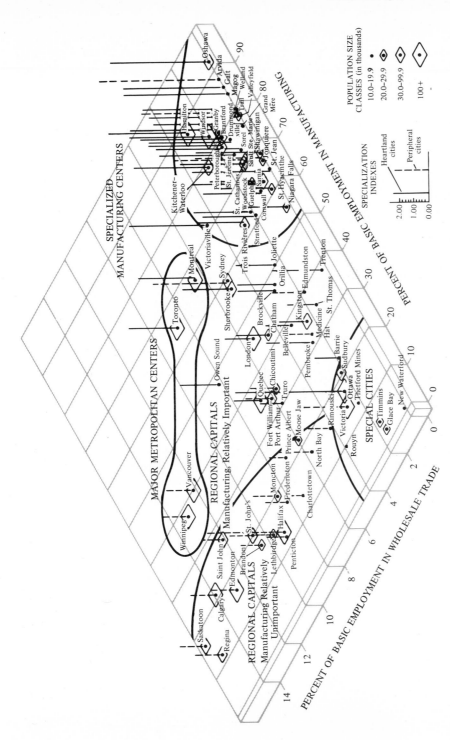

Fig. 7.3. City types in Canada. Specialization indexes are not shown for extraction centers because of their extremely high values. (*Source:* Maxwell, 1965, Fig. 5.)

The 20 cities in this group are heterogeneous in functional characteristics and can be thought of as transitional on the basis of the three indexes between city types 1, 2, and 3 above.

Concluding Remarks

The three approaches to functional town classification briefly reviewed here are representative of the alternative methods that have been used to identify the functional specialization of cities. Preferences for one method over another are often made on the basis of whether cities are assigned to a single class or to many. The argument for classification by a single, dominant function largely rests on the fact that the results are easier to use, and especially to map. Simplicity, however, would seem to be an attribute of declining importance in current geographic studies; and preferences based on this kind of argument are not particularly meaningful in the context of classification. It is undoubtedly more realistic to recognize that some cities specialize in several activities just as it is to recognize that the economy of others may be dominated by a single activity. Because of this, it would appear that classifications like Nelson's, which recognize multiple specialization, or the use of a single index of overall specialization, are potentially more useful and rewarding than those that do not.

There are, of course, many other reasons for preferring one classification over another. However, the final choice among alternatives should be based primarily on the "demonstrated greater relevance or predictive power of one classification in comparison to its alternatives, in the context of a well defined problem" (Duncan et al., 1960, p. 35). Despite the potential usefulness of the findings, it is unfortunate that both Harris' and Nelson's classifications were apparently undertaken more to illustrate method than to search or structure reality in a problem framework.

SPATIAL PATTERNS

The results of these classifications, when mapped, provide some useful information about patterns of functional specialization within the city system. The distribution of functional types identified by Harris (1943) are presented in Figure 7.4; maps of Nelson's (1955) manufacturing and mining cities are shown in Figures 5.1B and 5.3B. The distribution of the various city types emphasizes in a general way the differences between the heartland and hinterlands. Manufacturing cities, as noted in Chapter 5, are notably concentrated in the American manufacturing belt—in the heartland, with an extension southward in the Great Valley and along the Piedmont Plateau. Outside these areas, cities specializing in manufacturing are notably absent except in the Pacific Northwest. The distribution of retailing cities is quite different. These are generally located west of the manufacturing belt, and are particularly concentrated in a broad belt running north-south through the central part of the country, reflecting their role as central places in agricultural regions. Diversified cities, in which both trade and manufacturing are well developed, are well distributed throughout the eastern part of the United States, and occupy a pattern of spatial transition between the concentration of manufacturing cities and the band of retailing cities to the west of it.

Little comment is needed on the remaining patterns. Wholesaling cities are found mainly in the South and in the western parts of the country, and include smaller cities associated with the marketing of agricultural produce as well as larger hinterland regional centers such as San Francisco, Seattle, and Dallas. Transportation centers

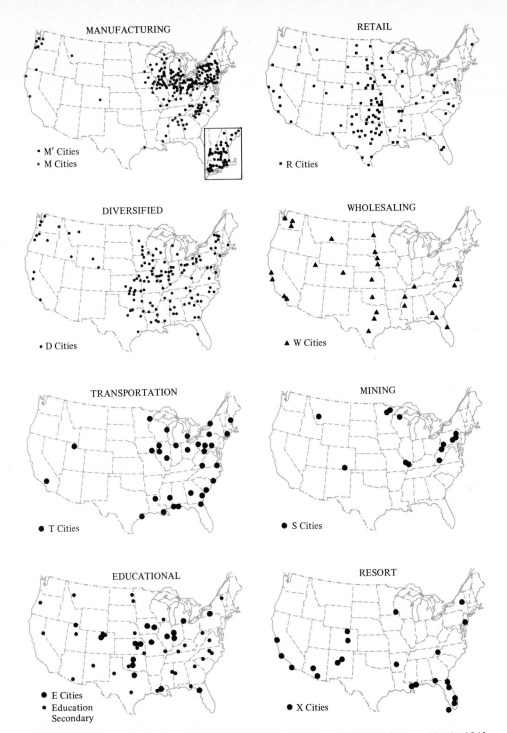

Fig. 7.4. Distribution of functional types of cities in the Harris classification. (*Source*: Harris, 1943, Figs. 2–9.)

include coastal and inland ports and railroad centers, many of which are focal points of movement within the heartland. The educational cities are mostly small places dominated by large state universities, particularly in the Midwestern states; and the pattern of resort and retirement cities in Florida, southern California, and the desert Southwest reflects the more recent influence of amenity factors on location and urban growth at the periphery.

Differences in the functional structure and specialization of cities in the heartland-hinterlands framework are more vividly revealed from Maxwell's study of Canadian cities. Generally speaking, specialization indexes increase with the importance of manufacturing in the economic base of cities (Fig. 7.4), and heartland cities are clearly more specialized than those in the hinterlands. All but four of the 31 specialized manufacturing cities and all but two of the 45 cities having manufacturing as the dominant function are located in the heartland. In contrast, cities in the hinterlands—except the mining centers and resource-oriented manufacturing cities—are generally less specialized and manufacturing is less important in them. Wholesaling, retail trade, and transportation are the dominant and distinctive activities in the economic base of hinterland cities.

Considerable regularity exists, therefore, in the pattern of urban functional specialization within the city system. In part this stems from peculiarities in the evolution of the urban patterns discussed in Chapter 2; in part from irregularities in the distribution of resources, population, and markets. Differences between the heartlands and hinterlands in North America have been reinforced by the continuation of a mineral-based economy well into the twentieth century and its translation into well-defined spatial relationships between the cores and peripheries in both countries.

MULTIVARIATE CLASSIFICATION

If the object of classifying cities is to group together those that have the greatest similarity in functional structure rather than simply to indicate a dominant function, then different methods must be used than those employed by Harris, Nelson, or Maxwell. For when deviations from an average are used as the basis for identifying specialization, important groupings are frequently hidden.

This problem can be illustrated with reference to the way Harris identified cities specializing in manufacturing, which is shown graphically in Figure 7.5. Using the critical values for employment and occupation data given in Table 7.1, all cities falling in the upper right-hand quadrant on the graph will specialize in manufacturing. However, close inspection of Figure 7.5 suggests that five distinct clusters can be identified on the graph. Each cluster contains cities that are most similar to each other in terms of the two stated criteria. Although groups of cities with similar functional structure can be readily identified when only two differentiating characteristics are used, as in Figure 7.5, the problem becomes quite complex when similarities in functional structure are identified on the basis of many urban characteristics taken together. When this is the case, more sophisticated multivariate methods of taxonomy have to be employed.

Basic Procedures

The procedures most commonly followed in the more complex kinds of classification are outlined in Figure 7.6. To start with, the data are arranged in the form of an $n \times m$ data matrix. In this there are m columns, each one of which corresponds to a differ-

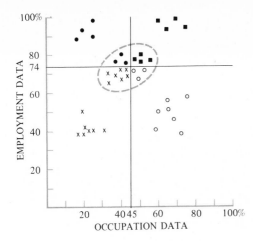

Fig. 7.5. Clusters of cities with similar kinds of functional specialization.

ent characteristic of the cities, while each of the n rows represents a different city. It was, of course, a data matrix similar to this that Nelson used as a starting point for his classification. That one had nine columns, one for each of the different activities, and 987 rows corresponding to the cities. Thus the percentage breakdown of a city's labor force was recorded along a row, as shown for Detroit (row 2) and New York City (row 3) in Figure 7.6. Variation among the cities in the proportions employed in the various activities is indicated by the column figures, and it was this information that Nelson was primarily interested in—first for the construction of the frequency distributions (Fig. 7.2), and then for calculating the arithmetic means and standard deviations.

Nelson's analysis of the matrix proceeded column by column. An alternative way of analyzing the matrix is to proceed with pairs of columns, calculating the correlation between them, and generating in this way a new set of data—a matrix of correlation coefficients. Multivariate classifications really start then with a correlation matrix. The way in which the analysis then proceeds depends largely on whether this matrix is generated from the column data or the row data (see Abler, Adams, and Gould, 1971, chap. 6).

In correlating the rows with each other, the interest is at the outset in the cities themselves rather than in their characteristics. The resulting correlation coefficients can be interpreted as measures of functional similarity; the larger the correlation, the higher the degree of similarity between a pair of cities. Since each city is correlated with itself and every other city, the result is an $n \times n$ correlation matrix. Thus for each city there are n coefficients, and these can be used as the coordinates to locate the city in an n-dimensional classification space. On the basis of the correlation coefficients, all of the cities can be plotted in an n space to result in a situation not unlike that shown in Figure 7.5, although of course since there are n instead of two dimensions, we cannot picture this graphically. Cities similar in functional structure can be identified by using an appropriate grouping technique. A good example of this approach in practice is Smith's (1965b) classification of cities in Australia.

Alternatively, the columns can be correlated with each other to yield an $m \times m$ correlation matrix in which the coefficients measure similarities in the way the characteristics vary among cities. A high correlation between any two characteristics (variables) indicates that they vary among the cities in a very similar way; conversely, a low coefficient indicates dissimilarity. Analysis of the matrix of correlation coefficients may reveal that many of the variables are not independent of each other, but that they are highly correlated and thus overlap in the story they tell about the cities. This suggests that running through the m characteristics there are a number of common threads that, if they can be identified, might be a useful basis on which to group and classify cities. Identification of these common threads—variously known as factors, components, or *dimensions*—is achieved by the use of multivariate techniques such as principal components or factor analysis. The number of factors identified will determine the dimensions of the classification space in which each city can be located by its factor scores. Application of a suitable grouping technique will then identify clusters of cities that are similar to each other with respect to these scores, and hence their character-

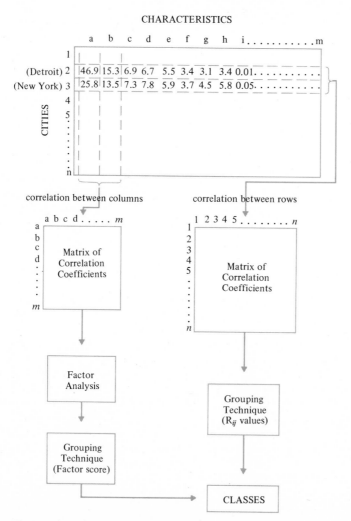

Fig. 7.6. Flow chart of procedures used in the multivariate classification of cities.

istics. Good examples of the uses of this approach are the classifications of British towns by Moser and Scott (1961); of American cities by Hadden and Borgatta (1965) and Berry (1972); and of Canadian cities by King (1966) and Ray and Murdie (1972).

BASIC DIMENSIONS OF CITY SYSTEMS

Classification of city types based on economic specialization identifies only one important source of variation within the city system. Cities also differ considerably from one another in their social and demographic conditions—in their social well-being (Smith, 1973). It also follows that variation should occur in the physical characteristics of the buildings in which the population is housed, which in turn also reflect the age of cities and their location in the time-space development of the system (Berry and Neils, 1970). When many different variables relating to the economic, social, demographic, and locational characteristics of cities are considered together, it is possible, by the use of the multivariate methods described above, to identify what are called the basic dimensions of variation in the city system.

Among the best-known of the early studies using this multivariate approach is that by Hadden and Borgatta (1965) of 644 American cities. In their study, restricted to places larger than 25,000, 65 variables were included, measuring demographic and employment characteristics, income, housing, education, economic activity, location, and age of city. The results of the factor analysis revealed that cities could be differentiated on 16 dimensions, the three most important being:

1. Socioeconomic status
2. Nonwhite population
3. Age composition

Factor scores on these and subsequent dimensions were then used to classify the cities. One of the interesting results of their analysis was the finding that the social conditions of cities were only weakly related to their economic specialization.

The main objective of Hadden and Borgatta's study was to determine the underlying dimensions of variation between cities, and in this way to contribute to the development of an empirical urban theory. As sociologists, however, they were not interested in the dimensions of geographical variation in the city system. In a subsequent map analysis of their results, Smith (1973) has presented some interesting insights into the way the most important dimension (socioeconomic status) varies spatially. This factor is all the more interesting because it can be interpreted as a kind of *deprivation index*, which indicates an important difference between cities in social conditions.

Cities with low indexes—the least deprived—were found to be concentrated in California, particularly around Los Angeles, and in the suburbs of the major cities in the Great Lakes region (e.g., around Chicago, Detroit, and Cleveland), with some scatter in the Plains States. The most deprived cities, on the other hand, are clustered almost without exception south of a line from Boston to El Paso, with the main concentration in the "Old South" and an extension northward in the older, poorer cities of the heartland, particularly in Pennsylvania and New Jersey. Urban deprivation thus shows a surprisingly high degree of regularity in variation across the nation, and although Smith did not attempt to explain this, it is interesting to note that the concentration of the worst cities in the South corresponds with the later levels of urbanization in that region (see Table 2.1).

Canadian and American Urban Dimensions

Comparing the results of studies undertaken in different countries is made difficult by the lack of a comparable data base and a standard definition of cities. However, two recent multivariate studies of cities in Canada (Ray and Murdie, 1972) and in the United States (Berry, 1972) are similar enough in their detail to enable general comparisons of the basic dimensions of the city systems in the two countries. The main types of variables included in the analyses and the dimensions of variation (the general factors) identified for the two systems are summarized in Table 7.5.

The American Pattern

Berry's factor analysis of cities in the United States indicated that nearly 80 percent of the variation between cities could be accounted for by 14 basic dimensions of differentiation (Table 7.5). Since these are uncorrelated with each other, one of the first things that is stressed is the lack of association between the socioeconomic characteristics of cities and their economic functions—a feature commented upon earlier by Hadden and Borgatta. Following Berry's presentation, it is convenient for purposes of discussion to distinguish between patterns of socioeconomic makeup on the one hand and those related to city functions on the other.

The most important dimension differentiating cities is their functional size (measured by, for example, numbers of people, employment levels, and size of labor force), which in turn reflects their position in the urban hierarchy, and indeed underlines the importance of the hierarchical component to the spatial organization of the city system. Moreover, there is a clear tendency for total manufacturing employment to vary with city size, emphasizing the importance of the market as a locational factor. The remaining socioeconomic dimensions generally reflect the trends in the evolution of the urban pattern noted in Chapter 2. Socioeconomic status (akin to the deprivation index in Smith's analysis, discussed above) points up the contrast between the rich suburbs around many of the larger metropolitan areas and the smaller towns in the isolated poverty regions (particularly in southwest Texas). The stage of families in the life cycle, which is very closely related to migration within metropolitan areas (see Chapter 11) and hence to differences between communities in their age structures, points up a major contrast between the young-family bedroom suburbs around the big cities and the concentration of the elderly in the retirement cities of the periphery. Cities in the manufacturing belt and in the South stand out on account of the high proportions of nonwhites in their population structure, the former reflecting the postwar migration from the southern regions. Differences in population growth point up the trend for deconcentration toward the periphery, with cities in California, the Southwest, and Florida scoring high on this factor, while the growth in employment confirms the importance of decentralization around the largest cities as a major process of contemporary change.

The second group of dimensions, those relating to the economic base of cities, single out many of the smaller cities that are still dependent on a single dominant activity, such as mining, military establishments, central-place functions, and colleges and universities. The spatial distribution of cities with these kinds of economic support corresponds in general to the maps shown in Figure 7.1, and suggests the nature of changes that have been taking place since Harris made his study 35 years ago. The principal change has perhaps been the intensification of the market in the location of manufacturing, which in turn is related to size of metropolitan area, position in the hierarchy, and regional concentration—with that in the heartland still relatively the most important. Increasingly the largest cities are becoming much more alike in economic structure, and the important differences in socioeconomic makeup are now very much intra-metropolitan. As was noted in the discussions of k values in Chapter 4, smaller cities are likely to be more specialized, and this is accounted for by the continued importance of traditional nonmetropolitan location factors, such as raw materials, and the concen-

Table 7.5.   BASIC DIMENSIONS OF THE CANADIAN AND AMERICAN URBAN SYSTEMS, 1960–1961

	Canada	United States
Number of cities included	113	1,762
Selection of cities	All cities over 10,000 in 1961	All cities over 10,000 in 1960
Number of variables	84	97
Types of variables:		
Economic	35	56
Housing	3	12
Demographic	11	17
Social	32	12
Locational	3	0
General factors: (in order of importance)	English-French contrasts	Functional size in hierarchy
	Prairie-type cities	Socioeconomic status
	Mining-service contrasts in economic base	Stage in family life cycle
	Postwar growth center	Nonwhite population
	British Columbia cities	Recent population growth
	Primary manufacturing cities	Economic base: college towns
	Ethnometropolitan centers	Recent employment growth
	Center-periphery contrasts	Economic base: manufacturing
		Female participation in the labor force
		Economic base: specialized
		Economic base: service centers
		Economic base: military
		Economic base: mining
		Elderly males in labor force
Variation explained:	70%	77%

SOURCE: From data in Ray and Murdie (1972) and Berry (1972).

tration of certain activities in areas of low labor costs (e.g., textile towns in poverty regions), as well as by the operation of noneconomic factors affecting the locations of, for example, colleges and military bases. Seen in the context of the changing nature of the city system, the traditional approach to functional town classification is of minimal and declining relevance (Berry, 1972).

The Canadian Pattern

Ray and Murdie's study of the dimensions in the Canadian city system revealed that 70 percent of the variation between cities could be explained by a smaller number of variables than was used by Berry. Although the variables resembled those used in his study, the nature of the dimensions that resulted point up the different course urbanization has taken in Canada. From our discussion in Chapter 2, it will be remembered that the growth of large cities there has occurred later and has been based in considerable part on a large-scale immigration in the postwar period. Moreover, the linear extension of the pattern means that considerable differences can be expected from one end of the country to the other—a differentiation in large part based on the pattern of resources, the history of colonization, and, of course, the variations between the French- and English-speaking regions. Thus, the major groups of dimensions in Canada relate to regional, cultural variations on the one hand and differences in the functional structure of cities on the other.

Three factors identify regional differences in the system. The contrast between Ontario and Quebec within the heartland is the most important of these, and is based on the marked cultural differences between cities in the two provinces in terms of language, religion, family size, educational level, and age structure of the urban population. The other two dimensions identify the cultural-economic distinctiveness of the cities in the Prairie Provinces, with their large Slavic population component, the high proportion of persons employed in farming and related activities, and the importance of immigration—especially from Germany and America—in their growth patterns, from those on the west coast. The British Columbia type of city has a local resource-oriented employment profile (e.g., fishing, timber, and shipping), and is characterized by a population largely born in the province itself, in Scandinavia, and in Asia.

The remaining five dimensions relate more to the nature of the Canadian space economy, in which the specialized functional structure of the smaller cities is a prominent feature. They include the contrast between the mining towns and service-distribution centers; primary manufacturing cities with their relatively high concentration of skilled workers; and the postwar growth centers. The importance of the largest metropolitan centers with their high proportion of foreign born (immigrants) is singled out, and the final dimension separates the cities of the heartland from those in the hinterland. That a comparable factor did not emerge from Berry's study is in large part due to the fact that spatial variables (distance of cities from reference points) were not included. The results of the Canadian study, then, emphasize some of the basic differences between the makeup of cities in the two countries.

CHANGES IN DIMENSIONS

Because of the processes operating, the changes taking place in the city system can be expected to be reflected in a modification of basic dimensions through time until the system reaches a stable state. On the other hand, in a number of other studies results have shown considerable stability of the basic underlying dimensions through time, and change in individual cities upward or downward in their scores on the main factors. This is, then, perhaps the main way the processes are reflected in the changing structure of the system. To investigate these kinds of questions, King (1966) analyzed the changing dimensions of the Canadian city system in the period 1951 to 1961. A total of 52 economic, social, demographic, and locational characteristics were measured for each city (see Table 7.6), and 106 cities were included in the analysis.

Urban Dimensions in 1951 and 1961

In 1951, 12 basic dimensions were revealed which together accounted for 83 percent of the total variance among the original variables. The first six components could be readily interpreted, and in order of importance they seemed to index:

1. The youthfulness of the female population in the nonmanufacturing and less densely populated cities.
2. The service role of many comparatively isolated places located outside of the province of Quebec.
3. The close economic orientation to primary activities of the frontier cities like Jonquiere, Que., and Timmins, Ont.
4. Manufacturing in smaller cities located outside of the metropolitan complexes, particularly those in Ontario.
5. Suburban communities, and the roles of cities as ports and as centers for the manufacture of transportation equipment.
6. Cities dominated by metals production (e.g., Hamilton, Ont.) and those with a run-down housing stock.

The comparable analysis for 1961 revealed dimensions that accounted for exactly the same amount of the total variation as in 1951 — 83 percent. Again the first six factors could be meaningfully interpreted and appeared to index:

1. Urban manufacturing, and especially textile manufacturing.
2. The differences in the population structure of cities located in Quebec from those in English-speaking Canada.
3. The socioeconomic structure of the Toronto and Montreal metropolitan areas.
4. Aspects of the residential character of many cities, and especially those with high socioeconomic status in Ontario.
5. The service function of many older and comparatively isolated communities, such as Quebec City, Halifax, N.S., and St. Johns, Newfoundland. It is interesting to note that the cities of Ontario generally rank low on this dimension, which is what one might expect in view of the importance of manufacturing activities in this part of the heartland.
6. Urban depression as one of the basic sources of variation between cities in the system.

Although comparison of dimensions at different time periods is thwarted by many technical problems, it is clear that the dimensions identified at the two dates are substantially different, and in fact exhibit considerable instability over time. Only two dimensions appear to be measuring the same general features of the urban system at

**Table 7.6.   SELECTED CHARACTERISTICS USED IN THE MULTIVARIATE
ANALYSIS OF CANADIAN CITIES, 1951 AND 1961**

Demographic Variables
  Percent women aged 15–39
  Percent total population aged 14 and under
  Percent total population French ethnic origin
  Number of males per 100 females
  Population immigrating from overseas in previous decade

Social Variables
  City population density
  Percent occupied dwellings single detached
  Percent occupied dwellings occupied over 10 years
  Percent occupied dwellings needing major repairs
  Median value of dwellings
  Percent wage earners earning over $4,000 annually

Economic Variables
  Percent total population to active labor force
  Percent total labor force in primary industry
  Percent manufacturing labor force in textiles, clothing, etc.
  Percent total labor force in manufacturing
  Percent labor force in proprietary, managerial, and professional occupations

Locational Variables
  Distance to nearest central city of a metropolitan area
  Having port facilities (Yes/No)
  Located on Canadian National Railway network (Yes/No)
  Number of cities in 100-mile radius
  Number of through highways

SOURCE: King (1966), Table 3.

both dates—factors 5 and 2 in 1951 closely resemble factors 4 and 5 respectively in 1961. The remaining factors, however, are substantially different, and suggest that the system is being modified by the ongoing processes of adjustment and change. Particularly important in this respect is the emergence by 1961 of a factor indexing the growing importance in Canada of Montreal and Toronto, while the metropolitan association of factor 4 in 1961 is considerably stronger than it was in the comparable factor (factor 2) in 1951. As we noted in Ray and Murdie's analysis, the postwar growth of the large cities in Canada is the major aspect of urban change.

City Groupings in 1961

In 1961, then, the 106 Canadian cities could be differentiated on the basis of their scores on each of 11 underlying dimensions. The use of these scores as coordinates enabled each city to be plotted in abstract, 11-dimensional classification space. Cities having roughly similar scores on the different dimensions clustered together. The application of a mathematical grouping technique then enabled these clusters of generally similar cities to be identified. In this way King suggested that the 106 cities could be classified into 11 distinct groups, as shown in Table 7.7. Perhaps the most interesting aspect of the resulting grouping is its fairly close correspondence to accepted broad regional divisions of Canada.

The first two groups contain what may be thought of as the eastern frontier industrial cities. The eight cities comprising group 1 generally have high scores on the first and second dimensions but rank low on the third. The low rank on the third dimension is also characteristic of the important metal-producing cities contained in group 2. Since the cities in this group, with the exception of Arvida, are all outside Quebec, they also rank low on dimension 2. This cluster of frontier industrial cities was also a notable feature in the grouping of cities in 1951. The fact that they have remained distinct over the decade 1951 to 1961 perhaps suggests that the urban system in Canada is not a highly connected one, but rather is relatively immature. These cities are therefore strongly dependent on the processing of natural resources or on a particular social and economic character that is distinctly different from that of the more diverse and mature cities found elsewhere in Canada.

The distinctive feature about cities in group 3 is their noticeable concentration in southern Ontario. The most outstanding feature is their high scores on the fourth dimension, that of high socioeconomic residential status. King suggests that these cities form a well-developed subsystem that is relatively homogeneous in terms of the urban characteristics included in the study. A similar regional concentration and homogeneity in structure is also typical of the cities in group 4, which for the most part contains the smaller cities in Quebec. Without exception, the cities in this group rank relatively high on the first two urban dimensions, while in both groups the regional contiguity effect is considerably more pronounced in 1961 than in 1951.

In contrast, the cities comprising groups 5, 6, and 7 are distinguished not so much by their regional concentration as by their type. Thus group 5 contains cities that function predominantly as service centers of one kind or another. As such they rank high on the fifth urban dimension—the service function of older and comparatively isolated communities. Groups 6 and 7 reflect the growing dominance of the two largest Canadian metropolitan areas, Toronto and Montreal. The two central cities themselves combine to form group 6, while their higher socioeconomic-status suburbs cluster together to form group 7. Interpretation of the remaining groups is not so easy in terms of either locational association or functional type. They can best be described as heterogeneous.

Thus whereas there has been a substantial shift in the basic underlying dimensions of the city system in Canada since 1951, the grouping of cities identified in 1961 appears to resemble in broad outline that identified in 1951. Of particular interest is the strong regional flavor of many of the groupings at both dates, which may be an indication of a "deviation amplifying process" (see Berry, 1964a) at work in the system and which is tending to accentuate the regional differences in Canada.

CONCLUSION

The more recent application of multivariate methods has enabled urban geographers to gain a much deeper understanding of the structure and variation of city systems, and has permitted better ways of classifying cities and identifying city types than was possible by the use of the simpler forms of taxonomy based on economic specialization. Moreover, results of factor analyses from many countries suggest that there is indeed a considerable degree of regularity in the evolution of urban patterns and in the differentiation within systems at various stages of development. As countries become technically more advanced, and the system is characterized by increasingly higher degrees of interdependence and integration, so the economic base of cities tends to become increasingly more independent of other structural characteristics. The hierarchy assumes greater significance, and position in the hierarchy is one of the most important sources of variation within the urban pattern of North America today. Socioeconomic differentiation is based principally on the social status and the age structure (stage in the life cycle) of urban populations, and as societies become technologically more advanced, these two factors operate independently of each other to give rise to well-developed patterns between cities, and to an ever increasing extent to marked differences in their internal structure.

Table 7.7.   CITY GROUPINGS IN CANADA, 1961

FRONTIER INDUSTRIAL CITIES

Group 1.
  Chicoutimi, Que.
  Rouyn, Que.
  Jonquiere, Que.
  Thetford, Que.
  Edmunston, N.B.
  Rimouski, Que.
  Hull, Que.
  Timmins, Ont.

Group 2.
  Arvida, Que.
  Glace Bay, N.S.
  New Waterford, N.S.
  Sault Ste. Marie, Ont.
  Trail, B.C.
  Sydney, N.S.
  Sudbury, Ont.

SOUTHERN ONTARIO RESIDENTIAL

Group 3.
  Barrie, Ont.
  Orillia, Ont.
  Trenton, Ont.
  Belleville, Ont.
  Chatham, Ont.
  St. Thomas, Ont.
  Owen Sound, Ont.
  Stratford, Ont.
  Niagara Falls, Ont.

  Brantford, Ont.
  Guelph, Ont.
  Brockville, Ont.
  Peterborough, Ont.
  Woodstock, Ont.
  Waterloo, Ont.
  Galt, Ont.
  Kitchener, Ont.

QUEBEC CITIES

Group 4.
  Cap de la Madeleine, Que.
  Grand'Mère, Que.
  Magog, Que.
  Victoriaville, Que.
  Sorel, Que.
  Drummondville, Que.
  Granby, Que.
  St. Jerôme, Que.
  Valleyfield, Que.

  Joliette, Que.
  St. Hyacinthe, Que.
  St. Jean, Que.
  Trois Rivières, Que.
  Jacques Cartier, Que.
  Montreal North, Que.
  St. Michel, Que.
  Cornwall, Ont.

SERVICE CENTERS

Group 5.
  Brandon, Man.
  Regina, Sas.
  Saskatoon, Sas.
  Lethbridge, Alb.
  Medicine Hat, Alb.
  Moose Jaw, Sas.
  Prince Albert, Sas.
  Penticton, B.C.
  Charlottetown, P.E.I.
  Fredericton, N.B.
  Truro, N.S.

  Pembroke, Ont.
  Calgary, Alb.
  Edmonton, Alb.
  St. Boniface, Man.
  Winnipeg, Man.
  Vancouver, B.C.
  North Bay, Ont.
  Ottawa, Ont.
  London, Ont.
  Kingston, Ont.
  Moncton, N.B.

METROPOLITAN COMPLEXES

Group 6.
  Montreal, Que.
  Toronto, Ont.

Group 7.
  Forest Hill, Ont.
  Leaside, Ont.
  Mount Royal, Que.
  Outremont, Que.
  Westmount, Que.

HETEROGENEOUS GROUPS

Group 8.
  Dartmouth, N.S.
  Levis, Que.
  Halifax, N.S.
  St. Johns, Nfld.
  Saint John, N.B.
  Eastview, Ont.
  Quebec City, Que.
  Verdun, Que.
  Hamilton, Ont.
  New Toronto, Ont.
  Mimico, Ont.
  Lachine, Que.
  Longueuil, Que.
  La Salle, Ont.
  St. Laurent, Que.
  Sarnia, Ont.
  Shawinigan, Que.

Group 9.
  Fort William, Ont.
  Port Arthur, Ont.
  New Westminster, B.C.
  North Vancouver, B.C.
  Victoria, B.C.
  Oshawa, Ont.
  St. Catherines, Ont.
  Windsor, Ont.

Group 10.
  Sherbrooke, Que.

Group 11.
  Sillery, Que.

SOURCE: King (1966), Table 4.

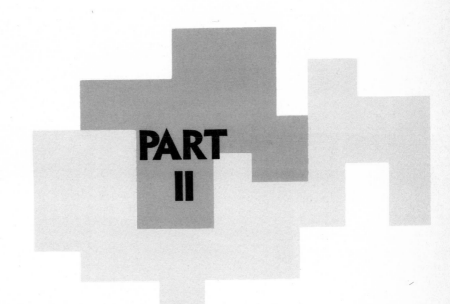

PART
II

THE INTERNAL STRUCTURE OF URBAN AREAS

8
URBAN GROWTH AND URBAN TRANSPORT

When analyzing the internal structure of urban areas, geographers are seeking to answer the locational question: Why are things located where they are? In the context of the current discussion, these "things" are the various land uses and activities that are characteristic of the North American city. At the outset it is important to recognize that the locations of these uses change over time; a high-grade residential area may be replaced by lower grade residences or vice versa. Change is, in fact, the essence of the North American city; it is in a continual state of flux. In order to begin the analysis of the internal structure of the North American city, we shall therefore first examine the process of change. As much of the ensuing analysis is concerned with the effect of accessibility on land use, our primary concern in this chapter will be to discern the influence of changes in transportation technology on the growth, structure, and form of the urban area.

A basic problem arising in an examination of the effect of changing technology on the urban area is that improvements in urban transportation tended to culminate and overlap each other at the end of the nineteenth and beginning of the twentieth centuries. Thus it is difficult to follow a strict temporal sequence in terms of discrete time periods. We shall, however, attempt to maintain the central temporal theme by examining some of the more important technical innovations in their historical sequence as they became important to the growth and form of the North American city (Adams, 1970). These changes will be examined in the following conceptual sequence: (1) the pedestrian city, (2) the railroad, (3) the streetcar, (4) rapid transit, and (5) the internal combustion engine.

THE PEDESTRIAN CITY

The central principle derived from our analysis of the economic base concept is that urban areas can grow only by producing and exporting goods, so that they may have the purchasing power to import the necessities and luxuries of their everyday life (Gilmore, 1953). The general conditions for rapid urban growth and large urban areas did not exist until the days of the Industrial and Agricultural Revolutions. The Agricultural Revolution made it possible for a few persons to produce a large food surplus, and the Industrial Revolution could take place only with the agglomeration of the surplus rural population into urban places to provide labor for factories. The fact that the existence and growth of urban areas depend upon the appropriation of a surplus product has been recognized for many decades, but this principle needs to be emphasized (Harvey, 1972). Before the Agricultural and Industrial Revolutions urban areas tended to be rather small in population size because the surplus product generated by society was small; after these "revolutions" the surplus generated was massive, and so urban areas became gargantuan. Urban development in North America coincided with these revolutions, so a few of the urban areas demonstrate a number of phases of growth. These urban areas are located primarily along the Eastern Seaboard of North America.

Compactness and Transport Costs

Even though the population of some of these cities during the early stages of the Industrial Revolution was quite large, the cities were quite compact. The reason for this compactness was that the costs of transportation for both people and goods were very high, owing to the primitive means of transportation available. This primitiveness was related to the sources of power available for intraurban transportation at that time. The two basic forms of power available were based on the strength and stamina of humans and horses. Human beings either walked, carried, or pulled goods and each other around, or horses performed this task. The horse-drawn omnibus was first used in North America in New York City about 1830, and in 1885, 593 omnibuses were licensed to operate over 27 routes in the city. The greater strength and durability of horses, of course, made them preferable to humans as power sources. But horses were expensive to buy and to maintain, and so even companies using horses for pulling omnibuses (where economies of large-scale use might prevail) were beginning to find by 1880 that this form of power was prohibitively expensive.

Horse Power

At that time "horses cost from $125 to $200 each, and a transit company had to own from five to eight times as many horses as cars" (Hilton and Due, 1964). But not only were horses expensive to buy, they were also expensive to maintain. In return for four to five hours of service each day, a horse would consume about 30 pounds of hay and grain and had to be provided with ancillary services such as stables, blacksmiths, veterinarians, and other facilities. On top of these costs was the additional fact that horses, like human beings, grow old and at all times are susceptible to injuries and diseases. For example, in 1872 the great epizootic, which involved an equine respiratory disease, killed more than 2,250 horses in three weeks in Philadelphia and disabled 18,000 horses in New York City. Disasters of this kind could obviously seriously disrupt an already slow and expensive form of urban transportation.

Home and Work in the Pedestrian City

People therefore did not, on the whole, move around the city as much as they do today. In fact, the large-scale movement of people within the city is a rather recent phenomenon (Vance, 1960). Before and during the early stages of the Industrial Revolution, people tended to live either close to or within the same building as their place of work. Only the wealthy could afford to move from one district to another as a daily event. Even then Warner notes that in Boston in 1850 "streets of the well-to-do lay hard by workers' barracks and tenements of the poor; many artisans kept shop and home in the same building or street; and factories, wharves, and offices were but a few blocks from middle-class homes" (Warner, 1962, p. 19). A lack of cheap transportation thus bound the city together into a dense compact unit. As a very few people traveled frequently between districts within the larger urban areas, each district was able to form its own identity. Therefore in the days of the pedestrian city, social distance and physical distance amounted to very much the same thing.

The Horsecar

Although the rich and the poor could live side by side, the innovation of the horsecar permitted the city to spread out along restricted lines and began the division of the middle classes from the poorer classes within the city. The first horse-drawn car on street rail lines in North America started regular operation in New York City in 1832. The economic success of this line led to the use of the horsecar in New Orleans, Chicago, Baltimore, St. Louis, Cincinnati, Pittsburgh, and Newark by 1860. Prior to the innovation of the horsecar, only the very wealthy could afford to live beyond the city and work in town, for only they could afford the maintenance of carriages. Thus the horsecar began the spatial separation of the middle and lower classes, with the wealthier families living at the periphery of the city in suburbs (Ward, 1964).

However, the expense and slowness of the horsecar virtually kept the city as a pedestrian place for most people until the 1880's. Up to that time many imaginative alternatives to the horsecar were investigated. One of the best was the steam engine, but it was cumbersome, noisy, and dirty, and above all tended to frighten horses, causing pandemonium and panic when emitting blasts of steam. An attempt at isolating the steam engine on elevated rails was undertaken with a reasonable degree of success in 1872 in New York City, along Greenwich Street between the Battery and Cortland Street. One of the chief problems confronting the widespread use of this type of system seems to have been that the center of gravity of the engine and the carriages was rather high, resulting in unfortunate mishaps on curves and sharp turns. For example, at a later date, the elevated railway curve 73 feet above 110th Street in New York City was known as "suicide corner."

Cable Cars

The most successful replacement for the horsecar was the cable car, which was first operated in San Francisco in 1873. These cars were probably introduced first in San Francisco because of the steep grades in certain sections, which precluded the possibility of citywide horsecar operations. Between 1877 and the mid-1890's, 48 cable railways were constructed in various cities in the United States, the most extensive system being in Chicago, which consisted of 82 miles of track. Two outstanding disadvantages of cable cars, however, led to their gradual decline. The first is their restricted speed of operation, for the car can move only as fast as the cable; and if the cable is moving fast, hooking and disengaging the car are difficult. The second disadvantage is the very high cost of construction, for the cables have to be laid underground. Thus the number of cable lines declined, so that today only San Francisco operates them, and this it does in order to protect and preserve one aspect of its unique image.

THE RAILROAD

We have previously mentioned that the steam engine had little impact on the internal movement of people within the North American city. Although the railroad had become the prime mover of goods and people between cities during the latter half of the nineteenth century, the steam engine proved much too cumbersome and dangerous to be applied to the daily ebb and flow of people and goods within urban areas.

Even as far as suburban commuting was concerned, it was also an expensive mode of transportation. Most railroad companies, which by 1880 received as much as 80 percent of their revenues from the transferral of goods, simply could not afford to allocate part of their rolling stock to the restricted daily transportation of people from suburban areas to the central city. There were, however, some companies that operated extensive commuter services that were highly profitable. For example, the Illinois Central Railroad began commuter services in the southern sector of Chicago in 1856, and by 1893 it handled nearly 14,000 commuters a day (a third of what it carries today). During the period of a fair in Chicago that year, the Illinois Central Railroad set a passenger record never since equaled: 500,000 passengers in one day.

Exurbs

The greatest impact of the railroad on urban structure and form was experienced with the growth of exurbs, or settlements beyond and spatially distinct from the immediate environs of the urban area. Vance (1964) notes that after 1864 in the San Francisco area there was a rapid growth of railroad towns, such as Burlingame, San Mateo, San Carlos, Belmont, and Atherton. All these exurbs had one characteristic in common: they were, among other things, the locations of estates of the wealthy who gained their livelihood in the city. Those of the city wealthy who chose to live in a rural environment located in and around the exurbs because they were able to purchase relatively large estates that permitted the creation of "an impression that the owner was of the country rather than of the city" (Vance, 1964, p. 43). These locations were made accessible by a method of transportation (the train) that was accepted as genteel.

Thus the railroad contributed to a further spatial stratification of society in that the wealthiest of all were now permitted (if they so chose) to live at considerable distances from the urban area yet maintain their vital social contacts and daily business interests in the central part of the city. The pattern of growth resulting from the influence of the railroads was quite restrictive, for it could occur only in nucleations along the radial lines of the railroad companies.

THE STREETCAR

Weber, writing in the last decade of the nineteenth century, noted with alarm the appalling congestion of cities in the Western world (Weber, 1963). We have observed that this appalling congestion could be attributed in large part to the technology of urban transportation available at that time. For most people it was still impossible to live very far away from their place of work or from alternative employment opportunities; and as a consequence, most people lived in areas of very high population density around the central business district (CBD). Furthermore, the public means of transportation were slow and space-consuming (a horse and carriage takes up more space than an automobile). These factors, along with narrow streets, resulted in terrible overcrowding. Weber's solution to this congestion was to advocate decongestion. This decongestion was not really feasible until the advent of the electric streetcar, or trolley (Smerk, 1967).

The Advantages of the Electric Streetcar

The electric streetcar was first used successfully on the Richmond Union Passenger Railway in Virginia in 1888 and was subsequently adapted by Whitney in 1889 in Boston. The immensely superior and efficient operation of the streetcar in Boston resulted in the building or ordering of more than 200 systems in North American cities in the following three years. By 1902, 97 percent of street railway mileage was electrically operated, whereas in 1890 70 percent of street railways had used animal power. In 1901 there were about 15,000 miles of electric railway in the United States (Hilton and Due, 1964). The innovation of the streetcar did not come a moment too soon for alleviating congestion in the city, for at the turn of the century the United States population was increasing at a rate of 1.3 million per year as a result of heavy immigration, increased life expectancy, and a relatively high birth rate. Most of this population increase was being experienced by the cities. Thus Vance states:

> It is hard to say whether the trolley produced the metropolis or vice versa. In any event, we may date the transformation of most American cities from the stage of simple urbanism to complex metropolitanism in the first or second decade following the introduction of trolleys [Vance, 1964, p. 50].

The electric streetcar was greatly superior to the other forms of urban transportation available at that time. In the first place, a streetcar system, though expensive, was economically feasible to construct within the city. Some horse-drawn cars were already running on rails along the main radials, and the electric streetcar could make use of these facilities. Furthermore, in the construction of new lines there was not the problem of excavating that there was with cable cars. The power source could be provided easily with overhead wires; and though they might look unsightly, few people were concerned with visual pollution in these bustling laissez-faire days. Compared with steam engines, the power source was much more efficient and could be applied quietly in creating motion. On top of these attractions, the streetcar could be quite fast, though this advantage was somewhat negated by the necessity for frequent stopping. All these advantages were enhanced by the relatively lower cost of transportation. In many cities the trolleys charged a flat rate, with no extra charge for transfering between lines. Thus it is not surprising that the trolley became the first form of public transportation to be used on a large scale by employees going to and from work.

The electric streetcar consequently made it possible for the population of urban areas to spread out and thereby to decrease residential densities. The spread that occurred was quite dramatic, and, as can be seen from the example of Toronto in Figure 8.1, changed the city from one that was quite compact up to 1886 to one that was spread out along quite definite paths by 1914. For the population to spread out, however, land had to be provided and serviced, and homes had to be built. The innovation of the trolley therefore led to great increases in land sales, land values, and land speculation, particularly along the areas adjacent to the main transportation arteries.

The Effect of the Electric Streetcar and Speculation

Warner (1962), in his seminal analysis of the effect of the electric streetcar on the suburban development of Roxbury, West Roxbury, and Dorchester—all in the southern sector and immediately adjacent to the central city of Boston—provides a quantitative estimate of the effect of this transportation innovation. Most of the land in these three independent towns, which became suburbs in the latter part of the nineteenth century, was beyond the zone of dense settlement in the "walking city" of Boston prior to 1850.

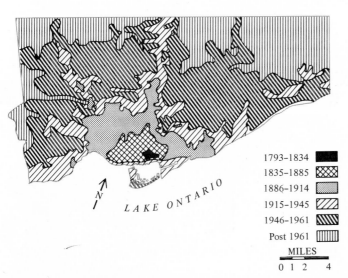

Fig. 8.1. Growth of metropolitan Toronto, 1793–1971. (*Source:* Modified from Kerr and Spelt, 1965, p. 97.)

In 1870, after the first 15 years of the horsecar, which prompted a tentative beginning of suburbanization in these towns, the population of these three towns stood at 60,000. By 1900 their combined population had boomed to 227,000. This increase in population was housed in 22,500 new buildings, of which 53.3 percent were single-family houses, 26.6 percent were two-family houses, and the remainder were multifamily dwellings. Developments of this kind could take place only through the expansion of streetcar lines and land development.

Thus throughout much of North America the expansion of "streetcar suburbs" involved close cooperation between the developer-speculator and the transit lines, which were often strategically placed and threaded through preplatted subdivisions. It was the developer, therefore, who determined the land use. If the developer thought an area of land was capable of supporting high-value housing, then the land was platted accordingly with large lots. Furthermore, the developer built according to his estimate of the tastes and values of the prospective buyers.

The Suburbanization of the Middle Classes

The vast majority of the prospective buyers were not the very wealthy. They were, infact, that mass of the total population commonly referred to as the middle class, which includes a wide variety of incomes and occupations. As the occupational structure of society in North America was becoming more complex with the progression of the Industrial Revolution, particularly placing a greater emphasis on organizational and managerial skills, the ranks of the middle classes were continually expanding. It was this broad group that was gaining in affluence, through (it was thought) the virtues of unfettered capitalistic enterprise, and which the streetcar "liberated" from the central city. As the land developer built for this middle class, it was not so much the expense of transport on the streetcar that prevented the lower classes from moving to the suburbs as the cost of housing and living in the suburbs. Although there were definitely certain groups that would not be permitted to buy in the suburbs, it was generally supposed that any person who could afford to pay middle-class suburban house prices could move into these areas. The fact that some groups could not afford to pay these prices because of a whole series of integrated discriminatory laws, mores, and traditions was rarely recognized (Ward, 1968).

Thus the streetcar not only affected urban form by encouraging residential development in the vicinity of the electric streetcar lines radiating from the central city; it also brought into focus the beginning of a spatial socioeconomic pattern considered to be symptomatic of the modern North American metropolis. The socioeconomic patterns involve house structures, the spatial separation of families by economic class, new health standards, and a weak community structure.

House Structures

Prior to this period of the mass suburbanization of the middle classes, urban wealth had attained a visible appearance through housing structures either by estates or by streets of well-designed row houses that achieved their prosperous effect through a repetition of more or less identical imposing fronts. In the new suburbs the gridded streets and subdivided lots, all with some small frontage on the street, resulted in a suburban style of individualized houses "arranged in such a way as to produce for the public the gratifying view of a prosperous street" (Warner, 1962, p. 151). These houses almost filled their entire lots and, though individually designed, were basically similar in style along each street. For example, they usually had structural features such as gables or shingles which were adapted from the homes of the more wealthy.

These suburban homes gave the appearance of being solid, prosperous, and family-oriented. They therefore gave a physical expression of the satisfaction and confidence of the middle-class owner in the economic underpinnings of the North American way of life. Home ownership was, however, not as frequent as this appearance of prosperity implied. The unregulated mortgage market of that time resulted in high down payments and short-term, nonamortizing mortgages that restricted home ownership. Only one-quarter of Boston's families owned their own homes in 1900. Furthermore, the pleasant semirural environment desired by the suburban dweller was rarely attained, for the vast majority of the subdividers and builders were not trained in architectural methods and construction techniques that would achieve and preserve this desired atmosphere.

Spatial Economic Differentiation

Thus the streetcar, by further stimulating and accelerating the rate of suburbanization, also indirectly affected the spatial socioeconomic differentiation of society. Because the suburbs, and suburban-style housing, specifically catered in large part to the middle class, and as this housing was in turn differentiated by street and area into price and style groupings, the population of the suburbs was spatially stratified according to income.

Warner (1962) notes that these income-graded neighborhoods rendered two important services to their residents. In the first place, the evenness of wealth found within local areas meant a uniformity and conformity in social and economic values. The middle classes found this acceptable, because it was felt to be highly desirable that these values be passed on to their children. If all people in the same area held the same values, then it would be possible to pass these values on to successive generations. Consequently the local educational system, churches, clubs and so forth came to reflect these values; and these institutions rarely publicly questioned them, because the apparent affluence of the middle class proclaimed them to be right.

This latter aspect interacts with the second important service rendered by income-graded neighborhoods to their residents. The evenness of wealth gave the adults in the community a sense of shared experience, for each family would be affected by the same economic forces and similar uncertainties. Thus, bank managers and doctors living on the more wealthy middle-class streets would hold the same views of social change and fervor for philanthropic missions. The less wealthy areas, on the other hand, would perhaps have a grouping of people with slightly different attitudes, particularly as they might be on the way up or trying to get ahead.

Warner indicates that this kind of socioeconomic variation was spatially expressed in concentric form (Fig. 8.2) in the southern sector of Boston in 1900. By this date the edge of the old pedestrian city of Boston was between two and two and a half miles from Boston City Hall (which was considered to be the center of downtown Boston). The range of lower-middle-class to middle-class housing extended to three and a half miles from the City Hall, and its outer limit is roughly demarcated by the outer limit of linear or radial street railway service. Beyond this band, the very wealthy were served by commuter railroads. With time, as the radial streetcar lines expanded and the crosstown services continued their interstitial infilling, the socioeconomic bands continued to move outward from the central city.

Rising Health Standards

This rapidly accelerating suburbanization of the middle classes had an important side effect on the provision of public services, such as parks and utilities, in the North American city. The frequent plagues and epidemics that were the scourge of nineteenth-century urban areas had given rise to a growing demand for better methods of garbage and sewage disposal, lighting, heating, water, and facilities for improving urban life. The rapid growth of the suburbs, following the innovation of the electric streetcar, provided an environment that encouraged the technological advances made in the provision of services and utilities of this kind, and often favored their installation by public or municipal authority.

New suburbs were therefore built and planned with these provisions in mind.

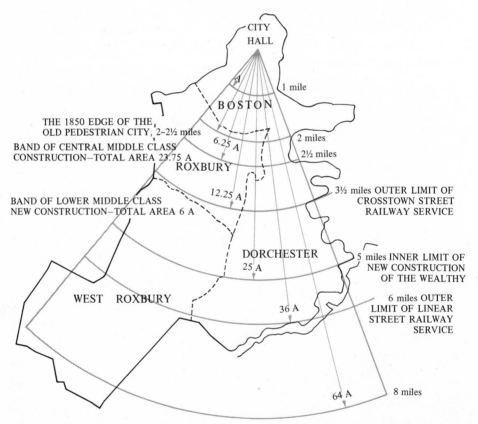

Fig. 8.2. Approximate class building zones of the three towns of Roxbury, West Roxbury, and Dorchester in 1900. On the map, A equals 357.4 acres. It is the area of a 64° segment of a circle whose radius is one mile. The other radii are marked in miles from Boston's City Hall and the areas given in terms of A. (*Source:* Warner, 1962, Fig. 9.)

Thus the land was subdivided in an orderly fashion, and often utilities were laid before the home builders began their work. These rising municipal standards were also followed by the home builders, who as a result of middle-class demand found it expedient to follow, and sometimes to lead, regulations concerning plumbing, gas fittings, and fire safety. Perhaps more importantly, the demands of the middle-class suburbs had an important feedback on the old central "walking" city itself, in that the provision of utilities and better housing became a matter of general metropolitan concern.

Community Structure and Government

The negative effects of the suburbanization of the middle classes counterbalance to a large degree these important positive benefits. These negative effects are most apparent with respect to metropolitan government. Although it might be thought that the collecting together of a group of people with similar aims, incomes, objectives, and tastes might produce a strong coherent community and political structure, the suburbanization of the middle classes achieved almost exactly the opposite. Warner (1962) contends that the philosophical basis of the suburb at the turn of the century was founded on the concept of the freedom of the family as a unit to pursue its own economic and cultural objectives. Of course, these objectives had to be within the acceptable norms of middle-class society. For example, belief in God and family attendance at church were undoubtedly a middle-class social and cultural norm at the end of the nineteenth century; but there was no stipulation as to which religion was generally acceptable, though undoubtedly some religions were less acceptable than others. This, of course, is not meant to imply that the suburban middle classes were the only churchgoers, but it is meant to suggest that the social action as much as the philosophical and ethical basis was extremely important among this group.

The important point is that a view of life centered on what was best for the individual family resulted in a lack of perspective in considering problems of other parts of the metropolitan area. Participation in local community politics was generally limited, and those aspects of political life that did achieve importance were generally quite parochial in nature. Thus, although some of the standards of the middle classes concerning health and welfare were percolating down to the lower classes, this was usually by accident rather than by public policy. Furthermore, the separation of the middle classes from the central city led to the isolation of this group from the growing and burgeoning problems of the central city. It could therefore be considered that the Industrial and Agricultural Revolutions, along with the decentralization made possible by the streetcar, gave birth to the spatial structure and self-defeating fragmentation of metropolitan interests that is so evident in North American cities today. Goheen (1970) argues strongly that there are very few elements of the modern city that are not also evident in the nineteenth-century industrial city, and that the social order and concepts of territoriality that emerged during this period were, in fact, innovations of that era.

RAPID TRANSIT

Rapid transit is a cross between the streetcar and the railroad. Although earlier systems used steam engines, rapid transit involves the application of the electric motor to a system involving rail lines placed in structures that are isolated from the rest of the city. Thus rapid-transit facilities are able to proceed at a faster pace than streetcars and can consist of more than one carriage, as with a train. Consequently rapid transit tends to be quicker and safer, and its carrying capacity can be expanded or restricted simply by the addition or removal of carriage modules. Although the system is quite rigid once it is constructed, with good planning it can be designed as an integrated part of the overall urban transportation system, for the rail lines may be elevated, on the surface, or sub-surface. The great density of activity at the center of the city immediately points to the advantage of the subsurface aspect of rapid transit.

As both the streetcar and rapid transit involved the use of the electric motor, it is not surprising that both methods of transportation were applied simultaneously to urban transportation. However, as rapid transit involved much greater fixed costs in its construction, its application was slower and more deliberate than that of the streetcar. Consequently rapid transit on elevated lines was first introduced into Chicago in 1892 by the South Side Elevated Railroad, using steam engines, which were replaced by elec-tric motor cars in 1897 and 1898. Boston's first rapid-transit facility started operation in 1891, and Philadelphia's in 1905. In New York City the first subway was put into opera-tion in 1904. Because of the high capital construction costs, few lines were built, with little attempt to facilitate crosstown movements. However, the development of rapid transit had a great impact on the form and structure of the city. This impact can be seen particularly in its emphasis on the radial or sectoral growth of the city, and by the rise of the area around local transit stations as centers of economic activity.

Sectoral Growth

Rapid transit is efficient only when it is moving large numbers of people daily. Consequently rapid-transit systems were constructed to connect the central business district (CBD), as the chief place of employment and commercial activity, with the principal areas of urban population. The direction of growth in most cases had already been defined by the horsecar, the cable car, and the streetcar. For example, in Chicago, rapid-transit routes on elevated lines (the El) followed a predetermined pattern estab-lished by the horsecar (Fig. 8.3) and cable cars (Fig. 8.4). The south- and west-side lines (Fig. 8.5) were constructed prior to the north-side lines, which followed the direction of growth marked by the cable and horsecar systems.

Rapid Transit in the North Sector of Chicago

As rapid transit was expensive to establish, few feeder lines were constructed, and the lines emphasized the radial nature of the preceding transportation systems. Thus, in the case of Chicago, a clear south, west, and north pattern of growth emerged as the rapid-transit lines pressed their systems to the periphery and began to precede urban development. Davis (1965) indicates three zones of development associated with the growth of the El in northern Chicago. In the first zone, within three miles of the CBD, the El had little effect as the land was already settled when the El began its operation in 1900. Between three and four miles from the CBD is transition zone that incurred a limited degree of building activity following the opening of the El. Beyond this zone the El provided a great impetus to urban development immediately following the opening of El services in 1900.

This urban development coincided with an increase in construction, in popu-lation, and in land values along the rapid-transit line. But these changes were greater farther away from the CBD. For example, ". . . land value changes were greater with El

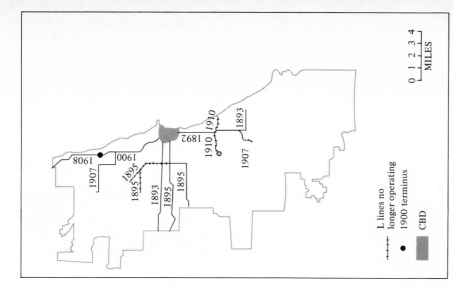

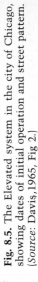

Fig. 8.5. The Elevated system in the city of Chicago, showing dates of initial operation and street pattern. (*Source:* Davis,1965, Fig 2.)

L lines no
longer operating
● 1900 terminus

CBD

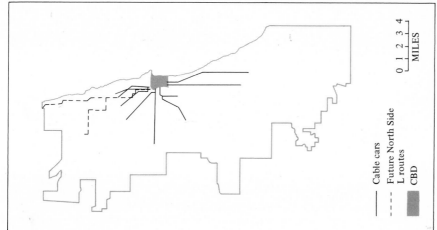

Fig. 8.4. Principal cable-car routes in the city of Chicago, 1893. (*Source:* Davis, 1965, Fig. 19.)

Cable cars
Future North Side
L routes

CBD

Fig. 8.3. Principal horse railways in the city of Chicago, 1890. (*Source:* Davis, 1965, Fig. 16.)

Horse railways
Future North Side
L routes

CBD

impact the farther one moved from the CBD, as zone 3 increased its land values by 66.40 percent more than zone 2 from 1892 to 1905" (Davis, 1965, p. 88). However, even though these changes increased with distance from the CBD, the intensity of construction, the density of population, and the value of urban land still decreased with distance from the CBD, though the curve was obviously becoming flatter.

Rapid Transit and the Growth of Outlying Centers of Economic Activity

A further aspect of rapid transit that differs from the streetcar and therefore adds a new dimension to urban spatial structure is that the system has discrete passenger loading and unloading points that are spaced farther apart than ordinary streetcar stops. Thus each station on a rapid-transit facility has a tributary area from which it draws its customers. Some tributary areas are much larger than others, owing to a coalescence of rapid-transit routes or a convergence of street transportation. Consequently there is apt to be business activity around each rapid-transit station, which, according to land-use theory, should be orderly and predictable.

Patterns of Development Around Rapid Transit Stations

Davis also empirically examined the impact of El stations on the pattern of new residential construction, land values, and population density in the northern sector of Chicago. Although the evidence showed some variation, it was generally found to be in accordance with land-use theory expectations. For example, in the case of residential construction,

> total block-by-block statistics for all forty-one El station areas . . . reveal that both the first and second block zones averaged 77.5 percent new settlement . . . while the third block zone trailed with 72.4 percent, and the fourth block zone was last with 71 percent [Davis, 1965, p. 177].

In terms of land values

> the average front-foot value of all the El station areas first block zones in 1911 was $68.70. This figure was 11.84 percent higher than that of the second block zone's average of $61.40, 41.94 percent higher than that of the third block zone's average of $48.40 and 95.67 percent higher than that of the fourth zone's $35.11 per front foot [Davis, 1965, p. 122].

Similar gradations were noted with population density patterns, the greatest changes being observed around those El stations farthest from the CBD.

THE INTERNAL COMBUSTION ENGINE

In 1903, when Henry Ford sought $100,000 to found the Ford Motor Company, he was able to raise only $28,000. Five years later, when W. C. Durant, the founder of General Motors, told an investment banker that eventually a half-million automobiles would be produced per year, the banker showed Durant to the door of his office (Moore, 1954). The application of the streetcar to intraurban traffic and its extension into interurban traffic, plus the use of rapid transit and the commuter railroad, led many persons to believe that the automobile had a limited future. However, the forces that these innovations had set in motion in reshaping and restructuring the city proved to be ideally suited to the internal combustion engine as applied to the automobile. All the facets of urban life that came to the fore with the innovation of the streetcar—the suburbanization of the middle class, the desire for travel and recreation beyond the city, the emphasis on individual and family group activities, the beginning of the outward migration of employment opportunities and crosstown commuting—could be developed a great deal further with the use of the automobile.

The rate of increase in automobile use in North America during the first few decades of the twentieth century has been quite dramatic. Table 8.1 presents data concerning the number of persons per registered automobile and taxi in the United States from 1900 to 1970. The measure is referred to as an automobile ownership ratio, and in 1900 there appears to have been approximately one automobile for every 10,000 people. By 1910 the rate of automobile ownership had increased fiftyfold; and from about 1922 onward there has been more than one automobile for every 10 persons in the United States. If the rate of automobile ownership continues to increase at the present rate, by 1980 there will be at least 120 million cars in the United States.

This rate of increase in automobile ownership is very strongly related to the ever increasing wealth in the United States. On a family basis, the wealthier the family, the greater the number of automobiles in that family. In 1970 nearly 43 percent of all households with less than $3,000 annual income owned one automobile, and 10 percent owned two; but 95 percent of all households with an annual income in excess of $10,000 owned one, and more than 50 percent owned at least two. As the proportion of families in the middle-income groups is expected to continue to rise, a much greater proliferation can be expected in the future in the use of the automobile and in increased mobility. This prediction is made notwithstanding fuel shortages and high gas prices, for these difficulties will not take the Americans and Canadians out of their automobiles; they will merely encourage them either to purchase cars with more efficient engines or to purchase new cars less frequently.

Table 8.1. **AUTOMOBILE OWNERSHIP IN THE UNITED STATES FOR SELECTED YEARS BETWEEN 1900 AND 1970**

Year	Auto Registrations (in thousands)	Population (in thousands)	Auto Ownership Ratio
1900	8	76,094	9,511.3
1910	458	92,407	196.6
1920	8,131	106,466	13.1
1930	23,035	123,077	5.3
1940	27,466	132,594	4.8
1950	40,339	152,271	3.8
1960	61,682	180,684	2.9
1970	89,230	203,810	2.3

SOURCE: U.S. Bureau of the Census, *Statistical Abstract of the United States, 1973*, pp. 5, 547. (Washington, D.C.: U.S. Government Printing Office, 1973.)

Previous discussion has indicated that the spatial distribution of wealth within the city is not even. Wealthier families tend to live at the periphery of the city, and the less wealthy tend to live toward the center. Thus the spatial rate of automobile ownership also varies, with a much higher rate of automobile ownership at the periphery. As it was the suburbanized middle class that first began the widespread use of the automobile for both work and social travel, it was at the periphery of the city that the impact of the automobile on urban structure and form began to be felt. This impact was accentuated by the fact that in areas of low population density mass-transit facilities could not hope to compete with the automobile. Thus it was at the fringe of the city that the automobile first began to shape the city (Vance, 1964).

The Automobile Shapes the City

The commuter railroad encouraged the growth of the upper-class exurbs, the streetcar stimulated the expansion of the middle class into the suburbs, and rapid transit further accentuated the radial growth of the city. The innovation of the automobile made possible an even greater physical expansion of the city, but most importantly it permitted the spread of population into areas between the major radial lines leading into the city. The ensuing continuing decrease in density of the suburban population has resulted in communities that are even more spread out than the streetcar suburbs and even more difficult to provide with a wide range of community services—except those facilities that had become entrenched as the norms of middle-class life. These include piped drinking water, sewage facilities (though many surburan homes have septic tanks), churches, and community schools. In terms of social and economic behavior, there has been an even greater emphasis on the individual family and the use by that family of modern technology in the home (particularly in the kitchen).

This modern suburban development is dependent almost entirely on the automobile for transportation, for public transport is infrequent, if available at all, in the suburbs. In many cases the male home owner finds it essential to use an automobile to get to work; and if he uses rapid transit or the commuter railroad, he either leaves his car at the railroad station, uses a car pool, or is driven there by his wife. Thus the automobile, in helping to create the modern interstitial suburb, has also helped to create a further demand for automobiles; for if one car is used in the daily journey to work, the wife must also have an automobile in order to shop, take the children to school, visit the doctor and the dentist, and pursue sundry social or philanthropic activities. It is partially in reaction to this suburban syndrome that the women's liberation movement has evolved.

The effect of the automobile on urban structure is not, however, felt only at the urban fringe. In order to speed traffic through the city and into the CBD, most North American cities are crisscrossed with limited-access highways and expressways. These make it possible for the suburban dweller to visit the CBD without seeing much of the old central city. Thus the conditions of the central city are hidden behind the concrete canyons of the expressway until dramatic events bring these conditions into the public eye. The insularity of the middle classes, first encouraged by the streetcar and rapid transit, has been greatly accentuated by the automobile.

The automobile has created a new urban form. The out-migration of people, commercial activity, and much of modern industry have changed the North American city from a phenomenon closely organized around a single central core to a metropolis in which the central core plays a less dominant part. Vance suggests that the North American city of the middle twentieth century has become noncentric, and that this is emphasized by the fact that the 1960 U.S. Census shows that the "greatest single movement of workers was from one outlying area to another, rather than from the periphery to the core" (Vance, 1964, p. 68).

The Effect of the Internal Combustion Engine on Other Modes of Urban Transportation

The internal combustion engine has not only had an impact on the shape of the city; it has also affected the other forms of urban transportation that had been developed immediately prior to it. In some cases the internal combustion engine has provided a cheaper and much more flexible replacement. Probably the best example of this is the Diesel-engine bus, which is a much more efficient machine that the streetcar. The streetcar, being confined to its rails and unable to move in and out of the regular flow of traffic in order to discharge and take on passengers, was rapidly outmoded with the innovation of the bus. However, the necessary fixed-cost capital outlays that had been incurred in the establishment of streetcar systems meant that they remained functioning long after they had, in effect, become obsolete. Thus it was not until 1945 that bus passenger traffic in the United States exceeded that of the streetcar (Table 8.2). Since 1945 there has been a great decline in streetcar traffic, so that by 1970 motor-bus traffic was 25 times greater than that of the streetcar. A minor innovation during this latter period was the trolley coach, which is, in effect, a cross between the motor bus and the streetcar, being dependent on electric wires but not confined to rails.

People are not the only commodities requiring mobility within the urban area. The inputs into and outputs from industries require shipment, and the multitude of goods and services of various kinds have to be transported to all parts of the urban area. Some commodities, such as water, gas, and electricity, can be provided with their own specific transport networks; but many others are not suitable to pipe or wire dispersion.

Table 8.2.   PASSENGER TRAFFIC BY STREETCAR, TROLLEY COACH, AND MOTOR BUS IN THE UNITED STATES, FOR SELECTED YEARS BETWEEN 1905 AND 1970 (IN BILLIONS OF TOTAL PASSENGERS)

Year	Streetcar	Trolley Coach	Motor Bus
1905	5.0		
1920	13.7		
1925	12.9		1.5
1930	10.5		2.5
1935	7.3	0.1	2.6
1940	5.9	0.5	4.2
1945	9.4	1.2	9.9
1950	3.9	1.7	9.4
1955	1.2	1.2	7.3
1960	0.5	0.7	6.4
1970	0.2	0.2	5.0

SOURCE: Owen (1966), Table 16, 1970 data from American Transit Association, *Transit Fact Book, 1970–1971,* Table 2.2.

The primary conveyor of material into and from most large cities is the railroad, though the application of the Diesel engine to motor vehicles has given rise to a rapidly growing interurban trucking industry in recent decades. The development of the interstate highway system in the United States and limited-access highways in Canada has further encouraged the growth of this intercity truck traffic.

The truck is, however, preeminent for the movement of goods within the city. Prior to the development of the internal combustion engine, within-city commodity movements were undertaken primarily with horse-drawn vehicles. Very little commodity movement was undertaken by streetcars, cable cars, or rapid transit, as all these systems are inflexible for local deliveries. Thus, though horses were quickly superseded for the movement of people, they remained in service much longer for the movement of goods. The development of the internal combustion engine was therefore vital for the efficient transport of goods within the rapidly expanding North American city, and has been an extremely important factor in permitting the decentralization of industry (Moses and Williamson, 1967).

CHANGING TRANSPORTATION TECHNOLOGY
AND THE NORTH AMERICAN CITY

From the preceding discussion it is possible to recognize three major periods of technological innovation in urban transportation in North America. These periods conform very closely to those suggested by Borchert (1967) as applicable to interurban transportation in North America.

1. The first period, prior to 1870, involved movement based primarily on the horse, or individual locomotion by foot. As a consequence the urban area was compact and can be described as a "pedestrian" city.

2. From 1870 to 1920, and particularly around the two decades at the turn of the century, the North American city witnessed dramatic technological innovations. These, in terms of urban transportation, involved the streetcar, cable car, and electric rapid transit. This was a period of great suburban expansion of North America with the strong development of urban radials. Although many forms of urban transportation existed at this time, the period can be characterized as that of the streetcar, as it was this innovation that led to some of the most dramatic changes in urban structure and form.

3. The third or present period, starting in 1920, brought the automobile to the fore as an important means of urban transportation. This last period is therefore designated as the automobile era.

Urban growth in North America has not been uniform through time. Some cities have grown predominantly in the nineteenth century and others in the twentieth century. It can be suggested that in general the cities of the South and West are newer and products of the twentieth century, while those of the East are more the products of the nineteenth century, In Table 8.3, 13 of the largest metropolitan areas in the United States and Canada are listed and the proportion of the population of each urban area in 1960 that was achieved during each of the three intraurban transportation eras. Thus Boston, by 1870, had achieved a population that was 27 percent of its 1960 population size. Between 1870 and 1920 it achieved a further 48 percent of its 1960 population size, and between 1920 and 1960 the additional 25 percent was added. Since people require space and housing structures in which to live, it might therefore be assumed that quite a large proportion of present-day Boston was built to house the pre-1870 population, and that an even larger area was consumed to house the population growth that occurred in the streetcar era. Farther down the table it can be observed that 85 percent of Los Angeles' growth occurred during the automobile era, only 15 percent in the streetcar era, and none at all prior to 1870. The table tends to substantiate the proposition that the larger cities of the West are the products of the automobile era, while those of the East are much more the products of the nineteenth century.

Borchert (1967) suggests that this variation in epochal growth expressed in Table 8.3 has very important implications for an understanding of urban obsolescence and renewal. Cities that grew primarily in those eras before the automobile will have a transportation system and a set of physical structures that are antiquated and invariably incongruent with respect to the automobile. Those cities that have grown up entirely within the automobile era will be noncentric and have a different structure and appearance from those that did not. This is because the bulk of

new construction has been concentrated, in any given epoch, not only in new neighborhoods and new suburbs but also in what have been, for all practical purposes, new cities. The residue of obsolescent physical plant has also become concentrated, not only in certain districts of most cities but in virtually the entire area of some [Borchert, 1967, pp. 328–329].

The impact of those technological innovations upon all aspects of urban structure and form has therefore varied greatly throughout North America. Although a general pattern of change can be observed in terms of technological innovations, each of which has specific impacts on the structure of the city, no one urban area will have exactly the same structure and form as another.

Table 8.3.   PERCENTAGE OF 1960 POPULATION OF SELECTED METROPOLITAN AREAS IN MAJOR HISTORICAL EPOCHS

SMSA	Pre-1870	1870–1920	1920–1960
Boston	27%	48%	25%
New Orleans	25	23	52
Philadelphia	24	38	38
Pittsburgh	17	56	27
New York	14	44	42
Washington, D. C.	10	19	71
Chicago	8	47	45
San Francisco–Oakland	7	26	67
Detroit	6	29	65
Toronto	4	29	67
Dallas–Ft. Worth	3	30	67
Seattle–Tacoma	0	42	58
Los Angeles	0	15	85

SOURCE: Borchert (1967), Table 3; other calculations by the authors.

9
THE LAND-USE SYSTEM

The accelerating growth and areal spread of the technological innovations in transport and communications, has involved the visible physical location, relocation, and expansion of land uses that comprise the fabric of these urban areas. This chapter is concerned with the major uses of urban land and with a discussion of various theories and descriptive models that can be used to understand the spatial variation in the intensity of urban land use. Central to the discussion is the fact that urban land use is in a continual state of flux, though some parts of urban areas tend to grow and change at a greater rate than others.

MAJOR GROUPS OF URBAN LAND USES

The land use of urban areas can be divided into six major categories. These are residential, industrial, commercial, roads and highways, public and semipublic land, and vacant land. Major studies inventorying the proportion of urban land in each of these uses have been undertaken by Bartholomew (1955), Niedercorn and Hearle (1964), and Montgomery (1969). In this section the main data that will be used are those presented by Niedercorn and Hearle, which were obtained from a questionnaire sent out under the auspices of the RAND Corporation to 63 large American cities, of which 52 returned replies. Information relating to urban areas in southern Ontario and Quebec will also be used.

Land use may be presented in either gross or net terms. Gross land use includes in each land-use category the area of streets abutting the land in question. Net land use treats streets as a separate land-use category. Niedercorn and Hearle found that most of the returned questionnaires gave estimates in net terms, and so Tables 9.1 and 9.2 provide a separate category for roads and highways. Four urban areas (Denver, Houston, Milwaukee, and Philadelphia) responded with gross estimates and consequently were dropped from the study. The 48 remaining cities are listed in Table 9.3.

Residential uses consume more land in American cities than any other type. According to Niedercorn and Hearle, 29.6 percent of all urban land and 39 percent of all developed land is devoted to residential use. This latter figure is very close to that provided by Bartholomew (1955) for central cities in the United States, where, for a sample of cities representing a much wider population range, he estimates that 39.6 percent of the developed land is devoted to residential activity. Residential land, in turn, can be divided into a number of subclasses. By far the dominant use of residential land is for single-family dwellings. Bartholomew estimates that 31.8 percent of the total developed area is in this use. Two-family dwellings, represented by the duplex, consume about 4.8 percent of the developed land, and multifamily apartments and tenements consume about 7.6 percent of urban land.

The second largest single category of land use is roads and highways. This class of use consumes nearly 20 percent of the total land found in the 48 urban areas responding to the RAND survey questionnaire. In terms of the developed land in urban areas, roads and highways comprise over a quarter of the total land use. This figure is higher for the parts of the city closest to the center of the city than it is for the periphery, where streets are spaced farther apart.

All other uses comprise a remarkably small proportion of the total land in urban areas. Industrial uses, involving heavy and light industry as well as railroad properties

---

**Table 9.1. MEAN PERCENTAGE OF LAND DEVOTED TO VARIOUS
USES IN 48 LARGE AMERICAN CITIES**

Type of Use	Total Land	Developed Land
Total developed	77.0%	100.0%
Residential	29.6	39.0
Industrial	8.6	10.9
Commercial	3.7	4.8
Roads and highways	19.9	25.7
Other public	15.2	19.6
Total undeveloped	23.0	—
Vacant	20.7	—
Underwater	2.3	—

SOURCE: Niedercorn and Hearle (1964), pp. 105–110.

Table 9.2.   CHANGES IN MEAN PERCENTAGE OF LAND USE

Type of Use	Mean Percentage of Land Devoted to Various Uses at Different Times in 22 Cities				Mean Percentage of Land Devoted to Various Uses at Different Times in 12 Cities			
	Percentage of Total		Percentage of Development		Percentage of Total		Percentage of Development	
	Early Data	Late Data	Early Data	Late Data	Early Data	Late Data	Early Data	Late Data
Total Developed	75.5	78.4	100.0	100.0	80.2	85.7	100.0	100.0
Residential	29.0	31.0	38.5	39.8	30.0	32.5	37.4	37.9
Industrial	8.5	8.5	11.0	10.4	10.0	10.6	12.4	12.4
Commercial	4.1	4.0	5.3	5.0	4.5	4.4	5.5	5.0
Roads and highways	20.7	19.8	27.9	25.4	20.3	21.0	25.4	24.5
Other public	13.2	15.1	17.3	19.4	15.4	17.2	19.3	20.2
Total Undeveloped	24.5	21.6	—	—	19.8	14.3	—	—
Vacant	23.3	20.4	—	—	18.4	12.9	—	—
Underwater	1.2	1.2	—	—	1.4	1.4	—	—

SOURCE: Niedercorm and Hearle (1964), pp. 105–110.

and airports, comprise 8.6 percent of the land available in urban areas. Commercial uses — involving wholesale, retail, and service activities — consume only 3.7 percent of urban land. General public uses — schools, public buildings, parks, playgrounds, cemeteries, and so on — comprise a little over 15 percent of urban land. In total, it seems that about 20.7 percent of urban land at present is vacant, and 2.3 percent is under water.

Land Use Changes

Thus far the discussion has involved a description of the average land uses in relatively large urban areas in the early 1960s. It is interesting to see the way in which land uses have changed through time. Table 9.2 is divided into a 22-city category and a 12-city category, showing changes in land use between two time periods. The 22-city table contains information from those cities that supplied data for two or more years. The average interval between these time periods is about 10.2 years. As a consequence, the data have been divided into an early group and a late group. From this table a number of points can be observed. First, residential and other public land uses have increased relative both to total area and to total developed land. Second, road and highway uses on the whole have decreased. Third, industrial and commercial uses have remained about the same, although declining slightly as proportions of developed land. These figures may well have been influenced by an increase in area of the cities through annexation of surrounding territory.

As a consequence, the 12-city table contains those cities that had not annexed any land between the early and the late period being discussed. The average interval in this subsample is about 9.8 years. The major point emerging from an analysis of this table is that the ratio of land in urban use to the total increased for all categories except commercial, which decreased slightly. Second, the largest increase was in residential land, and the next largest increase was in public land. Third, the proportion of total area remaining vacant has decreased substantially. In other words, the 22-city table is in fact

Table 9.3. THE 48 CITIES

Albany	Jersey City	Pittsburgh[b]
Baltimore	Kansas City (Mo.)	Portland (Ore.)
Birmingham	Long Beach[b]	Portsmouth (Va.)[b]
Boston[a]	Los Angeles[b]	Providence[a]
Buffalo[a]	Louisville	Rochester
Chicago[b]	Memphis	St. Louis[a]
Cincinnati[b]	Miami[a]	St. Paul
Cleveland[b]	Milwaukee	Sacramento
Columbus (Ohio)	Minneapolis[a]	San Antonio[b]
Dallas[b]	New Orleans	San Diego
Dayton[b]	New York[a]	San Francisco[b]
Denver	Newark[a]	San Jose
Detroit[a]	Oakland	Seattle[b]
Ft. Worth	Oklahoma City[b]	Syracuse
Hartford (Conn.)	Philadelphia	Washington, D.C.
Houston	Phoenix	Youngstown

[a] Twelve sample cities.
[b] Twenty-two sample cities (including those in the 12-city group).

influenced a great deal by annexation. As a consequence, it would appear that unless the city is annexing land, vacant land in central cities is fast disappearing. For those cities that cannot sprawl, a substantial growth of city population and employment will not be possible unless land-use densities are increased. Urban growth can be sustained only by an increase in density or by the consumption of more space at the periphery of the urban area.

The amount of space per person consumed for urban use varies according to the size of an urban area and with time (Maher and Bourne, 1969). These two characteristics can be illustrated by the use of land-consumption rates and land-absorption coefficients. *Land-consumption rates* measure the amount of urban land consumed per person at a particular date. For example, Feherdy (1971) quotes the following estimates of land-consumption rates for Montreal: 1952, 0.033 acres per person; 1961, 0.038 acres per person; and 1970, 0.042 acres per person. Though these rates represent quite high urban densities, it is apparent that the densities are decreasing over time. The changes in land consumption that are implied is measured by the *land-absorption coefficient*, which indicates the amount of new urban land consumed by each unit increase in urban population. For example, the Feherdy (1971) estimates can be used to calculate the following land-absorption coefficients for Montreal: 1952–1961, 0.054 new acres per additional person, and 1961–1970, 0.062 new acres per additional person. This increase in amount of space consumed over time is explained in greater detail with respect to urban population distributions in the next chapter.

The change in land consumption rates with city size is easy to document but requires some immediate explanation. Table 9.4 contains the average land-consumption rate for eight sizes of city ranging between 10,000 and 2 million population. The land-consumption rate decreases from 0.100 acres per person for cities of about 10,000 population to 0.057 for these of around 2 million. The indices have been estimated from a regression analysis of data obtained for 70 municipalities in southern Ontario and Quebec. The reason for this decrease in land-consumption rate with city size must be related to the higher degree of compactness required by large urban areas for their operation. Also, it is possible to build at greater densities in large cities, for there is usually sufficient demand to fill the specialized spaces of larger buildings.

The Location of Land Uses Within Urban Areas

Thus far we have determined the major uses of urban land and have implied that these uses consume disproportionate quantities of land in different parts of the city. In terms of developed urban land itself, the indication has been that much more land is developed within the central city than at the periphery. This situation is clearly evident in Chicago, where 90 percent or more of the land located within eight and a half miles of the CBD was developed in 1955, whereas beyond 16 miles less than 50 percent was developed for urban uses (Fig. 9.1). Thus it is evident that a very small proportion of the old, highly built-up part of the city is vacant (Browning, 1964).

The amount of developed land consumed for residential purposes at the center of the city is limited, however. Residential land in Chicago consumes 41.2 percent of the total developed land, but within two miles of the CBD less than 20 percent of the land is devoted to this use (Fig. 9.2). In this innermost zone the largest single use is the space occupied by streets, commercial activities, and transportation facilities. Streets and transportation facilities are major users of land in all zones, consuming respectively 31 percent and 11.7 percent of all developed land in Chicago. Commercial activities, on the other hand, use only 4.8 percent of all developed land within the city, but consume nearly one-quarter of all developed land at the center of the city. Manufacturing activities use only one-tenth of the land between four and 12 miles from the center of the city, and residential areas consume over one-third of the land in this area.

Table 9.4. LAND CONSUMPTION RATES FOR EIGHT DIFFERENT SIZES OF URBAN AREAS

Population Size of Urban Area	Land Consumption Rate
10,000	0.100
25,000	0.091
50,000	0.086
100,000	0.078
250,000	0.070
500,000	0.066
1,000,000	0.061
2,000,000	0.057

SOURCE: Yeates (1975), p. 3.21.

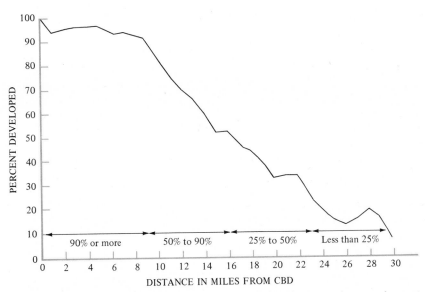

Fig. 9.1. Percentage of the total land in use by distance from the CBD, Chicago urban region. (*Source*: Browning, 1964, Fig. 1.)

ELEMENTARY LAND-USE THEORY

The ensuing chapters are concerned with a discussion of the various factors that affect the location of these various land uses. At the outset, however, it is important to develop a general theoretical base that casts some light on the distribution of the intensity of land use in urban areas. The major starting place for land-use theory is the work of Johann Heinrich von Thünin (1793–1850). Von Thünen's writings represent the first serious effort to systematize patterns in economic space (Hall, ed., 1966; Chisholm, 1962); and though his land-use theory was developed with respect to an agricultural environment, it has had great impact on the analysis of urban location problems.

Von Thünen envisaged the situation of a country with no connections with the outside world. A metropolis is located within an unbounded plain over which uniform soil and climatic characteristics prevail. Furthermore, transport possibilities are equal in any direction over this plain, though the costs of transportation increase with distance. The metropolis provides manufactured goods for the rural community, and the rural community provides the agricultural products for the workers in the metropolis. Prices for manufactured goods and agricultural products are stable and are set at the marketplace, which is the metropolis.

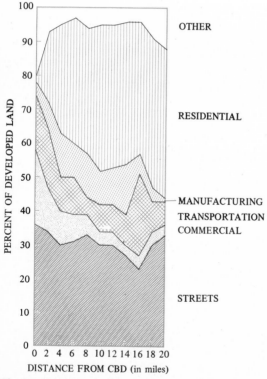

Fig. 9.2. Variations in the proportion of land in selected uses with distance from the CBD. (*Source:* based on Browning, 1964, pp. 34–35.)

Economic Rent

Assume that the price at the marketplace for one acre of wheat is four dollars. As all the land over the whole plain is equally fertile, one acre of wheat provides the same quantity at any location. Assume that there are three locations, A, B, and C (Fig. 9.3). A is closest to the marketplace, B is the next closest to the marketplace, and C is farthest from the marketplace. If the transportation cost for one acre of production of wheat from A to marketplace is 40 cents, A will receive $3.60 for one acre of production. B is farther away from the marketplace than A and his transportation cost can be assumed to be one dollar for one acre of production. The price that he actually receives, therefore, will be three dollars for one acre of wheat. C, the farthest away of all, has a transport cost of $1.50 for one acre of production. The price that he receives, therefore, is, in effect, $2.50 for one acre of production.

If all the farmers have equal standards of living and put in the same effort and have the same costs of production, they will all wish to locate at A or closer than A to the marketplace. C, for example, will perceive that he can make $1.10 more for exactly the same effort at A than at C. This difference, in effect, represents the economic rent of A with respect to C. In general terms, the economic rent can be defined as the difference in returns received from the use of a unit of land compared with that received at the margin of production. In this particular case, the difference is due solely to variations in distance.

Zonation of Land Use and Intensity Implications

In Figure 9.3 economic rent decreases with distance from the marketplace. The slope of the rent line is affected by the cost of transportation, which is in turn determined by the relative bulk, weight, and perishability of the commodity being transported, as well as by the distance that the commodity has to be transported. Assume now the existence of a second commodity, vegetables. Vegetables can be produced very

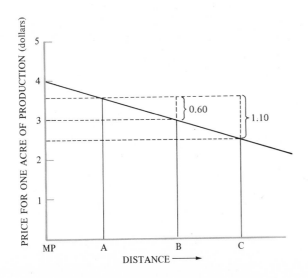

Fig. 9.3. Von Thünen's concept of economic rent. The economic rent of A with respect to C is $1.10, and of A with respect to B is $0.60.

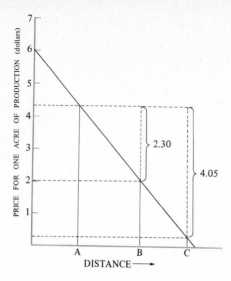

Fig. 9.4. Economic rent curves for vegetables. The economic rent of A with respect to C is $4.05, and of A with respect to B is $2.30.

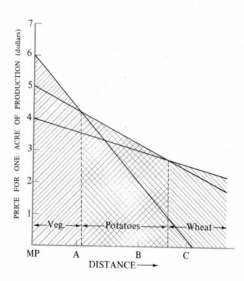

Fig. 9.5. Economic rent curves for three competing land uses.

intensively, but they are very bulky and perishable. As a consequence, the transportation cost for vegetables is very high. The price for the sale of one acre of production of vegetables is also high. Let us assume that this price is six dollars for one acre of vegetable production. Owing to the high transportation costs for transporting vegetables to the marketplace, the economic rent curve will be steep, as is indicated in Figure 9.4.

Assume the existence of another product, potatoes, for which the price at the marketplace is five dollars for one acre of production. The economic rent curve for this commodity is less steep than for vegetables, but steeper than that for wheat. This is because potatoes are not so highly perishable as vegetables, but they are more bulky than wheat. The farmer will always produce that crop which yields the highest price per acre. He will do this either out of choice or because he is forced to do it, because other farmers realize that they can produce that crop at a location and receive a greater return than he can for another crop at that particular location. As a consequence, vegetables will be produced closest to the marketplace, then potatoes, and then wheat (Fig. 9.5).

Thus the position of the crop vis-a-vis the marketplace is determined by the slope of its rent curve and the market price. Those crops with the steepest curves will always be located closest to the center, providing that the price is highest. The crops with a shallow rent curve will occupy the whole area if the price at the market is highest; otherwise they will occupy the more peripheral locations. By rotating the zones indicated in Figure 9.5, a series of land-use zones can be generated (Fig. 9.6).

Effect of Transportation Improvements

Transportation improvements result in a decrease in transportation cost for those areas located closest to the improved facility. The commodities that are most susceptible to improvements in transportation media are, of course, those that have the highest transportation cost. In Figure 9.7 the effect of water transportation on the surface configuration of land uses is shown. Because agricultural commodities can be hauled directly to the river's edge and thence moved to the city by inexpensive barge or boat, each zone of production becomes elongated in a direction roughly parallel to the stream. The innermost zone changes least because water transportation has little effect. However, for those commodities that are bulky, the innovation of water transportation is extremely important, as is indicated by the extension of the wood zone and the other crop zones along the water route.

Figure 9.8 presents an intuitive application of the land-use theory, at a high order of generality to the urban area. In this diagram the focus of accessibility is the central

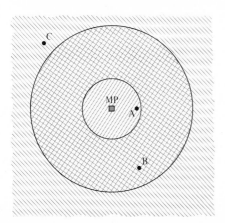

Fig. 9.6. Concentric land-use zones derived from rotating the economic rent curves shown in Fig. 9.5.

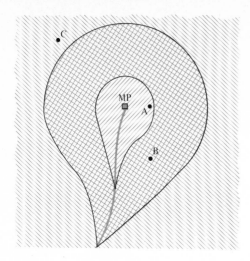

Fig. 9.7. Distortion in the concentricity of land-use zones resulting from an improvement in transportation.

business district, and four types of land use are arrayed with respect to this location. Those activities requiring the greatest centrality with respect to the urban market locate in the innermost zones, while those least susceptible to accessibility considerations locate at the periphery (Nourse, 1968). It must be remembered, however, that an urban area is not a surface over which transport is homogeneous in any direction; therefore considerable distortion to this highly generalized arrangement is to be expected. These distortions are discussed in detail in the ensuing chapters.

DESCRIPTIVE MODELS OF URBAN LAND USE

In this section we shall deal with three descriptive models of urban land use. The first is Burgess's concentric-zone model, which was formulated in the early 1920s (Park et al., 1925). The second is Hoyt's sector theory (1939), and the third is the Harris-Ullman (1945) multiple-nuclei model. Finally, we shall see how the land-use development of one urban area, that of Calgary, fits these models through time.

The Burgess Concentric-Zone Model

The concentric zone model suggests that the pattern of growth in the city can best be understood in terms of five concentric zones and a sixth lying beyond the immediate confines of the urban area (Fig. 9.9). This particular model was developed to try to explain the sociological pattern of the North American city and was based primarily on intensive research in the Chicago area during the early part of the present century. The six concentric zones are:

1. The central business district (CBD), which is considered to be the focus of commercial, social, and civic life, and of transportation. This area contains the department stores, smart shops, high office buildings, clubs, banks, hotels, theaters, museums, and so on, which are of importance to the whole urban area.

2. The fringe of the CBD. This second zone surrounds the CBD and is an area of wholesaling, truck, and railroad depots.

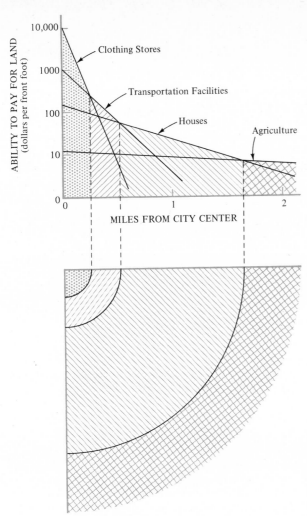

Fig. 9.8. Different activities require different levels of accessibility.

3. The zone in transition. This is a zone of residential deterioration that used to be quite wealthy, but as the city expanded and immigration occurred from rural areas and from overseas, this area became filled with low-income families and individuals. As a consequence, it contains the slums and rooming houses that are so common to the peripheral areas of the CBD. Business and light manufacturing encroach into this area because of the intensive demand for services and supply of cheap labor.

4. The zone of independent workingmen's homes. This zone consists primarily of industrial workers, who have escaped from the zone of transition. It might be regarded, therefore, as an area of second-generation immigrants and families who have had enough time to accumulate sufficient wealth to be able to purchase their own homes.

5. High-class residences. This is a zone of better residences containing single-family dwellings and exclusive restricted districts. There are a few high-income apartment buildings.

6. Commuters' zone. This is the outermost zone, containing a broad commuting area. These are the suburban areas containing satellite cities and middle- and upper-class residences along rail lines or rapid transit.

It can be perceived that the Burgess model is dynamic. It involves the concept of continuous immigration into the urban area and assimilation of these people into the "American way of life" via a process of wealth accumulation and family stability that enables them to move into the middle-income stream. The conceptual basis of the model is founded primarily on the socioeconomic scene of North America in the latter part of the nineteenth and the early twentieth centuries, when there was enormous immigration from Europe. Today the immigration into urban areas is primarily from urban and "small-town" North America; and in the United States this consists to a large extent of the immigration of blacks from the urban and rural South. The rate of assimilation of these people is extremely slow and has resulted in the major social problems of the American city today. In Canada, there is still large-scale immigration from the country to the major cities, for since 1945 at least one-fifth of the increase in population is attributable to this component.

The Sector Theory

The sector theory has been developed with respect to the movement of residential neighborhoods in the American city. Though it is primarily concerned with the movement of high-rent neighborhoods, it has implications for other types of housing as well. Basically, the theory states that high-rent areas follow definite sectoral paths outward from the center of the city as the urban area grows. Concomitantly, if one sector of a city first develops as a low-rent residential area, it will tend to retain that character over long distances as the sector is extended through the process of the city's growth. Thus

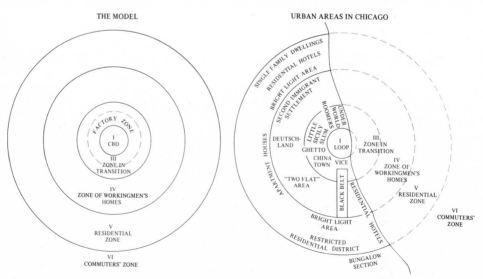

Fig. 9.9. The Burgess concentric-zone model of urban structure. (*Source:* after Park et al., 1925, Charts I and II.)

though the sector theory is basically applied to the location of residential areas, it is nevertheless a notable general descriptive statement. The details of Hoyt's model will be discussed in Chapter 10.

The Multiple-Nuclei Theory

Harris and Ullman (1945), recognizing the shortcomings of the concentric-zone theory and the sector theory, suggest that the city has developed a number of areas that group around separate nuclei. They also suggest that a grouping of specialized facilities has developed, such as retail districts, port districts, manufacturing districts, university districts, and so on. These activities tend to group together because they profit from cohesion, such as wholesale merchants and financial institutions. On the other hand, certain unlike activities are detrimental to each other, such as heavy industry and light industry, which are usually not found together, for the former is smoky and dirty and the latter is suburban in type, using electrical power. Also, in many cases towns grew by combining together, such as Minneapolis–St. Paul (Dickinson, 1964). As a consequence, one would expect to find a division of the city based upon grouping of certain activities. Such a grouping is indicated in Figure 9.10.

One of the problems of the three descriptive models just discussed is that they are overly simplistic. They try to explain a land-use pattern without clearly stating any assumptions. Also, it is very difficult to distinguish the different location decisions behind commercial and industrial development and residential location. A worthwhile descriptive model should include these decisions in the form of theories. Models of this type are developed and discussed later. In fact, Smith (1962), in a study of Calgary, states that these three models are not independent and that they all have some relevance.

The Internal Structure of Calgary

Hoyt's sector theory, however, seems to be most meaningful with respect to Calgary. The innermost of Burgess's five concentric zones—the CBD and the wholesale light manufacturing core—and the surrounding residential zone in transition are read-

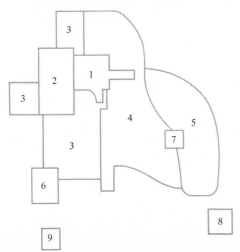

1 Central business district
2 Wholesale light manufacturing
3 Low–class residential
4 Medium–class residential
5 High–class residential
6 Heavy manufacturing
7 Outlying business district
8 Residential suburb
9 Industrial suburb

Fig. 9.10. The Harris-Ullman multiple-nuclei model of urban structure. (*Source*: Harris and Ullman, 1945, Fig. 5.)

ily apparent in Calgary, but the remaining zones are by no means clear. Broad general concentric patterns occur, but they are disrupted by radial cross zones of industry. Consequently the sector diagram of Calgary, Figure 9.11, includes most of the major elements of the land-use pattern in a way that would not have been possible in a concentric-zone diagram. Furthermore, the sector model does recognize the essential dynamics of Calgary's growth, which is the outward progression of generalized land-use types along radial lines of transportation. One of the major reasons for this is that residential land use has avoided areas of potential industrial value, such as the Bow Valley, and sectoral growth between the industrial areas has been encouraged by zoning.

There is evidence in the most recent diagram for 1961 that the Calgary pattern is breaking down into a more flexible multiple-nuclei pattern, with the CBD and wholesaling district and the Bow Valley industrial zone still being dominant. Newer industrial estates and residential areas are developing at the periphery of the city, causing the growth of further commercial business zones in that area. This trend is accelerating today, with many areas containing residential sprawl beyond the urban area.

A General Descriptive Model

Taking these various changes into consideration, it might be possible to develop a general descriptive model that pertains to the current era. This model is presented in diagrammatic form in Figure 9.12. The first zone is the central business district, which is the area of maximum vertical development of office buildings, the largest department stores, and numerous recreational, financial, and entertainment facilities. The second area can be described as the fringe of the CBD, which contains elements of a sector pattern radiating out from the city center. This area will be most prominent in those urban areas where there is a waterfront running through the downtown area. It contains blighted residences as well as wholesaling districts and industrial sectors.

The third area is the middle zone or the gray area as described by Hoover and Vernon (1959). In this area one finds a mix of activities, including high-rent apartment buildings and low-rent areas usually related to industrial sectors. There is also middle-income housing, particularly of the two-family variety, with the highest densities of housing prevailing toward the fringe of the CBD and the lowest densities at the periphery. The fourth zone is a concentric peripheral area consisting primarily of single-family residences of a middle-income variety. It is in this area that there has been great development of light industry, particularly of the kind that uses large quantities of electricity and needs enormous amounts of space for horizontal expansion. This type of industry is often truck-oriented and is therefore found on urban arteries and close to limited-access highways. The peripheral zone also contains large shopping centers, which need vast areas of space for parking and which serve both the gray area and the zones beyond this peripheral belt.

The fifth zone consists of radial suburbs that string out along older commuter railroads and the newer high-speed limited-access expressways and throughways feeding into the heart of the modern city. Upper- and middle-income suburbs are found closer to these transport arteries. Between these radial fingers one finds the interstitial zones. This area consists of a mix of subdivision housing, truck farming, and dairying activities. Residential subdivisions are rapidly taking the place of farmland, which is often held vacant by speculators. These subdivisions are developed by real estate promoters as high-income, middle-income, and low-income subdivisions, depending on

the intensity of development and array of services offered to the subdiv
area of the most rapidly expanding residential development in North A

LOCATION AND INTENSITY OF LAND USE

This section is concerned with a discussion of factors influencing the in
use. As it is believed that the value of land at a location is determined to
intensity of land use, and on the other hand that high land costs exert ve
sure to increase densities, this section will be concerned primarily wit

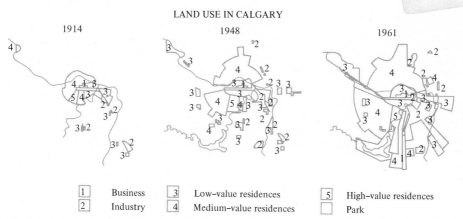

LAND USE IN CALGARY

Fig. 9.11. The sectoral distribution of land uses in Calgary, Canada, 1914, 1948, and 1961. (*Source*: after Smith, 1962, Figs. 6, 7, and 8.)

1	Business	3	Low–value residences	5	High–value residences
2	Industry	4	Medium–value residences		Park

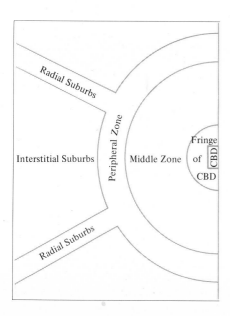

Fig. 9.12. Idealized structure of urban areas. (*Source*: after Taaffe et al., 1963, Fig. 1.1.)

factors of a spatial nature that influence land values are discussed in general terms and then applied specifically to the city of Chicago. Furthermore, the effect of zoning on land use and land values is discussed, and a specific case examined in north Chicago.

Land Value and Intensity of Land Use

A number of writers such as Hoyt (1933, 1960), Muth (1961), and Knos (1962) have indicated that there is a complex interrelationship between intensity of use and the structure of land values. This seems clear from the discussion of von Thünen's theory of economic rent and its relationship to the intensity of land use—the more intensive the use, the higher the economic rent pertaining to a piece of land. In von Thünen's model, this intensity of use depends on location in relation to the market. In a perfect economy, where every person is able to bid freely for a piece of land, the contract rent for a plot of land would be raised so that it would be equal to its economic rent. Of course, in many instances in the real world this true economic rent is never the real contract rent for a given location. Land ownership does not change very quickly, particularly in older established urban areas, and there is very rarely a perfectly competitive situation.

A Definition of Urban Land Value

The value of a piece of land should, however, be related to the use to which it is put. Urban land economists seem to be in general agreement about the way in which an individual or firm estimates the value of a given piece of land. It seems that the value of urban land results from a "discounting of future net income attributable to land by virtue of its location" (Wendt, 1957, p. 229). This theoretical definition of land value has been presented by Knos (1962, p. 7) as follows:

$$LV_i = \frac{R_i - C_i}{r}$$

where

LV_i = land value at any ith location

R_i = expected gross revenue to be received from the property, including the improvements. This expected gross revenue depends on the size of the market, the average income of the spending units within the market, and relative competition to be expected from other uses.

C_i = expected costs, such as local property taxes, operating costs, interest on capital invested in present and future improvements, and depreciation allowances on present and future improvements.

r = the capitalization rate, which is the average interest rate for all investments. This item is a function of current interest rates, allowances for expected risk, and expectations concerning capital gain.

Economic models of this kind occur in Wendt (1957), Hurd (1924), and Ratcliff (1949, 1957). The point that is geographically relevent in this rather classical economic definition of land value is that the expected revenues and the expected costs change with location (Wendt, 1961). Furthermore, the intensity of land use is now measured in monetary terms as the amount to be accrued from a particular location.

It is quite easy to envisage this kind of model applying to industry and commercial activities. The same kind of model can be developed for housing locations, though it may not be possible to measure all aspects of revenue and costs in monetary terms. For housing many intangibles must be taken into account. It is quite clear that transportation costs theoretically must play an important part in residential land-value determination. The farther a person is located from his place of work, the greater his expected costs because of increased transportation costs. However, this kind of theoretical discussion is offset by many individual preferences. A person may live miles away from his work place because of friends or relatives that the family does not wish to leave or because he simply prefers the district.

Thus it is the location of the site that is the chief factor in determining the value of land in an urban environment. The important question arising at this juncture is: Location with respect to what? Hurd (1924) neatly summarized the problem as follows: "Since value depends on economic rent, and rent on location, and location on convenience, and convenience on nearness, we may eliminate the intermediate steps and say that value depends on nearness. The next question is nearness to what?" (Hurd, 1924, p. 13). According to Pendleton (1962), nearness or accessibility to something really means distance, measured in some appropriate way. The question therefore can be restated as: Distance from what?

Accessibility and Land Value

If we presume that city growth spreads from a central core on a level plain, then in terms of commercial location the center of the city should be a major focus of high land values. The reason for this is that as the city develops and expands, the communication network of the urban area expands radially, thereby ensuring that all locations at equal

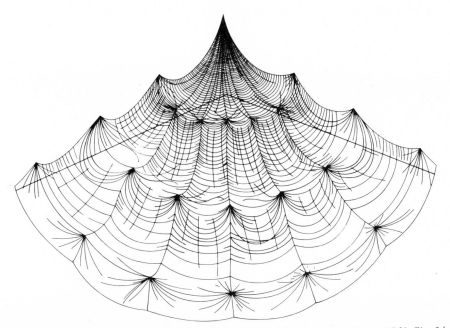

Fig. 9.13. Diagrammatic representation of urban land values. (*Source*: Berry, 1963, Fig. 3.)

distances from the center are equally accessible to the center of the city. As a consequence, the center of the city is the area of minimum aggregate travel cost for the whole urban area; and commercial activities requiring the largest hinterland possible, either as a labor source or as a market, will desire to locate close to the center. A concentrated grouping of those activities requiring central locations results in the formation of a central business district. Thus the peak-value intersection (PVI) or the corner of highest land value in the central business district is theoretically the point of minimum aggregate travel costs for the whole urban area.

As a city grows and expands, outlying business centers will be established; and the major arteries connecting these business centers with each other and with a central business district will become ribbons of commercial and business development. The land-value pattern should reflect varying accessibilities to these different centers in the hierarchy. Over the whole city relative accessibility to the central business district would be important for all areas, and individual parts of the city should reflect varying accessibility to outlying business centers. This particular situation is suggested in Figure 9.13, wherein the land-value surface is reflected as a circus tent, the highest point being at the CBD, with the ridge lines being the urban arteries of relatively greater land value, and the intersections giving rise to local peaks.

A Land Value Surface

The hypothetical structure of a land-value surface can be examined with respect to Chicago for the period between 1910 and 1960 (Yeates, 1965a). Land-value data can be obtained from Olcott's *Blue Book of Chicago Land Values*, which has been published annually since 1907. These valuations give a front-foot value for every block in the city. Corner valuations, except in a few instances, are not given, but have to be estimated from the front-foot estimates using certain rules laid down by Olcott. Thus, though within-block variations are difficult to analyze, between-block variations can be studied. Furthermore, Garner (1966) indicates that there is a very close correlation between assessed values and Olcott's estimates of land value.

The land-value maps (Fig. 9.14) are constructed from a sample of 484 front-foot land values located within the 1960 city limits of Chicago. In order to facilitate later statistical analysis, the data are normalized by means of a logarithmic transformation; and in order to facilitate comparison of the land-value maps between the time periods, the transformed data are converted into standard scores. The isoline interval chosen for each map is one standard deviation, so all maps can be compared because the intervals are comparable and related to their respective means.

A visual analysis of maps yields some interesting observations. Throughout the whole time period, the highest land values are found within and adjacent to the central business district, the center being the peak-value intersection at State and Madison, and from this area there is a sharp decline in all directions. This decline was logarithmically fairly uniform in 1910, but by 1960 it did not exhibit the same consistency. The contraction of the mean isoline and the general reduction of land values on the south side of the central business district are quite evident, as is the presence of residual outliers, which indicate the position of regional business and shopping centers. It could be suggested, therefore, that the effect of distance from, and consequently access to, the central business district on land values appears to have diminished in importance during

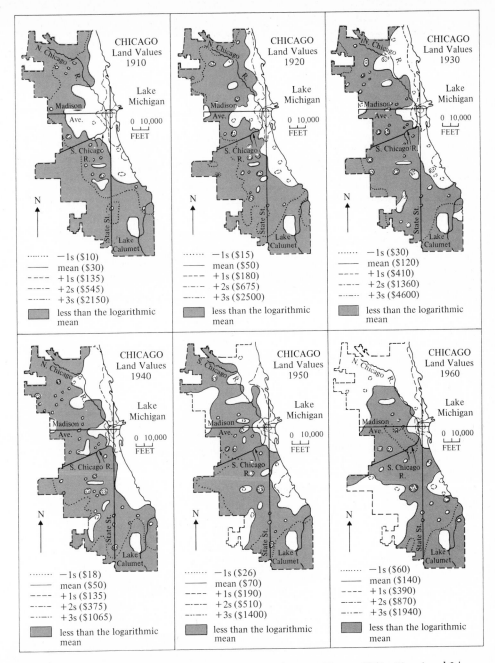

Fig. 9.14. Land-value surfaces in Chicago, 1910–1960. (*Source*: Yeates, 1965a, Figs. 1 and 2.)

the past 50 years, while the front-foot value of locations in the vicinity of outlying regional service centers has increased.

A further locational factor that appears to influence the general spatial distribution of land values is Lake Michigan, for relatively higher land values are found close to the lake shore. The 1950 and 1960 maps, however, suggest that land values within the vicinity of Lake Michigan on the north side of the city are generally increasing and higher than those on the south side, where values are declining. This is possibly a reflection of the nonwhite, low-income nature of the southern area, which discourages high-rise apartment speculation.

Land at the periphery of the city appears to be becoming relatively more valuable than land in the middle of the city. On the 1960 map, this tendency is much more strongly developed in the north than in the southwest and hardly present at all in the west. The great rise in land values at the periphery of the city in the north is probably a reflection of the high-income nature of this area. The absence of any rise to the west results from its being closer to the center of the city than the boundary to the north or south; and thus peripheral developments that are within the city on the north and south are absent in that area.

Thus it would seem that in the case of Chicago the effect of three specific locational factors should be examined. The first is the effect of variation in location with respect to the central business district, the center of which is defined as the intersection of State Street and Madison Street, the PVI of Chicago. The second is the effect of variation in the location of sites with respect to Lake Michigan. Lake Michigan appears to have been an area of amenity attractions, which have increased in importance during the past 50 years. The third is variation in location with respect to regional shopping centers. For the purpose of this discussion, those outlying shopping centers defined as "major regional center" and "smaller shoppers' goods centers" by Berry (1963) will be combined and classified as regional centers.

A fourth locational factor that might well be important, as defined in the theoretical analysis by von Thünen, is location with respect to transportation improvements. In this discussion the effect of the elevated-subway stations on land values is examined. This is the only variable that changes through time, because the rapid-transit system has changed considerably in elevated coverage during the last 50 years, maximum mileage having been attained in the 1930's. It is expected that this variable will prove to be more important in early years than in later years, because in the early part of the century people were more dependent on this form of rapid transit. In today's automobile society, the elevated-subway system is not quite so important.

Table 9.5.   CHICAGO LAND VALUES: CORRELATION COEFFICIENTS (R), COEFFICIENTS OF DETERMINATION (R^2), AND REGRESSION COEFFICIENTS, 1910 AND 1960

Year	R	R^2	C	M	E	S
1910	0.873	76.2%	−0.935	−0.469	−0.300	−0.035*
1960	0.335	11.2%	−0.250	−0.120	+0.029*	−0.124

*Not significantly different from zero at t (0.05).

A Descriptive Model of Urban Land Values

The factors influencing the spatial distribution of land values outlined above can be examined together in a multiple regression model. In general form, a multiple regression model can be represented as follows:

$$Y = a + b_{y1.234}X_1 + b_{Y2.134}X_2 + b_{Y3.124}X_3 + b_{Y4.123}X_4 + e$$

where

Y = the dependent variable
X_1, X_2, X_3, X_4 = four independent variables
b = regression coefficients pertaining to each independent variable
a = a constant, sometimes referred to as the Y intercept
e = an error term

An important feature of a multiple regression model is that the b coefficients indicate the change in the dependent variable associated with a unit change in an independent variable, with all the other independent variables in the equation being held constant. Thus, $b_{Y2.134}$ is read as "the change in Y per unit change in X_2 with X_1, X_3, and X_4 held constant." For the sake of convenience, this profusion of subscripts will be reduced in the ensuing discussion to the form b_1, b_2, b_3, and b_4.

The hypothesized model can be expressed with respect to the spatial distribution of Chicago land values as follows:

$$V_i = a - b_1C_i - b_2M_i - b_3E_i - b_4S_i$$

where

V_i = logarithm of the land value at any ith location
C_i = logarithm of distance of the ith location from the CBD
M_i = logarithm of distance of the ith location from Lake Michigan
B_i = logarithm of distance of the ith location from the nearest elevated-subway station
S_i = logarithm of distance of the ith location from the nearest regional shopping center
i = 1, 2, 3 . . . n, n being the sample size based on a systematic stratified random sample design of 484 points

The data have been transformed into logarithms in order to produce a situation that satisfies one of the major assumptions of tests of significance using the normal distribution; that is, that the residuals are distributed normally. The signs of the regression coefficients are negative because the discussion has indicated that land values should decrease with distance from the CBD, Lake Michigan, stations of the elevated-subway system, and regional shopping centers.

The above model has been tested with respect to the spatial distribution of land values in Chicago for 1910 and 1960. The multiple correlation coefficients, coefficients of determination, and regression coefficients are presented in Table 9.5. The model describes the 1910 land-value distribution extremely well. The four variables taken together explain 76.2 percent of the variation in land values. Furthermore, the signs of the regression coefficients are as hypothesized. As all the variables are measured in common distance units, the magnitudes of the regression coefficients indicate the relative importance of each variable in the equation. Clearly, the most important variable is distance from the CBD. Thus it may be concluded that in 1910 relative accessibility of locations to the CBD was the basic determinant of land values. Accessibility to Lake Michigan and stations on the elevated system were the second and third most important determinants of land values. In general, outlying regional shopping centers do not significantly affect the land-value surface.

The model for 1960 explains very little of the variation in land values, but the signs of the regression coefficients are as hypothesized, with one exception. The exception is the value of land with respect to distance from stations on the elevated-subway system. The regression coefficient pertaining to this variable is positive though not significantly different from zero. The change in sign and value of the regression coefficient provides some land-value evidence for the relative decline in importance of this form of rapid transit in Chicago. Although the signs of the other variables are as hypothesized, the values of the regression coefficients are much less than they were in 1910. Distance from the CBD is still the most important variable, but the relative accessibility of locations to Lake Michigan and regional shopping centers is now equally important.

Thus, as far as the growth of Chicago during the last half century is concerned, it would appear that centrifugal forces (Colby, 1933) have become paramount and are reflected in the changing land-value surface. Highway improvements and the almost universal use of the automobile, plus social changes resulting in a shorter work week and generally higher wages and salaries, have meant that families and entrepreneurs are less inclined to locate near the center of the city or close to their work places. Consequently the effect of accessibility to the central part of the city on land values is not so important as it has been in the past. Furthermore, whereas in 1910 commercial, business, and industrial activities as well as housing were relatively free to locate in any part of the city, during recent decades this freedom has been limited by zoning.

The Effect of Zoning

As a city grows it becomes increasingly obvious that land has to be set aside for certain uses and that certain elements in the land-use mosaic should be kept separate. Noxious industries should not be allowed to locate close to schools, and areas zoned for commercial use should be kept apart from housing developments. Areas set apart for housing should be zoned for intensity of development, because people buying property in a low-density, single-family area would not wish to see their district ruined by high-rise apartments, which would raise population densities and create social problems with which the district might be unable to cope. For these reasons, and many others, city governments increasingly zone land use to ensure the best development of the urban area.

Thus the growth and development of the city through time would seem to warrant an investigation of the effects of zoning on land-value variations. Of course, the extent to which zoning is rigorously applied varies from city to city in North America. Indeed, it has been said that "Houston, Texas, which has grown up without the exercise of any zoning powers at all, is little different from any other North American city" (Buchanan, 1963, p. 225). However, zoning has been in operation in Chicago since the 1930's, and its regulations have been followed with a degree of rigor since World War II.

Zoning and Land Values in Rogers Park, Chicago

In the Rogers Park district of north Chicago (Fig. 9.15) zoning has resulted in fairly uniform residential development (Yeates, 1965b). The most widespread land use in the area in 1960 is classified as general residence (Fig. 9.15), which means that apartment building is permitted over the whole area; and, in fact, three-story apartments are most common. The occupants of the apartments and single-family houses are generally of middle income and white. Two other considerable land uses consist of areas zoned for business and commercial use. The business areas demarcate zones of retail and shopping activities, whereas the commercial areas delineate zones occupied by financial activities, small workshops, and hotels. There are two other land uses found in the Rogers Park district, but the variations of land values in these areas are not very great.

The Rogers Park district is far enough away from the central business district in Chicago for that particular distance variable to have very little effect on the land-value surface. Comparison of Figures 9.16 and 9.17 indicates that the spatial distribution of land values in the business and commercial zones is affected by forces different from those in the residential zones. In Figure 9.16 there appears to be a very close relationship between land values in areas zoned residential and distance from Lake Michigan. The area bordering on Lake Michigan has, in fact, become an outstanding area of high land values for residential purposes for a number of reasons. In the first place, it has great amenity attractions; the beaches and bathing areas along the lake shore provide excellent facilities for Chicagoans during the hot and often humid summer. For city dwellers the open view and evening lake breezes make urban dwelling a little more pleasant. Furthermore, Lake Shore Drive and the elevated rapid transit facility running along the lake connect the CBD to suburbs north of the city limits of Chicago. Thus, locations along the lake shore are enhanced in value by the nearby presence of these transportation advantages.

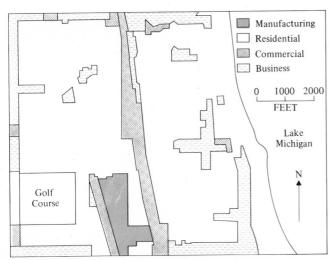

Fig. 9.15. Land-use zoning in Rogers Park, Chicago, 1961. (*Source:* Yeates, 1965b, Fig. 70.)

Figure 9.17 indicates that land values in business and commercial areas are not related to distance from Lake Michigan at all. In fact, there is very little reason for business or commercial activities to locate near the lake, as such a location would involve a truncation of their potential market area. It is reasonable to hypothesize that land values in business and commercial areas would, in fact, be most influenced by distance from the center of the outlying shopping areas. Figure 9.18 indicates that such an arrangement does, in fact, occur. The theoretical basis for this arrangement is discussed in Chapter 13.

Zoning and Planning

The evidence discussed with respect to changes in the spatial distribution of Chicago land values between 1910 and 1960 indicates the important effect of zoning on the land-value surface as cities grow. As the urban area expands and the population increases, it becomes more and more necessary to plan city services and land uses. Zoning is the method most commonly used to plan and control land uses and to separate various uses in order to maintain property values and appearance. The individual or firm is then allowed freedom of choice of location within the appropriate zoned area.

Theoretically, the optimum zoning is that which allows the land to be occupied by its highest and best use. The concept of highest and best use refers to the use that envisages the highest discounted future net income at a location. It would seem that the attainment of this goal by zoning would be extremely difficult. The aim, if the only goal is that of maximizing a taxable base, is sound. It is therefore necessary that a zoning board take very good care to satisfy the demand for each kind of land use. If too little commercial land is provided, for example, the land values in areas zoned commercial may be inflated; on the other hand, if too much land is provided, values may fall and submarginal commercial activities may enter.

In a growing urban area the problem of determining the amount of land to be zoned in each category takes on another dimension, that of trying to forecast future demand for a given general land use. It is in this situation that zoning and urban growth

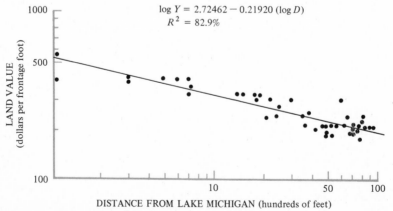

Fig. 9.16. Variation in residential land values with distance from Lake Michigan, Rogers Park, Chicago. (*Source:* Yeates, 1965b, Fig. 74.)

are particularly interrelated. Zoning is highly desirable, but as the urban area grows, the quantity and location of areas devoted to specific uses have to change. In too many cases, rezoning takes a great deal of time and numerous public hearings. The result is that the decision concerning land in the past is often stamped upon land in the present. Thus zoning may result in a slow adjustment to new conditions arising from urban growth. The urban geographer, by attempting to discern the factors that influence the internal structure of urban areas, is groping toward a theoretical base that will permit planning for the continuous readjustment of urban land use.

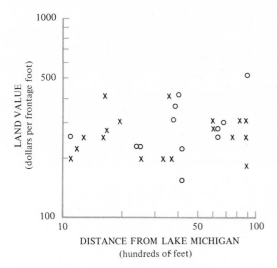

Fig. 9.17. Variation in business and commercial land values with distance from Lake Michigan, Rogers Park, Chicago. (*Source:* Yeates, 1965b, Fig. 75.)

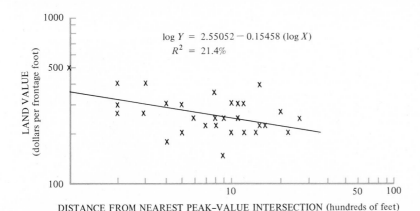

Fig. 9.18. Variation in business and commercial land values with distance from outlying shopping areas, Rogers Park, Chicago. (*Source:* Yeates, 1965b, Fig. 76.)

10
THE
LOCATION OF
RESIDENCES

We have observed in the previous chapter that residential land use consumes by far the largest proportion of the total developed land within urban areas. According to the data provided by Niedercorn and Hearle (1964), residential land use in large North American urban areas consumes 39 percent of the total developed land. This figure is supported by the information of Bartholomew (1955) for central cities in North America, though for smaller urban areas the proportion may be much higher. For example, in 70 municipalities with populations greater than 4000 in southern Ontario and Quebec, the average proportion of urbanized land devoted to residential use is 55.6 percent. In this chapter we shall be concerned with three particular aspects of urban residential location. In the first section the general location of people within urban areas is discussed, and some mathematical models concerning the distribution of population densities are presented. In the second section we shall discuss some general hypotheses that have been formulated with respect to various patterns of residential location in the North American city. In the third section we shall attempt to determine those factors that have the greatest influence in the locational decision.

THE DISTRIBUTION OF PEOPLE WITHIN URBAN AREAS

A brief analysis of population density maps of two North American cities reveals a few general characteristics (Fig. 10.1). Population densities on the whole seem to be greater at the center of the city than at the periphery, and the decline in the population density surface away from the center of the city is very steep at first and then flattens out. There are, of course, some departures from this general pattern. In particular, in some cases the density of population at the center of the city seems to be relatively low, increases to a peak, and then decreases away from the center, as previously described. Furthermore, there are noticeable instances where population densities tend to be relatively higher along the major radials leading into the central city. Aside from these departures, however, it seems that a very close relationship exists between population density distribution and general accessibility within urban areas.

Changes in Population Density Patterns

We have observed in Chapter 8 that as the city has grown and expanded, the distribution of people within the urban area has changed accordingly. In the early days of the pedestrian North American city, population densities were very high at the center

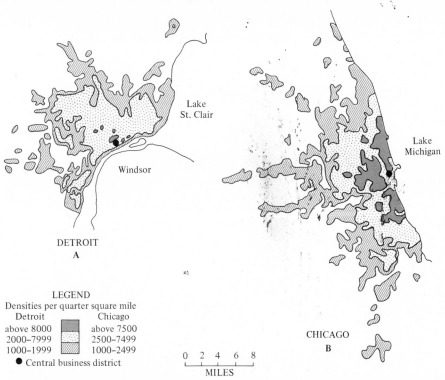

Fig. 10.1. Population density maps of (A) Detroit, 1953, and (B) Chicago, 1956. (*Sources: after Detroit Metropolitan Area Traffic Study*, 1955, Map 4, and *Chicago Area Transportation Study*, 1959, Map 12.)

of the city and decreased rapidly from the central focus of economic activity. With changing technology and the accompanying decentralization of economic activities, the population of the North American city has spread out accordingly. These changes are well illustrated with respect to Toronto, Montreal, and Ottawa in Figure 10.2. From these diagrams it can be observed that population densities were very high in the center

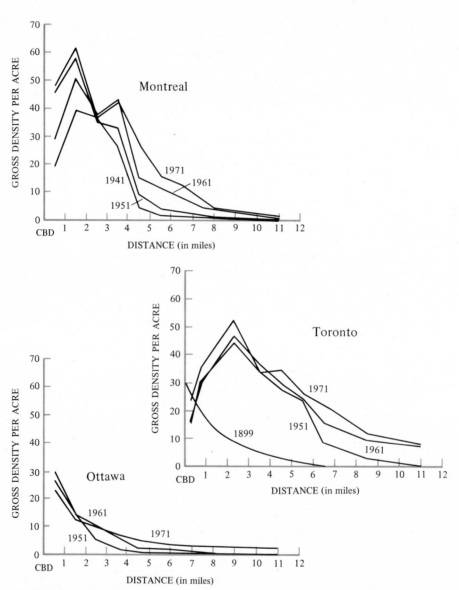

Fig. 10.2. Population density-distance relationships: Montreal, Toronto, Ottawa, various years. (*Source*: Yeates, 1975, Fig. 3.2.)

of the city some years ago, but in each case there has been a flattening of the curve over time. In the case of Toronto in 1899, population densities decreased rapidly with distance from the core to as far out as six miles. In 1951 the general increase in total population resulted in much higher population densities, but the general form of the curve was still the same, though population densities were tending to decrease at the center of the city. In 1961 this curve showed some signs of beginning to flatten out.

These recent changes in population density are well illustrated by the maps for metropolitan Toronto from 1951 to 1963 (Fig. 10.3). It can be observed that in 1951, population densities are very high in the center of the city, though there is a general decrease right at the center, which is the intersection of Queen and Yonge Streets, and that there is a general decline to the periphery. However, a very strong radial spread of relatively higher population densities is observed along the major radials, particularly leading to the north, northwest, west, and east. The map for 1956 indicates a contraction of the highest density area, but a general spreading out of densities ranging between 627 and 3200 persons per square mile and the beginnings of an in-filling between the major radials. This trend is continued through to 1961, particularly with an in-filling in the northwest between the major radials leading to the west and north. Finally, in 1963, the last map indicates that the area of lower population densities at the center of the city has expanded slightly and that the in-filling between the radials has continued apace. Concomitantly, densities along the radials have continued to increase, particularly at the periphery of the metropolitan area.

These changes are summarized quite well in the population growth-rate map in Figure 10.4. This map illustrates the variation in growth rate of population in metropolitan Toronto for the ten-year period between 1951 and 1961. During this period those areas closest to the center of the city decreased in population while the greater increases are found at the periphery of the city and in the interstitial areas to the northeast. Thus

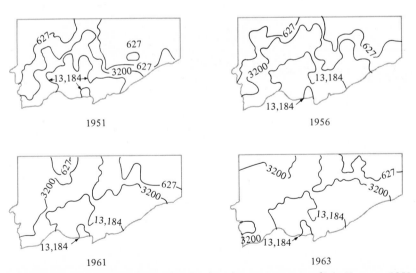

Fig. 10.3. Changes in population density distribution in metropolitan Toronto, 1951–1963. Population densities are measured in persons per square mile. (*Source:* Latham, 1967, from data on pages 53–59.)

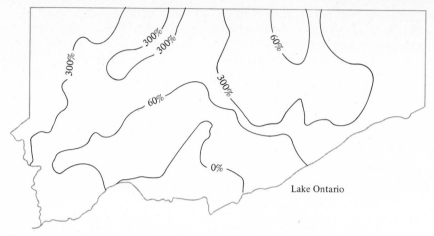

Fig. 10.4. Population growth rate in metropolitan Toronto, 1951–1961. The isolines show the percentage change during the period from 1951 to 1961.

the pattern of growth rates indicates a decline at the center of the city and high positive growth rates at the periphery. This pattern is typical of most North American cities, in which the population growth rate increases with distance from the center of the city rather than decreases with distance from the center of the city, as with population densities.

Some Mathematical Models of Urban Population Densities

One of the most stimulating attempts at postulating a general mathematical statement concerning the distribution of population densities within urban areas has been presented by Colin Clark (1951b). Having collected data for many urban areas throughout the world, he concludes that urban population densities are related in some systematic way to distance from or accessibility to the center of the city. Specifically, he suggests that urban population densities decrease in a negative exponential fashion (that is, decrease at a decreasing rate) with distance from the CBD. The formulation of this model is presented in equation form as follows:

$$D_d = D_o e - bd$$

where

D_d = population density at distance d from the CBD
D_o = a constant indicating the population density at distance zero; i.e., at the center of the city
$-b$ = a parameter indicating the rate of decrease of population with distance; i.e., the slope of the curve
d = the variable distance
e = base of the natural logarithms

In general terms, all that an equation of this type indicates is that population densities decrease rapidly at first with distance from the CBD and then tend to flatten out. This situation is expressed in Figure 10.5, which, as can be observed, is very close to the situation expressed in three time periods for Ottawa in Figure 10.2 and for portions of the curves for Montreal and Toronto. The curve presented in Figure 10.5 can be transformed into a straight line by the transformation of the population density variable into natural logarithms:

$$lnD_d = lnD_d - bd$$

where

lnD_d = natural logarithm of the population density at distance d from the CBD
lnD_o = natural logarithm of the constant

The evidence from various North American cities which Clark produces as support for this suggested model is presented in Figure 10.6, where the population densities are averages for annular rings, the loci of which are at the center of all the cities. The population density data are transformed into natural logarithms.

The Density Gradient and Time
From the data presented by Clark, it can also be observed not only that the densities decrease with distance from the center of the city, but that the lines are generally steeper in 1900 than in 1940. The steepness of the line is indicated by the parameter b, which represents the rate of decrease of population densities with distance from the center of the city. In all cases, the value of this parameter has decreased between 1900 and 1940. For example, in St. Louis the b parameter has a value of $-.75$ in 1900 but $-.45$ in 1940. If the value of b were zero, the population density curve would be flat, indicating that population densities were evenly distributed throughout the urban area.
Newling (1966) regards this as one of the most interesting features of Clark's data, and after examining information from other urban areas he concludes that the population density gradient decreases through time in a constant, systematic fashion. In

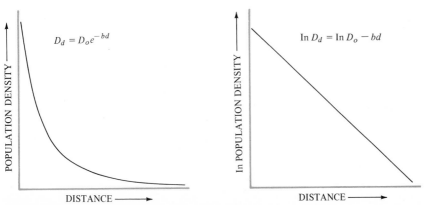

Fig. 10.5. Clark's model of urban population density.

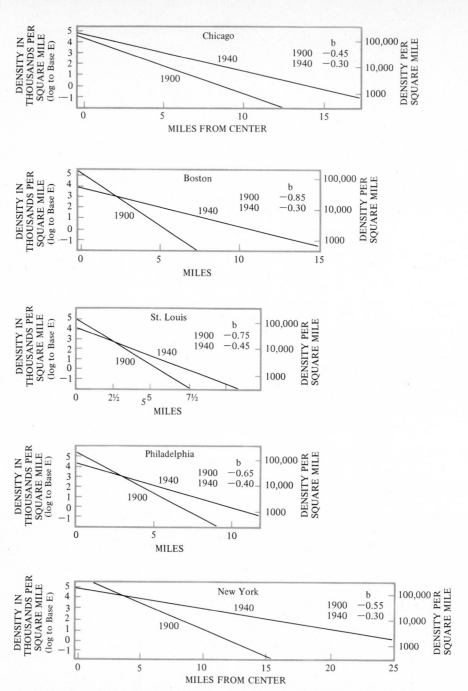

Fig. 10.6. Population density-distance relationships for selected cities in the United States, 1900 and 1940. (*Source:* Clark, 1951b, p. 492.)

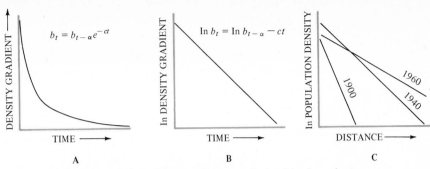

Fig. 10.7. Changes in the population density-distance relationship through time.

fact, he suggests that the mathematical form of this relationship is the same as that suggested by Clark relating population densities to distance from the center of the city. His hypothesis with respect to density gradient and time is expressed diagrammatically in Figure 10.7A and 10.7B, where it is suggested that the density gradient decreases rapidly through time in the earlier time periods, but then tends to decrease less rapidly as the value of the density gradient gets very small. This situation with respect to a particular hypothetical setting is expressed in Figure 10.7C with a very steep density gradient in 1900 but a shallower gradient in 1940 and a gradient that is very close to zero in 1960.

The equation for this relationship is expressed as follows:

$$b_t = b_{t-a}e^{-ct}$$

where

b_t = density gradient at time t
b_{t-a} = a constant, indicating the density gradient at an earlier period $t-a$
$-c$ = a parameter indicating the rate of decrease of the density gradient with time
t = the variable time
e = the base of the natural logarithms

This equation does not, of course, imply that time itself causes these changes, but that processes taking place over a period of time cause them. Some of these processes have been described in Chapter 8 with respect to innovations in urban transportation. Clark supports this argument by suggesting that the decline in the density gradient is related to changing transportation technology and particularly the introduction of the use of the automobile (Clark, 1957–1958).

Concurrent with this decline in density gradient has been the change in the density at the center of the city. The change in central densities does not, however, appear to be as consistent in North American urban areas as that for the density gradient itself (Berry, Simmons, and Tennant, 1963; Newling, 1964). In fact, it appears that the density at the center of the city increases for a period of time, and then decreases in recent years. This is well illustrated by the data prepared by Winsborough (1961) for Chicago. In Table 10.1 it can be observed that, whereas the density gradient has declined consistently since 1860, the central density rose and reached a peak somewhere between

Table 10.1. **CENTRAL DENSITY ESTIMATES AND DENSITY-GRADIENT PARAMETERS FOR CHICAGO, 1860–1950**

Year	Central Density (thousands per square mile)	Density Gradient (natural logarithms)
1860	30.0	−0.917
1870	70.8	−0.877
1880	96.6	−0.781
1890	86.3	−0.508
1900	100.0	−0.415
1910	100.0	−0.369
1920	73.0	−0.251
1930	72.8	−0.215
1940	71.1	−0.210
1950	63.7	−0.182

SOURCE: Data quoted by Newling (1966), p. 219, from Winsborough (1961).

1900 and 1910 and declined thereafter. On the other hand, the data for Toronto suggest that the central densities have remained fairly consistent (see Table 10.2).

The reason for these differences may well be related to the different epochs in which urban areas show their greatest growth (see Table 8.3). If an urban area grew rapidly in population when urban transportation technology permitted limited radial expansion of the city, then "piling up" would inevitably occur in the central locations. However, with changing technology, decentralization of activities has become possible, thereby permitting central densities to decline so that the greatest densities are now found at some distance from the central city and are perhaps moving outward in a tidal wave (Blumenfeld, 1954). It is in this context that Newling (1969) has modified Clark's model by suggesting a second-degree polynomial in order to take into account the central density crater (Fig. 10.8).

This general spreading of the urban population has a very important effect on future urban land-consumption rates. Not only are the populations of many urban areas going to continue to increase in the future, but the populations of these areas will spread out at a rate greater than the total population increase. The repercussions of this situation on the consumption of land for urban purposes is illustrated in Figure 10.9.

Table 10.2. **METROPOLITAN, TORONTO: POPULATION DENSITY-DISTANCE, RELATIONSHIPS, 1951–1963**

Date	$ln\ D_0$ Central Density	b Density Gradient	R^2
1951	4.73739	−0.21327	64.63
1955	4.86463	−0.19309	67.06
1961	4.81760	−0.15777	64.57
1963	4.80274	−0.14789	63.82

SOURCE: Latham (1967).

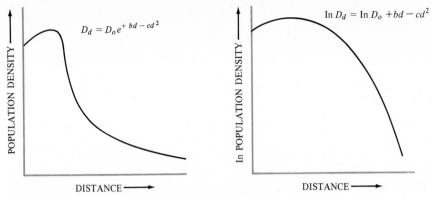

Fig. 10.8. Newling's model of urban population density.

These curves depict a situation for a metropolitan area that, at time t, has a population of two million. It is hypothesized that the threshold limit for urban population is at a density of 119 persons per square mile; so, with a central density of 40 persons per acre, the theoretical limit of the urban area is 7.7 miles.

   If the total population of the urban area at some future time $t+a$ remains two million, but the central density decreases to 30 persons per acre, the theoretical limit of the urban area will have moved out to a distance of 8.14 miles. Thus, purely as a result of the flattening of the population density curve, the land-consumption rate will have increased from 0.059 acres per person at time t to 0.067 at $t+a$. But if the total population of the urban areas increases to 3.2 million, and this increase is coupled with the

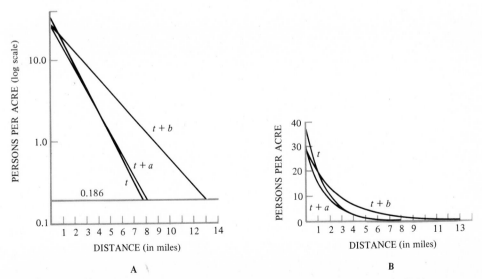

Fig. 10.9. The effect of a decrease in the slope of the population density curve on the land-consumption rate (*Source*: Yeates, 1965, Fig. 3.3.)

slope of the density curve at time $t+a$, then the theoretical limit will have moved out to a distance of 13.02 miles, as is illustrated by curve $t+b$ in Figure 10.9. The land-consumption rate now will have increased to 0.107 persons per acre, and in the period of time between t and $t+b$ the acreage of the metropolitan area would have tripled, while the urban population would have increased only 60 percent.

Population Growth Rate and Distance

We have observed with respect to Figure 10.2 that the recent growth of population in Toronto, Montreal, and Ottawa appears to be much greater at the peripheries of these urban areas than at the centers, and that at the centers of the cities, population densities are in fact declining. Newling (1966) suggests that this relationship is systematic throughout the urban area and that the form of this relationship can also be expressed in terms of an exponential equation. This equation takes the form

$$(1 + r)_d = (1 + r)_o e^{gd}$$

where

$(1 + r)_d$ = population growth rate at distance d, usually empirically defined as the population at distance d at time period t divided by the population at some earlier time period

$(1 + r)_o$ = a constant, indicating the population growth rate at the center of the city

g = a parameter indicating the rate of increase of the population growth rate with distance from the CBD

d = the variable distance

e = base of the natural logarithms

The hypothesized ideal relationship of the growth rate with respect to distance is expressed diagrammatically in Figure 10.10, and here it can be observed that the population growth rate is very low at the center of the city but increases at an increasing rate with distance from the center.

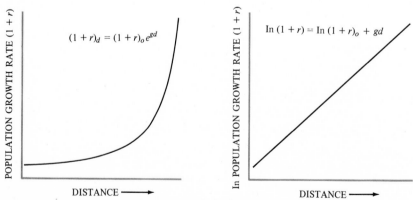

Fig. 10.10. Diagrammatic representation of the relationship between population growth rate and distance from the CBD.

There are two basic reasons for this pattern. The first is that as population densities tend to be low at the periphery of the city, any increase in population usually exhibits a high rate of increase. On the other hand, an increase of population in an area of large population will not show up high in terms of rate of increase. Second, the fertility rates at the peripheries of North American urban areas are much greater than at the centers of the cities. This is because at the periphery of the city, in the suburbs, the population is younger and the birth rate is a great deal higher than at the center of the city, where the population tends to be either older or in a pre-family-formation stage.

The Relationship Between the Population Growth Rate and Densities

If population densities decrease with distance from the center of the city and the growth rate increases with distance from the center of the city, then it is reasonable to assume that the growth rate decreases with population density.
Thus the relationship should take the form

$$(1 + r)_d = AD_d^{-k}$$

where

$(1 + r)_d$ = population growth rate at distance d
A = a constant, indicating the growth rate when the population density is close to zero
D_d = population density at distance d
$-k$ = a parameter indicating the rate of decrease in population density as the growth rate increases

In natural logarithmic form this equation can be expressed as
$$ln(1 + r)_d = ln\ A - k\ (ln\ D)_d$$

This relationship is expressed diagrammatically in Figure 10.11, which suggests

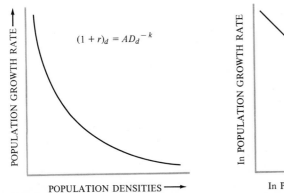
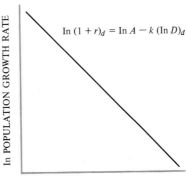

Fig. 10.11. Diagrammatic representation of the relationship between population growth rate and urban population density.

that areas of high population density have lower population growth rates than areas of low population densities. Thus at the periphery of the city, where there are low population densities, there are high growth rates; and at the center of the city, where there are high population densities, there are low growth rates.

The situation expressed by the equations relating the population growth rate to distance and the population growth rate to densities suggests, according to Newling (1966, p. 214), a "rule of intraurban allometric growth." The term "allometric" implies that each part of the urban area is growing in a related pattern to the growth of all other parts. In terms of urban populations, the population growth rate is related in a systematic fashion not only to distance from the center of the city, but also to the density of population itself.

The Urban Population of Toronto: A Case Study

We have, therefore, identified a number of models with respect to patterns of urban population densities and growth. Four of these are fairly simple, for they involve just two variables, and it might be useful to indicate how they may be applied in a particular situation. The four models are:

$$D_d = D_o e^{-bd} \tag{1}$$
$$b_t = b_{t-a} e^{-ct} \tag{2}$$
$$(1 + r)_d = (1 + r)_o e^{gd} \tag{3}$$
$$(1 + r)_d = A D_d^{-k} \tag{4}$$

These urban population models can be tested with respect to Toronto by using data that pertain to four time periods between 1951 and 1963. The data refer to the growth in population densities and were enumerated with respect to more than 300 equal-area hexagonal cells. Thus, although the data pertain to areas, each one of these is of the same size.

With respect to population densities in metropolitan Toronto, it can be suggested that the relationship postulated by Clark is good for metropolitan Toronto (see Table 10.2). It must be noted, however, that Latham and Yeates (1970) suggest that the second-degree polynomial modification postulated by Newling (1969) may be more explicit with respect to recent years. Nevertheless, continuing with the Clark model,

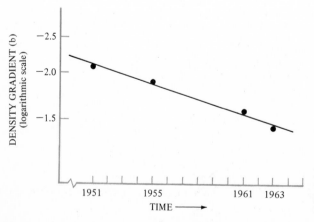

Fig. 10.12. Relationship between the slope of population density gradients and time in metropolitan Toronto.

the variances explained by the negative exponential model applied to each time period are quite high, ranging between 63 percent and 67 percent for the different time periods. The central density parameter has remained fairly constant but the b parameter has steadily decreased through time. Thus the Clark model fits the Toronto data for four time periods between 1951 and 1963 fairly well. In fact, the decline in value of the density gradient (b) conforms very closely to the model suggested by Newling. In Figure 10.12 the density-gradient values have been plotted against time on semilogarithmic paper, and each one of the points fits very closely to the "best-fit" line.

With respect to the population growth rate, models 3 and 4 are also applicable to the situation in metropolitan Toronto between 1951 and 1961. The relationship between the population growth rate and distance from the center of the city is significantly positive, but the proportion of the total variation explained is not very high ($R^2 = 12.4\%$). This is undoubtedly due to the great sectoral variation in growth rates exhibited in Figure 10.4. Interestingly, however, the negative relationship between the 1951–61 decadal growth rate and 1951 population densities is much higher ($R^2 = 45.7\%$). This latter relationship therefore has important implications for urban planners, who are vitally concerned with developing rational models of urban growth.

PATTERNS OF RESIDENTIAL LOCATION

Some general descriptive models of urban land use proposed by Burgess (1923), Hoyt (1939), and Harris and Ullman (1945) have been discussed in Chapter 9. These models allocate residential land use within the urban area according to different criteria. The Burgess model suggests that residential patterns will be concentrically spread throughout the city, with the highest income residential area at the periphery. Thus, in terms of residential types, the implication of the model is that many multifamily dwellings will be found close to the center of the city, with single-family dwellings on larger parcels of land at the periphery. However, Burgess's model applies specifically to the problem of assimilation of socioeconomic groups within the North American city. The Harris-Ullman model is a general description of the typical location of all types of land use. The model presented by Hoyt, however, relates specifically to the location of residential areas in North American cities.

The Sector Theory

Hoyt (1939) based his sector theory on an intensive study of the internal residential structure of 142 North American cities in the 1930's. From an analysis of the average block residential rental values of these cities, Hoyt presents a number of specific conclusions. Among these some of the most important are:

1. The highest rental area is located in one or more specific sectors on one side of the city. Generally these high-rent areas are in peripheral locations, though there are instances when a high-rent sector extends continuously out from the center of the city.

2. High-rent areas often take the form of wedges, extending in certain sectors along radial lines leading outward from the center to the periphery of the city.

3. Middle-range rental areas tend to be located on either side of the highest rental areas.

4. There are some cities in which large areas of middle-range rental units tend to be found on the peripheries of low-rent residential areas as well as high-rent areas.

5. All cities have low-rent areas, and these are frequently found opposite to the location of the high-rent areas, and usually in the more central locations.

On the basis of these observations, Hoyt rejects the concentric-circle theory of city structure and proposes a sectoral pattern as being more persuasive. Accordingly, he arranges the rent areas of 30 cities in an ideal pattern of concentric circles in order to show that the greatest variation is not between concentric circles, but between sectors (Fig. 10.13). Thus Hoyt states:

> From the evidence presented, therefore, it may be concluded that rent areas in American cities tend to conform to a pattern of sectors rather than of concentric circles. The highest rent areas of the city tend to be located in one or more sectors of the city. There is a gradation of rentals downward from these high-rent areas in all directions. Intermediate-rent areas, or those ranking next to the highest rental areas, adjoin the high-rent areas on one or more sides, and tend to be located in the same sectors as the high-rent areas. Low-rent areas occupy other entire sections of the city from the center to the periphery. On the outer edge of some of the high-rent areas are intermediate-rent areas [Hoyt, 1939, p. 76].

In fact, it appears that in no city studied by Hoyt was there a regular upward gradation of residential rental values from the center to the periphery in all directions.

Factors Influencing High-Grade and Low-Grade Residential Development

One of the specific concerns of Hoyt's early analysis of the structure and growth of residential neighborhoods in American cities is the location of high-rent residential areas. Following an analysis of the location of high-rent residential areas in a number of North American cities, he proposed a sector theory of neighborhood change. This theory states: "The high-rent neighborhoods of the city do not skip about at random in the process of movement—they follow a definite path in one or more sectors of the city" (Hoyt, 1939, p. 144). To illustrate this particular point, Hoyt presents cartograms showing the shift in location of high-rent residential areas in six North American cities (Fig. 10.14). The diagrams clearly indicate that the principle has some validity. For example, in Boston the high-rent residential area was originally located on the western side of the city and it remained in this sector to 1936 with a new area on the periphery to the southeast. Likewise in Minneapolis the high-grade residential area has always been in the southwestern sector.

Factors Influencing the Movement of High-Rent Residential Areas

Hoyt (1939) indicates the significance of studying the location and movement of high-rent residential areas when he suggests that "the movement of the high-rent area is in a certain sense most important because it tends to pull the growth of the entire city in the same direction." The high-rent residential area in North American cities always has its point of origin at the periphery of the CBD, near the retail, financial, and office activities. This point is always farthest removed from the side of the city that has industry or warehouses. The growth of the high-rent residential areas, and concomitantly the city, usually follows one or more principles.

The first of these is that the movement of high-rent residential areas tends to proceed from the given point of origin along established lines of travel or toward another existing nucleus of buildings or trading centers. Thus, in many North American cities there are well-known fashionable boulevards along or near which many of the wealthiest and best established families are located. Second, high-rent areas tend to be

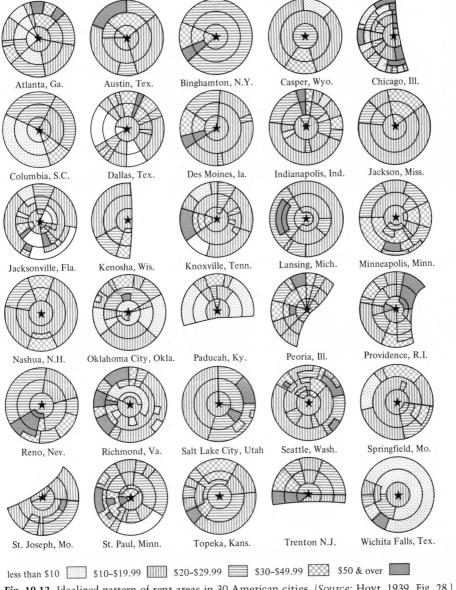

Fig. 10.13. Idealized pattern of rent areas in 30 American cities. (*Source:* Hoyt, 1939, Fig. 28.)

developed on high ground, free from the risk of floods, and to spread along lake, bay, river, and ocean fronts where such waterfronts are not used for industry. Well-known examples of this type of location are the Gold Coast along the waterfront of Lake Michigan in Chicago, Knob Hill in San Francisco, and the "upper-class highlands" in the Bel-Air district of Los Angeles. In a similar context, it is estimated that in Pittsburgh rental values increase by 10 cents for every foot in altitude (Blumenfeld, 1959).

High-rent residential districts also tend to grow toward the section of the city that has free, open country beyond the edges, and away from dead-end sections that are limited by natural or artificial barriers to expansion. The implication of this particular prin-

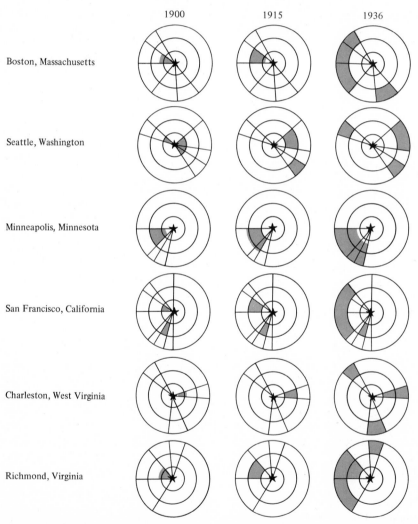

Fig. 10.14. The changing pattern of high-rent areas in six American cities, 1900–1936. (*Source:* Hoyt, 1939, Fig. 40.)

ciple is that there have to be possibilities for further growth and development as well as space for expansion. Thus the development of new golf courses and country clubs today acts as a lure for high-rent residential growth in many North American cities. Another lure is the homes of leaders of the community, for higher priced neighborhoods tend to develop around these. This principle recognizes the basic snob appeal of most high-rent residential locations, which follows from the quite human desire of most people to locate close to their peers. Thus in the early development of New York the homes of the Astors and the Vanderbilts were the forces that pulled the development of the city in a particular direction.

Trends in the location of office buildings, banks, and stores can also pull higher priced residential neighborhoods in the same general direction. The recent growth of outlying shopping centers in North American cities has resulted in the out-migration of a number of retail and service activities. Very often the establishment of a high-class shopping center in which well-known sophisticated department stores, banks, and so forth are located can result in the growth of adjacent upper-income districts by giving and aura of class to the surrounding area. Also the decentralization of office activities can result in the expansion of high-rent residential areas in a particular direction. Frequently these areas are linked by rapid transit lines, which themselves provide good locations for expensive high-rise apartments and condominiums.

Finally, real estate promoters may bend the direction of high-grade residential growth. This is, of course, one of the most important factors influencing residential growth within the city, particularly as the location of the high-rent residential areas appears to have such an important feedback effect on the location of other residential areas and economic activities as well. Ever since the days of the development of the streetcar suburbs, real estate promoters have been increasingly concerned with planning the development and growth of quality residential areas. The profits from such ventures are frequently quite high, particularly today when many promoters form companies that build complete communities, with shopping and business facilities and residential uses all forming part of an overall plan. This is because the highest profits are realized in the construction of the highest priced residential facilities. The profit margin for the lower priced residential units is much less, and so contractors are usually less inclined to build lower-income communities.

Factors Influencing the Location of Low-Income Residential Development

In general, it is frequently considered that the location of low-income residential areas is strongly influenced by the costs of commuting to work. This particular argument is well expressed by Alonso (1960) in his application of land-value theory to the location of residential areas in cities. His argument suggests that because the costs of transportation form a large part of the total budget of low-income families, but a comparatively smaller part of the total income of wealthier families, low-income families are much more susceptible to the costs of transportation and therefore consider this factor much more seriously in their locational decision. Low-income groups are therefore much more work-place oriented, and low-income residential areas are generally found much closer to the chief areas of employment within the city. If industrial employment is concentrated close to the CBD, the low-income residential areas will be on that side of the city closest to this area.

It has been noted, however, that there has been a dispersal of employment opportunities to the periphery of many cities (discussed in detail in Chapter 14). This, along with the widespread use of the automobile, has extended the zone of possible location of workingmen's homes to cover, in the case of small cities, almost the entire urban area; and in large cities, a great proportion of it. Under these conditions the individuals who suffer the most are those who cannot afford to purchase and maintain an automobile. The location of these people is very much constrained by the availability of public transportation; and in most cities in the United States, this is a facility that is declining in both quality and availability.

A second factor influencing the location of low-income residential areas is that they are very often occupied by those members of North American society who have suffered or still do suffer to a greater or lesser degree from discrimination, both in terms of employment and in terms of the possibilities of residential site selection. In numerous North American cities, blacks, Puerto Ricans, Indians, and so forth have suffered from job discrimination, lack of equal opportunity, and a limited availability of housing. As a result, the location of these individuals has become constrained to certain sections of the city. These groups then disperse outward from an original location in a clustered manner (Morrill, 1965b). The processes underlying this segregation and dispersion are discussed in the ensuing chapter.

A third factor influencing the location of low-income residential areas is concerned with the physical attributes of the urban space. The high-income people seek and can afford the better and most picturesque locations. The middle-income people take the next best, leaving the worst and poorest urban sites for the lowest income groups. Thus the low-income residential areas are frequently found on the worst-drained land and on the side of the city that is the least secluded. Very frequently these areas are also on the side of the city that suffers the most air pollution from surrounding industry, and in many cases the range and scale of the facilities serving the community are badly planned. There is very frequently a shortage of parks, the schools are the oldest and most overcrowded, and the medical facilities are poorly developed. All these conditions ensure that the area will continue to be occupied by the low-income groups.

It has frequently been observed that as time goes on, low-income groups tend to move in and occupy the land and houses or parts of houses previously occupied by the rich. This process is a basic element in Burgess's model and is observed also by Hoyt's sector model. In this latter case, as the high- and middle-income groups move outward along a given sectoral path, they are replaced by the low-income groups, who occupy the large houses by subdividing them. It is interesting to note that this process has been reversed in a number of urban areas, particularly in those residential areas that contain a number of well-built and well-designed homes that can be modernized. The catalyst for this type of change can be urban renewal, as in the case of Philadelphia, or the introduction of an avant-garde Bohemian element that gives the neighborhood an artistic appearance and therefore makes it more attractive, as in Greenwich Village, New York City. In a more recent era, Carey (1972) has described the hippie as the "vanguard of the middle class as well as its offshoot."

THE LOCATIONAL DECISION

The individual or family's locational decision is the result of a multitude of complex forces. From the individual or family's point of view, two aspects of this decision are paramount. The first involves the location of the house with respect to other features of the urban area, and the second relates to the characteristics of the dwelling unit itself. These two elements are not independent, for frequently the type of dwelling unit is related to its location. For example, single-family units are generally found at the peripheries of urban areas, whereas multifamily dwelling units are generally found in the central part of the city. Also, new units are found at the periphery and older units are generally found closer to the center. Thus these two elements of the location decision cannot be isolated from each other. We shall therefore examine the location decision in terms of the spatial elements of this decision. On the demand side, these may be described as the location of employment opportunities, the life cycle, social class, and life style, and on the supply side we shall refer to the supply of housing. As the effect of employment opportunities has been described previously, the discussion at this juncture will concentrate on the life cycle, social class, life style, and supply of housing.

The Life Cycle and the Locational Decision

North American society is a mobile society. In fact, it is estimated that 20 percent of the population of the United States changes residence annually (Simmons, 1968). On the average an individual family will move eight or nine times in a lifetime, and five of these moves are considered to be life-cycle moves; that is, moves related to the changing composition of the family of which the individual forms a part. Rossi (1955, p. 175) suggests that the majority of these moves are related to changing family requirements for living space, for, in his study, "among the three out of every five whose moves were undertaken voluntarily, the most frequently encountered motive for the shift lay in dissatisfaction with the amount of room available in their old dwellings." Thus, at certain periods in a family's existence a level of living-space stress occurs which is sufficient to cause that unit to decide to search for a new domicile and perhaps a new location. These causes of stress are included quite clearly in the Brown-Moore (1970) model of intra-urban migration as one of the elements in the decision to seek a new residence.

An individual passes through many stages in his life, which Erikson (1968) has categorized as infancy, early childhood, play age, school age, adolescence (teenage), young adulthood, adulthood (parents), and old age (Table 10.3). As the average length of life continues to increase and the birth rate to decrease, to these eight ages may be added late adulthood (with children having left home), sometimes referred to as the "swinging fifties." Although each of these stages gives rise to different problems to which social policy must be directed, the life cycle is important to residential location in at least three ways (Yeates, 1972).

First, as an individual passes through the life cycle, the type of house and the physical location that is optimally required varies. Second, most of the residential location decisions are made by the heads of the family, in accordance with their perception of the requirements of the family. These requirements may be difficult to reconcile or compromise because of the variations in stage within the life cycle in which the family members find themselves. For example, the location and space requirements of a teenager differ considerably from those of a child, and great stress may be created within a family when a teenager who wishes to be close to the wide array of experiences of big-city life finds himself removed to a suburb. Third, the length of each stage varies—five stages are crammed into the first 20 years of life, and three throughout the next 50. As a result, the decision makers in the family may become less responsive to life-cycle changes. This is frequently evidenced by a resistance to residential adjustment in later

Table 10.3.   CHANGES IN RESIDENCE RELATED TO
              STAGES IN THE LIFE CYCLE

Age	Stage	Moves
0	Birth	
	infancy, early	
	childhood, play	1
10	age, school age,	
	adolescence	
20		
	Young adulthood	
30	Adulthood	3
	(children)	
50	Late adulthood	
65	Retirement	1
75	Death	

Source: Based on Simmons, 1968, Fig. 4, and Erikson, 1968.

years due to sentimental attachment to a house and location that are no longer contiguous with the family's requirements.

Typically the situation in Table 10.3 may be characterized as describing the following situation: During the early years of a person's life, the individual's locational decision is made by his parents, who are the heads of the family. The one move that generally occurs during this period is determined by the parents. Frequently this move is in fact related to the requirements of the children; but generally speaking, the individual with whom we are concerned is not directly brought into the decision making. The next move, which generally occurs during the period of maturity, is frequently associated with the individual's gaining of independence, either as a result of leaving school and getting a job or going on to college. The next move comes with marriage. The individual has now once again become part of a family, and the decision making is not on the basis of the individual's requirements, but of the family's requirements. At this stage in life, the young family may have a large joint income when both husband and wife have jobs, and their locational decision may well be determined by a desire for proximity to good and varied recreational facilities. Thus the family may well be located in a downtown area where they can afford a reasonably expensive apartment because of their joint incomes (Bourne, 1968).

This conditional wealthy situation and its concomitant desire for a broad range of recreational amenities is usually changed by the arrival of children. Other factors now enter the locational decision. In particular, these are usually the changing housing requirements that the young couple considers to be associated with the raising of children. These housing requirements usually relate to single-family dwelling units with gardens or enclosed play areas and an elementary school within walking distance. Most parents generally believe that these conditions are available in the suburbs and not available in downtown areas. In particular it must be noted that the desire for locations within the districts of good schools is generally preeminent for the middle class. The last move mentioned in Table 10.3 may well be occasioned by a desire for more housing space as the family gets larger, a desire for less space when the children leave home, or simply retirement. These moves are, of course, detailed in a model form, and it will be clear that not all groups of North Americans fit into this general pattern. Probably the group that fits the model most easily is composed of middle-class white North Americans, but it should be evident that others incur similar life-cycle housing stresses.

Social Class and Residential Location

One of the fundamental realities of the social structure of North America is that there is a fairly rigid set of social classes. Social class in this environment is generally determined by occupation, education, and race, and to a lesser degree by income. There are two suggested characteristics that need to be emphasized: one concerns the type of housing and location preferred by different social classes, and one relates to changes that may occur as a result of mobility between classes.

The first suggested characteristic is that the higher social classes appear to demand better quality housing than lower social classes. This is because the percentage of a family's income that is spent on good-quality housing appears to be positively related to education (Michelson, 1970), and as education is one of the prime determinants of social status, quality preference must, to some degree, be positively related to social class. One must be very careful to consider the context of this statement. If two persons have the same income, the one with the highest level of education will usually (not always) spend more on housing than the person with the least education. The reason for this appears to be that the person with more years of education (and, therefore, higher social class) usually places a higher value on residential and environmental quality, and has a different concept of housing adequacy, than the less well-educated individual. This should not be extended to suggest that the lower-class families can therefore put up with poor-quality housing; it is simply an empirical finding.

The second suggested characteristic is that if a person or family attains a higher social rank (for example, through a change in occupation), this change may well be associated with a change in residential location. However, Lipset and Bendix (1959) suggest that only a small proportion of North Americans leave the social class into which they were born, so change in social class affects only a small proportion of residential location decisions. Most people who change their location of residence move to a part of the city that is of the same social class as that from which they originated. If there is a move upward, this is usually to an area of the city occupied by the next higher social class; a movement downward is usually to an area of the next lower social class. This situation is admirably expressed with respect to data from Rhode Island in Table 10.4. From this table it can be observed that 63.8 percent of all persons who moved from the highest social-class area moved to another high-social-class area, and that 51 percent who moved from the second highest social-class area moved to an area that was also of the second highest social class. Noticeably the values on the diagonal of the matrix are always very large, but decrease toward the lower social-class areas. Here 48 percent of the people who originated in the lowest social class moved to another area that was also of the lowest social class, and 17.4 percent moved up to the next higher (class 4) and 17.3 percent moved up two classes (to class 3). The general upward mobility of society

Table 10.4.   MOVES AMONG SOCIAL AREAS (IN PERCENTAGES)

Social Class (origin tract)	1	2	3	4	5
1 (High)	63.8	12.0	11.3	8.2	4.7
2	8.2	51.0	20.6	13.3	6.9
3	6.1	18.8	50.4	16.7	8.0
4	5.1	13.0	21.0	52.7	8.2
5 (Low)	4.1	13.2	17.3	17.4	48.0

SOURCE: Goldstein and Mayer (1961), p. 51.

is indicated by the fact that the largest percentages on the off-diagonals are to the left of the diagonal, whereas the smaller percentages are to the right (indicating downward movement).

Of course, this pattern is severely disrupted in many North American cities by ethnic patterns. In some instances particular ethnic or religious groups are very much restricted in their spatial location. Furthermore, some have a range of social ranks within their own particular areas which have very definite spatial locations. For example, in North America some urban areas have particular Jewish suburbs of various income levels and Catholic areas of particular income levels. Thus the process often works within minority groupings as well as among the majority. As the barriers between the ethnic and religious groups progressively disappear, it it likely that the locational criteria of social class based purely on the criterion of income will increase in strength.

Life Style and Residential Location

Life style refers to style of living, and it is based on the type of role emphasized by an individual or group. Michelson (1970) indicates that two elements, at a minimum, are included in life style. One element involves the types of behaviors that are performed, and the other the sphere of life that is emphasized. There are many types of behaviors, and most involve interaction with people, though the type of behavior emphasized categorizes the form of the interaction. For example, an achievement-oriented professor might be more concerned with fraternizing with administrative leaders within a university community than with assistant professors. There are usually considered to be five spheres of life that are central to any society: explanation of the supernatural, propagation, economic supply, socialization of the young, and political control. Presumably the achievement-oriented professor would be more concerned with political control than with socialization of the young.

The life style of an individual is based on his or her own personal characteristics as well as on certain behavior traits bestowed by the environment and economic circumstances. These self-developed and environmentally developed traits result in a person who very often needs to locate in a residential area that provides the style of living and form of interaction that are congruent with his or her life style. For example, a person who has grown up in the Italian community of Toronto may well have certain life-style requirements that constrain a residential location decision to the area occupied by the Italian community. Further, a person brought up within a black community may well have developed a life style that is distinctly incongruent with any white life style beyond the ghetto. There is considerable evidence to suggest that poor people, whatever their color, may develop a life style that makes them distinctly difficult to assimilate in any form of urban organization (Irelan, 1967).

Each person, therefore, has certain life-style constraints, and occasionally the constraints may be of sufficient force to influence a residential location. Again, however, the disclaimer must be added that the existence of a constraint should not be construed as a determinant of location by any planner or welfare agency. Furthermore, it should be noted that the degree to which an individual can permit a life-style preference to influence a locational decision depends very much on the stage in the life cycle and income. The life style adopted by a couple that is conditionally wealthy may have to be severely altered following the blessing of parental responsibilities.

The Supply of Housing

A very important element influencing the locational decision is the varying supply of housing available to the consumer. On the one hand, not all types of housing are built everywhere in an urban community. Modern high-rise apartments are frequently located downtown or close to limited-access expressways. Single-family dwelling units with large yards are not commonly found in the central city. Thus if a family desires a particular type of dwelling unit, it can locate only where that type of dwelling unit is available. Also the dwelling units themselves vary in age and style, and frequently they group in various parts of the city.

Dwelling units become available for occupancy through being vacated or through new housing stock. Vacated dwelling units can occur through the elimination of the family by death, but more commonly vacancies occur because the residents move somewhere else. Given the increase in the North American population, it is evident that housing space for new families can be provided only by increasing the stock through new construction. This new housing stock is usually located at the peripheries of the urban area, for land in sufficient quantities is available only in these fringe zones. This is reinforced by the fact that it is easier to obtain federally insured mortgages on new housing than for renovated older housing. Thus in a sense the federal governments in both the United States and Canada have encouraged the sprawl of the city and have done little to support the possible redevelopment of the central city (see Chapter 17).

The Filtering Process

The mobility of families from one housing submarket to another involves a filtering process (Smith, 1964). This process can be perceived in both economic and social terms. In an economic sense the process describes "the changing of occupancy as the housing that is occupied by one income group becomes available to the next lower income group as a result of a decline in market price. . ." (Ratcliff, 1949, p. 321). From the point of view of the house itself, this can be interpreted as the "change over time in the position of a dwelling unit or group of dwelling units within the distribution of housing prices and rents in the community as a whole" (Fisher and Winnick, 1951, p. 49). The implication of the economic view of filtering is that if the relative price of the housing decreases more rapidly than the quality, then the lower-income groups will be able to afford successively better quality housing.

The latter implication reveals the social interpretation of the filtering concept. A rapid rate of downward filtering in relative house prices will make possible an upward filtering of income groups into better quality housing. Conversely, a low rate of downward filtering in house prices would result in limited possibilities of upward filtering of income groups into better quality housing (Grebler, 1952).

Factors Affecting the Rate of Filtering

In general terms there are two factors affecting the rate of filtering: the rate of construction of housing and the demand, or rate of family formation. If the rate of new housing construction, implying a favorable mortgage market, is in excess of the demand, then it would be possible for the relative value of older housing to decrease quite quickly. The depth of the downward filtering of the housing stock varies according to the range in value of the new housing being constructed. If new housing were available primarily for the upper-income groups, then upward filtering would be possible for all income groups, with the low-income groups occupying the homes previously owned by the more affluent. The provision of only low-income housing would permit upward filtering only to the low-income groups.

The suggestion therefore arises that better housing for all can be encouraged by a vigorous rate of construction of middle- and high-priced housing. This will encourage a high rate of downward filtering of houses, and therefore a high rate of upward filtering in house quality for all socioeconomic groups. The ethical morality of providing new housing for only the wealthy, however, is dubious. Probably a better policy would be to provide new housing in all price ranges. The rate of upward filtering that results may be lower, but at least new housing would be available to some people in every income group.

If the demand is in excess of the supply, the value of the housing stock may decrease more slowly than the quality, and in extreme cases the values may well not decrease at all, and all types of homes may show a relative increase. Under these conditions the possibility for the upward filtering of socioeconomic groups into better quality housing is severely limited. In fact, there may be a downward filtering of socioeconomic groups into lower quality housing, with the higher-income groups preempting the homes previously occupied by the less wealthy. Under these conditions the lowest incomes suffer the most, as they are forced to occupy marginal or substandard dwellings at quite high rents (Lansing et al., 1969).

Thus the filtering concept has important policy and planning implications. In terms of policy, the intricate interrelationship of mortgage markets and the type of housing being provided has very important social implications. For the urban planner, the variation in the rate of filtering in different parts of the city is a vital indicator of neighborhood change, and therefore possible blight. Also it is evident that filtering is one of the chief processes involved in the re-sorting of people within the city into groups according to different criteria. The results of this re-sorting are described in the next chapter.

11
THE
SOCIAL GEOGRAPHY
OF URBAN AREAS

A quick windshield inspection of a cross-section of residential streets in any North American city reveals a variety of social, economic, and ethnic characteristics. In some areas the houses are new, large, and obviously occupied by high-income families. Other areas are older, consisting of walk-up apartments; children are playing on the streets, and the small local stores are owned by people with Germanic, Scandinavian, or other ethnic-sounding names. The differences between these two areas are based on a number of criteria, such as housing, density, and ethnicity; though in some instances a single characteristic may convey the image of the area. For example, in Kantrowitz's (1969) study of Puerto Ricans and blacks in New York City, a grouping of contiguous census tracts, each with more than a certain proportion of the population either black or Puerto Rican, was sufficient to define these two communities.

Urban social geography is, as the description suggests, social geography applied to the urban sphere. Therefore, the principles and concepts that have been developed in social geography in general are applicable to this unit of analysis. Probably the most succinct definition of social geography is that provided by Buttimer (1968), who suggests that it is the geographical study of social space. Social space in this context is a

251

melange of cultural, demographic, economic, ethnic, and other characteristics relating to the people that reside within an area. These characteristics can be examined geographically in three main ways:

1. Formally in terms of areas mapped with respect to specific social criteria, such as census tracts in which more than 50 percent of the population are, for example, Puerto Rican.

2. Functionally, in terms of flows to a particular point, or concentrations of particular activities to certain foci.

3. Circulatory, in terms of flows (goods, services, people) between people and other socioeconomic units.

Thus the geographic range of the social space that is defined depends upon the characteristics being selected and the form of analysis (formal, functional, or circulatory) being used.

Given this rather concise definition of social space, and the variety of forms of analysis that may be used, it is not surprising that urban social geography embraces many types of study, ranging from analyses of house types and social districts (Denis, 1972) to flows of telephone calls between subareas (Greer-Wooten and Marshall, 1972) to complex manipulations of a grab bag of socioeconomic characteristics relating to a number of cities (Davies and Barrow, 1973). Given the range of studies that may exist, it is perhaps useful to distinguish between two different types, and to propose that each can be characterized by the form of analysis emphasized. These two types can be grouped with respect to spatial emphasis into those relating to communities and those relating to neighborhoods.

COMMUNITIES AND NEIGHBORHOODS

Probably the best known early studies of the concepts of community and neighborhood were undertaken by Park, Burgess, and McKenzie at the University of Chicago early in the present century (see Burgess and Bogue, 1964). The basic assumption in their form of analysis was that the processes recognized by plant and animal ecologists as operating in the natural environment could be translated to the social sphere. Thus, human ecology developed as a science that is "fundamentally interested in the effect of position, in both time and space, upon human institutions and human behavior" (Park et al., 1925, p. 64). The immediate utility of the ecological approach was that the processes pertained to groups rather than individuals, and therefore could be applied to groups of people that are collected by the census into recording units of one kind or another. With the passage of time it is possible to disregard the biological analogies and focus on the theoretical orientations that have developed from the human ecology approach (Goheen, 1970).

The Community

The term "community" is one of the most widely used but difficult to understand terms in the literature of urban geography. We shall regard the community as a

social unit which consists of persons who share a common geographic area interacting in terms of a common culture and which incorporates a range of social structures which function to meet a relatively broad range of needs of all persons who make up the social unit [Popenoe, 1969, p. 70].

In this sense the community is comparable with the *quartier* in French urban areas (Caplow, 1952). In both these cases the community is a clearly defined area of sub-culture of the urban landscape having a distinctive appearance, with its own local industry and commerce, its housing forms, family types, collective attitudes, formal associations, and frequently its own dialect and folklore. In many settlements the community may well be bounded by the municipal limits of the entire region, while in large cities it may be just one part of the metropolis. Neighborhoods are regarded as smaller units found within a larger community.

Social Area Analysis

One approach at defining communities in urban areas has been through the technique of social area analysis, a method originally proposed by Shevky, Bell, and Williams (1949,1955). The method involves the application of a set of procedures for classifying census tracts with respect to three indexes: economic status, family status, and ethnic status. These indexes are derived from a set of hypotheses concerning the nature of societal change through time. Society is viewed as having changed from a rural to an urban-industrial state, and this change is represented by an increasing scale of complexity of social organization. The three postulates that provide the foundation for the indexes are presented in column 1 of Table 11.1.

The first hypothesis suggests that as society changes from a rural to an urban-industrial state, there is a change in the range and intensity of relations between families and individuals. The statistics considered by Shevky and Bell (1955) as interpretive of these trends involve the changing distribution of skills associated with industrialization. These refer, in particular, to the decreasing importance of manual productive occupations and a growing importance of clerical, supervisory, and management occupations. Thus society becomes differentiated by the derived construct economic status, or *social rank*. Columns 5 and 6 indicate the census tract data used by the social area analysts to determine the economic status of a particular census tract.

The second postulate suggests that the structure of the family is affected by the differentiation of functions that occur with the changing structure of productive activity. These are directly related to a decrease in the importance of primary production and a growing importance of activities of a secondary and tertiary nature. In the primary-rural state, the entire family is involved in a production process that is agrocentric. The urban-industrial family, on the other hand, is less unitary and may well be concerned with a number of kinds of occupations. The *family status* index therefore consists of derived measures (column 6 derived from column 5) concerning female fertility ratios, the proportion of women at work, and the ratio of single-family dwelling units to all others in a census tract.

Ethnic status, the third construct of the social analysts, is based on a hypothesis that the population becomes more complex with the increasing scale of urban-industrial activity and that this complexity is a result of mobility and a redistribution of the population in space. Thus there is, in effect, a tendency for the sorting out of population in terms of age, sex, and ethnic background. In North America this re-sorting is particularly marked by ethnic composition and color. The statistics used to compile this index of segregation relate particularly to race, country of birth, and citizenship. Those

Table 11.1. STEPS IN (SHEVKY) CONSTRUCT FORMATION AND INDEX CONSTRUCTION

Postulates Concerning Industrial Society (Aspects of Increasing Scale) (1)	Statistics of Trends (2)	Changes in the Structure of a Given Social System (3)	Constructs (4)	Sample Statistics (Related to the Constructs) (5)	Derived Measures (from Column 5) (6)
Change in the range and intensity of relations	Changing distribution of skills; lessening importance of manual productive operations — growing importance of clerical, supervisory, management operations.	Changes in the arrangement of occupations based on function	SOCIAL RANK (ECONOMIC STATUS)	Years of schooling, employment status, class of worker, major occupation group, value of home, rent by dwelling unit, plumbing and repair, persons per room, heating and refrigeration.	Occupation, schooling, rent. } Index I
Differentiation of function	Changing structure of productive activity. Lessening importance of primary production — growing importance of relations centered in cities — lessening importance of the household as economic unit.	Changes in the ways of living — movement of women into urban occupations — spread of alternative family patterns.	FAMILY STATUS (URBANIZATION)	Age and sex, owner or tenant, house structure, persons in household.	Fertility, women at work, single-family dwelling units. } Index II
Complexity of organization	Changing composition of population: increasing movement — alterations in age and sex distribution — increasing diversity.	Redistribution in space, changes in the proportion of supporting and dependent population, isolation and segregation of groups.	SEGREGATION (ETHNIC STATUS)	Race and nativity, country of birth, citizenship.	Racial and national groups in relative isolation. } Index III

SOURCE: After Shevky and Bell (1955), p. 4.

census tracts with high proportions of their populations consisting of a particular race, or coming from a particular country, are considered to be areas of high ethnic status.

The Social Areas of San Francisco, 1950

As an example of the use of social area analysis for defining the spatial location of different types of communities, the constructs are presented as defined by Shevky and Bell for San Francisco in Figure 11.1. These maps are part of a much larger study that, in fact, pertained to the whole San Francisco Bay Area in 1950. Figure 11.1A illustrates the spatial distribution of the social-rank construct and indicates that the highest social-rank tracts are on the western and northern parts of the peninsula, whereas the lower-ranked tracts are generally on the east, facing the bay. This, of course, reflects the historical development of San Francisco, for industry, commerce, and shipping activities are located on the bay.

The family status map (Fig. 11.1B) shows that the highest family status (or low urbanization) tracts are in the southern part of San Francisco, whereas the lowest family status (or high urbanization) areas are in the central and northern parts of the city. Finally, the tracts of greatest segregation are generally in the eastern part of the city, with the greatest concentration being in the core or downtown part in the northeast. A generalized composite of these three constructs (Fig. 11.1C) indicates the existence of a high-social-rank–low-family-status quadrant in the southwest, a high-family-status–low-social-rank area with some segregated tracts in the east and south, a high-social-rank–low-family-status area with a number of segregated tracts in the central and northern parts of the city, and a small area of low-family-status–low-social-rank tracts with some segregation in the old wharf area of the city in the central part.

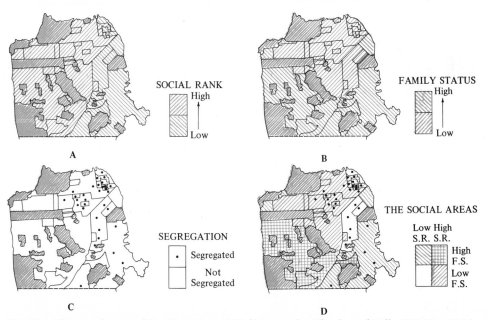

Fig. 11.1. The social areas of San Francisco, 1950. (*Source*: after Shevky and Bell, 1955, Fig. V.14.)

The Social Areas of Winnipeg, 1961

There have been some severe criticisms of social area analysis involving both the theoretical base and the statistics used in the methodology (Hawley and Duncan, 1957; Udrey, 1964). Although the social area analysts cite the works of Clark (1951a), Florence (1953), Ogburn (1933), and Wirth (1938) in support of their thesis, nevertheless they admit that "the theory, as presently stated, is too sketchy. It needs elaboration in both detail and scope" (Bell and Moskos, 1964, p. 416). The statistical objections to the method range from criticisms of census tracts as statistical units to the fact that the measures are chosen to support the constructs (Van Ardsol, 1961). With this latter point in mind, it is interesting to use all the census tract data available for urban areas to observe whether the constructs do conform to the basic underlying dimensions.

Nicholson and Yeates (1969) use principal components analysis to determine the basic dimensions of socioeconomic variation in Winnipeg in 1961. Each one of the 84 census tracts is characterized by 70 different variables, each of which is a percentage measure of a socioeconomic characteristic (Table 11.2). In effect, these variables comprise almost all the measured socioeconomic characteristics available in the census data (a few were deleted because of inappropriateness or lack of complete coverage). The analysis indicated that nearly 76 percent of the variation in the original 70 variables could be accounted for by five dimensions.

The first of these is a dimension describing census tracts consisting of many high- and middle-income families of British Isles ethnic stock, who belong to the Anglican or United church. The male labor force described by this component usually has completed high school, in many cases has a university education, and as a consequence is employed in professional, managerial, and technical occupations. Although only a few of the females work, those that do are often clerical or professional employees, and they earn relatively high salaries. The general affluence of the group defined by this component is indicated by the fact that it is well equipped with amenities such as automobiles and television sets. This dimension therefore defines a group that can be defined as high- and middle-income Anglo-Saxon Protestants, the characteristics of which conform very closely to those of the social-rank construct of the social area analysts.

The second dimension describes a group consisting of large but mostly young families living in single-family houses. Most of the adult population is married; most of

---

Table 11.2. SOCIOECONOMIC VARIABLES SELECTED FOR PRINCIPAL COMPONENTS ANALYSIS OF WINNIPEG, 1961

Socioeconomic Characteristics	Variable Number	Title
Population change	1	% annual population change, 1956–1961
Age structure		
	5	% female population, age 65 and over
Sex ratio	6	Sex ratio (females per 1,000 males)
Marital status	7	% population age 15 and over, single
	8	% population age 15 and over, married
Birthplace	9	% population born outside of Canada
	10	% population immigrated, 1946–1961
Ethnic allegiance	11	% population British Isles ethnic group

Socioeconomic Characteristics	Variable Number	Title
	12	% population French ethnic group
	23	% population Ukrainian (Greek) Catholic
	24	% population United Church of Canada
Educational status	25	% nonschool attenders, 15 and over, never attended school
	28	% nonschool attenders, 15 and over, attended university
Household size	29	% households occupied by 6 or more persons
	30	% households occupied by a single family
	31	% households with boarders
Family size	32	% families with 0–2 children
	35	Persons per family
Family age	36	% family heads under age 25
	39	Persons per room
Amenities	40	% households with flush toilet (exclusive use)
	43	% households with passenger automobile
Working women	44	% females age 15 and over in labor force (LF)
Male labor-force structure	45	% male LF wage earners
	53	% employed male LF, laborers
Female labor-force structure	54	% employed female LF, managerial
	60	% employed female LF, transportation and communication, primary and laborers
Wage and salary income	61	Average male wage and salary income
	62	Average female wage and salary income
	63	Wage and salary income per family
Family income	64	% families with incomes under $3,000
	67	% families with incomes $10,000 and over
Residential stability	68	% population, age 5 and over, nonmovers 1956–1961[a]
	69	% population, age 5 and over, movers from central city, 1956–1961
	70	% population, age 5 and over, movers from fringe area, 1956–1961

[a] Variables 68–70 are based on "estimates of population by mobility status (which were derived from a 20 percent sample of persons 15 years old and over residing in private households," Census of Canada, Dominion Bureau of Statistics, Migration, Fertility and Income by Census Tracts, Series CX, Bulletin CX-1, Catalogue 95-541 (1961), p. 1. The remainder of the variables are based on complete census returns.

them own cars; and although many have only a few years of education, they nevertheless receive middle-range incomes from work in transportation and communication activities or as craftsmen. There is a relative absence of elderly people and females in the labor force within this group. Thus the second component describes a group that can be defined as consisting of young middle-income families, the characteristics of which comprise those of the family status construct.

The third dimension consists of a group composed primarily of "other European" and Jewish people, many of whom have attended universities and are now employed in managerial capacities; and generally family incomes are greater than 10,000 dollars per year. This component can therefore be described as representing general non-AngloSaxon affluence. The fourth component consists of French-speaking Roman Catholics and large families, characteristics that obviously describe the French-Canadian ethnic group. The last dimension describes census tracts that contain a large proportion of eastern European and Ukrainian (Greek) Catholics, which have received few recent immigrants and which are undergoing a population decline. These tracts have relatively few young people in them and few large families or households, and obviously consist of a residual eastern European group. These last three components together define three distinct dimensions conforming very closely to the ethnic status construct of the social area analysts.

Neighborhoods

Communities subdivide into smaller areas called neighborhoods. Burgess illustrates the distinction by adopting a land-value definition of a community:

> The centers of local communities are to be found at the point of highest land value in the intersection of two business streets. . . . If high land values indicate the center of the community, the lowest land values generally define its periphera. But if the intersection of two business streets determines the trade center, these same streets divide it into neighborhoods [Park et al., 1925, pp. 148–149].

Each neighborhood has its own public school, its own church, its own social center, and frequently its own local shopping street. These characteristics usually act singly or in harmony as the focus of the neighborhood, the limits of which are usually set by the average length of convenient walking distance. It is interesting to note that Burgess comments favorably on the role of the neighborhood as a moral decision-making force.

The neighborhood, then, is the territory in which an individual lives his or her everyday existence. The human being, though he may be conditioned by his cultural heritage, can still be regarded as an animal with basic animal instincts concerning territory and space. Indeed, Chombart de Lauwe (1965) indicates that there is a complex interrelationship between an individual and the territory and space that is occupied. Thus the concept of territoriality and the physical dimensions of a neighborhood are fundamentally linked.

This linkage can be explained by defining the basic physical elements of the territoriality concept and examining some of the behavioral conditions that influence them (Bragdon, 1967). There are three physical elements of interest in neighborhood analysis. The first relates to the *boundary* of the neighborhood. Frequently this can be defined by a physical feature, change in house type, or a simple distance-decay effect on human interaction. Neighborhood boundaries occasionally can be zones of upheaval and conflict, such as between different ethnic groups or gangs. The second element relates to *usage*, for the physical extent of a neighborhood may vary according to the manner in which it is used. For example, the neighborhood for shopping may be quite different from that for children's play; and, in another context, the daytime neighborhood may be much more extensive than that occupied in the evening. Third, the extent of the neighborhood is controlled by the distance over which an individual can interact with others. This interaction may be social, political, or economic, and may involve unique physical distances in each case.

The behavioral conditions range from those arising as a result of simple sex differences to more cultural considerations. When the male is the sole provider, the territory occupied by the wife is quite different from that occupied by the husband. As a consequence, if a family moves, it is the wife who has to undertake the most severe neighborhood readjustment. Thus *sex* difference may be regarded as one condition influencing the territorial extent of a neighborhood. A second and more important behavioral consideration relates to the *life cycle*. An individual's perception of space varies according to his or her stage of development. Young children need prescribed spatial limits and are quite happy playing within a limited territorial range as long as the basic facilities for play, such as sandboxes, climbers, and so forth, are available (White, 1963). As the children grow, their territorial limits increase, and it is quite frustrating for a teenager to be confined by a lack of public transport to a homogenized green suburb. By retirement, though, the neighborhood becomes a controlling factor in an elderly person's field of social contact (Golant, 1972). The importance of the third behavioral condition, *social class*, is difficult to determine. The general impression is that the lower the class, the more prescribed the territory. But this is probably because lower-class individuals have little choice other than to reside in more hostile areas (Rainwater, 1966). The fourth factor, *culture*, is certainly extremely interesting, especially in those parts of urban areas where particular cultural groups predominate. Hall (1966), for example, cites a number of characteristics pertaining to various ethnic groups, and suggests that sight and sound should be included within the territoriality concept.

The automobile and the associated spreading out of the city have resulted in a change in the concept of the neighborhood beyond the central city. Although many subdivisions are constructed with some rudimentary knowledge of the neighborhood concept, frequently this goes only so far as religious institutions. Planned shopping centers are usually built to cater to a number of neighborhood subdivisions, and the busing of children to large economic high schools reinforces the fluidity of society. Thus the trend beyond the central city seems to be away from the neighborhood as a social unit and toward the community as a unit of organization. The problem that emerges frequently, however, is that people identify more readily with small spatial units than with larger ones. In these cases what is needed is some catalyst to foster neighborhood-community affiliation.

PATTERNS

The urban geographer is usually interested in the manner in which these socioeconomic areas are distributed within the city. Maps of social variation can be constructed by the use of a variety of methods. At one extreme can be distinguished the univariable map, and at the other extreme is the multivariable map. The most important aspect of this type of analysis is the search for order in spatial patterns, and the fundamental concern involves the development of some rationale to explain this pattern. This procedure should in fact be reversed, but research in urban social geography usually has not progressed from theory to patterns, but the other way around.

Uni- and Multivariable Patterns

Univariable patterns are those that are described on the basis of a single characteristic. In the context of regionalization they are synonymous with single-factor regions. Multivariable patterns describe regions based on a number of characteristics that have to be synthesized to define a single dimension.

Puerto Ricans in Manhattan

Figure 11.2A is based on the proportion of the total population in each census tract in Manhattan in 1950 which can be classified as Puerto Rican. Novak (1956) states that at that time only five of the 284 census tracts in Manhattan were between 40 and 76 percent Puerto Rican, and none exceeded 76 percent. These tracts are to the southeast of the black ghetto of Harlem, and for that reason form the core of an area that is referred to as "Spanish Harlem" or *El Barrio.* The reasons for this and other minor centers of concentration in Manhattan are considered by Novak to be twofold: (1) low-cost housing, where extended families can coexist or friends can live with others who speak the same language; and (2) the availability of public transportation, which is vital for the majority of Puerto Ricans who are employed in the downtown service trades.

A multivariable analysis of the 1960 census tract data for Manhattan (Fig. 11.2B) provides more detail concerning the socioeconomic characteristics of this Puerto Rican

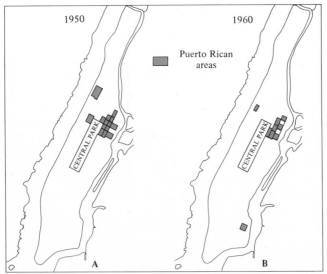

Fig. 11.2. The distribution of Puerto Ricans on Manhattan Island, New York City: (A) the 1950 pattern delimited by Novak; (B) the 1960 pattern delimited by Carey. (*Source:* adapted from Novak, 1956, Fig. 1, and Carey, 1966, Fig. 2.)

subgroup, and a modification of the distributional pattern described by Novak. As a result of a principal components analysis of 33 socioeconomic variables, Carey (1966) defines a Puerto Rican subpopulation factor as including many children of elementary and high school age, with the labor force employed in the garment trades and eating and drinking places, and generally unsound and overcrowded housing. The map illustrates that the Puerto Rican core area extends eastward to cover seven census tracts rather than five.

The Social Geography of Metropolitan Toronto, 1951 and 1961

One of the most comprehensive multivariate ecological analyses of an urban area has been undertaken by Murdie (1969) for Metropolitan Toronto using a principal components analysis of 86 socioeconomic variables. These variables concerned occupation, income, dwelling, ethnic background, language, religion, sex and school characteristics of census tracts. The results of this analysis indicate that there are nine significant dimensions of variation in both time periods. The dimensions that show the greatest consistency are those summarizing variations in economic status, family status, and recent growth. The remaining dimensions are also similar at both time periods, for

a factor describing ethnic status in the 1951 analysis separated into two independent factors in the 1961 analysis: Italian ethnic status and Jewish ethnic status. In contrast, two independent factors from the 1951 study which were identified as service-employment and household characteristics consolidated into one component comprising both household and employment characteristics in the 1961 analysis [Murdie, 1969, p. 76].

Thus, factors comparable to the social-area constructs are the dominant underlying dimensions of the original 86 socioeconomic variables in both 1951 and 1961.

The spatial relationships of these social areas or communities and ethnic groups of Toronto are expressed diagrammatically in Figure 11.3. It is to be noted that Murdie recognizes concentric zones distorted by the underlying pattern of transportation, with small families close to the center of the city and large families at the periphery. Juxtaposed with this concentric pattern is a zonal arrangement of census tracts of low- and high-economic-status families and individuals. Finally, clustered around the metropolis but conforming to the underlying concentric family status and zonal economic status patterns are certain ethnic groups.

Recurring Patterns

Evidence for the concentric, zonal, and clustered patterns presented by Murdie for Toronto has been recognized previously by a number of social area analysts. Anderson and Egeland (1961) concluded from social area analyses of Akron (Ohio), Dayton (Ohio), Indianapolis (Indiana), and Syracuse (New York) that family status was a concentric phenomenon and social rank sectoral. De Vise notes a rather more confusing pattern for metropolitan Chicago:

The rings are shown to contain towns of similar residential employment functions. Sectors, at least within the first two rings, are found to have towns of similar income characteristics. Zones, the composites of rings and sectors, are seen as areas of relatively homogenous functions and characteristics [De Vise, 1960, p. 6].

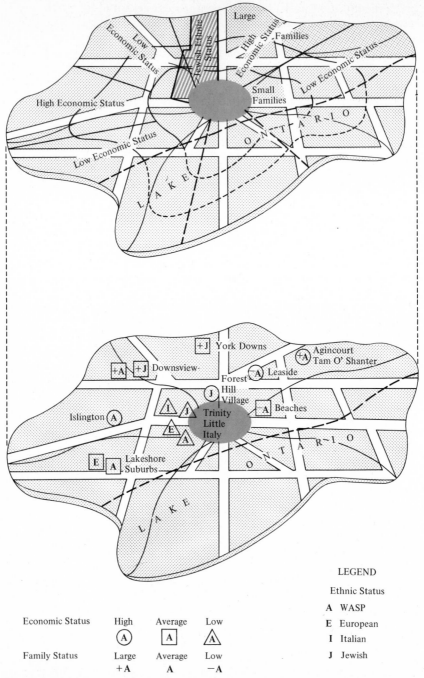

Fig. 11.3. "Communities" in Metropolitan Toronto. (*Source*: after Murdie, 1969, Fig. 29.)

These empirical studies, and others, have led Berry (1965) to hypothesize that, in general, there are three spatial patterns of socioeconomic variation. The first is the axial or sectoral variation of neighborhoods by socioeconomic rank. The second is the concentric variation of neighborhoods according to family structure. The third is localized segregation of particular ethnic groups in pockets, which conforms to some multiple-nuclei pattern.

These hypotheses are represented diagrammatically in Figure 11.4. Social rank varies from high to low, and its theoretical spatial distribution conforms closely to the locational mechanisms implicit in Hoyt's sector theory. The family status (or its inverse, urbanization) construct has its conceptual counterpart in Burgess's concentric-zone model. Finally the pockets of different ethnic or racial groups have to be explained by some other locational mechanism. The three patterns combine to produce a cartogram of a very complex mosaic.

Although a number of researchers have observed visually the recurring patterns indicated in Figure 11.4, few have attempted a quantitative analysis of the type of pattern existing. However, Murdie (1969), using analysis of variance, has undertaken such a quantitative analysis in Metropolitan Toronto. The economic-status components for both 1951 and 1961 proved to be sectoral, and the family-status components were chiefly zonal (Table 11.3). Both a zonal and a concentric pattern appear for the ethnic-status pattern in 1951, while the Jewish ethnic-status component in 1961 proved to be quite sectoral. This is due to increasing coexistence of this group with the high-economic-status sector.

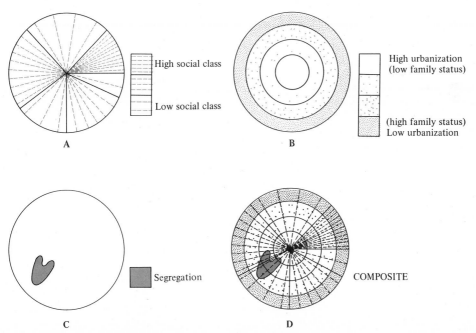

Fig. 11.4. An idealized spatial arrangement of indexes of (A) social class, (B) family status, (C) segregation, and (D) a composite view of the spatial variation in socioeconomic structure.

Table 11.3. **THE SPATIAL DISTRIBUTION OF SOCIAL AREA DIMENSIONS IN METROPOLITAN TORONTO, 1951 AND 1961**

Dimension	Primarily Sectoral	More Sectoral than Zonal	Both Sectoral and Zonal	Primarily Zonal
Economic status (1951)	Yes			
Economic status (1961)	Yes			
Family status (1951)				Yes
Family status (1961)				Yes
Ethnic status (1951)			Yes	
Italian ethnic (1961)		Yes		
Jewish ethnic (1961)	Yes			

Source: Murdie (1969), p. 164.

The approach to community definition described above is a simple example of the application of a factor analysis model to a mixture of data relating to census tracts. It is therefore one of the many studies in *factorial urban ecology* that have been presented over the past decade (Rees, 1971). The factorial ecology approach has been useful in that it has established, and mostly confirmed, the major constructs of urban social space as defined by the social area analysts (Timms, 1971). In a few cases some additional dimensions have been revealed as well, but on the whole the formal dimensions of social space revealed by these studies have been quite consistent. The factorial urban ecology approach, though useful, can now add little more to our understanding of the social geography of urban areas, for, apart from the well-known problems relating to the use of factor analysis in geographic research, the method has little more than refined our descriptive capabilities and reaffirmed the basic Shevky-Bell constructs at an aggregated level. This point has been well made by Berry (1971, p. 219) when he indicates that the field no longer requires "a stream of witless replications of methodologies and analyses long since generalized." The patterns exist, but it is not clear why they exist, for even though Burgess's and Hoyt's models provide partial explanations, they do not indicate why people behave or locate in the way that they do.

SOCIAL PROCESSES

We have previously emphasized the significance of social reorganization and territoriality as meaningful concepts in the understanding of community and neighborhood formation and differentiation. It is quite obvious that the urban geographer and, in a broader sense, the social scientist must develop a deep understanding of these concepts if they are to understand the spatial structure of the urban environment. Of equal importance is the development of an understanding of processes concerning change in these patterns. Changing patterns occur because of the changing socioeconomic characteristics of the population of urban areas. Generally, there are two ways in which this change can occur: either through a change in the people themselves, or through a displacement procedure.

Invasion-Succession-Dominance

One of the earliest and most enduring models concerning change has its roots in plant and animal ecology. In this model the process begins with a particular plant or animal occupying a given space or territory. An invasion then occurs, with the influx of a species foreign to the area; and if this invasion is successful, the species will eventually dominate the territory. This succession has its beginning on a frontier, an area of instability; wave after wave pushes on relentlessly until some form or system of organization has evolved that can maintain itself against external and internal attack" (Ford, 1950, p. 156). Successions are therefore the product of invasions, and although a temporary stability is achieved with each succession, a longer term stability is not achieved until the climax stage is reached.

This ecological process can be regarded as an analogy for social change if the plant ecologist's concept of an ultimate climax stage is disregarded. McKenzie (Park et al., 1925) suggests that intracommunity invasions can be grouped into two main classes: those involving land use change, and those involving change in type of occupant. Land use changes involve the transference of general uses, such as the replacement of a residential area by an industrial or business region. Changes of this type can usually occur only through rezoning. Occupancy changes refer in particular to the replacement of one type of residential group by another. The degree to which it is noticeable that a particular residential group is replacing another depends on the social distance separating them.

Social Distance

Social distance is a concept referring to the degree of separation between individuals, families, and groups. When applied to communities or neighborhoods, it refers to the way in which two or more community groups perceive each other. This perception involves a host of factors: economic, social, and psychological. If the social distance between groups or neighborhoods is large, then it will be difficult for members of one group to be assimilated into the other. If the social distance is great, and one group is trying to occupy the territory of another, then the change is noticeable and an invasion can be thought to be occurring. In situations where the social distance is not great, communities merge and there is little notion of replacement.

As the concept of social distance involves numerous perceptive features, it has proved very difficult actually to measure the social distance between groups. An early attempt was undertaken by Bogardus (1926), who analyzed the perception by native-born white Americans of other ethnic and linguistic groups in the United States in the 1920's. He hypothesized the following rank order of social relations as a scale for measuring the perception by the native-born white American group of the other groups:

1. To admit to close kinship by marriage
2. To have as friends
3. To have as neighbors on the same street
4. To admit as members of one's occupation within one's country
5. To admit as citizens of one's country
6. To admit as visitors only to one's country
7. To exclude entirely from one's country

Other important racial and linguistic groups residing in the United States were ranked along this qualitative scale by 450 native-born white Americans.

The results of the analysis showed that Armenians, blacks, Chinese, Hindus, and Turks were usually put in categories 6 and 7, while the English, French, Norwegian, and Scottish groups were generally put in categories 1 to 5. Thus the first group is socially rather distant from the native-born white American majority, whereas the latter group is a great deal closer. Assimilation, therefore, is rather more difficult for the former group than for the latter. It is to be remembered, however, that social distance varies within groups and geographically. Also, Bogardus analyzed the perception of a number of groups by members of only one group, not the way in which all the groups perceived each other.

Conditions Initiating Invasions

Invasions can occur as a result of many conditions. Probably one of the most important relates to changes in forms and routes of transportation. New transportation arteries affect accessiblity for the entire urban area, and their local impact can be quite dramatic. For example, Hoch (1957) indicates that the Edens Expressway in Chicago has had a positive effect on land values in areas bordering the route. On the other hand, declining or blighted transportation arteries can adversely affect the surrounding area. Obsolescence is also a debilitating factor that can change the entire image of a community or neighborhood and create opportunities for the invasion of a new occupational group or land use. On the other hand, the construction of new buildings or the redevelopment of an area can result in upgrading, which also provides a stimulus for invasion.

Some neighborhood invasions are created by real estate promoters, who can change the image of an area simply by good advertising and the emphasis of a few local features. One of the most notorious examples of the working of this mechanism is "block-busting." This procedure requires a situation where one particular group is living in a confined segregated area in which the demand for housing greatly exceeds the supply. Once sufficient piling up has occurred, the demand for new living space becomes so obvious and great that promoters can take advantage of the prejudices of the peripheral nonsegregated group by scaring it into panic selling. These properties are then purchased cheaply by speculators and renters, who subdivide the property and exploit the intense demand of the segregated group by greatly increasing unit space rents. It should be noted that the block-busting procedure often involves collusion and shared profits between white and black real estate speculators, and economic pressure on both white and black homeowners or renters. In effect, the scared whites end up paying for their prejudice, and the blacks, as usual, pay for their color.

Conditions Expressing Succession

Succession can therefore be expressed in many forms, such as:

1. Land ownership and value.
2. The appearance of residential structures, involving either rebuilding or renovation.
3. Transportation systems, particularly where one type of system replaces another, or where a particular system becomes blighted.

4. Media of communication, particularly newspapers, radio, and television.
5. Occupational groups.
6. Business, industrial, commercial, and financial enterprises.
7. Religious institutions and groups.
8. Cultural or ethnic groups.

Often a great deal of residual friction may occur if one particular group succeeds another in one aspect but fails to dominate in another. For example, one ethnic group may replace another, but the ownership of the buildings and media of communication may remain in the hands of the former. In this kind of situation the friction can be explosive, particularly if the succeeding group feels exploited in any way.

Segregation

Residential segregation can be expected to occur under two sets of circumstances. First, if a group is of an undesirable status, then the group will be involuntarily segregated. Second, voluntary segregation will occur if "proximity to members of the same group facilitates adjustment to the conditions of settlement in a new country or if members of an ethnic group simply view the residential proximity of members from the same group as desirable" (Lieberson, 1963, p. 5). In the first instance the process of segregation involves, in the North American context, "ghettoization," and in the second some form of grouping due to sentiment and symbolism.

Ghettos

Ghettos are common features of American urban life, for a vast majority of blacks, Puerto Ricans, and Mexican Americans are forced by a variety of pressures to reside in restricted areas where they are dominant (Taueber and Taueber, 1965). Morrill (1965b) suggests that it would be more accurate to state that almost every urban area, whatever the size, that has a considerable proportion of nonwhite inhabitants has a nonwhite ghetto. The term "ghetto" originally referred to the Jewish enclaves of eastern and southern Europe. In eastern Europe the Jewish area was not only distinct from the rest of the city, but ultimately physically contained by a wall built to confine the Jews to their defined area.

As applied to North America, a ghetto is a spatially contiguous area of the urban landscape in which the inhabitants have particular social, economic, ethnic, or cultural attributes that distinguish them from the majority of the inhabitants of the country in which they reside. Because of these differentiating characteristics, the inhabitants are, by and large, not permitted by the majority to reside beyond this well-defined area even if they wish, unless these differentiating attributes change sufficiently for them to be accepted (Rose, 1970). The ghetto is thus a result of external pressure rather than internal coherence. With the passing of time, however, certain ghettos may well develop a vibrant culture and an internal coherence that sustains the community to such an extent that the inhabitants would not wish to leave the ghetto even if they could.

This latter aspect of ghetto development is being reinforced as a result of the continuous deprivation, isolation, and exploitation of the black community. Black militants, who are frequently supported by the less militant, are stressing independence rather than integration, and Dr. Martin Luther King's concept of nonviolence is being replaced by the idea of self-defense. Integration proposals are frequently viewed by the black community as a further, but subtle, development of the white community's inherent racist sentiments. As a consequence, black people "are becoming increasingly unwilling to accept the assumptions of white culture, white values, and white power" (Skolnick, 1969, p. xxii). If the white community fails to overhaul its attitudes and procedures, which in many cases unwittingly give a racist impression, then the black ghetto will increasingly become an alienated and separate nation within North America (Kain and Persky, 1969).

Black Ghettos

The development of these views can perhaps be related to the phenomenal growth of black ghettos in large American metropolitan areas between 1910 and 1970 outside the South. Rose (1971) indicates that whereas in 1910, 12 of 18 urban places in the United States that had black populations of 25,000 or more were located in the South, by 1970 over half of the 70 or more urban places that had at least 25,000 blacks were located outside the South. This shift in relative location and composition of the black urban population is important because in the South the form and structure of the urban ghetto differs quite widely from that in urban centers beyond the South. Southern black urban ghettos are located in parts of the city that have for generations been set aside as black areas. They have, as a consequence, a clearly prescribed territory, and within the defined limits they have developed their own institutions and stratified residential structure. As a consequence, there is no question as to who lives where, who is serviced where, and the location of the black-white boundary. The present tense is used because even today these characteristics prevail.

Although a number of urban black ghettos outside the South have been in existence for a century or more, the prevailing characteristic is one of wholesale growth and establishment during the past four decades. The black people came to northern cities to find a situation quite different from that in the South. There was no clearly prescribed territory, but whites would not accept blacks into their neighborhoods, schools, community facilities, and so forth. The result was that the blacks occupied the most deteriorated or undesirable part of the urban area, and as immigration and growth caused pressure on land and housing, the ghetto expanded outward at the periphery, following lines of least resistance, which frequently resulted in a sectoral pattern. The result is a ghetto that has a number of territories (Rose, 1971). The ghetto *core* is an area in which more than 75 percent of the population are black, the ghetto *fringe* is between 50 and 74 percent black, areas that are 30 to 49 percent black represent the ghetto zone in *transition*, and areas less than 30 percent black which are immediately adjacent to the fringe or transitional zones are described as *temporarily stable*.

The importance of these definitions is that they indicate the areas of possible conflict that occur as the ghetto expands. The law decrees equality of opportunity and equal rights to purchase property, but the institutions involved are manipulated to make the process of assimilation difficult (Zelder, 1970). Frequently the gradient from the ghetto core to the zone in transition is steep, and with the advent of public housing schemes for low-income neighborhoods, the fringe area is often a zone of desolation and sterile reconstruction. Furthermore, the social and economic turmoil of ghetto expansion has severe negative repercussions on business, apart from insurance.

Employment in Ghettos

One of the most important problems found within ghettos is poverty, which is directly related to employment. Job opportunities are limited, and the result is a high unemployment rate, particularly among young people. Part of the employment difficulty is related to industrial and service decentralization, for with the ghettos located in the inner city, accessibility to jobs has decreased. Deskins (1969) indicates that in Detroit the accessibility of blacks to employment decreased between 1953 and 1965 as a result of decentralization, so that the black worker in 1965 was more disadvantaged in this respect than he was twelve years earlier.

The result of this situation has been an attempt to improve transport opportunities between the inner-city black ghettos and suburban employment centers. This cannot, however, be regarded as terribly successful, for in most cases public transport innovations from the inner city to suburban manufacturing centers have not been well patronized. A second remedy has been that of moving the homes of black people to the suburbs (Kain, 1968). There are, of course, a number of well-known examples of black suburbs (e.g., Maywood, outside of Chicago), but black people have, on the whole, not been part of the tremendous suburban sprawl that has occurred in the past quarter century. It is naive, however, to suppose that equality of access to housing could really alleviate this social problem.

Actually, it is not at all clear whether the suburbanization of blacks is really an answer to the employment question (Frieden 1972). Though many new jobs have been created in the suburbs, the vast bulk of jobs are still available in cities, and particularly in the traditional employment areas. These jobs may not have had as great a percentage increase as those in the suburbs, but the turnover rate and the small increases may provide more total opportunities. The task is to continue the process of making these, and suburban jobs, open to all, regardless of color. There is no doubt that the labor unions and trade certification committees could greatly assist this process of eliminating overt employment discrimination.

Sentiment and Symbolism

Firey (1945) suggests that two other conditions also result in clusters of particular ethnic groups, or members of a certain socioeconomic class: symbolism and sentiment. Symbolic features are described by Firey as being of particular importance when related to historic and aesthetic attributes. Beacon Hill in Boston and Society Hill in Philadelphia are good examples. Both areas are inhabited by high-income individuals who are consciously attempting to preserve the colonial and early American heritage of these areas. This end is achieved in the Beacon Hill district by strong local ordinances and the restricting of property sales to high-income, socially acceptable families who will preserve the atmosphere of their properties and the community.

The second condition involves sentiments that are often attached to a particular locale. Firey described this condition in great detail with respect to the Italian section of Boston's North End in 1940, a situation that resembles closely that of the eastern European ethnic groups in Winnipeg in 1960. This group consists particularly of first- and second-generation immigrants who live together in the North End in order to preserve family and group cultural characteristics. So significant is the family in the Italian milieu that it is not uncommon to find a building completely occupied by one extended family of grandparents, their children, their children's children, and so forth. The strength of the family lies, therefore, in its size and joint economic power. Frequently apartments owned by Italians are rented to their kin in order to keep the family members in close proximity. Subsequent generations, moreover, are slower than those of most other ethnic groups to break away from the old neighborhood, so the community regenerates itself and enjoys a remarkable stability.

Slums

One of the characteristics of ghettos and some segregated communities is that a large part of them are in slums. In a narrow sense, the term "slum" refers to housing characterized by dilapidated conditions, overcrowding, filth, and vermin. In a broader sense, however, the slum is a "genuine social community in the culture of poverty with all of the institutions of support and adjustment and accommodation new urban migrants as well as low-income groups need" (Wingo, 1966, p. 145). The fact that ghettos contain slums, and that slums are particularly associated with the zone of deterioration encircling the central business district, is not surprising, for the slum is the home of the poor and the stranger. The function of a slum, then, is to house these persons until they are absorbed into city life. This assimilation should be possible when the poor person has attained sufficient skills to achieve a higher wage level, and when the stranger has accepted the culture and behavior patterns of the urban dwellers, and is thus employable.

Stokes (1962) presents a simple model that attempts to sort out the variables that are thought to be determinants of slums and the culture of poverty (Lewis, 1966). These variables can be combined to provide a classification of slums, which in turn can be used to describe the complexity of public policy in this area. Stokes discerns two main groups of slum dwellers in terms of their psychological attitude toward the possibility of economic improvement. One group is composed of the slum dwellers who have hope; they think that they can better themselves and consequently they are employable. The second group consists of the slum dwellers of despair, who have a negative estimate of the outcome of any attempt at economic improvement. This feeling of despair can of course be brought about by a number of conditions—continuous failure, old age, and so on.

Apart, though intercorrelated with these psychological attitudes, are the socioeconomic conditions of the slum dweller. These conditons lead, in this simple model, to a postulate of the existence of an escalator class and a nonescalator class. An escalator group can move upward if it has the psychological attitude that enables it to do so. A nonescalator group is denied in some way the privilege of escalation, because of either caste, race, religion, color, or some other discriminating factor.

It is therefore possible to develop a simple classification of slums based on these psychological and socioeconomic variables. This classification is presented as a 2×2 matrix in Table 11.4, which identifies the following:

A. Slums of hope consisting of escalator classes
B. Slums of despair consisting of escalator classes
C. Slums of hope consisting of nonescalator classes
D. Slums of despair consisting of nonescalator classes

The suggestion is that a different strategy is necessary for each case. National policies concerning economic growth, equal opportunity, and minimum housing standards are basic prerequisites for a war on slums. Local area programs are necessary for each type of slum condition, particularly the B and D types.

Social Space and Locational Space

Factors involved in the individual's or family's locational decision therefore determines in aggregate the social geography of urban areas. Conceptually, Rees (1968) defines three elements related to the process, the first of which relates the decision-making unit to its position in social space. The axes of this space (Fig. 11.5) are socio-economic status and stage in the life cycle, which, for analytical purposes, are considered to be synonymous with the social-rank and family-status constructs as defined by the social area analysts. Life style is difficult to measure and to calibrate, and consequently is not included in the Rees diagram. Thus a unit located in position A in Figure 11.5A is fairly wealthy, with a small family, and is either in late middle age or young without children. A unit located at B is less wealthy, employed in a lower status occupation, and with fewer years of education. A unit positioned at C is a relatively large but low-income family, while a unit at D is a high-income, high-status, and relatively large

Table 11.4.   A CLASSIFICATION OF SLUMS

	Hope	Despair
Escalator	A. Rate of absorption depends on the growth of employment opportunities in the area. If the number of job-seekers is greatly in excess of available positions, then the surplus in this group will collect in slums. Thus steady national economic growth and expanding job opportunities will help hold this group to a minimum.	B. Can be regarded in most cases as a surplus that has lost hope. It may, for example, have been unemployed too long and lost any hope for economic betterment. Burgeoning job opportunities will not necessarily solve the problem of this group, for a degree of social reconstruction may be required along with job retraining. It is important, however, to prevent the feeling of despair from being imparted to the younger generation of this group.
Nonescalator	C. This group has hope of economic improvement, but there is a barrier that has to be overcome. If the barrier is linguistic, they must learn a new language; but racial, ethnic, and religious barriers are not so easily overcome. However, if the barrier can be broken down, this group will move into Group A and will be assimilated during the process of economic growth.	D. This is the most difficult slum type of all, as the problem will not pass away even if the barrier is dismantled and decent jobs are available. It is difficult to envisage any other policy than grass-roots social, economic, and cultural reconstruction, along with a growing national economy, as a strategy for tackling the problems of this group. Concomitantly there must be a policy that prevents a slum with these characteristics from being formed in the future. Many sections of black ghettos consist of Group D type; and a recession, along with a failure to implement equal employment laws, will only swell the numbers found in this category.

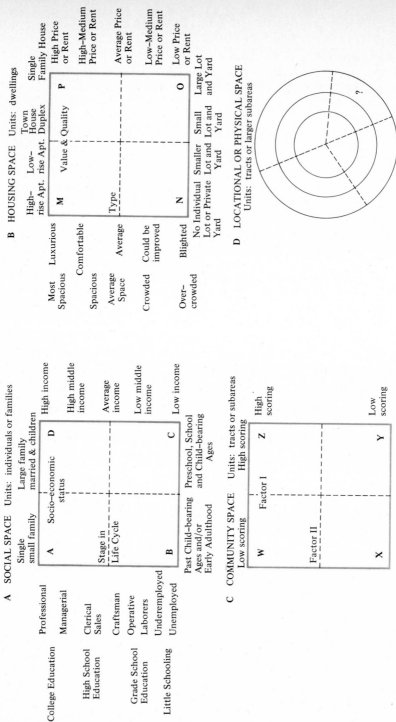

Fig. 11.5. The decision process and social areas. (*Source:* Rees, 1968, Fig. 4.)

272

family unit. Social space, in effect, therefore defines the demand matrix of the individual or family.

The second element refers to the supply of housing in terms of type, value, and quality. Thus in Figure 11.5B a dwelling unit positioned at M is a luxurious, high-priced, spacious high-rise apartment; whereas N defines a low-priced, blighted, and overcrowded apartment or tenement. A dwelling unit positioned at O, on the other hand, is a low-priced, blighted, single-family unit or duplex; whereas P defines high-priced, luxurious, spacious single-family unit.

The third element defines community space and is also a two-dimensional categorization (Fig. 11.5C). These dimensions are, as in Figure 11.5A, based on the economic-status and family-status constructs of the social area analysts, but they locate areas (census tracts or large subareas) rather than individual family units. The first factor refers to spatial units in terms of family status. Thus a family unit positioned at D in social space will most probably wish to buy or rent a dwelling unit positioned at P in housing space, which will imply a location at Z in community space. The geographical expression of this location varies according to the orientation of the city, but our locational space model (Fig. 11.5D) would suggest a position in the outer zone in one of the high-economic-status sectors.

The existence of the relationship between social space, housing space, and community space has been examined by Yeates (1972) with respect to experimental sample data for Winnipeg and Kingston. The results of this experiment were encouraging in that the various dimensions of the models could be calibrated quite easily, and they are interrelated in a predictable manner. There is a statistically significant association between a family's social space and its housing space, and these two are related significantly to community space. There are, however, a number of incongruencies, and these are related to inertia (Lansing and Mueller, 1967) and the difficulty experienced by low-income families in obtaining the housing that is congruent with their requirements as defined by their position in social space. Thus the social geography of urban areas is orderly owing to regularities in the operation of the land and housing markets and the fact that similar decision-making units (individuals or families) tend to make similar choices and desire a similar social and community environment. However, the groups that cannot participate freely in this process of selection are those that are restricted in their location and their ability to pay.

12
THE LOCATION
OF
COMMERCIAL USES

It has been noted previously that smaller central places are usually those whose primary function is to provide goods and services to consumers residing in areas surrounding them. As settlements get larger and the importance of the central-place function diminishes, the supply of goods and services to their resident populations becomes increasingly more important. In order to service these populations as efficiently as possible, commercial activities are spatially distributed within cities in general agreement with the distribution of population. In this chapter we shall discuss the intraurban pattern of commercial activities and examine some of the regularities that are apparent in the commercial structure of cities.

Although commercial activities are not great users of land within cities, the layout of commercial land use is such that business is brought into virtually every neighborhood in cities. In Chicago, 500 miles of continuous commercial frontage abut the section, half-section, and radial streets. A further 25 miles are scattered among predominantly residential neighborhoods, while another 30 miles of frontage make up the larger shopping centers at important street intersections, not to mention the frontage of the innumerable smaller shopping centers located at minor street corners and hidden away in the middle of residential areas.

Apart from the prominance of commercial land, it is also important in other respects. A sizable proportion of the total building space in cities is normally used by commercial activities. They are important generators of traffic flow within the urban area, and it is on trips to commercial land use that urban dwellers make most of their expenditures. It has been estimated that in Chicago, for example, over 16 percent of the city's total building space is used up by wholesale, retail, and service activities; that 28 percent (930,000 out of 3.28 million) of all vehicular trips and 25 percent (1.46 million out of 5.77 million) of all individual vehicular trips on an average weekday end on commercial land; and that on these trips to commercial land uses, Chicagoans make about 60 percent of their total consumer expenditures (Berry, 1963).

ELEMENTS OF COMMERCIAL STRUCTURE

The results from studies of the commercial structure of cities during the past quarter century suggest that the urban business complex can be disaggregated into three major elements or conformations. In turn, a number of subtypes within each of the major conformations can be recognized. A composite picture of these is presented in Figure 12.1. This classification is based on analysis of the locational requirements of the different business types within the urban area; that is, on the analysis of the functional characteristics of commercial areas rather than on their morphology or form. It should be remembered, however, that not all of these functional types may be present in all cities. Smaller cities in particular may lack some of the various ribbons or specialized areas, while at the same time not all the levels in the hierarchy of shopping centers may be fully developed. The commercial structure of larger cities will, however, approximate closely the suggested typology, and in metropolitan areas these elements become especially well developed (Table 12.1).

The general features of this commercial structure were laid down in most cities during the early part of this century. Until then, most of the commercial activity within cities was concentrated in the central business district, which, as a result, dominated the urban commercial pattern. But in the period from 1900 to 1935 considerable expansion of commercial activities took place in most cities outside this central area in conjunction with rapid urban growth. Most of the growth of commercial land use at this time was, however, unplanned; and in the absence of the strong influence of the automobile, it was conditioned largely by the disposition of the then existing surface transit network. It was also during this early period that the basic features of the land-value surface emerged in most cities (see Chapter 9).

Since World War II, the earlier developed structural skeleton has been intensified and added to in part. These more recent developments have resulted directly from the ascendance of the automobile and the increased consumer mobility associated with it. In turn, stemming from increased mobility, the growth of suburban residential areas has brought about peripheral expansion of commercial land use; and more recently integrated planned shopping centers have been grafted onto the unplanned, naturally evolved structure. This intensification of the outlying commercial structure (everything outside the central business district) is well illustrated in Chicago, where in 1958

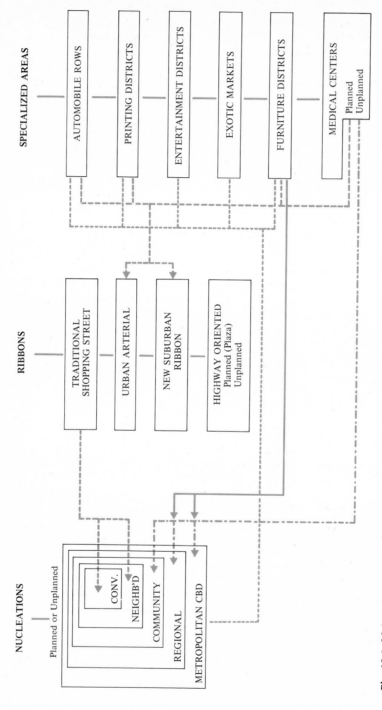

Fig. 12.1. Major components of the urban business pattern. (*Source:* Berry, 1963, Table 2.)

approximately 85 percent of total retail sales were made in commercial areas outside the central business district. The comparable figure in 1935, by which time the main features of outlying structure were well established, was about three-quarters of total retail sales. At the same time, however, the postwar period was also one of emerging problems and strains on the existing structure. This has been associated in part with the continued outward growth of many urban areas, and in part with the concomitant decline of the older, inner parts of cities. As yet, however, the basic elements of the urban commercial structure have been little modified by this, although pressure for change is undoubtedly building up.

The basic elements of the land-value surface within urban areas had jelled in most cities by the 1930s. The peak-value intersection and the disposition of the ridges of higher values along main arteries and minor peaks of value at the intersections of these are today very much as they were 25 years ago. Because of the need by most commercial uses for good accessibility to that part of the urban market served, a well-marked relationship appears to exist between the elements of commercial structure and these general features of the land-value surface. Generally the ridges of higher value are occupied by the various kinds of ribbon developments, while the minor peaks on the surface are associated with the more specialized retail and service businesses comprising the outlying shopping centers. As was pointed out in Chapter 9, the highest point on the surface of land values corresponds to the central business district and the very specialized and diverse commercial activities found in it. Moreover, the general tendency is for high-level centers in the hierarchy to be associated with minor peaks of higher value. But it should be remembered that this relationship is often blurred by the distorting influences of distance within the urban area.

Specialized Areas

Specialized areas is the name given to recognizable clusters of establishments of the same business type or of functionally interrelated business types within the urban area. They are usually freestanding in location, although they may be present in

Table 12.1.   CHICAGO'S OUTLYING COMMERCIAL STRUCTURE, 1961[a]

Type	Number of Ground-Floor Establishments	Front Feet of Buildings	Ground-Floor Area of Buildings (square feet)
1. Unplanned shopping nucleations (including small isolated nucleations)	5,782	165,497	14,777,145
2. Planned shopping centers	214	–	879,970
3. Ribbons (all types together)	45,172	1,108,680	91,074,000
4. Scattered uses	3,965	122,530	8,484,700
TOTALS	55,133	1,396,707	115,215,815

[a]Table includes only elements of the outlying commercial structure of the city. No data for the central business district are included; the data for the specialized areas are included in the four categories and are not shown separately.
SOURCE: After Berry (1963), Table 1.

incipient form within larger outlying shopping centers and well developed within the central business district (see Chapter 13). The dominant locational factor for this aspect of the commercial structure is accessibility to the portion of the urban market served. Hence it is not uncommon to find specialized areas established on major arterials within the urban area (e.g., automobile rows) or at points of focus within the public transport system (e.g., medical centers). Specialized areas normally have "just growed," like Topsy, at points within cities; they are mainly unplanned, although recently some planned concentrations have emerged, especially in connection with the provision of medical facilities.

Specialized areas are of many kinds, although the one most frequently encountered within cities is the automobile row. These rows are strung out along the main section and radial streets within urban areas, as is indicated for Toronto, for example, in Figure 12.2. They comprise contiguous strings of establishments selling new and used automobiles and facilities for parts, repairs, and servicing. Other types of specialized areas that have been identified, typical of other larger cities, include (1) medical districts comprising offices of doctors, dentists, and related medical facilities; the older, unplanned medical districts are often located at the upper-floor level within the outlying shopping centers, although in recent years the tendency has been for these to be either replaced or supplemented by newer, planned office accommodations away from shopping centers but at accessible locations near them; (2) printing districts, consisting of clusters of establishments performing printing and allied business services; these may not be associated with any particular sets of locations within the urban area although they are commonly distinguishing features in the area adjacent to the central business district, where they are well placed to serve the demand generated from the concentrations of various office functions there; (3) household-furnishing districts, comprising concentrations of furniture, household appliances, and related stores. The patterns of most of these in Toronto are presented in Figure 12.2.

Also included in specialized areas are the major large, independent, and discount stores found today within most North American cities. These are well distributed within most large cities in accordance with the distribution of population. They are normally situated at locations away from other elements of the business pattern, especially from the shopping centers, to which they sometimes offer serious competition. Although these do not constitute specialized areas in the true sense of the definition, they are distinctive, highly specialized features of the contemporary urban commercial scene and represent the trend to large-scale economies in modern retailing. Generally, these business types are found at arterial locations within urban areas, for they depend on automobile shopping. They are freestanding because the wide range of goods offered by them permit one-stop shopping visits and do not, therefore, necessitate linkages with other business types nearby.

Although many other types of specialized areas may be thought of—for example, the entertainment districts and exotic markets (such as Maxwell Street in Chicago, Grant Avenue in San Francisco, and Kensington Market in Toronto) listed in Figure 12.1—they all have one general feature in common, regardless of specific functional type: a concentration of establishments held together by close linkages between each other. They represent, therefore, the locational effects of the forces of scale economies, economies that—with the exception of the large independents—are external to individual establishments. By clustering together in this way, business types are able to take

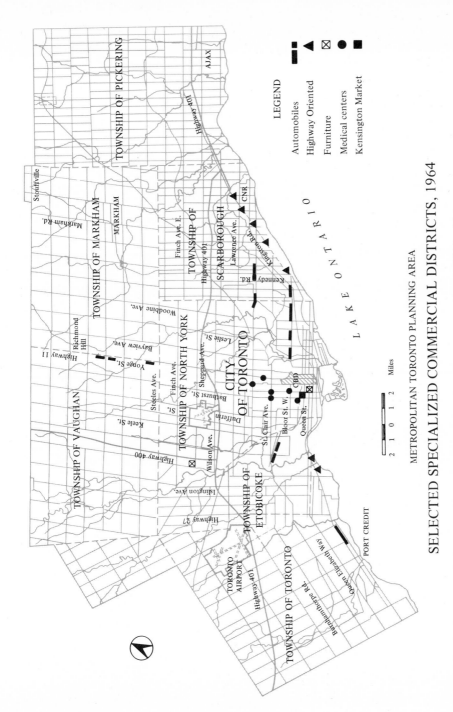

METROPOLITAN TORONTO PLANNING AREA

SELECTED SPECIALIZED COMMERCIAL DISTRICTS, 1964

Fig. 12.2. Specialized commercial areas in the Toronto area, 1964. (*Source:* Simmons, 1966, Fig. 8.)

advantage of economies of operation that would be denied them if they were located apart. Some savings may result from the nature of comparative shopping trips, as in the case of the automobile rows and furniture districts, or they may be the more usual kinds of savings associated with external economies in advertising and the sharing of common facilities.

The Ribbons

Ribbons, the second major element in the commercial structure of urban areas, are perhaps the most noticeable, since their constituents form the backdrop to most well-traveled routes through cities. Business types that have a tendency to locate in one or another of the types of ribbons are those that need a certain minimum degree of accessibility to the market served. They do not, however, require sites of maximum centrality within urban areas, and consequently can survive at locations along major arteries and urban highways. Although several different types of ribbons can be recognized, it is important to remember that the character of these is repeated from one part of the city to another. For the most part, the typical function of ribbons is to serve demands originating on the highways or to cater to one-stop, home-based shopping trips (Table 12.2). As such, they can be thought of as concentrations of commercial activities at common locations, but between which there is little if any functional interlinkage (Berry, 1959).

Highway-Oriented Ribbons

Highway-oriented ribbons have often been described as natural strip developments along major highways within urban areas. The business types located on this kind of ribbon truly serve demands originating on the highways themselves. Generally the greater the volume of traffic on the highway, the more important it is as a generator of demand, and consequently the greater the density of commercial development along it. For the most part, these ribbons are uncontrolled developments, although along some of the newer intraurban highways, planned service plazas have been constructed. Functions typical of the highway-oriented ribbons include gasoline and service stations, restaurants and drive-ins, ice-cream parlors, motels, and fruit-and-vegetable stands. These are essentially freestanding establishments between which there is very little functional linkage, which cater essentially to one-stop shopping trips originating from the transient market on the highways.

Urban Arterials

Functions generally associated with the urban-arterial ribbon development include things such as automobile repair shops, furniture and appliance stores, office-equipment sales, funeral parlors, lumberyards and fuel dealers, and a variety of building and household supplies, electrical repair services, plumbing establishments, and radio-television repairs and services. These types have two general characteristics: (1) they are for the most part large consumers of space; (2) they are associated with an infrequent demand calling for an occasional special-purpose trip or even a "home call." As a result of either or both of these characteristics, these activities need locations offering reasonable access to large portions of the urban market. However, they are generally assumed unable to pay the high rents for sites within the shopping centers at the intersections of the major urban arterials. Consequently, they function best outside the nucleated business centers where land values, and hence site rents, are generally lower. In many cases they form a continuation of commercial property along arterials between shopping centers. They exist because many different types of business seek out similar arterial locations for reasons of accessibility. However, as is the case for the functions typical of the highway-oriented ribbons, despite their common locations urban-arterial ribbons function independently of each other. There is normally little linkage between the different business types, which consequently can perhaps be best described as free-standing with common arterial locations.

Table 12.2.   SELECTED FUNCTIONS TYPICAL OF VARIOUS TYPES OF RIBBONS

HIGHWAY-ORIENTED RIBBONS

Gas stations
Restaurants   (Automobile service districts)
Motels
Fruit and produce stands

URBAN ARTERIALS

Building services and supplies
Lumberyards   (Space-consuming service districts)
Miscellaneous repairs
Radio-TV sales and repairs

Automobile repairs
Bars
Shoe repairs
Furniture
Automobile accessories   (Urban-arterial oriented)
Appliances
Fuel dealers
Gift and novelty stores
Food lockers
Florists

TRADITIONAL SHOPPING STREETS

Groceries
Laundromats
Bakeries   (Neighborhood streets)
Restaurants
Personal services

Missions
Secondhand stores
Bars and liquor stores   (Skid Rows)
Rooming houses

SOURCE: Berry (1959), Table 1.

Traditional Shopping Streets

Traditional shopping streets are distinctive features of the older parts of North American cities. They should be thought of as ribbon developments only in the sense of being morphologically similar to the other ribbon types. In functional structure, the traditional shopping streets are similar to the lower-level shopping centers. Typical business types in them include groceries, drugstores, laundries and laundromats, beauty salons, and barbershops. As such, they constitute small clusters of low-order convenience goods and services that are interjected into the arterial ribbons at minor street intersections. In older parts of cities, and especially near the CBD, many of these assume the form of skid rows. Thus, although their businesses share common locations with those of other ribbons, they differ in that they cater to home-based trips, which may be of a multiple-purpose nature. Hence there is more linkage between business types in these kinds of ribbon developments than in any of the others.

New Suburban Ribbons

New suburban ribbons are included largely for the sake of completeness, although their functional structure does differ somewhat from that of the two types of ribbons mentioned so far. They are more recent developments associated particularly with postwar suburbanization. As such they are typically found in the newer, peripheral parts of urban areas and especially in suburbs adjacent to central cities. Their functional character is derived from the inclusion of more exotic uses, catering to demands from new residential areas, along with business types that are typical of the urban arterial ribbons discussed above. Hence, more business types of the drive-in variety (e.g., banks, restaurants, and so on) are included in this variety of ribbon development.

Although the different types of ribbon development are associated with different locations within urban areas, it is not unusual to find them intertwined within any particular city. Notwithstanding this, however, it has been suggested that a clear differentiation exists between ribbons that are adjacent to shopping centers and those that are isolated within the urban area. The former constitute a frame around the nucleation they adjoin, whereas the latter are separated from them and are more or less freestanding. This difference in location is reflected in a difference in functional structure and size. For example, an investigation of these types in Chicago found that sample quarter-mile ribbons abutting nucleations had on an average 91 establishments and 33 different business types, occupied 2,550 front feet, and had a ground-floor area of 175,000 square feet. Isolated quarter-mile ribbons, on the other hand, contained on an average only 27 business types, occupying 55 establishments, accounted for only 1,670 feet fronting on the street, and had a ground-floor area of 130,000 square feet. In the ribbons close to nucleations most of the activities of the ribbon types discussed above are represented, and particularly those typical of the urban arterials. In fact, it is these that are mainly responsible for the intensification of ribbon development close to the nucleations (Berry, 1963). By comparison, the isolated ribbons in Chicago were found to be far more devoted to stretches of convenience businesses in association with highway-oriented activities and to restaurants, bars, liquor stores, and so on than the adjacent ribbons. The service uses so typical of the arterials are noticeably absent from these less intensive ribbon developments.

The Nucleations

The third major conformation in the commercial structure of cities comprises the various types of nucleated shopping centers. These consist of clusters of retail and service activities at important street intersections within the urban area. They usually constitute foci at the intersection of two or more ribbon developments, where high vehicular and pedestrian traffic intensity provides the focus for growth. On primary streets they may arise at intervals within ribbon developments, while in some cases, and especially the smaller centers, they may string out as local shopping streets. But regardless of their specific location, the nucleated centers are associated with high degrees of centrality within the urban transportation system, which is reflected in the locational correlation between them and the peaks of higher land values at street intersections within the urban area.

Shopping centers in the urban area are the equivalent of the central places in predominantly rural areas. As such, it is generally agreed that they form a hierarchy comparable to that found in rural areas and discussed in Chapter 7. Consequently the same structural features of hierarchical organization are present, and the same general forces giving rise to hierarchical organization operate (Getis, 1963). However, because of the higher density of population in urban areas and the marked variation in levels of demand associated with differences in the social structure of cities, the hierarchy of urban shopping centers differs in some respects from its rural counterpart. These differences include the types of goods and services provided, the spacing of centers within the urban area, and the size of trade areas served by them.

The hierarchy of shopping centers in cities is dominated by the central business district. This contains many kinds of commercial functions, including concentrations of offices and administrative buildings, warehouses, and places of entertainment as well as retailing. Beyond the central business district there are at least four levels of centers. In order of decreasing size these are

1. Regional centers
2. Community centers
3. Neighborhood centers
4. Isolated store clusters

It should be remembered, however, that the number of levels in the hierarchy depends very much on the size of the urban area. In smaller cities the central business district itself may be only functionally equivalent to the higher level regional centers typical of larger cities, and the levels below this will be adjusted downward accordingly. However, within larger cities and especially within metropolitan areas, the four levels of outlying business centers indicated in Figure 12.1 are normally a very clearly established element in urban commercial structure. Because the CBD and outlying shopping centers are in some ways the most important aspects of urban service provision, they will be discussed separately.

The Central Business District

The CBD is usually the largest single concentration of commercial activity within an urban area. Not surprisingly, it has been studied extensively from a wide variety of viewpoints, and geographers have long regarded it as a rather special region within cities for analysis. Yet despite the attention that has been focused on the CBD, there is still today little agreement as to what constitutes the central business district of a city, and hence where its boundaries should be drawn. The central district, central region, city center, central areas, the 100 percent zone, or simply "downtown"—these are but some of the many terms used to refer vaguely to the heart of the city.

Regardless of this multiplicity in terminology, most people are familiar with the characteristic features of the downtown area. It is the area of greatest concentration and variety of retailing in the city; the tight cluster of the city's tallest buildings there gives rise especially to the distinctive skylines of North American cities; and it is the largest single focus of vehicular and pedestrian traffic in the city. The functions located in the CBD serve not only the local urban community but also the people living in the surrounding areas, and often even the wider regional and national scene. Concentration would appear to be its single most visible distinguishing characteristic; and consistent with the intensity of land use there, land values reach disproportionately higher levels than those prevailing in the rest of the urban area. It is these features that the U.S. Bureau of the Census has in mind in defining the CBD as comprising one or more tracts in the central part of a city that constitute "an area of very high land valuation, an area characterized by a high concentration of retail businesses, offices, theaters, hotels, and service businesses, and an area of high traffic flow."

The Core-Frame Concept

Cursory examination of the central area of a city brings out the fact that it is far from homogeneous in structure. In particular, there is a marked variation in intensity of land use between its innermost and outermost parts. This change in the intensity of land use is at the same time associated with a change in the types of activities carried on within the central area. Differences in the intensity and in the types of use in the CBD are what underlie the recognition of its two component parts—the inner core area and the surrounding frame (Horwood and Boyce, 1959). The distinction between these two areas is presented diagrammatically in Figure 12.3. The boundary separating them is difficult to determine exactly, and the one should be thought of as gradually merging into the other. The frame, moreover, overlaps the area that has been described as the middle zone or gray area in models of urban structure (see Chapter 9).

The general properties of the *core* of the CBD are presented in Table 12.3. This is the area within the CBD used with greatest intensity, largely devoted to offices and retail trade. Epigrammatically it can be thought of as being devoted to "people, parcels, and paper work." It is characterized by multistoried buildings that reflect the tendency for vertical as opposed to horizontal expansion. Walking distances are critical in restricting the spread of the core, and great reliance is placed on the elevator for interaction within it. The highest retail sales density per unit ground area in the urban area occurs here. In addition, it is the focus of convergence for mass-transit systems, and the area of highest density of daytime population within the city. Of particular importance are the specialized retail and office activities found here. In many respects the core is the heart of the decision-making machinery for the entire urban business community.

The *frame* is an area of mixed land use surrounding the inner core. Its general properties are listed in Table 12.4. Typical activities include business services, wholesaling with stocks, warehousing, light manufacturing, and various kinds of transport facilities, such as trucking and intercity transportation terminals. Intermingled with

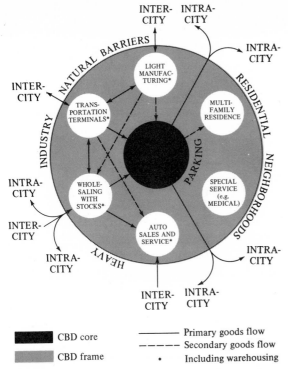

Fig. 12.3. Diagrammatic representation of the core-frame concept. (*Source*: Horwood and Boyce, 1959, Fig. 2.6.)

thesé are low-quality residences, especially aging multifamily houses, tenements, and transient rooming houses. The general character to which such an admixture of land uses gives rise can best be described as blighted. It is this zone that has furnished the sites for many of the urban renewal projects currently being undertaken in larger, older cities across the land.

The mixture of activities gives rise to a less intensive use of land than in the core. Buildings are not so tall and are generally restricted to the walk-up scale. Sites may be only partially built upon, and many vacant sites exist that are often devoted temporarily to parking. Although the vertical scale may not be so exaggerated as that of the core, the horizontal scale is more extended and is geared to the handling of goods and accommodation of the motor vehicle. In fact, it is the motor vehicle that has largely been responsible for the creation of the frame, in that it brought with it greater locational freedom for a wide range of commercial activities and business services. Hence many activities were able to take advantage of inner locations close to the core of the CBD, but for which site rents are appreciably lower.

Subfoci are well developed in the frame; but unlike those typical of the core, they are not characterized by well-developed functional interlinkages. They are, for the most part, oriented outward to the rest of the urban area and beyond. Some of the uses within the frame, however, have important linkages with complementary activities in the core. This is particularly true of warehousing, a wide range of business services such as printing, and of course the facilities that transport people and goods to and from the concentration of activities in the core. Thus, although the core and the frame are two distinct and independent functional areas, they do not stand entirely apart; they are to a certain extent integrated functionally.

Delimiting the CBD

The problem of delimiting the boundary of the CBD is, as is true for all regional studies, a difficult one because the edge of the central business district is a zone of transition. Admittedly, sharp breaks may occur around the CBDs of some cities whenever

Table 12.3.   GENERAL PROPERTIES OF THE CBD CORE

Property	Definition	General Characteristics
Intensive land use	Area of most intensive land use and highest concentration of social and economic activities within metropolitan complex	Multistoried buildings Highest retail productivity per unit ground area Land use characterized by offices, retail sales, consumer services, theaters, and banks
Extended vertical scale	Area of highest buildings within metropolitan complex	Easily distinguishable by aerial observation Elevator personnel linkages Grows vertically rather than horizontally
Limited horizontal scale	Horizontal dimensions limited by walking-distance scale	Greatest horizontal dimension rarely more than one mile Geared to walking scale
Limited horizontal change	Horizontal movement minor and not significantly affected by metropolitan population distribution	Very gradual horizontal change Zones of assimilation and discard limited to a few blocks over long periods of time
Concentrated daytime population	Area of greatest concentration of daytime population within metropolitan complex	Location of highest concentration of foot traffic Absence of permanent residential population
Focus of intracity mass transit	Single area of convergence of city mass transit system	Major mass transit interchange location for entire city
Center of specialized functions	Focus of headquarters offices for business, government, and industrial activities	Extensive use of office space for executive and policy-making functions Center of specialized professional and business services
Internally conditioned boundaries	Excluding natural barriers, CBD boundaries confined only by pedestrian scale of distance	Pedestrian and personnel linkages between establishments govern horizontal expansion Dependency on mass transit inhibits expansion

Source: Horwood and Boyce (1959), Table 2-1.

large obstacles such as parks, clusters of government buildings, or extensive railroad facilities prevent horizontal expansion. These are exceptional cases, however, and variation from one city to another prohibits their use as a basis for any standardized delimitation procedure. Largely because of this, the criteria used to delimit the CBDs of individual cities have been a matter of local judgment set within the context of local problems. It is therefore not surprising to find that a wide variety of measures have in the past been used in determining the boundary of the CBD. These include land values, trade figures, population distribution, building heights, traffic flows, pedestrian counts, and several indexes based on land use. Regardless of the particular index used, however, it will be represented by a surface of intensity that declines with distance from a maximum somewhere within the core to a minimum at the outermost boundary of the frame.

The *central business index method*, proposed by Murphy and Vance (1954a), is generally recognized as a useful method of delimiting the CBD, especially for comparative purposes. The method rests on the analysis of detailed mapping of all land uses in the central areas of cities within which the true CBD is thought to lie. The city block

Table 12.4.   GENERAL PROPERTIES OF THE CBD FRAME

Property	Definition	General Characteristics
Semi-intensive land use	Area of most intensive nonretail land use outside CBD core	Building height geared to walk-up scale Site only partially built on
Prominent functional subregions	Area of observable nodes of land utilization surrounding CBD core	Subfoci characterized mainly by wholesaling with stocks, warehousing, off-street parking, automobile sales and services, multifamily dwellings, intercity transportation terminals and facilities, light manufacturing, and some institutional uses
Extended horizontal scale	Horizontal scale geared to accommodation of motor vehicles and to handling of goods	Most establishments have off-street parking and docking facilities Movements between establishments vehicular
Unlinked functional subregions	Activity nodes essentially linked to areas outside CBD frame, except transportation terminals	Important establishments have linkages to CBD core (e.g., intercity transportation terminals, warehousing) and to outlying urban regions (e.g., wholesale distribution to suburban shopping areas and to service industries)
Externally conditioned boundaries	Boundaries affected by natural barriers and presence of large homogeneous areas with distinguishable internal linkages (e.g., residential areas with schools, shopping, and community facilities)	Commercial uses generally limited to flat land Growth tends to extend into areas of dilapidated housing CBD frame uses fill in interstices of central focus of highway and rail transportation routes

SOURCE: Horwood and Boyce (1959), Table 2–11.

is used as the basic areal unit, and two indexes (the central business height index and the central business intensity index) are calculated for each block from the land-use data. Calculation of these indexes, however, requires an initial classification of land uses into CBD and non-CBD types. The distinction used by Murphy and Vance was quite arbitrary and is shown in Table 12.5.

The *central business height index* (CBHI) is simply obtained by dividing the total floor area occupied by CBD uses in each block by the total ground-floor area of the block. The figure obtained in this way can be thought of as an indication of the number of floors of CBD use that would exist in the block if these uses were spread evenly over it. For example, if a block has a CBHI of 2.5, the amount of floor space devoted to CBD uses would be enough to cover the entire block with the equivalent of two and one-half stories. In reality, of course, this amount of CBD floor space might be concentrated in a part of the block only, the rest of it being devoted to non-CBD uses. The shortcoming of this index is that it fails to take into account the proportion of the total floor area of the block devoted to CBD uses. To overcome this, a *central business intensity index* is obtained by dividing the total floor area in the block devoted to CBD uses by the total floor area of the block itself. When multiplied by 100, the central business intensity index (CBII) represents the percentage of the total floor area (all floors combined) devoted to CBD uses.

These two indexes can be thought of as the coordinates that locate each block within a two-dimensional classification space. This is shown in Figure 12.4. For example, on the graph point A represents a block for which the CBHI and CBII values are 1.5 and 25 percent respectively; similarly, point B represents a block with values of 0.5 and 75 percent. Murphy and Vance decided arbitrarily that for a block to be classified as forming part of the CBD, it should have a CBHI value of at least 1.0 and a CBII value of at least 50 percent. According to this definition, the CBD would include all the blocks falling within the upper right-hand shaded quadrant on the graph. To apply the method meaningfully it was found necessary, however, to include some blocks as part of the CBD even though they did not have large enough CBHI or CBII indexes, such as those that are surrounded by CBD blocks.

It should be remembered that the boundary resulting from the application of the central business index method does not represent the boundary of the CBD, but only an

---

Table 12.5. NONCENTRAL BUSINESS DISTRICT USES[a]

Permanent residences (including apartment houses and rooming houses)
Government and public (including parks and public schools, as well as establishments carrying out city, county, state, and federal government functions)
Organizational institutions (churches, colleges, fraternal orders, etc.)
Industrial establishments (except for newspapers)
Wholesaling
Vacant buildings and stores
Vacant lots
Commercial storage and warehousing
Railroad tracks and switching yards

[a] All other uses are considered as CBD uses.
SOURCE: Murphy and Vance (1954a), Table 2.

approximation to it; but it is most probably a fair approximation. The main advantages of the method lie in its simplicity and particularly its standardized approach to delimitation, which is essential if comparisons are to be made between central business districts. Its main disadvantages stem from the elements of subjectivity inherent in the selection of values for the indexes and in the classification of central business uses, for a different boundary would result if lower or higher values for the CBHI and CBII were to be used and if a different set of activities were defined as central business uses. The classification of uses excludes, for example, some of the functions listed as typical of the frame of the CBD (Davies, 1960). Consequently the boundary resulting from the method will generally fall short of the outer limit of the frame, but it will include more than just the core alone.

Characteristics of Central Business Districts

The central business index method is a good example of a classification procedure that has been used not only for delimitation, but also as the basis for further analysis. Murphy and Vance used the method to delimit the boundaries of the CBD's of nine medium-sized cities, and used the results to develop broad generalizations concerning the size and land-use structure of downtown areas (Murphy and Vance, 1954b). Selected size characteristics of the nine central business districts are listed in Table 12.6. The most noticeable feature in the table is the considerable variation in the size of the CBD between the nine cities. The figures in column 5 of the table indicate that CBD's vary in size from 75.5 acres in Mobile to 207.7 acres in Tulsa; the average size based on this measure is indicated as 120 acres. Variation in the size of individual CBD's can be understood only from detailed study of their historical development and local conditions. However, it does appear that size is partly related to population of the incorporated city in which it is located, although there does not appear to be any regular relationship between CBD size and population of either the local SMSA, the city's trade area, or the population of the urbanized area in which it is located.

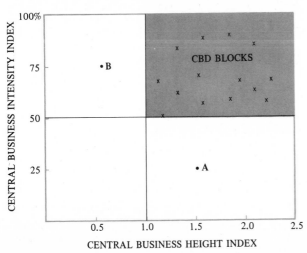

Fig. 12.4. The classification space for delimiting the CBD by the Murphy-Vance method.

Table 12.6. SELECTED SIZE CHARACTERISTICS FOR NINE CENTRAL BUSINESS DISTRICTS

Place (1)	Population Size, 1950[a] (thousands) (2)	Acreages in CBD: Total Floor Space (3)	Acreages in CBD: Ground-Floor Area (4)	Central Business: Floor Space (acres) (5)	Summary Indexes[b]: CBHI (6)	Summary Indexes[b]: CBII (7)
Grand Rapids, Mich.	277	195.5	58.9	142.5	2.4	72.9
Salt Lake City, Utah	277	255.4	120.8	186.4	1.5	73.0
Worcester, Mass.	219	176.7	59.6	120.0	2.0	67.9
Phoenix, Ariz.	216	138.8	76.8	113.8	1.5	82.0
Sacramento, Calif.	212	228.4	108.8	167.0	1.5	73.1
Tulsa, Okla.	206	251.8	79.8	207.7	2.6	82.5
Mobile, Ala.	183	107.1	50.4	75.5	1.5	70.5
Tacoma, Wash.	168	122.4	52.4	98.6	1.9	80.5
Roanoke, Va.	107	124.5	53.3	103.1	1.9	82.8
Average (median)	212	176.7	59.6	120.0	1.9	73.1

[a] Population figure for the urbanized area, 1950.
[b] The CBHI is calculated by dividing the total floor space devoted to central business uses (column 5) by the total ground-floor space (column 4); the CBII is obtained by dividing the total floor space devoted to central business uses (column 5) by the total CBD floor space (column 3).
SOURCE: Murphy and Vance (1954b), after Table 1.

The variation in the size of the CBD is paralleled by considerable variation in structure. Table 12.7 shows the proportion of total central business district floor space devoted to the main categories of land use for the average of the nine CBD's. The importance of the service-financial-office-use category is clearly revealed, and this category occupies about 44 percent of total floor space. Retailing ranks second (32 percent), and noncentral uses rank third (24 percent) as users of the CBD floor space. Considerable variation is also shown to exist between different land-use types within each of the three major categories. It should be noted, however, that some variation occurs in the proportion of each CBD devoted to the three main categories and their subtypes. Roanoke, Tulsa, and Phoenix have the smallest proportions of noncentral uses. All three cities are relatively young; and by the time they were built, there was little demand for space in the CBD except for true central uses. Conversely, nearly one-third of the CBD of Worcester is devoted to noncentral uses, particularly to public and organizational uses. Variation in the proportion of the CBD devoted to the other two categories is also marked and can be understood only from detailed study of the individual cities themselves. In part, the land-use structure reflects the functional specialization and hinterland characteristics of each city.

Commercial Nucleations Beyond the CBD

That the outlying commercial nucleations within cities are consistently related to the hierarchy of central places in rural areas is shown in Figure 12.5. Centers within the urban area form part of the overall systematic relationship between trade areas, population served, levels in the hierarchy, and the density of population. Differences in the

Table 12.7.   LAND-USE CHARACTERISTICS OF AN AVERAGE CBD[a]

Central Uses	Proportion of the Total Floor Space in CBD	Total Space in Category
Service-financial-office uses	44.0%	100.0%
General offices	12.7	29.0
Transient residences	11.7	27.0
Parking	7.0	16.0
Headquarters offices	5.0	11.0
Service trades	4.0	9.0
Financial	3.0	7.0
Transportation	0.6	1.0
Retail business	32.0%	100.0%
Variety	9.4	29.0
Household	5.3	17.0
Miscellaneous	5.3	17.0
Clothing	4.2	13.0
Foodstuffs	3.9	12.0
Automotive	3.9	12.0
Noncentral uses	24.0%	100.0%
Public-organizational	11.7	49.0
Vacant	5.5	23.0
Residential	3.5	14.0
Wholesale	1.8	8.0
Industrial	1.5	6.0

[a] Average for the nine central business districts listed in Table 12.6.
SOURCE: After Murphy and Vance (1954b), Figure 25.

structure of the hierarchy within urban areas compared with central places may, however, be expected on account of much higher densities of demand. Because of the more extreme market condition in urban areas

1. Business types are able to enter the hierarchy at lower levels than in rural areas.
2. The higher density and diversity of demand makes possible a far greater degree of specialization between establishments of the same type, and this tendency increases with the population size of cities.
3. The urban market is considerably more diversified on account of marked differences in the socioeconomic characteristics and ethnic groupings between various parts of the city.

The effect of these conditions is to make centers at any given level in the urban hierarchy considerably more complex and less rigid in their functional structure than those at comparable levels in the rural central-place system. A general impression of the functional structure of the different-level outlying shopping centers is given in Table 12.8. Centers at the two lowest levels are essentially of the convenience type.

The *street-corner* developments constitute the most ubiquitous element of the pattern of nucleated centers; consequently they are scattered throughout residential neighborhoods to ensure maximum accessibility to consumers residing within a two-or three-block radius of the cluster. They normally comprise from one to four business types of the lowest threshold types, and the grocer-drugstore combination is most common. *Neighborhood nucleations* are characterized by the addition of higher threshold convenience types, which supply the major necessities to consumers living in local areas of the city. Grocery stores, small supermarkets, laundries and dry cleaners, barbers and beauty shops, and perhaps small restaurants are the most usual business types represented.

Centers at the higher levels in the hierarchy are distinguished by their shopping goods, which are added to the convenience functions of the lower-level centers. In addition they provide a range of personal, professional, and business services. *Community nucleations* provide less specialized shopping types, like variety and clothing stores, small furniture and appliance stores, florists, jewelers, and in many cases a post office.

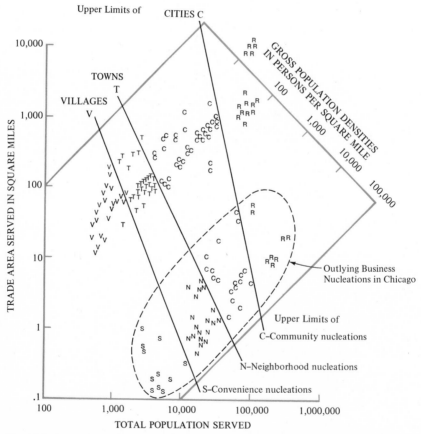

Fig. 12.5. Systematic variations in the hierarchy of urban shopping centers and rural central places. (*Source:* Berry, 1967a, Fig. 2–9.)

Supplementing these are a range of more ubiquitous services and entertainment facilities.

The highest level *regional nucleations* are set above the community centers not so much by the types of business they perform as by the number and variety of activities they provide for large segments of the urban area. Increased specialization of business types thus becomes the keynote. In some very large North American cities, the population has become so spread out that the position of the CBD with respect to retailing and entertainment has declined so that it now offers an array of services no more extensive than those of regional nucleations. The CBD of Los Angeles is a good example, though the financial nucleus still retains its importance. As far as retailing is concerned, the Los Angeles CBD is little more than a regional nucleation serving some distinctive socio-economic groups.

Table 12.8.   A REPRESENTATIVE SAMPLE OF BUSINESS TYPES TYPICAL OF OUTLYING SHOPPING NUCLEATIONS

Street Corner
  General stores
  Groceries
  Drugstores

Neighborhood
  Supermarkets
  Bakeries
  Barbershops and beauty salons
  Laundries, laundromats

Community Centers
  Variety stores
  Clothing stores
  General furniture stores
  Florists
  Jewelers
  Real estate agents
  Banks

Regional Centers
  Department stores
  Shoe stores
  Camera shops
  Sporting goods stores
  Other, more specialized types (i.e., music stores)
  Professional services

SOURCE: After Berry (1959), Table 1.

As indicated in Figure 12.1, outlying nucleations may be either planned or un-planned. Most of the older centers within central cities are of the unplanned sort and have grown up around major street intersections. But in the more recently developed suburbs, and also in those parts of central cities that have undergone redevelopment within the past decade, nucleations are increasingly planned on a unitary, integrated basis. Planning, however, affects largely the design of centers, and to a lesser extent their location, and has little effect on their functional structure. Hence both planned and unplanned centers at any given level in the hierarchy may be expected to provide essentially the same kinds of retail and service businesses. Planned centers do differ in their structural characteristics, however, as will be indicated below.

Regardless of whether centers are planned or unplanned, they share the same de-grees of centrality within urban areas. By clustering together at discrete locations, busi-ness types are able to capitalize on the tendency of consumers to make single, home-based trips, shopping from store to store within centers for the bundle of goods they expect to be offered by them. Functions at any one level are thus linked together into nucleations by the desire of consumers to visit several establishments on a single shop-ping trip.

The Hierarchy of Nucleations in the City of Chicago

Specific details of the structure of outlying shopping centers can best be illustrated by a study of outlying nucleations undertaken in the city of Chicago (Berry, 1963). In this study the structural characteristics of 64 outlying nucleations were analyzed by the use of factor analysis. The resulting typology indicated that a four-tier hierarchy existed within the city limits. The distribution of these nucleations within the city is shown in Figure 12.6. The basic size characteristics of an average center at each of the four levels are presented in Table 12.9. The general features are consistent with what

Table 12.9. **AVERAGE SIZE CHARACTERISTICS OF UNPLANNED SHOPPING NUCLEATIONS IN THE CITY OF CHICAGO, 1961**[a]

Level of Center	Number	Ground-Floor Establishments	Business Types	Ground-Floor Area (square feet)	Front Feet	Estimated Sales[b] ($ millions)
Major regional centers	4	196	60	566,627	6,562	60
Shopping goods centers	14	114	43	314,693	3,170	32
Community centers	25	73	37	161,250	2,075	25
Neighborhood centers	21	41	25	90,125	1,200	18

[a]The median is used as the average for all characteristics.
[b]Sales data, obtained from a special tabulation of the Census of Business, 1958, do not relate exactly to the nucleations as they were delimited in the study, but to a group of census tracts most closely approximating them.
SOURCE: Berry (1963), from data presented in Table 6.

was discussed regarding the rural central-place hierarchy in Chapter 6. Low-level nucleations are more ubiquitous in the urban area than high-level centers, although from the table this is apparently not the case for the neighborhood nucleations. This discrepancy results from the way in which nucleations were identified in the Chicago study. From the relationship previously noted between the location of nucleations and the minor land-value peakings within the city, only those retail clusters with peak land values of more than 750 dollars per front foot were selected. Consequently, many of the smaller neighborhood nucleations and all of the street-corner developments were omitted from

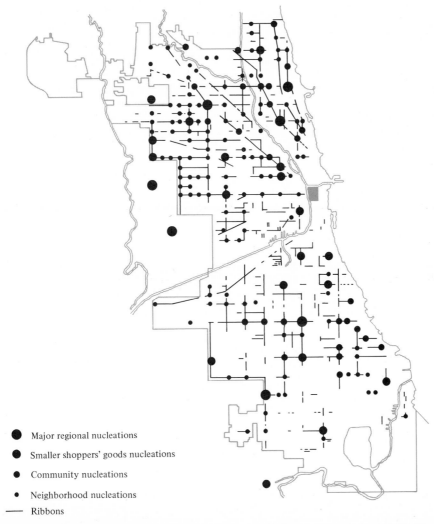

● Major regional nucleations

● Smaller shoppers' goods nucleations

● Community nucleations

• Neighborhood nucleations

— Ribbons

Fig. 12.6. The hierarchy of shopping nucleations in the city of Chicago. (*Source*: Berry, 1963, Fig. 10.)

the analysis. Had these been included, the regularity would have been as expected from the nature of hierarchies.

Other features of the table are much as expected. High-level nucleations have more business types and more establishments, account for greater frontages, and occupy larger ground-floor areas than low-level centers. Sales generated at each level follow the same general sequence, and data showing numbers of persons employed, size of trade area, and number of shopping trips would tend to emphasize the regularity with size of nucleation.

Table 12.10 indicates the way in which functions most typical of each level enter into the hierarchy. The difference between the essentially convenience-goods nature of the neighborhood nucleation and to a lesser extent the community nucleation is clearly revealed. The shopping-goods centers and major regional centers are particularly characterized by the addition of shopping goods. Nucleations at each higher level in the hierarchy perform all the functions of the lower-level centers in addition to a set of high-threshold, more specialized types, which set them above the low-level centers in the hierarchy. However, because of the greater opportunities within the urban area for remaining in business, it is not uncommon to find some high-threshold types in lower-level centers. This gives rise to rather more complex functional patterns at centers in cities than those typical of rural areas. Comparison of Table 12.10 and Table 6.4 will give some idea of how certain functions enter centers at lower levels in urban areas than in rural central places.

Nine of the largest *planned centers* within the Chicago city limits and a number of larger planned centers in suburbs immediately adjacent to the city were also included in the analysis. When the same method of classification is used, a similar four-tier hierarchical arrangement is also indicated for them. However, some noticeable differences exist between the planned centers and their unplanned equivalents. Apart from the obvious differences in their architectural features, the planned centers are generally smaller in content and structure. They offer fewer business types, have fewer establishments—which are, however, normally larger in size than those in unplanned centers—and have smaller total ground-floor areas than their unplanned counterparts at the same levels.

Major planned regional centers contain an average of between 50 and 70 establishments, have about 40 business types, and occupy ground-floor areas exceeding 400,000 square feet. Planned shopping-goods centers have between 30 and 40 stores, 25 to 30 functions, and ground-floor areas of 150,000 square feet. The comparable figures for the community- and neighborhood-level centers are respectively 25 establishments, 20 business types, and 100,000 square feet of floor space, and 17, 15, and 50,000 square feet.

The implication from these figures is that, at any given level in the hierarchy, planned centers provide fewer business types than unplanned centers; yet above it was stated that planning had little effect upon the functional structure of shopping centers. What happens is that the same core functions at each level are provided, but many of the peripheral uses are absent. Thus in planned shopping-goods centers—and to a lesser extent in the major planned regional centers—the peripheral uses such as army and navy stores, furniture stores, bars, liquor stores, insurance agents, and movie houses typical of the unplanned centers at this level are missing. In addition, planned centers normally do not have any extensive upper-floor uses. Hence the upper-floor medical-

Table 12.10. ORDER OF ENTRY OF FUNCTIONS IN THE HIERARCHY OF UNPLANNED NUCLEATIONS IN THE CITY OF CHICAGO, 1961

	Nucleations			
	Neighborhood	Community	Shopping Goods	Major Regional
Core Neighborhood Functions	Groceries Variety stores Men's and boys' clothing Women's clothes Eating places Drinking places Drugstores Liquor stores Jewelry Currency exchanges Laundries Beauty salons Barbershops	Supermarket Yes	Supermarket Yes	Supermarket Yes
Functions Added at the Community Level		Hardware Department stores Candy stores Bakeries Family shoes Furniture Radio-TV Real estate agents Physicians Optometrists	Yes	Yes
Functions Added at Smaller Shopping-Goods Nucleations			Butchers Millinery Children's wear Men's shoes Women's shoes Appliances Music stores Gift and novelty stores Banks Movies Dentists	Yes
Functions Performed Only by Major Regional Nucleations				Family clothing stores Custom tailors Drapery stores Miscellaneous home furnishings Stationers Florists Camera stores

SOURCE: Berry (1963), Table 19.

dental complex, common at larger unplanned centers, is not represented, unless specific provision has been made in planning the center for a professional office building.

The same may be said for the planned community and neighborhood centers. At the former, the doctor-dentist-lawyer complex found at the upper floors of unplanned centers is missing, as are such business types as bars, radio-TV sales and repair stores, and so on. On the other hand, planned community centers tend to offer certain shopping goods not found at the unplanned centers, including junior department stores, gift and card shops, and certain of the clothing functions. Neighborhood centers are much the same whether planned or unplanned, although the newer ones usually have supermarkets instead of grocery stores and often provide a gas station and laundromat—functions noted as typical of the ribbons in unplanned areas of the city.

The reduction in number of business types at planned centers is related to the reduced number of establishments at them, for shopping-center developers seek to restrict competition between stores within the center by controlling the amount of functional duplication. Hence there is usually only one establishment of a given business type at each planned center, although at the larger centers the amount of duplication increases to cater adequately to the larger number of consumers who visit them. The generally larger size of establishments reflects the technological changes currently taking place in retailing toward larger economies of scale, especially in such functions as drugstores, supermarkets, and variety stores. Elimination of duplication together with these trends in retailing results in the tendency for larger store sizes in planned centers.

The Effects of Income Differences on the Hierarchy

We have observed in the previous chapter that one of the distinguishing features of a large urban area is the considerable variation in socioeconomic conditions between its various parts. At least a simple distinction can be made in most cities between areas of high and middle income and those with low incomes. When these areas occupy considerable portions of cities, as they do in the larger metropolitan areas, the differences in purchasing power and the related nature of demands may be expected to influence the structure and functional components of nucleations in them.

Accordingly, unplanned shopping nucleations occur in different ways in the low-income parts of a city than they do in the high-income areas. In the high-income parts of a city, shopping goods are provided by major regional nucleations located at strategic points and by the smaller shopping-goods centers located around the edges of the trade areas of the larger nucleations. Convenience goods are provided by the high-level community nucleations and smaller neighborhood nucleations. In contrast to this normal development, Table 12.11 provides example information indicating that low-income neighborhoods lack both the highest-level major regional centers and also for the most part the community-level nucleations, but have a greater proportion of the low-level neighborhood centers. Consequently in these areas the hierarchy is simpler and comprises essentially only two levels: the smaller shopping-goods centers that provide most of the shopping goods required by the low-income consumers and a larger number of neighborhood nucleations that provide the basic necessities. The effect of the lower incomes, therefore, is to eliminate the larger nucleations providing greater varieties of goods, more specialized stores, and greater opportunities for a full range of shopping choice.

**Table 12.11.   DIFFERENCES IN THE OCCURRENCE OF
NUCLEATIONS IN AREAS OF THE CITY OF CHICAGO**

Class of Nucleation	Area Served	
	High Income	Low Income
Major regional	4	–
Smaller shopping- goods nucleations	5	9
Community nucleations	22	3
Neighborhood nucleations	7	14
TOTALS	38	26

SOURCE: Berry (1963), Table B1.

The effect of the lower incomes is not only confined to the types of nucleations located in the various socioeconomic areas of a city. It also underlies some considerable changes in their structural characteristics. For example, shopping-goods nucleations in low-income areas are noticeably smaller than their counterparts in the high-income areas. Although there appears to be little difference in the size of the community-level centers in the two areas, there is a considerable difference at the neighborhood level, for in the low-income part of a city, the neighborhood centers are the largest nucleations exclusively concerned with selling convenience goods. In line with this more important role, centers at this level are slightly larger in the low-income areas than their equivalents in the high-income parts of a city.

Another important difference between nucleations in the high-income and low-income areas relates to the size of establishments. In the nucleations serving the low-income parts of a city, establishments tend on an average to be larger than those at centers in the high-income areas. This is especially true for such functions as army and navy stores, men's and women's clothing stores, millinery shops, shoe stores, furniture stores, radio-TV stores, and liquor stores. Several reasons may be offered for this tendency. First, lower rents within centers coupled with greater availability of space enable individual stores to operate on a less rent-intensive basis. Second, demand is lacking for the smaller specialized stores, so that a few larger stores offering a more general bundle of goods provide the goods and services offered. Third, many of the retail properties in the older parts of a city were laid out on a larger scale than those in the relatively newer parts of the city.

Lastly, lower levels of demand result in greater duplication rates at nucleations in the low-income areas. As areas have undergone transition from high- to low-income levels, the more specialized functions in the centers have been unable to stay in business and so have left. The space that they left behind is eventually taken over by more ubiquitous functions, which were previously located in the ribbons. In this way the nucleations are able to remain full, but with substantial duplication of the low-threshold functions. However, as incomes continue to fall and trade areas shrink, so the number of business types is reduced at nucleations, resulting in high vacancy rates and eventually in occupation of former retail property by alien uses.

STRUCTURAL RELATIONSHIPS IN THE URBAN HIERARCHY

It is reasonable to assume that the number and types of retail service activities in urban areas are constantly being pushed and pulled toward an equilibrium situation; that is, to a high level of adjustment to the demands of the consumers served. But this state of balance is hard to reach because the supply of goods and demands for them are constantly changing. However, at any given stage in the evolution of the hierarchy of nucleations, an approximation to the equilibrium conditions might be expected to occur even if perfect development is never obtained. Certain areas of the city will have more or less retail and service activities because people and their incomes are more mobile than retail and service businesses.

This idea of a tendency toward equilibrium was, of course, implied by the regularities noted in the structure of the central-place hierarchy and discussed in Chapter 6. Because the same underlying mechanism, leading to the formation of a hierarchical structure, operates in the case of nucleations within urban areas, it is to be expected that analogous kinds of regularities will be characteristic of the hierarchy of nucleations as well. The essential features of the structural relationships in the urban case can be outlined as follows: The total sales of a nucleation ($) in the hierarchy will depend on the total population served by it (P). In turn, the number of business types (BT) it provides will depend on its total sales; the larger the total sales of a center, the more business types it should provide. Since high-level nucleations have more business types and establishments (and these occupy a larger floor area) than lower-level centers, it can also be argued that the number of establishments (E) at a nucleation will be related in some ways to its number of business types. It follows from this that variation in the ground-floor area (G) at nucleations will generally depend on the number of establishments, other things being equal (Berry, 1963).

The correlation coefficients for the relationships between variables in the high-income part of the city (Table 12.12, part A) indicate the close agreement to equilibrium conditions found there. But in contrast, the equivalent relationships in the low-income areas are considerably less well developed (Table 12.12, part B). In each case the correlation coefficients are smaller than those in the high-income area, indicating the lower level of adjustment in the retail structure in the poorer part of the city. Table 12.12, part C, gives the same relationships for the planned centers, which are typified by lower correlations than the equivalent unplanned nucleations in the high-income areas. Planned centers are less commonly found in the poorer areas of cities except where they form part of redevelopment schemes.

The fact that a considerable part of the commercial structure of Chicago, like that of other cities, is not in equilibrium is a reflection of the processes of change going on in cities. Changes in the commercial structure of cities in North America are currently being influenced by factors such as

1. The increased mobility associated with the automobile and the more complicated shopping patterns it brings about.

2. Changing purchasing levels and tastes associated with rising incomes.

3. The increasing tendency to control commercial developments through the zoning mechanism, which if anything tends to reinforce the trend toward larger, integrated centers.

4. Changes in the technology of retailing itself with its emphasis on increasingly large-scale operations.

5. The actual physical changes associated with urban renewal.

There are also likely to be long-run changes in commercial structure associated with escalating energy costs, but at this stage the impact of this influence on structure seems difficult to ascertain. Nevertheless, because of these kinds of influences, the commercial structure of cities is in a constant state of change, even though in part it may exhibit the characteristics of short-term stability and equilibrium.

Table 12.12. STRUCTURAL EQUATIONS FOR SHOPPING NUCLEATIONS IN CITY OF CHICAGO

Equation	Correlation[a]
(A) Unplanned Nucleations in the High-Income Areas	
1. $\$ = 18,652,258 + 145\ (P)$	0.630
2. $BT = 201.8 + 32.48\ (\text{Log }\$)$	0.715
3. $\text{Log }E = 1.111 + 0.020\ (BT)$	0.956
4. $\text{Log }G = 3.268 + 1.043\ (\text{Log }E)$	0.932
(B) Unplanned Nucleations in the Low-Income Areas[b]	
1&2. $BT = -32.7 + 13.161\ (\text{Log }P)$	0.467
3. $\text{Log }E = 1.242 + .018\ (BT)$	0.830
4. $\text{Log }G = 3.145 + 1.126\ (\text{Log }E)$	0.910
(C) Planned Centers	
2. $BT = -83 + 14.848\ (\text{Log }\$)$	0.640
3. $\text{Log }E = .843 + .0263\ (BT)$	0.948
4. $\text{Log }G = 3.261 + 1.2567\ (\text{Log }E)$	0.922

[a] The Pearson product moment correlation coefficient is used. The closer the value of this is to 1.0, the higher the degree of correlation.
[b] Equations 1 and 2 are combined in the lower-income areas on account of the lack of sales data.
Source: Berry (1963), from Tables 49–51.

13
PATTERNS WITHIN COMMERCIAL AREAS

Nucleations, ribbons, and specialized areas have a spatial extent and constitute small uniform regions suitable for analysis at a more elemental level. These conformations have been treated in the previous chapter as if they were points on maps and graphs, and differences between their functional structure have been stressed at the aggregated level. In this chapter we are concerned with some aspects of the internal structure of these conformations. Of particular interest are the differences in the location of business types within commercial areas and the small-scale land-use patterns to which these differences give rise. These patterns may be found to some extent in all retail conformations, but distinctive arrangements of business types are most noticeable within nucleations, and especially within the older, unplanned ones. It is at these that the economic forces influencing the intensity of land use discussed in Chapter 9 operate unhindered by social, political, and architectural (in the case of newer planned shopping centers) constraints to give rise to significant land-value–land-use relationships.

LAND VALUES AND LAND USE

The development of an economic theory concerning the internal structure of retail nucleations depends upon a clear understanding of the interrelationship between land values and land use. Such an interrelationship is usually present in all unplanned nucleations, but the arrangements are most visible in the CBD, for it is here that the average level of land values is usually highest and the variation in values the greatest. Thus, while much of the ensuing discussion will focus upon land-use–land-value relationships in some CBD's, it must be understood that the general priciples may be transferred to most nucleations at the regional and lower level. For example, the counterparts to the peak-value intersections of the CBD are the minor peak-value intersections found within outlying unplanned nucleations. This situation has been discussed in some detail in Chapter 9.

Land Values Within Nucleations

The land-value gradient within the CBD is concave but does not assume the form of a smooth curve. Rather it is stepped, indicating that the surface of values is discontinuous. Normally there is a very steep drop in values within a short distance from the PVI, but thereafter the decline is more gradual. Hence land values decrease with distance away from the PVI but at a decreasing rate. Neither is the gradient symmetrical about the PVI. Land values decline more sharply in some directions than in others. Usually this decline is less rapid along the longitudinal axis of the CBD than in the direction at right angles to it.

These features of the land-value surface within the CBD are shown for the small city of Dubuque, Iowa, in Figure 13.1. The gradients represent slices across the CBD in a north-south and east-west direction intersecting at the PVI. On the graphs, actual land values expressed as dollars per front foot have been translated into percentages of the value at the PVI—the 100 percent value. The north-south gradient along the main axis of the CBD is notably higher than that cutting across the CBD in the east-west direction at comparable distances from the PVI. Note also the steepness of the decline in values; there is a very marked drop-off in values within a short distance from the PVI in an east-west direction, and there is an even more pronounced decline in the gradient toward the west. Conversely, it is as though the gradients have been stretched out along the north-south axis of the CBD. If anything, values along this section appear to decline more rapidly with distance in the northerly direction. Regardless of these minor directional variations of the land-value surface, the dominant aspect of the relationship is clearly shown: there is a marked decline in value in all directions within relatively short distances of the PVI. The marked drop-offs in values that are noticed can be used to define the break between the nucleations and the ribbons.

The discontinuous land-value *surface* indicated by the stepped characteristic of the value gradients for the CBD of Dubuque has two marked features. First, there is a very small core area immediately adjacent to the PVI comprising locations with values as high as approximately 75 percent of the peak value. This innermost area stands in contrast to the rest of the CBD, which is characterized by values below this level. Second, most locations in the downtown area have values of less than about 25 percent of the peak value. From our understanding of the relationships between intensity of land use and land values, we might expect from this that the greater part of the CBD is associated with a relatively low level of use intensity.

That this picture is typical of land-value patterns in the CBD's of the medium-and small sized cities is indicated by the data in Table 13.1. These data show the amount of land associated with various levels of land value in six of the CBD's investigated by Murphy and Vance and discussed in the previous chapter. The difference between the small inner hard-core area of high values and the generally low level of the value surface for the greater part of the CBD is clearly indicated by the figures in column 2 of the table. These figures represent percentages of the total land area in the different value classes for all six CBD's combined. Just over 1 percent of the total area is associated with values as high as 90 percent of the peak value. In marked contrast to this, just over 40 percent of the total area in the six downtown districts has land values of less than 10 percent of that at the peak-value intersection. Perhaps the most significant aspect of the land-value pattern illustrated by these figures is that approximately nine-tenths of the total area of these six CBD's consist of land values of less than 50 percent of the peak value.

Land Use Within Nucleations

In Chapter 9 a direct relationship was suggested between the surfaces of land values and land use. The implication of this is that low-value sites are generally not so intensively used as high-value sites. Since in the CBD the high-value sites occupy central locations around the PVI, the intensity of use should reach its highest level there and should decrease with distance outward to the edge of the activities at different locations. This was illustrated in the discussion of elementary land-use theory in Chapter 9.

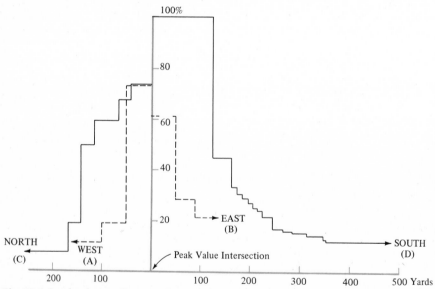

Fig. 13.1. Land-value gradients in the CBD, Dubuque, Iowa, 1960.

From this kind of argument it is expected that an analogous kind of pattern will be typical of the distribution of commercial activities around the PVI within the CBD.

Evidence suggesting this to be the case has been presented by Murphy, Vance, and Epstein (1955) in their study of the internal structure of eight CBD's. In their analysis, a grid with four 100-yard divisions centered on the PVI was superimposed over the innermost part of each CBD. The proportion of each of the four zones devoted to various activities was then calculated and used to compare the land-use pattern at different distances from the PVI. Because the investigators did not extend the grid beyond a distance of 400 yards from the PVI, only about one-half of the area of the nine CBD's was included in the analysis.

Variation in the proportions of each of the four zones devoted to three main categories of land use (retail business, offices, and noncentral users) are presented in Figure 13.2. In the diagrams the total area of each zone is represented by the vertical column, and this is divided into percentages on the vertical (the Y) axis. The bar graphs shown are based on the average land-use pattern for eight CBD's. Separate graphs are given for (A) the average of all floors combined, (B) first floor, and (C) all upper floors combined.

All Floors by Zones

The zone immediately surrounding the PVI represents the quintessence of the characteristics that are associated with the core of the CBD. This is the area of greatest concentration of vehicular and pedestrian traffic. It includes the inner core of highest land values arising from the extremely intense level of competition for the use of land, and this is where we should normally expect to find the tallest buildings in the downtown area. It is perhaps not surprising to find that this innermost zone is dominated by various retail business uses, which account for about 55 percent of the total floor space (Fig. 13.2A). Offices are the second most important users of land in this zone and occupy

Table 13.1. LAND VALUES AND AREAS WITHIN SIX CENTRAL BUSINESS DISTRICTS[a]

Values as a Percentage of the Peak Lot	(1) Total Area in Acres Within Six CBD's Combined	(2) Percentage of the Total Area Within the Six CBD's	(3) Mean Area in Acres Within Each Land Value Class
100.0–90.0	4.07	1.16	0.68
90.0–70.0	6.57	1.88	1.10
70.0–50.0	16.20	4.63	2.70
50.0–30.0	33.45	9.80 ⎫	5.58
30.0–10.0	134.83	33.60 ⎬ 92.34%	22.48
Less than 10.0	153.58	43.94 ⎭	43.61

[a]The six central business districts are those at Phoenix, Sacramento, Grand Rapids (Mich.), Tacoma (Wash.), Salt Lake City, and Worcester (Mass.).
SOURCE: After Murphy et al. (1955), Table 1.

about one-third of available space there. As expected, the activities classified as non-central uses are only poorly represented and account for just under 12 percent of the total area of the first zone.

Beyond this first zone there is a regular change in the proportion of the total area devoted to each of the three sets of activities. Most significant is the marked decrease in the proportion devoted to retail business as distance increases away from the PVI. In the outermost zone, only about a quarter of the total area is devoted to retailing, and there it becomes the least important of the three main types of activity. This reduction in the area devoted to retail uses in the outermost zones is counterbalanced by the increased importance of both office functions and noncentral uses. Offices are well represented in all the zones beyond the first, and in zones 3 and 4 account for about half of the available floor area where they become the dominant use. Although noncentral uses are more important toward the periphery of the downtown area, they are nowhere a very important user of land within its first 400 yards. They are best represented in zone 4, where they occupy just under a third of the space—a slightly higher proportion than that occupied by retail business.

Ground and Upper Floors by Zones

When all floors are combined together in this way, however, interesting patterns in the vertical distribution of the three main types of land use are covered up. Figure

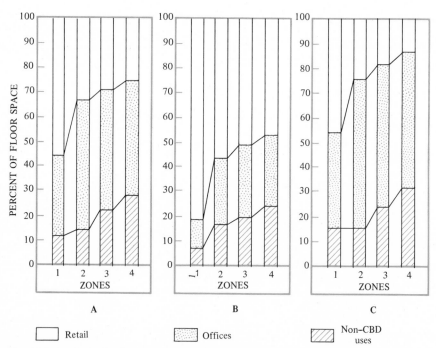

Fig. 13.2. Land uses by distance zones within the CBD: (A) average for all floors combined, (B) first-floor uses, and (C) average for all upper floors combined. (*Source:* after Murphy et. al., 1955, Fig. 3.)

13.2B shows the arrangement of uses at the ground-floor level only. The intensive use of street-level frontage by retail businesses is clearly shown in this diagram. This set of activities dominates in all four zones; in the innermost area it accounts for as much as 82 percent of the total ground-floor area. Even in zone 4, retail business occupies just under half of the availability frontage. The noncentral uses are poorly represented at this level and reach their maximum representation in the outermost zone, where they account for about a quarter of the ground-floor space. The remainder of the available space at ground-floor level is devoted to office uses, which become particularly important in zones 3 and 4, where they account for one-third of all ground-floor property.

The use of upper-floor space (all upper floors combined) is much as might be intuitively expected: office functions are by far the most important users of space (Fig. 13.2C). This is especially true in the three outermost zones, where offices account for well over one-half of the available floor space. Noncentral uses become slightly more important at the upper floor than at ground level, but even in outermost zone 4 they account for only about one-third of the total area. Retail business is dominant at the upper-floor level only in zone 1, where its importance is half of what it is at street level. The 45.5 percent of combined upper-floor space devoted to retail business in this innermost zone most probably reflects the multistory department and variety stores that are typical retail functions in the high-value area immediately adjacent to the peak intersection. Outside this compact area, very little upper-floor space space is devoted to retailing, and in zone 4 this activity accounts for less than 15 percent of total floor space.

The above description of the arrangement of land uses presents the average picture of the internal structure of the CBD. The specific patterns within any individual CBD can be expected to differ in particulars for two important reasons: first, individual functions will vary in importance from one CBD to another; and second, because the CBD is the commercial heart of the city, it will reflect in a general way the functional specialization of its surrounding urban area. Thus Tulsa, Okla., which experienced rapid growth resulting from the development of the nearby midcontinent oilfield, was built primarily as an office center serving the oilfield interests. Offices, therefore, dominate the CBD of Tulsa, though most of the business types are distributed in a predictable manner.

The Relationship Between Land Values and Land Use

It is clear from the discussion so far that both land values and the locational patterns of various activities are related to distance from the PVI within the CBD. One of the major shortcomings of the 100-yard zone method used by Murphy and Vance in their analysis of the internal structure of the CBD is that it does not permit explicit recognition of the relationship between these two patterns. The simplicity of the method is offset by its more serious limitations arising from the rigid geometrical nature of the grid. It is insensitive to variation in the size and shape of the CBD and hence to the marked distance and directional variation in the pattern of land values and associated patterns of land use.

The shortcomings are vividly revealed when the 100-yard zones are superimposed on the pattern of land values, as is done in Figure 13.3 for the CBD of Dubuque. Because of the elongated shape and restricted size of this downtown area, the first 100-yard zone from the PVI extends to the edge of the CBD in all directions except to the south. As a result, it contains locations that differ considerably in land value, ranging from the peak value itself to locations with values as low as 32 percent of it. Similar diversity to the land-value structure within the first 100-yard zone is clearly apparent for the other zones as well. Consequently the use of such a rigid framework for land-use analysis tends to cover up the real locational patterns of activities within this business nucleation by grouping together in the same zone uses that ought to be separated from each other, and separating uses that perhaps go together. Obviously a more flexible framework for analyzing the arrangement of land uses is to be desired. Despite the general argument that land-value data are difficult to obtain and to interpret, it would seem logical to place the analysis of land use within a framework of zones comprising locations with generally similar land values.

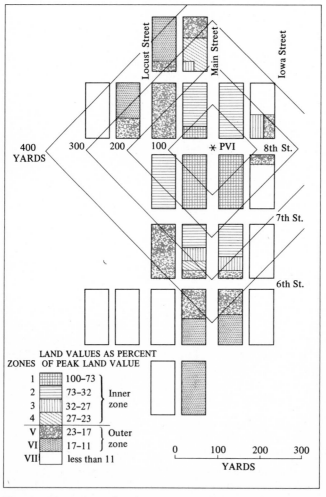

Fig. 13.3. The "100-yard grid" superimposed on the CBD of Dubuque, Iowa.

Such a framework has been used as the basis for the construction of Figure 13.4, which shows the arrangement of activities at the ground-floor level by land-value zones within the CBD of Dubuque. These zones were derived from the application of a method called linkage analysis to the front-foot values expressed as a percentage of the peak land value. By the use of this simple grouping procedure, locations that are most similar to each other in land value are grouped together to form a class, which when mapped is expressed spatially as a zone of similar land values. In this way the zones used as the basis for the analysis of land use are explicitly related to distance from the PVI.

Seven land-value zones were generated, as shown in the graph. These may be combined in a second round of grouping into two broader regions, designated as the inner and outer zones of the CBD. The inner area may be thought of as corresponding to the core of the downtown district, while the outer area is most probably the innermost part of the surrounding frame of the CBD. That these two regions are meaningful in terms of their structure is clearly apparent from the diagram. The inner area, which comprises all locations with values higher than approximately 25 percent of the peak value, is characterized by a concentration of retail business types and a marked absence of service, financial, and office uses. In contrast to this, the outer zone with its lower values has a more diversified structure characterized by a mixture of retail businesses and office functions.

Considerable variation exists in the land-use structure of the zones that comprise these two broader regions. On the higher-value land in zones 1 and 2, clothing and variety stores dominate, and together these business types account for 80 and 65 percent of zones 1 and 2, respectively, As distance increases away from the PVI, and land values become lower, other business types become more important. Thus in zone 3, household goods and a variety of other types classified as miscellaneous become the dominant retail business types, in association with banks and other financial services. Food stores are added to these activities to become a significant feature of zone 4, and they dominate the diversified structure of zone 5. In the outermost zones with values below 16 percent of the peak value, parking lots and automotive types become significant features of the land-use pattern. Notice that the clothing and variety types are not represented at all in the low-value peripheral area of the CBD in Dubuque.

The Land Value–Land Use Theory Restated

The evidence from the analysis of the CBD of Dubuque clearly suggests that there is a marked degree of order in the arrangement of land uses within business nucleations. The decline in land values with distance from the PVI is clearly associated with a change in the type of land use. This pattern is the combined result of a multitude of decisions made by individual entrepreneurs about location within the downtown area. Although the basis on which these decisions are made is not perfectly understood, it was suggested in Chapter 9 that the quality of locations measured by the rent to be paid for their use is a major factor.

The pertinent aspects of the mechanism underlying the land-value–land-use relationship can be briefly summarized as follows: Each activity is able to gain some utility from every site within the downtown area. Site utility will vary both between locations within the CBD and between different activities. In general, whatever the specific relation of site utility to a particular activity, it will be largely reflected in the rent that that activity must pay in order to use the site. The greater the perceived utility of a site for a

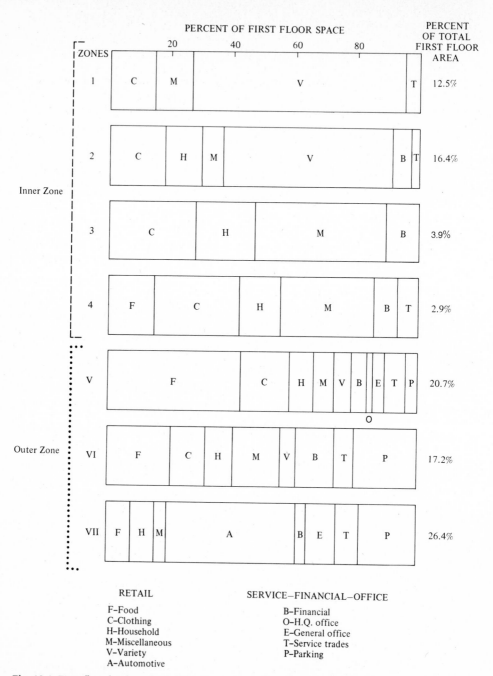

Fig. 13.4. First-floor land use by land-value zones within the CBD of Dubuque, Iowa.

given use, the higher the rent. In the long run, competition in the urban land market is presumed to sort out activities between locations to give rise to distinctive arrangements of land use. Conceptually the final pattern should be one in which each site is occupied by the highest and best use; that is, the use that can maximize the utility, and hence the rent, of every site. This process of land-use competition is, of course, identical to that referred to in Chapter 9. In the urban area, however, this process is operationally much more complex.

What, then, determines the utility of a given location within business nucleations? Although this is a difficult question to answer, evidence suggests that the numerous factors involved can be summarized under two headings: availability and accessibility. Availability refers generally to the existence of suitable sites from the physical standpoint. Factors involved in this might be the size and shape of the lot, the nature of the existing structure built upon it, and whether both of these are suitable for an intended purpose. Accessibility, on the other hand, refers to the locational quality of the site and particularly to its spatial relationship with other downtown features.

Accessibility means different things to different activities. But whatever the activity, accessibility is viewed in terms of nearness, proximity, or convenience to something else. For example, in the case of retail businesses, convenience to shoppers and the retail sales potential associated with them will be major factors determining site utility. The concentration of shoppers varies within any unplanned nucleation. For obvious reasons it is greatest at street level, and we have seen above how retail business dominates ground-floor use, especially within the innermost parts of the CBD. But more important than this, perhaps, is the decline in concentration of shoppers with distance away from the PVI, for pedestrian and vehicular traffic is greatest at the center. As distance increases away from this central location, the concentration of shoppers, and presumably therefore sales potential, declines. It is to be expected, therefore, that strong centripetal forces operate in the location of retail businesses, pulling them toward the innermost part of the downtown area. Competition for site use is intensified, and rents become high there.

Not all types of retail business have the same ability to pay high rents for the use of the more central sites. Rent-paying ability depends very much on sales turnover and markup. Because of this, certain uses are able to outbid all others for the most desired sites. For example, in the analysis of Dubuque's CBD, the evidence suggests that the clothing and variety department store types are most able to acquire the prime sites adjacent to the PVI. Other uses are forced to occupy sites at increasingly greater distances from it. This latter point is well emphasized in Figure 13.5, for variety and clothing stores appear to be the most centrally located and are clustered together, whereas transient residences and automobile and household-goods functions are located at the periphery of the CBD.

At the same time, however, we might imagine a variety of opposing centrifugal forces acting within business nucleations that tend to pull some kinds of activities toward the periphery. These forces are largely related to the space demands of different activities. For example, furniture stores need larger floor areas for display purposes than do most food stores or clothing stores. The same is true for new and used automobile showrooms. Moreover, these kinds of activity probably have lower sales turnover than, say, department stores. Consequently they are pulled toward the periphery of the nucleation, where rents per unit area are lower and where they are able to outbid

Fig. 13.5. Distribution of selected business types within the CBD of Tulsa, Okla. (*Source*: Murphy et al., 1955, Figs. 12 and 15.)

other activities for the use of land. It is in this way that the general factors of availability and accessibility are interrelated to give rise to well-ordered patterns in the distribution of retail and other commercial activities within business nucleations.

Specialized Areas Within High-Order Nucleations

Thus far, the discussion concerning land uses and land values in business nucleations has used examples of patterns within the central business districts of small- and medium-sized cities. At this scale, distinct relationships beween the location of different commercial activities and distance (measured in terms of land values) are a prominent feature of their internal structure. Similar relationships also underlie the internal structure of the downtown areas of larger cities. However, because of the larger spatial dimension and greater functional complexity of the CBD in large cities, these relationships may not initially be as clearly apparent. One of the reasons for this is that functional specialization becomes a distinctive feature of the land-use pattern in high-order

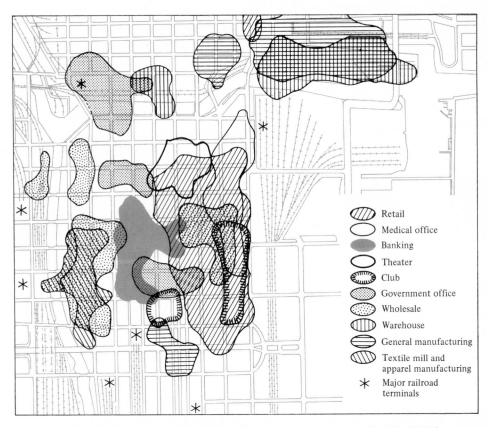

Fig. 13.6. Functional areas within the CBD of Chicago. (*Source*: Berry, 1967a, Fig. 2–23.)

nucleations, such as large CBD's. These specialized areas are superimposed on the underlying distance regularities, which as a result may become blurred.

Two general types of specialized areas may be recognized within central business districts. First there are what may be called functional areas that consist of local concentrations of different business activities that are functionally interrelated. Second, tiny clusters develop comprising different establishments of the same business types. These are generally small-scale concentrations and may develop within the larger functional areas. Both types are examples at different scales of the effects of the forces of agglomeration discussed in Chapter 14.

Examples of some functional areas in the CBD of Chicago are presented in Figure 13.6. The area shown on the map includes both the core (the Loop) and the frame of the central business district. At this scale retail business emerges as one of the many different functional areas in the CBD core. Other examples in the core might be financial districts, theater districts, and medical centers. In the surrounding frame, separate districts devoted to wholesaling, transportation facilities, warehousing, and small manufacturing and service industries (e.g., printing) may emerge as functional areas. In some cases this kind of a real specialization may extend over several city blocks; in others a particular set of activities may be concentrated on a particular street in the CBD; in still others the functional area may be contained within a specific block. Many of them are so strongly developed and important to the urban, even national community that the districts or streets in which they are located have become household names. To take a rather special case, many of the functional areas of Manhattan are known throughout America, even the world. Wall Street is synonymous with the financial community there; Park Avenue with the headquarter offices of many of America's largest corporations; Madison Avenue goes with advertising agencies; and Fifth Avenue is associated with high-quality retailing.

Examples of clusters of similar types of activities are perhaps best developed within the retailing area of large CBD's. Thus a characteristic feature of these is the marked concentrations on certain streets or blocks of activities such as clothing stores, shoe stores, and furniture and automobile showrooms (Getis and Getis, 1968). Similar clusters of services and places of entertainment may develop, as for example of theaters (Broadway in Manhattan), legal offices, restaurants, and so on. In some cases these may overlap with each other to give rise to more complex kinds of specialized areas.

Although specialized areas may be best developed within the CBD's of larger cities, they are by no means absent from the smaller business nucleations. However, at this smaller scale they may be only incipient developments lacking any distinct spatial extent. Certainly at this scale clothing stores tend to cluster together and usually in conjunction with the larger department stores. An example of the more weakly developed specialized areas that may be observed generally within smaller CBD's is given for the city of New Brunswick, N.J., in Figure 13.7. The area shown on the map includes more than the CBD proper, which if delimited by the Murphy and Vance index method would most probably extend only for one block, perhaps two blocks, along George Street, the central axis. Weak concentrations of hardware stores, household-goods stores, and clothing stores can be clearly delimited here. In the vicinity of the railroad station a small complex of transportation-oriented activities has developed, including hotels, eating places, the bus station, and a variety of dingy entertainment activities. Perhaps the best examples of specialized areas in this business nucleation are the tight

cluster of legal services adjacent to the group of civic buildings, especially the Middle-
sex County courthouse, with which they are functionally linked, and the more recently
developing concentration of professional offices, especially of doctors and dentists, at
the edge of the area along Livingston Avenue.

   The distribution of specialized areas within the CBD and other large business
nucleations does not necessarily bear any relationship to distance from the PVI. This is
because they develop from a separate set of forces than those embodied in the land-
value–land-use relationship discussed above. Specialized areas result from the forces of
agglomeration generally founded upon the external economies of scale made possible
when functionally interrelated activities are located in close juxtaposition with one
another. For some activities these economies may stem from the sharing of common
facilities; for example, this is often the case in medical centers, where patients may be
referred to specialists in the complex or use is made of a central X-ray facility, and so
forth. For other activities the economies may come from the possibility of face-to-face
contact with other functions in the cluster. The important point to remember is that
the economies are external to the individual activities or establishments, and savings
are made by being part of a larger complex of similar or interrelated activities. In this

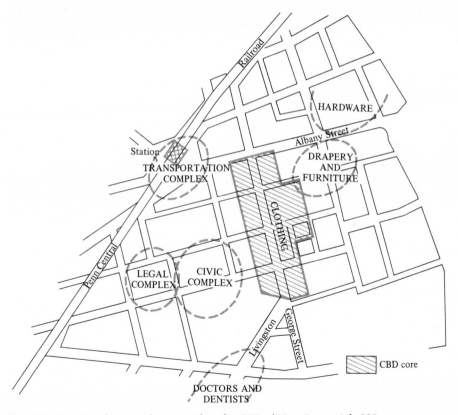

Fig. 13.7. Incipient functional areas within the CBD of New Brunswick, N.J.

context, then, accessibility takes on a slightly different meaning than nearness to the PVI. For activities forming the various types of specialized areas, it is the accessibility or proximity to similar kinds of activities that is important and which determines site utility and eventually land value.

In the case of clusters of similar types of retail businesses within the broader retail area, another important agglomerating factor operates. This is related to the different kinds of shopping and buying habits associated with different types of goods and services. These habits have an important effect on the location of certain business types and are to a large extent responsible for differences in site utility. Thus, some kinds of goods are purchased on impulse—for example, chocolates. Hence it is not uncommon to find candy stores located at points that truly maximize accessibility to shoppers in high-order nucleations, such as near transportation terminals or close to a peak-value intersection. We know from our everyday experience, however, that impulse buying does not lead to the development of clusters of candy stores; this business type is generally well distributed within shopping centers. Clusters of similar kinds of retail business types develop only when purchase of the goods they provide involves considerable selection and comparison. This aspect of comparative buying is a particularly important aspect of shopping for clothes or for other goods, such as automobiles and furniture, which involve less frequent purchase but considerable outlays of money. For these kinds of goods, shoppers usually want to shop around in order to compare price, style, and quality before making the final purchase.

It is this feature of shopping around that, it is argued, results in the clustering together of similar types of retail businesses. For in shopping around, the customer, if he obeys the principle of least effort, will want to minimize his time and effort on the shopping trip. At the same time, the astute entrepreneur will realize that it is to his advantage to ensure that his goods are included in the selection and comparison process. It is to his advantage to locate close, even next door, to other stores offering similar kinds of goods. Over the long run, small clusters of, for example, clothing or shoe stores may build up within the downtown retail area. In the case of these business types, accessibility does not relate only to the general concentration of shoppers in the immediate vicinity of the PVI, but also to other establishments of the same kind. Site utility is greater within the cluster than outside it, and hence higher rents must be paid for site use. If these higher rents represent a savings in transportation costs, as implied in Chapter 9, it is in terms of shoppers' time and effort involved in comparative buying. Hence the formulation at this microscopic level is consistent with the general model for land values presented previously.

A MODEL OF THE INTERNAL STRUCTURE OF BUSINESS NUCLEATIONS

The relationship between land values and the location of business types suggests that land-use patterns in shopping nucleations are consistent with the general theory of tertiary activity developed in Chapter 6. The structural features of the hierarchy of nucleations are translated into spatial patterns in the different level centers. Business types are allocated to different levels in the hierarchy according to their threshold size; high-threshold types are found only at high-level nucleations while low-threshold types occur at all levels. If threshold size is directly related to rent-paying ability, then the same allocation process possibly operates within the different level nucleations to give rise to well-developed patterns. According to this hypothesis, high-order business types would tend to be located at high-value locations close to the peak-value intersection of the nucleation, while low-threshold types would be displaced outward onto low-value land.

The hypothesis of a direct relationship between threshold size and land value is intuitively appealing but difficult to establish. Evidence recently presented suggests that there tends to be a general relationship between the two variables (Garner, 1966). The argument can be simplified as follows: High-order business types require locations with high degrees of centrality within the overall urban commercial complex. Centrality is measured in terms of accessibility to consumers. Within shopping centers, centrality may be thought of in terms of accessibility to the local concentration of shoppers. We have already noted that the density of shoppers within centers declines with distance from the peak-value intersection of a nucleation. This is illustrated in Figure 13.8A for a section along Ashland Avenue in Chicago. Note how the density of pedestrians drops off sharply from the two main business intersections at 63rd and 79th Streets. The differences in desirability of sites within centers which arises from these differences in pedestrian traffic are great enough to result in marked variation in land values. As shown in Figure 13.8B, the decline in land values around the two intersections mirrors the pattern of consumers walking along the street. High-threshold business types can, then, ensure maximum centrality within centers if they gravitate toward the peak-value intersection where site utility is greatest for them, and where they can best satisfy their thresholds. But to do so, of course, they must pay higher rents. Low-threshold types will not generally be able to compete with these high-order business types for the use of these prize locations and will be pushed farther out into low-value locations.

The hypothetical pattern in the internal structure of outlying business centers, to which this argument gives rise, is formalized in Figure 13.9 for the three levels of centers. The innermost sites with their high land values are occupied by the set of high-threshold functions that are typical of centers of this level. Thus, within community nucleations these functions are the high-threshold community-level functions; at the

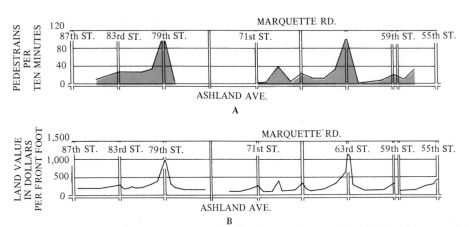

Fig. 13.8. Pedestrian counts (A) and land-value profiles (B) along a part of Ashland Avenue, Chicago. (*Source*: Berry, 1967a, Fig. 2–21.)

regional nucleations they are higher threshold regional-level functions. Business types typical of each low-level center in the hierarchy are located at successively low-value sites consistent with their lower thresholds. Thus in community centers the inner-core area of high values is occupied by community-level functions surrounded on low-value

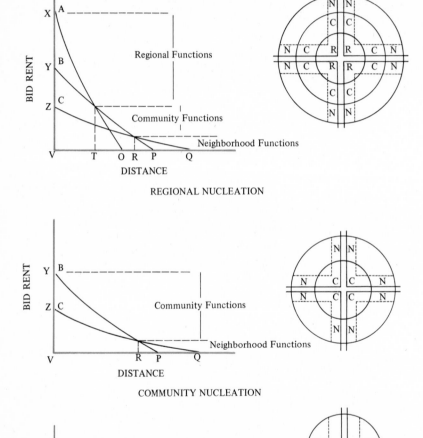

Fig. 13.9. Hypothetical patterns of the internal structure of regional, community, and neighborhood-level shopping nucleations. (*Source*: Garner, 1966, Fig. 20.)

peripheral sites by the low-threshold neighborhood functions. At the regional level, the locational sequence runs regional-community-, and neighborhood-level functions on land of successively lower value. Similar zoning by threshold type might be expected within the CBD, although the pattern there is most certainly more complex—perhaps so complex as to destroy the simplicity of the pattern typical of outlying centers. It is, however, well to remember that when the "simplicity of land use patterns is destroyed . . . this does not mean that the order and system are destroyed. It means that the order imposed by the influence of economic distance takes on increasingly more complex forms" (Dunn, 1954, pp. 61–62).

Table 13.2 indicates that the arrangement of business types within regional-level centers in Chicago generally agrees with the model. In the table, business types are ranked by their average values expressed in percentage form and are classified down the right margin according to the level of center at which they are typically found.

Distortions to the Expected Pattern

The expected arrangement is, however, somewhat blurred at the larger regional-level nucleations (Table 13.2). Though the high-order regional types tend to be concentrated toward the upper part of the list, they are joined by low-order types. Neighborhood-level types are not all concentrated at the lower end of the list, as we might expect; neither are all the community-level types placed among those in the middle of the table. There appears to be considerable scatter of the different groups of activities through the list. Of the many factors responsible for these distortions, three are of particular importance: space demands, product differentiation, and agglomeration economies.

In discussing patterns in the high-order nucleations, we noted that business types that need large amounts of space tend to be located at peripheral sites where they can afford it. This factor is not taken into account in the model. It is clear from Figure 13.10, however, that a strong correlation exists between average front-foot land value and the average size of stores for a sample of business types in the regional center at 63rd and Halsted Streets in Chicago. Candy stores are generally small and are associated with high-average land values consistent with the tendency for them to locate as close to the peak-value intersection as possible, where they can tempt the large numbers of shoppers into buying on impulse. In contrast, the high-order furniture and household-appliance stores with their larger showroom space tend to be pushed outward onto the low-value land consistent with the comparative buying associated with the goods they sell.

Product differentiation refers to qualitative differences between establishments selling the same type of goods. Our methods of classification implicitly assume that all men's clothing stores or supermarkets are identical in the nature of the goods they sell—that they are all of the same quality. In reality, however, the competitive nature of retailing tends to bring about a variety of tangible (e.g., price) and intangible (e.g., level of service) differences between individual establishments of the same business type. When these differences affect the cost structure of establishments, they are reflected in threshold size. Thus, each establishment can be thought of as having its own threshold size. As a result, there is a range of threshold sizes reflecting the product differentiation between establishments of the same business type, and in turn a considerable variation in rent-paying ability and hence location in nucleations. The average figures in the table mask this variation and, because of the way they are calculated, may even result

Table 13.2.   THE INTERNAL STRUCTURE OF REGIONAL NUCLEATIONS IN THE CITY OF CHICAGO

SIC Code		Description	Percent Value
R	5634	Apparel accessory	56.2
R	5633	Hosiery stores	53.7
C	5441	Candy	49.1
R	5662	Men's shoes	49.0
C	5311	Department stores	48.7
C	5651	Family clothes	44.1
R	5663	Women's shoes	43.7
R	5664	Children's shoes	41.7
C	5621	Women's clothes	41.3
C	5331	Variety stores	41.3
N	5912	Drugstores	40.8
C	5665	Family shoes	39.3
C	5612	Men's clothes	38.4
C	5971	Jewelers	35.3
R	5641	Children's clothes	32.7
R	5632	Corsets and lingerie	32.5
R	5699	Miscellaneous clothing	32.0
R	5722	Household appliances	31.8
N	5462	Bakeries	31.8
N	605	Currency exchanges	30.9
C	783	Motion-picture theaters	30.5
C	5499	Delicatessens	28.8
R	7949	Sports promoters	28.2
N	5812	Eating places	28.0
C	60	Banks	27.6
C	5732	Radio & television	26.2
C	6159	Loan offices	25.8
R	5631	Millinery stores	25.3
N	8099	Optometrists	25.1
R	5996	Camera stores	25.1
C	5997	Gift and novelty shops	24.5
R	64	Insurance agencies	24.1
C	7631	Watch repairs	24.0
N	5251	Hardware	23.5
C	5712	Furniture	23.4
N	5411	Grocers	22.8
R	5713	China and glassware	22.4
N	5422	Meat markets	22.2
C	5921	Liquor stores	22.1
N	801	Medical services	22.1
R	5952	Sporting-goods stores	21.9
C	5392	Army and navy stores	21.5
R	7221	Photographers	20.5
N	65	Real estate agents	20.1
R	5714	Drapery stores	19.8
C	5733	Music stores	19.6
N	5813	Bars	19.6
N	7231	Beauty salons	19.3
N	10	Supermarkets	19.0
N	7211	Dry cleaners	18.9

Table 13.2 (cont.)

	SIC Code	Description	Percent Value
N	7241	Barbers	18.3
C	5943	Stationery stores	18.3
N	7215	Laundromats	17.7
C	5231	Paint and glass stores	17.7
R	5715	Floor covering	15.1
N	7251	Shoe repairs	14.7
R	5719	Miscellaneous furnishing	14.5
N	5423	Fish and sea foods	14.2
C	5992	Florists	13.9

Note: R, C, and N indicate regional-, community-, and neighborhood functions, respectively.

in the upward and downward movement within the table to give rise to apparent distortions to the regularity.

   This factor, which distorts the pattern that might be expected from the operation of the model, has been discussed extensively with respect to the very high-order centers, particularly CBD's. Forces of agglomeration, such as the desire for face-to-face contact, comparative shopping, economies arising from joint advertising, and so forth, give rise to specialized areas in most downtown districts and in many regional centers. The downtown areas of small cities and the regional centers of large metropolitan areas usually exhibit signs of incipient specialized clusters, particularly those relating to entertainment and clothing. In fact, in some large metropolitan areas, centers that contain community-level functions frequently exhibit an extent of incipient clustering comparable to that for the CBD's of small cities.

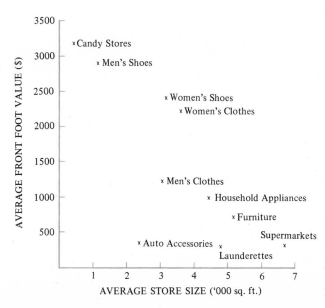

Fig. 13.10. Relationship between average front-foot land values and store size for selected business types in the 63rd and Halsted regional-level shopping nucleation, Chicago. (*Source:* from data in Berry and Tennant, 1963, p. 3.)

The Internal Structure of Planned Nucleations

Planned shopping centers have become a significant feature in the commercial structure of most urban areas. It has been indicated previously that they can be included within the hierarchical structure of commercial nucleations within an urban region, though they tend to have fewer establishments at a particular level than their unplanned counterparts. Their internal structure cannot, however, be analyzed in quite the same way as unplanned nucleations.

This is because planned centers involve a different set of marketing principles. A planned center will contain some fundamental features of attraction that will determine its market hinterland and therefore its potential position in the hierarchy of nucleations. For example, if a center is to be built containing just one large supermarket, it is fairly clear that the total number of customers that this facility could attract would place the center at about the convenience level. Thus the range of additional establishments that may be included within the center will be limited by the market attractiveness of that one dominant facility, and they will be located immediately adjacent.

If, on the other hand, a shopping center is planned to contain a large supermarket *and* a full-range, well-known chain department store, then the range of attraction of the center is considerably greater. The volume of customers attracted to the center will be quite large, and as a consequence the range and number of additional establishments that may be supported will be considerably greater. Furthermore, the internal structure of the center can be designed to take advantage of the joint attraction of the two dominant facilities. The common pattern is for a linear center to be constructed, with the department store at one end and the supermarket at the other. With these two facilities in the same center, the customers can enjoy one-stop shopping, and will, providing the distance is not great, actually walk from the department store to the supermarket and vice versa. Thus a line of heavy pedestrian traffic is created, and the smaller stores can locate in between. Frequently the mid-location is designed as an area of attraction, and refreshment facilities along with commercial amusements are provided.

The largest planned shopping centers contain at least two well-known full-range department stores, a glossy supermarket, and, increasingly, one or two movie houses. The market attractiveness of a center with these high-order facilities is very great, placing it at the regional level in most instances. In some medium-sized cities a center of this kind may well rival and replace the CBD. The large volume of customers creates sufficient business for a wide array of additionsl service establishments, ranging all the way from specialty clothing stores to restaurants and barbers. The internal structure of centers of this kind is, again, designed to take advantage of the possibility for one-stop shopping generated by the major facilities. For example, the existence of three major facilities usually leads to the construction of a three-pronged shopping center, and the junction of the three prongs may be designed as an arboreal retreat surrounding a fountain or waterfall.

Thus the internal structure of planned centers is related to the possibility for one-stop shopping and the pedestrian flow that may be generated between specific high-order facilities. The attractiveness of these major facilities is extremely important, for it is these that determine the commercial success of the center. Consequently, many planned shopping centers have been developed by large department stores that gained their original reputation and prestige from prominant downtown locations.

CHANGES IN LAND-USE PATTERNS

Patterns within nucleations result from the operation of some complex, and often conflicting, sets of locational forces. The nature of these forces, however, is constantly changing with time. Hence, order in the internal structure of business nucleations may never be perfectly developed, because the arrangement of land uses is in a constant state of flux. The present distribution is only a stage in an evolutionary process that can never be completely understood. Some of its causes are permanent, some are no longer active, while others are just beginning to function.

Changes in land-use patterns may arise as a result of regional economic growth or decline, physical impacts, social replacement, and life-style developments. Perhaps responses to regional economic growth are the most important, for if the potential volume of sales in a market area changes, the number, range, and type of business that can be supported in a nucleation adjusts accordingly. For example, if a retail nucleation fails to attract the volume of business that it once did, the threshold business level required by the higher order functions may not be attained. These functions will not go out of business immediately, but they may reduce their range of services and offer different products. Certainly they will not be able to afford the level of upkeep that they exhibited prior to the change.

The result of this type of regional economic decline is, initially, an appearance of physical blight in the center of the nucleation, which is soon transmitted like a contagious disease to adjacent buildings. Eventually some businesses may vacate and be replaced by lower order functions. These changes at specific locations are generally referred to as the *sequent occupance* of a location, and this is particularly common in older buildings downtown. In areas of decline, there may be a gradual contraction of the nucleation, and vacant premises or sleazy uses may appear at the periphery. Of course, if there is regional economic growth, exactly the opposite may occur, and higher order functions may wish to locate in the center and displace the previous occupants.

Thus nucleations may well change their boundaries over time, and sometimes these changes are effected by external physical factors. Changes within nucleations that have been influenced by physical factors have been well documented by Murphy, Vance, and Epstein (1955) with respect to CBD's. They noticed that the CBD itself is not stable through time, but that its boundaries gradually shift. The CBD expands in one direction and contracts in another, usually the opposite direction. The advancing front is called the "zone of assimilation" and the retreating front the "zone of discard." They note that the zones of discard reflect the repelling influences of industrial land and transport facilities, whereas the zones of assimilation are usually in the direction of better quality housing and general urban growth.

In effect, the zones of discard and assimilation represent an invasion-succession process, for activities that were characteristic of a former pattern are gradually replaced by a new and different set of activities. Activities indicative of assimilation include specialty shops, automobile showrooms, drive-ins, banks, headquarter offices, and newer hotels. In contrast, the zone of discard is invaded by pawnshops, discount clothing stores, bars, "greasy spoons," and questionable "joints." The upper floors of the buildings in this area are usually vacant, and the premises quickly become fire traps and the homes of rats, roaches, and rare diseases.

Land uses may also change as a result of social changes in the hinterland of the nucleation, even though the total level of demand (as measured by people and money) remains fairly constant. In this context, "social" is defined as relating to ethnicity, color, or a particular behavioral pattern. University students have their own particular tastes in stores, and as these tastes change over time, so the stores that serve them must change. If one particular social group is replaced by another, the commercial activities serving the area generally change in response to the new market. The stores may be owned by the same people, but different facilities have to be provided. Land-use changes as a result of shifts in social composition of the hinterland population may be quite traumatic, particularly for the vestigial original inhabitants, who perceive their habitual way of life disappearing.

Land-use changes in response to changing life styles are extremely important, but difficult to delineate except by impression. The impact that needs to be emphasized concerns the manner in which suburban life styles have come to dominate most urban areas. The features concerning commercial activities that this life style emphasizes are one-stop shopping, shopping as a family activity, and shopping as entertainment. The result is that the business nucleations have to be attractive to the family as a whole, not just to one person in the family. Certainly, it would appear that enclosed air-conditioned and centrally heated shopping centers fill these requirements the best. During specific periods in the year, street malls may suffice, but on the whole, the enclosed center has the greatest attraction. With these trends it is not surprising that many lower order planned and unplanned centers are showing signs of deterioration, and downtown renovations are directed toward linking buildings by overhead, underground, and covered walkways. Given the great increases in energy costs that have occurred since 1970, it could be predicted that one-stop attractive facilities of this kind will receive even greater preference in the future.

Nevertheless, accepting that there will always be elements of change, a measure of order in land-use patterns within business nucleations is quite evident. The order, however, is never perfectly attained because of a constant change in the importance of different locational forces. Land-use patterns are consequently in a state of constant change. The array of activities found within shopping centers results from the continuance of previous patterns and the active formation of new groupings of businesses, and occasionally new types of activities. Despite the general inertia characteristic of many activities within nucleations, a shift of activities among alternate locations is always taking place somewhere.

14
THE
LOCATION OF
MANUFACTURING

Although manufacturing land occupies a small proportion of total urban land, it contains a very important aspect of the urban economy, for on this land are located production facilities that provide employment for a large proportion of a city's labor force (see Fig. 14.1 and Table 9.1). In the Pittsburgh region, for example, although manufacturing production facilities occupy less than 15 of the region's 4487 square miles, on an average workday more than one-third of the region's work force pours into this area, and the activities of these industries generate more than two-fifths of the total earned income of the region (Lowry, 1963b). It is therefore extremely important to develop an understanding of the factors influencing the location of industry within urban areas, for these manufacturing activities are centers of a large proportion of total urban economic activity.

Many studies of the manufacturing structure of cities have been made, yet the geographic literature is rather sparse on the subject of industrial location models at the urban level (Hamilton, 1967; Rowland, 1959). While general industrial location theory can be used to indicate fairly well the metropolitan area in which a firm can best locate, it provides a less adequate framework for indicating where in an urban area industry should be situated (Goldberg, 1970). There is, in fact, an important difference in scale, for the problem of manufacturing location within an urban area becomes that of choosing a particular site. Thus Kitagawa and Bogue (1955) distinguish between location theory as a framework to place a factory at a given metropolitan area and site considerations to locate the industry within the metropolitan area. The problem that arises in a discussion of site considerations is that it is difficult to express them in terms of a general model of the intraurban location of manufacturing. However, an attempt will be made in this chapter to provide a framework for such a model, though before this can be presented it is necessary to have some discussion of factors influencing site selection in both a spatial and historical framework.

LOCATIONAL REQUIREMENTS OF MANUFACTURING PLANTS

Factors determining where in an urban area a manufacturing concern can most profitably operate fall mainly into three broad groups (Lowry, 1963b):

1. Characteristics of the site itself, including such buildings as may be already on it when it is being considered as a location.
2. Characteristics of the neighborhood or immediate surroundings of the site.
3. Accessibility characteristics, such as access to customers, suppliers, and labor.

Although it may be assumed that a manufacturing concern will seek the most profitable location, it must be remembered that this consideration comes up when the location is being sought. Furthermore, it is possible that for many concerns "profitable" really means "survival," particularly for new firms just starting. Indeed, it should be noted that "most human decision making, whether individual or organization, is concerned with the discovery and selection of satisfactory alternatives; only in exceptional cases is it concerned with . . . optimal alternatives" (March and Simon, 1958, pp. 140–141).

At this juncture it is also necessary to distinguish between plants and firms, for the locational requirements may well be affected by this distinction. A firm is regarded as an independent entity, either publicly or privately owned; and in much of the industrial location literature, it is synonymous with the entrepreneur. A plant is a manufacturing unit (establishment) located on a particular site. Thus a firm can consist of one or many plants. In the latter case, the plants may be distributed at many locations that may be adjacent or dispersed throughout an urban area or over a very large area (a country, a continent, or the world). When a firm consists of many plants, the important locational distinction is that the firm may be seeking to maximize or obtain satisfactory profits from the combination of plants, not from a single plant. Furthermore, for firms with a large number of plants, this maximization procedure is with respect not only to the short term but to the long term as well. Thus a firm with many plants may have a number running at a loss if the potential long-term prospects at those particular locations indicate the investment to be sound. As much of the following discussion is with respect to plants, this important distinction must be borne in mind.

Site Characteristics

Firms or plants may seek sites with particular characteristics. For example, a few may desire a particular type of water that requires a well at a particular site; others may use mineral materials derived from a particular site. In this latter case, the weight-loss principle is obviously the determining factor. However, in general terms, the site characteristics of importance to most plants concern the amount, flatness, and cost of the land, and the type of building found upon it.

Physical and Cost Characteristics

The amount of level land available and its cost are two of the most important factors determining the location of a plant within an urban area. Some types of industry require large quantities of fairly level land, for the production process may be of the conveyor-belt or integrated type. For this type of industry the employment density of the site is fairly low. Table 14.1 lists the ten largest users of industrial land in the Pittsburgh region and the site employment density for each manufacturing type. The largest users of space are the iron and steel, railroad equipment, electrical-industrial apparatus, and metal-can industries, for in all of these the employment-density ratio is very low. Thus it is clear that industries requiring large amounts of space per plant and per employee usually locate only in those areas where land is cheap and not in general demand. On the other hand, industries requiring relatively little space per plant and per employee could locate in the more intensely developed parts of urban areas.

Land Cost

Our discussion of land values in Chapter 9 suggested that the cost of land at the edge of the city is generally less than that within the city, and a great deal less than that at the center of the city. The cost of a site is further increased if the purchaser has to buy a building that has been erected previously on the lot. Thus an industrialist who wishes to buy land per se is usually looking for vacant serviced lots. The serviced aspect is particularly important, for the provision of water, electricity, sewage disposal, and access

---

Table 14.1. AVERAGE SITE AREA IN USE AND EMPLOYMENT DENSITY BY MANUFACTURING ESTABLISHMENTS, PITTSBURGH REGION, 1960–1961

SIC Code	Industry Type	Employment Density (persons per 1,000 sq. ft.)	Average Site Area in Use (in millions sq. ft.)
331	Blast furnaces, iron and steel works, rolling mills	2.2	13.5
291	Petroleum refining	14.3	3.2
282	Plastics materials, etc.	6.1	3.1
325	Structural clay products	49.8	2.9
374	Railroad equipment	1.1	1.9
373	Ship and boat building	4.1	1.7
321	Flat glass	3.5	1.7
362	Electrical-industrial apparatus	1.0	1.3
341	Metal cans	0.9	0.9
329	Abrasives, asbestos, etc.	14.9	0.6

SOURCE: Lowry (1963b), p. 65.

routes reduces an expensive overhead. The evidence available indicates that the price of industrial land varies according to the degree to which it is serviced and the size of the lot, as well as its location within the urban area. Bearing these details in mind, Stuart (1968) suggests that the average price of industrial land within the city of Roanoke, Va., in 1964 (population 160,000) was 6000 dollars per acre, compared with 4200 dollars per acre in the suburban ring, and suggests that the difference between city prices and suburban prices is greater in larger urban areas.

Buildings

Some types of manufacturing establishments seldom have a plant specifically designed for their purpose, but prefer to rent or lease floor space in existing buildings. Rental buildings or loft space are attractive for those enterprises with uncertain futures and particularly for those not using heavy equipment or materials, which are thus able to use secondhand space. Vacant space of this type is most plentiful around the CBD, and it is common to find numerous small firms clustered together in the frame of the CBD.

The types of industries located in this kind of premise are usually those that have some functional link with CBD activities. Lowry (1963b) indicates that the following are typical of this group in the Pittsburgh area:

Service industries to the printing trades
Ophthalmic goods
Jewelry, silverware, and plated ware
Costume jewelry, costume novelties, etc.
Publishing and printing of periodicals
Photographic equipment and supplies
Men's and boys' furnishings, etc.
Miscellaneous apparel and accessories
Manufacture of manifold business forms
Miscellaneous manufacturing industries
Miscellaneous plastics products
Pens, pencils, etc.

From the above list it can be observed that printing and publishing activities in general and the clothing industries (including accessories) are the two dominant groups. In most urban areas the total employment in these industries is relatively small, but in the large metropolises these industries are extremely important, as they form a vital adjunct to the regional office and service activities located in the core of the CBD.

Taxes

Another important factor influencing the location of industry that involves land, buildings, and profits are taxes (Due, 1961). The importance of differential taxation rates between central cities and suburban areas has been emphasized by Campbell (1958), who indicates that 14 percent of factories that left New York City between 1947 and 1955 gave taxes as their prime reason for doing so, and for another 25 percent taxes were a secondary factor. State differences in industrial taxation in the New York region have also been emphasized by Hoover and Vernon (1959). Prior to 1958, New York City had both a corporate tax and a tax on gross receipts, while New Jersey had only a property tax. New Jersey, therefore, was favored as a location by firms with high profits and high property needs.

Tax differentials are therefore an important economic aspect of the locational decision, though they usually represent only a very small component of the total costs or expenditures of most manufacturing firms. However, it seems to be the manufacturer's perception of taxes that is important, for although they may form a small proportion of his costs, they nevertheless loom large in his decision-making matrix (Williams, 1967). This may be because low taxes are synonymous with freedom in the entrepreneur's mind. Nevertheless, the higher taxes on land and buildings in central cities, as well as business taxes, do seem to have an effect on the location of firms and plants.

Neighborhood Characteristics

Much industrial activity is noisy and dirty, and these characteristics give rise to air and water pollution and blight. Although industry is but one cause of air pollution, the local effect of a particular plant or group of plants can be quite overwhelming. This is because man in his industrial life uses the air as a sewer, into which he discharges dust, soot, ash, and gaseous chemical effluents. One of the most devastating examples of this latter kind of pollution exists in and around Sudbury, Ont., where sulfurous and nitrous fumes have completely destroyed the vegetation of an area of many hundreds of square miles. Local air pollution can therefore be a deterrent to other industries, particularly the clean light industries that use electricity. As these industries are usually modern and fast growing, and thus are welcomed by most communities as a desired addition to the urban economy, any local factor discouraging their location has severe repercussions.

Some industrial activity also results in neighborhood frictional blight. It is evident in most urban areas that the "incompatibility of manufacturing with most other land uses has contributed to the formation of industrial clusters within which neighbors are not overly critical" (Lowry, 1963b, p. 66). This clustering of plants has been made formal in most urban areas by zoning ordinances. But the potential use of land bordering these industrial zones is limited, and the demand for such land is relatively low. Consequently, inexpensive and low-rent residential structures, occupied by low-income families, usually are found in these areas. However, since the advent of electricity and natural gas as sources of industrial energy, it is possible for some plants to conduct their operations intermingled with other land users, and in many cases commercial despoilation is greater than that of the modern industrial plant.

It may be suggested that although neighborhood characteristics may not now play a major role in the selection by industrialists of manufacturing sites, it is almost certain that their importance will increase as other locational constraints are eased. A major reason for this expectation is derived from the fact that the proportion of female, professional, and highly skilled workers in the manufacturing labor force is continually increasing. In order to recruit and retain these people as employees, industrialists will be forced to pay attention to the environment surrounding the plant. Thus, the availability of labor, as an input material to the firm, may well be determined in part by the characteristics of the neighborhood.

Accessibility

In Chapter 5 we have emphasized the effect of accessibility on the location of manufacturing between urban centers. Here we are concerned with the effect of accessibility on the location of industry within urban areas. The term "accessibility" in this context covers a number of factors influencing location decisions. Generally, these include accessibility to materials, accessibility to labor supply, and accessibility to markets. These factors, taken together, are commonly considered to be the most important influences on location decisions.

Accessibility to Material Inputs

The sensitivity of a plant to accessibility to materials is related to the weight loss and bulk of the input concerned. Many fuel inputs are very bulky and incur weight loss in the manufacturing process; as a consequence, plants requiring this kind of input tend to locate adjacent to the cheapest means of transportation available. This is either water or rail, with water transportation usually being the cheaper, particularly if the commodity has to be hauled over long distances. For example, in Pittsburgh the iron and steel industry has a vast intake of coal and iron, and shipments of these commodities are twice the weight of outbound product commodities. Thus these, and a few other heavy industries, depend on cheap barge transportation, and they locate along the navigable waterways in the Pittsburgh area. Table 14.2 indicates for these industries the high weekly tonnage of inbound shipments by barge, which contrasts sharply with the general absence of outbound shipments using water transportation.

Table 14.2. PRINCIPAL MANUFACTURING INDUSTRIES IN THE PITTSBURGH REGION USING WATER TRANSPORTATION (RANK ORDERED BY TOTAL VOLUME)

Industry	Average Weekly Tonnage of Barge Shipment per 100 Employees		
	Total	Inbound	Outbound
1. Blast furnaces and steelworks	250	220	30
2. Producers of lubricating oils and greases	2,294	2,294	0
3. Producers of ready-mixed concrete	1,555	1,111	444
4. Producers of paving mixtures and blocks	1,510	1,483	27
5. Producers of ground or otherwise treated minerals and earths	470	470	0
6. Petroleum refining	305	305	0
7. Producers of plastics materials, etc.	199	193	6
8. Zinc smelting and refining	—[a]	—[a]	—[a]
9. Cement, hydraulic	74	7	67
10. Industrial inorganic chemicals n.e.c.	34	34	0

[a] Figures not disclosed to avoid revealing information of individual operations.
Source: Lowry (1963b), p. 67.

If good water transportation is not available, rail is usually used, particularly as it is the most preferred form of shipment for the outbound products of industries with high weight-loss material inputs. Those industries with low weight-loss material inputs are obviously less tied to cheap transportation facilities, and are therefore able to use either rail or truck transportation. In the latter case, the industry has a high degree of locational freedom, and plants can be established with a minimal consideration of accessibility to material inputs.

Accessibility to Labor

The effect of labor differentials within urban areas on the location of industry is partly related to city size. In small urban areas labor differentials are relatively unimportant, but in large urban areas they may be extremely important for certain industries. This is most particularly the case for light manufacturing industries employing large numbers of low-wage, unskilled, married female labor, for married women generally have a much more restricted commuting range than men. Industries that fall into this category are those concerned with canning and preserving, confectionery, electric measuring instruments and test equipment, and household appliances.

Some industries locate within certain areas because of particular skills. This is especially true of the clothing trades in large metropolitan areas, where certain groups have developed traditional skills in needlework, cutting, and designing. For example, Kenyon (1964) notes that the great growth of the apparel industry in New York City in the 1880's is related in part to the arrival of thousands of Jewish immigrants from eastern Europe who, in reality, initiated the needle trades in New York. The high level of skills introduced by these people was extremely important in making New York City the center of the clothing industry in North America, and the dominant influence of this group continues today.

Unionization also seems to be a factor influencing the locational decision of some firms, particularly with respect to suburban and central city locations. Stuart (1968) notes that some nonunion plants in Roanoke, Va., chose suburban sites so as to place a distance barrier between themselves and the unionized plants in the central city. This is particularly true if the company is labor-intensive and is using low-wage workers.

Accessibility to Markets

There are two aspects of the marketing process that are of interest to the urban geographer. The first involves the destination of the product, and the second involves the geographic range of sales. In Chapter 5 we observed that in any economy goods can be produced and purchased by each industrial group. In a closed urban system the flows all occur within one area; but in an open system, where all urban areas are linked, goods can flow between urban areas as well as within an urban area. Thus the geographic range of sales of a plant may be local or worldwide.

Interindustry Linkages

The flow of a product from one industrial group to another gives rise to interindustry linkages. In these cases the output of one firm forms the input of another. Thus it would be logical to expect that firms with a high degree of interdependency would, other things being equal, tend to cluster within an urban area. However, whether the possibility of interindustry linkages really effects micro-location decisions is difficult to determine (McGregor, 1974). In a highly generalized study, Richter (1969) indicates that on a metropolitan-area basis geographic associations are more prevalent among linked than nonlinked sectors of the urban economy. This study does not, however, examine the existence and need for interindustry linkages on a plant-by-plant basis in a particular area. Karaska (1969) uses input-output methodology to estimate the degree to which certain sectors of industry are interlinked in the Philadelphia region and concludes that external linkages are much stronger. He does not, however, identify a group of plants that require physical proximity.

The Geographic Range of Markets

The geographic range of sales of most plants is usually very wide, and for a few it may be worldwide. For example, in a study pertaining to a few small towns in southern Ontario, it is estimated that only 1.56 percent of the outputs of manufacturing industries were sold locally, 21.78 percent were sold to Metropolitan Toronto, 30.93 percent to the rest of Ontario, 33.71 percent to the rest of Canada, 9.96 percent to the United States, and 2.06 percent to the rest of the world (Yeates and Lloyd, 1970). The total population of the local area referred to in this case is only 100,000 persons, and one would expect that as the population of an area increased, the proportion of local sales would also increase.

Industries that serve a local area have been referred to in Chapter 4 as nonbasic industries. Their products are usually perishable, bulky, or custom-made, and thus small-scale operation is practical. Plants of this type include those concerned with bottled beverages, dairy products, baked goods, commercial printing, ready-mixed concrete and concrete products, and so forth. In Pittsburgh this type of industry usually sells more than 70 percent of its output to the local region, whereas the electrical industries commonly sell less than 20 percent of their output to the local area (Table 14.3). Furthermore, it is interesting to note from Table 14.3 that industries making the greatest use of rail transportation are those that ship most of their output beyond the local Pittsburgh region. We have previously noted that the type of transportation used depends a great deal on the weight loss incurred; consequently some industries use water for the transportation of inputs and rail for outputs. Examples of these are plants classified as blast furnaces, steel works, and rolling mills.

It is in this context of transportation that the contrast between suburban and city plants is most outstanding. Plants located within the city tend to make use of rail transportation much more than plants in suburban locations, which tend to transport by truck. These differences are detailed in Table 14.4 for Roanoke, Va., the contrasts being particularly evident if comparisons are made with the total shipment pattern for the metropolitan area. Furthermore, the table indicates that whereas there is a great difference between the proportion of materials moved into and from the city by rail, this difference is very minor in the suburban ring.

THE SPATIAL EVOLUTION OF MANUFACTURING

In terms of contemporary transportation facilities and communications media, it would seem that a manufacturer is fairly free to locate in any part of an urban area, provided that land in sufficient quantity is available. Thus any pattern of industry observed in

Table 14.3.   PRINCIPAL MANUFACTURING INDUSTRIES OF THE PITTSBURGH REGION, BY MEANS OF TRANSPORTATION USED AND PERCENTAGE OF SALES WITHIN THE REGION

Rank in Use of Truck Relative to Rail Transport	Percentage of Sales Within Pittsburgh Region				
	0–9	10–19	20–34	35–69	70–100
Most truck-oriented	Instruments for measuring, etc.[a]	Metal stampings	General industrial machinery Heating apparatus and plumbing fixtures	Apparel, etc.[a] Nonferrous foundries Special industrial machinery, except metalworking Abrasives, asbestos products, etc.	Dairy products Commercial printing[a] Misc. nonelectrical machinery Concrete, gypsum, and plaster products[b]
Relatively truck-oriented		Paints, etc.[a] Electric lighting and wiring equipment	Construction, mining, and materials-handling machinery	Household furniture Structural clay Paperboard containers and boxes Misc. food preparations	Newspapers Beverages[a] Meat products Bakery products Millwork, etc.
Relatively rail-oriented	Electrical industrial apparatus[a] Electrical transmission and distribution equipment	Ship and boat building and repairing Plastics materials[b] Misc. primary metals industries	Screw-machine products Misc. fabricated metal products Nonferrous metals, rolling, etc.[b] Industrial chemicals[b] Plastic and rubber products	Fabricated structural metal products[b] Metal-working machinery and equipment	
Most rail-oriented	Pressed and blown glass Flat glass Canning and preserving[a] Petroleum refining Railroad equipment Metal cans	Pottery, etc. Cutlery, hand tools, etc. Misc. products of petroleum and coal[b] Motor vehicles and equipment Blast furnaces, steel works, and rolling mills[b]	Iron and steel foundries		

[a]Indicates industries reporting largest use of air freight or express relative to employment.
[b]Indicates industries reporting significant use of water transportation.
SOURCE: Lowry (1963), p. 69.

Table 14.4. CONTRASTS IN TRANSPORTATION MODES USED BETWEEN
THE CITY AND SUBURBAN RING, ROANOKE SMSA, 1964

Zone	Percent Materials Moved In			Percent Product Moved Out		
	Rail	Truck	Air	Rail	Truck	Air
City	32.7	66.9	0.4	23.1	74.9	2.0
Suburban ring	16.4	82.4	1.2	15.4	82.1	2.5
SMSA total	22.5	73.8	0.7	10.7	78.1	2.2

Source: Stuart (1968), p. 31.

the present, such as that for Minneapolis–St. Paul (Fig. 14.1), has to be perceived as a product of differential locational forces prevailing in the past, some of which are no longer of importance. Noting the apparent confusion and geographic chaos in the distribution of manufacturing in the modern city, Pred comments that

> ... beneath this superficial disorder and confusion, certain spatial regularities can be discerned if the structure of metropolitan manufacturing is viewed in terms of its evolution, the local friction of distance, and broad industrial categories which express similar locational tendencies [Pred, 1964, p. 165].

This evolution can be expressed in terms of technological change in the organization of manufacturing industry and major transportation innovations, both of which intertwine historically to constrain locational patterns. These can be classified as

1. The pattern before the Industrial Revolution
2. The early Industrial Revolution waterway era
3. The middle Industrial Revolution railway era
4. The late Industrial Revolution highway era

In each of these eras certain locational forces tend to predominate, but no one locational force is exclusive to any particular era.

Preindustrial Revolution

In the colonial or preindustrial era in North America, the population of towns was very small, and the manufacturing that took place usually occurred within an area corresponding today to the center of the metropolis. This area usually corresponded to a zone adjacent to a waterfront, for nearly all colonial towns were located close to river and sea transportation. The preeminence of the waterfront as a manufacturing area derived from the fact that in every colonial town the principal industries were those concerned with shipbuilding and the preparation of provisions or naval stores for export (Bridenbaugh, 1950). Thus shipbuilding was early established as the chief waterfront activity in seventeenth-century Boston, New York, and Philadelphia; and it was even of importance in centers founded later in nonmaritime locations, such as Pittsburgh and Cleveland.

The types of activity undertaken usually occurred in small workshops, which were often the places of residence as well as the places of work. These workshops clustered around the waterfront and the incipient commercial and retail centers, all of which vied for the best business locations. Eventually, in some towns, the commercial and retail centers grew to sufficient proportions to make it possible for local manufacturers to produce for these local businesses. In this way small clothing establishments, weavers' shops, and leather-working plants grew to provide goods for the quasi CBD as well as the waterfront. Thus, with urban growth, manufacturing activity can be regarded as being located with respect to the CBD and the waterfront. As these areas were often juxtaposed, the spatial differentiation of manufacturing location was not immediately obvious, but in time this distinction became extremely important.

The Early Industrial Revolution

The early nineteenth-century development and spread of settlement in North America followed very closely the pattern of waterways, for the river systems had an obvious advantage over muddy roads and rutted tracks. This advantage was reflected by the choice of manufacturing to locate along waterway sites and, for example, is one reason for the location of various industrial enterprises along the forked branches of the

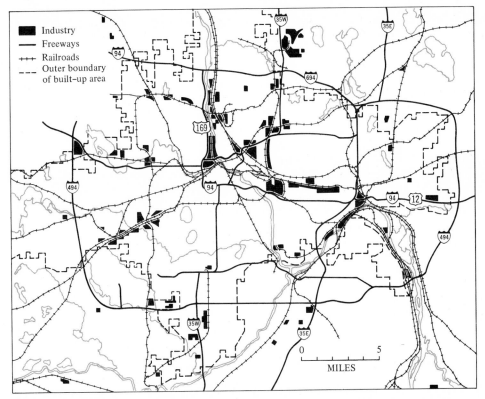

Fig. 14.1. The distribution of industrial land uses in Minneapolis–St. Paul, Minn. 1970. (*Source*: *Focus* [published by the American Geographical Society of New York], 1970, after Map 1.)

Chicago River (Solzman, 1966). Thus the advantages of the waterfront in maritime urban locations were paralleled by settlements in the interior, many of which were located close to water transportation.

Technological innovations and expanding markets resulted, however, in a greater complexity and proliferation of manufacturing, which, in the American experience, "became apparent with the introduction of the factory system, power-driven machinery, interchangeable parts, and other mass-production techniques during the later eighteenth and early nineteenth centuries" (Pred, 1964, p. 167). The power source was frequently water, particularly with respect to wool and textile mills, and this requirement "often dictated location at rural waterfall sites, such as in Waltham, Mass., and in Paterson, N.J. . . ." (Pred, 1964, p. 167), locations that have since become industrial areas within the Boston and New York metropolitan areas. A further aspect of this changing technology is that water became not only important for transportation and as a power source, but also as a material input to the production process. Thus for those industries using large quantities of water, waterway locations were extremely important. In this regard, most of the blast furnaces in operation by 1825 in the Pittsburgh area had riverside locations outside the city and formed industrial nucleations as the city grew in response to the burgeoning urban economy.

Thus water sites were extremely important areas for the early development of manufacturing, and their importance has continued through to today. However, it is possible that "in giving due weight to the necessity for water in industrial processes we have overemphasized its strategic importance in industrial location" (White, 1960). This overemphasis may well have resulted from the continuing expansion of manufacturing at the center of the city, for "the factory system was a city development" (Taylor, 1951, p. 233). We have previously noted that these industries were often juxtaposed with waterfront locations, and so in many instances it is difficult to determine whether CBD industrial expansion or waterway industrial expansion was the primary growth trend. Furthermore, the limited physical mobility of the working force constrained industry to locate in the central part of the city.

The Middle Industrial Revolution

The rapid development of the North American railroad network in the middle and late nineteenth century reinforced the advantages of central areas in most urban concentrations. This was particularly due to the fact that the railroad companies established their terminals either within the CBD or as close to the CBD as possible, and these terminals became break-of-bulk points that offered direct access to a large geographic supply and market area. Thus a mélange of wholesaling and manufacturing establishments became located around rail terminals, which, in the process of serving each other, developed a complex network of commodity and information flows. Pred (1964, pp. 167–168) notes that the "railroad was particularly influential in the evolution of the manufacturing districts near the core of midwestern metropolises; e.g., by the 1870s The Flats of Cleveland and the Union Stockyards of Chicago were prominent features in their respective urban landscapes."

New manufacturing technology continued to increase at an exponential rate through the nineteenth century, resulting in an increasing scale of operation of factories that continually required more land on which to expand. Small factories could not realize the efficiencies of production gained by the larger factories, and many were forced to amalgamate or close down in the face of increased competition. The larger factories could not find enough cheap space in the traditional railroad terminal or waterfront locations, and thus they were forced to decentralize. This decentralization was not possible without innovations in public transportation (detailed in Chapter 8) which permitted the urban area to spread, and without the provision of cheap industrial land, particularly by railroad companies.

Belt-Line Railroads

As the private-enterprise–constructed railroad system in North America continued its development during the latter part of the nineteenth century, the trunk-line railroad companies realized that the interchange of rolling stock between systems was essential for the continued expansion of the industry. This need was particularly noticeable within large urban areas, where many companies might operate lines and share terminal facilities. It was to serve this need that belt-line railroads were established, along with classification yards, either by a consortium of railroad companies or by independent operators. The belt-line railroad could stay in business only if it offered multichange facilities that were cheaper than single-stage transfers between trunk-line companies. In order to offer cheap facilities and additional traffic inducements, the belt-line railroads also encouraged industry to locate along their tracks and adjacent to their classification yards.

The Chicago Belt-Line Railroad

A classic case of belt-line railroad manufacturing locations is to be found in Chicago. The Belt Railroad Company (BRC) began industrial promotion almost from the day it was opened for traffic in the 1880's (Pinkepank, 1966). The inducements were similar to those offered by the trunk lines to industry locating along their tracks: cheap land and direct rail access. However, the BRC inducements were greater in that they offered freedom of access to all of Chicago's trunk-line railroads, and thus an industry would be free to use the facilities of trunk-line companies that offered the most favorable rates. The plentiful supply of cheap, transportation-serviced land was particularly important for those industries that could not obtain land for new plants or for expansion near the center of the city.

In fact, up to the 1880's manufacturing in Chicago has concentrated around the Chicago River near the present Loop (CBD) district.

> This area soon became crowded, and the Chicago River itself would not accommodate the larger lakeboats. The mouth of the Calumet River arose as a rival to the downtown area for industrial location, and BRC was active in promoting this new industrial site, since the Calumet district was on BRC rails [Pinkepank, 1966, p. 40].

The largest industrial district promoted by BRC, however, is the Clearing Industrial District adjacent to Clearing Yard, which is operated by BRC. This city of factories was developed by a land syndicate in the 1920's and 1930's as a planned industrial community, with its own street, water, and sewage services.

Thus the decentralization of manufacturing began during the latter half of the nineteenth century and is directly related to transportation innovations and changing technology, which increased the scale and diversity of manufacturing in growing urban areas. However, the rate of decentralization was limited by the general lack of low-cost urban transit facilities, which kept many manufacturers close to the traditional work and residential areas around the CBD. For example, as late as 1910, 75 percent of the manufacturing employment in Manhattan was in the small area south of 14th Street (Pratt, 1911). This pattern of downtown manufacturing concentration was not noticeably broken until the advent of mass public transportation, the internal combustion engine, the truck, the highway, and the widespread use of electricity for power in manufacturing. These are some of the features that are characteristic of the late Industrial Revolution.

The Late Industrial Revolution

Although there is no degree of uniformity in the rate of decentralization of industry within urban areas, nevertheless the present century has witnessed a general centrifugal movement of manufacturing activity (Colby, 1933; Moses and Williamson, 1967). For example, for the period 1939 to 1947, the standard metropolitan areas of 13 economic regions in the United States showed extensive suburbanization in three regions, and no consistency of change in the other seven (Kitagawa and Bogue, 1955). This lack of uniformity appears to be partly a function of time, for in some urban areas decentralization began earlier than in others. Weber (1963), for example, notes decentralization tendencies in New York City before the turn of the present century, though Chinitz indicates quite clearly that this decline is relative (Table 14.5). Whereas the proportion of manufacturing employment in Manhattan declined, particularly between 1889 and 1919, total employment in Manhattan continued to increase. The great growth in manufacturing employment has been in the counties adjacent to New York City but within the metropolitan area. In more recent years, the proportionate decline of employment located in Manhattan has been matched by an absolute decline in numbers. This is not, of course, total employment, but refers only to production workers.

Forces of Change

Thus far we have discussed intraurban location in terms of the competitive advantages of various areas, particularly with respect to transportation facilities and the availability of space. Kitagawa and Bogue (1955) list numerous factors of a centrifugal

---

Table 14.5. ESTIMATES OF THE CHANGING DISTRIBUTION OF PRODUCTION WORKERS IN THE NEW YORK METROPOLITAN REGION, 1869–1970

Year	Number of Employees (thousands)	Manhattan (percent)	Rest of Metropolitan Region (percent)
1869	240.3	54.7	45.3
1889	683.0	52.2	47.8
1919	1,158.6	33.2	66.8
1956	1,483.3	25.4	74.6
1970	1,889.9	17.6	82.4

SOURCE: Chinitz (1960), p. 131, and comparative estimates for 1970 calculated from 1970 census (PHC [1]–145).

(Table 14.6) and centripetal (Table 14.7) nature that can result in a decentralization or centralization of industry in particular urban areas. However, although all of these forces can be regarded as extremely relevant in particular situations, one factor that has strong spatial implications is the continuing changing nature of industry itself.

Innovation and Uncertainty

Innovation implies uncertainty with respect to all phases of production and marketing (Hund, 1959). These uncertainties force newly established firms to keep their capital outlays at a minimum and to direct their sales efforts toward large concentrated

---

Table 14.6. CENTRIFUGAL FORCES IN INDUSTRIAL LOCATION

1. Topography. A central city located in hilly country with narrow valleys may have little land suitable for factory sites.
2. Late manufacturing development. Cities that have had little manufacturing and are now belatedly attracting factory development may have little room for such activities except beyond the city border.
3. Manufacturing type. Certain types of manufacturing, such as oil refineries, steel mills, meat-packing plants, and aircraft factories with test-flying fields, may create nuisances to such a degree that location beyond the city's boundaries is imperative.
4. Nonfocused transportation. Along a harbor front, navigable river, canal, or belt railroad, the advantages for manufacturing are spread out for a long distance.
5. Annexation difficulties. Some central cities are in sections of the country where annexation of surrounding land is essentially impossible.
6. Extensive highway transportation facilities. With well-designed freeways and other modern highway facilities, factory development is less restricted to the central city.
7. Government policy. Some metropolitan areas experienced much of their manufacturing growth with the development of plants during World War II and were thus subject to government policy of avoiding concentration.
8. Tax laws. In some metropolitan areas, manufacturing plants have been located outside the central city in order to avoid paying the high taxes of the city or taxes to both the city and the state.
9. Failure of former factories. As old manufacturing operations located in the central city die from obsolesence or other causes, their facilities and space are often converted to parking or other nonmanufacturing uses.
10. Zoning. Where the zoning ordinance of the central city fails to set aside enough land or large enough parcels of land for manufacturing, development in suburban areas is encouraged.
11. High land values in central city. The high costs of factory sites inside a city may result in industries' locating just outside the city.
12. Satellite manufacturing cities. In some cases manufacturing may be highly concentrated in the central city and in one or two adjacent satellite cities that are not quite large enough to be classed as central cities but may have had their factories as long as the central city itself.
13. Promotion by railroads. In some standard metropolitan statistical areas, railroad companies have promoted manufacturing growth on sites strung out along their rights of way and therefore extending out of the city.
14. Rural labor force. In some instances a substantial rural and suburban labor force may tempt industrialists to move their factories to suburban locations.
15. Factory design and space requirements. The relatively large space needs of new factories for plant construction, parking facilities, etc. often favor a suburban location.
16. A single-industry city. When a city is essentially a single-industry city, new manufacturing may actually be discouraged by the dominant firm and may be forced to occupy suburban positions.

SOURCE: Modified from the list in Kitagawa and Bogue (1955), pp. 121–123.

Table 14.7.   CENTRIPETAL FORCES IN INDUSTRIAL LOCATION

1. Topography. In a hilly area the central city may contain the only land suitable for most types of manufacturing. Swamps and lowlands subject to flooding also may keep industry inside a city. Or all the waterfront area suitable for port activities and water-oriented industries may be inside the city's boundaries.
2. Utilities. Factories require water, sewage disposal, gas, electric power, and fire protection. These may be available only from the central city, which may be reluctant to provide facilities for suburban areas.
3. Early industrialization. Some cities founded as industrial centers grew up around factories, thus producing a centralized pattern of manufacturing.
4. Use of old buildings. Industry sometimes expands by taking over old warehouses or old factory buildings left by earlier industries. Such developments would result in centralization of manufacturing.
5. Growth through expansion of existing plants. In some standard metropolitan statistical areas most of the expansion of manufacturing volume has come about through expansion of old, well-established firms located in the central city.
6. Single-industry or single-firm towns. Where a single industry or single firm dominates manufacturing employment, it is often located within the city limits and is closely identified with the central city.
7. Zoning. The early adoption of a zoning program that made liberal provision for manufacturing has favored centralization in some cities.
8. Original area of city. Other things being equal, we should expect that a city whose boundary was liberally drawn to begin with would have a relatively low degree of suburbanization of manufacturing.
9. Annexation. Some states have liberal provisions by which central cities can annex adjacent territory. Such additions bring industries inside the city's boundaries, thus reducing the percentage of workers outside the central city or cities.
10. Type of manufacturing. Some types of manufacturing, such as jewelry and garment manufacture, seek a central location to be near other industries, near suppliers, or near a market.
11. Focused transportation. Where transportation facilities are highly focused upon the city but only limited outside the city's boundaries, industries are likely to be centralized.
12. Cheap labor from slum areas. In some large cities factories develop to use the cheap labor from slum areas at the edge of the central business district. This favors location of manufacturing within the city's central area.

SOURCE: Modified from the list in Kitagawa and Bogue (1955), pp. 123–124.

---

markets where advertising costs can be minimized. Although the per capita probability of acceptance of an innovation may be equal for all populations, the total probability of acceptance in a large urban area will be greater than in a small area. Furthermore, it may well be possible that large urban areas have a higher per capita probability of acceptance of innovations than small urban areas, for the inhabitants may have become conditioned through time to accept new things because they are more frequently exposed to them. Uncertainty in production techniques tend to result in the locating of firms toward the center of urban areas where there is the greatest concentration of other small firms and rentable space. In these areas firms can expand and contract fairly easily, can gain a degree of security through accepting contracted work, and can subcontract work if they are going through a successful period. Also, it is in these central areas that labor is cheapest and easiest to hire and lay off.

All these aspects of central locations that reduce the penalties of innovation cannot be incorporated into the accounting structure of the firm. The entrepreneur realizes the advantages of these central locations in a perceptual sense, but he cannot estimate in monetary terms the economies derived from these advantages. Economies of this type are commonly referred to as external economies and are generally defined as a favorable effect on one or more persons or firms that results from the actions of other persons or firms. External diseconomies are the opposite: they refer to the harm done to individuals or firms by the actions of others. Thus in cases of uncertainty, the external economies that can be derived from central locations are extremely important factors influencing the firm to locate around the CBD.

If the firm is successful with respect to both sales and production techniques, then the degree of uncertainty is reduced. The firm will now be able to raise capital more easily in the money market and will be able to reduce costs by large-scale production. The required increased scale of production can often be achieved only by more space and buildings constructed specifically to house the production process that has been developed (Kenyon, 1960). Thus the firm is now free to locate in areas other than the "incubator" of the central part of the city. Consequently, as uncertainty is reduced, the location horizons of the firm expand.

The types of firms that are involved in the process outlined above are essentially those involved with the high-growth industries. These are industries involved with plastics, communications equipment, motor vehicle components, and electrical goods. All of these industries are spatially flexible, for they are not tied to any one mode of transportation, and they use electrical machinery in their production processes. Thus the construction of highways has facilitated the outward movement of firms of this type.

Industrial Parks

Industrial districts and industrial parks have been important agents in the process of decentralization. Although they were first developed in North America in conjunction with railroads, they are now commonly associated with freeways, and are especially located near the interchanges of freeways.

> An "organized" or "planned" industrial district is a tract of land which is subdivided and developed according to a comprehensive plan for the use of a community of industries, with streets, railroad tracks, and utilities sold before sites are sold to prospective occupants [Pasma, 1955, p. 1].

Industrial parks have been developed in a number of urban areas for a variety of reasons. They are often established as antidotes to the depressing appearance of established industries in old urban areas. Very often it is hoped that these parks will attract new industry to the town, and for this purpose the park may be equipped with standard factory shells that are rented at low cost. There are, therefore, many types of industrial parks, ranging from those developed by private companies, such as the Hershey Industrial Park in Hershey, Pa., and the National Cash Register Company in Dayton, Ohio, to those established by municipalities. In some cases the parks are established as parks in the garden-city sense (Howard, 1945), while in many cases they are simply tracts of land at the edge of the city that have been zoned for industry and are partially serviced.

The Components of Decentralization

Total figures relating to changes in the location of plants and manufacturing in a particular urban region do not reveal the components of the change. It is therefore necessary to develop a simple model of change which incorporates the array of possible causes and shifts. Steed (1973) has developed such a model, which is of significant use in analyzing plant location dynamics. This model can be expressed in equation form as follows:

$$x = b - d + m - e$$

where

x = the net change in the number of plants
b = the number of births
d = the number of plants closing down completely
m = the number of plants migrating to an area
e = the number of plants emigrating from an area

Steed (1973) applied this model to the change in the distribution of manufacturing in 13 subareas within the greater Vancouver area for the two time periods 1954 to 1957 and 1964 to 1967. The 13 subareas were chosen so as to isolate the city core from several other foci (e.g., North Vancouver and Burnaby) and suburban areas around the city. Briefly, the innermost and historic industrial area exhibited by far the largest decrease in total number of plants between 1955 and 1965, whereas the greatest absolute increases were experienced in the outer zone, particularly along the north area of the Fraser River, and in East Vancouver and Burnaby.

Application of the model outlined above indicates that the absolute decline in the central part of the region was related to heavy out-migration during the early part of the 1955–1965 period. During the 1954–1957 period this subarea generated one in three of the region's migrant plants, and though a number stayed within the downtown area, a large number moved to other locations within the region. By the end of the period the situation was more stable, for though the heavy out-migration persisted, it was offset by a high plant birth rate and fewer mortalities.

The areas of greatest net increase received their gains primarily through new plant births, and secondarily as a result of plant immigration. On the average, about one-third of the net increase was due to immigrating plants, while two-thirds was the result of the establishment of entirely new plants in the region. Most of the immigrating plants were emigrants from the downtown area.

Thus, in the Vancouver case, the apparent decentralization of industry was primarily the result of the entry of new plants. These new plants located either in the inner industrial core or in the outer growth areas. The plant births in the inner core were, however, offset by a large number of deaths and emigrants, whereas the growth areas did not exhibit these symptoms. The inner core, therefore, continued in its role as an incubator of new plants, and retained a high degree of importance. The growth areas gained in importance, primarily because it is here that space is available, though in the Vancouver region industrial space is extremely expensive. The application of the model is therefore quite instructive, even in the Vancouver situation, where the total manufacturing picture is one of great absolute growth during the past two decades.

THE ELEMENTS OF INTRAMETROPOLITAN MANUFACTURING LOCATION

Having observed the way in which transportation and technological evolution have placed their stamp on the industrial pattern of North American cities, we must now interpret the entire industrial pattern of cities from a locational point of view. Chinitz (1960) has defined industrial plants as

1. Those serving markets that are predominantly local
2. Those serving markets of national extent
3. Those plants localized by external economy considerations

All of these categories can, of course, be subdivided, but the basic aspect of the classification is that each has particular, though not exclusive, locational tendencies. Using this approach as a basis, Pred (1964, p. 174) has grouped metropolitan manufacturing into "seven flexible types, each of which should be characterized by distributional patterns with a unique set of attributes . . ." though within each type a random element may well be present. These are

1. Ubiquitous manufacturing industries concentrated near the CBD
2. Centrally located communication-economy industries
3. Local market industries with local raw-material sources
4. Nonlocal market industries with high-value products
5. Noncentrally located communication-economy industries
6. Nonlocal market industries on the waterfront
7. Manufacturing industries oriented toward national markets

Ubiquitous Manufacturing Industries Concentrated Near the CBD
    Industries are classified as ubiquitous when their market area is coextensive with or part of the metropolis in which they are located. They are concentrated near the edge of the CBD partly because they are intricately linked with wholesaling firms in the wholesaling district, and partly because they wish to minimize distribution costs to the entire urban area. The industries in this group are usually associated with food processing in one way or another, as the old warehousing and multistory factory buildings located in this area are particularly useful for the storage of both raw materials and finished products.

Centrally Located Communication-Economy Industries
    Industries grouped in this category have a particular need to realize the external economies of face-to-face communication with the purchaser immediately prior to manufacturing. In this case, as the purchasers are located usually within the CBD, the industries have to locate as close as possible to this area. Industries found within this group, such as the job-printing and garment industries, are usually composed of small plants that are prepared to pay relatively high rents for central locations. These high rents are, of course, merely a small part of the costs of central locations, for in addition to these are the costs of "congestion on the streets, and the higher cost of handling freight at the plant because of inadequate facilities" (Chinitz, 1960, p. 42). External

economies, other than communication, offset these costs through advantages such as centrally located freight-forwarding agencies, communal warehousing facilities, and unionized labor pools that permit the individual plant to have a flexible working force.

Local Market Industries with Local Raw-Material Sources

The manufacturing industries grouped in the category of those with local raw-material sources include

1. Those whose chief raw material is fairly ubiquitous, such as ice manufacturing and the concrete brick and block industries.

2. Those whose raw materials are the by-product(s) of local manufacturing industries, such as those using the by-products of petroleum refining.

3. Those industries that process locally produced semi-manufactured goods, such as the metal-plate and polishing industry.

Industries in each of these categories are found dispersed over the entire urban area, for the fact that all input assembly and product distribution take place within the urban area means that truck haulage is the chief means of transportation. Furthermore, as trucking has been "one of the most powerful of several propulsive forces uprooting industry from its established locations within the congested core of the metropolitan area" (Fellman, 1950, p. 77), industries in this category tend to be noncentrally located.

Nonlocal Market Industries with High-Value Products

Industries manufacturing high-value products are oriented toward truck or air-freight transportation rather than rail or waterway facilities. As a consequence, they too are dispersed in locations around the urban area, particularly in those metropolises crisscrossed by freeways, such as Los Angeles. Industries of this type are frequently located in newer industrial parks that are built around airports close to adjacent freeway interchanges. A recent example of rapid manufacturing growth of this type is in the suburban Montreal community of Pointe Claire, adjacent to Dorval airport, where employment in the industrial park increased by over 52 percent between 1960 and 1970. Industries with high value-added products include the machinery and chemical industries, such as computer and drug-manufacturing firms. Chinitz (1960) notes that small plants in this group may locate centrally for external accessibility purposes, but Pred (1964) emphasizes that the locational pattern of these small firms tends to be diminished by the apparent peripheral distribution of the larger factories within this group.

Noncentrally Located Communication-Economy Industries

The manufacturing industries in the fifth group embrace those firms that tend to cluster in noncentral locations in order to realize external economies of communication, particularly with respect to innovations and possible contracts. Such industries are generally highly scientific or technical, and they do not cluster in order to be close to their purchasers but to observe each other's activities and progress. A typical example of a concentration of this type is along Route 128 around Boston, adjacent to which are located many electronic, research, and technical consulting firms. Similar clustering is observed by Pred (1964) in San Francisco with respect to the electronic components industry, and it is to be noted that both these locations are adjacent to prominent urban highways.

Nonlocal Market Industries on the Waterfront

Many industries in the sixth group are very transportation-conscious, because the weight loss incurred in manufacturing or the orientation of markets of firms in this category are vital considerations. Industries in this group are those involved with petroleum refining, sugar refining, and others that use nonlocal water-carried materials.

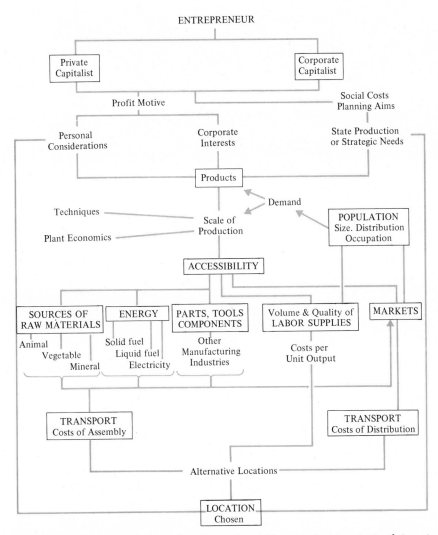

Fig. 14.2. A model of the factors influencing industrial location decisions in North America. (*Source*: after Hamilton, 1967, Fig. 10–1.)

Obviously the shipbuilding and -repairing industry is also constrained to waterfront areas. It is to be noted that not all waterfront industries use the waterfront; in many cases they happen to be there for other reasons. Indeed, it is observable that many manufacturing firms that occupy waterfront property do not use the waterway for transportation. But good examples of recent growth associated with waterfront areas exist in the Vancouver region, Seattle, and San Diego.

Manufacturing Industries Oriented Toward National Markets

Group seven consists of those industries, such as iron and steel and motor-vehicle manufacturing, that have extensive national market areas and are greatly influenced by high transport rates on their bulky finished products. In order to be close to their national markets and to facilitate transportation without too many railroad transfers, these industries tend to locate on the side of the metropolis facing the greatest proportion of the national market. Because these industries have large space requirements, they are located at some distance from the center of the city; but their labor requirements constrain their location to the vicinity of good highways as well as rail facilities.

Thus the pattern of intraurban industrial location is a product of myriad decisions, the bases of which vary in time and space. Change in the structure and organization of manufacturing through time, the continuing technological revolution, change in consumer preferences, change in governments and laws—all these factors, and many others, have contributed to the spatial arrangement of industry within urban areas that the geographer can describe but finds difficult to explain. The complexity of Hamilton's (1967) industrial location-decision model (Fig. 14.2) illustrates the problem very well, for to each of the decisions should be attached a probability statement that varies not only for every entrepreneur, but also for each entrepreneur in time. However, the locational approach has permitted us to analyze the observed spatial regularities, for the sum total of many individual and often conflicting decisions does appear to be economically rational.

15
INTRAURBAN MOVEMENTS

Modern intraurban travel involves a variety of modes that developed at different periods in time. Though some modes of travel are declining while others are increasing in importance, the modal picture at any given period in time involves an urban transportation system of great variety. This system involves the suburban railroad, the subway or elevated rapid transit, buses, the automobile, trucks, taxis, and walking. Information based on origin and destination surveys in Chicago, Washington, D.C., and Detroit suggests the automobile accounts for between 74 and 82 percent of total vehicle trips within the city, that trucks account for between 10 and 13 percent, and that taxis account for between 1 and 3 percent (Table 15.1). Information concerning vehicle trips for other modes is lacking.

The relative importance of these modes can, however, be gauged with respect to the movement of persons within urban areas (person trips). From Table 15.2 it can be observed that for the three large urban areas of Chicago, Washington, and Detroit, automobile drivers made up the great majority of all person trips. As automobile passengers contribute the second largest proportion, total automobile trips comprise about three-quarters of all person trips. Buses account for between 15 and 20 percent, and rail rapid transit and the commuter railroad account for only 8 percent between them.

347

Table 15.1. THE RELATIVE IMPORTANCE OF DIFFERENT TYPES OF VEHICLE TRIPS

Mode		Percent of Total Trips
Automobiles	resident, internal	74–82%
	resident, external	2– 6
	nonresident	2– 9
		unknown
Buses	internal	10–13
Trucks	external	1– 2
	through	0– 1
Taxis		1– 3

Source: Martin et al. (1961), p. 23.

THE MOVEMENT OF PEOPLE

It is evident from the preceding discussion that although person and vehicular travel can be discussed separately, they cannot be regarded as mutually exclusive, for each overlaps the other. As approximately 75 percent of person travel is also included within vehicular travel, it can be concluded that person trips comprise the greater part of the total traffic within urban areas. The volume of this traffic is staggering. The average daily number of person trips regardless of origin in the Chicago area (*Chicago Area Transportation Study, 1959*) in 1956 (population 5.17 million) totaled 10.5 million, and in the Toronto area (*Metropolitan Toronto and Region Transportation Study*, 1966) in 1964 (population 2.7 million) the average daily trip volume was approximately 4 million. These trips involve a number of origins and destinations and can occur at any time throughout the day.

Table 15.2. THE RELATIVE IMPORTANCE OF DIFFERENT TYPES OF PERSON TRIPS

Type of Person Trip		Percent of Total Trips
Automobile drivers	resident, internal	41–53%
	resident, external	1– 4
	nonresident	1– 8
Automobile passengers	resident, internal	22–26
	resident, external	1– 4
	nonresident	1– 4
Bus		15–20
Subway-elevated rail rapid transit		5
Commuter railroad		3
Walk		unknown

Source: Martin et al. (1961), p. 23.

The Components of Urban Travel

Person trips are undertaken for a variety of purposes and involve a multitude of origins and destinations. Commonly, these can be grouped into four main categories:

1. Trips to and from home
2. Trips to and from work
3. Social and recreational trips
4. Trips for shopping, school, and personal business purposes

A diagrammatic representation of the flow pattern involving these four categories is presented in Figure 15.1, which uses data derived from the *Metropolitan Toronto and Region Transportation Study*.

Figure 15.1 indicates that nearly all trips in the Toronto area involve the home as either origin or destination. One-half of all trips are from home to work and return, and another very large proportion is from home to shops and schools and return. It is estimated that school trips, which can be repetitive in a day, exceed the proportion of work

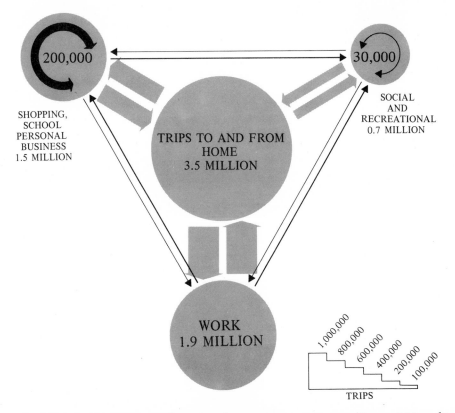

Fig. 15.1. The predominance of home-based trips within urban areas. (*Source: Metropolitan Toronto and Region Transportation Study*, 1966, Fig. 40.)

trips; but the Toronto data include only school trips made in a vehicle. Thus shopping trips are very numerous . Nearly 17 percent of all trips involve the home and some social or recreational destination and return. Although the origin and destination of nearly all the person trips are the home, a number (almost 10 percent) are not. These are usually three-stage trips, such as home-work-shopping-home, and can include a few involving all four categories.

This type of daily flow pattern can be examined in more detail by using information for Chicago. Table 15.3 presents the proportions of total traffic in an average week-day in 1956 which can be allocated to 64 possible combinations of trip purposes. In the aggregate 43.3 percent of the total 9.9 million internal person trips originated at the home, and a further 43.5 percent ended at home. Most of these trips were single purpose, the dominant flow being home-work (16.6 percent) and work-home (15.9 percent). Another quite large flow involves home–social-recreational (9.3 percent) and social-recreational–home (10.4 percent). A reasonably large flow involves shopping and general personal business activities, while all other flows are small. The number of triangular trips seems to be very small. Slightly more trips go to work than come home directly from work, while slightly more trips return to home from shopping than go to shop from home. Thus, though a number of flows are triangular trips, such as home-work-shop-home, the proportion is very small, probably about 5 percent. This fact of directional symmetry permits the transportation planner to deal with trips in one direction only, for he can be fairly confident that over a 24-hour period directional travel on individual streets is equal, with outward and returning movements balancing one another.

Time-Distance Variations

A second general feature of these person trips is that their length varies according to their purpose. Figure 15.2 presents a highly agregated view of the difference in trip

Table 15.3. TRIP PURPOSE AT ORIGIN RELATED TO TRIP PURPOSE AT DESTINATION EXPRESSED AS A PERCENTAGE OF ALL INTERNAL PURPOSE TRIPS

Trip Purpose at Destination

Trip Purpose at Origin	Home	Work	Shop	School	Soc.-Rec.	Eat Meal	Pers. Bus.	Serve Pass.	Total
Home		16.6	4.1	1.7	9.3	0.8	7.6	3.2	43.3
Work	15.9	3.1	0.2	0.1	0.2	0.5	0.4		20.4
Shop	4.3	0.1	0.5		0.2	0.1	0.2		5.4
School	1.6	0.1		0.1					1.8
Social-recreation	10.4	0.1	0.2		1.6	0.4	0.4	0.1	13.2
Eat meal	1.0	0.4	0.1		0.2		0.1		1.8
Personal business	6.9	0.2	0.4		1.0	0.2	1.5		10.3
Serve passenger[a]	3.4				0.1			0.3	3.8
TOTAL	43.5	20.6	5.5	1.8	12.7	2.1	10.2	3.6	100.0

[a]Includes "ride" trips.
SOURCE: *Chicago Area Transportation Study*, (1959), p. 37.

length (measured in minutes) between work and nonwork trips. The polygon is positively skewed, the extended tail illustrating the relative infrequency of long trips. In Toronto in 1964 the average duration of nonwork trips seems to have been about 21.4 minutes, while work trips averaged about 27.8 minutes. Thus in the Toronto area the average worker in 1964 seems to have spent about one hour a day commuting. This difference between work and nonwork trips suggests that purpose has a strong influence on trip length. Evidence from Chicago (1956) indicates that shopping trips are usually short, averaging about 2.8 miles in length, and that the longest trips are made to work, with an average length of 5.3 miles (C.A.T.S., 1959).

The form of travel or mode, like person trips, also varies by length. These variations are illustrated in Table 15.4, where the average length of each person trip by mode is estimated from the total miles of travel for each mode. The average length of each trip in Chicago in 1956 is estimated as 4.2 miles, and the average length of trips on three of the modes is less than this. The shortest trips of all are made by auto passengers, followed by bus passengers and auto drivers. The longest trips of all are made by suburban railroad users, who average about 13.3 miles per trip. As most of these trips are work trips, it can be concluded that suburban railroad users commute, on the average, about 27 miles per day.

Travel Pattern Variations

These variations in modal trip length and frequency imply great variations in travel patterns. Rapid-transit facilities, such as the suburban railroad and elevated-subway facilities, focus dramatically on the CBD. Although these rapid-transit facilities

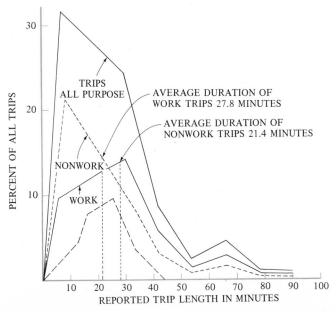

Fig. 15.2. Frequency distributions of all-purpose, nonwork, and work trip lengths, Toronto. (*Source: Metropolitan Toronto and Region Transportation Study*, 1966, Fig. 42.)

Table 15.4.   AVERAGE INTERNAL PERSON TRIP LENGTH (STRAIGHT LINE) BY MODE

Mode of Travel	Person Trips	Miles of Person Travel	Average Length[a]
Auto driver	4,810,886	18,878,000	3.9
Auto passenger	2,706,114	9,593,000	3.5
Suburban R.R.	248,851	3,300,000	13.3
Subway-elevated	479,780	3,444,000	7.2
Bus	1,686,007	6,112,000	3.6
Total	9,931,638	41,327,000	4.2

[a]Airline miles.
Source: *Chicago Area Transportation Study*, (1959), p. 47.

represent a small proportion of all person trips (in Chicago, less than one-twelfth), they nevertheless comprise the great majority of all trips to the CBD (in Chicago, over 45 percent). As the lengths of these trips tend to be long and focused on a single area, there is a strong radial pattern. This radial pattern is emphasized by the location of the transportation facilities along corridors of intense land usage.

Bus passenger trip patterns contrast strongly with those of rapid-transit facilities, for bus trips crisscross and overlap each other within a relatively small area. The routes are mainly located within central city limits and between the older, more densely settled suburban communities. Furthermore, the routes do not tend to be focused, though buses do carry a considerable passenger volume into the CBD. Automobile drivers and automobile passengers display similar trip patterns that, like the bus, are nonfocused, but unlike the bus, spread out into suburban areas beyond the city limits. Within these suburban areas, automobile passenger traffic tends to predominate.

The Daily Cycle

In Toronto, 40 percent of all person trips were concentrated within four hours of the day (M.T.A.R.T.S., 1966). This uneven distribution of daily trips is the result of a concentration of particular purposes throughout the day. Figure 15.3 indicates that this purpose concentration is primarily the result of work trips, which, in the diagram, are double-peaked. The first peak occurs in the morning between 6:30 and 8:30 A.M. and involves home-work trips. The second peak is in the evening between 4 P.M. and 6 P.M. and involves work-home movements. This twice-daily peaking, involving unidirectional flows, is especially severe near areas of large employment; and it is in these locations that the rush hour is particularly severe. Other trips are distributed relatively evenly throughout the nonsleeping hours, though there is a concentration in the evening between 7 P.M. and 9 P.M., which presumably corresponds to travel for shopping and social purposes.

In the same way that person trips are concentrated in certain hours of the day, so is the demand for various modes of travel concentrated in certain hours. Some modes, in fact, are in much greater demand at certain times of the day than others. This is well illustrated by Figure 15.4, which presents the hourly percentages of total daily trip volume for five modes of travel on an average weekday in Chicago in 1956. The demand for

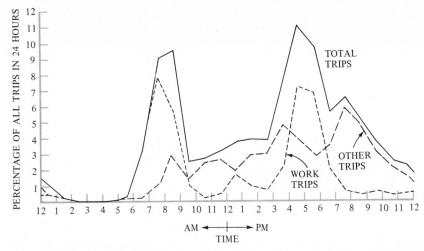

Fig. 15.3. The daily cycle of person trips, Toronto. (*Source: Metropolitan Toronto and Region Transportation Study*, 1966, Fig. 41.)

travel, which we have seen is satisfied (within limits) by a transportation system consisting of a rapid-transit system, a system of buses, and a road network system for automobiles, has a counterpoint in time consisting of a layering of service patterns. In Figure 15.4 automobile travel is the base, its use being spread relatively evenly throughout the day, though there is a definite concentration of use in the morning and evening rush hours. Buses have much sharper peaks, and in the subway-elevated and suburban railroad systems the peaking of activity is even more dramatically evident. We shall observe in a later chapter that this peaking of activity is basically the most difficult problem concerning the provision of mass transportation facilities.

Fluid Fields

This double peaking of traffic-flow intensity during an average weekday is also apparent when the hourly distribution of internal person trips is examined by trip purpose. The data presented in Figure 15.5 indicate that in Chicago in 1956 the purpose of travel varied throughout the day. In fact, there appear to be four major concentrations of trip purposes, each one of which has important implications with respect to mode of travel and trip length.

The morning period presents two major concentrations of traffic flow, both of which are home-based. The primary flow is home-work, and the secondary flow is home-school. Both these patterns are nodal in character in that they concentrate the flow toward a few centers of employment and learning. Thus, if most of the employment in a town is situated in one locality, the employment field will be clearly demarcated by the travel patterns of the labor force. If the employment locations are dispersed throughout the city, the fields will be much more diffuse. The journey to school fields will be fairly discrete, though school hinterlands will be larger for the largest schools and will embrace those of the lower order elementary schools.

The evening period is marked by an overwhelming concentration of traffic toward the home. This movement takes place primarily between 3 P.M. and 6:30 P.M. and consists predominantly of school-home and shop-home trips in the period before 4 P.M. (the prerush rush hour) and work-home trips between 4 P.M. and 6:30 P.M. As homes are spread throughout the city, there are no obvious fields of flow during this period of time.

After 6:30 P.M., however, fields do become evident, with a concentration of activity in social-recreational trips, which is the fourth major trip purpose during the average weekday. Although the social-recreational purpose covers a variety of trips, the concentration of entertainment and retail activities within certain areas does imply a focusing of traffic to these nodes. Furthermore, whereas the three earlier concentrations involve a variety of transportation modes, this particular activity tends to be much more automobile-dominant.

Thus the temporal variation in internal person-trip volume is matched spatially by a fluid pattern of traffic fields. The ever changing nature and modal composition of these fields reflect the daily cycle of human activity within urban areas, and it is this changing activity that is the lifeblood and purpose of urban life. In the ensuing sections we shall specifically examine work and shopping trips, as these are the basic components of urban travel.

THE JOURNEY TO WORK

The daily journey to work is not only an important area of study because of its magnitude; it is also important because it is a common experience of many people (Liepman,

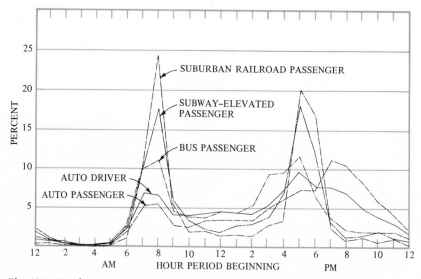

Fig. 15.4. Hourly percentage of total daily trip volumes by mode of travel, Chicago. (*Source: Chicago Area Transportation Study*, 1959, Fig. 24.)

1944). The fact that the journey to work is an experience should not be lost in any mechanistic discussion of its spatial ramifications. Commuting takes time, and to many people this is time wasted in a life of finite length. To others it is not merely that time is wasted, that so many hours are lost in the day; it is the general nervous fatigue of daily travel that is most difficult to withstand. In fact, it could be suggested that it is the mass ebb and flow of human beings in packed public transportation facilities and overcrowded highways that makes for much of the depersonalization of everyday life. Thus any changes in the journey-to-work patterns, trip lengths, and modes of travel are important to catalog and understand.

Journey-to-Work Patterns

Although the greatest area of employment concentration is in the CBD, we have observed that employment locations are widely dispersed throughout the city. In fact, we have observed that a general decentralization of employment opportunities has taken place in recent years and that this out-migration shows no sign of abating. Thus it is imperative to have some knowledge of the changing journey-to-work patterns associated with this dispersal. The information available, however, is limited, and the examples used are confined to a series of snapshots at a given point in time (Taaffe et al., 1963).

These snapshots are presented in six maps (Fig. 15.6) based on data collected by the *Chicago Area Transportation Study* in the spring and summer of 1956. The dots on the maps relate to grid cells a half-mile square, and the dots indicate whether one or more commuters traveling to a particular employment location originated in that cell.

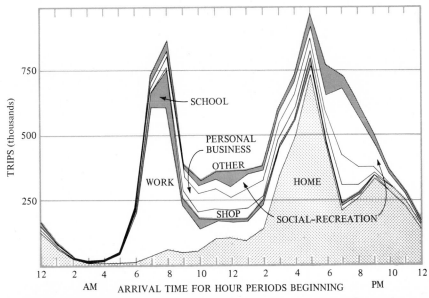

Fig. 15.5. Hourly distribution of internal person trips by trip purpose, Chicago. (*Source: Chicago Area Transportation Study*, 1959, Fig. 15.)

Thus the visual impression gained from the dot maps overstates the degree of dispersion of the journey-to-work patterns, since it could be expected that the number of commuters in half-mile-square grid cells close to employment locations would be considerably greater than from other cells farther away. Bearing that consideration in mind, however, we are able to compare the change in dispersion pattern of commuters to different destination districts within the same sector in a traverse from the CBD to the periphery.

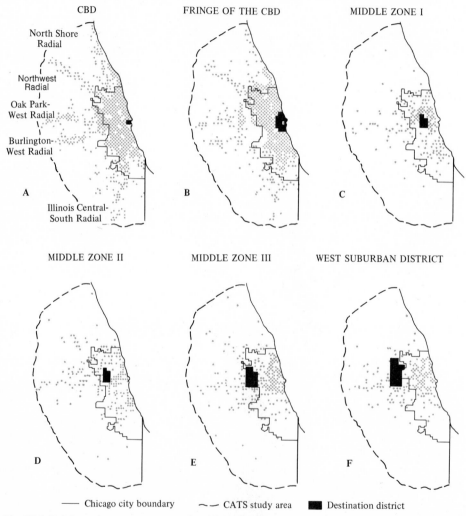

Fig. 15.6. Origins of commuters to selected work-place zones, Chicago region, 1956. (*Source:* Taaffe, Garner, and Yeates, 1963, Fig. III–3.)

A Sectoral Traverse: Chicago

The six maps displayed in Figure 15.6 indicate the origin cells of work trips to six employment areas in the western sector of Chicago in 1956. These employment areas are:

1. The central business district.
2. The fringe of the central business district.
3. Three areas in the middle zone or gray area (see Fig. 9.12):
   middle zone I
   middle zone II
   middle zone III
4. The west suburban district, which is part of the peripheral ring.

The CBD Commuter Pattern

Figure 15.6A shows the distribution of the commuter origin cells for work trips to the central business district. The dots cover most of the urbanized area of Chicago, and, in fact, most of the blank spaces on the map represent nonresidential areas. All of the radial suburbs are clearly delineated, for the suburban population is able to use both the rail and highway routes along these fingers. Thus rail and highway commuting to the CBD are both dominant.

The Fringe of the CBD Commuter Pattern

The second zone corresponds roughly to the fringe of the CBD area as delimited and discussed in Chapter 9. This destination area has a journey-to-work pattern (Fig. 15.6B) which is roughly similar to that for the CBD. The radials are well defined, though the intensity of the dot pattern is not quite so great as that for the CBD pattern. Within the city of Chicago almost every cell is the origin of at least one commuter to this zone, and the pattern seems to be even more intense than that for the CBD. Thus though Figures 15.6A and 15.6B are very similar, there is a minor difference in that the fringe of the CBD pattern tends to be less dispersed.

The Middle-Zone Commuter Pattern

The greatest change in commuting patterns occurs for origin cells in the middle-zone employment areas (Fig. 15.6C, D, E). The first of these maps (Fig. 15.6C) presents a pattern to a middle-zone destination district that is at the edge of the fringe of the CBD. The pattern illustrates that in this zone the advantages of the concentration of transportation facilities at the CBD have been lost, particulary in those areas and radials that are not within the western sector. There are very few origin cells in the northern and southern suburban radials; and the city itself is considerably less thoroughly covered with origin cells, particularly to the north and south of the destination district. Although relative concentrations are difficult to discern in these maps because magnitudes are ignored, it is possible to note that the Figure 15.6C pattern is less dispersed than that for the CBD.

Essentially the same pattern prevails as the destination areas move outward in the middle zone of the western sector. The origin cells for commuters to middle zone II (Fig. 15.6D) and middle zone III (Fig. 15.6E) are not so dispersed as those for the CBD, though the location of commuters along more than one radial becomes evident. This is particularly true for two other western radials, the Burlington-west radial and the northwest radial. Furthermore, the concentration of employment cells in the western sector of the city is greater. Thus the adjacent area in the city becomes rather more important as a source of commuters to middle zone III.

The West Suburban District Pattern

The changes observed through the middle zone are repeated in the west suburban district pattern (Fig. 15.6F), which is part of the peripheral ring. The adjacent radial (the Oak Park–west radial) and the adjacent area within the western sector in the city are particularly important, but the areas to the north and south are barely represented. Furthermore, it is interesting to note that the Burlington-west radial and the northwest radial are less well represented as origin areas for commuters to this peripheral location than for employment districts in the middle zone.

Thus the sectoral traverse indicates that for employment districts farther away from the center of the city the frictional effect of distance is greater. This increasing friction of distance, which has also been noted elsewhere (Hoover and Vernon, 1959; Wolforth, 1965), is due to the lack of a concentration of transportation facilities in these areas compared with the concentration of transport facilities at the center of the city. Table 15.5 indicates that approximately 84 percent of the west suburban commuters drive or are driven to work, whereas only 30 percent of the CBD commuters use these modes. Mass-transit facilities account for almost 70 percent of the commuters entering the CBD as opposed to less than 10 percent for the west suburban district. This contrast suggests that the mass-transit modes facilitate much longer work trips to the center of the city, and that their concentration in the CBD permits a wide dispersion of commuters.

The Components of Journey-to-Work Patterns

The discussion of the various journey-to-work patterns of different employment areas in the preceding section emphasizes that the dispersion of the patterns decreases toward the periphery. These patterns are, however, aggregates of individuals and families who locate according to a variety of criteria. These criteria have been discussed in

Table 15.5. MODE OF COMMUTER TRANSPORTATION TO THE CBD AND WEST SUBURBAN DISTRICTS, CHICAGO, 1956

Mode	CBD (percent)	West Suburban (percent)
Auto drive	24.4	65.4
Auto passenger	5.7	18.3
Railroad	16.6	0.7
Elevated-subway	24.4	1.3
Bus	28.4	7.4
Walk to work	—	6.2

Note: The modes "taxi" and "at home" are missing.
Source: Taaffe et al. (1963), p. 9.

detail in Chapters 10 and 11, but they also provide an important framework for an appreciation of the components of commuting fields. These components include transportation and distance, race, sex, and occupation and income.

Transportation and Distance

There is little doubt that one of the factors influencing the dispersion of the commuting field is distance (Lapin, 1964; Wolforth, 1965; Duncan and Duncan, 1960), the perception of which is strongly influenced by the alternative modes of transportation available. Commuting by automobile along expressways and freeways is easier than along congested urban arterials, and riding the commuter railroad can be quite a pleasurable experience. Lansing (1966) notes from a sample interview of drivers that 53 percent enjoyed the journey to work, 34 percent didn't care one way or the other, and only 13 percent expressed dislike of it. He suggests, however, that there is a limit for quite a large proportion, as 36 percent indicated a definite maximum time for the journey to work beyond which commuting would be time lost (Lansing, 1966).

It is interesting to consider the factors that might influence this threshold time limit, for intuitively one would suggest that through time this threshold limit is increasing. Undoubtedly technological changes in urban transportation have had a great effect, for ultimately the result has been to make intraurban movement less arduous. A more important facet, however, may probably be that the provision of new housing stock is much greater at the peripheries of urban areas than elsewhere (Meyer et al., 1965). Thus the head of the household has become willing to offset better living conditions against an increase in time spent in the daily journey to work. Undoubtedly the general reduction in the length of the working week has had an important effect on this kind of decision.

Occupation and Income

As people of higher income and the higher status occupations tend to live farther from the center of the city, it could be expected that the length of the journey to work for these groups would be greater than for others. Table 15.6 presents information that supports this contention with respect to commuting to the CBD of Chicago in 1956. The trip lengths are measured in airline miles, and the median distances only are listed. Thus 50 percent of the workers classified as proprietors and managers traveled 8.7 airline miles or more to their employment in the CBD, and 50 percent traveled less than this. The occupational groups are ranked in descending order of occupational class, and the median miles tend to decrease as the class of occupation decreases. It is noticeable, however, that there is no such regular arrangement of commuting distances by occupational class at the periphery of the city.

This apparent difference between CBD and non-CBD commuting lengths may account for the inconsistencies noted by Lansing (1966) in the literature concerning this problem. For example, Lapin (1964) suggests that the work trips for middle-income clerical, sales, and blue-collar workers are relatively long, while Lowry (1963a) and Duncan (1956) both support the contention that persons with higher incomes live farther away from their job locations. Thus the decentralization of employment opportunities discussed specifically with respect to manufacturing in Chapter 14 and commercial activities in Chapter 12 necessitates a continuous reassessment of the influence of occupation and income on the journey to work (Simmons, 1968).

Table 15.6. COMPARISON OF MEDIAN TRAVEL DISTANCES OF VARIOUS OCCUPATIONAL GROUPS TO THE CBD AND WEST SUBURBAN DISTRICT, CHICAGO, 1956

	Median Miles	
Occupational Group	CBD	West Suburban
Professionals and technicians	8.5	3.9
Managers and proprietors	8.7	4.0
Clerical and kindred workers	7.2	2.2
Sales workers	7.6	2.8
Craftsmen	6.2	4.7
Operatives and kindred workers	4.9	3.0
Service workers	5.1	1.4
Laborers	3.9	3.6

SOURCE: Taaffe et al. (1963), p. 88.

Race

Residential segregation obviously distorts the work-trip length preference of non-white commuters and makes this group a separate component of the aggregate commuting pattern (Taaffe et al., 1963). In one sense residential segregation limits the range of employment opportunities of nonwhite workers, for the direction of public transit or radial highways may restrict travel in certain directions. For example, whereas 14 percent of all CBD commuters in Chicago in 1956 were nonwhite, only 6 percent of the commuters to the west suburban district were nonwhite. Whether this is due to the lack of industries requiring low-wage labor or the lack of low-wage labor discouraging the location of industry of this type is not clear. It is clear, however, that residential segregation does result in race forming a separate and distinct component of the journey-to-work pattern (Kain, 1968). This component obviously suffers disadvantages as new industry is increasingly being located beyond the central city, though, as has been pointed out in Chapter 11, these disadvantages may not be so great as they seem.

Sex

There seem to be significant differences in the commuting patterns of male and female workers. In 1956, of the commuters to the Chicago CBD, 68 percent were male and 32 percent female, whereas 77 percent of the west suburban district commuters were male and only 23 percent female (Taaffe et al., 1963). This tendency for a lower percentage of female workers in peripheral employment centers seems to be fairly well established in other studies as well (Reinemann, 1955; Hoover and Vernon, 1959; Burtt, 1961).

There are perhaps three main reasons for the apparent concentration of female employment in the CBD: the need for the private automobile for peripheral-area employment, the relative attraction of CBD amenities, and the types of employment available. Automobiles are not always available to female workers. Many young unmarried women do not own automobiles, chiefly because clerical work and service activities (the chief sources of female employment) generally pay low wages. In addition, the American dating system requires that the automobile be provided by the male, not the female of the species. Married women are often without an automobile because their husbands use the family car for their own commuting. Thus low-cost public transportation facilities concentrate the direction of female commuting to the center of the city.

In addition to these fundamental economic advantages of the CBD for women are the attractions to the bright lights and greater array of shopping, social, cultural, and recreational amenities of the downtown area, particularly for single women. Not to be discounted is the real (or imaginary) function of the CBD as a marriage market. In fact, Burtt quotes an example of a downtown Boston firm that carefully recruited its female help from the suburban area to which it was about to relocate. When the relocation took place, however, many of the girls resigned and went to work for another downtown firm, even though every effort was made to keep them with the company (Burtt, 1961). Thus it is not surprising that the average length of commuter trips to the CBD by females is slightly longer than that for males, though for the urban area as a whole it is less.

The most important reason, however, is related to the employment opportunities for females. The types of employment available in non-CBD locations are much more male-oriented than those within the CBD, for the downtown area is the location of skyscraper office buildings for the headquarters of companies, and major department stores. Both these activities use female labor intensively, whereas the activites located elsewhere use female labor in limited quantities. The result is that the CBD contains the greatest single concentration of employment opportunities for women in an entire urban region, and this, of itself, creates inequalities. Not only do women have to travel relatively great distances to work, using public transit, but women with children in suburban areas have little access to the opportunities of this highly focused market. In

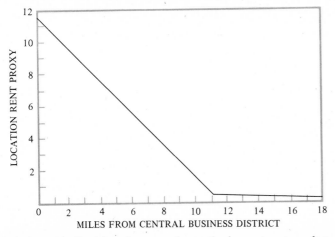

Fig. 15.7. Idealized location rents for work places at various distances from the CBD. (*Source:* Kain, 1962, Fig. 2.)

fact, the only real alternate sources of female employment are in the regional shopping centers and some of the peripheral industrial parks.

A Model of Journey-to-Work Trip Length

We have observed that the journey-to-work trip length can be measured in a number of ways: time, distance, airline distance, cost, and so forth. For the development of a journey-to-work model, Kain uses elapsed time; that is, the actual time spent by a person in commuting from his home to his place of work (Kain, 1962). The data relate to Detroit and are based on information received from interviews of a stratified random sample of households of the white work force conducted in 1953, which has been aggregated to 254 work-place zones.

The Hypotheses

The statement developed by Kain for use in a large multiple-equation model of household location and trip-making behavior is expressed in equation form as follows: (15.1)

$$ET_j = a + b_1 SR_j + b_2 MP_j + b_3 Y_j + b_4 P_j + b_5 SW_j + b_6 PT_j \qquad (15.1)$$

where

ET_j = mean elapsed time in hours and tenths spent by the workers of the jth work-place zone in reaching work

SR_j = percentage of the jth zone's workers residing in single-family residential units

MP_j = proportion of the workers in the jth zone that are male

Y_j = mean income of the jth work zone

P_j = a proxy variable for the price of residential space for workers in each zone, calculated as 11.5 minus the airline distance from the CBD, where 11.0 is the maximum distance. The location rent curve implied by this statement is presented in diagrammatic form in Figure 15.7, though the values will increase with distance rather than decrease

SW_j = percentage of the workers of the jth work-place zone belonging to families that have a single wage earner

PT_j = the proportion of the workers of the jth work-place zone that use public transit

$a, b_1 \ldots b_6$ = empirically determined constants

The hypotheses developed by Kain are quite consistent with our preceding discussion, and can be listed as follows:

1. Work-trip length is positively correlated with the proportion of workers living in single-family dwelling units. The rationale for this is that the worker offsets greater time spent in getting to work against the advantages of single-family residential locations.

2. The average length of the journey to work should be greater in those zones that have a high proportion of male workers. We have noted that female trips to the CBD have a tendency to be longer than male trips, but that for the whole urban area they are shorter. Kain contends that the reason for this is that the labor-force attachment of women is generally weaker than that for men. This is because working women often belong to families that have low space preferences, and more than a single wage earner.

3. If, in the multiple-regression model, the effect of residential space consumption (SR_j), the price of residential space (P_j), and transit usage (PT_j) are held constant, then it could be expected that higher income households would make shorter work trips in terms of elapsed time. This is because higher income households can afford to use higher speed modes of transportation, which also cost more.

4. The proxy location-rent variable should be positively correlated with trip length. This is because "workers would make longer journeys-to-work at every level of space consumption as the price of residential space increased, since the savings in location rents would be great enough to make longer journeys-to-work economically rational" (Kain, 1962, p. 45).

5. Zones with large proportions of families having a single wage earner should have greater time spent in the journey to work.

6. Zones with high proportions of transit users should have higher mean elapsed times for the journey to work than zones with low proportions of transit users. This is because public transportation and getting to and from public transportation tend to be time-consuming procedures.

The Results

Table 15.7 gives the coefficient of multiple determination (R_2) for equation 15.1. The regression equation explains 65 percent of the total variation in the dependent variable, which is mean elapsed journey-to-work time. The standard error of estimate of the regression equation is quite small, so the results can be viewed with a degree of confidence. Also presented in Table 15.7 are the regression coefficients pertaining to the independent variables and their standard errors. These indicate that all the regression coefficients, except the one pertaining to single-family residence (SR_j), can be regarded as significantly different from zero at the 0.05 percent confidence level.

The signs of the regression coefficients for the proportion using public transit, the proportion male, and the location-rent proxy are all positive. These all conform to the hypothesized relationships. The negative signs of the regression coefficients pertaining to the income and single wage-earner variables also behave as expected. Thus the multivariable model, expressed in equation 15.1 and empirically examined with sample data from Detroit, combines in a rather interesting way many of the factors that we

Table 15.7. ESTIMATED COEFFICIENT OF DETERMINATION, REGRESSION COEFFICIENTS, AND STANDARD ERRORS FOR EQUATION 15.1

Variable	*SR*	*MP*	*Y*	*P*	*SW*	*PT*
Regression coefficient	−0.0006	0.0020	−0.0010	0.006	−0.0006	0.0040
Standard error	0.0004	0.0004	0.0005	0.002	0.0003	0.0005
Coefficient of determination	0.65	Intercept	0.304	Standard error of estimate		0.06

Source: Kain (1962), p. 46.

have discussed as influences of journey-to-work trip lengths. It can, however, be readily appreciated that the model provides only a partial statement of a very complex situation.

THE JOURNEY TO SHOP

Shopping trips differ from the journey to work in the following important ways:

1. They account for only a small part of the total pattern of urban movement. Whereas, for example, journeys to work account for about 20 percent of the total person trips by destination in Chicago, shopping trips only account for just over 5 percent of the total (see Table 15.3). This number of shopping trips is an underestimate, for many walking trips to nearby corner stores have not been counted.

2. They are typically much shorter in terms of time and distance. Shopping trips are more sensitive to the frictional effects of distance than are work and other types of trips. In Chicago, for example, shopping journeys averaged only 2.8 miles, compared to 4.3 miles for social-recreational trips and 5.3 miles for journeys to work (C.A.T.S., 1959).

3. They are much less regular in time. The marked concentration of commuting flow during the morning and evening rush hours is not typical of shopping patterns, which for the most part occur fairly evenly throughout the day, and particularly in the period 10 A.M. to 2 P.M. The intensity of shopping may increase to give minor peaks at suburban centers between 4 and 8 P.M. on Thursdays, Fridays, and Saturdays.

4. Unlike commuting, which takes place between the same set of origins and destinations each day, shopping trips are spatially dispersed. The distance and direction traveled from day to day varies depending on the specific demands to be satisfied. Thus on some days consumers may undertake major shopping excursions to the more widely spaced higher level centers, on others only short trips may be made to purchase convenience goods from local centers, and occasionally a longer trip may be made to the CBD. The wide range of shopping opportunities within the urban area, coupled with the varying frequency, nature, and intensity of demand for different goods and services, gives rise to very flexible patterns of shopping journeys.

Types of Shopping Trip

Shopping trips can be classified in a number of ways; for example, by type of good(s) purchased (the distinction between convenience goods and shopping goods is particularly important in this respect), by mode of travel, and so on, depending on the purpose of study. For general purposes it is important to distinguish between the following three types of shopping trips:

1. *Single-purpose trips*, during which a stop is made at one kind of retail or service establishment on a trip that starts and ends at the same location, usually the home. These are the most frequently undertaken sorts of shopping trip and are particularly important in the purchase of convenience items (e.g., groceries). Normally they are characterized by a visit to only one establishment; but when comparison buying is associated with the good in question, a number of establishments of the same type may be visited. Distance minimization is often an important influence on this kind of trip, hence the distances involved are normally relatively short.

2. *Multiple-purpose trips*, during which stops are made at more than one kind of retail and or service establishment, and hence a variety of goods are purchased on the same trip. They are especially important in connection with visits to larger business centers. In general they are less frequently undertaken and involve relatively longer distances than single-purpose trips.

3. *Combined-purpose trips*, during which shopping is undertaken during a journey being made for some other purpose, for example, in conjunction with the journey to or from work. They account for a relatively small proportion of the total volume of shopping journeys (see Table 15.3). The frequency with which they are undertaken varies considerably between households, and longer distances are usually involved than for journeys made expressly for shopping.

Differences between the three types of shopping trips are well illustrated by the results of two of a number of studies of household travel behavior. One is the classical study undertaken in Cedar Rapids, Iowa (Garrison et al., 1959), and the other is a more recent analysis of shopping travel behavior in Kingston, Ontario (Steele, 1972). In the Cedar Rapids study, 95 households kept travel diaries for a 30-day period, and 51.5 percent of the trips were single-purpose, 24.7 percent were multipurpose, and 23.8 percent were combined work-shopping trips. In the Kingston study, 88 households kept detailed travel diaries for a seven-day period for every member of the family, and 58.2 percent of the trips were single-purpose, 28.6 percent were multipurpose, and 13.2 percent were combined work-shopping trips. Not only are single-purpose shopping trips more frequent; they also tend to be shorter. For example, in the Cedar Rapids study, the median length of single-purpose trips was 1.8 miles, whereas multipurpose trip lengths had a median value of 3.4 miles, and combined work-shopping trips tended to be 4.3 miles in length. Generally, consumers from high-income households will travel farther for shopping purposes than consumers of lower economic levels. This is partly because the demands of individuals of higher economic levels are generally greater, and partly because they have better means of transportation at their disposal and therefore can experience relatively lower shopping travel costs than individuals from low-income groups (Huff, 1961).

The Notion of Trip Utility

For the consumer, the distinction between these three types of shopping trip is largely a matter of the differences in trip utility associated with them. Any trip can be thought of as having an associated reward for the individual undertaking it. For shopping journeys perhaps the most useful way of assessing reward is in terms of getting what one wants. However, we have already noted that movement between points in space involves costs. For shopping journeys these not only include the usual transportation and opportunity costs, but also the additional costs incurred once the consumer has reached the center: parking cost and the intangible costs associated with time, effort, and personal comfort related to the level of congestion within the center and its stores. In a very simple way, then, the notion of trip utility can be thought of as the difference between the reward from the trip and the costs incurred in making it. A particular shopping trip is worthwhile from the individual's viewpoint when the rewards are at least equal to the costs of making the trip. Hence consumers may not be concerned as much with minimizing trip costs as they are with maximizing trip utility. It is largely because of this that the distance-minimization hypothesis by itself is not a sufficient basis for understanding shopping patterns.

The benefits associated with multiple- or combined-purpose shopping trips are illustrated diagrammatically in Figure 15.8. In the example a consumer requires four goods available from separate locations, as shown. On the one hand the consumer could undertake four single-purpose trips and in this way obtain the goods from separate locations at an imagined cost of 10 units (Fig. 15.8A). Alternatively he could obtain all four goods on the same journey more cheaply by undertaking a multiple-purpose trip, either by visiting each location in turn like a traveling salesman (Fig. 15.8B) or by traveling to a large center where all four goods are found in association (Fig. 15.8C). Clearly the multiple-purpose trip is a strategy that is likely to yield higher shopping-trip utilities because the effort or cost of travel is spread over a number of goods to result in lower unit costs. The potential savings from multiple-purpose trips are such that consumers will often travel much longer distances than necessary to larger centers where the goods and services they require can be obtained together.

The Influence of Retail Structure

That the shopping patterns of urban residents should be affected by the distribution of business types within the city follows from the discussion of the urban commercial structure in Chapter 12. There it was noted that business types occur in the landscape more or less frequently depending on their threshold requirements. This in turn results in their being more or less ubiquitously distributed within the urban area. Thus lower order convenience types are widely scattered throughout the urban area in close correspondence with the density and distribution of population, while higher order types needing higher centrality tend to be concentrated at increasingly fewer locations. Some very specialized types with very large threshold requirements may occur only downtown or in regional nucleations. Because of this, the average distances separ-

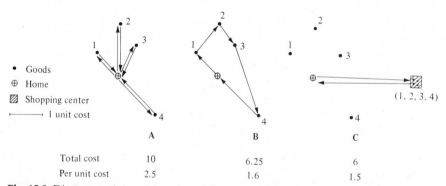

	A	B	C
Total cost	10	6.25	6
Per unit cost	2.5	1.6	1.5

Fig. 15.8. Diagrammatic representation of the costs of different types of shopping trips: (A) single-purpose trips, (B)"traveling salesman" multiple-purpose trips, and (C) regular multiple-purpose trips.

ating consumers from an establishment of a given business type tend to increase directly with its order in the hierarchy of centers.

The result is that consumers need travel only relatively short average distances to acquire frequently demanded, lower order goods, but are more or less obliged to travel longer average distances to obtain the less frequently demanded, higher order shopping goods and more specialized services. Data from the survey of household travel behavior in Cedar Rapids, Iowa, shown in Table 15.8, indicate this to be generally true for single-purpose trips, but less so for multiple-purpose trips. On these, longer distances are traveled to purchase the same set of goods, and this is particularly noticeable for convenience goods. An important effect of the multiple-purpose trip is, therefore, to blur the distance relationships between buyers and sellers which are implicit in the spatial distribution of business types. When trips of all kinds are grouped together, the average distances traveled to obtain different order goods and services range from 1.9 miles for groceries to 4.7 miles for visits to department stores. Similar aggregate relationships are evident in other cities—for example, Detroit, where the average distances traveled to grocery stores and department stores were 2.0 and 4.8 miles with elapsed journey times of 8.9 and 22.8 minutes respectively (*Detroit Metropolitan Area Traffic Study*, 1955). This kind of evidence suggests that the spatial patterns explicit in the commercial structure of cities operate to give rise to fairly regular distance relationships in aggregate patterns of consumer behavior from city to city, often despite marked differences in their population size and areal extent.

This is not, however, meant to imply that consumers always shop at their nearest shopping opportunity. The averages may indicate that trip lengths appear to vary in accordance with the level of the good being sought, but these averages conceal a wide array of preferences (Rushton, 1969 and 1971b; Clarke, 1968). These preferences are related to individual travel habits and the experiences that have evolved with living in an urban area. Furthermore, the large proportion of shopping trips that are multipurpose frequently relegate distance considerations to a position of secondary importance. The growing preference for shopping in planned centers adds another dimension to this situation, for the trip becomes multipurpose but involves a single stop. Thus, it is important to include behavior-space considerations in any discussion of shopping trip patterns.

Behavior-Space Perception

Shopping trips are the result of a consumer decision process. Although we do not know very much about the way consumers in fact make their decisions, they are undoubtedly influenced to a degree by distance and travel costs. For a more complete understanding of shopping patterns, we must consider other factors. Particularly important among these are the so-called sociopsychological factors affecting spatial behavior (Cox and Golledge, 1969). Unlike the rational economic man so important in our abstract conceptual arguments, the real-world consumer does not have perfect knowledge about the city's commercial structure. His knowledge is imperfect and is restricted at any given time to the opportunities for shopping he has learned about from his experience of living in the urban area. It is this part of the retail structure that constitutes his behavior space. Each consumer can be thought of as having his own, highly personalized behavior space, the extent of which will depend primarily on his level of mobility and attitude to space.

Table 15.8.   AVERAGE DISTANCES TRAVELED TO SHOP FOR DIFFERENT ORDER GOODS
AND SERVICES BY TYPE OF SHOPPING TRIP, CEDAR RAPIDS, IOWA

Business Types	(1) Total Number of Trips	(2)[a] Average Distance	(3) Number of Single-Purpose Trips	(4)[a] Average Distance	(5)[b] Number of Multiple-Purpose Trips	(6)[a] Average Distance
Grocery stores	264	1.9	157	0.5	107	4.1
Beauty salons	17	4.0	4	0.7	13	5.0
Bakeries	34	3.3	5	0.9	29	3.6
Drugstores	160	3.0	57	1.1	103	4.1
Barbers	18	3.6	5	1.7	13	4.4
Appliances	12	4.9	2	1.7	10	5.6
Banks	62	5.0	6	2.1	56	5.2
Furniture stores	18	3.5	3	2.4	15	3.7
Dentists	13	3.0	6	2.4	7	3.4
Clothing stores	52	4.6	4	2.5	48	4.7
Theaters	108	4.4	67	2.9	41	3.4
Department stores	151	4.7	11	3.0	140	4.1

[a] Average distances in miles are for round-trip journeys.
[b] Multiple-purpose trips include multiple-purpose shopping trips and all other combined shopping trips.
SOURCE: Garrison et al., (1959), after Table 11-8.

The way in which the consumer operates within his behavior space depends on his perception of the opportunities it contains for the satisfaction of a given need. This perception can be thought of as comprising two sets of images, those pertaining to the contents of the space and those relating to the ease of movement within it. Both of these will be conditioned by the individual's value system, which is influenced by things such as income level, age, sex, race, occupation, and education level, besides such intangible qualities as his ethical and moral code, personality, and mental synthesizing abilities (Huff, 1960). The way in which these are interrelated to give rise to shopping patterns is suggested in Figure 15.9. Although the value system, and hence the images consumers have of the retail structure, will be in part idiosyncratic, the scanty

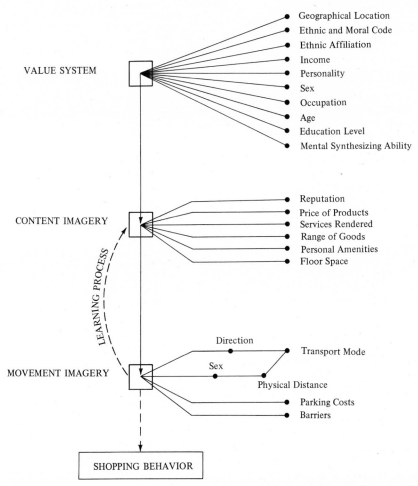

Fig. 15.9. Suggested relationships between consumer images and shopping behavior. (*Source*: Huff, 1960, Fig. 6.

evidence available to date suggests that a certain proportion of these images are common to groups of individuals (Lynch, 1960). Because of this it is possible to make meaningful generalizations about the shopping patterns of, for example, high- and low-income groups, young and old shoppers, and so on.

Content Imagery

Content imagery is related to the value the consumer attaches to the various shopping areas and individual establishments comprising his behavior space. It is presumably on the basis of these value images that consumers express preferences for some shopping areas over others, or for the goods of one retailer over those of another. The preceived differences between shopping centers appear to be related to things such as level of discomfort experienced while shopping, the general attractiveness of the center, the quality and choice of goods offered there, and the size of the nucleation as measured by floor space (Fig. 15.9). It is partly on the basis of these attitudes that many consumers choose to shop at newer, planned shopping centers instead of at the older, unplanned ones. Table 15.9, which shows the results of attitude surveys among shoppers in Columbus, Ohio, and Houston, Tex., suggests some of the ways in which consumers perceive differences between suburban shopping centers and downtown.

Images of particular retail or service outlets are based on things like the breadth of merchandise offered, price, personal amenities, window display, services rendered, and the store's reputation (Garner, 1969). Thus, although a consumer may be aware of a number of centers and specific retail/service establishments of a given type, on the basis of his content imagery he may consider some of them unsuitable for the satisfaction of his own particular needs and wants. These will be disregarded, and consequently we can think of his shopping activities as being restricted to those alternatives for which he has well-developed preferences. If the wants cannot be satisfied by searching among these, the consumer may then extend his shopping activity to other stores for which at the time his awareness and preferences are not so well developed.

Movement Imagery

Movement imagery relates to the images consumers have of the relative location of centers and stores and the difficulties of undertaking shopping journeys to them. A significant factor in these is the way in which distance between home and shop is perceived, and it is largely on the basis of this that the concept of accessibility takes on a specific meaning in the shopping context. The perception of distance depends on a number of factors, including the means of travel available, real physical distance, the sex of the individual, and the relative direction of the shopping facility. The limited and arguable information available indicates that short distances are estimated more accurately than long ones (Bratfisch, 1969); females estimate distances more accurately than males (Lee, 1970); and if the direction of travel is away from the CBD, distances are underestimated, but if the direction of travel is toward the CBD, distances are overestimated (Golledge et al., 1969).

The perception of distance will also depend on the way barriers to movement are perceived within the urban area. These may be formed either by natural features, such as rivers, which can be bridged only at certain points, or man-made features, such as large areas of industrial land use and railroad tracks. Increasingly important, however, are the perceived barriers to movement arising from the social and ethnic structure of the urban area. Unfortunately, and to an increasing extent in the larger cities, these tend to constrain the behavior space of many individuals, not only for shopping but for other activities as well. On the basis of his movement imagery, therefore, the consumer may further discriminate between otherwise acceptable shopping opportunities and in this way reduce still further the set for which he develops well-formed preferences.

An immediate effect of the consumer's content and movement imagery is that it gives rise to individualistic shopping patterns within the urban area in which the importance of distance minimization may be still further reduced. This is particularly important in connection with the purchase of shopping goods and may even be characteristic of trips for lower order convenience items. For example, in a survey of shopping

Table 15.9.   ATTITUDES OF CONSUMERS TO SHOPPING DOWNTOWN AND AT SUBURBAN SHOPPING CENTERS IN COLUMBUS, OHIO, AND HOUSTON, TEXAS

Shopping Satisfaction Factors	Columbus Percentages for		Houston Percentages for	
	Downtown	Suburban Centers	Downtown	Suburban Centers
Greater variety of styles and sizes	86.3	2.3	87.6	4.0
Greater variety and range of prices and quality	81.1	1.7	83.1	5.0
More bargain sales	65.5	2.7	70.8	6.7
Best place to meet friends from other parts of the city for a shopping trip together	66.9	11.5	65.1	16.0
Better places to eat lunch	61.3	7.9	49.0	26.7
More convenient to public transportation	52.5	14.2	44.4	17.8
Cheaper prices	46.6	7.9	51.5	8.6
Goods more attractively displayed	44.1	16.3	67.9	6.5
Better place to combine different kinds of shopping and other things one may want to do	56.3	29.7	72.3	20.6
Easier to establish a charge account	30.1	5.2	33.5	7.3
Better place for a little outing away from home	38.5	33.2	50.2	28.5
The right people shop there	10.3	21.5	15.3	15.5
Cost of transportation less	15.7	59.3	4.0	72.4
Keep open more convenient hours	16.3	62.6	9.1	51.6
Less walking required	16.3	69.9	13.6	72.4
Easier to take children shopping	2.5	47.6	1.6	60.9
Less tiring	9.3	75.0	9.0	75.4
Takes less time to get there	12.3	78.9	9.6	78.8

Note: Percentages for each city do not equal 100 percent since two other choices, "undecided" and "no concern," are not shown.
Source: Jonassen (1955), after Table 20.

habits in Christchurch, New Zealand, it was found that for purchases of groceries, meat, and vegetables, only 63.1, 66.4, and 52.1 percent respectively of the total families interviewed habitually frequented their nearest stores for these goods (Clark, 1968). Table 15.10 clearly shows that many consumers travel considerably farther on shopping trips than they need to from a purely distance-minimization standpoint. Although the pattern revealed by these particular data cannot be interpreted solely on the basis of behavior-space perception, consumer preferences and movement imagery are likely important factors in accounting for the discrepancy between the two sets of distance figures.

The Learning Process

The consumer's imagery of the retail structure is a potent factor affecting his shopping patterns. These images are not static, however, but are continually changing through time as the consumer develops greater awareness of the urban area. The consumer experiences a learning process (Downs, 1970). There is a continuous input of sensory information from the urban environment; however, not all of this is stored ad infinitum, or until it may be needed. Much of it may be rejected at once as being irrelevant or because it contributes nothing new to the images already developed. The rest makes its mark, impresses, and is incorporated into the individual's behavior-space perception. Thus, although aggregate shopping patterns may be fairly stable over periods of time, the patterns for many individuals may be subject to continual adjustment and change through time.

A number of factors are involved in the learning process. Two important ones are the length of residence in an area and the changes taking place in the urban retail structure referred to in Chapter 12. That length of residence in an area affects the individual's behavior space is obvious and can perhaps best be illustrated by what happens when people migrate into an urban area, or move from one part of it to another. New-

Table 15.10. **DIFFERENCES BETWEEN LENGTH OF SHOPPING TRIPS AND DISTANCE TO THE NEAREST ESTABLISHMENT FOR SELECTED GOODS.**

| | Distances in Miles to | | | |
| | Center Visited | | Nearest Center | |
	Mean	S.D.	Mean	S.D.
Canterbury, N.Z.				
Groceries	.71	1.21	.23	.15
Vegetables	.95	1.12	.31	.18
Meats	.70	0.99	.29	.20
Cedar Rapids, Iowa				
Groceries	.60	—	.19	—
Supermarket	.78	—	.70	—
Clothing	1.30	—	1.23	—
Restaurant	1.65	—	0.32	—

SOURCE: Clark (1968), Table 5, p. 393 and Marble and Bowlby (1968), Table 1, p. 62.

comers to the city must learn about the shopping opportunities from scratch. The rate at which they learn will vary from individual to individual and may be largely influenced by the value system. For these people, the more distant, larger centers with their greater number of establishments and functions will be particularly attractive in the early stages, since the probability of getting what they want will be highest at them. People relocating within a different area of the same city will already be familiar with parts of its retail structure, but they will probably have to learn about the new opportunities in the local area. Old-timers in the city can be expected to have fairly well-established images developed during their longer periods of familiarity with the city. Hence individuals can be expected to be in different stages of the learning process. This can be thought of as another important factor influencing their particular behavior spaces and shopping patterns.

That changes in the city's retail structure will also influence the learning process is equally self-evident. New stores are continually being added to the retail structure; old and familiar elements are forever disappearing, either under the bulldozer or because of changes in function, even management. Whole shopping areas change their character, particularly when there is invasion of the surrounding neighborhood by different social and ethnic groups, and consequently they may not continue to offer the same kind of opportunities for shopping to the traditional clientele (Pred, 1963). These ongoing changes in the retail structure will influence the images held by consumers and will bring about changes in them through time. The result is that behavior space perception is subject to varying degrees of modification, which will be reflected in individual, and in some cases aggregate, shopping patterns.

Trade Areas

Shopping journeys undertaken by consumers from dispersed origins tend to focus on specific retail/service establishments or shopping areas. They consequently involve a centripetal element that gives rise to trade areas. Unlike the comparable areas associated with rural service centers, those for nucleations within the city are considerably more complicated. In the densely built-up urban areas, consumers have a much greater range of alternative shopping opportunities available to them within the maximum distance they are prepared to travel. Although they may have well-developed preferences for certain of these, they visit none exclusively, but rather will visit many of them at some time or other in the course of their shopping behavior.

In this way consumers can be thought to have probabilities of visiting the various centers. The probabilities of visiting a given center will be influenced by the consumer's content and movement imagery, and consequently they are difficult to determine empirically. It has been shown, however, that a useful approximation to the probabilistic nature of trade areas can be obtained on the basis of center size and distance (Huff, 1963). A hypothetical example of the trade areas for three centers is shown in Figure 15.10. The overlapping influence of different shopping centers, the break points between centers (which occur where the contours of equal probability intersect), and the general decline of center influence with distance are clearly shown. The latter is well illustrated from the results of a study of regional shopping centers in the San Francisco Bay Area, where it was found that although 17 percent of the customers come from more than 10 miles away, one-half of the customers live within three miles of the center visited (Vance, 1962).

Despite this probabilistic nature of trade areas, it is still very useful to indicate their size and shape in a more general way to show the dominant area served by a nucleation. An example is given in Figure 15.11. The trade-area boundaries on the maps include about 80 percent of the centers' regular customers. The resulting patterns indicate quite explicitly the hierarchical nature of the centers discussed in Chapter 12 and and the nesting of trade areas discussed in Chapter 7. The convenience-goods trade areas (Fig. 15.11A) are relatively small and form a mesh over the city. Boundaries overlap, especially in the more densely built-up parts of the city, and the size of the trade area appears to be generally related to the size of the center. At the higher order shopping-goods level, many of the smaller centers drop out, consistent with the notion of the hierarchy, and fewer larger centers dominate the trade-area pattern (Fig. 15.11B). The way in which the smaller trade areas nest within the larger ones is clearly revealed when the maps are superimposed. The patterns also indicate the influence of the barriers to movement shown by the gray areas, on the size and shape of trade areas.

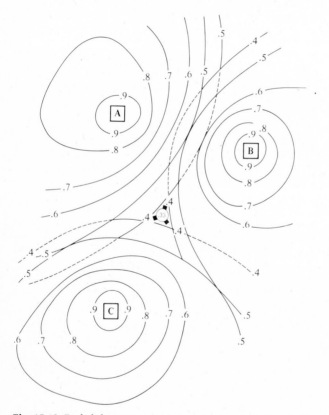

Fig. 15.10. Probability contours for consumers shopping in three centers. (*Source*: Berry, 1967a, Fig. 2.16.)

A Shopping Model

Most models used to describe and predict intraurban shopping patterns are direct descendants of the gravity model discussed in Chapter 3. As such, they deal with aggregate patterns of interaction between shopping areas and various residential zones in the city. They differ from the original Reilly (1931) formulation in three important respects:

1. Movement for all kinds of goods is considered.

2. The interaction between a continuous distribution of population and shopping opportunities is described.

3. The dependent variable is, initially at least, specified as a probability, thereby including the notion that consumers choose between many shopping centers.

As developed by Lakshmanan and Hansen (1965), the probability that a consumer resident in zone i patronizes a center in zone j is given as:

$$P_{ij} = \frac{A^a_{ij} / d^\beta_{ij}}{\sum_{j=1}^{n} A^a_j / d^\beta_{ij}} \qquad (15.2)$$

where

A_j = the attractiveness of shopping center located in zone j
d_{ij} = the distance between residential zone i and center j
a and β = empirically derived exponents

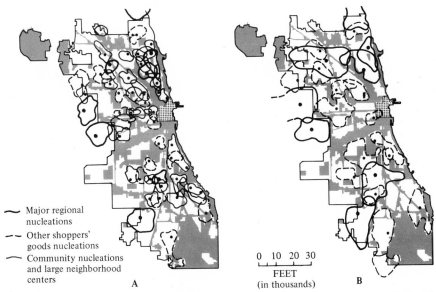

— Major regional
  nucleations

-- Other shoppers'
  goods nucleations

— Community nucleations
  and large neighborhood
  centers

0 10 20 30
FEET
(in thousands)

A   B

Fig. 15.11. Shopping trade areas in Chicago: (A) convenience goods trade areas and (B) shoppers' goods trade areas. (*Source:* Berry, 1963, Figs. 11 and 12.)

When the right-hand side of the equation has been multiplied by the total consumer retail expenditure in residential zone i, the model will estimate the total amount of consumer expenditure from that zone spent at center j. If the total population of residential zone j is multiplied by P_{ij}, the model will estimate the total number of consumers traveling from zone i to center j.

The above model states that the probability of a consumer traveling from zone i to shop at center j is (1) directly proportional to the size of the shopping center at j, and (2) inversely proportional to (a) the distance between i and j, and (b) the competition from other centers (the expression in the denominator of equation 15.2). For its aplication, the exponents in the equation must be estimated and the variables indexed. The first problem is essentially a technical one, but it is critical for the successful operation of the model, the effectiveness of which depends largely on the specific value given to the exponent of distance (β). The second problem is largely one of definition and is concerned with quantifying distance and the rather vague concept of the attractiveness of centers. Distance is usually measured by airline miles, although other measures such as driving time may be used. Attractiveness is a more difficult concept to handle, however, and most studies use some measure of size of shopping center for this. Size can be measured in a number of ways, including total floor area, number of functions or establishments, and total sales, if this is known.

The success of the model is normally measured by a correlation between observed flows and those generated from the model; and despite the simplicity of the equation, its application in planning studies has been highly satisfactory by this standard. In the Baltimore region, for example, the correlation between shopping flows known to exist from an origin-destination study and those generated from the model was very high ($R^2 = 91\%$). Nevertheless, large discrepancies between observed and expected patterns may often result, and modifications to improve the model's efficiency are continually being suggested. Huff (1963) has suggested that the model be disaggregated by type of good to take into account the observation that consumers are prepared to travel longer distances for higher order, specialized commodities. More recently, the notion of competition between claimants at shopping centers has been introduced, and a modification of the distance variable to incorporate this into the model has been suggested. It is not difficult to think of other ways of making the model more realistic, but regardless of the refinements made, the results from using this kind of model will always be highly generalized because of its aggregative nature.

Thus, journey-to-work and journey-to-shop patterns are influenced by a host of factors. The arrangement of commercial activities and work places within the urban area affect movements in a similar fashion, but individual trip decisions rest upon an additional host of personal as well as socioeconomic characteristics. Concomitantly, the predominance of trips for sociorecreational purposes, which take place primarily in the evening, are also affected in their direction and frequency by the arrangement of entertainment facilities in the urban area and individual behavioral characteristics. Trips to local movie houses or bowling alleys are shorter and more frequent than those to theaters or night clubs located in downtown areas. Consequently, the movement concepts presented with respect to work and shopping trips are underlying forces determining most trips in urban areas.

PART

III

THE URBAN DILEMMA

16
POLLUTION
AND URBAN
TRANSPORTATION
PROBLEMS

During the present century, the urban population of North America has increased at a much faster rate than that of more rural areas. As a consequence, a far greater proportion of the total population of North America is now living in urban areas than even 30 years ago. Depending upon how the word "urban" is defined, the population of North America is now almost 80 percent urban, and by the year 2000 this proportion should exceed 90 percent. This concentration of the population into vast urban regions creates a number of problems, of which pollution and urban transportation are outstanding examples. Others, such as metropolitan government, finance, housing, and regional inequalities, are discussed in other chapters.

Pollution and urban transportation are linked to a degree insofar as the gathering together of a mass of people in one area and their demands for transport are bound to create environmental problems. These range from the irritating and stupid predilection of many Americans and Canadians for throwing paper, cans, and wrappers of many kinds from their cars and bicycles as they idly move along, to the shocking use of the air, streams, and lakes as sewers for industrial and domestic waste.

Much of this waste, whether it be in the form of gum wrappers and beer cans or detergents and gaseous effluents, is the product of a grossly overindulgent society. Every generation passes on its successes and failures to the one succeeding. The successes are valued and used, but the problems have to be solved. The post–World War generation is passing on the advantages of wealth, stability, and opportunity, but with this heritage is included not only obvious inequalities, but a colossal indifference to environmental hazards that arise from overconsumption. Not only are we using our sources of raw materials and energy at a frightenly fast rate, we are also wrecking and altering the environment. Interrelated with environmental pollution is the problem of urban transportation, for one of the habits that has been allowed to develop is that of the overuse of petroleum as the source of power for personal and public transportation. This is seen most clearly in the use of the automobile for personal transportation and the polluting effects of air transport. The fact that petroleum has become society's habit is clearly demonstrated by the way in which people react to impending shortages, and their willingness to pay almost any price for a tank of gas.

It is, however, necessary to emphasize that though the problems of pollution and urban transportation are related, they overlap only to a degree. It is therefore necessary to consider the various aspects of pollution arising from urbanism and the urban transportation question separately. It must also be recognized that the ensuing discussion is a brief review of these questions, and that the various issues have been discussed quite widely over the past decade. Recent excellent collections concerning urbanism and the environment include those by Detwyler and Marcus (1972), Manners and Mikesell (1974), and Berry et al. (1974); and recent discussions of urban transportation issues are summarized quite well by Owen (1972). The pollution issues that will be discussed in the ensuing sections relate to air, water, and noise, while the urban transportation section is devoted to an examination of the basic problem and an evaluation of some current myths.

POLLUTION AND THE URBAN ENVIRONMENT

Man has been changing and altering his environment for thousands of years (Manners and Mikesell, 1974). Marshes were drained during the days of the Roman Empire, and villages and cities have always existed close to rivers and streams, which have been used as open sewers. In fact, the first realization that pollution caused the spread of deadly diseases was with respect to urban water supplies. When enough people are collected together and allowed to use the environment in the way that only they see fit, the supplies of water and air are seriously affected. Thus, the first forms of urban management were simply to provide administrative services for water supplies and sewage disposal; it is only during the past century that urban management has been pressed into services beyond the merely physical.

Water Pollution

Pollution occurs when a resource is so altered that it cannot be used for something else. Thus water is regarded as polluted if substances are added to it which affect its use for drinking, washing, swimming, fish and other biotic life, and industrial purposes. Many of these uses, however, conflict, for water that is ideal for industrial use has characteristics that make it deadly for human and aquatic life. For example, for most industrial applications it would be desirable to obtain water containing no dissolved oxygen, yet for human and aquatic consumption such water could be disastrous. Nevertheless, given the need for water for human consumption and biotic life, we must assume that it should be as pollution-free as possible.

Water can be regarded as polluted if it contains a variety of solids, organic materials, and infectious and toxic agents and nutrients, or if its temperature and appearance are affected. These polluting agents can be introduced by a variety of means, such as agriculture, normal geomorphological processes, and airborne agents, as well as from urban development and urban-related activities. The urban sources are in many cases the most important, though chemicals used for weed and pest control and fertilization in agriculture are building up in many rivers and lakes to an alarming degree.

The Effects of Urbanization on Water Pollution

Urban areas have a detrimental effect on water supply and water quality directly through their physical mass, and indirectly through the activities that are included within the urban scene. The process of building and paving the surface results in a greatly decreased rate of infiltration of rainwater, and the channeling of this water into conduits and storm sewers effectively reduces the amount that enters subsurface natural reservoirs. Furthermore, areas that are under construction and in which the normal vegetation cover has been removed are subject to massive erosion. Thus, river basins that are experiencing high rates of urbanization experience severe disruptions in water flow and changes in sedimentation. Not only is the flow subject to more extreme fluctuations, but the amount of material borne by the stream or river is greatly increased. This results in severe silting up of channels, and, eventually, possible despoilation in the areas of deposition.

For example, in recent years the land area adjacent to the western portion of Lake Ontario has been subject to a high rate of urban development. A study by Ongley (1973) has indicated that those river basins in which urban development has been most rapid experienced two to three times the rate of sedimentation that has been experienced by those subject to less intense urban development. Much of the material contained in these streams and rivers is deposited in Lake Ontario, with the result that the large natural reservoir is increasingly filled with dissolved and suspended sediment. Furthermore, the silting up of bays may ruin the habitat of aquatic life not only by covering the rocks and sources of food, but by adding material that uses the oxygen in the water.

Though there are many features of water quality that affect its use for various purposes, one of the most important characteristics is the amount of dissolved oxygen that it contains. Oxygen in water is used for a variety of purposes: it supports all forms of fish life, it is required for plant growth, it is necessary for human consumption, and it is consumed as materials degrade. It is this latter use that can lead to the ruination of water for the support of human and aquatic life and can result in the spoiling of lakes. If too much material that requires oxygen for degrading is introduced into a body of water, the foreign materials use up the oxygen at a faster rate than it can be introduced. As the quantity of dissolved oxygen decreases, the amount of degradable material continues to increase, so that eventually the water becomes choked in vegetable, chemical, and mineral material that it can no longer absorb or support. Large parts of Lake Erie have become choked in this manner, and, to all intents and purposes, this water is useless as a life support.

The two most important sources of material that not only affect the color, potability, mineral content, and so forth of water, but also add constituents that consume dissolved oxygen, are industrial and municipal wastes. These are indirectly associated with urbanization, for they are not really caused by urban construction, but occur as a result of economic activities and human life within urban areas.

Industrial Use and Contamination of Water

In 1968 manufacturing industries in the United States used almost 15.5 trillion gallons of water, the chief users being the chemical, paper, and the petroleum and coal industries (Berry et al., 1974). Nearly two-thirds of this water was used for cooling purposes, the remainder being involved in some form of processing (Table 16.1). There is, however, a wide variety in the use of water by industry type, for three of the four biggest volume users use water for cooling, whereas the chemical industry actually uses water in the production process. This concentration on cooling is, of itself, important in the consideration of pollution, for the heating of water and its return at a higher temperature to a river or lake result in contamination and modification of the area into which the water is discharged.

The use of water in the production process, however, causes the greatest pollution. Though some water is actually incorporated into the production of a few industries, such as soft drinks, beer, and so forth, in most cases the water is used to flush away residue materials. It is for this reason that the paper, textile, and chemical industries are the greatest sources of pollution. These wastes embrace a wide variety of pollutants, ranging from suspended solids to toxic agents and radioactive material. These types of pollutants not only are potential health hazards, but also interfere with the use of the water for recreation and increase the rate of erosion on piers and boats. If chemical nutrients, such as nitrogen and phosphorous, are added, the water may become fertilized, and this stimulates the growth of weeds and algae, which in turn consume excessive quantities of oxygen in the water. Needless to say, the addition of any kind of material may result in discoloration, foaming, floating sludge and slime, and a peculiar taste.

Table 16.1.   WATER USE BY INDUSTRY TYPE, 1968

Industry	Intake (billions of gallons)	Cooling	Process	Other
Food and kindred products	811	52.6	35.8	11.6
Textile mill products	154	15.3	70.7	14.0
Paper	2252	28.9	65.6	5.5
Chemicals	4476	78.9	16.4	4.7
Petroleum and coal	1435	85.7	6.6	7.7
Rubber	135	70.9	17.6	11.5
Primary metals	68	28.4	54.8	16.8
Machinery	189	72.0	15.3	12.7
Electrical equipment	127	38.4	36.8	24.8
Transportation equipment	313	25.6	20.2	54.2
All manufacturing		65.5	27.8	6.7

SOURCE: Berry et al., (1974), p. 95.

Municipal Use and Contamination of Water

All urban areas require an adequate supply of safe drinking water, which may be obtained from groundwater, lakes, rivers, and reservoirs. Frequently this water is recycled, implying that it is used a number of times either in the same urban system or by a number of systems, as the water moves along its course. The need for safe water, and the increasing involvement in recycling, makes the purifying processing before and after use vital, and the effect of untreated or partially treated sewage on water quality and aquatic life may be devastating.

In fact, municipal waste and sewage are the second largest polluters of water, after manufacturing. As urban areas get larger and larger, the amounts of waste sewage that are handled by municipal sewers increase at an exponential rate. It is wrong, however, to assume that all of this waste is domestic in origin, for about 55 percent come from homes and commercial establishments, whereas about 45 percent come from industries (Berry et al., 1974). Although most of this waste is organic, there are considerable quantities of chemicals, in the form of detergents and mineral matter.

Full and complete waste treatment is, therefore, vital. Proper waste treatment requires a good sewage system that is connected to a plant that is capable of handling peak volumes. Unfortunately, not all the urban population of North America is served by a sewage system, and a considerable proportion that is so served is not provided with adequate facilities. In the United States in 1970, nearly 73 percent of the population was served by sewers, whereas almost 80 percent of the population resided in urban areas. Frequently the sewage system serves as an artery for the transmittal of storm overflow as well as waste material, and in times of heavy rain or quick thaw the treatment plants are overloaded, and the waste material is either treated inadequately or passed straight through to the receiving area. Thus many systems are required to fill two purposes, and in times of peak flow neither purpose is adequately served.

This situation would not be so bad if, during normal flow, the waste material was adequately removed from the water. There are three levels of treatment employment by municipal plants, and very few go to the highest level. *Primary* treatment involves the collection of waste in large tanks, and utilizes settling by gravity for the removal of the material. This form of treatment removes no more than 30 percent of the waste in the water, yet about one-third of all sewage systems in the United States still employ primary treatment or less. *Secondary* treatment involves a biological process for speeding up decay and filtering through a sand and rock bed. This procedure not only permits oxygen to be dissolved into the water, but may result in the removal of up to 90 percent of the waste material. Two-thirds of all sewage systems in the United States employ treatment up to the secondary level. *Advanced* treatment, involving more filtering and chemical absorption procedures, may result in the removal of up to 99 percent of the waste matter. There are, however, very few systems that employ waste-removal techniques up to the advanced level, for natural processes are considered adequate to handle existing waste beyond the secondary level. This may be true where large water bodies are involved, but it is not acceptable if the receiving area is small, or if there is a concentration of particular chemicals that remain in the effluent.

Thus there is very little doubt that urban areas could invest more deeply in facilities that would reduce the quantities of polluted water that now exist in North America. The first systems of waste removal and water treatment for drinking purposes were introduced to control the spread of diseases, such as typhus, which were rampant in the nineteenth and early twentieth centuries. Now the sheer volume of effluent can kill indirectly, but just as effectively. Furthermore, the aquatic life that is destroyed may be difficult to replace, and the waters that are contaminated ruin their use for recreational purposes as well as future consumption. Municipalities must invest more in waste disposal and treatment, but they can do so only if more efficient means for financing urban areas are introduced (Chapter 18).

Air Pollution

On the average, each person inhales about 15,000 quarts of air per day. This is 10 times the weight of food and water consumed daily by the average person, and it is therefore rather surprising that mass concern and legislative action concerning the control of air pollution is rather recent. Legislation concerning the purification of water and the adulteration of food precedes that for air by a number of decades. As a result, it has taken catastrophic events of dramatic proportions to publicize the need for cleaner air. This is because people get used to "normal" air pollution, and the effects of many abnormal incidents of air pollution are never recorded.

One case in America that has been recorded and is cited in many reports of the U.S. Department of Health, Education, and Welfare is that of Donora, Pa., a town of some 14,000 people located in a deep valley about 30 miles south of Pittsburgh (Heimann, 1967). On the morning of October 27, 1948, the residents of Donora arose to find themselves enveloped in a fog resulting from a temperature inversion. Fogs are not unusual in this area, but this particular fog was quite intense and lasted for four days, until the afternoon of October 31. In that period of time there were 17 deaths in a community that normally experienced an average of two deaths in an equivalent period at that time of year. Many persons became ill, experiencing sore throat, chest constriction, headache, breathlessness, a burning sensation of the eyes, lacrimation, vomiting, and so on. Elderly people proved to be particularly susceptible to this abnormal air pollution, and subsequent autopsies showed acute lung irritation.

Events of this kind are not uncommon in the memories of most urban dwellers, but rarely have they been so carefully recorded and their cause so directly established. However, although it is the increased death rate, eight times above normal, that wins headlines and prompts responsible individuals to act, it is the continuing normal despoilation of our air that is of primary concern. It is sad that many of the inhabitants of Los Angeles have become used to being unable to see the hills around them and have accepted watering eyes as part of everyday urban living.

Sources of Air Pollution

Pollutants present in the air are normally divided into two categories, primary and secondary. Primary pollutants are those emitted directly from identifiable sources, while secondary pollutants are the result of the interaction of two or more primary components, or the reaction of primary components with normal constituents in the atmosphere. Thus if man is to control air pollution, the source of the primary pollutant must be identified.

Natural Air Pollution

The major sources of air pollutants are man and the natural physical environment (Table 16.2). Man can do very little to control the regular and irregular flow of pollutants derived from volcanoes, breaking seas, and plant pollen, but he can diminish the dust content of the atmosphere derived from windstorms and fires. The construction of roads and buildings in semiarid areas usually results in a removal of the natural vegetation cover, which is difficult to replace. The result is often widespread wind erosion and dust storms. Forest and brush fires are even more hazardous to the atmosphere, for they lay waste to an area for a considerable period of time.

Man-Made Air Pollution

Combustion processes are a major source of primary pollutants of both the particle and the gaseous varieties. The most common forms of particle pollution in urban areas are ash and soot, pollutants that are easily visible, for they soil buildings, plants, and people and provide obvious obstructions to sunlight. Very small particles have important secondary effects on the climate of urban areas, for they can act as nuclei for the condensation of atmospheric water vapor, thus causing a further decrease in visibility through mists and fogs. It would therefore appear that urban areas significantly affect their own climates, particularly with respect to fogs (Table 16.3) and decreases in visibility. This climatic modification occurs, in general, as a result of:

1. The increased *area* of buildings that is exposed to light, heat, wind, and so forth.

2. The amount of surface area that has a high rate of conductivity, that is, cools fast and warms quickly.

3. The heat generated in the urban area from traffic, industries, buildings, and so forth.

4. The impervious nature of the surface which increases runoff and accelerates snow thaw (Terjung, 1974).

Table 16.2.   THE SOURCE OF PRIMARY POLLUTANTS

SOURCES OF PRIMARY POLLUTANTS

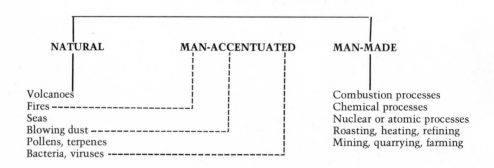

NATURAL	MAN-ACCENTUATED	MAN-MADE
Volcanoes		Combustion processes
Fires		Chemical processes
Seas		Nuclear or atomic processes
Blowing dust		Roasting, heating, refining
Pollens, terpenes		Mining, quarrying, farming
Bacteria, viruses		

Source: Bryson and Kutzbach (1968), p. 9.

Gaseous pollutants are also derived from the combustion of fuels, particularly coal and fuel oil. These gases are primarily sulfur dioxide and various nitrogen oxides, which by themselves are fairly harmless, though they can and do accelerate erosion and wear when combined with moisture. It is, however, the secondary reaction of these gases with other pollutants in the atmosphere that gives rise to the two best-known types of air pollution. Colloquially, these can be referred to as the London type and the Los Angeles type.

The London type of air pollution is common to many cities that still have a nineteenth-century form of industry and domestic heating, using coal as the energy base. Coal combustion generates quantities of sulfur dioxide, which reacts to form sulfur trioxide in the atmosphere. The sulfur trioxide combines with droplets of water vapor to produce small droplets of sulfuric acid around minute particles of dust and ash. In humid conditions these droplets produce haze and fog, and when they are coated with an oily film or other pollutants, they produce the "pea-soup" fogs for which the London area was famous. Apart from a reduction in visibility to such an extent that on occasion one could not see one's outstretched hand, these acid water droplets are an irritant to the bronchial tubes and are highly corrosive.

The Los Angeles type (or the oxidation type) of air pollution is directly related to the widespread use of the internal combustion engine, which, even in its modern form, incurs a loss of about 15 percent in fuel energy. Haagen-Smit (1964) suggests that this represents an annual loss of about three billion dollars, which can be interpreted as excess use of three billion dollars' worth of energy fuel. Through this loss the internal combustion engine releases large amounts of nitrogen oxides and hydrocarbons, which, together with other pollutants, incur a photochemical reaction in sunlight to produce smog. From Figure 16.1 it can be observed that one of the key elements in this reaction is the group of hydrocarbons. Smog obscures views, damages plants, irritates eyes and throats, has an unpleasant odor, increases corrosion, and may well adversely affect health.

Thus it would appear that the principal man-made causes of air pollution are:

1. Heavy industry, such as iron and zinc smelting and steel manufacturing, which produce dust and iron, zinc, and copper oxides.

2. The internal combustion engine, which produces nitrogen dioxides and a variety of hydrocarbons.

Table 16.3.   CLIMATIC CHANGES PRODUCED BY CITIES

Climatic Element	Comparison with Rural Environs
Clouds	5–10% more
Fog, winter	100% more
Fog, summer	30% more
Precipitation	
Total amount	5–10% more
Days with 0.2 in. (or less)	10% more

SOURCE: Bryson and Kutzbach (1968), p. 11.

3. General coal combustion, which in some areas adds greatly to the quantity of suspended particles in the atmosphers.

4. Petroleum refining, which produces hydrocarbons and suspended oily particulates.

Thus the causes and the sources of much urban air pollution are well known.

Effects of Air Pollution

We have previously referred to some of the effects of air pollution, particularly those effects that are dramatic and evident to the urban dweller. However, studies in Great Britain, Japan, and the USSR, as well as the United States, have catalogued a variety of effects of normal everyday air pollution on health, agriculture, property, safety, and the weather. Some of these effects can be measured in financial terms; others have to be viewed in a nonmonetary or aesthetic sense.

Air Pollution and Health

The major effect of air pollution may well be on health. The cost of illness, decreased strength, and a shortened life span cannot be measured in dollars, but there is sufficient evidence to indicate that normal air pollution does adversely affect people's health. In particular there is strong evidence to suggest that air pollution is associated with (1) acute nonspecific upper respiratory disease, (2) chronic bronchitis, (3) chronic constrictive ventilatory disease, (4) pulmonary emphysema, (5) bronchial asthma, and (6) lung cancer. There are many other diseases or illnesses that may also be associated with air pollution, but the evidence is inconclusive in this respect.

Air Pollution and Agriculture

The effects of air pollution on agriculture vary according to the variety of plants and the mix of pollutants in the atmosphere. Some classic cases have occurred with respect to sulphur dioxide at Copper Hill, Tenn., and in the state of Washington with respect to the smelter across the Canadian border at Trail, British Columbia. Ozone has been found to affect grape leaves in California and tobacco leaves in the eastern part of the United States, and it has injured spinach, alfalfa, rye, barley, orchard grass, tobacco, petunias, radishes, clover, beans and parsley in New Jersey.

Fluorides, which are primarily of industrial origin, have also caused extensive

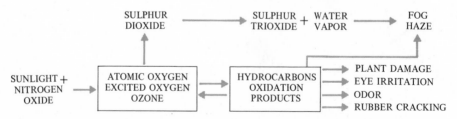

Fig. 16.1. The Los Angeles type of air pollution. (*Source:* Haagen-Smit, 1964, p. 30.)

damage, particularly to cattle foraging on fluoride-contaminated vegetation. Hydrogen fluoride, in particular, is very damaging to crops, particularly corn and peaches. Agricultural economic losses from air pollution are very difficult to measure, but the best estimate available indicates losses reaching hundreds of millions of dollars per year.

Air Pollution and Property

Air pollution accelerates the deterioration of materials, structures, and machines of all kinds. Sulphur dioxide in particular attacks metals and converts limestone, marble, roofing slate, mortar, and other carbonates containing stone to water soluble sulphates, which can then be leached away by rain. Dust and ash settles on buildings, enters all structures, including homes, and has to be continually removed if the property value is to be maintained. Ozone in smog causes excessive cracking in rubber, as well as deteriorating dyes, fabrics, and other synthetic material. The total cost of this type of pollution, including its depreciating effect on property values, is estimated to be about 65 dollars per person per year, which, in the United States, represents an annual cost of over 14 billion dollars.

The effect of normal air pollution on urban areas in North America is therefore very high. Dramatic accidents involving instances of rapidly forming fogs on highways and airline landing strips are well documented. More difficult to estimate is the aesthetic and psychological effect of air pollution on man. No real permanent health effects have been demonstrated from smog-induced stinging and tearing of the eyes, but there is no doubt that it is uncomfortable and disturbing. Dirty buildings, smog-filled skies, dying flowers, and rapidly depreciating property values certainly detract from the pleasures of urban living.

Solutions to Air Pollution

The two major causes of urban air pollution therefore appear to be industry and automobiles. Pollution from both these sources can be controlled if sufficient emphasis is placed on legislative controls and preventive measures. Before 1940, Pittsburgh was a classic case of a city polluted by industrial wastes (Friedlander, 1965). For 40 years Pittsburgh had relied upon the self-control efforts of industry to solve the problem, but the results of self-regulation were negligible. As a result, Pittsburgh adopted city and country ordinances against air pollution from industry and domestic sources, and the results are outstanding. In 1965 the average sootfall in Pittsburgh was only 30 tons per square mile per month, compared with 60 tons per square mile per month in New York City.

The methods used to achieve this reduction in air pollution were undoubtedly costly to the operators. Smoke-control devices (such as the electrostatic precipitator) had to be installed on industrial stacks, and homeowners had to use smokeless fuels or install gas or oil furnaces. With the exception of installations in private residences, all fuel-burning equipment is subject to periodic inspection by the local bureau of air-pollution control.

Pollution in Pittsburgh has therefore been controlled by strong local action, but pollution control from industry in other areas has not been introduced so effectively. For example, the Chicago area has been plagued by a continuous barrage of soot and smoke from the steel mills of Hammond and Gary, which are located 15 miles to the southeast in northern Indiana. On many days of the year the sky in this area is black and the sootfall tremendous. The present average monthly sootfall is 43 tons per square mile; but on many days of the year when the smoke from steel mills is wafted in the direction of Chicago, the rate of sootfall is three to four times greater. Although the steel producers in the Calumet region of Chicago are installing 50 million dollars' worth of control equipment, the steel mills of northern Indiana cannot be coerced in the same way, for they are in another state. Thus, cases of interregional and interstate air pollution can be effectively controlled only by federal action.

Air pollution between two urban areas at the junction of international boundaries is even more difficult to control. Though there have been many joint U.S. and Canadian reports on air pollution in the Detroit-Windsor area, they have not been accompanied by comparable legislation (Brazel, 1973). Whereas Windsor achieved an 80 percent reduction in particle emission between 1968 and 1972, this has not been accompanied by a reduction in pollution in the air. This is because the prevailing movement of air is from the west and south, and polluted air from Detroit is transported over this portion of southwestern Ontario. The situation cannot, therefore, be resolved by action in Windsor alone, for similar action has to occur in the Detroit metropolitan area before any pollution reduction can be noticed.

The contribution of automobiles to air pollution has been shown to be quite large, particularly with respect to the formation of smog. The key elements emitted by automobiles are nitrogen oxides and unburned hydrocarbons. So far state laws—for example, those in California—have been concerned with eliminating the amount of unburned carbons by requiring the addition of a few simple devices (such as afterburners) to cars. The problem of nitrogen oxide emission has not, however, been tackled, though further engine modifications could radically reduce the emission of this pollutant as well. This combined approach could radically reduce smog to a fairly tolerable level. There is little doubt that, if the automobile industry were prepared to spend a fraction of the amount on engine modifications that it spends on advertising to reduce those emissions, the problem of urban air pollution would be greatly reduced, though not eliminated.

Thus urban air pollution exists because man insists on treating the atmosphere as a sewer. Of course, the question arises whether people are prepared to pay to have clean air. In many cases it appears that we are prepared to accept dirty air as part of the price of urban living, and it may well be that after a while we get used to it. It must be remembered, however, that air pollution, though at its greatest in urban areas, is really a global problem. We all breathe air from the atmosphere, and as the population of the world expands, it is a finite resource that is being consumed and polluted at an ever increasing rate.

Noise Pollution

At this moment, three electric typewriters are clattering in the office, a truck is unloading fill outside the window, traffic is roaring to and from the local hospital, and the Big Band is warming up in the music building. Ordinarily these sounds are quite pleasant, because they indicate that people are well, going about their business, and activities are humming along. But these sounds are occasionally disrupting, and when sound becomes annoying and disruptive it becomes noise pollution. There are times when noise is quite pleasant (though one would wish that rock bands could perform at a less deafening level), and in these instances the noise is wanted. It is the unwanted noise that disrupts, and urban areas are replete with maddening noises.

Noise in urban areas can be classified spatially into two groups: (1) noise from stationary sources, and (2) noise occurring in transport corridors (Berry et al., 1974). Noise from stationary sources includes noise from industry, building sites, blasting, entertainment facilities, and so forth. It is therefore possible to pinpoint the location of these sources and, if they become sufficiently unbearable, to control at site. Transport corridor noise arises from rapid transit, railroads, automobile traffic, aircraft, boats along rivers, and so forth. This type of noise can be either periodic or constant. Urban arterials appear to emit a fairly constant noise, for the traffic is usually constant throughout the day. At nighttime it may be less frequent, and at this time it becomes periodic. Periodic noise is probably more annoying, and when it occurs at regular intervals it can approach the destroying level of the Chinese water torture.

The Sources of Noise Pollution

The chief sources of noise in sites external to buildings are automobiles, trucks, aircraft, and people or animals. Following studies in a number of field areas, Bolt et al. (1967), note that 80 percent of the test sites recorded automobiles as the "most frequent" source of noise, while 10 percent record aircraft as the most frequent, and the remaining 10 percent regarded trucks and other persons or animals as the most frequent. This, of course, reflects the general dispersal of noise from automobiles around an entire urban area. The proportionate distribution of the sources described as the "next most frequent" is, however, more interesting. People and animals were cited as the next most frequent source of noise pollution at 40 percent of the field sites. Aircraft were cited as the next most frequent sources at 25 percent of the sites, and automobiles, trucks, and other sources were cited at the remainder. Thus, the evidence would seem to suggest that the major sources of external noise pollution are automobiles and trucks, followed by aircraft, and people or animals.

Noise Pollution from Automobiles and Trucks

Automobiles can be noisy to passengers traveling within them, and to people living or working adjacent to roads. Presumably, if people wish to travel in automobiles that are noisy internally, that is their business; if they dislike it, they should not purchase noisy vehicles. However, the imposition of noisy automobiles on others is more serious. The basic sources of external noise in automobiles are engines, exhaust systems, and tires. The amount of noise emitted from these sources varies with speed, so one method of noise control is to limit speed. Other controls may be exerted via muffler inspection and soundproofing around engines. Most states and provinces have noise-emission regulations, but these are very general and related primarily to new automobiles. There is very little control exerted over the sound of vehicles when they are in use.

Trucks tend to be more noisy than automobiles, and for similar reasons. They are, however, more localized in their noise effect, for in most urban areas they are banned from roads other than arterials or limited-access highways, except for local deliveries. Trucks are, however, extremely noisy at night or in the early morning, for at these times the general background level of noise in an urban area is at a low level, and the sound waves appear to carry a greater distance. This is accentuated by the fact that many deliveries occur at night or in the early morning as stores and warehouses stock up for the day's sales. Inhabitants of the central areas of cities are particularly affected by garbage trucks and intercity road haulage.

Noise Pollution from Aircraft

Areas within and around airports are particularly affected by noise, and the location of this type of pollution is quite predictable. The areas affected by aircraft noise are controlled by the location of the runways and takeoff and landing patterns. Landing angles tend to be shallower than takeoff angles, so the noise levels related to landing tend to be more extensive. These are indicated in the predicted noise levels for the proposed second Toronto airport (Figure 16.2). The noise contours in Figure 16.2 are expressed in a composite noise rating (CNR) which combines the physical characteristics of sound along with time and frequency of occurrence. This index is supposed to reflect the noise to individuals stemming from aircraft operations. Aircraft noise levels around airports increased greatly with the use of jet engines and aircraft that require

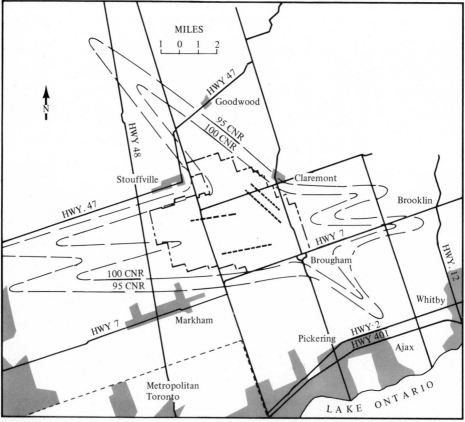

Fig. 16.2. Noise exposure forecast contours: proposed, and now halted, second Toronto airport. (*Source*: Hauer, 1972, p. 185.)

longer and shallower landing paths. The newer, larger aircraft, requiring much bigger engines, are quieter, however, for sound-control mechanisms can be included in their construction. Furthermore, a considerable proportion of landing noise is, in fact, controlled by the pilot, and the noise emanating from the larger engines is much more pilot-controllable than that from smaller planes.

Thus, the areas affected by aircraft noise in the future may not be so extensive as they are at the moment. This is quite interesting, for one of the reasons why new airports are built is that a large residential population has become affected by serious sound problems. This was, for example, a major reason for the decision to investigate the need for a second Toronto airport, and one cannot escape the impression that once a bureaucracy is asked to investigate a need, the process soon becomes one of justification of and planning for a new airport.

Noise Pollution from People and Animals

Radios blare forth, children scream, parents yell, dogs bark, and cats fight at night. These and other human and animal noises are apt to create severe sound problems. There is little that one can do to control these noises except to request that people be more considerate, and to require that buildings be constructed with more than sufficient soundproofing. There are, of course, minimum construction standards with respect to sound, but these standards usually relate to "normal" noise levels. Shrieking, crying, and barking are not, however, normal noises, and people at parties rarely speak at their normal voice levels. Furthermore, walls are rarely sealed correctly, and gaps and cracks are invariably left at joints. Sound waves travel through these crevices, thus nullifying the soundproofing standards of the substances incorporated within the walls and ceilings. As a consequence, noise emanating from people and animals can be reduced only by self-control, animal control, and greater care in construction.

Effects of Noise Pollution

Noise pollution has been defined previously as unwanted noise. This definition implies that its effect is mainly one of annoyance, but there is much more involved than that. This type of pollution may also be deleterious to health and learning, and may have economic effects as well. As far as health is concerned, the persistence of a high level of noise can be harmful to hearing, and can give rise to temporary headaches. The amplified din of rock bands and quadraphonic sound projection are now part of youth culture. The evidence is quite clear, however, that persistent high-volume sound does result in impaired hearing. This is recognized in some areas of employment. For example, the ground staff at airports are required to wear protective devices, and workman's compensation can be claimed for loss of hearing resulting from work in noisy atmospheres.

There is little doubt that some people involved in a "cerebral" activity (such as reading or writing) are greatly disturbed by noise. Academic life is full of stories involving people who seem capable of working through any kind of noise, and those who are greatly disturbed by the smallest sound. Learning seems to be less effected by continuous noise than random noise, though again the level of impairment varies according to the person concerned. Furthermore, it varies according to the task or subject matter. If a person is greatly interested in what he is doing, he may be able to concentrate regardless of the environment, but if a textbook has to be read, then any sound may assume the dimensions of that emanating from a drag-strip racing car.

There is considerable evidence to suggest that noise can have certain economic effects. Colony (1967) has demonstrated that property adjacent to limited-access highways may be as much as 30 to 40 percent cheaper than comparable property located elsewhere. The percentage decrease tends to be greater for high-value properties than for those at the cheaper end of the scale. Similarly, houses adjacent to airports may be 10 percent less in value than those located elsewhere, and the rents of apartments adjacent to elevated rapid-transit lines may be less than those located a block away. Certainly, the negative environmental impact of elevated rapid-transit facilities can have a severe effect on the business immediately adjacent.

Noise pollution is, then, prevalent in urban areas, but some would contend that noise inside buildings is more harmful than that emanating from external sources. People living in apartment buildings complain more than anything else about unwanted noise. Offices are full of little noises, such as scraping of chairs, casual conversations, and so forth, which, apart from typewriters and office machines, help to create a tense environment. But urban transport seems to be the most prevalent source of environmental pollution, and, as a consequence, it deserves special consideration. This consideration is directed toward urban transport as a whole, for improvements in transport within cities may well have other environmental benefits as well.

THE URBAN TRANSPORTATION PROBLEM

For most individuals living within urban areas, the urban transportation problem is the major and continuing source of frustration. This frustration is directed in particular toward the automobile, for it is this means of transportation that promises the greatest freedom and excitement, but at the same time offers a major constraint. The result has been on the one hand passionate outcries against the further proliferation of use of automobiles and the construction of highways, while on the other hand the per capita use of automobiles has been steadily increasing. These passionate outcries often assume an emotional tone: "In short, the American has sacrificed his life as a whole to the motorcar, like someone who, demented with passion, wrecks his home in order to lavish his income on a capricious mistress, who promises the life he can only occasionally enjoy" (Mumford, 1961, p. 235). Less emotionally, but in more specific terms, it is often considered that "the price being paid for the privacy and convenience provided by the automobile is enormous" (Hamilton and Nance, 1968, p. 19). This price includes congestion, high accident rates, air and noise pollution, the dominance of the city by expressways and freeways, and urban sprawl. However, it may well be that we blame automobiles for too much (Jacobs, 1961), and what is really needed is a clear assessment of urban transportation requirements and trends. To do this we must of course discount one element in all the automobile passion, and that is the advertising-induced perception of it as a fountain of youth, a sex symbol, or a surrogate for power.

Two elements of transportation are available for the movement of cargo (people or goods) around urban areas. One element involves private transportation facilities such as automobiles, trucks, and self-locomotion on foot. The second element, public transportation, is available in a variety of forms such as taxis, buses, and rapid transit. We have previously observed how these facilities are used in the modern North American city and that even when public transportation was dominant there was a tendency toward decentralization of the population. This decentralization has made it possible for people to obtain larger living spaces and more modern housing. Previous discussion has also indicated that there are two major constituents of the daily flow of people within urban areas. One is the peak travel and the other is the off-peak travel, and the solution to the transportation problem lies in an assessment of both these components.

Off-Peak Travel

Off-peak travel involves the greatest number of hours in the day. The people involved in this movement are usually concerned with a wide variety of activities, such as shopping and social visiting. With the spreading out of the urban population and the decentralization of many urban activities, the origins and destinations of these trips appear to be extremely dispersed, and as a consequence it can be argued that the best means of transportation available is the automobile. This contention is reinforced by an analysis of personal preferences, which indicate that even when there is public transportation available, there is a much greater tendency to use a private means of transportation. Furthermore, it appears that movement around urban areas during these off-peak hours is not really all that difficult. Even in large urban areas, such as Los Angeles, it is quite possible for people to move from one part of the city to another in a short space of time using the automobile and freeways.

One problem that emerges during these off-peak hours involves the provision of parking space in areas where the destinations of many individuals are concentrated. Parking, however, appears to be a necessity for which individuals in an affluent society, such as that in North America, are prepared to pay; and if necessary, to pay quite high rates. Those individuals who cannot afford to pay high rates simply do not frequent or visit only occasionally those areas in which parking is expensive. If business does find that high parking rates reduce the level of demand for its services, then it will have to subsidize the parking or persuade the local government that it is a social good to provide free public parking subsidized through taxes. Furthermore, if the residents of an urban area consider that adequate parking should be provided, and that it should be free, then they too can persuade the local government to provide these facilities.

A second consideration, which is common to both peak and off-peak travel, is the increasing costs of fuel. Following the initial shock of high prices and gasoline shortages, many were predicting severe impacts on existing patterns of automobile usage. While there is no doubt that the shortages did drive some commuters from their automobiles and into public transportation (where it was available), and recreational or shopping travel was reduced, the overall effect does not appear to be greatly changed travel behavior. After all, how can travel behavior change if the disposition of land uses and alternate forms of travel do not alter? The modern dispersed metropolis is a product of decades of decentralization and modern travel patterns are the products of years of automobile use. The most obvious trend as a result of increasing cost of energy is away from large cars with big engines to smaller cars with smaller engines. But, even then, North American intermediate-sized cars are huge by normal European standards. One could therefore predict that increased energy costs and gasoline shortages will have little impact on activity patterns within urban areas, for current patterns can be maintained with more efficient and smaller vehicles.

Peak Travel

Urban transportation becomes a problem when rush-hour traffic occurs. We have previously noted that this rush-hour traffic occurs for approximately five hours in any given day, and it consists of individuals going to and from work. The problem becomes particularly acute in those areas where there is a large number of work places concentrated in a few locations. Under these conditions the desire of many individuals to use automobiles results in severe congestion on highways and traffic jams of mammoth proportions on the peripheries of business areas.

It could be considered that an urban area with severe traffic jams has three choices. The first is to permit traffic jams to continue; that is, do nothing. The second is to build more highways, so that there is enough space for vehicles to enter and leave places of work. The third condition is to provide some other means of transportation that will cater to the vast number of individuals that need to be moved.

Alternative 1: Do Nothing

The first alternative, to do nothing, has as many repercussions as doing something. For example, if nothing is done, the electorate may become so frustrated as to demand reform and vote against the administrative structure that it considers responsible for the situation. The economic impact may also be dramatic, for continuous overcrowding could well cause a stagnation of activity in the area concerned because people will refuse to work and firms to locate or expand within the congested area. Thus the "do nothing" alternative is a negative attitude, and in a philosophical sense is antiurban in that the chief function of urban areas is to encourage and promote contact between people.

Alternative 2: Private Transportation Only

The second alternative involves the assumption that people do not want to use public transportation at all. The question that arises then concerns the possibility of building enough freeway and highway space to cater to rush-hour automobile traffic without creating severe traffic jams and long delays. If areas of employment are dispersed, this may well be a solution, though of course it is an expensive solution, particularly when rights of way have to be obtained. If people really wish to use their automobiles to go to and from work, it would seem reasonable, given modern construction techniques, to build double-deck and triple-deck expressways or freeways in dispersed urban areas, such as Los Angeles.

Urban areas with great concentrations of employment in particular locations, such as in central business areas, cannot, however, adopt a private transportation solution because there would be no way possible of creating enough freeway space. The question that arises then concerns the degree to which this heavy traffic can be handled while still using as much private transportation as possible.

Personal Transit

One private system recently proposed is called "personal transit," which, in effect, operates like a railroad but transports individuals or groups to stations of their own selection. The vehicles used for this transportation are similar to automobiles, but they are electrically propelled and run on tracks called guideways, which seem to be rather similar in concept to those used in Autopia in Disneyland. It is envisaged that "the passenger will enter a waiting car at a station, touch his destination on a keyboard and then be carried to the designated station with no further action on his part" (Hamilton and Nance, 1968, p. 21). As the guideways would be designed to carry both private automobiles and public transit cars, it would be possible to extend the system out to the suburbs and control the entire flow and speed through the use of computer-controlled flow mechanisms.

For the suburbs it is suggested that individuals could be taken to the guideway stations by using the dial-a-bus system, which would in effect be a large taxi that could be called to a person's home by dialing the rapid-transit station. As the calls come in, a computer would continually optimize the route pattern of the buses in the system. For short-distance travel in high-density central areas, the best mode of transportation probably would be on foot or moving sidewalks. This would greatly speed up the flow and reduce the density of traffic and eliminate the need for taxis and buses for short-distance travel. It is suggested that people could be encouraged to use the public transit capsules by charging exorbitantly high amounts to private automobiles using the guideway system and for parking.

Alternative 3: Public and Private Transportation

The third alternative is public mass transportation, for this involves the use of facilities that are capable of moving vast numbers of people within very limited spaces and in a short space of time. There are several difficulties, however, that emerge in the use of these systems in North America. The first is that some urban areas that have not developed public transit systems, and particularly mass-transit systems, find it very expensive to adopt their use once the urban area has reached sizable proportions. For example, Los Angeles considered spending 2.5 billion dollars on a rapid-transit–commuter-railroad system that was rejected by the electorate. Furthermore, it is questionable that such expenditures are justified in large decentralized urban areas, particularly when the private transit system previously mentioned may well be much less costly to institute. For those urban areas that have mass-transit systems, it may well be worthwhile to consider renovating and modernizing these systems out of public funds in order to make them more efficient.

One of the reasons why these systems have to be modernized is that they are considered by the vast majority of individuals to be an inferior form of transportation and are therefore used only when the automobile alternative proves for some reason or another to be impossible. If highways are not constructed to serve areas of dense employment and mass-transit facilities are available, then mass transit becomes the only alternative; but this alternative is really the same as the first, the drawbacks of which we have already discussed.

Thus for those urban areas that have mass transit, the aim should be to improve the service, make it more comfortable, and try to raise it from an inferior good to one that is comparable to the use of the automobile. In the first instance, public transit will have to be made more personal, more pleasing, and physically safe for travel. But unfortunately, even if this were accomplished, the problem remains that some people dislike traveling with individuals that they consider to be of a lower socioeconomic status or of a different ethnic group or color. This latter problem can be solved only through time and really involves the reeducation of the urban population to perceive public transit in a favorable light. Of course, elements of personal transit can also be incorporated, such as the dial-a-bus system in the suburbs, which will also help to overcome the reluctance of most North Americans to walk more than three blocks.

It therefore seems highly desirable to have a mixture of public and private transportation within any urban area. This can be viewed not only as an economic-optimum solution but also as a social-optimum solution. Many people in the urban community cannot for some reason or another drive or own automobiles, such as the elderly, schoolchildren, and the unemployed, and these people simply must be provided with a rational alternative. If no alternative is provided, then, in terms of social welfare, some form of private transportation should be provided for them; otherwise a large segment of the urban population will be prevented from moving around the urban area. There have been many designs for the solution of urban transportation problems in different cities, all of which involve the outlay of large sums of money; but in no case are the sums of money excessive when compared with other expenditures by central governments (such as defense).

Balanced Systems: Spreading the Peak

Urban transportation systems should, therefore, be designed to respond to two features. One is the fact that there are various densities of demand, and in the most dense areas high-capacity carriers are more efficient than those of low capacity. Conversely, in less dense areas, low-capacity carriers are preferable, for high-capacity vehicles become economic dinosaurs in situations of this type. The second feature is the peaked nature of much urban travel, and any transport system should attempt to cater to this peak.

The matter of various densities in origins and destinations can be facilitated if a balanced system is developed. There are four basic modes of transportation that can be incorporated into a balanced design. These are:

1. The private automobile for travel in low-density areas and for "captive" car users elsewhere. It is envisaged that the size of cars will be reduced as a result of high costs of energy, and this should help toward ameliorating some parking problems. Smaller engines can be made reasonably pollution-free.

2. Public transportation in the form of buses, trolley coaches, and streetcars, to facilitate movement to, within, and from medium-density sections of urban areas (10,000 to 25,000 persons per square mile) and downtown areas. These are more ubiquitous means of transportation, and can be used for crosstown travel as well as periphery-downtown travel.

3. Rapid transit to cater to long- and intermediate-distance movements between medium-density and downtown areas, as well as short-distance movements within the CBD. Rapid-transit lines are expensive to construct, but if they can be built or expanded when city pride is at stake (such as for the Olympic Games), then they can be designed for implementation without this type of excuse. The Bay Area Rapid Transit System (BARTS), connecting downtown San Francisco with other communities around the bay area, is a good example of a new facility designed to connect urban communities in a regional framework.

4. Suburban railroad lines to provide transportation from fairly low-density suburban areas to the CBD. Automobiles and buses can provide access to the suburban terminals.

Of course, the four-mode balanced system can be implemented only in very large metropolitan areas, for in smaller cities and towns the first and second elements are all that may be required.

The peaking problem cannot be solved by providing more and more facilities. The magnitude of the situation is indicated for rapid transit in Figure 16.3, where the arrivals during the evening rush hour at the King Street (Toronto) subway station are about six times the normal level. This is an extreme case, for the average over the downtown stages is about three times the normal off-peak traffic. The fact that most people arrive at and leave their work at about the same time results in overloads on all modes of transportation, and this form of congestion can be resolved only by spreading the peak. It would be economically unjustifiable even to try to cater to the peak. Many places of work are, however, finding it possible to stagger work hours, but the scheduling of the stagger is quite complex and requires a detailed analysis of the major foci of peaking. Relatively small changes in work hours, of at most about 30 minutes, can result in great reductions in the magnitude of congestion. The scheduling of the stagger should therefore be planned, for office complexes can work against each other if the decisions are unilateral. Pricing, as a form of peak-spreading, is more complex, and the results are probably not commensurate with the costs of implementation.

The problems of environmental pollution and transportation therefore require careful planning over large regions. The methods for implementing planning designs and control legislation need to be enforceable and to have teeth. Policies and legislation of this type have proven difficult to enact in North America, but it is necessary to forgo certain individual and corporate freedoms in order to achieve the necessary environmental benefits and transport efficiencies. These freedoms will have to be forgone because urban societies need a higher level of organization and control in order to survive.

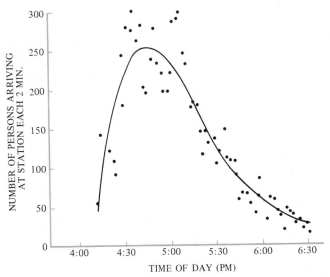

Fig. 16.3. The peaking of evening rush-hour arrivals at the King St. subway station, Toronto. (*Source:* Plewes and Yeates, 1972, p. 209.)

17
URBAN HOUSING PROBLEMS AND PUBLIC POLICY

The one urban problem that, over the last 150 years, has repeatedly attracted the attention of urban reform movements in North America is the housing conditions of the urban poor. Despite the concern and reforms, one has to take only a cursory glance at the housing stock in the inner city of any large North American city to see that the "housing problem" is still with us, and that a substantial number of people continue to live in housing conditions that can be described only as deplorable, given the general level of national affluence.

In the United States, the passage of the National Housing Act on 1934 marked the beginning of a federal commitment to provide decent housing. In 1949 the U.S. Congress made the commitment explicit in a now famous statement:

> the Congress hereby declares that the general welfare and security of the nation and the health and living standards of the people require . . . the realization as soon as is feasible of the goal of a decent home and suitable living environment for every American family.

In an attempt to attain this goal, a bewildering array of housing legislation has been enacted in the past 25 years. Although the overall condition of the nation's housing has improved, within many cities there are individual neighborhoods and areas within the inner city where the housing situation continues to deteriorate. In addition, it is sometimes unclear as to the extent to which public policy has helped achieve the overall improvement in conditions.

In the latter part of this chapter we shall attempt to evaluate the impact of public policy on the housing problem. However, in order to understand the problem, we must first sketch its empirical dimensions and explain why the private housing market has failed to produce "a decent home and suitable living environment for every American family."

THE COMPONENTS OF THE HOUSING PROBLEM

In 1970 there existed in the United States 68.6 million dwelling units. At the same time, there were 62.9 million households in the nation, counting both families and unrelated individuals. Therefore, at least in the aggregate, it seems that the housing problem was not one of an absolute shortage of housing units. But figures on the number of dwelling units say nothing of the quality of the units, nor do they indicate the level of satisfaction their occupants derive from their use.

Most housing analysts identify three main aspects of the housing problem. First, there is still a substantial number of people who are living in poor-quality housing measured by absolute standards. Second, minority groups suffer relatively severe housing problems as a result of the existence of a dual housing market based on discrimination. Finally, housing provided by the private market is too expensive for low-income families. Let us look at each of these three facets of the problem in turn.

The Absolute Quality of Housing

When we talk of housing quality we are really trying to measure the quality of service offered by a given residential unit. Housing quality is extremely difficult to define, let alone measure, because quality is obviously multidimensional in character. A housing unit can be classified as substandard or of poor quality if it is structurally unsound or in a state of disrepair. Similarly, it can be substandard if the unit is lacking in basic amenities, such as plumbing and heating equipment. Even though a unit might be structurally sound and contain the basic amenities, it might still be deemed inadequate if it is overcrowded. Structural defects, lack of amenities, and overcrowding are directly related to the internal characteristics of the housing unit itself. A broader and more realistic definition of housing quality would be one that incorporated the myriad factors associated with the attractiveness of the neighborhood as a place to live. Such a definition would encompass measures of the physical and social environment within the neighborhood as well as its accessibility to employment, shopping, and recreational facilities.

The only source of comprehensive data on housing quality is provided by the Census of Housing, and this pertains only to the quality of housing services provided by the unit itself and not to neighborhood amenities.

Data on the overall physical condition of housing are the most subjective and the least reliable of the census data pertaining to quality. In the 1950 census, housing units were categorized as either "dilapidated" or "not dilapidated," and in the 1960 census as either "sound," "deteriorating," or "dilapidated" on the basis of the census enumerator's appraisal of the extent of disrepair. The 1970 census was conducted by mailed questionnaire and the topic of overall housing condition was omitted because of the large degree of subjectivity required to make a judgment. The accuracy of the judgments of housing quality made by census enumerators have been questioned. For example, the 1961 Canadian census reported the following figures for housing in six low-income tracts in Montreal: 7 percent in need of major repair, 30 percent in need of minor repair, and 63 percent in good condition. A more detailed city survey of the same six tracts conducted a year later found that 16 percent were "not inhabitable," 48 percent were "repairable," and only 30 percent were satisfactory—a very rapid rate of deterioration (Dennis and Fish, 1972)!

To measure adequacy of basic amenities the census records the presence or absence of a long list of amenities such as water supply, bathroom facilities, lavatory facilities, method of heating, and cooking facilities. In general, plumbing facilities have been singled out as the most relevant amenity measure for an overall evaluation of housing conditions. The census and housing agencies in the United States combine information on structural condition and information on plumbing facilities to classify units as either "standard," in which case the unit is not dilapidated and contains all enumerated plumbing facilities, or "substandard," which includes units that are dilapidated and/or lacking one or more of the plumbing facilities.

Even if a housing unit is structurally sound and contains all the basic amenities, it is still inadequate for its present tenants if it is overcrowded. To measure overcrowding, the census divides the number of persons by the number of rooms in each dwelling unit to provide a persons-per-room ratio. A unit with a ratio of 1.01 or more generally is classified as overcrowded.

Statistics on housing conditions such as those discussed above may be used both to measure changes over time in the quality of the housing stock and to compare housing conditions between geographical areas or groups of people. Table 17.1 contains selected data on housing conditions which summarize recent trends in the quality of housing in U.S. cities. The table contains the absolute and relative numbers of overcrowded and substandard housing units (units that lack complete plumbing facilities or are judged dilapidated by the enumerator) in metropolitan areas as recorded by the census in 1960 and 1970. According to these generally accepted measures of housing conditions, the quality of urban housing has shown a marked improvement in recent years. For all categories there has been a significant decline in the percentage of both overcrowded and substandard units. Although the table reveals that conditions are improving just as fast in black-occupied housing as in white, the condition of black housing is still far inferior to that of white housing, particularly in terms of the proportion of overcrowded central city units.

Racial Segregation and Housing Problems

The differences between the quality of white-occupied and black-occupied housing which were noted in the previous section are one sympton of another aspect of the housing problem: the prevalence and persistence of racial segregation in the housing markets of most, if not all, U.S. cities. Another manifestation of racial segregation which impinges upon the housing problem is the question of price discrimination.

In most U.S. cities the housing decisions of white households coupled with the actions of real estate entrepreneurs result in a housing market that is effectively divided into at least two distinct submarkets: a white housing market and a black housing mar-

Table 17.1. HOUSING CONDITIONS IN METROPOLITAN AREAS BY RACE, 1960 AND 1970

| | Overcrowded (Occupied by 1.01 or more persons/room) | | | | Substandard[a] (Dilapidated or lacking complete plumbing facilities) | | | | Percentage Change in Proportion 1960–1970 | |
| | 1960 | | 1970 | | 1960 | | 1970 | | | |
	Number[b]	%[c]	Number[b]	%[c]	Number[b]	%[c]	Number[b]	%[c]	Overcrowded	Substandard
All Races										
SMSA's	3,694	10.3	3,304	7.5	3,576	10.0	2,417	5.5	−27%	−45%
Central city	2,023	10.6	1,761	8.2	1,988	10.4	1,300	6.1	−23%	−41%
Outside central city	1,671	9.9	1,542	6.9	1,588	9.5	1,117	5.0	−30%	−47%
White										
SMSA's	2,762	8.5	2,486	6.4	2,549	7.8	1,764	4.5	−25%	−42%
Central city	1,358	8.3	1,126	6.4	1,293	7.9	862	4.9	−23%	−38%
Outside central city	1,404	8.7	1,360	6.4	1,256	7.8	902	4.2	−26%	−46%
Black										
SMSA's	811	24.1	818	17.3	1,027	30.5	653	13.8	−28%	−55%
Central city	618	22.8	635	16.6	694	25.6	438	11.4	−27%	−56%
Outside central city	193	29.5	183	20.2	333	51.0	215	23.8	−32%	−53%

[a] In 1960 the number of dilapidated units were enumerated directly by the census; in 1970 the number of dilapidated units were estimated by the census from other data.
[b] In thousands.
[c] Percentage of all occupied units.
SOURCES: U.S. Bureau of the Census, Census of Housing, 1960 and 1970.

ket. It has been suggested that the existence of two distinct submarkets has led to blacks' and whites' paying different prices for structurally identical rental units in similar neighborhoods. King and Mieszkowski (1973) offer three explanations for such price differences based on racial discrimination and market segregation. The first explanation is that white landlords and real estate brokers are reluctant to rent or sell to blacks and will do so only if they receive a markup of the price charged a white tenant. This can be defined as pure racial price discrimination in housing, since blacks and whites purchase identical bundles of housing services, but blacks pay more.

A second reason why the prices of structurally identical housing units differ within a housing market is that blacks and whites may have a preference for the racial composition of their neighborhoods. From the assumption that blacks and whites have tastes for integration and segregation respectively, it follows that a consistent pattern of spatial price variation will occur across housing markets even when all other factors are held constant. Specifically, white rents on the white side of the black-white boundary will be lower than in the interior of the white area, while black rents on the black side of the boundary will be higher than in the interior of the black area.

The third explanation is that segregation effectively closes the white market to increases in black housing demand and funnels the increased demand into a submarket that has a relatively small and fixed housing stock, thus leading to an increase in the price of black housing in the ghetto relative to white housing in all white areas.

There have been a number of empirical studies designed to measure the extent to which segregation influences housing prices. In general, the evidence points to the conclusion that in fact blacks do obtain fewer housing services per dollar spent than whites do.

One study found that renters paid 8 percent less and homeowners paid 5 percent less in all-white residential areas than in all-black areas, even after the influences of a large number of structural, neighborhood, and public service variables were held constant (Kain and Quigley, 1970). Another found that blacks pay 2 to 5 percent more than whites for housing of any given quality (Muth, 1969), while King and Mieszkowski (1973) found that in New Haven there was evidence of substantial price discrimination (7 percent along the boundary between black and white areas) and that blacks in the heart of the ghetto pay 9 percent more than whites in the interior of all-white areas for equivalent rental dwellings. That segregation and not pure price discrimination accounted for the latter figure was implied by the fact that whites in the ghetto paid the same prices as blacks for housing.

The impact of the changing racial composition of a neighborhood on housing costs and property values has also received considerable attention. The empirical evidence gathered in a number of studies tends to refute the popularly held belief that an influx of blacks into a neighborhood reduces property values except where panic selling by whites creates a sudden excess supply and a short-term decrease in prices (Muth, 1969; Kain and Quigley, 1970).

The Cost of Housing

There are two aspects of expenditures and costs that impinge upon the housing problem: the proportion of family expenditures required to attain suitable housing and the absolute cost of new housing.

For a considerable proportion of the low-income urban population the housing problem is one of cost of housing when matched against low incomes, although in many instances low incomes and high costs may be combined with poor-quality housing and/or overcrowding. Statistics on housing expenditures as a fraction of household income (called *shelter/income ratio*) are compiled to reveal whether some households spend excessive proportions of their incomes to obtain adequate housing. For many years a shelter/income ratio of 25 percent has been viewed by policy makers and economists as the critical value beyond which families suffer hardship.

Low-income North Americans spend a far larger proportion of their income on housing than do high-income North Americans. Table 17.2 gives shelter/income ratios for Canadian families in 1969, and the statistics are similar for the United States. Fifty-eight percent of Canadian families in the bottom quintile (bottom 20 percent) of the income distribution spent more than 25 percent of their income on shelter, while 90 percent of the families in the top quintile of the income distribution spent less than 20 percent of their income on shelter. Many low-income families are now paying far more for housing than they can actually afford, with the result that money is shifted from food and other essential family needs to meet the cost of housing.

Another major source of dissatisfaction with housing in recent years has been the high cost of new construction. The cost of new housing is so high that it has been estimated that in the United States only families in the upper third of the income distribution can afford to live in new housing. For example, in 1967 the President's Committee on Urban Housing estimated that a new two-bedroom apartment built without subsidy in Detroit, the city with the lowest costs among the large cities, would have had to rent for 2,719 dollars a year. If 25 percent is accepted as a reasonable shelter/income ratio, then a family required earnings of 10,876 dollars per year to live in such an apartment. Yet in 1967 only 34.5 percent of families living in central cities had incomes in excess of 10,000 dollars. Therefore, approximately two-thirds of the families living in large U.S. central cities are unable to afford new commercially financed housing. The situation in Canada is even worse; it was recently estimated that less than 5 percent of the families living in Metro Toronto could afford to purchase new single-family housing in the first half of 1974.

The inability of most families to afford new housing obviously determines the way in which new construction is absorbed into the housing stock; new housing, unless subsidized by government, enters the market near the upper end of the rent distribution and causes a series of adjustments by which older housing filters down into lower rent classes. Therefore, a very large proportion of the housing units catering to the low-income market are old filtered-down dwellings, a fact that to a large degree explains the poor quality of much low-income housing. This and other features of the housing market which tend to produce poor-quality low-income housing are discussed in more detail in the following section.

THE HOUSING MARKET

The general spatial arrangement of land uses and areas of varying residential quality within cities has been described in an earlier chapter. Here we wish to examine how the housing market functions to produce the mixture of "good" and "bad" housing that is found in every North American city. This question will be addressed in two ways. First of all, a general "adaptive" model of the urban housing market is discussed to demon-

Table 17.2. NUMBER OF CANADIAN FAMILY UNITS WITH SPECIFIED SHELTER/INCOME RATIOS, ALL COMMUNITIES AND ALL FAMILY TYPES, 1969

Income Distribution (quintiles)	Income Interval $	Average Income $	Family Units (thousands)		Shelter/Income Ratio				
					Over 50 %	50–40 %	40–25 %	25–20 %	Under 20 %
1st	under 3,000	1,858	No.	976.8	141.8	168.5	262.1	200.0	204.5
			%	100	14	17	27	20	21
2nd	3–6,000	4,541	No.	1,282.3	18.1	50.9	201.9	185.0	828.3
			%	100	1	4	16	14	65
3rd	6–8,000	6,974	No.	1,025.6		17.9	124.7	108.8	775.2
			%	100		2	12	11	75
4th	8–12,000	9,705	No.	1,523.8			90.1	152.2	1,281.6
			%	100			6	10	84
5th	over 12,000	16,657	No.	1,046.0				109.1	936.9
			%	100				10	90
All			No.	5,854.5	159.9	237.3	678.8	755.1	4,026.5
			%	100	3	4	12	13	68

Source: Dennis and Fish (1972), p. 60. Compiled from Statistics Canada, "Family Expenditures 1969," unpublished.

strate how housing quality responds to changes in supply and demand at a macro level. This is followed by a more detailed examination of some of the actors in the urban housing market and the ways in which they influence the quality of individual housing units and individual neighborhoods within the city. However, before we embark on any analysis of the housing market, it is important to discuss briefly some of the difficulties that are encountered when the housing market is analyzed in a normative micro-economic framework; difficulties that stem from the rather special characteristics of housing when it is viewed as a commodity.

Imperfections in the Housing Market

There is a variety of housing characteristics that a potential buyer or renter of housing considers when selecting a particular dwelling unit as a home. These characteristics include not only the internal characteristics of the housing unit, such as space and household equipment, but also such factors as the accessibility of the unit to employment, shopping, and recreational opportunities, its proximity to undesirable features of the urban environment such as sources of pollution and high-crime areas, and the general social and physical environment of the neighborhood in which the residence is located. Such characteristics serve to describe a set of uses to which a residential site is put by the occupant and can be collectively used to measure the use value of a given dwelling unit. The use value of a given property is different for different households, since different households attach varying degrees of importance to each of the factors that go to make up the use value. Similarly, the use value of a given property to a given family will vary over time, since one of the most important factors influencing use value is stage in the life cycle.

In addition to a use value, the dwelling unit also will have an exchange value, since housing is a scarce resource and households must compete in the housing market for the limited available supply. Exchange value is determined via the price mechanism that underlies the housing market (Harvey, 1972). In economic analysis it is usually assumed that use value and exchange value are equivalent at the margin, by which it is meant that the purchaser or renter when determining exchange value will bid exactly that extra quantity of money which represents the value to him of obtaining an extra quantity of use value, be it extra space, accessibility, or a slightly better neighborhood. However, this assumption is reasonable only if we have a market situation that is kept in a perfectly well-ordered state. While in reality there is no such thing as the economist's perfect market, there are several important reasons for asserting that the housing market is more imperfect than most other commodity markets.

1. A house is not a mobile commodity. A given housing unit is fixed in space and therefore is highly susceptible to external economies and diseconomies, since its spatial relationships with other elements of the urban environment may change although no change occurs in the unit itself. In addition, the immobility of supply necessitates a search by demand for that supply and in effect the housing market has no marketplace.

2. Shelter, which is one of the principal uses to which a housing unit is put, is nonsubstitutable. Everyone must purchase the commodity irrespective of price.

3. Housing is one of the most durable of commodities, and this means that present housing needs must always be substantially met out of a supply designed for past housing needs.

4. Housing is a commodity that changes hands infrequently, and when an exchange takes place, the transaction costs involved, in the form of lawyers' fees, mortgage fees, and real estate fees, are relatively high. Therefore, the marketing mechanism contains a barrier to free exchange.

5. Because housing is such a permanent feature of the built environment and because it is relatively expensive, housing is itself a form of stored wealth which individuals use to preserve their own equity. This is a very important point. It means, for example, that the purchase of a house is not geared simply to use values, but also to its future market exchange value. It becomes important for the individual property owner to preserve the market value of his house because it represents much of his lifetime savings. It also means that a certain proportion of the housing stock will be "used" by investors, landlords, and real estate operators to generate income or increase their net worth. Mortgage rates, interest rates, tax depreciation laws, speculation, and future expectations with respect to use values all affect the housing market in ways that have nothing at all to do with the actual use value of the property to the person living in it.

Therefore, housing is a rather special nonhomogeneous commodity and there are difficulties in analyzing the housing market within a normative microeconomic framework.

Demand and Supply Aspects of Housing Quality

In the previous section it was pointed out that since housing is relatively expensive and durable, it follows that, at any specific time, almost the whole of the demand for housing must be met from the existing stock of housing. In an average year, new construction adds only 2 to 3 percent to the nation's housing stock, and part of that simply offsets demolitions. In addition it was noted that, because of the high cost of new construction, much of the new housing added in any given year enters the market at the upper end of the price range. However, adjustments on the supply side occur not only through the addition of newly constructed units but also through adjustments in the quality of existing units and hence in their rent levels. In other words, the existing housing supply is "adapted" to the pattern of housing demand.

For example, as housing is abandoned by one income class as it moves on to newer housing, it will generally be adapted by alteration of its quality to meet the needs of another, lower income class. Since shelter is a nonsubstitutable commodity, the basic function of the housing market is to match households with the existing stock of housing, and since income is one of the principal determinants of housing demand, this amounts to matching up a distribution of households, differentiated by income, with a distribution of housing units, differentiated by cost. As new construction enters the market at the upper end of the price scale it attracts tenants from the upper levels of the income distribution and this occasions a whole series of readjustments in the matching of households to housing units. The complex process by which this rematching takes place has been referred to in Chapter 10 as filtering. While the term "filtering" tends to be used in a variety of contexts by housing analysts, here it is used to describe the process whereby housing formerly occupied by a higher income class is vacated and becomes available at a lower cost to tenants with lower incomes.

Assuming no change in population or the level of household incomes during the process, filtering occurs in the following way: It begins with a higher income group moving into newly constructed housing. The owners of the units that are vacated will have to reduce rents in order to attract tenants from the next lower income class. The tenants attracted will, in turn, vacate other units whose rents, in turn, will be reduced to attract a still lower income class. Thus a whole series of rent reductions and concomitant moves will take place, and housing previously occupied by one income class will filter down to the next lower income class.

How are owners able to reduce their rents? Just as tenants can move from one rent class into the next, so owners can move their buildings from one rent class to another by remodeling, by dividing units, or by reducing the levels of operating and maintenance costs for the unit. This will lower the quality of housing services produced by the unit. Normally the owner of a unit will expand his operating and maintenance costs as long as each dollar of additional expense generates more than a dollar of additional gross income from rents. Therefore, one way of adapting a unit to meet the rent-paying ability of a low-income household is to reduce the levels of operating costs and investment in repairs and hence the quality of housing services offered. Probably the most obvious way of moving a unit to lower rent levels is to reduce the size of the unit through remodeling.

Filtering is often suggested as the best method of improving the housing conditions of the poor. While filtering is capable of improving housing standards in terms of the permanent physical characteristics of a unit, it cannot improve housing standards as they are related to maintenance and operating costs, since these vary directly with the rent level the owner is attempting to establish. Therefore, improvements in housing standards which occur through filtering are likely to be in terms of the unit's physical design and equipment rather than in terms of the level of maintenance and operating services offered. In addition, if one thinks in terms of occupancy rather than physical standards, units that filter down may well move into the "overcrowded" category. Thus, viewed from the supply side, the urban housing market is bound together by the adaptability of its structures.

Turning to the demand side, the consumer will generally trade off quality against quantity when choosing a home. For a given rental outlay a household can obtain a smaller unit of higher quality or a larger unit of lower quality. Since quality and quantity compete for the consumer's housing dollar, if attempts are made to improve quality, such as strict housing code enforcement, without changing the level of housing expenditure, it will result in increased overcrowding. Conversely, the problem of overcrowding could be reduced by increasing the supply of low-quality, low-priced housing. Thus, two of the major objectives of public policy in the field of housing, improved quality and reduced overcrowding, come into direct conflict with each other, given the constraint of a fixed level of household income and rent-paying ability.

As noted earlier, one of the principal determinants of housing demand is household income. The response of housing expenditures to changes in income is measured by the elasticity of demand, which is defined as percentage change in expenditure divided by percentage change in income. Empirical studies suggest a very strong relationship between income on the one hand and housing quality and overcrowding on the other (Muth, 1969). While these results suggest that an overall increase in real income will markedly reduce the incidence of substandard and overcrowded housing, they also imply that substandard housing will continue to persist where poverty persists. Consequently, it could well prove to be extremely difficult to eradicate inadequate housing from the central city with its concentration of low-income households.

Housing Market Actors and the Quality of Housing

In the preceding section we discussed how the interplay of housing demand and supply at the macroscale results in a low-income inner-city housing stock that in large part consists of filtered-down, poor-quality housing. At the microscale economic forces also govern the actions of a number of individual actors in the housing market. Such actors can have a profound impact on housing quality, and their actions often help to explain variations in housing quality on a local scale, such as between neighborhoods within the central city or even between streets within the same neighborhood. Let us consider how the actions of some of the principal actors in the housing market—property investors, real estate agents and developers, and financial institutions—can affect housing quality.

There are two alternative strategies that a property investor interested in making money from housing can adopt. Either he can purchase a property outright, using his own capital, or he can buy a property with the aid of mortgage financing and a minimum of his own capital. If he adopts the first strategy, he will earn an income from the capital invested in the form of rent. If he adopts the second strategy, the rent is used to service the mortgage, allowing the investor to increase the net worth of his holdings over time. The choice of strategy has important implications for the future quality of the property involved. If he adopts the first strategy, the investor is seeking to maximize the current income generated through rent over a fairly short time horizon, and as a consequence will tend to minimize operating and maintenance costs, which in turn will lead to the fairly rapid deterioration of the property. Alternatively, the choice of the second, more long-term strategy will result in a high level of upkeep and maintenance.

The investor's choice of strategy is dependent upon a number of factors, including the general availability of mortgage financing in the neighborhood in which investment is being considered, the degree of risk associated with investment in the neighborhood, and the relationship between operating and maintenance costs and the income levels of the typical tenants who live in the area (Harvey, 1972). Lack of mortgage financing, high levels of risk resulting from anticipated social or planned change in the neighborhood, and the ability to maximize the difference between rent and operating costs will all lead to the choice of the first strategy. It is interesting to note that the conditions leading to the adoption of the first strategy and the subsequent deterioration in the housing stock are precisely those most generally encountered in central-city low-income neighborhoods.

It has also been demonstrated that, in a neighborhood consisting of rental property owned by a number of different property investors, it is always to the benefit of any individual landlord to underinvest slightly in his property relative to every other investor in the area (Davis and Whinston, 1961). Obviously if all investors act in such an economically rational manner there will be quite rapid deterioration in the housing stock, since each will be competing with the others to cut down on investment. It is noticeable that blocks of rental housing completely under the control of one or two landlords are usually kept in substantially better condition than comparable blocks in which property is held by numerous landlords, each of whose behavior is somewhat unpredictable.

Therefore, in a large measure the poor quality of inner-city rental housing is not the result of excessive exploitation by slum landlords; the fact that slum housing is not excessively profitable is supported by evidence such as the high rate of abandonment of housing in the inner city cited by Harvey (1972). Rather, it results from rational profit-maximizing behavior on the part of investors who, because of the set of conditions that exists in the inner-city housing submarket, must seek to maximize their profits through extracting the maximum current income over a short-run period instead of increasing their net worth through the purchase, maintenance, and improvement of the property, as would be typical in more affluent, stable neighborhoods where the investor feels more confident about the future security of his investment.

Real estate agents receive income for their services as intermediaries between buyers and sellers by charging transaction fees, which are usually a percentage of selling price. Since the real estate agent's income depends largely on his sales volume, there is a built-in incentive for him to encourage increased turnover in the housing stock. Increased turnover can be stimulated by either ethical or unethical means. One of the best examples of the latter is the process of block-busting, which occurs when a real estate agent works with a developer to assemble land for redevelopment and which can have a dramatic effect upon housing quality in the chosen area.

The following is a brief synopsis of the block-busting process as described in a document designed to help Toronto citizens resist such artificially induced deterioration in their neighborhood (Pollution Probe, 1972). Through a real estate agent the developer begins to purchase properties as they become available in an area he has selected for future development. The real estate agent or a hired manager then begins to operate the acquired homes as low-income apartments or rooming houses. The properties begin to deteriorate fairly rapidly, since few or no repairs or maintenance are performed. The long-time owner-occupiers in the neighborhood see the area deteriorating. At this stage the real estate agent begins to call on owners to persuade them to sign options, or he buys and gives a mortgage back to the vendor. This minimizes the cash outlay on the part of the developer. As more owners move out, their houses are turned into rental units for deterioration. As deterioration continues, the area becomes a fire risk, and as fire insurance companies refuse to renew fire insurance policies, more owners are persuaded to sell out to the developer. Toward the end of the land assembly the developer may even begin to demolish housing in order to encourage the remaining owners to sell. The overall effect of such a process is the rapid deterioration of a neighborhood in a relatively short time and the development of concentrated pockets of extremely poor-quality housing within the city.

Financial institutions such as banks and savings and loan associations control and regulate the flow of funds into the housing market, and therefore can have a significant impact on the quality of housing through their spatial investment strategy within the city. In a recent study of mortgage markets and the investment strategies of various financial institutions in Baltimore, Harvey and Chatterjee (1974) concluded that there was a highly structured relationship between household characteristics, particularly income, and the availability of mortgage funds in appropriate price categories. The large institutions avoid direct involvement with low-income and old housing because the latter are characterized by high risks and low rates of return.

The withdrawal or denial of mortgage funds to a particular neighborhood can effectively kill the property market in that neighborhood. Owners wishing to sell homes find it impossible to sell to a new owner-occupier because the would-be buyer cannot obtain a mortgage. Therefore, the owner is forced either to become a part-time landlord himself or to sell the house to a professional property investor, who in turn is forced to adopt the strategy that involves the short-term maximization of income through rent, which, as we have seen, leads to deterioration. Similarly, homeowners or businessmen in the neighborhood who wish to carry out extensive remodeling or repairs to their properties find it impossible to secure loans or second mortgages, and the result is further deterioration.

This problem is particularly severe in U.S. cities, where the health of the low-priced housing market appears to be directly tied to the fate of the state savings and loan institutions servicing particular neighborhoods. State S & L's are oriented to local neighborhoods and operate on a nonprofit basis. As Harvey and Chatterjee (1974) note, if these institutions collapse, or come to have strong profit motivation, then the housing market in the price range below 15,000 dollars in the neighborhood suffers irreparable damage, since the larger financial institutions are reluctant to operate in this market.

URBAN HOUSING POLICY IN NORTH AMERICA

Now that the nature and some of the causes of urban housing problems have been identified, attention will be focused on the efforts of public policy to solve the problems. There is now fairly general acceptance in North America of the need for public intervention in the private housing market, stemming either from the fact that people find the housing conditions of the poor morally shocking in an affluent society or because they fear that such conditions are a threat to the very existence of that society. Such public concern with urban housing standards has produced a wide variety of government housing programs. The primary purpose of this section is to examine the development of housing policy in the United States, to describe some of the more important federal housing programs, and to assess their impact. In order to place the discussion in a more general context, the first section describes a general typology of national housing policies based upon the extent and nature of government intervention in the private market, and the final section briefly examines solutions to the housing problem derived from analytical viewpoints that are fundamentally different from the liberal interventionalist paradigm that underlies current North American policy making.

National Urban Housing Policies

In a detailed study of European housing policy, Donnison (1967) identified three general approaches to tackling housing problems which had been adopted by governments.

1. The assisted free-market approach, associated with countries in the early stages of urbanization and industrialization, such as Turkey, Greece, and Spain. The goal of the assisted free-market approach is simply to increase total housing production, with little concern paid to the type of housing produced. This goal is attained through a variety of incentives to private industry and institutional reforms that enable the government to channel more funds into housing. Programs such as tax subsidies, mortgage insurance schemes, the creation of special mortgage lending institutions, and direct government lending are used to encourage the private housing industry to increase its output of new housing.

2. Social housing programs combined with free-market production, associated with the more advanced industrial societies such as Great Britain and Switzerland. The state continues to rely on the private market to produce the majority of new housing and intercedes only to aid those who cannot afford privately produced housing. Government social housing programs are designed to service specific groups in the population and are usually viewed as exceptional and temporary interventions in the free market. The state is neither assumed to be responsible for the housing conditions of the whole population nor expected to develop and implement a long-range, comprehensive housing policy.

    3. Comprehensive housing policy. In a few countries, such as Sweden and France, the state has expanded its activities in the housing market to a point at which it can be regarded no longer as simply intervening in an otherwise normal market. Such governments now shape and control the housing market to such an extent that their housing responsibilities have assumed a national and comprehensive form, and housing policies are integrated with other social policies in order to attain an overall set of national goals.

    In both the United States and Canada there are a large number of government housing programs, but it is virtually impossible to find a well-articulated statement of an overall national housing policy. The lack of an overall policy is underscored by the title of a recent report on Canadian housing: *Programs in Search of a Policy* (Dennis and Fish, 1972). However, upon examining past and current housing legislation, one is led implicitly to the conclusion that U.S. and Canadian housing policy is still by and large a purely assisted free-market approach and includes only a very few social housing programs.

    Housing programs that have been introduced in both the United States and Canada to overcome imperfections in the private housing market are many and varied. While some programs, such as building codes, antidiscrimination laws, and zoning ordinances, are purely regulatory in nature, the majority of programs have entailed subsidies designed to achieve one or more of the following objectives.

1. Increase the supply of housing
2. Reduce the price of housing
3. Reduce the cost of construction
4. Increase the availability and reduce the cost of housing credit
5. Increase the purchasing power of housing consumers

Any comprehensive examination of the entire range of North American housing programs is impossible in the present context, but, the following section contains a brief description and evaluation of some of the more significant U.S. housing programs introduced in recent years.

Postwar Federal Housing Programs in the United States

    Postwar housing programs in the United States can be divided into three chronological periods. Before 1960 urban renewal and low-rent public housing programs were the principal instruments of national housing policy. These programs essentially consisted of subsidies linked to new construction, which in turn was linked to slum clearance. Subsidies were provided to the supplier of housing rather than to the consumer. The second phase, which came into vogue in the 1960's and includes programs such as

NHA, Sections 221(d)3, 235, and 236, severed the tie between subsidies and slum clearance, but, in the sense that benefits for specific income classes were still specifically linked to occupancy of newly constructed housing units, the programs were still very much part of a new construction strategy and therefore strongly resembled earlier and more conventional public housing programs.

The third and most recent period, while producing little in the way of concrete legislation, can be characterized as one in which thinking on housing policy has been directed away from supply-side subsidies linked to the construction of new units toward demand-side subsidies linked to low-income households which will enable them to compete more effectively in the market for existing units.

The principal programs in each of these three phases are discussed in the ensuing sections. Each program is discussed in terms of its initial objectives, its actual mechanics in terms of such items as participation, qualification, and size of subsidy, and an evaluation of its success in attaining its objectives. This discusssion draws upon an excellent compendium of U.S. housing programs to which the reader seeking additional information is referred (Aaron, 1972). The reader interested in a similar survey of housing programs in Canada is referred to Dennis and Fish (1972).

Public Housing and Urban Renewal

Strictly speaking, the term "public housing" refers only to units that are owned and operated by local public housing authorities. The first federal involvement with public housing dates back to the 1930's, when public housing projects were initiated with the primary aim of stimulating employment rather than from a concern with housing conditions. Under the 1937 Housing Act the federal government agreed to contribute up to 100 percent of the capital costs for public housing projects, thus enabling local housing authorities to set low rent levels. While, at the outset, rents were set to cover operating and maintenance costs, rapid increases in these costs led to the amendment of public housing legislation in 1969 to provide federal subsidies for operating costs. Households wishing to gain admittance to public housing units must have incomes below an established maximum (the maximum income for admittance varies locally but is generally only marginally above the federally defined poverty line), and as soon as their incomes rise to 25 percent above the maximum level for admission they must vacate the units.

These income qualifications, which are designed to confine program benefits to the lowest income group, have led to a number of problems, since they foster racial and economic segregation within neighborhoods. In addition, since the construction of public housing is at the discretion of local housing authorities, the fact that the suburbs have shown a marked reluctance to participate in the program has led the majority of public housing to be built in the central city. Thus public housing programs have helped to maintain economic segregation at the macrogeographic scale as well as creating segregation at the neighborhood level. To place the public housing program in perspective, it might be noted that according to the 1970 census there were just under 900,000 units of public housing in existence, which constituted less than 1.5 percent of the nation's housing stock.

In an effort to overcome the problem of de facto segregation produced by large publicly owned multifamily projects, a leasing program (Section 23 of the Housing Act) was introduced in 1965. Section 23 allows local housing authorities to lease units in privately built and operated buildings and sublet them at reduced subsidized rents to the usual public housing recipient. The purpose of this program was to scatter public housing tenants among conventional private buildings and existing neighborhoods rather than concentrate them into segregated and socially stigmatized housing projects. It was intended that 30 percent of the funds to be used in expanding the stock of public housing units would be used for acquiring leased units.

In the early 1950s there was a move to hold down federal expenditures on public housing in order to curb inflation, and government programs were directed toward attracting private capital and investment into the housing sector. This is another instance where housing programs were used to tackle cyclical macroeconomic problems in the nation's economy. Title 1 of the 1949 Housing Act enabled the federal government to channel subsidies through local agencies to make the private redevelopment of blighted areas economically feasible.

Under Title 1 local public redevelopment authorities assembled and cleared chosen sites and then sold the land at a loss to a private developer. The federal government paid two-thirds of the difference between the cost of acquiring, clearing, and servicing the site and the price at which it was sold for redevelopment. In order to qualify as a renewal project the site had to be in predominantly residential land use either before or after redevelopment, but not necessarily both. Therefore, the program was designed to increase new private construction in the older and more run-down sections of the central city by reducing the cost of construction through the subsidization of the cost of the land component. A secondary purpose of the program was the improvement of housing conditions through the removal of slum housing on the one hand and the stimulation of the filtering process through the construction of new middle- and upper-income housing units on the other. In practice, far more sites were in residential use before redevelopment than after, and urban renewal became characterized by the demolition of low-income, low-quality residential neighborhoods and their replacement with commercial buildings or private middle- to upper-income rental units. In fact, slum clearance and urban renewal had the effect of actually reducing the total supply of housing, and of low-income housing in particular. For example, between 1949 and 1968, 439,000 housing units were demolished under Title 1 renewal schemes, and during the same period only 124,000 new housing units were constructed.

As a result, in the late 1960s urban renewal programs came under increasing criticism, with critics charging that the programs were resulting in bulldozed low-income neighborhoods, creating innumerable social problems for displaced low-income families, and that public money was being used to subsidize private commercial redevelopment. Consequently, in 1969 the Congress amended the urban renewal legislation to require that each redevelopment authority provide one new standard low- or moderate-income housing unit for each such unit demolished. However, by 1970 urban renewal activity had been reduced to a very low level in most cities.

Subsidized Private Housing

In the mid 1960s, as disaffection with the urban renewal and public housing schemes became prevalent, a series of subsidy programs was introduced which, although still aimed at stimulating new private construction, severed the connection between federal subsidies and slum clearance. By and large these programs, including Sections 221(d)3, 235, and 236 and the rent-supplement program, were aimed at reducing rent or ownership costs so that moderate- or low-income households could afford to live in new or rehabilitated housing of reasonable quality. Since the programs contained subsidies to private developers, they received widespread political support from the construction industry, and program funding was comparatively more generous than it had been for the public housing programs.

Section 221(d)3, often referred to as the "below market interest rate" (BMIR) program, was introduced as part of the 1961 Housing Act and was a principal tool of federal housing policy until it began to be phased out after the introduction of Sections 235 and 236 in 1968. The program was designed to reduce the rental costs of new, privately constructed units built for middle- and lower-income families by subsidizing interest rates. Funds were supplied through regular financial institutions to qualified builders at a BMIR of 3 percent and the Government National Mortgage Association (GNMA) then purchased the mortgage from the financial institution at the current market interest rate. The benefits of the program were in the form of reduced rents for tenants made possible by the subsidized interest rates; for example, if market interest rates were at 9 percent the loan at 3 percent made possible an estimated 37 percent reduction in rent.

Section 221(d)3 was aimed at assisting households with incomes in the 4000–6000-dollar range. The maximum family income limit for admission to units built with BMIR funds varied geographically, but were on the order of one to one and a half greater than those for admission to public housing. In general, the program had little impact on the nation's housing problem, with only about 150,000 housing units constructed under it. Critics of 221(d)3 argued that in practice it was a very shallow subsidy program that benefited the lower middle class but did nothing for the poor, and that it was inflexible in that the subsidy to a family with an income of 10,000 dollars was identical to the subsidy to a family with an income of 2,000 dollars. The main difficulty with the program from the government's point of view was that the full cost of housing subsidized under 221(d)3 appeared as a budget expenditure as soon as GNMA purchased the mortgage and was not spread over the life of the subsidized unit, as in the case of public housing.

Initially the rent-supplement program requested by President Johnson was intended to correct some of the deficiencies of Section 221(d)3. Specifically, it was intended to reach households whose incomes were too high to qualify them for public housing but too low to enable them to afford housing built under 221(d)3. Under the proposed plan, the federal government would pay property owners the difference between the fair market rent and the share paid by the tenant, which was to be 20 percent of the tenant's income. The program was enacted only after significant modification as part of the 1965 Housing and Urban Development Act. In its final form the program was restricted to families with incomes below rather than above limits for entry to public housing, the tenant's share of rent was fixed at 25 percent of income rather than 20 percent, and the tenant's share was to constitute at least 30 percent of fair market rents.

The chief innovation of the rent-supplement program was the fact that for the first time subsidies were graduated according to the recipient's income. As the tenant's income rose, his rent would increase until it reached market level, but with rising income the tenant would not have to vacate the unit as he would in public housing. It was hoped that projects built under the rent-supplement program would promote economic heterogeneity within projects by allowing a mixture of newly admitted households with very low incomes and older established families with somewhat higher incomes. Like 221(d)3, the rent-supplement program turned out to have limited appeal, with only about 45,000 units constructed in the first five years of the program and with the principal beneficiaries being families who were on average poorer than those living in conventional public housing.

Twin programs, Sections 235 and 236 of the National Housing Act, directed at home ownership and rental housing respectively, were enacted in 1968 and eventually replaced Section 221(d)3 as the government's principal housing policy instrument. In many ways the two programs resemble the rent-supplement program as it was originally proposed. To be eligible for assistance under Section 236 a household must have an income that is less than 135 percent of the public housing admission income level. The tenant pays at least 25 percent of his income in rent and the government pays a subsidy for each tenant which is equal to the lesser of (a) the difference between the market rent based on the mortgage costs actually incurred and the rent that would result if the mortgage rate were only 1 percent, or (b) the difference between market rents and 25 percent of the tenants's income. This means that the government subsidy declines as the tenant's income increases.

Section 235 is similar in design to 236 but is geared to home ownership rather than rental accommodation. Subsidies are paid to homeowners to help them meet the monthly carrying costs of a conventionally financed mortgage on either a new or existing single-family dwelling. The homeowner commits at least 20 percent of his income toward the cost of carrying the mortgage and the federal government supplies a subsidy that is equal to the lesser of (a) the difference between the homeowner's monthly payments and the actual monthly carrying costs including insurance and property tax, or (b) the difference between the cost if the mortgage rate was 1 percent and the monthly carrying cost not including property taxes and insurance.

Therefore, Section 235 is designed to help lower-income families become homeowners by subsidizing their mortgage payments and keeping their monthly housing payments at a manageable level. In addition, the government hopes that if it guarantees a market for low-cost housing through such a subsidy program, then builders will respond by building more homes in the lower price range. In general, to qualify for assistance under Section 235 a family must have an income that is less than 135 percent of the maximum income limits for initial occupancy of public housing. However, in order to foster economic integration, Section 235 administrators can allocate up to 20 percent of their available funds to families whose incomes are above the 135 percent limit but below 90 percent of the income level allowable for occupants of Section 221(d)3 projects for moderate-income families.

Data assembled by Aaron (1972) suggest that in 1971 most families that benefited from Sections 235 and 236 programs had annual incomes in the 4000–8000-dollar range and subsidies accounted for 40 to 50 percent of the actual cost of housing. At the outset, both programs received substantial funding and stimulated a considerable amount of subsidized construction. For example, in 1971 alone approximately 130,000 units were subsidized under each program. For a variety of reasons, most of the new housing generated by the program was located in the suburbs, whereas units funded in the central cities were largely older, renovated buildings.

"Demand Side" Subsidies

In the early 1970s the new construction subsidy programs, particularly 235 and 236 programs, came under renewed criticism. The federal government was concerned about rapidly increasing expenditures on housing programs while at both the local and national levels there were a number of well-publicized scandals centered on the quality and profit margin of housing constructed under 235 and 236. In addition, existing programs were not having an appreciable impact on the housing problems of the poor with incomes of less than 5000 dollars and were tending to accentuate rather than diminish residential segregation by income class; for example, new construction under Section 235 was concentrated in the suburbs, thus encouraging the lower middle class to leave the inner city, with the result that the inner city became more uniformly poor. Housing analysts, both inside and outside the government, began to have serious doubts about the general validity of the new construction policy implicit in the subsidy programs introduced in the 1960s. This growing discontent with existing housing programs culminated in the 1973 decision of the Nixon administration to freeze most federal housing programs until a reappraisal of the rationale underlying the programs had been undertaken.

Although no concrete legislation has been forthcoming, it is evident that recently there has been a marked shift in thinking with respect to housing subsidies. The shift has been away from the idea of linking subsidies to new construction, and toward the more conservative notion (in the sense that it would reduce direct government intervention in the market) of a "demand side" subsidy to poor households. Such a subsidy, which could be in the form of either vouchers or a direct cash transfer payment, and which is similar in concept to the federal food stamp program, could be spent on old, new, or renovated housing of the household's choosing. A "demand side" subsidy is most clearly consistent with the adaptive model of the housing market discussed earlier and rests on the assumption that if subsidies in the form of rent vouchers are used to increase the purchasing power of low-income households to an adequate level, then the private market will respond and supply adequate standard-quality housing.

Proponents of housing allowance programs argue that such programs would be far more equitable than the present system of subsidies tied to specific housing units, since under the latter a relatively small number of families receive relatively large benefits and the majority of low-income families, equally qualified, receive nothing, whereas the former would provide smaller benefits but would reach all eligible households. In addition, since subsidies paid to families are geographically mobile, such a program would prevent funds from becoming locked into one neighborhood and thus would avoid the risk of serious public investment errors, such as the disastrous Pruitt-Igoe public housing project in St. Louis. Critics argue that a housing allowance program is likely simply to drive up housing prices, since it will increase demand while having no direct impact upon supply. One way of trying to avoid simply driving up prices would be to tie the housing allowance program to an effective rent-control program, but recent experience with rent control in New York City and Vancouver is not encouraging.

ALTERNATIVES TO A LIBERAL INTERVENTIONALIST HOUSING POLICY

The housing subsidy programs described above have formed the backbone of federal housing policy in the United States for the last 20 years. Collectively, they can be viewed as constituting a typically liberal interventionalist housing policy. Implicit in this policy is an unquestioned acceptance of the private housing market as an indispensable institution and implicit a steadfast faith in the "filter-down process" for improving the housing conditions of the poor. Government intervention in the free market has been largely limited to subsidies to private builders in order to overcome imperfections and assist the market to operate more smoothly. Thus, subsidies were first directed at stimulating new construction and hence filtering, and more recently housing allowances have been suggested as a means of increasing the effective purchasing power of low-income households in the private housing market.

It is extremely important to realize that the prevailing liberal response to the urban housing problem represents only one general analytic view of the problem. In concluding, it might be instructive to examine briefly how the analyses and proposed solutions of the housing problem change when viewed from different analytic perspectives, specifically perspectives derived from, on the one hand, a conservative view of society, and, on the other hand, a radical view.

Analyses of the housing problem that are derived from a conservative view of society, exemplified by writers such as Banfield (1974) and Kohler (1973), argue that housing problems are the result of too much government intervention in the private market rather than too little. Government regulatory devices such as zoning, building and housing codes, and rent controls are seen as factors that increase the cost of housing, block the efficient operation of the market, and prevent the private market from meeting the low- and moderate-income families' housing needs. The conservative analyst places more faith in the free market than his liberal counterpart, and views the filtering process as the only efficient mechanism for solving the housing problems of the poor. He argues that building public or subsidized low-income housing is inefficient, since its effective life is much shorter than that for new housing constructed for the top of the price range. Similarly, the conservative argues that income supplements to low-income families will not solve the problem either, since they would simply push up the price of housing still further and the supplement would be creamed off as excess profit. In summary, conservatives view the solution to the housing problem as lying in the removal of government restrictions on the private market, which would enable the market to produce housing at a low enough cost to satisfy the demand from low-income households.

The radicals' analysis of urban housing problems, as exemplified by Gordon (1971), is based on a relatively simple argument: that the structure of North American social and economic institutions makes it impossible to solve the absolute and relative physical housing problems within the context of these institutions. They argue that the housing market is based upon the concept of scarcity, and in order to sustain the market a scarcity of good housing is maintained through institutional controls, and thus the housing market will continually spawn inadequate housing. The radical analysis suggests that only radically increased efforts by the government to provide adequate housing for the poor will have any real impact on solving the problems, and that this is unlikely to happen since the radical theory of the capitalist state implies that the government will not directly aid the poor.

Liberals and conservatives claim that such arguments are absurd, since the government has already provided substantial housing assistance to the poor. The radical response is that housing programs have never been directly concerned with the poor.

The early programs were used to provide a countercyclical category of direct federal expenditure while the liberal subsidy programs have been used to the primary benefit of three groups: (*a*) the financial institutions, by eliminating risk on capital and guaranteeing profitable returns on investment; (*b*) the construction industry, by providing additional profits through government servicing of land or subsidies to build low-income housing; and (*c*) the middle class, who seem to have derived the most benefits from NHA financing schemes. Similarly, with the public housing program

> Congress has never appropriated enough money to make public housing work, local public housing authorities have not even spent what little money the federal government has authorized, and those to whom our institutions have given control over public housing have no intention of redirecting the program in order to improve its contribution to the low income housing stock [Gordon, 1971, p. 361].

It has been charged that local housing commissioners act as a brake on programs since they represent a microcosm of middle-class, white views about the poor, their housing, and the responsibilities of government (Hartman and Carr, 1969).

Since the radical views the housing market and related capitalist institutions as the fundamental cause of the housing problems of the poor, solutions to the problem lie in the replacement of capitalist institutions by socialist institutions. One radical solution would be the abolition of private property rights with respect to housing and land. Housing would be produced and controlled by the state and allocated to households on the basis of need. Partial steps toward a solution which have been suggested or tried in various countries include the municipalization of all rental housing, as in Cuba, since this is the area where most of the problems of low-income families occur (Jenkins, 1972), and the large-scale public ownership and control of land (Massey et al., 1973), of the kind that has occurred on a smaller scale in Sweden, Holland, and Canada.

Since this chapter has been concerned with housing problems and housing policy as it has evolved in North America, it has been concerned almost exclusively with the kind of liberal-conservative analysis and prognosis which dominate not only political thought but also a large amount of intellectual analysis in North America. It is as well to remember that there are alternative solutions based on alternative modes of analysis and views of society, and to bear in mind that "it is not the experts, but the laymen, who hold the key to the urban future. The basic decisions to be made are political ones" (Richardson, 1972, p.8).

18
POLITICAL FRAGMENTATION AND FISCAL SQUEEZE

The policies needed to solve the kinds of problems discussed in the previous chapters are increasingly governmental ones; solutions require action by some government entity, whether it be at the federal, state, or local level. In many cases these may require little more than new rules or the alteration of existing ones, such as building codes and zoning ordinances. Increasingly, however, they require larger investments in facilities and services, income transfers to needy people, and the payment of subsidies to achieve specified goals (Netzer, 1974). The extent to which these are possible depends not only on the willingness of governments to implement corrective policies, but in large part on their abilities to pay the substantial and mounting costs involved. In the last resort, then, the problems of providing adequate levels of public services in cities and the solutions to many of today's pressing urban problems are linked to the fiscal situations of particular local governments.

The problem is not, however, only an economic one; it is also to an increasing extent a geographical one, since local government activity is very closely tied to the kinds of spatial frameworks within which funds are raised and decisions made. In almost all cities, this framework is highly fragmented and confused, since the decentralization of people and activities outward from the old core cities has brought about a corresponding decentralization and proliferation of local government units. The proliferation of local government entities, the associated fragmentation of decision making, and the marked disparities in the distribution of needs and resources are therefore some of the major characteristics of present-day metropolitan structure. In this chapter we turn to a discussion of some of the salient features in the spatial organization of local governments in urban regions and the problems of financing local government activity, and to questions of fiscal and administrative reform in the metropolitan context.

THE CHANGING ROLE OF URBAN GOVERNMENTS

Although the role of the federal and state or provincial governments in solving urban problems has increased dramatically in the last decades, the task of providing services in cities and solving their problems is still today very much the main responsibility of local governments in North America (Table 18.1). In fact, the relative importance of local governments as providers of urban services is greater in Canada and the United States than in any other major country. This stands in stark contrast to the situation at the turn of the century, when local governments had generally small budgets and played a relatively minor role in the economic, cultural, and social life of cities. The one exception was in education. School districts had been created as independent units in the political structure of most states at an early date because of the conviction that public education should have its own financial base and be independent of the policies and politics of other local government units, such as the municipalities and counties.

There was generally little desire on the part of urban residents to participate in local government, which as a result was delegated to those individuals who were prepared to undertake the administration of the developing urban areas. In many instances, these individuals were prepared to undertake the responsibility in order to attain the rewards associated with positions of power. This power was maintained in a comparatively democratic system through the judicious deployment of patronage, influence, and bribes. This was, for example, the heyday of Tammany Hall in New York City, the leaders of which tended to regard the direction of the city as a personal commercial venture and "the style of the time was to regard governmental programs as sources for exploitation and plunder" (Wood, 1961, p. 5).

At that time, therefore, it was not considered that local governments—or for that matter national government—should guide and stimulate the development of the city. Although a body of laws had been growing concerned with restricting private property rights, particularly those relating to offensive trades and industries in residential areas, these laws were often minimaly enforced and frequently ignored. In fact, the laissez-faire doctrine as applied to government of any form was "the less government, the better," and, as enunciated in President Grover Cleveland's second inaugural address, it was generally considered quite proper that while "the people should patriotically and cheerfully support their government, its functions do not include the support of the people."

A Period of Change

From 1910 to 1935, a substantial change occurred in the powers of local government as their service functions were significantly expanded and extended into new areas. At the same time a concomitant change occurred in the urban community toward local government. Continuing urban expansion, and changes in technology and the national economy, translated themselves into "more public expenditures, more taxes, [and] more governmental intervention" (Wood, 1961, p. 9). Accompanying the widespread use of the automobile, fundamental changes were taking place in the form and structure of cities, as was noted in Chapter 8. The need arose for extensive programs dealing with the construction of new streets and roads, street lighting, water lines and sanitary sewers, storm drainage systems, electricity networks, and so on—and the responsibility for much of this activity lay with local governments. In addition, the continually rising levels of incomes and expectations resulted in a greater demand for schools and hospitals, for better law enforcement and fire prevention; and local governments were increasingly being forced by the electorate to encourage and prompt the private sector to help provide facilities in addition to those publicly owned or operated.

A major stimulus to the changing power and responsibility of local government was the Great Depression, which shattered established procedures for government action. The economic collapse increased the demand by the electorate for positive action by all levels of government to alleviate the crisis. These pressures were felt most acutely at the local level, and the inherent weakness of the administrative and financial structure of local government rapidly became apparent. Most local governments were in a relatively weak financial position, and the capital costs incurred in the growth of their service function had largely been financed by large-scale borrowing. In fact, between 1913 and the early 1930's the yearly interest payments alone on loans to local governments in the United States rose from 167 million dollars to a staggering 1.5 billion dollars. It was as a result of these weaknesses that the actions of the federal government in Washington had to be extended in order to alleviate the ever increasing problems, for the financial power of most local governments was severely limited.

The Present Situation

Despite considerable spatial variation in the extent of their obligations and responsibilities, particularly between Canada and the United States, each local government has its own corporate powers, which most commonly include the right to sue and be sued, the right to obtain and dispose of property, and the authority to provide services and to enforce regulations, especially zoning ordinances and building controls. Local governments have the power to raise revenue by imposing charges or collecting taxes. Many municipalities now function as agents of social change through the operation of fair housing and public accommodation laws (Lockard, 1968). Today, then, more than ever before, local governments in both Canada and the United States wear "the powerful mantle of public authority, including the power of financial exaction from the citizenry and the ability to affect people's lives beneficially or harmfully" (Bollens and Schmandt, 1975, p. 42).

Since World War II, both the financial responsibility and the number of local government units in urban areas have been increasing at a rapid rate. In the past 25 years, state and local government has been the fastest growing sector of the national economy. Whereas the United States' Gross National Product (the national output of goods and services) is three times larger than it was 20 years ago, state and local government expenditures have increased sixfold in the same period (Netzer, 1974). Today nearly two-thirds of the total expenditure occurs in metropolitan areas. This rise in public expenditure is related to rising price levels, the increased population of urban areas, and the problems these have created—but for the most part because the scope and quality of state-local government services have been greatly expanded. For an increasingly large segment of the urban population, the activities of local governments are decisive factors in determining the quality of life in the city.

LOCAL GOVERNMENT EXPENDITURES

In 1970–1971, governments in the United States spent a total of 250 billion dollars for civilian purposes; that is, excluding the costs of defense, space and international programs, veterans' aid, and related activities. Well over 75 percent of this amount was spent in urban areas or was made on behalf of urban-area residents (mental hospitals in the countryside serving urban people is a good example). In spite of the growing involvement of the federal and state governments, local governments are still directly responsible for about 40 percent of all civilian public expenditure—a figure that will most certainly rise in the coming decade.

Expenditures for selected urban services, and the way these were financed in 1970–1971, are shown in Table 18.1. The various activities are classified in a way now conventional among economists, who distinguish between three major objectives in the use of taxes and expenditures (Musgrove, 1959):

1. The reduction of economic fluctuations in the economy (omitted from Table 18.1)
2. Income-redistribution activities
3. Resource-allocation activities

Following Netzer (1974), a third category has been added in Table 18.1, the expenditures for public schools—not because the objectives are different, but because public education is both an income-redistribution and a resource-allocation activity. The responsibilities of local governments in financing urban services are striking. After grants from federal and state sources are deducted, they end up financing from their own resources about a quarter of the income-redistributive activities, just over one-half of local school costs, and nearly all of the resource-allocation activities. In all, a formidable task of fund raising is placed on the shoulders of urban local governments in the United States. In 1973 they raised by various means approximately 500 dollars per capita of the urban population (Netzer, 1974), and the situation is roughly similar in Canada. The scope and quality of urban services in the North American city are consequently very much the results of local government initiative, and marked variations in the levels of services provided are increasingly related to the ability to raise the money.

LOCAL GOVERNMENTS IN ABUNDANCE

The growing involvement of local government in the life of the city has been accompanied by a marked growth and proliferation in the kinds of local government areas. In general, younger metropolitan areas have fewer units and simpler spatial patterns than older ones. Political fragmentation is generally more pronounced in the older cities of the heartlands than it is in the hinterland cities, although regardless of location, the complexity of urban government is, as a general rule, directly related to population size. For example, in 1972 the 27 SMSA's with fewer than 100,000 inhabitants had an average of 20 local government units of all kinds. In contrast, the 33 SMSA's with more than one million inhabitants averaged 268 separate jurisdictions. The most prolific SMSA was Chicago, with a total of over 1170 units, followed by Philadelphia (852), Pittsburgh (698), New York (538), and St. Louis (483). By comparison, Los Angeles, with a population of 2.8 millions in 1970, had only 232 local government units. There are, of course, many discrepancies. Metropolitan Baltimore, with over two million inhabitants, had only 29 local governments in 1972, whereas—to take an extreme case—Madison, Wis., with a population of about 290,000, had over 80. Despite these exceptions, in general the pattern of local government in urban areas is today fantastically complex.

The numerical profusion of governmental entities in urban regions is made even more complicated by the many kinds of jurisdictions that occur. First there are the elected governments of the municipalities (including villages, incorporated towns, cities, and boroughs), towns and townships—which are a distinctive feature in New England and the Middle and North Central census regions—and the counties. Second, there is a multiplicity of special districts—the ad hoc special-purpose bodies such as school, fire, police, health, library, zoning, and housing districts. These are by far the

Table 18.1.   THE FINANCING OF SELECTED URBAN SERVICES, 1970–1971

Services	Expenditures by Governments Actually Providing the Services (in billions)			Source of Funds		
	State	Local	Combined	Federal[a]	State	Local
Income Redistribution						
Welfare	$10.5	$ 7.7	$12.2	54%	35%	11%
Health	5.4	5.8	11.2	7	47	46
Housing	0.5	2.5	2.6	63	5	32
TOTAL	$16.4	$16.0	$26.0	—	—	—
Public Schools						
TOTAL	$ 0.5	$41.3	$41.8	10	39	51
Resource Allocation						
Police, corrections, and fire service	$ 2.0	$ 7.4	$ 9.4	2	22	76
Transportation	0.3[b]	3.4	3.7	5	11	84
Water supply & treatment	N.A.[c]	6.1	6.1	8	2	90
Local parks & recreation	N.A.[c]	2.1	2.1	2	5	93
Sanitation	—	1.4	1.4	—	—	100
Libraries	0.1	0.7	0.8	10	13	77
TOTAL	$ 2.4	$21.1	$23.5	—	—	—

[a] Includes only direct federal aid to state and local governments.
[b] Excluding highways.
[c] The state government expenditure for urban water supply and for urban parks is small and difficult to separate from published data.
SOURCE: Adapted from Netzer (1974), Table 8.2.

most numerous in urban areas today (64 percent of the total number of local government entities in the United States in 1970), and despite the trend of consolidation in recent years, the number of special districts has been growing at an alarming rate as the scope of public service provision has been enlarged. The special districts add to the confusion of urban spatial organization because they typically cut across differing social and economic groups, and overlap with each other and the underlying layer of other political divisions. Most local government units are relatively small in population size, area, or both; large units (e.g., counties) are the exception to the rule. The confusing and highly fragmented pattern of local government in the North American city is, then, very much a "geo-political science fiction" (Soja, 1971).

FINANCING LOCAL GOVERNMENT ACTIVITY

National, state, and local governments are very keen competitors for the tax dollar, and over the years a rough division of revenue sources has developed among the three tiers of government. The federal government in both countries raises the bulk of its revenue from personal income taxes, corporation taxes, and payroll taxes. It is able to impose relatively high rates of taxation of these kinds because the national territory is completely under its jurisdiction. Smaller geographical units, such as the states, provinces, and especially the cities, cannot take full advantage of this source of revenue in an open economy in which people, businesses, and capital are free to move among its various geographical parts. The nonuniform levy of a substantial income tax by states or cities would certainly give rise to marked tax differentials in different parts of the country, and people and businesses would undoubtedly "vote with their feet" by moving in large numbers to those places where tax advantages were greatest.

As a result, the lowest tiers of government have had to look to other sources of revenue. The states and provinces rely heavily on sales and gross receipt taxes. Local governments are eventually left with taxes on property as the main source of revenue, and since the turn of the century the general property tax has been acknowledged as the almost exclusive domain of local governments. The two other important sources of local revenue for urban governments are various kinds of nonproperty taxes (e.g., municipal payroll and sales taxes) and service or user charges. In both the United States and Canada, then, urban governments have rather limited powers of taxation, and the other ways of raising funds locally are restricted and severely constrained. Nevertheless, local governments in metropolitan areas are still able to raise considerable sums as shown for selected central cities in Table 18.2.

The Property Tax

The general property tax is essentially agrarian in origin and has provided the historical basis of local government support since colonial times in the United States. It is still the most productive source of public revenue in North America after federal income and excise taxes. Although its importance to local governments has declined relatively in recent decades because of the increase in tax-sharing with higher tiers of government, it nevertheless still accounts for about 75 percent of all local tax revenues and about 40 percent of the aggregate incomes of urban governments. The relative importance of the property tax varies markedly from city to city, and often between different municipalities within the same metropolitan area. In New England the property tax alone provides between 80 and 90 percent of all local revenues (Table 18.2), whereas in smsa's with payroll taxes—for example, Pittsburgh—it accounts for only about 60 percent of total revenue (Bollens and Schmandt, 1975). In 1973 nearly 66,000 local government units, about 18,000 of them in metropolitan areas, used the property tax as the dominant source of revenue to finance the local share of public school costs and to pay for a major portion of the local share of most other governmental activity (Table 18.3).

Taxes levied on property are of course a good and sound measure of taxation as long as the value of property is fairly assessed and that property itself is a true measure of an individual's or family's wealth. But increasingly throughout North America this is not so, particularly when taxes are also imposed on income at the state or provincial and federal government levels. Local property taxes are therefore decidedly unpopular, and in a recent survey they were thought to be the "most unfair tax in the fiscal system" (Advisory Commission on Intergovernmental Relations, 1972).

The property tax is unpopular because it is imposed at relatively high rates in real money terms. Although bills typically average only between 2 and 3 percent of the market value of property, this corresponds to a flat-rate income tax, for example, of 10 percent or more after exemptions and in urban areas to a sales tax of 25 percent or more. It is consequently a decidedly regressive tax—that is, the burden as a percentage of income is much higher for low-income people than for the wealthy, because housing is such a large component of consumer spending for low-income groups. For example, whereas the property tax on owner-occupied single-family houses averaged 4.9 percent of family income in the United States in 1971, it was *twice* as high for the lowest income homeowners as it was for those with incomes above 10,000 dollars, for whom the tax averaged less than 3.7 percent (Netzer, 1974). It is perhaps not surprising, therefore, that in many urban areas it is the middle- and lower-income homeowners' votes

Table 18.2. SELECTED CENTRAL CITY GOVERNMENT FINANCES, 1972

Source of Revenue[a]

City	Total General Revenue	From State and Local Governments	From Federal Government	Property Taxes	Sales and Gross Receipts	Other	Charges and Miscellaneous
New York City	7,538.9	3,447.7	132.3	2,011.5	744.6	506.8	696.0
Chicago	740.3	80.4	107.3	274.0	128.6	46.7	103.3
Los Angeles	594.3	84.9	15.7	177.8	97.8	61.9	156.3
Philadelphia	705.1	65.4	156.4	115.6	2.3	258.1	107.3
Detroit	500.7	77.7	96.1	144.3	10.7	93.1	78.8
Houston	154.0	2.6	4.0	68.5	38.2	3.1	37.5
San Francisco	531.8	146.2	39.0	191.7	45.3	11.9	97.7
Boston	402.4	72.4	18.4	247.9	–	3.3	60.4
St. Louis	162.8	10.6	8.6	35.5	24.9	50.3	33.1
Seattle, Wash.	138.0	28.7	13.4	23.7	18.1	11.1	43.1

[a]All figures in millions of dollars.
Source: U.S. Bureau of the Census, *Statistical Abstract of the United States, 1973*, Table 684. (Washington, D.C.: U.S. Government Printing Office, 1973.)

that are perpetually rejecting new school bond issues and other new expenditure proposals that might cause an increase in the taxes levied on property.

As a high percentage of annual housing costs to consumers, the property tax suffers from another important disability: it has a deterrent effect on the consumption of
housing, particularly where housing conditions are at their worst, in the central cities.
This situation is aggravated by the high proportion of rented units. Landlords can, and
by and large do, pass the burden of the tax on to renters by increasing rents. Unlike
homeowners, however, renters cannot offset the higher costs of housing by using federal income tax advantages; nor in the central city can they treat higher rents as a direct
payment for a package of local services enjoyed—good schools, parks, and adequate
police protection, for example—as is generally the case for suburban residents. If property taxes were substantially lower, rents could be reduced and housing consumption
would be expanded in response to increased demand, particularly for better quality
housing for middle-income families. In turn, the filtering process would make more and
better quality housing available for low-income city dwellers. In central cities, then, the
property tax has the added disadvantage that it "imposes a serious impediment to the
needed rebuilding of the central-city housing stock, an impediment that is increasing
not decreasing with time as property taxes rise. There is much evidence that, in the
large central cities, these rates have been climbing steeply during the past decade" (Netzer, 1974, p. 249).

Nonproperty Taxes

Faced with rising costs and mounting public needs, local governments have
increasingly had to tap other local sources of revenue. Since World War II taxes have
been levied by local governments on a range of things, including motor vehicles, gasoline, business gross receipts, cigarettes, alcoholic beverages, payrolls, and retail sales
(Davies, 1965). Only the last two forms have provided a significant source of revenue,
and their use has mainly been restricted in metropolitan areas to the large central cities.

The municipal payroll tax has proved to be a significant source of revenue in
those cities where it has been introduced, including New York City, Philadelphia, St.
Louis, and Baltimore. In New York City alone, receipts from the levy exceed 500 million dollars (Deran, 1968). As the system is commonly employed, residents are taxed on
income earned regardless of source, while nonresidents are taxed on that portion of
their income earned within the municipality. The main attraction of the tax for the
central cities is that it enables them to exploit a source of "extraterritorial" revenue,
namely, that from commuters working in the municipality, for whom the central city
government provides services and facilities, which the nonresident working population
otherwise enjoys without contributing toward their costs.

The local sales tax is the most important source of nonproperty tax revenues
(Table 18.2), and is now employed by over 2000 local governments in more than 13
states. As with the municipal payroll tax, it enables municipalities to tap nonresidents
for revenue, but has the added advantages of revenue productivity and ease and low cost
of administration. However, like the property tax, it is decidedly regressive and a general nuisance to the shopper. Moreover, in certain situations it can penalize local merchants, because in a large metropolitan area consumers are often able to avoid the levy
by shopping in adjacent territories.

Service Charges

The third major source of local government revenue is the charges levied on the users of public services. These defray a substantial part of the costs of providing many services; about 20 percent of the income-redistribution and 30 percent of the resource-allocation activities of local governments are financed through user charges (see Table 18.3). About 75 percent of the local government costs of supplying water is recouped from user charges and 20 percent of the outlays for refuse collection and transportation (excluding highway construction) (Netzer, 1974). Service charges are based on the quantity of service used or the benefits received by urban residents. If thought of as a tax, they would doubtless be thought of as regressive, but then so would, for example, electricity and telephone service charges imposed by the private sector. The charges are justified on the grounds that the individual himself decides just how much or how little of a particular service he wishes to use. This decision can be made within the framework of the allocation of his resources to bring him maximum satisfaction. User charges, then, can be thought of as an example of the application of the market mechanism in the public sector.

Service charges cannot be applied to all local public services. They are, for example, inappropriate in the case of "pure public goods," defined as services that no one can be denied, whether they pay for them or not, and for which the benefits to one person do not in any way preclude enjoyment of the same benefits by others. An example is the visual attractiveness of urban open space and parks. Although there are not very many goods and services in this category, their very nature requires that they be provided by the public sector, since no rational person would pay a price for something provided by the private sector if he can enjoy it free. Service charges are also inappropriate for redistributive activities and whenever the service provides social rather than private benefits. Thus, although the costs of financing libraries could be defrayed in part by user charges, libraries are financed from taxes because they serve an

Table 18.3.   **THE FINANCING OF LOCAL GOVERNMENT EXPENDITURE, 1970–71 (IN BILLIONS OF DOLLARS)**

Source of Funds	Income Redistribution	Public Schools	Resource Allocation	Totals
Total local gov't direct expenditure	16.0	41.3	45.8	103.1
Financed by:				
Federal and state aid	7.9	20.2	9.1	37.2
User charges	3.2	2.1	12.6	17.9
Other (taxes, loans, etc.)	4.9	19.0	24.1	48.0

Note: The figures relate to *all* local governments in the United States.
SOURCE: U.S. Census Bureau, *Government Finances in 1970-1971*, (Washington, D.C.: U.S. Government Printing Office, 1972.)

educational, and hence social, function. User charges are also difficult to apply when cost-benefit relationships are inexactly specified, as in the case of pollution control. Consequently, the possibilities of imposing service charges are considerably more restricted than levying taxes, and they are best used when private needs are being satisfied — particularly when the product or service would be significantly wasted if it had zero price (for example, unmetered water). Although there is undoubtedly scope for intensifying the use of service charges, and some public finance experts argue that there are good grounds for doing so (Wilson, 1966), their very nature causes them to be a relatively unimportant source of revenue compared to taxation.

FRAGMENTATION AND PROBLEMS

The shortcomings of the various ways by which local governments raise funds, even the regressivity of the property tax itself, would be less pronounced if only they were applied on uniform basis throughout metropolitan area. The fact that they are not is due in large part to the proliferation and fragmentation of local government areas. Two main kinds of problems stem from this: (1) *fiscal* — those related to the existing methods of financing local government activities — and (2) *organizational* — those arising from the difficulties of coordinating the various local government responsibilities within metropolitan areas. The second class of problems is in fact very much a result of the first, since in order to raise funds, local governments are often forced to pursue conflicting rather than cooperative policies in service provision.

Fiscal Problems
Fiscal Imbalance

The major problem arising from the fragmentation of local government structure is without doubt the tremendous disparity between revenue resources and expenditure needs between different units within urban areas. This leads to significant spatial variation in the level and quality of public services provided from place to place within cities, and also to marked disparities in the level of tax rates that can, and do, influence patterns in the location of economic activity within metropolitan areas in undesirable ways. The segregation of resources and needs is most pronounced between the central cities and the suburbs, although not all suburban communities enjoy favorable resource bases. Increasingly the problem of fiscal imbalance involves "all units and their fiscal position in the metropolitan matrix" (Bollens and Schmandt, 1975, p. 136). Nevertheless, the worsening fiscal squeeze on the central cities stands out as one of the most acute problems stemming from the fragmented pattern of local government in the larger metropolitan areas.

Central cities are almost without exception characterized by insufficient funds and resources relative to the demands for services they must try to satisfy. The building stock is generally old and dilapidated, and the high densities make it increasingly a major fire risk, thereby necessitating higher levels of fire protection. High crime rates are translated into higher costs of providing police protection. Median family incomes are appreciably lower than in the suburbs — a situation aggravated by higher unemployment rates. The massive concentration of the poor in central cities is of course a major source of demand for services. In this regard, it is interesting to note that the high levels of concentration of poverty in the central cities are not unrelated to the difficulties low-income people have in finding low-cost housing in suburban areas, a situation that is made worse by the tendency of many communities to use their powers of zoning to keep low-income groups out. Central cities, then, not only abound with problems, but increasingly they are charged with the responsibility of solving them on behalf of the whole metropolitan area.

The demand for and costs of providing health and welfare services—and especially various forms of public assistance—are high. Whereas about 10 percent of local govenment tax revenues are on average spent on income-redistributive activities, in the central cities the figure approaches 25 percent and is steadily rising as prices increase and in-migration from lagging regions continues. To politicians it is often difficult to see why the demand for further investments continues to grow. Whether or not inflation continues, there is administrative mismanagement, even some mis-appropriation of funds—budgets will almost certainly continue to rise, and fast! At the same time, the opportunities for increasing tax revenues are severely limited, especially since an increasingly large amount of economic activity has, as we have noted, decentralized from the core areas. As it is, tax rates in·central cities are higher relative to personal income than in the suburbs, and to increase taxes on the poor to give them more services hardly makes sense.

Central city governments are, then, located in the viselike grip of rapidly rising expenditures and falling revenues, such that expansion in health and welfare programs, education, and other services is seriously constrained in a situation where existing levels of service provision are generally grossly inadequate and deteriorating. The contrast with the generally high revenue-expenditure ratios characteristic of most suburban municipalities is one of the most iniquitous features in the contemporary spatial organization of metropolitan areas.

Spillovers
Existing arrangements for local government taxation cannot adequately cope with spillovers, the effects of which are accentuated by the proliferation of small geographic entities. Spillovers, or externalities, arise because the actions of individuals or groups (e.g., local governments) at one location affect the utility of those at other locations (Mishan, 1970). Thus, they are an expression of interdependencies in spatial organization and as such are typically geographic (Tullock, 1970). Spillovers arise in many ways, can assume many forms, and may be either positive or negative in their effects. Thus the benefits of many kinds of local government services spill over the boundaries of (are external to) the units providing them, and the costs of solving many problems within urban areas—and especially social ones—spill over the boundaries of the units that are ostensibly responsible for their resolution (Cox, 1973). For example, a high quality of police protection in one jurisdiction is commonly reflected in lower crime rates in neighboring communities, and a well-developed school system in one district enhances the general well-being of the urban complex as a whole.

The problem of spillovers is significant whenever the external benefits of providing services are very large in relation to the internal ones and the services are financed by taxes. This is particularly the case for education and those activities for which the costs and benefits cannot be confined to small spatial units—for example, pollution control, recreational facilities, and public transportation systems. Under these conditions, it is unreasonable to expect that adequate levels of service will be provided, for voters in a community are unlikely to be willing to pay higher taxes to finance services whose benefits are largely realized by others.

The situation is different, of course, when service charges are employed. These overcome some of the problems of geographic spillovers, since costs can be recouped from users who benefit regardless of where they reside whenever they make use of the particular service. But since most local revenue is raised by taxation, spillovers are an important factor contributing to inequalities in the levels of service provision between the different parts of metropolitan areas.

Organizational Problems

The very nature of many urban problems is such that within an economically and socially integrated metropolitan community, they cannot be handled effectively by a large number of local governments acting in isolation. In an intensive study of the political economy of the New York metropolitan region—an area covering 6,914 square miles and containing a population of 16,139,000 in 1960—the extent of local government fragmentation led one writer to conclude that here one could observe "one of the great unnatural wonders of the world; that is, a governmental arrangement perhaps more complicated than any other that mankind has yet contrived or allowed to happen" (Wood, 1961, p. 1). He was, of course, referring to the fact that the metropolitan region governed itself in 1960 by 1467 distinct political units, each one of which had its own power to raise and spend money in areas of jurisdiction that have developed more by chance than by design.

Although this high degree of political fragmentation can be defended on the grounds of continuing the democratic tradition of home rule, it can also be deplored as being hopelessly unsuited to the realities of modern metropolitan life. From the governmental point of view, the metropolitan whole should be very much more than the sum of its administrative parts. And because it is not, many urgent problems—for example, land-use planning and service provision—have remained difficult to solve, and will inevitably continue to be so unless existing conditions are radically changed.

Fiscal Zoning

A major hindrance to rational land-use planning within metropolitan regions is the practice of fiscal zoning by local governments. With their heavy reliance on the property tax as the major source of local revenues, a typical response by local governments to meet increased costs—or to hold outlays to a reasonable level—is to use their powers of zoning for fiscal ends. Different types of land use demand different kinds of services, and at the same time are capable of making different-sized contributions to the public purse. Thus, whereas commercial, and industrial uses—especially "clean industry" such as modern plants and research laboratories—and high-income families living in expensive homes are often able to contribute in taxes two or three times the costs of services they require, residential property of moderate value pays only a fraction of the cost of public services it requires. This is particularly the case for education, since the cost of providing schools is heavily supported, as we have seen, by the property tax.

Fiscal zoning is therefore an extremely important instrument of local government. When practiced it more often than not leads to a conflict of interests between policies aimed at short-term gains for individual communities and the longer-term gains for the urban area as a whole. For in the attempt to speed up the process whereby benefits are derived from the use of land, communities may make decisions that are in their immediate interests but run counter to the proper development of the wider urban environment. It is largely as a result of such decisions that, for example, islands of high-value residential property become surrounded by industrial sections, or enclaves of industrial activity persist in areas apparently economically unsuitable for their location, which result in irrationalities in the overall urban land-use pattern and the promotion of negative spillover effects.

With this goal of attracting what are for them the most beneficial land uses, a kind of "beggar thy neighbor" policy has become a significant feature of much local government behavior in metropolitan areas. This is especially so in attempts to bolster sagging tax bases by attracting industry to a community. The inevitable community boosting and the often exaggerated claims of locational advantage and sense of political power that go with such strategies have frequently led in the past to open hostility between neighboring areas. Thus strong pressures build up to go it alone, and decisions are often made without regard for adjoining communities and almost never with regard to the metropolitan-wide spatial organization.

Conflicting Programs

The problems arising from fragmented local government in metropolitan areas are most clearly revealed in the conflicting programs of service provision, especially those administered by the boards of the special districts. The complicated nature of the organization of special districts in a large city is clearly illustrated by information recently provided for the Toronto metropolitan area (Yeates, 1975). The six municipalities comprising the area under the jurisdiction of the Toronto Metropolitan Council (see Fig. 18.1) contained, in 1968, 94 special-body governments. These can be classified into six groups on the basis of their major roles. Twenty-seven bodies were concerned with the provision of *services* (S); 24 with *management* (M); 17 were *regulatory* (R) bodies; 13 operated more or less as *business enterprises* (E); 11 were *advisory* (A); and two bodies were engaged in *promotion* (P). Nineteen of the boards played a metropolitan-wide role under the auspices of the Toronto Metropolitan Council; the remainder were of a more local nature, discharging their responsibilities within the boundaries of the six municipalities. The variety of types of districts and an idea of their different responsibilities can be appreciated from Table 18.4.

The proliferation of special districts makes it difficult if not often impossible to develop common policies or programs for the benefit of metropolitan areas as a whole. Of course, not all services provided by local governments require region-wide policies and cooperation between the various units. Many services, and problems too, are of a purely local nature, and the existing system of local government is largely capable of handling them. Often smaller units are an advantage because they permit greater citizen participation and community involvement, as for example in the case of neighborhood planning (Wolpert et al., 1972).

For other kinds of service provision, and particularly those for which economies of scale are important, larger areal units are required. For example, water filtration and purification systems are much more cost-efficient if they are built with a larger capacity than a smaller one. In this particular case, there are very few concerns of a noneconomic nature that matter other than flouridation of the water supply, so it would be appropriate to allow the size of plant and its service area to be determined purely on the basis of cost minimization. It is important, therefore, to distinguish between the provision of local as distinct from regional or area-wide services. An attempt to do this is made in Table 18.5, in which an impressionistic scale is used to rank functions from most to least local.

The need for larger units and cooperation between them in the form of region-wide policies thus becomes increasingly more urgent as one moves down the list of functions in Table 18.5. In this regard Toronto is fortunate in having a metropolitan government structure to oversee the provision and coordination of some of these higher-order activities. But Toronto is the exception rather than the rule, and in most

Table 18.4. SPECIAL DISTRICTS IN METROPOLITAN TORONTO, 1968: SELECTED EXAMPLES

METROPOLITAN TORONTO

S School Board
S Separate School Board
S Retarded Children's Education Authority
S Library
S Regional Conservation Authority
S Toronto and York Roads Commission
S Children's Aid Society
S Catholic Children's Aid Society
M Housing Company Limited
M Civic Garden Centre Board of Management
M Board of Management of the O'Keefe Center

R Planning Board
R Courts of Revision
R Licensing Commission
R Board of Commissioners of Police
E Toronto Transit Commission
E Canadian National Exhibition Association
P Industrial Commission
P Convention and Tourist Bureau

CITY OF TORONTO

S Board of Health
S Public Library Board
S Board of Education
M Historical Board
M Runnymede Hospital Board of Directors
M George Bell Arena Board of Management
M Ted Reeve Arena Board of Management
M Stanley Park Stadium Property Board of Management
M North Toronto Memorial Arena Board of Management
M University Settlement Recreation Centre Board of Management
M Good Neighbours Club Board of Management

R Planning Board
R Committee of Adjustment
R Housing Standards Appeal Committee
E Electric Commissioners
E Parking Authority
E Housing Authority
E City of Toronto Limited Dividend Housing Corporation
E Toronto Harbour Commissioners
A Redevelopment Advisory Council

BOROUGH OF ETOBICOKE

S Board of Health
S Public Library Board
S Board of Education
S Combined Roman Catholic Separate School Board
M Community Centres Board
M Cemetary Board

R Planning Board
R Committee of Adjustment
E Hydro Commission
A Historical Board
A Safety Council

SOURCE: Yeates (1975), Table 8.2. The letter code is explained in the text.

other cities the lack of a corresponding body means that friction and noncooperation between local governments in the provision of region-wide functions is usually pronounced. Since each local entity is more likely to be concerned with preserving its own authority than anything else — and quite understandably so from a political viewpoint — it is perhaps not surprising to find that the existing arrangements tend to work against the broader regional interests to result in marked inefficiencies from the viewpoint of the urban area as a whole.

Public Awareness and Control

In addition to the problems of coordination and economic efficiency resulting from the proliferation of special districts, those of public awareness and control of public bodies are equally significant. There is little doubt that, in general, the public is simply not aware of the numbers of different units of local government that influence their daily lives. This is, of course, well evidenced by the very low voter turnout experienced in elections for representatives to those boards that require such democratic procedures. This lack of public awareness is quite serious, for the operation of the bodies responsible for the special districts then falls into the hands of those who perceive the concern as being of direct interest to them and particularly their economic activity. It is therefore not surprising that many special district boards are dominated by financial, insurance, and real estate interests, which view such representation as important for business protection as well as public relations.

This limited public awareness goes far to explain the rather poor degree of public control that is often exercised over what are, after all, public bodies. As public bodies they should be concerned primarily with the public interest, and they should ensure that this interest is served and that the avenues for interaction between the governed and the governments are visible and clear. One of the methods for achieving this is,

Table 18.5.   RANK ORDER OF URBAN SERVICES ON THE BASIS OF THEIR LOCAL IMPORTANCE

	Rank	Function
Most Local	1	Fire protection
	2	Public education
	3	Refuse collection and disposal
	4	Libraries
	5	Police
	6	Health
	7	Urban renewal
	8	Housing
	9	Parks and recreation
	10	Public welfare
	11	Hospital and medical care
	12	Transportation
	13	Planning
Least Local	14	Water supply — sewage disposal
	15	Air pollution control

Source: Advisory Commission on Intergovernmental Relations (1963), p. 11.

theoretically at least, to increase the numbers of citizens who are appointed or elected to the special bodies in cities. Unfortunately, because of the number of *ex officio* members, duplication of appointments, and duplication of business interests represented on the boards or commissions, the degree of public control is much less than it appears (Yeates, 1975). The result is that the vast bulk of the community is not represented, and furthermore, is totally ignorant of the fact that it is not represented. In fact, it would appear that the operating dictum of many local government bodies is that "what the public does not know it cannot worry about."

At the heart of the problem of metropolitan land use and service provision is, then, the dilemma of local finance and fragmentation of local government units, which neglects the facts of interdependence within the total metropolitan community (Chinitz, 1965). The solution to the problem is complex and obviously requires very careful consideration. Clearly there is a need to formulate some kind of region-wide policy in which revenue sharing, control over land use, and heightened coordination between local governments are but some of the many important ingredients. It would appear, however, that little opportunity exists for this under present arrangements in which

> each government is preoccupied with its own problems, and collectively the governments are not prepared to formulate general policies for guiding economic development or to make generalized responses to the financial pressures generated by urbanization. They are neither in a position to establish and enforce public criteria for appropriate conditions of growth nor to provide public services that the private sector requires on a regionwide basis. By their organization, financing, and philosophy, they foreswear the opportunity for the exercise of these larger powers [Wood, 1961, p. 113].

TOWARD SOLUTIONS

Wood's conclusions are perhaps a little pessimistic and harsh in view of the heightened extent to intergovernmental cooperation that has taken place in metropolitan areas in the last decade. Nevertheless, the fact remains that much of this has not led to any drastic reduction in the scale of metropolitan problems, which still loom as large as ever. In fact, in view of the problems created by the proliferation of local governments — not least of all the financial ones — the remarkable thing is that major disasters have, so far, been averted. The question remains, however, of how long they can be forestalled. As disruptible forces mount, it is clear that some kind of change in the organization of local government within metropolitan areas is needed. To this end, some argue that finances are at the root of the problem. Given a rational distribution of funds and perhaps a realignment of responsibilities, they feel that the problem would sort itself out without any major change in the pattern of local government. These are the advocates of fiscal reform.

Although there is much to support this line of argument, it would most probably result only in a postponement of other sorts of crises. For the problem is not only one of the availability and distribution of funds, but also one of lack of coordination in the provision of region-wide services and functions. It does not follow that an equable distribution of money would bring about better cooperation in the way it is spent. Because of this, others argue that more fundamental changes in governmental organization are needed to establish an administrative machinery capable of effectively mobilizing the metropolitan region's resources. These are the advocates of local government reform. In the last resort, it would appear that any lasting solution will require elements from both approaches.

Fiscal Reforms

Several strategies exist for reducing the financial burden of local governments, especially those of the central cities. A number of economists have advocated greater revenue sharing by the federal government. They argue that since the federal government receives enormous revenue bounties but has only limited responsibilities for civilian expenditure, whereas the major burdens fall on the state, provincial, and local governments with their severely limited tax-raising capabilities, "there is no escaping the logic of putting the power of the federal income tax at the disposal of beleaguered state and local governments" (Heller, 1969, p. 101). To this end, the so-called Heller-Pechman plan is widely advocated.

Under this scheme, the federal government would route into a special trust fund a percentage (2 percent was originally mentioned) of the federal individual income tax receipts, which would be channeled to the states at fixed intervals. The distribution between states would be based on population totals—so much per head. As a means of ensuring that the claims of local government are met, a fixed proportion of the states' receipts—perhaps as much as 50 percent—would be legally required to pass to local units and the financial plight of urban areas would be given top priority in the allocation process. The funds should be used at the discretion of each state and local government, subject to the usual auditing and accounting procedures and compliance with federal legislation, and subject to the constraint that the funds must not be used for activities already separately subsidized by the central government (e.g., highway construction). An important start to this end was made in the form of revenue-sharing legislation sponsored by President Nixon in October 1972, which provided for the sharing of 30 billion dollars of federal revenue for the five-years ending December 31, 1976, on the basis of a formula that reflected mainly population and state-local tax-raising differentials. Similar proposals have been made for a greater degree of revenue sharing between states and local governments (see Netzer, 1974).

Opponents to revenue sharing, particularly that involving the central government, see a realignment of responsibilities as a better way of solving the problems. One such scheme, aired by the editors of *Fortune* magazine (February 1971), proposed that the federal government assume the entire cost of most of the income-redistribution programs currently financed at the state-local levels, including medicaid, unemployment insurance, aid for dependent children, old-age assistance, and vocational rehabilitation. This would lift about 15 billion dollars off the backs of local governments. The state governments should assume full responsibility for financing elementary and secondary education, thereby relieving the burden of crushing costs on the cities and local school districts, but also removing inequalities in educational opportunities and quality between different jurisdictions within metropolitan areas. If this were done, then the advantages of fiscal zoning as they relate to reducing school costs would of course disappear. The editors also favored the retention of an overhauled property tax as the main local source of revenue for local governments.

Others argue strongly against the retention of the property tax in any form, saying that its positive attributes are insignificant compared to its defects—and especially its regressivity. An interesting and workable alternative to the property tax has been suggested by some economists, notably by Netzer (1974)—namely, a land-value tax: a tax on the value of bare sites regardless of the buildings placed on them. The tax is the economist's ideal: it is neutral in its economic effects and it is equitable. The arguments favoring a land-value tax, which is already widely used in western Canada, Australia, and New Zealand, are that it does not change land-use incentives; in this sense it is economically neutral, since, unlike the existing property tax, it does not discourage investment in buildings. Second, land values, as we saw in Chapter 9, are mainly the result of location within the framework of investment in public facilities, population growth, and community development—and not the result of any action by individual landowners. Hence it is fair that the community recoup these "unearned increments" by taxation, and then use them for public purposes; in this sense the tax is equitable. A land-value tax would especially benefit the central cities by encouraging the redevelopment of deteriorating property and inefficiently developed sites there. However, until these kinds of fiscal reforms are implemented, the present crisis in local government finance and the fiscal squeeze are likely to continue.

Toward Government Area Reforms

Several strategies have been implemented to improve the working of local government within metropolitan areas. They can for convenience of discussion be divided into two classes:

1. The simpler forms of voluntary cooperation; for example, service agreements and the creation of metropolitan councils.
2. The more complicated two-tier arrangements; for example, metropolitan districts, comprehensive county plans, and federal systems, which usually involve surrender of some local government power.

Voluntary cooperation has been promoted by a variety of public and private bodies as an effective mechanism for solving problems without relinquishing local control. This approach can therefore be viewed as a defensive strategy against more thorough forms of government reorganization in cities. Two main forms of voluntary cooperation may be recognized.

Service Agreements

Under these, the provision of a service (for example, water supply) by one community may be shared with adjoining ones or a facility may be built and operated by two or more governments. So far this kind of approach has been most successful in providing local services, those at the lower end of the spectrum in Table 18.5, such as libraries and public health facilities. Although service agreements are a step in the right direction, many are essentially temporary. Frequently they amount to little more than a kind of stand-by arrangement between governments for mutual aid at times of crisis. The piecemeal nature of most arrangements means that they would have to be extensively operated throughout metropolitan regions if they were ever to become an effective solution to region-wide problems. Moreover, since they are founded for the most part on the provision of a service for money, many communities are unable to take advantage of the opportunities available because of their already inadequate financial resources.

Metropolitan Councils

These do not have any governmental powers, but function as multipurpose advisory bodies to make recommendations concerning cooperation and coordination toward the solution of metropolitan problems. They have been established in a number of cities since the mid-fifties, including Detroit, Philadelphia, and the San Fransisco Bay area. Their main strength is the forum they represent for discussing problems and acting as a unified spokesman in these matters with branches of state and federal government. However, they lack bite. Their real effectiveness is limited by their general lack of power; for many, this is their strong point.

The weaknesses of service agreements and metropolitan councils has led to other approaches based on the premise that local needs and services should be handled at the local level and that only certain kinds of broader, area-wide functions should be handled by various forms of metropolitan government. Schemes in this category are therefore based on a two-tier arrangement. Three types of two-tier approaches may be recognized.

Metropolitan Districts

These are the mildest of the three. Although they may operate over an entire metropolitan area or major parts of it, they are normally restricted in scope to one service or a very small number of activities. They have been most frequently established to provide area-wide coordination of sewage disposal and port facilities, although they commonly exist to look after airports, mass-transit facilities, parks and recreational land, and water supply. Despite their restricted functional scope, and perhaps because of it, metropolitan districts have an impressive record for alleviating pressing metropolitan problems with which they are concerned.

This record is in part responsible for their relatively rapid spread, and today there are about 125 such districts in the United States. Moreover, they can be set up relatively easily, since they are not generally empowered to levy taxes. Most metropolitan districts are therefore profit-making concerns, which raise funds through tolls and service charges. As such their scope is restricted to those functions that can be made to pay — although the very nature of these is that they do not. Thus the Port of New York Authority has a greater outstanding debt than most states. This restricted role is commonly the basis of arguments against metropolitan districts, for since they are confined to one function, a fragmented approach to the solution of metropolitan-wide problems is still said to exist. Nevertheless, metropolitan districts will certainly continue to play an extremely useful and important role in solving area-wide problems.

The Comprehensive Urban County Plan

This second important form of two-tier government is based on the reallocation of responsibility for certain functions from all municipalities to a county. In this way a kind of single metropolitan government is created to look after area-wide problems while local service provision remains in the hands of existing local governments. Thus a certain measure of metropolitan control is obtained without the need to create yet another unit of government. However, although a county plan is an attractive proposition on paper, the possibilities for its application are restricted to those metropolitan areas that fall completely within the boundaries of a single county. Even where one-county metropolitan areas exist, comprehensive agreements are often difficult to implement. Bollens and Schmandt (1975) list five major obstacles: The approach is not legally sanctioned in many states; for it to work effectively, existing county governments need to be extensively restructured; the governing body is difficult to constitute; it is difficult to decide which functions should be assigned to the county government; and the financial powers of most counties are inadequate. In view of these difficulties, it is perhaps not surprising that the concept has become a reality in only one locality: metropolitan Miami in Dade County, Fla., where the one-county approach has been operating with considerable success since its inception in 1957.

Federation
    The third form of two-tier approach, federation, is very similar to the one-county concept, and in fact in the case of a one-county metropolitan area the two are virtually indistinguishable. This approach can be almost considered, then, as an extension of the previous concept to regions consisting of more than one county. In this situation a new intercounty governmental unit is created to look after area-wide functions, while local municipalities are left in charge of local service provision. The idea of creating a single government for an entire metropolitan area through federation has been an appealing one in the United States since the end of the nineteenth century. However, because of the many legal problems involved in its implementation, there have been only three serious attempts to federate: Boston (as early as 1896), Alameda County (Oakland, Calif.), and Allegheny County (Pittsburgh)—all of which ended in failure. By the mid-fifties, interest in the approach had virtually vanished as attention shifted to the other two kinds of two-tier concepts.

Metropolitan Toronto: An Example of Federation
    While the interest in the idea of federation flagged in the United States, it was taken up in Canada, where on January 1, 1954, it was adopted as the solution to the problems of rapid growth in the metropolitan Toronto region. Events leading up to this decision began initially as long ago as 1912 with the decision by the city of Toronto to curtail its long-time policy of annexing adjacent territory when it became fairly well settled. The costs of providing services to the newly acquired areas had become too great. As the fringe areas continued to grow in population, so separate municipalities were established to cater to local needs. By 1930, 13 such municipalities had been created, and these continued to grow in population size, so that by the outbreak of World War II several serious problems had emerged in the region. At the root of these was the familiar problem of insufficient community finances (Smallwood, 1963). Although some municipalities had managed to attract a favorable mix of land uses, others had rapidly developed as dormitories for workers of the central city. For these the cost of providing community services rapidly became a major problem, and the quality of service provision deteriorated. This became acute with respect to education facilities, water supply, and sewage disposal. In an attempt to alleviate what had obviously become an area-wide problem, the city of Toronto filed an application to the provincial government in 1950 calling for consolidation of the 13 municipalities into a single gov-

ernmental entity. The resulting metropolitan government area created in 1954 is shown in Figure 18.1.

As a result of federation, the Municipality of Metropolitan Toronto was established to perform such area-wide functions as water supply, sewage disposal, property assessment, construction of arterial highways, parks, and planning (see Table 18.3). The original city and 12 suburbs were retained as local units to carry out functions not assigned to the metropolitan government, such as provision of local parks, libraries, schools, fire departments, and various aspects of public health. In 1967 the pattern of local government units was simplified when the original 13 municipalities were consolidated into six municipal governments, comprising the city of Toronto and the boroughs of Etobicoke, North York, Scarborough, East York, and York. As a result, the two-tier system was considerably simplified and responsibility for welfare services and education were transferred from these new units to the Metropolitan Council. The latter move has achieved in Toronto what advocates of state responsibility for education in the United States hope for—namely, the elimination of disparities in education financing and provision of a uniform standard of schooling throughout the metropolitan area.

Since its inception the new government has flourished and major accomplishments have been made on several fronts. In the areas of education, water supply, and sewage disposal, many of the earlier problems have been arrested if not eradicated; a metropolitan park district of many thousand acres has been established; an extensive expressway system has been launched; an attempt has been made to control air pollution; a system of unified law enforcement has been implemented; and public transportation has been consolidated and improved. Naturally, the new form of region-wide

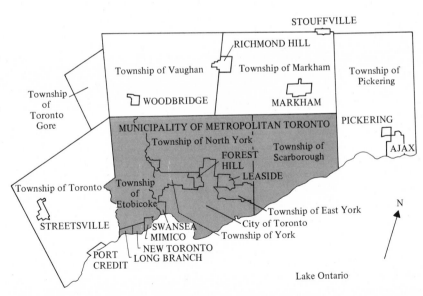

Fig. 18.1. The Municipality of Metropolitan Toronto, 1954.

government has not been without its critics, who point especially to the lack of success in the fields of health and welfare, housing and urban renewal, and particularly the problems that still remain related to the assimilation of a large number of immigrants from overseas. Despite these and some early failings, notably in planning, the metropolitan form of government is firmly established as part of the political organization of Toronto.

Thus, from the brief review of the various strategies open to advocates of metropolitan government and increased cooperation, the two-tier approaches, and especially federation, are appealing. They offer a workable compromise between the politically impossible supergovernments controlling everything and the metropolitan councils controlling nothing. Their main value lies in the fact that they offer a new system that does not require the complete dissolution of the old. Combined with tax-sharing agreements, they offer hope of finding workable solutions to the problem of the proliferation of governments within metropolitan areas. For as long as local governments are forced to balance their books within their own boundaries, it is unrealistic to expect them to surrender their parochial interests in favor of regionalism. However, regionalism must inevitably become a more important part of our thinking if, as Gottmann (1961) suggests, the new order in the organization of inhabited space is to be megalopolitan. For without greater concern for and sacrifice in the interests of the larger whole, the outlook for the urban future is very bleak indeed.

19
TOWARD URBAN AND REGIONAL POLICIES

The essence of urbanization is the increased concentration of people and activities in space. As we have seen in the previous chapters, many of today's urban ills have become most pronounced where concentration is greatest—in the largest cities and urban regions. The problems of contemporary urban development are not, however, restricted to the mounting social costs of metropolitan growth. The forces of concentration, by their very nature, create regional imbalance; they accentuate disparities between growth centers and the so-called depressed or lagging regions within nations. All of these problems are separate yet interrelated; each represents a different malady of urban development, yet the solutions to one affect the others.

Moreover, it is becoming increasingly clear that the nature of these kinds of problems and their solutions range far beyond the boundaries and capabilities of individual cities and regions. They very quickly become a matter of national concern, and as such involve central governments—especially since only these have the power of redirecting public and private investment decisions to influence urban growth patterns. This explains why throughout the world pressures are mounting for central governments to "do something"—to devise policies for national urban growth (Rodwin, 1970). In this

443

chapter we turn our attention to questions relating to the need for such policies, drawing upon the experiences of other countries to illustrate the difficulties of formulating and implementing strategies for guiding urban growth at the regional and national scales.

FUTURE URBAN PATTERNS

The need for urban growth strategies is not predicated on the basis of current problems alone, but also on the patterns of urban concentration that can be expected in the future. The difficulties of solving urban problems at the present scale of urban development suggest that their solution will be even more problematic and certainly more costly in the future if the concentration of population in a few mammoth megalopolitan regions continues. Moreover, there is no telling what new problems concentration at increasingly large geographical scales will create.

There is no reason to believe, given the continuation of present trends, that the growth of more extensive urban regions will not be the dominant feature of the urban pattern in the future as increasingly larger numbers of people become urban. This is not, of course, an exclusively North American problem. At present the population of the world is about 65 percent rural and 35 percent urban, but according to Doxiadis (1966), this will change to about 95 percent urban and 5 percent rural in the course of the next hundred years as the urbanization of the Third World countries gathers momentum (Berry, 1973b, ch. 3). This change, together with a projected increase in the world's population to between six and seven billion by the year 2000 and more than 12 billion by a hundred years from now, will mean the rapid expansion of urban areas in all countries. In fact, the much discussed world population explosion is being accompanied by an urban explosion of mammoth proportions.

Increasing Urbanization

It is realistic to expect that North America will share in this experience, and that the largest metropolitan areas will become significantly larger in the future. Just how large they may possibly become is suggested by projections made some years ago by Pickard (1959), shown in Table 19.1, which gives figures for the past, present, and future for the 10 largest metropolises in the United States. In aggregate, these accounted for one-fifth of the total population in 1910; about one-quarter in 1970; and should account for roughly one-third of an expected national population totaling over 300 million by the year 2000. By then it is anticipated that 70 percent of the population of the United States will be living in urbanized areas larger than 100,000 population and 53 percent in complexes of over one million inhabitants.

These projections are, of course, based on the extrapolation of existing trends, and despite the sophisticated methods used, the future is very much an unknown quantity. For example, it is difficult to foresee what kinds of technology will exist by the year 2000, and the current trend of rapidly increasing energy prices cannot be discounted as a factor of vital significance for future patterns of spatial organization. The projections are, moreover, based on assumptions of continued high rates of economic growth, the validity of which may be seriously questioned in view of the current experience. Nevertheless, whatever the future, the continued growth of the largest metropolises can be achieved only by a significant increase in their spatial extent. In fact, the size of the

Table 19.1. TEN LARGEST METROPOLISES IN THE UNITED STATES, 1910, 1970, AND 2000

1910 Census Metropolitan Area	Population (in millions)	1970 Census Standard Metropolitan Statistical Area	Population (in millions)	2000 Projection for Supermetropolitan Area	Population (in millions)
New York	6.7	New York	11.5	New York	23.0
Chicago	2.5	Los Angeles	7.0	Los Angeles	20.0
Philadelphia	2.0	Chicago	6.9	Chicago	11.0
Boston	1.6	Philadelphia	4.8	Detroit	9.5
Pittsburgh	1.0	Detroit	4.2	Chesapeake-Potomac	9.5
St. Louis	0.8	San Francisco–Oakland	3.1	Delaware Valley	8.5
San Francisco–Oakland	0.7	Washington, D.C.	2.9	San Francisco Bay	7.5
Baltimore	0.7	Boston	2.8	S. E. Florida	6.5
Cleveland	0.6	Pittsburgh	2.4	New England	6.5
Cincinnati	0.6	St. Louis	2.4	Cuyahoga Valley	5.0
TOTAL	17.2		48.0		107.0
% of U.S.	19.0%		26.0%		33.0%

SOURCE: Projection from Pickard (1959), p. 43.

population concentrations envisaged makes it difficult to think in terms of current metropolitan area definitions, even in terms of "urban daily systems," hence some new names for these megalopolitan regional complexes are introduced in Table 19.1.

The New York supermetropolitan area will still be the largest by the year 2000, but by then this will, of course, embrace the southern part of New York State, northeastern New Jersey, and southwestern Connecticut. A close second will be the Los Angeles area of southern California, which will have extended north to Santa Barbara, merged to the south with the northward thrusting San Diego, and extended in the east to San Bernardino and the desert fringe. Chicago and Detroit will exhibit similar growth, but not of such dramatic proportions as Los Angeles.

A number of large metropolitan areas will have completely merged. The Chesapeake-Potomac supermetropolitan area comprises the merging of Washington and Baltimore; the Delaware Valley supermetropolis will be a combination of Philadelphia, Trenton, and Wilmington; present-day San Francisco–Oakland will expand to include San Jose; Southeast Florida City will include Miami–Palm Beach; the New England supermetropolis will cover most of eastern Massachussetts and Rhode Island, while the Cuyahoga Valley metropolitan area will be formed by the merging of Cleveland with Lorain, Elyria, and Akron. All of these supermetropolitan areas will be larger (except Cuyahoga Valley) than the Chicago smsa was in 1960.

Urban North America in 2060

According to Doxiadis (1966, p. 112), the urban pattern of North America about a hundred years from now will consist of "some great concentrations of megalopolises interconnected by elongated strips of settlement along the major highways of the future." The macrogeographic aspects of this pattern are indicated in Figure 19.1, in which are outlined twelve major supermetropolitan areas. These are:

1. The northeastern Atlantic Seaboard, an area stretching from New Hampshire to North Carolina and representing the expanded megalopolis in the region today.

2. Chipitts, the area stretching from Milwaukee through Chicago, Detroit, and Cleveland to Pittsburgh.

3. Southern Ontario–St. Lawrence lowlands surrounding the twin-growth areas of Montreal and Toronto.

4. Ciloubustonis, consisting of an agglomeration of Cincinnati, Louisville, Columbus, Dayton, and Indianapolis.

5. Minneapolis-Duluth in the upper Midwest.

6. California, from Eureka to Tijuana, Mexico.

7. The Puget Sound lowland, including Portland, Seattle, and Vancouver.

8. Central Colorado, including Denver, Colorado Springs, and Pueblo.

9. Florida, covering the entire southern half of the Florida peninsula and stretching north through Jacksonville to coastal Georgia.

10. The coastal "Old South," including Baton Rouge, New Orleans, Mobile, and Pensacola.

11. Houston–Dallas–Fort Worth in Texas.

12. The mouth of the Rio Grande, incorporating a small area around Brownsville, Tex., but including a larger part of northeastern Mexico, in particular Monterrey.

Thus the supermetropolitan areas of both the American and Canadian heartlands will have merged to form a continuous urbanized region, but the most significant change in the pattern will be the continued decentralization or urban growth toward the periphery which will result in major concentrations in California, along the Gulf Coast, and in the Florida peninsula.

An idea of the population totals likely to be contained within the largest of these concentrations can be obtained from some more recent figures made available by Pickard (1970). Although the bases for his calculations are not exactly the same as those shown in Figure 19.1, there is nevertheless a fairly high level of correspondence between Pickard's definitions and those used by Doxiadis. Thus, the heartland super-

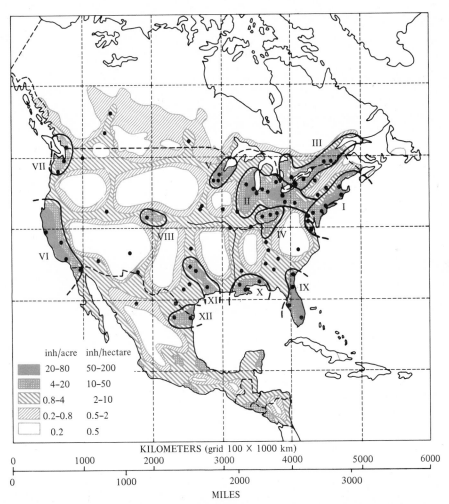

Fig. 19.1. A view of urban North America, 2060. (*Source*: Doxiadis, 1966, Fig. 49.)

metropolis (I and II in Fig. 19.1) will contain about 118 millions; California about 38 millions; Florida 14 millions; and the regions of the Gulf Coast together about 20 millions. Over one-half of all Americans will consequently be living in four massive concentrations by the year 2000, while most of the remainder will be residing in places larger than 100,000. Only about 12 percent of the total population will be living in the intermetropolitan peripheries. Put another way, 77 percent of all Americans will be living on about 11 percent of the land area (excluding Alaska and Hawaii). Similar high levels of concentration will also be typical of Canada.

The apparent inevitability of the future urban pattern resembling this, and the high levels of concentration and congestion that it implies, raise a number of important questions concerning its desirability. Two are particularly important: First, concerning the future regional balance of population distribution, is it desirable that population be massed in a few mammoth megalopolitan areas along the coasts and lake shores? Second, concerning the future rural-urban balance, is it in the national interest to continue to depopulate small towns and rural America to build bigger but not necessarily better cities? Within the context of these kinds of questions, the alternatives are clear enough: ". . . the 300 millions can be highly concentrated in a few 'megalopolises' or they can be distributed more evenly as among regions and dispersed in a more nearly balanced way among large metropolitan areas, middle-sized cities, and thriving small towns and villages. Which do we want?" (Sundquist, 1970, p. 89).

THE TRADITIONAL BELIEFS

The question of whether to seek a different distribution of population and economic activity or to let existing processes run their course to an almost certain urban pattern along the lines of that shown in Figure 19.1 is one of whether or not to implement urban and regional policies and intensify planning action. The ways in which central governments have answered this question vary considerably among nations. In many countries, particularly those of western and eastern Europe, policies to guide and steer urban growth are generally well established and widely accepted as both necessary and desirable; by and large in North America they are not. Here the extent of central government intervention has, until very recently, been limited in scope, and the pervading attitudes are that laissez-faire best serves the interests of individuals and the nation. In both Canada and the United States this attitude rests on the traditional beliefs in the principles of "privatism" and reliance on the market mechanism to shape the development of cities and patterns of urban growth (Warner, 1968).

The environment for urbanization in North America, then, has traditionally been that of free enterprise within a decentralized market-directed system. Decisions are made by individuals and groups within the framework of the free interplay of the forces of supply and demand, and status and power gained through success in the competitive system have been instrumental in determining the course of urbanization. The instruments of collective or government action have been used principally to protect the central institutions of the market and to ensure the continued dispersion of power, while the legal system is essentially regulatory and functions to preserve the existing values (Berry, 1973b). Economic efficiency in particular has been the major factor motivating decisions about location and land use. Under this system of "free-enterprise dynamics," the growth and prosperity of cities in North America have depended to a high degree on the aggregate successes or failures of thousands of individual enterprises rather than on collective action, while their internal structure has been shaped to a large extent by the essentially unbridled actions of land speculators, large investors, and profit-motivated builders.

In view of the traditional values, it is understandable that the role of the central governments in shaping the course of urbanization has been minimal in Canada and the United States, and that any serious concern with questions of urban and regional policy by and large have been neglected. This is not to imply that governments have done nothing toward this end. However, what little activity there has been has arisen out of the necessity to solve acute problems of the moment. Moreover, policies and programs have largely been uncoordinated, often contradictory, and initiated very much in the wake of the economic forces that create growth and the problems that are associated with it. Urban and regional policies have consequently been "curative"—a reaction to past trends and existing processes; they have been neither future-oriented nor goal-oriented.

Referring to the situation in Canada, Lithwick (1970) has drawn attention to the fact that no explicit policies guide urban growth there, and stresses that the first priority is not to decide what kinds of policies are required, but rather to agree on whether an urban policy is needed at all. The situation is very much the same in the United States. There, recent debate on urban policy, which was brought into the limelight with the publication by the Advisory Commission on Intergovernmental Relations of the reports *Urban and Rural America* (1968) and *Urban America and the Federal System* (1969), culminated in 1970 with the passage of Title VII of the Housing and Urban Development Act. Under this, the president was charged with presenting a biannual report to Congress to assist in the development of a national urban policy. The first report presented by President Nixon's Domestic Council in February 1972 tacitly recognized the traditional role of privatism and clearly advocated its continuation as the main force guiding future urban development:

> Patterns of growth are influenced by countless decisions made by individuals, families, and businesses . . . aimed at achieving the personal goals of those who make them [These] decisions cannot be dictated. . . . In many nations, the central government has undertaken forcefully comprehensive policies to control the process of growth. Similar policies have not been adopted in the United States for several reasons. Among the most important is the distinctive form of government which we value so highly . . . it is not feasible for the highest level of government to design policies for development that can operate successfully in all parts of the nation.

Growing Disbeliefs

Although laissez-faire and privatism are deeply rooted in the cultures of North America, and indeed have in many respects served the national interests well, there is a growing conviction that the market mechanism by itself is not able to provide the solutions to the problems that urban growth generates. Indeed, it may very well be that the urban problems will be aggravated in the future if the market mechanism is permitted to run its course unchecked. For whenever there are "sluggish or inflexible adjustments to price signals, differences between private and public costs, and inadequate or wrong information, these market mechanisms work badly. And for groups living outside the economy or for groups which are unresponsive to economic rewards and penalties, they do not work at all" (Rodwin, 1970, p. 3). The market mechanism would not, therefore, appear to be capable of altering the direction and scale of future urban growth patterns, largely because by its very nature it tends to promote metropolitan concentration of employment and population, and in so doing it accentuates rather than diminishes regional imbalances, particularly as these result from lack of job opportunities and social investment. The inability of the market mechanism to check the growth of very large metropolitan areas is consequently one of the important cornerstones in arguments advocating the need for policies to guide and regulate urban development (Hansen, 1970).

Proponents of laissez-faire argue that the solution to the growth of large cities is guaranteed by the operation of the market mechanism, since cities reach a size or state of maturity after which they no longer become attractive to job-creating activities. Hence their population growth rates drop off to reach the levels of smaller places. Although this may possibly be the case with the central cities, it is certainly not for entire metropolitan regions. Nevertheless, the argument continues, "free market" forces of locational competition regulate the development of very large cities, and thus there is no need for policies to guide urban growth by steering urbanization toward areas outside the large urban concentrations. Although there is some merit to this kind of argument, it is overly optimistic, and it can be questioned on several grounds, not least on the basis of current experience. Current trends do not seem to support the contention of the operation of a self-regulating mechanism. Rather, they convincingly suggest that physical and social conditions of the largest cities may reach disaster proportions long before diseconomies of scale deter further population growth in them.

Questions relating to the economies and diseconomies of scale and size of urban concentration are not easy to answer; the empirical evidence is at best conflicting. Some writers argue that even the largest cities are by no means too big — and perhaps are not even big enough — in the sense of marginal costs exceeding marginal productivity (Alonso, 1968; Mera, 1973). Others argue the opposite, that many cities are today far too big and that the disadvantages of continued growth will outweigh the advantages by far (Lynch, 1965; Hoover, 1968). Regardless of the particular viewpoint, the growing evidence of diseconomies of scale and the serious problems these have created in large cities can hardly be disputed. Congestion imposes high costs, not least for transportation. Highways are more expensive to build in densely built-up areas, and longer distances between homes and jobs not only impose added costs on commuting but also create extra demands for transport improvements. Services are more costly to provide and infrastructure costs are generally higher in larger metropolitan areas — a situation aggravated by extensive sprawl. Pollution and the need for massive urban renewal have become very real problems, as we have seen in the older central cities. In short, everything points to the operation of a kind of circular-cumulative decay process in the largest metropolitan areas which, once triggered, continues in an accelerating downward direction (Baumol, 1967). External costs in large cities really do seem to grow disproportionately as a function of population size.

The increasing social costs of large cities do not arise only from the high levels of population concentration, but also from the excessive concentration of manufacturing in them. Obviously the two are interrelated. Real costs are not just a matter of plants and operation; they very much involve the added costs to the community arising from the pollution and highway congestion they create, the extra services they require, and so on. True benefits accrue in the form of jobs, but increasingly it appears that decentralization forces have created a marked spatial imbalance in supply and demand, particularly for the residents of the inner cities (Harvey, 1973). In many cases the supposed benefits of added jobs in large cities fall far short of the added costs they generate to the community as a whole and the contribution that firms make to the public purse. The continued concentration of manufacturing and white-collar jobs in large metropolitan centers also increases migration to them, which adds to social costs. Many in-migrants are not suited to big-city life; they are too ill, too poor, or just too old to adjust. Growing numbers of newcomers end up on welfare or turn to less desirable ways of getting a living. These costs too are transferred in large part to the community. If these kinds of hidden costs were included in the economic calculations of choosing between alternative locations, then for the whole society as a general rule it is probably far less economical to let smaller cities die by allowing the growth of very large metropolitan concentrations to proceed unchecked.

The arguments allowing the market mechanism free rein are perhaps a little easier to accept in the context of regional differences. Proponents of laissez-faire claim that the market mechanism takes care of the problems of regional imbalances since it encourages migration out of the lagging regions and evens out income differences. There is indeed some support for this view, since the trend during the past 50 years in the United States, at least, has been for per capita incomes in the various regions to converge. Moreover, since the price system in a market economy is the best available automatic regulatory device for achieving efficiency, it should induce an optimal spatial allocation of resources. Therefore regional imbalances are to be expected and may be justified on the basis of overall national efficiency. However, the economic rationale on which these kinds of arguments rest may be seriously questioned (Richardson, 1972a), and in any case, equity is now increasingly thought to be as important as efficiency. The social costs associated with marked regional inequalities in unemployment or income levels are usually high and quickly become politically unacceptable.

URBAN AND REGIONAL POLICY

A policy is a definite course or method of action selected from among alternatives, and in light of given conditions, to guide and determine present and future developments. It specifies the kinds of programs that are required to change the present situation to satisfy a set of specified goals. Policy making can consequently be likened to a trip: "The origin is the current situation; the destination the goal; the route selected is the policy; and the vehicle used is the program" (Till, 1974). The essence of any policy is therefore its goal orientation and its future orientation.

Policies aimed at containing, for example, the excessive growth of large cities cannot be implemented in isolation, but rather must be set in a broader context. In highly urbanized countries, this wider framework is that of the urban and regional distribution of national population. The population of a country is one of its basic resources, and people cannot be divided into social and economic entities. Individuals are simultaneously members of households in a social setting and employees in an economic setting. Hence just as the supply of labor is an important part of the urban environment from the viewpoint of industrialists, so the variety of job opportunities forms part of the total social environment from the point of view of the individual. Job opportunities combine with living conditions, service, education, welfare provision, and recreational amenities to determine the total living conditions or quality of life of particular urban centers in particular regions. Hence, because "these factors [together] influence migration and ultimately the distribution of population, and these in turn market conditions, the population distribution is clearly the focal point of this complex set of inter-relationships" (European Free Trade Association, 1974, p. 17).

National urban policy would focus primarily, then, on creating a desired distribution of population, employment, and welfare services between different cities in different regions within the country. An urban policy can consequently be defined as "an explicit statement of the purpose of urbanization, its pace, its character, and the values that are to prevail" (Berry, 1973b, p. 73). The programs needed to achieve this would obviously shift much of the initiative for urban growth away from private interests to governments, hence would impose on public authorities an obligation to plan the physical, economic, social, and spatial character of urban and regional life within national territories.

To this end, national policy would probably include decisions about the preferred size and spatial distribution of urban settlements together with the transportation links between them. A key element might be policies to regulate the location of economic activity, since differences in job availability are usually one of the basic causes of regional inequality and a prime force motivating migration. The dispersion of urban-economic growth coupled with containment policies to curb the growth of the largest cities would be a central feature of the overall strategies required, perhaps to create a situation of "concentrated decentralization" within the country. Key cities in lagging regions could be expanded or created *de novo* to help promote regional growth and prosperity, while in the prosperous, congested urban regions new towns might be created to accommodate new population growth or the overspill resulting from the renewal of existing metropolises (Meyerson, 1967).

The task of devising and implementing comprehensive urban policies is extremely complex. Agreement on the goals to be achieved is not likely to be easily reached. Moreover, such a policy would require the integration of spatial planning with other aspects of government activity not usually associated with it, such as economic and social policies. Hence integrating and coordinating programs would be a difficult task requiring new administrative machinery and close cooperation between existing agencies at different levels of government. Some idea of the interrelationships between strategies at different levels is suggested in Table 19.2, which shows the main goals and considerations that have been used in attempts to contain the growth of London, England (Foley, 1963).

In view of the complexities, it is not surprising to find that very few countries have been bold enough actually to implement a truly national urban policy; South Africa and Israel are the two most commonly cited (Schackar, 1974). In most other countries only limited policies relating to urban and regional growth have been devised. The nature and extent of these, and indeed their success, have varied from country to country, largely depending on the pervading values and attitudes toward urban policy making and planning.

Table 19.2.   MAIN GOALS AND CONSIDERATIONS USED IN ATTEMPTS TO CONTROL THE GROWTH OF LONDON

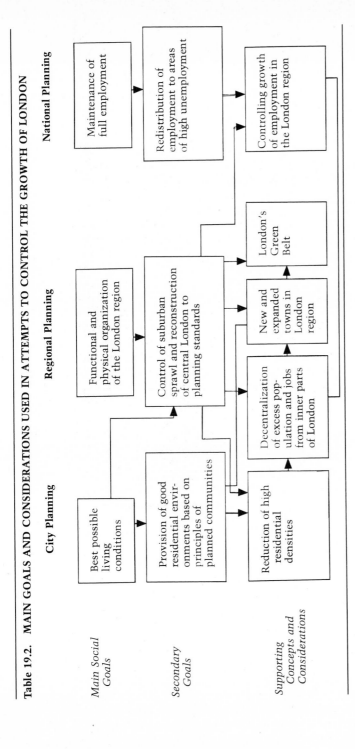

Planning Approaches

In reviewing the human consequences of urbanization in various countries of the world, Berry (1973b) suggested that a sequence of four modes of urban policy making and planning may be recognized. The main features of each of these styles are shown in Figure 19.2. On each of the diagrams, a distinction is made between two kinds of inputs that produce change in the city system, and two kinds of outputs that may result. The inputs are (1) external forces, such as inflation, the birth rate, and fluctuation in the GNP, whose causes are beyond the control of policy makers, and (2) the policies and programs chosen by public authorities. The outcomes can either be (3) undesirable problems created by the growth and change of the city system itself or (4) the desired outcomes specified by the goals and objectives. The different approaches to urban policy making are represented in Figure 19.2 by appropriate rearrangement of these four items.

A. *Ameliorative problem solving.* The simplest and commonest approach can be thought of as "planning for the present." Nothing is done until the problems arising from the dynamics of change in the city system reach crisis proportions or levels below this that are politically unacceptable. Then a course of action is devised and resources are allocated accordingly. Explicit goals are not specified, and the major objective is to scale problems back down to acceptable levels of tolerance. Hence this approach is past- rather than future-oriented. Moreover, as a strategy it is reactive and consequently can achieve little more than a haphazard modification of the future pattern of urban growth.

B. *Allocative trend-modifying.* This is the future version of planning for the present. It is based on the projection of existing trends into the future to forecast the problems that are likely to arise. Regulatory mechanisms are then devised to modify and make the *best* of trends and, one hopes, bring about a problem-free future without altering any of the existing values.

C. *Exploitive opportunity-seeking.* This is an extension of the foregoing approach, since the main objective is to make the *most* of the future by capitalizing on existing trends. Hence analyses are made not to identify future problems, but rather to identify new growth opportunities. Resources are then allocated so as to take advantage of what is expected to happen in the future.

D. *Normative goal orientation.* This, the ideal approach, can be thought of as planning from the future, in that goals are set in accordance with the kind of future that is desired. Policies are then designed and plans implemented to guide the city system toward these goals. If necessary, the existing system is changed to make sure that the goals are attained.

It is difficult to associate any single one of these approaches to urban policy making with any particular country. In reality, a mixture of all styles is usually present, although, depending upon the predominant beliefs, one or two of them usually take precedence over the others. Thus, normative planning can be applied only in countries in which the government has sufficient control and power to ensure that the policies *will* produce the desired results. Hence it is highly developed in the Soviet Union, although it also plays an important role in planning in democratic countries with strong central government traditions, such as Sweden, France, and Britain. In Canada and the United States, policy making is based on the first two approaches. As a result, planning is

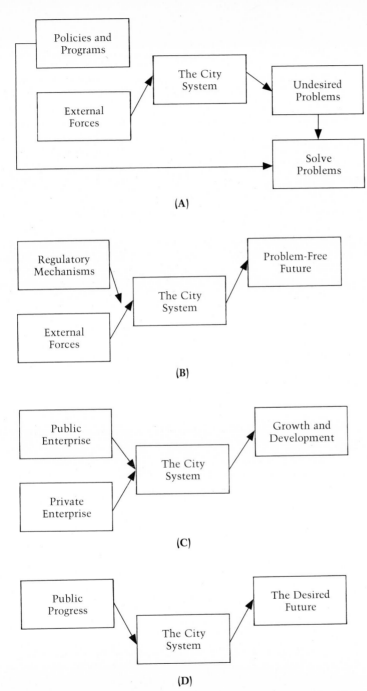

Fig. 19.2. Four styles of planning. (*Source*: after Berry, 1973, Fig. 18.)

essentially reactive or regulatory. Hence the future urban pattern of North America will almost certainly be based on the continuation of past trends—perhaps that shown in Figure 19.1—unless a substantial change in attitudes emerges in coming decades to shift the emphasis to a more goal-oriented approach. With this background, it is easier to understand why urban and regional policies in North America are the way they are and why other countries have often been able to achieve far more.

LAGGING REGIONS AND URBAN GROWTH POLICY

We have noted previously that urban growth is closely related to economic growth and that cities are intimately tied to their surrounding regions. The city system itself in advanced countries can in fact perhaps be thought of as a form of spatial organization adopted by the industrial economy to achieve its growth goals. The natural process of urban-economic development can be expected to bring about uneven patterns of growth as the city system unfolds and concentration in a few regions occurs. The continued polarization of growth together with structural changes in regional economies, however, inevitably leads to marked spatial imbalances in economic health and general well-being, and lagging or depressed areas emerge.

Lagging regions are characterized either by above-average unemployment and/or marked instability of employment or by below-average family incomes and high levels of out-migration. Often these may occur in combination. When these become pronounced, political pressures usually force central governments to do something to aid regional development. Area development policies can be built around two main strategies. Attempts may be made to induce people to move out of the depressed regions by promotion migration to the more prosperous regions. Alternatively, attempts can be made to attract economic activity and capital away from the prosperous to the lagging regions.

The Case Against Migration Policies

Policies aimed at increasing migration out of lagging areas may be appropriate if unemployment rather than underemployment is the main problem. The economic arguments for this approach are that the movement of labor from the depressed regions to prosperous regions creates a better balance between the regional labor supply and employment opportunities, and this in turn increases total national output because the aggregate level of employment is increased or because labor is transferred from low- to high-productivity industries. As a result, differences in income levels between regions should diminish as labor supplies are reduced in the lagging regions and wage levels are at least slowed down as a result of the increased availability of labor in the more prosperous regions. Such a policy, it can be argued, is therefore consistent with national efficiency.

Although this strategy may have the merit of promoting economic efficiency, it can be seriously questioned on the basis of its practicability and on social grounds. In a democratic society in which the central government cannot force people to move from one region to another, it is impracticable. Of course, various incentives can be used to encourage people to migrate—for example, education and retraining expenses, direct financial assistance to cover costs of travel and removal, housing subsidies and allowances to defray other resettlement costs, and so on. However, not only are these expensive, but it seems that they are not notably successful in encouraging migration—at least, not at the high levels that would be required to make an out-migration policy effective.

Most people attach a "psychic income" to living in their own area where they are in contact with family and friends, and even when they are unemployed many prefer to accept the hardships of remaining there rather than moving out. For migration imposes severe stresses and strains on individuals. Moreover, it probably adds to the social costs of receiving areas, and since these are likely to be the already congested urbanized regions where, as we have seen, social costs are already high, this is undesirable. Substantial out-migration also affects the lagging regions themselves, where it is a prime factor in bringing downward multiplier effects into play as thresholds decline, services thin out, and investments become increasingly underutilized. Policies to improve the well-being of lagging regions by encouraging large-scale migration are therefore not only impracticable, they are generally not thought to be socially desirable, and they are seldom politically acceptable (Morrill and Wohlenberg, 1971).

The Case for Industrial Relocation

A major aspect of regional policy in many countries is in fact to reduce interregional migration, especially migration to the prosperous regions. Attempts to do this are usually based on strategies designed to encourage the flow of capital and economic activity to the lagging areas. The economic arguments for this are not convincing (see Richardson, 1972a, chap. 15), but in social terms a strong case can be made to support the practice of bringing jobs to the workers. First there are the social benefits to be gained from utilizing wasted human resources—the unemployed and the nonparticipants in the labor force who might work if jobs were available. Moreover, by attracting capital to the lagging regions in sufficient amounts, pressures for migration are reduced, thereby improving the chances for individuals to satisfy their locational preferences. Furthermore, this strategy aids the regional balance in the distribution of population and may help reduce external diseconomies in the prosperous, congested urban regions. The strategy of stimulating lagging regions by encouraging investment and growth in them while at the same time deterring growth in the prosperous regions thus forms a central part of regional policies in many countries today.

Area Development Policies in the United States

Although individual states have been active in promoting economic growth within their boundaries for a long time, federal policies to aid lagging regions are a recent development in the United States. They date essentially from 1961, when the Area Redevelopment Act was passed and a new agency was established within the Department of Commerce—the Area Redevelopment Agency (ARA). This body was to be responsible for assisting lagging regions in four main ways:

1. By providing loans (initially totaling 150 million dollars) to business enterprises, subject to reasonable assurances of repayment and that the firms aided were *not* relocating from other areas. Hence loans were restricted to new activities, to firms opening branch plants in the designated areas, and to those already established there but operating under full capacity.

2. By giving loans and making grants totaling 175 million dollars for the construction of public facilities.

3. By helping to cover the costs of labor-retraining programs.

4. By giving various kinds of technical help and through research.

The basic unit for defining areas eligible for assistance under the program was the Bureau of Employment Security Areas, although in some cases a number of smaller cities and counties were used instead. High levels of unemployment and low levels of median family income were the criteria used to identify areas in need of redevelopment. Delimiting these areas was a political problem from the start. When the legislation was first proposed, it was intended that about 20 major labor areas and 50 smaller industrial areas should benefit from the program. This figure was later revised to include a further 200 communities with stagnating economies, and shortly after the act was passed a total of 800 areas had been declared eligible for aid. Two years later, in 1963, the number had exceeded 1000, and these were widely scattered across the nation (see Fig. 19.3).

The new program had many shortcomings. One of the most important was that the aid could not be confined to the neediest areas, but because of the large number of designated areas it had to be scattered widely among many poor communities. Consequently the limited amount of aid that was available to each of the areas was not enough to add up to any real opportunity to strengthen their local economies significantly. Moreover, about two-thirds of the projects supported and investments made were in smaller cities and rural communities with fewer than 50,000 inhabitants.

The Area Redevelopment Act expired in 1965. Rather than eliminate the program, however, an attempt was made to modify it through the passage of the Public Works and Economic Development Act, which more than doubled appropriations to ARA and at the same time transformed it into the Economic Development Administration (EDA). The most important change relating to urban growth policy under the new program was in the definition of areas eligible to receive assistance; larger areas were now favored and the total number of areas was significantly reduced. In addition, a strategy was adopted of spreading the effects of assistance throughout a region by channeling aid into a small number of urban growth centers.

Three types of areas were designated for assistance, as shown in Figure 19.3. The basic unit was still the *redevelopment area*, and to satisfy conflicting political interests there had to be at least one of these in every state. The intermediate units within a state were the newly created multi-county *Economic Development Districts*. These had to be sufficiently extensive (on average five to 15 counties) and with sufficient basic resources to allow for effective economic planning, and also had to have at least one urban center with fewer than 250,000 inhabitants which had potential for relatively self-sustaining growth. The most significant innovation was the designation of multi-state *Economic Development Regions* and the establishment of regional planning commissions to direct and coordinate a comprehensive program of public investment and planning activity in them. In addition to the regional commission for Appalachia (established under a separate act in 1965), five others were set up: New England, the Upper Great Lakes, the Ozarks, the "four corners" area in the Southwest, and the Coastal Plains area (see Fig. 19.3).

It is generally recognized that the ERA-EDA experiment has by and large been ineffectual; because of the lack of a clear strategy the benefits were not as great as they might have otherwise been. The scale of the programs was trivial in relation to needs and was too scattered to be of any substantial value. An important restriction was the exclusion of firms wanting to relocate in the designated areas from eligibility to receive aid. Although the urban growth center concept was a significant innovation in the later programs, its application was weakened by the vague definition used in identifying growth centers and the ambiguity in the criteria used in their selection (see Berry, 1973a).

Moreover, the ways of delimiting areas eligible for assistance meant that programs were not able to attack the problems of the most critical areas—the lagging areas of the metropolitan central cities. Neither did the programs come to grips with the problems of the nation's most critical lagging region, the deep South. Hence the migration of blacks from the South continued and the growth of ghettos was converting the central cities into a new kind of lagging region, "at once more visible and more explosive than the social quagmires from which their impoverished residents have come" (Rodwin, 1970, p. xiv). Only a national urbaneconomic development policy designed to create new economic and social opportunities for the nonwhite population of the growth centers in the South as well as in the ghettos of the cities of the North and West could hope to cope with the situation.

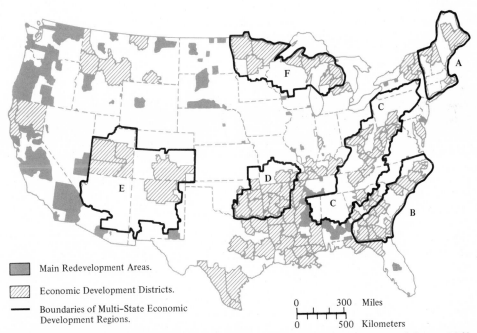

Fig. 19.3. Designated areas of the Economic Development Administration, United States, 1968. The Multi-State Economic Development Regions are New England (A), Coastal Plains (B), Appalachia (C), Ozarks (D), "Four Corners" (E), and Upper Great Lakes (F). (*Source*: U.S. Department of Commerce.)

Regional Policy in Canada

Explicit federal area development policies are a recent innovation in Canada too, where they began in 1963 with the passage of the Area Development Act and the establishment of the Area Development Agency (ADA) within the Department of Industry. Prior to this, limited cooperation between the federal and provincial governments had been taking place under the provisions of the 1961 Agriculture Rehabilitation and Development Act, directed specifically at the problems of rural poverty, and the 1962 Atlantic Development Board, which was established to help in the general economic development of the Maritime Provinces in eastern Canada. Under ADA, 35 areas embracing about 8 percent of the labor force were designated to receive assistance. With one exception, these were all located in eastern Canada, and were identified, as in the United States, by high levels of unemployment.

The Canadian approach, however, differed substantially from that adopted in the United States in two important respects. First, with its principal aim of combating local unemployment, aid under the program was restricted to the location of manufacturing industry, and second, the aid was made available not in the form of repayable loans but as tax concessions. Approved firms locating in a designated area were exempt from income taxes for the first three years of operation and could write off the cost of new buildings and machinery at rates ranging between 20 and 50 percent within an initial five-year period.

In 1965 a major change occurred in policy with the passage of the Area Development Incentives Act. The number of designated areas was increased from the previous 38 to 81, and these were more widely scattered across the country. In addition to high unemployment rates, account was now also taken of underemployment as it was reflected in low median family incomes. The form of assistance was also altered; "tax holidays" were abolished and capital grants were implemented to help cover initial investment costs in plant and buildings. Changes were again made in 1969 when the Regional Development Incentives Act was passed. The Department of Regional Economic Expansion, which was created under this act, would in the future be responsible for the coordination of the various activities of the federal government in an attempt to create a more holistic approach to the problem of the lagging regions. The most interesting aspect of their program from the viewpoint of urban and regional policy was that in the future aid was to be chaneled into urban growth centers (Brewis, 1969).

Of the many criticisms that may be leveled at the area development programs in both the United States and Canada, one stands out as being especially important. The policies were not tailored to suit the particular needs of the various regions, but rather a blanket strategy for all regions was adopted. Different regions have different development possibilities and of course varying needs. Some regions might have benefited more from investments in tertiary activity than in manufacturing or government services—for example, the regions with good potential for tourism. Some regions may be short of trained labor and aid should perhaps be concentrated on this at the expense of other programs. Other regions need greatly improved communication to function efficiently, while still others require massive investments in public services and infrastructure. Although some atttempt to do this kind of thing was made in the American programs, they nevertheless operated within the framework of a general set of solutions, and to this extent they might have been inappropriate, for "the problems of every depressed region should be analyzed in detail, their main depression characteristics indicated, a list of objectives drawn up and priorities determined, and comprehensive plans formulated and/or individual policy instruments applied which achieve the chosen objectives most efficiently" (Richardson, 1972a, p. 230).

GROWTH CENTER STRATEGIES

Experiences to date suggest that aid to lagging regions, and particularly aid intended to stimulate industrial growth, cannot be widely dispersed or dissipated on many small activities, but rather must be concentrated at a few locations. This is in large part because the nature of urban growth has changed in an important respect. Whereas in the past, regions created cities, as we saw in Chapter 2, today cities make regions. A strategy based on this observation which is increasingly being recommended is that of developing growth centers in the lagging regions, and often in the prosperous regions as well when the objective is to reduce congestion and sprawl by spreading growth out in a controlled pattern (see, for example, Hansen, 1970, 1971a, 1971b; Kuklinski, 1972). The essential idea behind a growth-center strategy, which is itself an outgrowth of the "growth pole" concept initially developed by French economists (see Darwent, 1969; Boudeville, 1968; Lausen, 1969), is to encourage the development of a network of urban centers within the lagging regions and to help them to become self-sustaining centers of industrial and service growth (Berry, 1973a). Although the need for this was explicitly recognized in the later area development programs in both the United States and Canada, attempts to create viable growth centers were unsuccessful. Two problems in particular may help explain this: the way urban places were chosen as growth centers, and the difficulties of triggering growth in them.

A critical factor in choosing cities as growth centers is their size. In the United States, the growth centers were generally far too small (in 1968 the 88 growth centers had a median population of only 38,000). Consequently, they could not hope to have any significant influence on their hinterlands and hence could not justify public investments in them for regional development purposes (Morrill, 1974b). Results of recent research suggest that cities and their labor force areas need about 250,000 inhabitants before they can function effectively as growth centers. Above this size, the evidence suggests that they become viable parts of the urban system and have the conditions necessary for self-sustained growth (Berry, 1968b). The figure of 200,000–250,000 was, it will be remembered, the size at which Thompson (1965a) thought that the urban size ratchet effect first took effect, and the chances of decline were minimal. On the other hand, there is a considerable body of evidence suggesting that from the viewpoint of government services, at least, the optimal size of cities is far less than this (Neutze, 1967; Richardson, 1972b). Scale economies in public utilities, for example, appear to be greatest either in small places or in large agglomerations (Hirsch, 1968), suggesting that places of 250,000 may encounter diseconomies of scale in the public sector. The effects of this, however, would probably be more than offset by the external economies accruing to the private sector, and especially the urbanization economies for industry (Hansen, 1971b).

The problem of achieving self-sustained growth at growth centers is a more complex one, although in theory it is simple enough; namely, to trigger the circular-cumulative growth process referred to in Chapter 4. In part this is a locational problem. Growth centers need strong connections and linkages with the areas surrounding them.

Moreover, they should already be growing relatively rapidly, and hence possess good prospects for developing and creating new jobs. However, the crux of the matter is attracting the right kinds of industry to them, so that a favorbale industry-mix effect is created. In this respect, stable high-wage export-oriented industries rather than rapid-growth industries are probably best because of their ability to support a well-developed service base. Moreover, to be a viable growth point, a center should probably have a national "propulsive" industry, or a group of industries that have local productive linkages with other industries in the region in order that growth can be diffused through the surrounding area.

Inducing such industries to locate at growth centers is one of the main goals of regional policies. The problem is a difficult one to solve because of the very strong pressures that exist for industries to locate and expand in cities in the already prospering regions. However, recent changes in technology and communication suggest that, as was noted in Chapter 5, the importance of locational costs in the overall cost matrix have been substantially reduced so that many industries with plants of optimal size can operate really at a wide variety of locations in different regions with only minimal differences in production costs. If this is the case, then attractive government incentives may be able to divert industry away from the existing concentrations to the growth centers, although the extent to which this attempt is successful may depend very much on whether or not restrictions are placed at the same time on the further growth of existing cities.

There are many kinds of incentives that may be used. Interest-free loans, capital grants, and tax concessions are among the most commonly used. In Sweden, transportation costs have been subsidized in attempts to attract industry to the remote northern part of the country. In Britain a whole battery of incentives has been used since World War II to assist industries in the lagging regions and to attract industry to them, including government aid to older staple industries in these regions either to slow down their rate of decline or to modernize them. Industrial estates have been built, factories constructed in advance of demand, and rents subsidized. Large investment grants, construction grants, and even grants to help purchase land for sites have frequently been used. For a short period, employment premiums were offered as a subsidy to labor costs, while various kinds of labor-retraining schemes have been introduced. At the same time these incentives were coupled with various restrictions on the further growth of employment in southeast England, and in this way a powerful comprehensive regional policy was developed. As a result of all these measures, expenditure by the British government to encourage employment in the development regions increased from about 200 million dollars in 1966–1967 to 650 million dollars in 1968–1969. Yet despite this effort and expense, the problems of creating sustained growth in the lagging areas have not yet been solved (see Manners, 1972).

Growth centers have been explicitly built into planning strategies in various countries. The latest regional development scenario for the province of Ontario accents the need to structure growth that is spontaneous on the one hand and to stimulate growth where necessary on the other. To this end three types of growth center have been suggested: *Primate centers* — the fast-growing large cities such as Toronto, Hamilton, Kitchener-Waterloo, Thunder Bay, and Ottawa. Associated with these are the *linked centers* — cities close to the major centers that can be developed as secondary and tertiary employment centers. Finally, beyond the zones of metropolitan concentration, a number of *strategic centers* have been proposed as places for industrial and service development. In this way it is hoped that employment opportunities in key urban places will be available throughout the province by 1981 (Thoman, 1974).

Growth Centers in France

At the national level, growth centers have recently become an important element in French regional policy. The Fifth National Plan (1966–1969) explicitly recognized that the most effective way of handling regional growth problems was to build up a system of large growth centers throughout the country. These were to be established to counterbalance the excessive concentration in the Paris region, but would also help solve one of the major problems in the French city system—namely, the lack of influential high-order cities at the top of the urban hierarchy. To this end the concept of equilibrium metropolises was introduced. Four criteria were used to select these: city size, level of service and infrastructure to support economic activity, the special functions cities performed in the system, and the nature and extent of their hinterlands. After careful analyses, the eight cities shown in Figure 19.4 were chosen as the national growth centers—a growth strategy that took account of the need to stimulate urban and regional growth in the peripheries yet at the same time the need to contain the already excessive growth in the Paris region. Large-scale public investments were to be made in the eight growth centers to balance as much as possible the influence of Paris, thereby creating a situation of equilibrium in the urban system, and it was planned to increase their combined population from the 6.5 million in 1969 to 16.5 million in the following 25 years.

NEW TOWNS

An alternative strategy to developing existing places as viable growth centers is to build entirely new ones. Several attempts have been made in the United States to create new

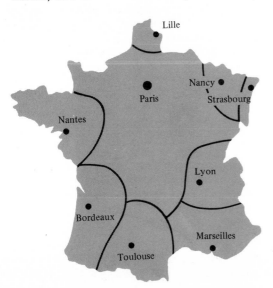

Fig. 19.4. Equilibrium metropolises: national growth centers and their hinterlands in France.

towns of sorts during the past 50 years. Early "new towns" were often little more than planned residential extensions to existing metropolitan areas—for example, Sunnyside Gardens in New York City (1924–1928) and Chatham Village in Pittsburgh (1932). The first community actually started as an independent entity was Radburn, N.J., in 1928. Serious attention was first given to the idea of building new towns during the Depression years of the 1930s, when the federal government initiated the Greenbelt Towns program. Originally it was hoped to build about 300 of these throughout the country. Actually only three ever materialized: Greenbelt, Md.; Greenhills, Ohio; and Greendale, Wis. (Arnold, 1971). Among the better known recent examples of new town development are Reston, Va., and Columbus, Md., both of which are located in the vicinity of Washington, D.C. (Turner, 1974).

Apart from the limited federal involvement during the 1930's and some postwar activity in connection with the atomic energy program, new towns in America have resulted from private initiative—from consortiums comprising builder-developers, large national corporations, large landowners, and big mortgage lenders. To the extent that there is public involvement, "it involves reducing the risks to the entrepreneur in exchange for some mild regulation of the development style" (Berry, 1973b, p. 68) under provisions in the 1968 Housing Act. However, state governments are more active and are becoming interested in the idea of new towns; New York has designated three under its Urban Development Corporation program (at Amherst, Lysander, and Welfare Island), while several other states are considering legislation to promote new town construction.

New towns in the United States are for the most part, however, not really new towns in a strict sense, but rather new residential communities. There is a big difference between the two, for "a new town is an attempt to break the pattern of urban growth, and at the same time to shift development to different places and to control it. A new community is a way of ordering the business of land development at the fringe of American metropolitan areas" (Eichler and Kaplan, 1967, p. 24). Hence in the United States, at least, what is thought of as a new town is primarily a physical planning device for what essentially amounts to controlled suburban development. As such these towns are of course hardly suited as growth centers, even less so since industry is not usually regarded as one of their primary functions.

New Towns in Britain

The situation has been quite different in Britain, where an ambitious program of new town construction has been operating since 1946 (Edwards, 1964). In Britain, however, a new town is narrowly and precisely defined as a town built under the provisions of the 1946 New Towns Act by a Development Corporation (a public body that is directly responsible to Parliament) at a location designated by the Secretary of State for the Environment (formerly by the Minister of Housing) and directly financed by the Treasury. The British new towns are therefore fully under the control of the central government during their early years, and, moreover, they have all been built to perform specific planning functions. Most commonly these have been to provide houses and jobs for "overspill" populations from large urban agglomerations whose growth is being restrained by planning policies, and to promote economic and social development in the depressed areas or lagging regions. They are planned to be reasonably self-sufficient and to grow through a carefully phased program of attracting industry in step with their population growth (Thomas, 1969). This has been achieved by the use of various kinds of incentives and inducements, both to industry and to in-migrants. Hence in Britain, new towns have been built for specifically social purposes as part of a wider national urban and regional policy (Hall, 1972).

At the beginning of 1971 there were 28 of these new towns in Britain, containing a total of 1.5 million inhabitants (over half of whom have moved to the new towns from other cities) and over 35 million square feet of new factory space and a further 4 million square feet of office space (Clawson and Hall, 1973). The distribution of the new towns in shown in Figure 19.5. They have all been created, then, not by private enterprise, but by the central government, and not for profit, but to solve some specific problem of the region in which they are located. Their specific role varies in part depending on when they were first started and in part on where they are. The chronology of new town construction enables them to be classified into two well-defined groups: the original 14 new towns designated in the period 1946–1950 (now referred to as the Mark I new towns) and those that were started later than 1961.

London's New Towns

Of the first batch of new towns, eight were designated around Greater London to provide for the orderly decentralization of population and jobs from the central city. They formed part of a comprehensive planning effort after World War II to contain the growth of the London region, the principal ingredients and goals of which are sketched in Table 19.2. At the national level, the main goal was the maintenance of full employment, and to attain this it was considered appropriate to reduce regional imbalances in employment opportunities. To this end, industry and other employment were encouraged, by the kinds of incentives discussed above, to move to or expand in the regions with high unemployment rates—the so-called development regions shown on Figure 19.5. In connection with this, certain restraints were placed on the location of industry, and later on offices, in the Greater London region. At the regional level, the main planning goals related to the physical organization of the built-up area of London, and it was as part of this effort that the eight new towns were designated around the London conurbation. The main concern at the local level was the creation of the best possible living environments through coordinated physical city planning. The remainder of the original new towns, with one exception (Corby), were built as part of regional development policies to stimulate the economies of the regions that had lagged behind the development of the rest of the country during the interwar years (Madge, 1962). These were then in a sense growth centers.

The Second-Generation New Towns

The second-generation new towns date from 1961, and differ from their earlier counterparts not so much in the role they were intended to play as in their location and especially in their size. Ten of the 13 towns designed after 1961 were conceived primarily to help decentralize population from the major conurbations; the remaining three fulfilled this role in part but were also designed with regional development in mind. The main difference is that these newer towns have for the most part been located farther away from the bigger cities to prevent them from becoming commuting communities, as some of the earlier London new towns had tended to become, and most of them are now planned to have considerably larger populations from the start (Diamond,

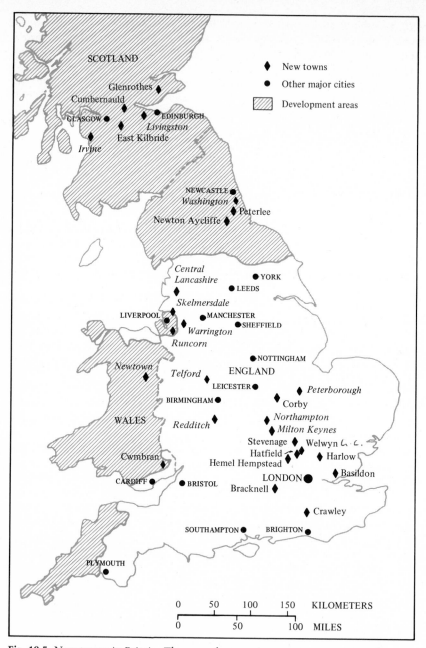

Fig. 19.5. New towns in Britain. The second-generation new towns are in italics.

1972). Several are expected to have well over 150,000 inhabitants when completed, and Milton Keynes, the latest of the London overspill towns, has a target population of 250,000—the size most generally believed to be appropriate for a growth center.

The new towns in Britain were not originally conceived as growth centers per se, but functioned in part in this capacity. The earlier ones in particular were, however, too small to be effective growth centers; they had populations ranging only from 25,000 to 60,000. Moreover, they were often too close to larger cities. Nevertheless, and despite some problems with the new towns program, the British experience has been a bold experiment and has contributed positively to broader policies of urban and regional development in which the growth-center concept has played an important role.

WHITHER THE FUTURE?

A considerable body of theory now exists concerning urban and regional development, and a substantial literature on the subject is available. Moreover, there is now a wealth of experience in devising and implementing urban policies in many countries. Lessons have been learned and mistakes made, to be sure. But despite this, positive attempts have been made to come to grips with the complex problems involved and many successes have been scored. The question is whether this has any relevance for the future urban pattern in North America. If it has, it will require some radical changes in attitudes in both the United States and Canada to be of any positive use. For North American society is at present inherently incapable of being goal-oriented for deep-seated reasons. Yet without this change, planning—as distinct from plan-making—can never become a reality. What substitutes for planning and urban regional policy in North America is a complex set of

> uncoordinated, often contradictory, essentially random public policies and programs provided in the wake of strong economic forces which set the agenda for urban growth. Thus, if in the past urbanization has been governed by any conscious public objectives at all, these have been on the one hand, to encourage growth, apparently for its own sake; and on the other, to provide public works and public welfare programs to support piecemeal, spontaneous development impelled primarily by private initiative [Berry, 1973b, p. 73].

The question is whether this attitude toward such an important problem, if allowed to continue, is sufficient to ensure that the North American way of life will still exist for future generations.

20
THE
FUTURE
CITY

Regardless of the changes in the distribution of population that could possibly result from greater involvement in planning and policy making in North America, one thing is very clear: the majority of North Americans will in future continue to live in large cities and city regions. The problem remains, therefore, of improving the environments of these massive concentrations so that life can be greatly improved for the greatest number of people. It is quite obvious that urban life will not be very meaningful for most people if:

1. The general standard of housing for everyone fails to rise, especially for those presently living in the ghettos and slums of the inner cities.

2. There are not equal opportunities and access to these opportunities for all in terms of education, medical care, and cultural and recreational amenities.

3. The transportation system within urban areas continues to be congested.

4. The quality of the environment continues to deteriorate through pollution of all kinds, lack of adequate sewage facilities, and other essential public services.

5. General distrust and disillusionment grow as a result of the apparent outright rejection of humanistic values by governments and individuals with economic power.

6. Crime, particularly organized crime, increases its hold on society.

Many of these conditions are interrelated to varying degrees, so what in fact is needed is a program to tackle some of these issues in a comprehensive manner at the city-region scale. Of course, items 5 and 6 in the above list require a fundamental ethical change in society which is beyond the scope of an urban program, but is nevertheless predicated upon it. Individual packages—such as urban renewal, metropolitan transportation studies, and special mortgage facilities for the low-income groups—have attempted to ameliorate some of the problems, as we have seen in the previous chapters; but they have in fact raised more problems than they have solved. Many of the principles and concepts discussed in this book will, we hope, help lead us toward the development of sound policies and programs, particularly since a major part of these are spatial in nature. In this concluding chapter, we turn our attention to the problems of large cities, and especially to scenarios concerning the form of the city of the future and its livability.

FUTURE CONDITIONS

In their comprehensive review of planning and urban growth in the United States and Britain, Clawson and Hall (1973) have listed what they feel are the principal considerations that will have to be incorporated in developing the future city. First, most of the population increase is not likely to be accommodated in whatever new towns may be built in the future, but rather will need to be housed in suburbs to existing cities. Hence decentralization and suburbanization are likely to be as important as they have been in the past in shaping future urban growth. Per capita real incomes will most certainly continue to rise and the trends toward more single-person households and more than one living space in cities per household will accelerate. Rising incomes will express themselves in higher demand for material goods and services for private consumption, but there will also be greater demands to divert a greater proportion of the rise in living standards into the production of *public* goods and services of all kinds. These trends will inevitably mean that demands on land will be greater in scale and variety than ever before, and that cities will have to be transformed to meet the change in life styles and consumption patterns that can be expected to develop. As a result, greater attention will have to be given to questions relating to the proper use of land and the equitable distribution of activities, especially public ones, within cities.

Use of Innovations

At the same time, innovations will be required, particularly in construction and in transportation. The massive increase in urban population expected in the coming decades can be catered to only by a tremendous increase in construction activity. Though there have been a number of technological improvements in the construction industry, and a few instances of undoubted increases in productivity, there is little doubt that this branch of industry has demonstrated an inability to become as productive as others. This is in part due to the instability of the construction industry, which tends to have a marked cyclical pattern; but it is also due to the nature of the industry, which has to cater to the individual potential homeowner as well as to the ambitious downtown redeveloper. However, the future pressure on the construction industry promises to be so great that innovations in both techniques and production management will have to be incorporated in the future. These innovations range all the way from prefabricated units to the on-the-spot utilization of continuously poured cement for large structures.

A second type of innovation necessary for the future city is a different form of urban transportation. The massive construction and reconstruction of urban areas that is going to be required will make innovation and experimentation feasible. Since there are now doubts concerning future energy sources and increased prices seems inevitable, it is perhaps reasonable to assume that although the automobile will still play an important part in moving people and goods within cities, the best alternative is the development of some form of personal transit system as suggested in Chapter 16. This type of system involves interfacing *cybernetics*—the science of communication and control—with individual transport vehicles. Such an interfacing could well be financially feasible in the short term, given the colossal overexpenditure on personal transportation incurred today. It is difficult to envisage that an individual really requires a 420-cubic-inch internal combustion engine for personal or even family mobility, particularly when the average speed of urban travel is usually less than 25 miles per hour.

THE FORM OF FUTURE CITIES

The fact that increasingly large numbers of people will be concentrated in massive city regions, and that the form of these will have to be transformed to accommodate changing life styles, means that ways will have to be found to ensure that the overall physical environment of urban areas is improved (Doxiadis, 1970). A number of strategies are involved to this end, including city beautification programs, improvements in the quality and availability of housing, changing the distribution of service provision, and so on. But more importantly, the problem of alleviating the negative aspects of suburban sprawl will be one of the top priorities: "The city is here, will remain, and we must learn how to control its form to our ends" (Clawson and Hall, 1973, p. 272). Without this, the problems of rearranging the fabric within the city will remain as large as ever. Planning the form of cities has received considerable attention in the literature, much of which is concerned with three alternative basic city forms: the linear, the circular, and the sectoral arrangements (Reynolds, 1961).

The Linear Plan

The linear plan is of European origin and became particularly well known when it was proposed as a planning framework for London, England, by the MARS group (Modern Architectural Research Society). The MARS plan featured an arrangement of land uses around a main spine of communication (Foley, 1963). Along this main spine are arrayed the major areas of employment and economic activity (Fig. 20.1). The residential areas are located along right-angle offshoots from this main spine and are linked one with the other by the main spine itself or a circumferal belt. Urban growth is facilitated by a simple extension of the spine and the creation of right-angle residential offshoots.

There are several obvious advantages to a plan of this type. In the first place, it does provide a rational procedure for urban growth. Second, it presents a very clear distinction between major land uses, and it does provide a feasible means of interconnection. Third, it emphasizes centrality and the location of major city-serving activities in an elongated downtown area. Finally it provides for open spaces within an orderly arrangement of land uses that are equally accessible from all residential areas. The major fault in the plan is that it is perhaps too geometric and formal. As applied to London, the major objection was that its implementation would lead to a rather drastic destruction of historical buildings and re-sorting of land uses on a very large scale. These objections do not, of course, apply to many North American cities, and certainly not to new urban areas.

The Circular Plan

The circular plan form is developed from a communication system based on ring roads and radials. The radials focus upon a nucleus to a central business area, which is surrounded by a ring and from which the radials spring (see Fig. 20.2). One major advantage of a plan of this type is that it clearly fosters the development of neighborhood units between each radial and ring. Furthermore, the plan conforms very closely to the natural evolution of most urban areas, for they have tended to follow this radial-concentric growth. The major drawback becomes apparent, however, when open spaces are being considered, for there are really only two choices — a green belt or wedges between the radials.

Green belts have in fact been encouraged as a major device, both for controlling urban sprawl and for providing recreational space for inhabitants of urban areas. In many instances a green belt is considered to be a barrier to urban growth, containing the

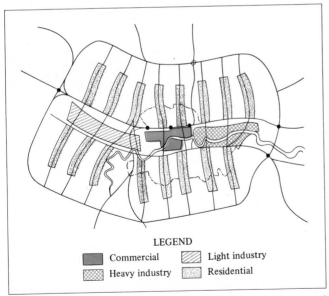

LEGEND

Commercial Light industry
Heavy industry Residential

Fig. 20.1. A linear urban plan. The MARS group's proposal for London, England. In this plan, commercial and industrial areas are concentrated in a core paralleling the river Thames, and residential areas are placed in strips perpendicular to the core. (*Source*: Reynolds, 1961, Fig. 17.)

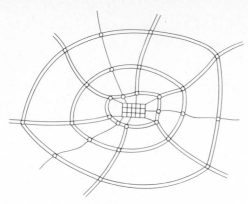

Fig. 20.2. A circular urban plan.

city and at times providing land for essential services that cannot be located within the urban area, such as hospitals or sanatoriums (Coleman, 1969). However, the simple introduction of a green belt usually results in the leap-frogging or urban sprawl over the zoned area, so that the green belt becomes a barrier crisscrossed by a variety of modes of communication.

Although green belts seem to be an article of faith among many planners, it is doubtful whether they have the great utility attributed to them. Frequently green belts are provided regardless of the type of land involved. It is possible, for example, that potentially good recreational areas may be excluded from a green belt and developed for residential purposes or even commercial activities, simply because they have not been zoned within the green belt. On the other hand, flat, boring, nonrecreational areas may well be included within a green belt because they fall within a planner's geometric conception of design. Thus though one of the philosophical bases of a green belt, that of providing land for recreational purposes, may be quite sound, it is quite feasible to cater to this need without designating an entire ring as a barrier.

One great drawback to green belts is that they are most accessible to people living on the fringe of urban areas and therefore offer an unfair amenity advantage to people living in these peripheral zones. As a means of circumventing this problem, some planners have modified the green-belt concept by proposing wedges that penetrate the urban area to provide open spaces for those people living within the central zone. This modification, however, seems at best a makeshift support to the green-belt concept.

The Sector Plan

The sector plan concentrates on radials as the dominant framework within which urban development and growth take place. The radials focus upon the urban core, which provides the nucleus for the urban area. The chief lines of communication use avenues along the spine of each radial, and minor nucleations of commercial activities are spaced along each like beads on a string. Probably the best-known plan of this type in Europe is the Copenhagen Finger Plan, and the most discussed similar design in North America is that for Washington, D.C.

In the latter case the plan envisages the development of six radials from central

Washington, D.C., one following the Washington-Baltimore corridor and the others connecting the major outlying satellite areas in Maryland and Virginia. Along each of these radials a number of new towns are planned, each of which will offer its own array of services, but they will all be linked to Washington, D.C., as the focus of economic activity for that region (Fig. 20.3). Where the radials connect major urban areas, the radial will in fact become a corridor of movement and will itself become an elongated ribbon of economic activity. Between the radials or corridors, open land for farming and recreational activities will be preserved.

This plan is basically one that prevents sprawl but channels growth into distinct

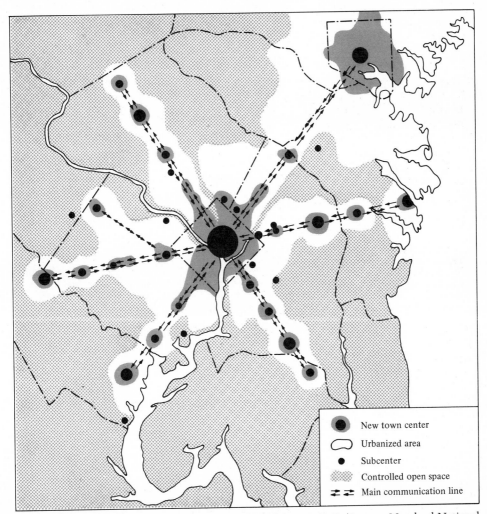

Fig. 20.3. The suggested radial corridor plan for Washington, D.C. (*Source*: Maryland-National Capital Park and Planning Commission, 1964, p. 20.)

avenues. Urban growth can take place by extending the radials as well as intensifying the land use, both within the central capital area and along the radial corridors closest to the core. The whole system, of course, depends on the use of high-speed urban transportation. The spine of each corridor will therefore consist of limited-access freeways and rapid transit, as well as railroads for moving bulky goods. It is envisaged, of course, that this mixture of transportation facilities would be designed as a whole rather than as separate units, for they could individually mar the landscape of each corridor. Furthermore, each radial node will have to be planned carefully in terms of optimum size and internal structure.

Thus the sector plan has many advantages over the linear and circular forms. In the first place, it provides a clearly defined framework for urban growth. Second, it permits the development of urban nuclei in economic modules, so that they do not become too large for the scale of human organization to be overwhelmed. Third, sprawl is avoided, for the areas between the corridors act as buffer zones. Fourth, the hierarchical nodal principle of human organization is kept intact, for not only does each radial settlement focus upon its own central core, but the entire system concentrates on the major focus. Ultimately, of course, all these major foci themselves concentrate on the highest order focus of all. Thus, the system is intuitively appealing to the urban geographer, for it recognizes the spatial interrelatedness of the entire urban system. The feasibility of the plan depends, however, on the efficiency of the transportation system involved.

BASIC ELEMENTS OF THE SECTOR PLAN

The basic elements of the sector plan are fourfold. The first of these is the system of communication which ties the components parts together. The other three are the component parts themselves. The chief component part is the focus of activity, the central city. The third element consists of the nodes along the radials, which are the units that cater to overall growth as well as to major residential and minor business, commercial, and industrial activities. The fourth element consists of the area between the radials, the open land that it is envisaged will be used for farming and recreational purposes. The planning for each of these elements is vital if the whole system is to be viable.

The Communication System

Although it can be envisaged that in the future the necessity for personal movement may well decrease, it is nevertheless considered that people will still wish to move around the urban area. The necessity for personal movement, particularly for work purposes, may well decrease as a result of the increasing use of sophisticated communication technology used to control the production or office process. In fact, in this sense we may well see a return to the "pedestrian" city, as the work place and the home may be one and the same thing, or at least not very far apart in physical terms, for communication resources may be pooled to form local or neighborhood communication centers. They may be far apart in reality; but the various media of communication available, such as television, telephones, sonic data phones, remote off-and-on line computer terminals, and so forth, will reduce the importance of distance and the daily journey to work in man's life.

However, interpersonal communication, without the use of electronic devices, is very necessary for many business activities, and vital for social, cultural, and recreational purposes. It is envisaged that these latter activities will absorb an increasing share of an individual's life in the future. To facilitate these activities, it is expected that several modes of transportation will be necessary. In the first place, the automobile, or some future substitute, will continue to provide the necessary personal or private transportation that most individuals require. Rapid transit will be most efficient for the transportation of people from the smaller nodes along radials to the central city. The mass transportation of people between nodes on different radials would be best undertaken by bus.

For the transportation of goods, it is difficult to envisage any other alternative to rail and truck. The trade-off between truck and rail for the shipment of goods in the future depends on the continuing effort of the railroad industry to compete, and the degree to which trucks are to be permitted to use limited-access highways. Obviously the medium- and long-haul advantage of the railroad industry could be restored and emphasized if trucks were banned from all limited-access highways. As this event is both doubtful and unwise in a competitive economy, what is really needed is some rationalization of the alternatives available. This can be accomplished in part through design of the facilities to be used for the different modes of transportation.

Transport Facilities

The transportation system involves, at one level, movement between central cities. Intercity rail lines and limited-access highways can be used for this purpose. They may run in conjunction or parallel with each other and will provide the arteries of heavy traffic. A second level of movement will be that connecting the nodes along the radials with central cities and connecting the nodes on different radials. Here design becomes preeminent, and it is considered that these should be parkways, from which trucks are banned, but buses permitted. Also, rapid transit is to be developed to carry passengers between the radial nodes and the central cities. It is considered that the location of these routes can be designed in conjunction with the parkways, perhaps using the right of way along, beneath, or above the median strip. Parkways are also to be used to connect nodes on different radials, and the bus will be the mode of mass transit for this kind of linkage.

The third level of transportation is that involving within-node and within-central-city circulation. Here we can envisage the use of parkways, rapid transit, bus, and urban arterials. These latter facilities can accommodate quite heavy volumes of traffic if commercial land use is not allowed to locate continuously on either side of the route. This type of commercial strip, consisting, as it has been observed, of freestanding enterprises, results in congestion owing to the multitude of separate entrances and parallel parking. Highway-oriented enterprises of this type should be clustered into planned centers adjacent to the highway with parking space and with well-designed entrances and exits from the parking area. Land-use clustering of this type will go far toward reducing congestion along urban highways.

The Central City

The central city poses the biggest problem in future urban planning. It is the area in which the accumulated fixed investment of capital is the greatest, and it is also the most obsolete area. In most cases it is difficult to envisage anything other than urban renewal on a massive scale, for in most cases a radical re-sorting of land uses is required.

This type of urban renewal is usually undertaken by public agencies, for private redevelopment is usually impossible. Reasons for this have been listed by Bourne (1967) as:

1. The units of ownership are too small in most central areas for present redevelopment uses. Thus time has to be spent in accumulating suitable contiguous lots, and this is a complicated procedure.

2. The physical and social environments in many areas are unattractive as centers of both employment and residence.

3. The value of land in many areas is excessively high, for it is frequently inflated by overoptimism on the part of the owners, taxation, or inappropriate zoning. Furthermore, land valuations are frequently based on assessments that are not realistic in terms of current conditions.

4. Various legal and financial constraints act as obstacles to renewal, such as zoning, financing, and land titles. For example, the land titles may be in multiple ownership and difficult to trace.

5. Neighborhood and community resistance to change is often sufficiently strong to delay or prevent proposed renewal schemes.

6. The shortage of housing for low-income families and racially segregated groups makes it difficult to remove the existing deteriorated housing which they occupy.

L. S. Bourne's (1967) study of Toronto indicates that the private redevelopment that does exist takes place primarily in the most favorable areas. These are in the higher-income sectors close to subway stations. This is because private redevelopment tends to be middle- and upper-income oriented, and not directed toward families with small children. It is the task of city planning to coordinate private redevelopment opportunities with those designed for the good of the urban area as a whole.

One of the better examples of city planning on a large scale can be seen in Philadelphia (Mitchell, 1960). The relative success of urban renewal and restructuring on a large scale in this case is associated with many factors. In the first place, general comprehensive planning, associated with a desire for government reform, had been pushed by a variety of people for a number of years. Second, the large number of professional planners available in the area (many of whom were, and are, associated with the University of Pennsylvania) were complemented by the interest of a number of citizens' advisory groups. Third, during the last two decades Philadelphia has been fortunate in having a succession of mayors who have been able to provide the necessary leadership. Finally, the availability of federal funds on quite a large scale during the late fifties and early sixties provided the necessary financial base for the execution of much of the program.

The Philadelphia Physical Development Plan

There are two main aspects of the Philadelphia physical development plan that are the bases of the objectives and proposals. The first of these ". . . is concerned with maintaining the eminence of Philadelphia as the central city in a growing metropolitan area," and the second involves ". . . improving the quality of the city's environment as a place in which to live and conduct business" (Row, 1960, p. 177). In order to achieve these aims, two sets of objectives are derived: economic objectives and people objectives. The economic objectives are aimed at improving the competitive position of

Philadelphia among the major cities of North America, and the people objectives are concerned with the residential-cultural environment of Philadelphia.

Economic Objectives

The economic objectives of the Philadelphia plan are fourfold. First, the plan aims to maintain the downtown area as the major focus of offices, high-order retail and wholesale activities, cultural amenities, and professional and financial activities. This needs imaginative land use and dramatic architecture. Place de Ville in Montreal is a fine example of an attempt at dramatic but functional renewal on a large scale. Second, there is emphasis on the improvement of major transport facilities that link the primary facilities of the city to each other, to the surrounding residential areas, to the region and the world beyond. Third, the need of industry for space within the city is being met. New industry and the expansion of existing industry are vital for urban growth, and a variety of sites are being made available, close to the city center, in the middle of the city, and at the periphery. Finally, an adequate distribution of tertiary activities is being achieved by the construction of lower-order shopping centers within the city, as well as at the periphery of the urban area. Within many of these centers are to be located smaller cultural and recreational facilities to serve the local community.

People Objectives

A major objective of the Philadelphia plan is to improve the average quality of housing. In some cases this implies demolition of whole blocks; in others, thinning out to reduce densities. Unfortunately, improvements of this type have the effect of removing people from homes, so that alternative residences must be available. In most cities, as nearly all areas due for demolition are occupied by the poor, and in the United States these are invariably minority groups, such action is fraught with pitfalls. In fact, it seems that relocation of people in the execution of a plan is the most serious problem and must be approached with the greatest sensitivity and understanding.

With the renewal of large areas of the city and the reconstruction of all or parts of entire sections, it may well be possible to emphasize or create local identity. This is being approached through the organization of the residential area into functional units of three levels: districts, communities, and neighborhoods. Public services of different types are located at each functional level. For example, a major hospital would be located at the district level, and the community-level focus would include facilities such as a library, a satellite health clinic, and a community-level shopping center. Playgrounds and parks are located at every level in the organizational hierarchy.

Nodes Along the Radials

The nodes located along the radials are the areas basically designed to cater to urban growth. In many instances these can be designed as new towns or expanded smaller towns. Their size should be limited to some upper limit, perhaps of the order of 200,000 to 250,000, and they should not merely be satellites of the central city. Rather they should have a balanced structure, in terms of both land use and inhabitants.

The Internal Structure of New Towns

The internal structure of these new towns should be designed in accordance with the highest possible environmental ideals. These should include proper segregation of land uses and an equitable location of activities and service facilities; and possibly the concept of neighborhood units should be a key feature in the pattern of spatial organization. Although the European new towns are in no way utopian in their physical layout, they are certainly a vast improvement over towns that have grown up naturally. The principal features in the layout of a British new town are illustrated in Figure 20.4, which shows the plan for the town of Crawley, one of the eight new towns built around London to accommodate population from the inner parts of the central city. The residential parts are in this case divided into several distinct neighborhoods, each with a few thousand inhabitants. Each neighborhood is equipped with schools, churches, a community center, local shopping center, and playground areas. The dwellings are of several types: apartments, row houses (town houses), and duplex and single-family units, and they are built at fairly low densities in order to ensure the provision of gardens and sufficient areas for children to play. The houses are grouped away from the major roadways, which are used as the dividing lines between the various neighborhoods.

The manufacturing base of the community is zoned in specific areas either close to the CBD, or in a specific sector close to the principal lines of communication to areas beyond the town. These areas are, in fact, conceived as industrial parks, with their own amenities and integrated design. The CBD is designed to provide the highest-order service facilities for the community. As a consequence, it is the focus of administration, commerce, specialized shopping, and entertainment. It is planned as a distinct element with malls, plazas, and associated parking facilities, and is accessible from all the neighborhoods.

The transportation system of the town links these various parts together with a hierarchy of service routes. Footpaths connect the residential areas within the neighborhoods to the schools and neighborhood shopping areas. Residential streets are not designed for heavy traffic, as there are numerous circles and crescents. The major roads within the community connect the residential areas to the factory areas and town center. Finally, these roads connect into major highways which link the community to the national intercity network. Thus there is an internal coherence in traffic design and transport facilities. A major problem with British new towns, however, is that those conceived between 1945 and 1950 are designed to cater to an expected automobile ownership ratio of about 1:15 rather than 1:6, which became the norm during the 1960's.

Megastructures and Platform Cities

Much of the large-scale construction that needs to take place in these radial areas (and in the central cities) may well occur in the form of huge buildings of interlinked complexes. Projected prototypes for this kind of very large-scale development are Market East in Philadelphia and the John Hancock Center in Chicago. The Market East structure is, in effect, an elongated (seven-block-long) miniature platform city, with integrated rapid-transit, bus, truck, and automobile parking facilities arrayed along the lower levels of the structure. The long towers rising from this platform base contain the potential residential, office, industrial, and commercial facilities. The narrowness of the structure and the high density of land use that it implies ensure an abundance of open space in adjacent areas along the entire length. An even greater density of land use is envisaged by the proponents of megastructures. These are envisaged as tall buildings

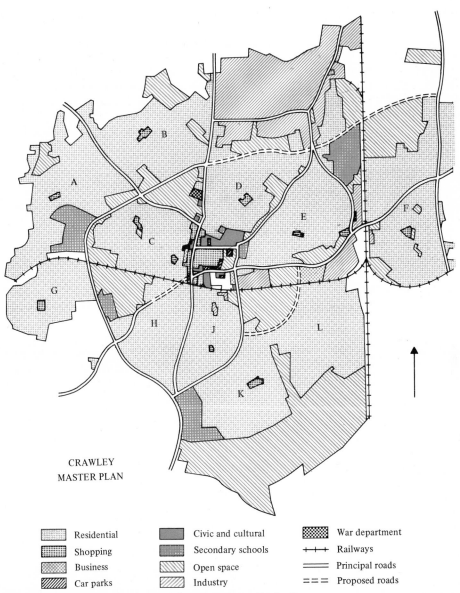

CRAWLEY
MASTER PLAN

Residential	Civic and cultural	War department
Shopping	Secondary schools	+++ Railways
Business	Open space	Principal roads
Car parks	Industry	Proposed roads

Fig. 20.4. The master plan for Crawley New Town, England.

(such as the World Trade Center in Manhattan), occupying a minimal amount of land, serviced at their base by many kinds of public transport media, and within which are located all the facilities desired by the urban dweller.

Interstitial Areas

The interstices between the radials are clearly defined to prevent sprawl and provide open spaces. The land can be used for a number of purposes: agriculture, recreation, and the location of special facilities. The agricultural activities located within this area should be of the intensive variety, such as truck farming and horticulture, providing fresh commodities for the adjacent urban market. Recreational space would need to be provided in abundance, and a wide variety of uses should be developed. Among the special facilities located in this area would be sanatoria and convalescent homes. It is obvious that great care must be taken to conserve and preserve these interstitial areas. The pressure to use the land for urban construction would be great, and as a consequence it may well be necessary to develop a number of programs concerned with conserving the land. The economic returns should not be viewed in terms of direct economic benefits, but rather in terms of social utility to the urban community as a whole.

LAND-USE CONTROLS

None of the plans discussed above can be realized without proper planning and control over land use. This is required in two respects: to contain sprawl and to ensure the best possible arrangement of land uses within the built-up areas. In North America, planning and land-use control are unfortunately frequently divorced from each other. Good plans have been made, but the planner's power to implement them is frustrated by the fact that he does not have very much control over zoning, the cornerstone of land-use control.

Zoning is a complicated business. It is by and large a device to guide development, not to stop it, although it is interesting to recall that it was first used for purely restrictive purposes, to protect the private property of a local group against "speculative developments and unwanted newcomers"—namely, Chinese laundries in California. As such, zoning can be thought of as an essentially negative form of land-use control and it provides little positive incentive to use land the way planners seek to do. This is particularly the case when land is not already developed, since zoning cannot stop development of unused land or hold it in its original state. Although zoning is an effective tool to protect the values of developed property, it is an inadequate tool to guide land-use change. Moreover, since zoning decisions can be changed, and often are when demands are strong enough, it is not a binding control.

Present land-use control practices will therefore have to be substantially modified if planners are to be able to secure a better arrangement of land use within cities. At the root of the problem is land speculation. Measures to reduce the amount of financial gain from land would probably go a long way toward making zoning a better weapon. Several means can be used to this end. Land could be purchased directly by local governments and resold when needed for development and with the right to examine carefully the kind of development that is to take place. Alternatively, the free market could be retained but with some control, possibly in the form of a tax on markups. Taxes on idle land would help prevent land from being held for speculation, while the introduction of a land-value tax would encourage the use of sites for the highest and best use. However, in the last resort, what is needed most is the integration of the work of the planner with the control of land use to ensure that developments proceed in the best possible way.

ACCESS TO RESOURCES IN THE CITY

Of crucial importance for the livability of the future city is a vastly improved distribution of activities within it. The city is a gigantic man-made resource system. It is also a localized resource system, since the resources that individuals make use of are not ubiquitous but are localized in space. Hence their use is affected by accessibility and proximity (Teitz, 1968). Since these in turn will differ depending on the relative location of individuals with respect to the various activities entering into the daily life pattern, the distribution of activities, and changes in this distribution, have an important effect in determining the real income of individuals (Harvey, 1973). The need to consider the availability and accessibility to resources in the future city is consequently an extremely important one.

At present there is considerable imbalance in the availability and accessibility of resources in most cities. We have noted in Chapter 18 that one of the reasons for this is the fragmented structure of local government in cities and the disparity between needs and financial resources, which result in considerable spatial differences in the level and quality of service provision. But the situation is not only restricted to public services; imbalance is just as pronounced for private services. The case of the availability of health-care facilities in cities is often cited. Tracts with higher median incomes tend to be served, for example, by greater numbers of physicians than those with lower average incomes. And when allowance is made for these income differences, black tracts are generally far worse off than white ones. Physicians' services have a tendency, therefore, to be least available where they are most needed—in the parts of the city occupied by low-income black people (Cox, 1973; see also De Vise, 1973).

Another well-known situation of this sort is that relating to the changing location of jobs and homes within large metropolitan areas. As industry decentralizes to the suburbs, and the poor are increasingly concentrated in the inner cities, the spatial imbalance between the supply and demand for employment—especially from low-income residents—has become acute. Generally speaking, they are denied access to job opportunities in the suburbs because of the lack of an "inside-out" mass-transit system. As a general rule, then, spatial imbalance in the supply of and demand for services and jobs within cities seems to favor the rich to the detriment of the poor. Hence there is a much greater need to stress equity and less efficiency in the future city.

Constraints on Accessibility

The problems of creating equitable distributions of various kinds of activities, not least of all public facilities, is not, however, purely a locational one. It also involves the need to reduce the constraints on individuals imposed by the way society is organized, and inherent to individuals themselves. In satisfying his needs and wants, the individual has to move from one location to another. However, the freedom to do this is often limited by three main types of constraints: capacity constraints, coupling constraints, and authority constraints (Hägerstrand, 1970; Pred, 1974b).

Capacity Constraints

These limit the individual's action space through both his own biological makeup and the tools at his command. Among the latter, command over transportation is a most important one. Owing to his need for sleep, each individual can be thought of as conducting his everyday life on an island, the size of which varies with the distance he can travel and still have time to return home for the night. Clearly this is a function of his mobility. From a time-space point of view, therefore, the daily action space of the individual assumes the form of a prism, as shown in Figure 20.5. The time-space walls of the prism will vary from day to day in accordance with the activities engaged in, but the individual cannot appear outside the walls of the prism, and in this sense it is very much the individual's daily prison too.

Coupling Constraints

These to a large degree govern the paths the individual can take inside the daily prism (Fig. 20.5). They define "where, when, and for how long the individual has to join other individuals, tools, and materials in order to produce, consume, and transact" (Hägerstrand, 1970, p. 14). A grouping of paths (for example, a meeting or a classroom activity) can be called a bundle. The important point is that many bundles follow predetermined timetables that limit the individual's spatial degrees of freedom once he has chosen his places of work and residence. As this relates to access to resources, it means that an individual "bound to his home-base, can participate only in those activities . . . which have both ends inside his daily prism and which are so located in space and time that he has time to move from the end of one to the beginning of the following one" (Hägerstrand, 1970, p. 15). Thus in Figure 20.5, for example, the individual can participate in either activity 1, 2, or 3, but not in all three. Moreover, he is denied access to activity 4 because its end lies outside the walls of his daily prism. It would appear we are extremely vulnerable to even small adjustments in timetables (e.g., opening times, public transport departure times, and so on). Hence in planning the future city much greater attention needs to be given to the problem of locating activity bundles in time and space in such a way that the capacity constraints of the individual are respected.

Authority Constraints

These exist because events are under the control of individuals or groups in society. As a result, spatial organization is characterized by the existence of domains of various kinds to which individuals are often denied access by rules, regulations, even discrimination. An obvious example is the fact that people living in one local govern-

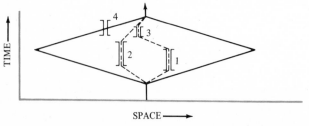

Fig. 20.5. An individual's daily prism and time-space constraints on access to activities.

ment jurisdiction are denied access to certain kinds of facilities—for example, libraries—in other jurisdictions (domains), even though those facilities may be more accessible to them. As a result they may not have good access to the facility in their own domain because its location does not permit a visit at the time they can make it. Hence there is also a need to reduce the effects of all kinds of authority constraints as they pertain to access to resources in the future city.

We have sketched in this last chapter some of the problems facing the future city. Clearly there is a need to specify the goals for future developments at the city-region scale and also to ensure that the machinery exists to attain those goals. Technology is no drawback in this respect, for the technology is available in North America to produce or do almost anything that man desires. What is needed is some assessment of the kind of society that is required, so that the technology and know-how can be used to create the conditions conducive to the development of that society. This is very much a question of having the will to face up to the problems. This is undoubtedly the task of man in North America at this time, for he needs the will to become as deeply involved in the family of man as he is in his own family—that is, if the future that can be is to become more than a pale reflection of what might have been.

REFERENCES

AARON, H. J. 1972. *Shelter and Subsidies: Who Benefits from Federal Housing Policies?* Washington, D.C.: Brookings.

ABLER, R., J. S. ADAMS, AND P. GOULD. 1971. *Spatial Organization: The Geographer's View of the World.* Englewood Cliffs, N.J.: Prentice-Hall.

ACKERMAN, E. A. 1963. "Where Is a Research Frontier?" *Annals of the Association of American Geographers,* 53:429–440.

ADAMS, J. S. 1970. "Residential Structure of Midwestern Cities." *Annals of the Association of American Geographers,* 60:37–62.

ADVISORY COMMITTEE ON INTERGOVERNMENTAL RELATIONS. 1963. *Performance of Urban Functions: Local and Area Wide.* Washington, D.C.: U.S. Government Printing Office.

———. 1968. *Urban and Rural America: Policies for Future Growth.* Washington, D.C.: U.S. Government Printing Office.

———. 1969. *Urban America and the Federal System.* Washington, D.C.: U.S. Government Printing Office.

———. 1972. *Public Opinion and Taxes.* Washington, D.C.: U.S. Government Printing Office.

ALEXANDER, J. W. 1954. "The Basic-Nonbasic Concept of Urban Economic Functions." *Economic Geography,* 20:246–261.

484

ALEXANDERSSON, G. 1956. *The Industrial Structure of American Cities.* Lincoln: University of Nebraska Press.

ALONSO, W. 1960. "A Theory of the Urban Land Market." *Regional Science Association, Papers and Proceedings,* 6:149–157.

_____. 1968. "Urban and Regional Imbalance in Economic Development." *Economic Development and Cultural Change,* 17:1–14.

ANDERSON, T. A., AND J. A. EGELAND 1961. "Spatial Aspects of Social Area Analysis." *American Sociological Review,* 26:392–398.

ANDREWS, R. B. 1953. "Historical Development of the Base Concept." *Land Economics,* 29:161–171. Reprinted together with other relevant articles in R. W. Pfouts, ed. 1960, *The Techniques of Urban Economic Analysis.* New York: Chandler Davis.

ARNOLD, J. L. 1971. *The New Deal in the Suburbs: A History of the Greenbelt Towns Program.* Columbus: Ohio State University Press.

AUROUSSEAU, M. 1921. "The Distribution of Population: A Constructive Problem." *Geographical Review,* 11:563–592.

BANFIELD, E. C. 1974. *The Unheavenly City Revisited.* Boston: Little, Brown.

BARTHOLOMEW, H. 1955. *Land Uses in American Cities.* Cambridge: Harvard University Press.

BAUMOL. W. J. 1958. "On the Theory of Oligopoly." *Economica,* 24:187–198.

_____. 1967. "Macroeconomics of Unbalanced Growth: The Anatomy of Urban Crisis." *American Economic Review,* 57:415–426.

BECKMANN, M. 1958. "City Hierarchies and the Distribution of City Size." *Economic Development and Cultural Change,* 6:243–248.

BELL, W., AND C. C. MOSKOS. 1964. "A Comment on Udry's Increasing Scale and Spatial Differentiation." *Social Forces,* 62:414–417.

BERGSMAN, J., P. GREENSTON, AND R. HEALY. 1972. "The Agglomeration Process in Urban Growth." *Urban Studies,* 9:263–288.

BERRY, B. J. L. 1959. "Ribbon Developments in the Urban Business Pattern." *Annals of the Association of American Geographers,* 49:145–155.

_____. 1960. "The Impact of Expanding Metropolitan Communities upon the Central Place Hierarchy." *Annals of the Association of American Geographers,* 50:112–116.

_____. 1961. "City Size Distributions and Economic Development." *Economic Development and Cultural Change,* 9:573–588.

_____. 1963. "Commercial Structure and Commercial Blight." Research paper 85, Department of Geography. Chicago: University of Chicago Press.

_____. 1964. "Approaches to Regional Analysis: A Synthesis." *Annals of the Association of American Geographers,* 54:2–11.

_____. 1964b. "Cities as Systems Within Systems of Cities." *Regional Science Association, Papers and Proceedings,* 13:147–163.

_____. 1965. "Internal Structure of the City." *Law and Contemporary Problems,* 30:111–119.

_____. 1966. "Essays on Commodity Flows and the Spatial Structure of the Indian Economy." Research paper 111, Department of Geography. Chicago: University of Chicago Press.

_____. 1967a. *Geography of Market Centers and Retail Distribution.* Englewood Cliffs, N.J.: Prentice-Hall

_____. 1967b. *Strategies, Models and Economic Theories of Development in Rural Regions.* Washington, D.C.: U.S. Department of Agriculture.

_____. 1967c. *Functional Economic Areas and Consolidated Urban Regions of the United States.* Washington, D.C.: Bureau of the Census.

——. 1968a. "Metropolitan Area Definition: A Re-evaluation of Concept and Statistical Practice." Working paper no. 28. Washington, D.C.: Bureau of the Census.

——. 1968b. "A Summary of Spatial Organization and Levels of Welfare: Degree of Metropolitan Labor Market Participation as a Variable in Economic Development." *E.D.A. Research Review*, July 1–6. Washington, D.C.: Department of Commerce.

——. 1970. "The Geography of the United States in the Year 2000." *Transactions of the Institute of British Geographers*, 51:21–54.

——. 1971. "Introduction: The Logic and Limitations of Comparative Factorial Ecology." *Economic Geography* (supplement), 47:209–219.

——. 1972. *City Classification Handbook: Methods and Applications*. New York: Wiley.

——. 1973a. *Growth Centers in the American Urban System*. Cambridge, Mass.: Ballinger.

——. 1973b. *The Human Consequences of Urbanization*. London: Macmillan.

——, H. G. BARNUM, AND R. H. TENNANT. 1962. "Retail Location and Consumer Behaviour." *Regional Science Association, Papers and Proceedings*, 9:65–106.

—— AND W. L. GARRISON. 1958a. "Functional Bases of the Central Place Hierarchy." *Economic Geography*, 34:145–154.

—— AND ——. 1958b. "A Note on Central Place Theory and the Range of a Good." *Economic Geography*, 34:304–311.

—— AND ——. 1958c. "Recent Developments of Central Place Theory." *Regional Science Association, Papers and Proceedings*, 4:107–120.

—— AND ——. 1958d. "Alternate Explanations for Urban Rank-Size Relationships." *Annals of the Association of American Geographers*, 48:83–91.

—— AND F. E. HORTON. 1970. *Geographic Perspectives on Urban Systems*. Englewood Cliffs, N.J.: Prentice-Hall.

—— AND E. NEILS. 1970. "Location, Size, and Shape of Cities as Influenced by Environment Factors." In *The Quality of the Urban Environment*, ed. H. S. Perloff, pp. 257–302. Baltimore: Johns Hopkins University Press.

——, S. J. PARSONS, AND R. H. PLATT. 1968. *The Impact of Urban Renewal on Small Businesses*. Center for Urban Studies. Chicago: University of Chicago Press.

—— AND A. PRED. 1964. *Central Place Studies: A Bibliography of Theory and Applications*. Philadelphia: Regional Science Association.

——, J. R. SIMMONS, AND R. TENNANT. 1963. "Urban Population Densities: Structure and Change." *Geographical Review*, 53:389–405.

—— AND R. TENNANT. 1963. "Chicago Commercial Reference Handbook." Research paper 86, Department of Geography. Chicago: University of Chicago Press.

—— et al. 1974. "Land Use, Urban Form and Environmental Quality." Research paper no. 155, Department of Geography. Chicago: University of Chicago Press.

BLUMENFELD, H. 1954. "The Tidal Wave of Metropolitan Expansion." *Journal of the American Institute of Planners*, 20:3–14.

——. 1955. "The Economic Base of the Metropolis." *Journal of the American Institute of Planners*, 21:114–132.

——. 1959. "Are Land Use Patterns Predictable?" *Journal of the American Institute of Planners*, 25:60–64.

BOGARDUS, E. S. 1926. "Social Distance in the City." In *The Urban Community*, E. W. Burgess, pp. 48–54. Chicago: University of Chicago Press.

BOLLENS, J. C., AND H. J. SCHMANDT. 1975. *The Metropolis*. New York: Harper & Row.

BOLT, B. et al. 1967. *Noise in Urban and Suburban Areas: Results of Field Studies.* Washington, D.C.: U.S. Government Printing Office.

BOLTON, R. E. 1965. *Defense Purchases and Regional Growth.* Washington, D.C.: Brookings.

BORCHERT, J. R. 1967. "American Metropolitan Evolution." *Geographical Review*, 57:301–323.

_____. 1972. "America's Changing Metropolitan Regions." *Annals of the Association of American Geographers*, 62:352–373.

BOUDEVILLE, J. R. 1968. *Problems of Regional Economic Planning.* Edinburgh: Edinburgh University Press.

BOURNE, L. S. 1967. "Private Development of the Central City." Research paper 112, Department of Geography. Chicago: University of Chicago Press.

_____. 1968. "Market Location and Site Selection in Apartment Construction." *Canadian Geographer*, 12:211–226.

_____ AND G. GAD. 1972. "Urbanization and Urban Growth in Ontario and Quebec: An Overview." In *Urban Systems Development in Central Canada*, ed. L. S. Bourne and R. D. MacKinnon, pp. 7–34. Toronto: University of Toronto Press.

BRAGDON, C. R. 1967. "Territoriality: An Ecological Concept for Urban Planning." *Planning Comment*, 4:29–42.

BRATFISCH, O. 1969. "A Further Study of the Relation Between Subjective Distance and Emotional Involvement." *Acta Psychologica*, 29:244–255.

BRAZEL, A. 1973. "International Air Quality Control in the Detroit-Windsor Area." *Proceedings of the Association of American Geographers*, 5:25–30.

BREWIS, T. N. 1969. *Regional Economic Policies in Canada.* Toronto: Macmillan.

BRIDENBAUGH, C. 1950. *Cities in the Wilderness: The First Century of Urban Life in America, 1625–1742.* New York: Knopf.

BROWN, L. AND F. E. HORTON. 1970. "Functional Distance: A Note on an Operational Approach." *Geographical Analysis*, 2:76–83.

_____ AND E. MOORE 1970. "The Intra-Urban Migration Process: A Perspective." *Geografiska Annaler*, 52B:1–13.

_____, J. ODLAND, AND R. G. GOLLEDGE. 1970. "Migration, Functional Distance, and the Urban Hierarchy." *Economic Geography*, 46:472–485.

BROWNING, C. E. 1964. "Selected Aspects of Land Use and Distance from the City Center: The Case of Chicago." *Southeastern Geographer*, 4:29–40.

_____. 1974. "Population and Urbanized Area Growth in Megalopolis." Studies in Geography, no. 7. Department of Geography. Chapel Hill: University of North Carolina.

BRUSH, J. E. 1953. "The Hierarchy of Central Places in Southwestern Wisconsin." *Geographical Review*, 43:380–402.

BRYSON, R. A., AND J. E. KUTZBACH. 1968. *Air Pollution.* Washington, D.C.: Association of American Geographers.

BUCHANAN, C. D. 1963. *Traffic in Towns.* London: Her Majesty's Stationery Office.

BUNGE, W. 1962. *Theoretical Geography.* Lund Studies in Geography, ser. C, 1. Lund, Sweden: Gleerup.

BURGESS, E. W. 1923. "The Growth of the City." *Proceedings of the American Sociological Society*, 18:85–89.

_____ AND D. J. BOGUE. 1964. "A Short History of Urban Research at the University of Chicago Before 1946." In *Contributions to Urban Sociology*, ed. E. W. Burgess and D. J. Bogue. Chicago: University of Chicago Press.

BURGHARDT, A. F. 1971. "A Hypothesis about Gateway Cities." *Annals of the Association of American Geographers*, 61:269–285.

BURTT, E. J., JR. 1961. "Changing Labor Supply Characteristics Along Route 128." Research report 14. Boston: Federal Reserve Bank of Boston.

BUTTIMER, A. 1968. "Social Geography." *International Encyclopedia of the Social Sciences*, 6:134–145.

———. 1974. "Values in Geography." Resource paper no. 24. Washington, D.C.: Association of American Geographers, Commission on College Geography.

CAMPBELL, A. K. 1958. "Taxes and Industrial Location in the New York Metropolitan Region." *National Tax Journal*, 11:195–218.

CAPLOW, T. 1952. "Urban Structure in France." *American Sociological Review*, 17:544–550.

CAREY, G. 1966. "The Regional Interpretation of Manhattan Population and Housing Patterns Through Factor Analysis." *Geographical Review*, 56:551–569.

———. 1972. "Hippie Neighborhoods and Urban Spatial Systems." Paper read to the 134th meeting of the American Association for the Advancement of Science.

CARROLL, J. D., AND H. W. BEVIS. 1957. "Predicting Local Travel in Urban Regions." *Regional Science Association, Papers and Proceedings*, 3:183–197.

CARROTHERS, G. A. P. 1956. "An Historical Review of the Gravity and Potential Concepts of Human Interaction." *Journal of the American Institute of Planners*, 22:94–102.

Chicago Area Transportation Study, vol. 1 1959.

CHINITZ, B. 1960. *Freight and the Metropolis*. Cambridge: Harvard University Press.

———. 1965. "New York: A Metropolitan Region." *Scientific American*, 213:134–148.

——— AND R. DUSANSKY. 1972. "The Patterns of Urbanization Within Regions of the United States." *Urban Studies*, 9:289–298.

CHISHOLM, M. 1962. *Rural Settlement and Land Use*. London: Hutchinson.

CHOMBART DE LAUWE, P. 1959. *Famille et habitation*. Paris: Editions du Centre National de la Recherche Scientifique.

———. 1965. *Des hommes et des villes*. Paris: Payot.

CHORLEY, R. J. 1964. "Geography and Analogue Theory." *Annals of the Association of American Geographers*, 54:127–137.

——— AND P. HAGGETT, eds. 1967. *Models in Geography*. London: Methuen.

CHRISTALLER, W. 1966. *Central Places in Southern Germany*, trans. C. W. Baskin. Englewood Cliffs, N.J.: Prentice-Hall.

CLARK, C. 1951a. *The Conditions of Economic Progress*. London: Macmillan.

———. 1951b. "Urban Population Densities." *Journal of the Royal Statistical Society*, A; 114:490–496.

———. 1957–1958. "Transport: Maker and Breaker of Cities." *Town Planning Review*, 28:237–250.

CLARK, W. A. V. 1968. "Consumer Travel Patterns and the Concept of Range." *Annals of the Association of American Geographers*, 58:386–396.

CLAWSON, M., AND P. HALL. 1973. *Planning and Urban Growth*. Baltimore: Johns Hopkins University Press.

CLAYTON, C. 1974. "Communication and Spatial Structure." *Tijdschrift voor Economische en Sociale Geographie*, 65:221–227.

COLBY, C. C. 1933. "Centrifugal and Centripetal Forces in Urban Geography." *Annals of the Association of American Geographers*, 23:1–20.

COLEMAN, A. 1969. *The Planning Challenge of the Ottawa Area*. Ottawa: The Queen's Printer.

COLONY, D. C. 1967. *Expressway Traffic Noise and Residential Properties*. Traffic Research Foundation. Toledo: University of Toledo.

Cox, K. R. 1965. "The Application of Linear Programming to Geographic Problems." *Tijdschrift voor Economische en Sociale Geographie*, 56:228–236.

———. 1973. *Conflict, Power, and Politics in the City*. New York: McGraw-Hill.

——— AND R. G. GOLLEDGE, eds. 1969. *Behavioral Problems in Geography: A Symposium*. Studies in Geography, 17. Evanston, Ill.: Northwestern University Press.

DARWENT, D. 1969. "Growth Poles and Growth Centers in Regional Planning." *Environment and Planning*, 1:3–31.

DAVIES, D. 1965. "Financing Urban Functions and Services." *Law and Contemporary Problems*, 30:127–161.

DAVIES, D. H. 1960. "The Hard Core of Cape Town's Central Business District." *Economic Geography*, 34:53–69.

DAVIES, W. K. D., ed. 1972. *The Conceptual Revolution in Geography*. London: London University Press.

——— AND G. T. BARROW. 1973. "A Comparative Factorial Ecology of Three Canadian Prairie Cities." *Canadian Geographer*, 17:327–353.

DAVIS, C. A., AND A. D. WHINSTON. 1961. "The Economics of Urban Renewal." *Law and Contemporary Problems*, 26:105–118.

DAVIS, J. L. 1965. *The Elevated System and the Growth of Northern Chicago*. Studies in Geography, 10. Evanston, Ill.: Northwestern University Press.

DENIS, P.-Y. 1972. "The Development of the Various Districts." In *Montreal: Field Guide*, ed. L. Beauregard, pp. 78–88. Montreal: Presses de l'Université de Montréal.

DENNIS, M., AND S. FISH. 1972. *Programs in Search of a Policy: Low Income Housing in Canada*. Toronto: Hakkert.

DERAN, E. 1968. "Tax Structures in Cities Using the Income Tax." *National Tax Journal*, 21:147–152.

DESKINS, D. R. 1969. "Interaction Patterns and the Spatial Form of the Ghetto." Department of Geography, special publication no. 3. Evanston, Ill.: Northwestern University Press.

Detroit Metropolitan Area Traffic Study, Part 1, 1955.

DETWYLER, T. R., AND M. G. MARCUS, eds. 1972. *Urbanization and Environment*. Belmont, Cal.: Duxbury Press.

DE VISE, P. 1960. *A Social Geography of Metropolitan Chicago*. Chicago: Northeastern Illinois Area Planning Commission.

———. 1973. "Misused and Misplaced Hospitals and Doctors." Resource paper no. 22, Commission on College Geography. Washington, D.C.: Association of American Geographers.

DIAMOND, D. R. 1972. "New Towns in Their Regional Context." In *New Towns: The British Experience*, ed. P. Self. London: Town and Country Planning Association.

DICKINSON, R. E. 1948. "The Scope and Status of Urban Geography." *Land Economics*, 24:221–238.

———. 1964. *City and Region*. London: Routledge & Kegan Paul.

DODD, S. C. 1950. "The Interactance Hypothesis: A Gravity Model Fitting Physical Masses and Human Behavior." *American Sociological Review*, 15:245–256.

DONNISON, D. V. 1967. *The Government of Housing*. London: Penguin Books.

DOWNS, R. 1970. "Geographic Space Perception: Past Approaches and Future Prospects." In *Progress in Geography*, ed. D. Board vol. 2, pp. 65–108. London: Edward Arnold.

DOXIADIS, C. A. 1966. *Urban Renewal and the Future of the American City*. Chicago: Public Administration Service.

———. 1970. "The Future of Human Settlements." In *The Place of Value in a World of Facts*, ed. A. Tiselius and A. Nilsson, pp. 307–338. Stockholm: Almqvist & Wiksell.

Due, J. F. 1961. "Studies of State-Local Tax Influences on the Location of Industry." *National Tax Journal*, 14:163–173.

Duerr, W. A. 1960. *Fundamentals of Forestry Economics*. New York: McGraw-Hill.

Duncan, B. 1956. "Factors in Work-Residence Separation: Wage and Salary Workers." *American Sociological Review*, 21:48–56.

——— and O. D. Duncan. 1960. "The Measurement of Intracity Locational and Residential Patterns." *Journal of Regional Science*, 2:37–54.

Duncan, O. D., W. R. Scott, S. Lieberson, B. D. Duncan, and H. H. Winsborough. 1960. *Metropolis and Region*. Baltimore: Johns Hopkins University Press.

Dunn, E. S. Jr. 1954. *The Location of Agricultural Production*. Gainesville: University of Florida Press.

———. 1960. "A Statistical and Analytical Technique for Regional Analysis." *Papers and Proceedings, Regional Science Association*, 6:97–112.

Edwards, K. C. 1964. "The New Towns of Britain." *Geography*, 69:279–285.

Eichenbaum, J., and R. L. Morrill, eds. 1974. "New Directions in Urban Geography." *Antipode*, 6.

Eichler, E. P., and M. Kaplan. 1967. *The Community Builders*. Berkeley: University of California Press.

Erickson, R. A. 1974. "The Regional Impact of Growth Firms: The Case of Boeing, 1963–1968." *Land Economics*, 50:127–136.

Erikson, E. 1968. *Identity, Youth, and Crisis*. New York: Norton.

European Free Trade Association. 1974. *National Settlement Strategies: A Framework for Regional Development*. Geneva.

Federal Reserve Bank of Kansas City. 1952. "The Employment Multiplier in Wichita." *Monthly Review*, 37:1–13.

Feherdy, Y. 1971. *Etat global de L'occupation du sol de Montreal*. Montreal: Service d'Urbanisme.

Feller, I. 1973. Determinants of the Composition of Urban Inventions." *Economic Geography*, 49:47–58.

Fellman, J. D. 1950. "Truck Transportation Patterns of Chicago." Research paper 12, Department of Geography. Chicago: University of Chicago Press.

Firey, W. 1945. "Sentiment and Symbolism as Ecological Variables." *American Sociological Review*, 10:140–148.

Fisher, E. M., and L. Winnick. 1951. "A Reformulation of the Filtering Concept." *Journal of Social Issues*, 7:45–55.

Florence, P. S. 1953. *The Logic of British and American Industry*. London: Routledge & Kegan Paul.

Foley, D. 1963. *Controlling London's Growth*. Berkeley: University of California Press.

Ford, R. G. 1950. "Population Succession in Chicago." *American Journal of Sociology*, 56:156–160.

Fox, K. A., and T. K. Kumar. 1965. "The Functional Economic Area: Delineation and Implications for Economic Analysis and Policy." *Regional Science Association, Papers and Proceedings*, 15:57–85.

Frieden, B. J. 1972. "Black in Suburbia: The Myth of Better Opportunities." In *Minority Perspectives*, ed. L. Wingo. Baltimore: Johns Hopkins University Press.

Friedlander, G. D. 1965. "Airborne Asphyxia: An International Problem." *Spectrum*, 9:13–14.

FUCHS, V. R. 1962. *Changes in the Location of Manufacturing in the United States Since 1929.* New Haven: Yale University Press.

GARNER, B. J. 1966. *The Internal Structure of Retail Nucleations.* Studies in Geography, 12. Evanston, Ill.: Northwestern University Press.

_____. 1967. "Models of Urban Geography and Settlement Location." In *Models in Geography,* ed. R. J. Chorley and P. Haggett, pp. 303–360. London: Methuen.

_____. 1969. "The Analysis of Qualitative Data in Urban Geography: The Example of Shop Quality." *Techniques in Urban Geography.* London: Institute of British Geographers Urban Studies Group.

GARRISON, W. L., et al. 1959. *Studies of Highway Development and Geographic Change.* Seattle: University of Washington Press.

GETIS, A. 1963. "The Determination of the Location of Retail Activities with the Use of a Map Transformation." *Economic Geography,* 39:1–22.

_____ AND J. GETIS. 1968. "Retail Store and Spatial Affinities." *Urban Studies,* 5:317–332.

GIBBS, J. P. 1963. "The Evolution of Population Concentration." *Economic Geography,* 39:119–129.

GILMORE, H. W. 1953. *Transportation and the Growth of Cities.* New York: Free Press.

GOHEEN, P. 1970. "Victorian Toronto 1850–1900: Pattern and Process of Growth." Research paper no. 127, Department of Geography. Chicago: University of Chicago Press.

GOLANT, S. M. 1972. "The Residential Location and Spatial Behavior of the Elderly." Research paper 143, Department of Geography. Chicago: University of Chicago Press.

GOLDBERG, M. A. 1970. "An Economic Model of Intrametropolitan Industrial Location." *Journal of Regional Science,* 10:75–79.

GOLDSTEIN, S., AND K. B. MAYER. 1961. *Metropolitanization and Population Change in Rhode Island.* Providence: Planning Division, Rhode Island Development Council.

GOLLEDGE, R. G. 1967. "Conceptualizing the Market Decision Process." *Journal of Regional Science,* 7:239–258.

_____, R. BRIGGS, AND D. DEMKO. 1969. "The Configuration of Distance in Intra-Urban Space." *Proceedings of the American Association of Geographers,* 1:60–65.

_____, L. A. BROWN, AND F. WILLIAMSON. 1972. "Behavioural Approaches in Geography: An Overview." *Australian Geographer,* 12:59–79.

GORDON, D. M. 1971. *Problems in Political Economy: An Urban Perspective.* Lexington, Mass.: Heath.

GOTTMANN, J. 1961. *Megalopolis.* New York: Twentieth Century Fund.

GREBLER, L. 1952. *Housing Market Behavior in a Declining Area.* New York: Columbia University Press.

GREEN, C. M. 1965. *The Rise of Urban America.* London: Hutchinson.

GREEN, H. L. 1955. "Hinterland Boundaries of New York City and Boston in Southern New England." *Economic Geography,* 31:283–300.

GREER-WOOTEN, B., AND J. MARSHALL. 1972. "The Urban System." In *Montreal: Field Guide,* ed. L. Beauregard, pp. 157–169. Montreal: Presses de l'Universite de Montreal.

GRIGG, D. B. 1965. "The Logic of Regional Systems." *Annals of the Association of American Geographers,* 55:465–491.

HAAGEN-SMIT, A. J. 1964. "The Control of Air Pollution." *Scientific American,* 210:3–9.

HADDEN, J. K. AND E. F. BORGATTA. 1965. *American Cities: Their Social Characteristics.* Chicago: Rand McNally.

HAGERSTRAND, T. 1968. *Innovation Diffusion as a Spatial Process* (with postscript and translation by A. Pred). Chicago: University of Chicago Press.

———. 1970. "What About People in Regional Science?" *Regional Science Association, Papers and Proceedings*, 24:7–21.

HAGGETT, P. 1965. *Locational Analysis in Human Geography*. London: Edward Arnold.

———. 1972. *Geography: A Modern Synthesis*. New York: Harper & Row.

——— AND R. J. CHORLEY. 1969. *Network Analysis in Geography*. London: Edward Arnold.

HALL, A. D., AND R. E. FAGEN. 1956. "Definition of System." *General Systems*, 1:18–28.

HALL, E. T. 1966. *The Hidden Dimension*. New York: Doubleday.

HALL, P. 1966. *The World Cities*. New York: McGraw-Hill.

———, ed. 1966. *Von Thünen's Isolated State*. Oxford: Pergamon Press.

———. 1972. *The Containment of Urban England*, 2 vols. London: Allen & Unwin.

HAMILTON, F. E. I. 1967. "Models of Industrial Location." In *Models in Geography*, ed. R. J. Chorley and P. Haggett, pp. 361–424. London: Methuen.

HAMILTON, W. F., AND D. K. NANCE. 1968. "Systems Analysis of Urban Transportation." *Scientific American*, 221:19–27.

HANSEN, N. 1970. "A Growth Center Strategy for the United States." *Review of Regional Studies*.

———, ed. 1971a. *Growth Centers and Regional Development*. New York: Free Press.

———. 1971b. *Intermediate-Size Cities as Growth Centers*. New York: Praeger.

HARRIS, C. D. 1943. "A Functional Classification of Cities in the United States." *Geographical Review*, 33:86–99.

———. 1954. "The Market as a Factor in the Localization of Industry in the United States." *Annals of the Association of American Geographers*, 44:315–348.

——— AND E. L. ULLMAN. 1945. "The Nature of Cities." *Annals of the American Academy of Political Science*, 242:7–17.

HARTMAN, C., AND G. CARR. 1969. "Housing Authorities Reconsidered." *Journal of American Institute of Planners*, 35:18–24.

HARTSHORNE, R. 1939. *The Nature of Geography*. Lancaster, Pa.: Association of American Geographers.

HARVEY, D. W. 1969. *Explanation in Geography*. London: Edward Arnold.

———. 1972. "Society, the City, and the Space-Economy of Urbanism." Resource paper no. 18. Washington, D.C.: Association of American Geographers, Commission on College Geography.

———. 1973. *Social Justice and the City*. London: Edward Arnold.

——— AND L. CHATTERJEE. 1974. "Absolute Rent and the Structuring of Space by Governmental and Financial Institutions." *Antipode*, 6:22–36.

HAUER, E. 1972. "Noise and Airport Planning." In *Readings in Airport Planning*, ed. R. Soberman, Toronto: University of Toronto, CUCS.

HAWLEY, A. A., AND O. D. DUNCAN. 1957. "Social Area Analysis: A Critical Appraisal." *Land Economics*, 33:337–345.

HAYNES, K. E., D. L. POSTON, JR., AND P. SCHNIRRING. 1973. "Intermetropolitan Migration in High and Low Opportunity Areas: Indirect Tests of the Distance and Intervening Opportunities Hypotheses." *Economic Geography*, 49:68–73.

HEIMANN, H. 1967. *Air Pollution and Respiratory Disease*. Public Health Service publication 1257. Washington, D.C.: U.S. Government Printing Office.

HELLER, W. W. 1969. "Should the Government Share Its Tax Take?" *Saturday Review*, March 22, pp. 101–103.

HELVIG, M. 1964. "Chicago's External Truck Movements." Research paper no. 90, Department of Geography. Chicago: University of Chicago Press.

HILTON, G. W., AND J. F. DUE. 1964. *The Electric Interurban Railways in America*. Stanford: Stanford University Press.

HIRSCH, W. Z. 1968. "The Supply of Public Services." In *Issues in Urban Economics*, ed. H. S. Perloff and L. Wingo, Jr., pp. 509–511. Baltimore: Johns Hopkins University Press.

HOCH, I. 1957. "Rising Land Values Found Along Edens." *Cook County Highways*, 4:3–5.

HODGE, G. 1965. "The Prediction of Trade Center Viability in the Great Plains." *Regional Science Association, Papers and Proceedings*, 15:87–118.

HOOVER, E. M. 1963. *The Location of Economic Activity*. New York: McGraw-Hill.

_____. 1968. "The Evolving Form and Organization of the Metropolis." In *Issues in Urban Economics*, ed. H. S. Perloff and L. Wingo, Jr., pp. 237–284. Baltimore: Johns Hopkins University Press.

_____ AND R. VERNON. 1959. *Anatomy of a Metropolis*. Cambridge: Harvard University Press.

HORTON, F., AND D. REYNOLDS. 1971. "Effects of Urban Spatial Structure on Individual Behaviour." *Economic Geography*, 47:36–48.

HORWOOD, E. M., AND R. R. BOYCE. 1959. *Studies of the Central Business District and Urban Freeway Development*. Seattle: University of Washington Press.

HOWARD, E. 1945. *Garden Cities of Tomorrow*. London: Faber & Faber.

HOYT, H. 1933. *One Hundred Years of Land Values in Chicago*. Chicago: University of Chicago Press.

_____. 1939. *The Structure and Growth of Residential Neighborhoods in American Cities*. Washington, D.C.: Federal Housing Administration.

_____. 1960. *Dynamic Factors in Land Values*. Technical Bulletin 37. Washington, D.C.: Urban Land Institute.

_____. 1961. "The Utility of the Economic Base Method in Calculating Urban Growth." *Land Economics*, 37:51–58.

HUDSON, J. C. 1969. "Diffusion in a Central Place System." *Geographical Analysis*, 1:25–58.

HUFF, D. L. 1960. "A Topographic Model of Consumer Behavior." *Regional Science Association, Papers and Proceedings*, 6:159–173.

_____. 1961. "Ecological Characteristics of Consumer Behavior." *Regional Science Association, Papers and Proceedings*, 7:19–28.

_____. 1963. "A Probability Analysis of Shopping Center Trading Areas." *Land Economics*, 53:81–90.

HUND, J. M. 1959. "Electronics." In *Made in New York*, ed. M. Hall, pp. 241–325. Cambridge: Harvard University Press.

HURD, R. M. 1924. *Principles of City Land Values*. New York: Record and Guide.

IKLE, F. C. 1954. "Sociological Relationship of Traffic to Population and Distance." *Traffic Quarterly*, 8:123–136.

INGRAM, D. R. 1971. "The Concept of Accessibility." *Regional Studies*, 5:101–107.

IRELAN, L. M. 1967. *Low Income Life Styles*. Washington, D.C.: Department of Health, Education, and Welfare.

ISARD, W. 1956. *Location and Space Economy*. New York: Wiley.

_____. 1960. *Methods of Regional Analysis*. New York: Wiley.

_____. 1974. *Introduction to Regional Science*. Englewood Cliffs, N.J.: Prentice-Hall.

_____ AND R. KAVESH. 1954. "Economic Structural Interrelations of Metropolitan Regions." *American Journal of Sociology*, 60:152–162.

JACOBS, J. 1961. *The Death and Life of Great American Cities*. New York: Random House.

JAMES, P. E. 1931. "Vicksburg: A Study in Urban Geography." *Geographical Review*, 21:234–243.

JANELLE, D. G. 1969. "Spatial Reorganization: A Model and Concept." *Annals of the Association of American Geographers*, 59:348–364.

JENKINS, R. 1972. "Socialism and the Cities." *Socialist Commentary*, September 1972, pp. 15–19.

JOHNSON, J. H. 1967. *Urban Geography: An Introductory Analysis.* Oxford: Pergamon.

JOHNSTON, R. J. 1968. "Choice in Classification: The Subjectivity of Objective Methods." *Annals of the Association of American Geographers*, 58:575–589.

JONASSEN, C. T. 1955. *The Shopping Center Versus Downtown.* Bureau of Business Research. Columbus: Ohio State University Press.

KAIN, J. F. 1962. *A Multiple Equation Model of Household Locational and Tripmaking Behavior.* Memorandum RM-3086-FF. Santa Monica, Calif.: RAND Corporation.

———. 1968. "Housing Segregation, Negro Employment, and Metropolitan Decentralization." *Quarterly Journal of Economics*, 82:175–197.

——— AND J. J. PERSKY. 1969. "Alternatives to the Gilded Ghetto." *Public Interest*, 14:74–87.

——— J. M. QUIGLEY. 1970. "Measuring the Value of Housing Quality." *Journal of the American Statistical Association*, 65:532–549.

KAISER, E. J. 1974. *Promoting Environmental Quality Through Urban Planning Controls.* Washington, D.C.: U.S. Government Printing Office.

KANTROWITZ, N. 1969. "Ethnic and Racial Segregation in the New York Metropolis, 1960." *American Journal of Sociology*, 74:685–695.

KARASKA, G. J. 1969. "Manufacturing Linkages in the Philadelphia Economy: Some Evidence of External Agglomeration Forces." *Geographical Analysis*, 1 (4):354–369.

KASPERSON, R. E., AND M. BREITBART. 1974. "Participation, Decentralization, and Advocacy Planning." Resource paper no. 25. Washington, D.C.: Association of American Geographers, Commission on College Geography.

KENNELLY, R. A. 1954–1955. "The Location of the Mexican Steel Industry." *Revista Geografica*, 15, (41):109–129; (42):199–213; (43):60–77.

KENYON, J. B. 1960. "Industrial Localization and Metropolitan Growth: The Patterson-Passaic District." Research paper 67, Department of Geography. Chicago: University of Chicago Press.

———. 1964. "The Industrial Structure of the New York Garment Center." In *Focus on Geographic Activity,* ed. R. S. Thoman and D. J. Patton, pp. 159–166. New York: McGraw-Hill.

KERR, D. 1968. "Metropolitan Dominance in Canada." In *Canada: A Geographical Interpretation,* ed. J. Warkentin, pp. 531–555. Toronto: Methuen.

——— AND J. SPELT. 1965. *The Changing Face of Toronto.* Ottawa: The Queen's Printer.

KING, A. T., AND P. MIESZKOWSKI. 1973. "Racial Discrimination, Segregation and the Price of Housing." *Journal of Political Economy*, 81:590–606.

KING, L. J. 1966. "Cross-sectional Analysis of Canadian Urban Dimensions: 1951 and 1961." *Canadian Geographer*, 10:205–224.

KITAGAWA, E. M., AND D. J. BOGUE. 1955. *Suburbanization of Manufacturing Activity Within Standard Metropolitan Statistical Areas.* Oxford, Ohio: Scripps Foundation.

KNOS, D. S. 1962. *Distribution of Land Values in Topeka, Kansas.* Center for Research in Business. Lawrence: University of Kansas Press.

KOHLER, H. 1973. *Economics and Urban Problems.* Lexington, Mass.: Heath.

KUKLINSKI, A., ed. 1972. *Growth Poles and Growth Centers in Regional Planning.* The Hague: Mouton.

LAKSHMANAN, T. R., AND W. G. HANSEN. 1965. "A Retail Market Potential Model." *Journal of the American Institute of Planners*, 31:134–143.

LAMPARD, E. E. 1968. "The Evolving System of Cities in the United States: Urbanization and Economic Development." In *Issues in Urban Economics*, ed. H. S. Perloff and L. Wingo, Jr., pp. 81–139. Baltimore: Johns Hopkins University Press.

LANE, T. 1966. "The Urban Base Multiplier: An Evaluation of the State of the Art." *Land Economics*, 42:339–347.

LANGTON, J. 1972. "Potentialities and Problems of Adopting a Systems Approach to the Study of Change in Human Geography." In *Progress in Geography*, ed. C. Board et al., pp. 125–179. London: Edward Arnold.

LANSING, J. B. 1966. *Residential Location and Urban Mobility.* Survey Research Center, Institute for Social Research. Ann Arbor: University of Michigan Press.

_____, C. W. CLIFTON, AND J. N. MOIZAN. 1969. *New Homes and Poor People.* Ann Arbor: Institute for Social Research.

_____ AND G. HENDRICKS. 1967. "How People Perceive the Cost of the Journey to Work." *Highway Research Record*, 197:44–55.

_____ AND E. MUELLER. 1967. *The Geographic Mobility of Labor.* Ann Arbor: Institute for Social Research, University of Michigan.

LAPIN, H. S. 1964. *Structuring the Journey to Work.* Philadelphia: University of Pennsylvania Press.

LATHAM, R. F. 1967. "Urban Population Densities and Growth, with Special Reference to Toronto." Unpublished master's thesis, Queen's University, Kingston, Ont.

_____ AND M. H. YEATES. 1970. "Population Density Growth in Metropolitan Toronto." *Geographical Analysis*, 2:177–185.

LAUSEN, J. R. 1969. "On Growth Poles." *Urban Studies*, 6:137–161.

LEE, T. 1970. "Perceived Distance as a Function of Direction in the City." *Environment and Behavior*, 2:40–51.

LEONTIEF, W., et al. 1953. *Studies in the Structure of the American Economy: Theoretical and Empirical Explanations in Input-Output Analysis.* London: Oxford University Press.

LEWIS, O. 1966. *La Vida: A Puerto Rican Family in the Culture of Poverty — San Juan and New York.* New York: Random House.

LIEBERSON, S. 1963. *Ethnic Patterns in American Cities.* New York: Free Press.

LIEPMAN, K. 1944. *The Journey to Work.* London: Routledge & Kegan Paul.

LIPSET, S. M., AND R. BENDIX. 1959. *Social Mobility in Industrial Society.* Berkeley: University of California Press.

LITHWICK, N. J. 1970. *Urban Canada.* Ottawa: Central Mortgage and Housing Corporation.

_____ AND G. PAQUET. 1968. *Urban Studies: A Canadian Perspective.* Toronto: Methuen.

LLOYD, P. E., AND P. DICKEN. 1972. *Location in Space: A Theoretical Approach to Economic Geography.* New York: Harper & Row.

LOCKARD, D. 1968. *Toward Equal Opportunity: A Study of State and Local Antidiscrimination Laws.* New York: Macmillan.

LÖSCH, A. 1954. *The Economics of Location*, trans. W. H. Woglom. New Haven: Yale University Press.

LOWRY, I. S. 1963a. "Location Parameters in the Pittsburgh Model." *Regional Science Association, Papers and Proceedings*, 11:145–165.

_____. 1963b. *Portrait of a Region.* Pittsburgh: University of Pittsburgh Press.

LYNCH, K. 1960. *The Image of the City.* Cambridge: M.I.T. Press.

———. 1965. "The City as an Environment." *Scientific American*, 213:192–201. New York: Knopf.

McFARLAND, J. R. 1966. "The Administration of the New Deal Green Belt Towns." *Journal of the American Institute of Planners*, 32:217–225.

McGREGOR, J. R. 1974. "Manufacturing Linkages as a Location Factor." Professional paper no. 5, Department of Geography and Geology, Indiana State University.

MACKAY, R. 1958. "The Interactance Hypothesis and Boundaries in Canada: A Preliminary Study." *Canadian Geographer*, 11:1–8.

MADDEN, C. H. 1956. "On Some Indications of Stability in the Growth of Cities in the United States." *Economic Development and Cultural Change*, 4:236–252.

MADGE, J. 1962. "The New Towns Program in Britain." *Journal of the American Institute of Planners*, 28:208–219.

MAHER, C. A., AND L. S. BOURNE. 1969. "Land Use Structure and City Size: An Ontario Example." Research paper no. 10. Toronto: University of Toronto.

MANNERS, G., ed. 1972. *Regional Development in Britain*. London: Wiley.

MANNERS, I. R., AND M. W. MIKESELL, eds. 1974. *Perspectives on Environment*. Publication no. 13. Washington, D.C.: Association of American Geographers.

MARBLE, D. F., AND S. R. BOWLBY. 1968. "Shopping Alternatives and Recurrent Travel Patterns." In *Geographic Studies of Urban Transportation and Network Analysis*. Studies in Geography no. 16. Evanston: Northwestern University Press.

MARCH, J. G., AND H. A. SIMON. 1958. *Organizations*. New York: Wiley.

MARCHAND, B. 1973. "Deformation of a Transportation Surface." *Annals of the Association of American Geographers*, 63:507–521.

MARTIN, B. V., F. W. MEMMOTT, AND A. J. BONE. 1961. *Principles and Techniques of Predicting Future Demand for Urban Transportation*. Cambridge: M.I.T. Press.

MARTIN, F. 1969. "La Théorie de la croissance urbain par étape." *Développement Urbain et Analyse Economique*. Paris: Cujas.

MARYLAND-NATIONAL CAPITAL PARK AND PLANNING COMMISSION. 1964. *On Wedges and Corridors: A General Plan for the Maryland-Washington Regional District in Montgomery and Prince George Counties*.

MASSEY, D., R. BARRAS, AND A. BROADBENT. 1973. "Labour Must Take Over Land." *Socialist Commentary*, July 1973, pp. 9–11.

MAXWELL, J. W. 1965. "The Functional Structure of Canadian Cities: A Classification of Cities." *Geographical Bulletin*, 7:79–104.

MAYER, H. M. 1954. "Urban Geography." In *American Geography: Inventory and Prospect*, ed. P. E. James and C. F. Jones, pp. 142–166. Syracuse: Syracuse University Press.

MERA, K. 1973. "On the Urban Agglomeration and Economic Efficiency." *Economic Development and Cultural Change*, 21:309–324.

Metropolitan Toronto and Region Transportation Study 1966. Toronto: Government of Ontario.

MEYER, J. R., J. F. KAIN, AND M. WOHL. 1965. *The Urban Transportation Problem*. Cambridge: Harvard University Press.

MEYERSON, M. 1967. "National Urban Policy Appropriate to the American Pattern." In *Goals for Urban America*, ed. B. J. L. Berry and J. Meltzer, pp. 69–84. Englewood Cliffs, N.J.: Prentice-Hall.

MICHELSON, W. 1970. *Man and His Urban Environment*. Reading, Mass.: Addison-Wesley.

MIERNYK, W. H. 1965. *The Elements of Input-Output Analysis*. New York: Random House.

MISHAN, E. J. 1970. *Technology and Growth*. New York: Praeger.

MITCHELL, J. B. 1960. "Planning and Development in Philadelphia." *Journal of the American Institute of Planners*, 26:155–261.

MONTGOMERY, D. A. 1969. *Urban Land Use in Ontario: Areas and Intensities.* Toronto: Department of Municipal Affairs, Community Planning Branch.

MOORE, D. A. 1954. "The Automobile Industry." In *The Structure of American Industry,* ed. W. Adams, pp. 274–325. New York: Macmillan.

MOORE, E. 1972. *Residential Mobility in the City.* Washington, D.C.,: Association of American Geographers, Commission on College Geography, Resource paper no. 13.

MORRILL, R. L. 1965a. *Migration and the Spread and Growth of Urban Settlement.* Lund, Sweden: Gleerup

_____. 1965b. "The Negro Ghetto: Problems and Alternatives." *Geographical Review,* 55:339–361.

_____. 1974a. *The Spatial Organization of Society.* North Scituate, Mass.: Duxbury Press.

_____. 1974b. "Growth Centers–Hinterland Relations." In *Proceedings of the Commission on Regional Aspects of Development,* ed. R. S. Thoman, vol. 2: *Applications,* pp. 215–240. Washington, D.C.: International Geographical Union.

_____ AND E. H. WOHLENBERG, 1971. *The Geography of Poverty in the United States.* New York: McGraw-Hill.

MORRISSETT, I. 1958. "The Economic Structure of American Cities." *Regional Science Association, Papers and Proceedings,* 4:239–256.

MOSER, C. A., AND W. SCOTT. 1961. *British Towns.* Edinburgh: Oliver & Boyd.

MOSES, L. F., AND H. F. WILLIAMSON, JR. 1967. "The Location of Economic Activity in Cities." *American Economic Review* 52:211–222.

MULLER, P. O., AND G. J. DIAZ. 1973. "Von Thünen and Population Density." *Professional Geographer,* 25:239–241.

MUMFORD, L. 1961. *The City in History.* New York: Harcourt Brace Jovanovich.

MURDIE, R. A. 1965. "Cultural Differences in Consumer Travel." *Economic Geography,* 41:211–233.

_____. 1969. "Factorial Ecology of Metropolitan Toronto, 1951–1961." Research paper 116, Department of Geography. Chicago: University of Chicago Press.

MURPHY, R. E. 1974. *The American City.* New York: McGraw-Hill.

_____ AND J. E. VANCE, JR. 1954a, "Delimiting the CBD." *Economic Geography,* 30:189–222.

_____ AND _____. "A Comparative Study of Nine Central Business Districts." *Economic Geography,* 30:301–336.

_____, _____, AND B. J. EPSTEIN. 1955. "Internal Structure of the CBD." *Economic Geography,* 31:21–46.

MUSGROVE, R. A. 1959. *The Theory of Public Finance.* New York: McGraw-Hill.

MUTH, R. F. 1961. "The Spatial Structure of the Housing Market." *Papers and Proceedings of the Regional Science Association,* 7:207–220.

_____. 1969. *Cities and Housing.* Chicago: University of Chicago Press.

MYRDAL, G. 1957. *Rich Lands and Poor.* New York: Harper & Row.

NELSON, H. J. 1955. "A Service Classification of American Cities." *Economic Geography,* 31:189–210.

_____. 1957. "Some Characteristics of the Population of Cities of Similar Service Classifications." *Economic Geography,* 33:95–108.

NETZER, D. 1968. *Impact of the Property Tax: Its Economic Implications for Urban Problems.* Washington, D.C.: U.S. Congress, Joint Economic Committee.

_____. 1974. *Economics and Urban Problems.* New York: Basic Books.

NEUTZE, G. M. 1967. *Economic Policy and the Size of Cities.* Clifton, N.J.: Kelley.

NEWLING, B. E. 1964. "Urban Population Densities and Intraurban Growth." *Geographical Review,* 54:440–442.

———. 1966. "Urban Growth and Spatial Structure: Mathematical Models and Empirical Evidence." *Geographical Review*, 56:213–225.

———. 1969. "The Spatial Variation of Urban Population Densities." *Geographical Review*, 59:242–252.

NICHOLSON, T. G., AND M. H. YEATES. 1969. "The Ecological and Spatial Structure of the Socio-Economic Characteristics of Winnipeg, 1961." *Canadian Review of Sociology and Anthropology*, 6:162–178.

NIEDERCORN, J. H., AND E. F. R. HEARLE. 1964. "Recent Land Use Trends in 48 Large American Cities." *Land Economics*, 40:105–110.

NOURSE, H. O. 1968. *Regional Economics.* New York: McGraw-Hill.

NOVAK, R. T. 1956. "Distribution of Puerto Ricans on Manhattan Island." *Geographical Review*, 46:182–186.

NYSTUEN, J. D. 1963. "Identification of Some Fundamental Concepts." *Papers of the Michigan Academy of Science, Arts, and Letters*, 48:373–384.

——— AND M. F. DACEY. 1961. "A Graph Theory Interpretation of Nodal Regions." *Regional Science Association, Papers and Proceedings*, 7:29–42.

OGBURN, W. F. 1933. *Recent Social Trends in the United States.* New York: McGraw-Hill.

OLSSON, G. 1964. *Distance and Human Interaction.* Philadelphia: Regional Science Research Institute.

ONGLEY, E. D. 1973. "Sediment Discharge from Canadian Basins into Lake Ontario." *Canadian Journal of Earth Sciences*, 10 (2):146–156.

OWEN, W. 1966. *The Metropolitan Transportation Problem.* Washington, D.C.: Brookings.

———. 1972. *The Accessible City.* Washington, D.C.: Brookings.

PARK, R. E. 1929. "Urbanization as Measured by Newspaper Circulation." *American Journal of Sociology*, 35:60–79.

———, E. W. BURGESS, AND R. D. MCKENZIE. 1925. *The City.* Chicago: University of Chicago Press. Reprinted in 1967.

——— AND C. NEWCOMB. 1933. "Newspaper Circulation in Metropolitan Regions." In *The Metropolitan Community*, ed. R. D. McKenzie. New York: McGraw-Hill.

PASMA, T. K. 1955. *Organized Industrial Districts: A Tool for Community Development.* Washington, D.C.: Area Development Division, Office of Technical Services, U.S. Department of Commerce.

PENDLETON, W. C. 1962. "The Value of Accessibility." Unpublished Ph.D. dissertation, University of Chicago.

PERLOFF, H., AND L. WINGO. 1961. "Natural Resource Endowment and Regional Economic Growth." In *Natural Resources and Economic Growth*, ed. J. J. Spengler, pp. 191–212. Washington, D.C.: Resources for the Future, Inc.

———, E. S. DUNN, JR., E. E. LAMPARD, AND R. F. MUTH. 1960. *Regions, Resources and Economic Growth.* Baltimore: Johns Hopkins University Press.

PFOUTS, R. W. 1960. *The Techniques of Urban Economic Analysis.* New York: Chandler Davis.

PHILBRICK, A. K. 1957. "Principles of Areal Functional Organization in Regional Human Geography." *Economic Geography*, 33:299–336.

PICKARD, J. P. 1959. *Metropolitanization of the United States.* Washington, D.C.: Urban Land Institute.

———. 1970. "Growth of Urbanization in the United States." In *The Modern City*, ed. H. W. Rasmussen and C. T. Haworth, pp. 5–15. New York: Harper & Row.

PINKEPANK, J. A. 1966. "Serving Twelve Masters." *Trains*, 26:36–46 and 42–49.

PLEWES, J., AND M. YEATES. 1972. "The Urban Rush Hour: An Analysis of the Yong St., Toronto, Subway System." *Traffic Quarterly*, 26:209–229.

Pollution Probe. 1972. *Rules of the Game.* Toronto.

POPENOE, D. 1969. "On the Meaning of Urban in 'Urban Studies.' " In *Urbanism, Urbanization, and Change*, ed. P. Meadows and E. H. Mizruchi, pp. 64–75. Toronto: Addison-Wesley.

PRATT, E. E. 1911. *Industrial Causes of Congestion of Population in New York City.* Studies in History, Economics, and Public Law. New York: Columbia University Press.

PRED, A. 1963. "Business Thoroughfares as Expressions of Urban Negro Culture." *Economic Geography*, 39:217–233.

_____. 1964. "The Intrametropolitan Location of Manufacturing." *Annals of the Association of American Geographers*, 54:165–180.

_____. 1965. "Industrialization, Initial Advantage, and American Metropolitan Growth." *Geographical Review*, 55:158–185.

_____. 1966. *The Spatial Dynamics of U.S. Urban Industrial Growth, 1800–1914: Interpretive and Theoretical Essays.* Cambridge: M.I.T. Press.

_____. 1967. *Behaviour and Location, Part I.* Lund, Sweden: Gleerup.

_____. 1969. *Behaviour and Location, Part II.* Lund, Sweden: Gleerup.

_____. 1971. "Urban Systems Development and the Long-Distance Flow of Information Through Preelectronic U.S. Newspapers." *Economic Geography*, 47:498–524.

_____. 1973. "The Growth and Development of Systems of Cities in Advanced Economies." *Lund Studies in Geography*, B, 38:7–32. Lund, Sweden: Gleerup.

_____. 1974a. "Major Job-Providing Organizations and Systems of Cities." Resource paper no. 27. Washington D.C.: Association of American Geographers, Commission on College Geography.

_____. 1974b. "Urbanization, Planning Problems and Research: A Review of Swedish Geography." In *Progress in Geography*, ed. C. Board et al., vol. 5, pp. 1–76. London: Edward Arnold.

PYLE, G. F. 1969. "The Diffusion of Cholera in the United States in the Nineteenth Century." *Geographical Analysis*, 1:59–75.

RAINWATER, L. 1966. "Fear and the House-as-a-Haven in the Lower Class." *Journal of the American Institute of Planners*, 32:23–31.

RATCLIFF, R. U. 1949. *Urban Land Economics.* New York: McGraw-Hill.

_____. 1955. "Efficiency and the Location of Urban Activities." In *The Metropolis in Modern Life*, ed. R. M. Fisher, pp. 125–148. Garden City, N.Y.: Doubleday.

_____. 1957. "On Wendt's Theory of Land Values." *Land Economics*, 33:360–363.

RAY, D. M. 1965. "Market Potential and Economic Shadow." Research paper 101, Department of Geography. Chicago: University of Chicago Press.

_____. 1969. "The Spatial Structure of Economic and Cultural Differences: A Factorial Ecology of Canada." *Regional Science Association, Papers and Proceedings*, 23:7–23.

_____. 1972. "The Economy [of Ontario]." In *Studies in Canadian Geography: Ontario*, ed. L. Gentilcore, pp. 45–63. Toronto: University of Toronto Press.

_____ AND R. A. MURDIE. 1972. "Canadian and American Urban Dimensions." In *City Classification Handbook*, ed. B. J. L. Berry, pp. 181–210. New York: Wiley.

REES, P. H. 1968. "The Factorial Ecology of Metropolitan Chicago, 1960." Unpublished master's thesis, University of Chicago.

_____. 1971. "Factorial Ecology: An Extended Definition, Survey, and Critique of the Field." *Economic Geography* (Supplement), 47:220–233.

REILLY, W. J. 1931. *The Law of Retail Gravitation.* New York: Knickerbocker Press.

Reinemann, M. 1955. "The Localization and the Relocation of Manufacturing Within the Chicago Urban Region." Unpublished Ph.D. dissertation, Northwestern University.

Reynolds, J. P. 1961. "The Plan." *Town Planning Review*, 32:151–184.

Richardson, B. 1972. *The Future of Canadian Cities*. Toronto: New Press.

Richardson, H. W. 1972a. *Regional Economics*. London: Weidenfeld & Nicolson.

———. 1972b. "Optimality in City Size, Systems of Cities, and Urban Policy." *Urban Studies*, 9:29–48.

Richter, C. E. 1969. "The Impact of Industrial Linkages on Geographic Association." *Journal of Regional Science*, 9 (1):19–28.

Robson, B. T. 1973. *Urban Growth*. London: Methuen.

Rodgers, A. 1957. "Some Aspects of Industrial Diversification in the United States." *Economic Geography*, 33:16–30.

Rodwin, L. 1970. *Nations and Cities*. Boston: Houghton-Mifflin.

Rose, H. M. 1970. "The Development of an Urban Subsystem: The Case of the Negro Ghetto." *Annals of the Association of American Geographers*, 60:1–17.

———. 1971. *The Black Ghetto*. New York: McGraw-Hill.

Rossi, P. H. 1955. *Why Families Move*. New York: Free Press.

Roterus, V., and W. Calef. 1955. "Notes on the Basic-Nonbasic Employment Ratio." *Economic Geography*, 31:17–20.

Row, A. 1960. "The Physical Development Plan." *Journal of the American Institute of Planners*, 26:177–185.

Rowland, D. T. 1959. *Urban Real Estate Research*. Washington, D.C.: Urban Land Institute.

Rushton, G. 1969. "Analysis of Spatial Behavior by Revealed Space Preferences." *Annals of the Association of American Geographers*, 59:391–400.

———. 1971a. "Temporal Change in Space Preferences Structures." *Proceedings of the Association of American Geographers*, 1:129–132.

———. 1971b. "Postulates of Central-Place Theory and the Properties of Central-Place Systems." *Geographical Analysis*, 3:140–156.

Schackar, A. 1974. "National Urbanization Policy: A Case Study of Israel." In *Proceedings of the Commission on Regional Aspects of Development*, ed. R. S. Thoman, vol. 1: *Methodology and Case Studies*, pp. 757–778. Washington, D.C.: International Geographical Union.

Senate Committee on Public Works. 1963. *A Study of Pollution*. Washington, D.C.: U.S. Government Printing Office.

Shevky, E. and W. Bell. 1955. *Social Area Analysis: Theory, Illustrative Applications, and Computational Procedures*. Stanford: Stanford University Press.

——— and M. Williams. 1949. *The Social Areas of Los Angeles: Analysis and Typology*. Los Angeles: University of California Press.

Simmons, J. 1964. "The Changing Pattern of Retail Location." Research paper no. 92, Department of Geography. Chicago: University of Chicago Press.

———. 1966. "Toronto's Changing Retail Complex: A Study in Growth and Blight." Research paper no. 104, Department of Geography. Chicago: University of Chicago Press.

———. 1968. "Changing Residence in the City: A Review of Intra-Urban Mobility." *Geographical Review*, 58:622–651.

———. 1972. "Interaction Among the Cities of Ontario and Quebec." In *Urban Systems Development in Central Canada*, ed. L. S. Bourne and R. D. MacKinnon, pp. 198–219. Toronto: University of Toronto Press.

——— and R. Simmons. 1969. *Urban Canada*. Toronto: Copp Clark.

SIMON, H. A. 1955. "On a Class of Skew Distribution Functions." *Biometrica*, 42:425–440.

SKOLNICK, J. H. 1969. *The Politics of Protest*. New York: Ballantine Books.

SMAILES, A. E. 1953. *The Geography of Towns*. London: Hutchinson.

SMALLWOOD, F. 1963. *Metro Toronto: A Decade Later*. Toronto: Bureau of Municipal Research.

SMERK, G. M. 1967. "The Streetcar: Shaper of American Cities." *Traffic Quarterly*, 21:569–584.

SMITH, D. M. 1969. "Industrial Location and Regional Development: Some Recent Trends in North-West England." *Environment and Planning*, 1:173–192.

———. 1971. *Industrial Location*. New York: Wiley.

———. 1973. *The Geography of Social Well-Being*. New York: McGraw-Hill.

SMITH, P. J. 1962. "Calgary: A Study in Urban Pattern." *Economic Geography*, 38:315–329.

SMITH, R. H. T. 1965a. "Method and Purpose in Functional Two Classification." *Annals of the Association of American Geographers*, 55:539–548.

———. 1965b. Functions of Australian Towns." *Tijdschrift voor Economische en Sociale Geographie*, 56:81–92.

SMITH, W. 1964. "Filtering and Neighborhood Change." Research report no. 24, Center for Research in Real Estate and Urban Economics. Berkeley: University of California Press.

SOJA, E. W. 1971. "The Political Organization of Space." Research paper no. 8, Commission on College Geography. Washington, D.C.: Association of American Geographers.

SOLZMAN, D. M. 1966. "Waterway Industrial Sites: A Chicago Case Study." Research paper no. 107, Department of Geography. Chicago: University of Chicago Press.

SPELT, J. 1972. *The Urban Development in South-Central Ontario*. Toronto: McClelland & Stewart.

SPILHAUS, A. 1969. "Technology, Living Cities and Human Environment." *American Scientist*, 57:24–36.

STAFFORD, H. A., JR. 1963. "The Functional Bases of Small Towns." *Economic Geography*, 39:165–175.

STEED, G. P. F. 1973. "Intrametropolitan Manufacturing: Spatial Distribution and Locational Dynamics in Greater Vancouver." *Canadian Geographer*, 17:235–258.

STEELE, J. K. 1972. "Consumer Behaviour Shopping Activity Patterns in Kingston." Unpublished master's thesis, Queen's University, Kingston, Ont.

STEIGENGA, W. 1955. "A Comparative Analysis and a Classification of Netherlands Towns." *Netherlands Journal of Economic and Social Geography (T.E.S.G.)*, 46:106–112.

STEVENS, B. H., AND C. A. BRACKETT. 1967. *Industrial Location: A Review and Annotated Bibliography of Theoretical, Empirical and Case Studies*. Philadelphia: Regional Science Research Institute.

STEWART, C. T. 1958. "The Size and Spacing of Cities." *Geographical Review*, 48:222–245.

STEWART, J. Q. 1950. "Potential of Population and its Relationship to Marketing." In *Theory in Marketing*, ed. R. Cox and W. Alderson. Homeward, Ill.: Irwin.

STOCKING, G. W. 1954. *Basing Point Pricing and Regional Development*. Chapel Hill: University of North Carolina Press.

STOKES, C. J. 1962. "A Theory of Slums." *Land Economics*, 38:187–197.

STOUFFER, S. A. 1940. "Intervening Opportunities: A Theory Relating Mobility and Distance." *American Sociological Review*, 5:845–867.

STUART, A. W. 1968. "The Suburbanization of Manufacturing in Small Metropolitan Areas: A Case Study of Roanoke." *Southeastern Geographer*, 8:30–39.

SUNDQUIST, J. L. 1970. "Where Shall They Live?" *Public Interest*, 18:88–100.

TAAFFE, E. J. 1956. "Air Transportation and United States Urban Distribution." *Geographical Review*, 46:219–238.

———. 1962. "The Urban Hierarchy: An Air Passenger Definition." *Economic Geography*, 38:1–14.

———. 1974. "The Spatial View in Context." *Annals of the Association of American Geographers*, 64:1–16.

———, B. J. GARNER, AND M. H. YEATES. 1963. *The Peripheral Journey to Work*. Evanston, Ill.: Northwestern University Press.

TAEUBER, K. E., AND A. R. TAEUBER. 1965. *Negroes in Cities*. Chicago: Aldine.

TAYLOR, G. 1942. "Environment, Village, and City." *Annals of the Association of American Geographers*, 32:1–67.

TAYLOR, G. R. 1951. *The Transportation Revolution: 1815–1860*. New York: Harper & Row.

TEITZ, M. 1968. "Towards a Theory of Public Facility Location." *Proceedings of the Regional Science Association*, 21:35–51.

TERJUNG, W. H. 1974. "Climatic Modification." In *Perspectives on Environment*, ed. I. R. Manners and M. W. Mikesell, pp. 105–151. Publication no. 13. Washington, D.C.: Association of American Geographers.

THOMAN, R. S. 1974. "Ontario's New Regional Development Plan: A Review." In *Proceedings of the Commission on Regional Aspects of Development*, vol. 1: *Methodology and Case Studies*, ed. R. S. Thoman, pp. 795–828. Washington, D.C.: International Geographical Union.

THOMAS, E. N. 1960. "Some Comments on Functional Bases for Small Towns." *Iowa Business Digest*, 1:10–16.

———. 1961. "Toward an Expanded Central Place Model." *Geographical Review*, 51:400–411.

THOMAS, R. 1969. *London's New Towns*. London: P.E.P.

THOMPSON, W. 1965a. "Urban Economic Growth and Development in a National System of Cities." In *The Study of Urbanization*, ed. P. M. Hauser and L. F. Schnore, pp. 431–490. New York: Wiley.

———. 1965b. *Preface to Urban Economics*. Baltimore: Johns Hopkins University Press.

———. 1968. "Internal and External Factors in the Development of Urban Economies." In *Issues in Urban Economics*, ed. H. S. Perloff and L. Wingo, pp. 43–62. Baltimore: Johns Hopkins University Press.

TIEBOUT, C. M. 1956. "The Urban Economic Base Reconsidered." *Land Economics*, 32:95–99.

———. 1960. "Community Income Multipliers: A Population Growth Model." *Journal of the Regional Science Association*, 2:75–84.

TILL, T. A. 1974. "National Transportation Policy: The Need for a Clear Concept." *Proceedings, Transport Research Forum*, 25:18–22.

TIMMS, D. W. G. 1971. *The Urban Mosaic: Towards a theory of Residential Differentiation*. Cambridge: The University Press.

TULLOCK, G. 1970. *Private Wants, Public Means*. New York: Basic Books.

TURNER, A. 1974. "New Communities in the United States." *Town Planning Review*, 45:259–273.

UDRY, J. R. 1964. "Increasing Scale and Spatial Differentiation: New Tests of Two Theories from Shevky and Bell." *Social Forces*, 42:403–413.

ULLMAN, E. L. 1954. "Amenities as a Factor in Regional Growth." *Geographical Review*, 44:119–132.

———. 1956. "The Role of Transportation and the Bases for Interaction." In *Man's Role in Changing the Face of the Earth*, ed. W. L. Thomas, pp. 862–890. Chicago: University of Chicago Press.

———. 1957. *American Commodity Flow*. Seattle: University of Washington Press.

_____ AND M. F. DACEY. 1962. "The Minimum Requirements Approach to the Urban Economic Base." In *Proceedings of the I.G.U. Symposium on Urban Geography, Lund, Sweden, 1960*, ed. K. Norborg. Lund, Sweden: Gleerup.

_____ AND _____. 1969. *The Economic Base of American Cities*. Seattle: University of Washington Press.

VAN ARDSOL, M. D. 1961. "An Investigation of the Utility of Urban Typology." *Pacific Sociological Review*, 4:26–32.

VANCE, J. E., JR. 1960. "Labor-shed, Employment Field, and Dynamic Analysis in Urban Geography." *Economic Geography*, 36:189–220.

_____. 1962. "Emerging Patterns of Commercial Structure in American Cities." In *Proceedings of the I.G.U. Symposium in Urban Geography, Lund, 1960*, ed. K. Norborg, pp. 485–518. Lund, Sweden: Gleerup.

_____. 1964. *Geography and Urban Evolution in the San Francisco Bay Area*. Institute of Governmental Studies. Berkeley: University of California Press.

VANCE, R. B., AND S. SMITH. 1954. "Metropolitan Dominance and Integration." In *The Urban South*, ed. R. B. Vance and N. J. Demerath. Chapel Hill: University of North Carolina Press.

WARD, D. 1964. "A Comparative Historical Geography of Streetcar Suburbs in Boston, Massachusetts, and Leeds, England: 1850–1920." *Annals of the Association of American Geographers*, 54:477–489.

_____. 1968. "The Emergence of Central Immigrant Ghettoes in American Cities 1840–1920." *Annals of the Association of American Geographers*, 58:343–359.

_____. 1971. *Cities and Immigrants: A Geography of Change in Nineteenth Century America*. New York: Oxford University Press.

WARKENTIN, J., ed. 1968. *Canada: A Geographical Interpretation*. Toronto: Methuen.

WARNER, S. B., JR. 1962. *Streetcar Suburbs: The Process of Growth in Boston*. Cambridge: Harvard University Press.

_____. 1968. *The Private City*. Philadelphia: University of Pennsylvania Press.

WARNERYD, O. 1968. *Interdependence in Urban Systems*. Gothenburg: Regionkonsult Aktiebolag.

WARNTZ, W. 1965. *Macrogeography and Income Fronts*. Philadelphia: Regional Science Research Institute.

WATSON, J. W. 1955. "Geography: A Discipline in Distance." *Scottish Geographical Magazine*, 71:1–13.

WEBER, A. 1929. *Theory of the Location of Industries*. Chicago: University of Chicago Press (translation of 1909 German edition).

WEBER, A. F. 1963. *The Growth of Cities in the Nineteenth Century*. Ithaca, N.Y.: Cornell University Press (reprint of 1899 volume).

WEBER, D. 1958. "A Comparison of Two Oil City Business Centers: Odessa-Midland, Texas." Research paper no. 60, Department of Geography. Chicago: University of Chicago Press.

WENDT, P. F. 1957. "Theory of Urban Land Values." *Land Economics*, 33:228–240.

_____. 1961. *The Dynamics of Central City Land Values: San Francisco and Oakland, 1950–1960*. Real Estate Research Program, Institute of Business and Economic Research. Berkeley: University of California Press.

WHEBELL, C. F. J. 1969. "Corridors: A Theory of Urban Systems." *Annals of the Association of American Geographers*, 59:1–26.

WHITE, G. F. 1960. "Industrial Water Use: A Review." *Geographical Review*, 50:412–430.

WHITE, L. E. 1963. "Outdoor Play of Children Living in Flats." In *Living Towns*, ed. L. Kuper. London: Grosset.

WILLIAMS, W. V. 1967. "A Measure of the Impact of State and Local Taxes on Industrial Location." *Journal of Regional Science,* 7:49–60.

WILSON, A. G. 1974. *Urban and Regional Models in Geography and Planning.* London: Wiley.

WILSON, J. Q. 1966. "The War on Cities." *Public Interest,* 3:27–44.

WINGO, L. 1966. "Urban Renewal: A Strategy for Information and Analysis." *Journal of the American Institute of Planners,* 32:144–148.

WINSBOROUGH, H. H. 1961. "A Comparative Study of Urban Population Densities." Unpublished Ph.D. dissertation, University of Chicago.

WIRTH, L. 1938. "Urbanism as a Way of Life." *American Journal of Sociology,* 44:1–24.

WOLFORTH, J. R. 1965. *Residential Location and Place of Work.* Series in Geography no. 4. Vancouver: University of British Columbia Press.

WOLMAN, A. 1965. "The Metabolism of Cities." *Scientific American,* 213:179–190.

WOLPERT, J. 1965. "Behavioral Aspects of the Decision to Migrate." *Regional Science Association, Papers and Proceedings,* 15:159–169.

———, A. MUMPHREY, AND J. SELEY. 1972. "Metropolitan Neighborhoods: Participation and Conflict over Change." Resource paper no. 16, Commission on College Geography. Washington, D.C.: Association of American Geographers.

WONNACOTT, R. J. 1963. "Manufacturing Costs and the Comparative Advantage of United States Regions." Study paper no. 9, Upper Midwest Economic Study. Minneapolis: University of Minnesota.

WOOD, P. A. 1969. "Industrial Location and Linkage." *Area,* 2:32–39.

WOOD, R. C. 1961. *1400 Governments.* Cambridge: Harvard University Press.

YEATES, M. H. 1963. "Hinterland Delimitation: A Distance Minimizing Approach." *Professional Geographer,* 15:7–10.

———. 1965a. "Some Factors Affecting the Spatial Distribution of Chicago Land Values, 1910–1960." *Economic Geography,* 41:55–70.

———. 1965b. "The Effect of Zoning on Land Values in American Cities: A Case Study." In *Essays in Geography for Austin Miller,* ed. J. B. Whittow and P. D. Wood, pp. 317–333. Reading, England: University of Reading Press.

———. 1972. "The Congruence Between Housing Space, Social Space, and Community Space, and Some Experiments Concerning Its Implications." *Environment and Planning,* 4:395–414.

———. 1975. *Main Street: The Windsor-Quebec City Urban Axis.* Toronto: Macmillan of Canada.

——— AND P. E. LLOYD. 1970. *Impact of Industrial Incentives: Southern Georgian Bay Region, Ontario.* Ottawa: The Queen's Printer.

ZELDER, R. E. 1970. "Racial Segregation in Urban Housing Markets." *Journal of Regional Science,* 10:93–105.

ZIPF, G. K. 1949. *Human Behavior and the Principle of Least Effort.* New York: Addison-Wesley.

INDEX

*Illustrations are indicated by italics.

505